FROMMER'S

BUDGET TRAVEL GUIDE

SOUTH AMERICA
ON $40 A DAY '93-'94

by Arnold and Harriet Greenberg
with Susan Bittencourt

PRENTICE HALL TRAVEL

NEW YORK • LONDON • TORONTO • SYDNEY • TOKYO • SINGAPORE

Dedicated to

Frank P. Cammisa, Jr.,

the "Baedeker" of orthopedic surgeons,

and a class act

FROMMER BOOKS
Published by Prentice Hall General Reference
A division of Simon & Schuster Inc.
15 Columbus Circle
New York, NY 10023

ISBN 0-671-84761-9
ISSN 0277-7827

Design by Robert Bull Design
Maps by Ortelius Design and Geografix Inc.

FROMMER'S EDITORIAL STAFF
Editorial Director: Marilyn Wood
Editorial Manager/Senior Editor: Alice Fellows
Senior Editor: Lisa Renaud
Editors: Charlotte Allstrom, Thomas F. Hirsch, Peter Katucki, Sara Hinsey Raveret,
   Theodore Stavrou
Assistant Editors: Margaret Bowen, Lee Gray, Chris Hollander, Ian Wilker
Managing Editor: Leanne Coupe
Editorial Assistants: Gretchen Henderson, Bethany Jewett

Special Sales

Bulk purchases of Frommer's Travel Guides are available at special discounts. The publishers are happy to custom-make publications for corporate clients who wish to use them as premiums or sales promotions. We can excerpt the contents, provide covers with corporate imprints, or create books to meet specific needs. For more information write to Special Sales, Prentice Hall Travel, Paramount Communications Building, 15 Columbus Circle, New York, NY 10023.

Manufactured in the United States of America

CONTENTS

LIST OF MAPS vii

1 BEFORE YOU LEAVE HOME 1

1. Information, Entry Requirements & Money 3
2. Health & Insurance 7
3. What to Pack 8
4. Getting There 9

2 CARACAS, VENEZUELA 11

1. Introducing Caracas & Venezuela 11
2. Orientation 14
3. Getting Around 16
4. Where to Stay 20
5. Where to Dine 27
6. Attractions 38
7. Sports & Recreation 42
8. Savvy Shopping 43
9. Evening Entertainment 45
10. Easy Excursions 47
11. Margarita Island 48
12. Suggested Itineraries 51

SPECIAL FEATURES
- What's Special About Caracas 12
- What Things Cost in Caracas 14
- Fast Facts: Caracas 18
- Did You Know . . . ? 39

3 RIO DE JANEIRO, BRAZIL 52

1. Introducing Rio & Brazil 52
2. Orientation 54
3. Getting Around 57
4. Where to Stay 62
5. Where to Dine 72
6. Attractions 82
7. Special & Free Events 87
8. Sports & Recreation 88
9. Savvy Shopping 88
10. Evening Entertainment 91
11. Easy Excursions 94
12. Salvador 95
13. Suggested Itineraries 100

SPECIAL FEATURES
- What's Special About Rio 53
- What Things Cost in Rio 53
- Fast Facts: Rio 58
- Did You Know . . . ? 83

4 MONTEVIDEO, URUGUAY 105

1. Introducing Montevideo & Uruguay 105
2. Orientation 108
3. Getting Around 109
4. Where to Stay 113
5. Where to Dine 117
6. Attractions 123
7. Sports & Recreation 126
8. Savvy Shopping 126
9. Evening Entertainment 128
10. Punta del Este 131
11. En Route to Buenos Aires 133

SPECIAL FEATURES
● What's Special About Montevideo 106
● What Things Cost in Montevideo 106
● Fast Facts: Montevideo 110
● Did You Know . . . ? 124

5 BUENOS AIRES, ARGENTINA 134

1. Introducing Buenos Aires & Argentina 134
2. Orientation 138
3. Getting Around 140
4. Where to Stay 144
5. Where to Dine 149
6. Attractions 156
7. Sports & Recreation 161
8. Savvy Shopping 163
9. Evening Entertainment 166
10. Suggested Itineraries 171

SPECIAL FEATURES
● What's Special About Buenos Aires 135
● What Things Cost in Buenos Aires 136
● Fast Facts: Buenos Aires 142
● Did You Know . . . ? 157

6 SANTIAGO, CHILE 174

1. Introducing Santiago & Chile 174
2. Orientation 175
3. Getting Around 179
4. Where to Stay 183
5. Where to Dine 186
6. Attractions 193
7. Sports & Recreation 198
8. Savvy Shopping 199
9. Evening Entertainment 201
10. Easter Island 203
11. Suggested Itineraries 205

SPECIAL FEATURES
● What's Special About Santiago 175
● What Things Cost in Santiago 175
● Fast Facts: Santiago 179
● Did You Know . . . ? 194

7 ASUNCION, PARAGUAY 210

1. Introducing Asunción & Paraguay 210
2. Orientation 212
3. Getting Around 214
4. Where to Stay 216
5. Where to Dine 218
6. Attractions 222
7. Savvy Shopping 225
8. Evening Entertainment 226
9. Suggested Itineraries 227

SPECIAL FEATURES
- What's Special About Asunción 211
- What Things Cost in Asunción 212
- Fast Facts: Asunción 214
- Did You Know . . . ? 224

8 LA PAZ, BOLIVIA 231

1. Introducing La Paz & Bolivia 231
2. Orientation 232
3. Getting Around 234
4. Where to Stay 237
5. Where to Dine 241
6. Attractions 246
7. Sports & Recreation 249
8. Savvy Shopping 250
9. Evening Entertainment 252
10. Suggested Itineraries 255
11. Moving On 260

SPECIAL FEATURES
- What's Special About La Paz 232
- What Things Cost in La Paz 232
- Fast Facts: La Paz 234
- Did You Know . . . ? 247

9 QUITO, ECUADOR 261

1. Introducing Quito & Ecuador 261
2. Orientation 262
3. Getting Around 264
4. Where to Stay 268
5. Where to Dine 271
6. Attractions 278
7. Sports & Recreation 282
8. Savvy Shopping 282
9. Evening Entertainment 285
10. The Galápagos Islands 288
11. Suggested Itineraries 290

SPECIAL FEATURES
- What's Special About Quito 262
- What Things Cost in Quito 262
- Fast Facts: Quito 266
- Did You Know . . . ? 281

10 BOGOTA, COLOMBIA 298

1. Introducing Bogotá & Colombia 299
2. Orientation 302
3. Getting Around 304
4. Where to Stay 307
5. Where to Dine 310
6. Attractions 317
7. Sports & Recreation 322

SPECIAL FEATURES
- What's Special About Bogotá 299
- What Things Cost in Bogotá 300
- Fast Facts: Bogotá 305
- Did You Know . . . ? 318

8. Savvy Shopping 322
9. Evening Entertainment 325
10. Easy Excursions 328

11 WHERE COLOMBIANS PLAY 331

1. Cartagena 332
2. Santa Marta 345
3. San Andrés Island 351

12 PANAMA CITY, PANAMA 354

1. Introducing Panama City &
Panama 355
2. Orientation 356
3. Getting Around 359
4. Where to Stay 361
5. Where to Dine 364
6. Attractions 369
7. Sports & Recreation 374
8. Savvy Shopping 375
9. Evening Entertainment 377
10. Easy Excursions 380

SPECIAL FEATURES
● *What's Special About
Panama City 355*
● *What Things Cost in
Panama City 356*
● *Fast Facts: Panama
City 359*
● *Did You Know . . . ? 369*

13 LIMA, PERU 384

1. Introducing Lima & Peru 384
2. Orientation 386
3. Getting Around 388
4. Where to Stay 392
5. Where to Dine 397
6. Attractions 405
7. Sports & Recreation 409
8. Savvy Shopping 410
9. Evening Entertainment 413
10. Easy Excursions 417
11. Suggested Itineraries 419

SPECIAL FEATURES
● *What's Special About Lima
& Peru 385*
● *What Things Cost in
Lima 386*
● *Fast Facts: Lima 388*
● *Did You Know . . . ? 406*

14 CUZCO & MACHÚ PICCHÚ 422

1. Introducing Cuzco & Machú
Picchú 423
2. Orientation 425
3. Getting Around 426
4. Where to Stay 428
5. Where to Dine 431
6. Attractions 434
7. Savvy Shopping 437
8. Evening Entertainment 439

SPECIAL FEATURES
● *What's Special About
Cuzco & Machú
Picchú 423*
● *Fast Facts: Cuzco 426*

9. Easy Excursions 440
10. Moving On 443
11. Machú Picchú 443

APPENDIX 447

A. Useful Vocabulary 447
B. Metric Measures 452

INDEX 454

General Information 454
Destinations 455

LIST OF MAPS

SOUTH AMERICA 5

ARGENTINA
Argentina 137
Buenos Aires 141

BOLIVIA
La Paz 235

BRAZIL
Brazil 55
Rio de Janeiro 59
Copacabana & Leme 69
Ipanema & Leblon 71
Salvador, Bahía 97

CHILE
Chile 177
Santiago 181

COLOMBIA
Colombia 301
Bogotá 303

ECUADOR
Quito 265

PANAMA
Panama City 357

PARAGUAY
Asunción 213

PERU
Lima 389
Cuzco 427

URUGUAY
Uruguay 107
Montevideo 111

VENEZUELA
Venezuela 13
Caracas 17

INVITATION TO THE READER

In this guide to South America, we have selected what we consider to be the best of the many fine budget and other establishments we came across while conducting our research. You, too, in the course of your visit to South America, may come across a hotel, restaurant, shop, or attraction that you feel should be included here; or you may find that a place we have selected has since changed for the worse. In either case, let us know of your discovery. Address your comments to:

Arnold and Harriet Greenberg
Frommer's South America on $40 a Day '93–'94
c/o Prentice Hall Travel
15 Columbus Circle
New York, NY 10023

DISCLAIMERS

(1) We have made every effort to ensure the accuracy of the prices as well as of the other information contained in this guide. Yet we advise you to keep in mind that prices fluctuate over time and that some of the other information herein may also change as a result of the various volatile factors affecting the travel industry.

A major problem with regard to prices is the frequent—and sometimes dramatic—fluctuation in the exchange rate between the local currency in many South American countries and the U.S. dollar. We therefore give prices *only in U.S. dollars.* We also advise the reader to add 15%–20% to the prices quoted throughout, particularly during the second year (1994) of the lifetime of this edition.

(2) The authors and the publisher cannot be held responsible for the experiences of the reader while traveling.

SAFETY ADVISORY

Whenever you are traveling in an unfamiliar city or country, stay alert. Be aware of your immediate surroundings. Wear a moneybelt and keep a close eye on your possessions. *Be especially careful with cameras, purses, and wallets—* all favorite targets of thieves and pickpockets. Every society has its criminals (though some more than others—see **"Fast Facts: Safety"** in each chapter). It is therefore your responsibility to exercise caution at all times, in heavily touristed areas no less than in secluded areas (which you should avoid, particularly after dark).

ADDRESSES

In giving addresses, we have used the local Spanish and Portuguese designations. Some are easy to guess at, but others require a quick translation: **Avenida,** avenue; **bulevar,** boulevard; **calle,** street; **carrera,** avenue or boulevard; **cuadra,** city block; **local,** suite; **praça,** plaza or place; **rambla,** avenue; **rua,** street; **transversal** (calle transversal), cross street.

CHAPTER 1

BEFORE YOU LEAVE HOME

1. INFORMATION, ENTRY REQUIREMENTS & MONEY
2. HEALTH & INSURANCE
3. WHAT TO PACK
4. GETTING THERE

The southern half of the Americas—thought by some North Americans to be a semiprimitive continent one step away from revolution—is actually one of the world's great travel oases. It offers sights and attractions, adventures, and experiences that cause the offerings of many other areas to seem pale and insignificant. Think, for instance, of what you can do and see in a 21- to 30-day trip to South America:

- Begin by sunning and swimming at Rio de Janeiro's Ipanema Beach, with its stunning women in string bikinis who have been immortalized in song.
- Then move on to Buenos Aires to dine on a superb ¾-inch-thick steak after enjoying a Teatro Colón performance of *Aïda,* more polished than what you may have seen at Milan's La Scala.
- If you ski, test the challenging slopes of Portillo, not far from Santiago, the former scene of the World Alpine Ski championships.
- Visit Rapa Nui (Easter Island) and climb into the center of a volcano to inspect the mute monoliths that rest there, oblivious of time.
- Next explore a jungle village only hours by bus from La Paz, a mountain city where the temperatures are 40 degrees F cooler than they are in the community below.
- Explore Ecuador's Galápagos Islands and come away with your own theory of evolution.
- Make a dramatic visit underground into a church set in a salt mine outside Bogotá.
- Take a cruise through the Panama Canal, which to this day remains an incredible engineering achievement.
- And, finally, take a climactic journey into the blood-stirring world of the Incas high in the Peruvian Andes, where life is as it was five centuries ago; there you'll see an incredible marvel—Machú Picchú, the legendary "Lost City of the Incas."

To add excitement, you can come to Rio in February and immerse yourself in the most frenzied Carnival atmosphere you will ever hope to see. Or at any time of the year in any South American city, you can shout yourself hoarse at one of the innumerable *futbol* (soccer) matches that draw up to 200,000 partisan fans.

In addition, consider the hypnotic beauty of these cities*:

Quito where it is springlike all year round, despite its equatorial location, and from where you can make a 1-day excursion to a stunning Indian market or a towering volcano.

Lima where in 1535 the conquistadors spawned a sea-level Spanish colonial city (after razing the gold-rich Inca mountain cities) and where today the suburbs are stylish and sophisticated.

Asunción where the residents are as warm and welcoming as those in Copenhagen.

La Paz where the Indians still marvel at the mighty iron birds that roar in and out of this 2½-mile-high city (highest capital in the world) and where the open-air stalls make European flea markets seem tame.

Caracas where from Mount Avila you can have a stunning view of the city and, when it is running, take a cable-car ride down 7,000 feet to the Caribbean beaches.

Margarita where the blue sky and sandy beaches rival those of any other Caribbean isle at half the price.

Cartagena where blue water and sandy beaches surround the walled colonial part of the city.

For shoppers, good buys are everywhere—in alligator, lizard, suede, alpaca, silver, gemstones, hand-woven wool rugs, and intricately designed wood-carvings—at prices that are far lower than those in the United States.

Even though tourism has risen dramatically in the last few years, we are surprised that South America remains a distinct third-choice destination (after Europe and Asia) for U.S. and Canadian travelers.

South America is exotic, cosmopolitan, history-rich, scenically stunning, and lower-priced than Europe. And, yes, you jaded budget travelers who never thought you'd see the day—the budget hotels here come with private baths.

At the drop of a tourist brochure, U.S. travelers skip off to Europe, the Caribbean, the Near East, and Japan; there are even 21-day Rotary charters to Beijing. But until the last 2 years, South America was largely ignored. Of the 9 million or so U.S. travelers who went abroad in 1990, more than 3 million went to Europe; South America attracted fewer than 1 million.

An often-asked question is how Rio and Buenos Aires compare with Paris and Rome. Let's begin by making one point clear: South America is not Europe. While Buenos Aires does resemble Paris in certain respects and even New York in others, it possesses a unique flavor, stemming in part from gaucho influences and the hybrid crosscurrents of its Spanish, Italian, and German immigrants. Rio is not like any other city, for it boasts a year-round carnival atmosphere in Copacabana Beach and a low-key, good-natured populace. Some travelers insist that Rio is much like Rome, but this is a superficial view, deriving largely, we suspect, from a similar climate (both are extremely hot in summer) and the similar leisurely pace of life. The differences, while sometimes intangible, are nonetheless real and significant. Romans immerse themselves in their proud history and therefore have a tendency to look back rather than ahead. Cariocas look neither back nor ahead but instead focus on the present.

Every major South American city is distinctive, with something unique to offer. In some cities, such as Lima, you'll find a fascinating contrast between the modern way of life and the lingering Spanish colonial and Indian cultures. In La Paz the 2½-mile-high elevation affects the way you walk, breathe, and just plain exist. This city is perhaps geographically like some areas in Switzerland but certainly not culturally so, since half the population is proudly Indian. Even Montevideo, often likened to Geneva, has been undergoing an inflationary surge that the well-ordered Swiss would never tolerate. Quito, gentle and quiet like Copenhagen, is far more beautiful, and its people are more earnest about life.

Several other differences should be stressed: Europe is far more developed economically than is South America. Thus, European currencies are relatively more stable than those of Bolivia, Brazil, Chile, Peru, and Uruguay. Since the purchasing power of U.S. dollars fluctuates drastically at times, *don't try to anticipate exact prices*. Read our currency section carefully and do your homework.

Unlike Europe, South America is not equipped to cope with annual floods of tourists. There are not enough hotels, pensions, or restaurants. However, since South

IMPRESSIONS

South America is bounded at its northern end by an isthmus and at its southern end by a strait. . . . An isthmus and a strait are . . . the most interesting things with which geographical science has to deal.
—JAMES BRYCE, SOUTH AMERICA, 1912

Modern Latin America . . . far from being romantic or remote, is very much a part of the world the rest of us live in. . . . But none of it is in the least like the stereotypo which the rest of the world has come to accept.
—J. HALCHRO FERGUSON, LATIN AMERICA, 1963

"You must not judge people by their country," a lady advised me. "In South America, it is always wise to judge people by their altitude."
—PAUL THEROUX, THE OLD PATAGONIAN EXPRESS, 1979

America is still relatively virgin travel terrain, you will find many advantages; for example, almost all hotels offer rooms with private baths (even many rock-bottom budget ones).

Don't expect much help from travel agents regarding South American budget travel; those with whom we have talked know very little about nonluxury travel in South America.

1. INFORMATION, ENTRY REQUIREMENTS & MONEY

SOURCES OF INFORMATION

Before you go to South America, you can obtain travel information as well as basic information about the different countries by calling or writing to their respective embassies in Washington, D.C. Their addresses are:

ARGENTINA Embassy of Argentina, 1600 New Hampshire Ave. NW, Washington, DC 20009 (tel. 202/939-6400).

BOLIVIA Embassy of Bolivia, 3014 Massachusetts Ave. NW, Washington, DC 20008 (tel. 202/483-4410).

BRAZIL Embassy of Brazil, 3006 Massachusetts Ave. NW, Washington, DC 20008 (tel. 202/745-2700).

CHILE Embassy of Chile, 1732 Massachusetts Ave. NW, Washington, DC 20036 (202/785-1746).

COLOMBIA Embassy of Colombia, 2118 Leroy Place NW, Washington, DC 20008 (tel. 202/387-8338).

ECUADOR Embassy of Ecuador, 2535 Fifteenth St. NW, Washington, DC 20009 (202/234-7200).

PANAMA Embassy of Panama, 2862 McGill Terrace NW, Washington, DC 20008 (tel. 202/483-1407).

PARAGUAY Embassy of Paraguay, 2400 Massachusetts Ave. NW, Washington, DC 20008 (tel. 202/483-6960).

PERU Embassy of Peru, 1700 Massachusetts Ave. NW, Washington, DC 20036 (tel. 202/833-9860).

URUGUAY Embassy of Uruguay, 1919 F St. NW, Washington, DC 20006 (tel. 202/331-1313).

VENEZUELA Embassy of Venezuela, 1099 30th St. NW, Washington, DC 20007 (tel. 202/342-2214).

ENTRY REQUIREMENTS

DOCUMENTS The only official papers you'll need in order to travel in South America are a valid U.S. or Canadian passport, required by all countries; tourist cards, required by some countries; and a visa, required by Brazil. These are all simple to obtain, if you allow enough time.

Arranging for a **passport** is routine. Pick up your application at the State Department Passport Office (or at designated post offices and county courthouses) in any good-size city. The fee is $42 for a new passport and $35 for a renewal; the passport will be valid for 10 years. You will need two 2½- by 2½-inch passport photos. The wait for your passport is at least two weeks from the date of application.

The acquisition of **tourist cards** is easily arranged through your airline when you purchase your ticket. Most are free, although some require a nominal fee. You can pick up tourist cards in South America from your airline when you check in for your next destination. Always carry extra small photos with you.

A U.S. citizen needs a **visa** to visit Brazil; it can be obtained from any Brazilian consulate by mail or in person. To obtain a visa, you need a round-trip ticket (or letter from a travel agent giving your scheduled dates of arrival and departure), a photo, and a valid passport. The visa must be used within 90 days from its date of issuance; it is good for 90 days from the first day it is used and allows multiple entries within that period. Canadian citizens do not need visas.

As for **vaccination certificates,** smallpox vaccinations are no longer required. You might want to get a typhoid shot (if you usually get one when traveling) as a precaution. Readers planning trips to the jungles of Brazil should consider a yellow fever shot. A tetanus shot might also be advisable. Consult your local health department.

CUSTOMS Before deciding what to buy in South America, acquaint yourself with U.S. Customs regulations. Current regulations permit U.S. citizens to bring back up to $400 in duty-free merchandise per person (including children). Many articles, however, are not subject to duty (see "Savvy Shopping" for each country). You may also bring in one quart of liquor if you are over 21.

Shipping Purchases Home No matter what you purchase, if you plan to ship it instead of carrying it with you, be sure to total up the price of air or ocean freight and the cost of having the merchandise delivered from the airport or dock to your home. It cost us $38 to have some light furniture delivered from JFK Airport to Manhattan.

Depending on what you purchase, your overall expense may be twice as much. You can save money by carting the stuff home yourself and using ocean freight instead of air freight.

You can avoid unpleasant surprises by calculating in advance what it will actually cost you to get that table or alpaca rug from the store to your living room. Don't let the merchant put you off when you ask about freight charges. He or she knows, or certainly can find out quickly, what the approximate freight cost is. As a guide, just remember that it will cost you, for example, $28 to ship by air 22 pounds of furniture from La Paz to JFK Airport in New York. Ocean freight charges run somewhat less.

MONEY

CASH & CURRENCY Each country in South America has its own currency, with its own value in relation to the U.S. dollar. But many South American currencies tend to fluctuate in value, sometimes sharply and almost overnight. This tendency can

N

0 | 1000 mi
0 | 1600 km

SOUTH AMERICA

GALAPAGOS ISLANDS
(Ecuador)

Caribbean Sea

Atlantic Ocean

Santa Marta
Cartagena
Panama City
PANAMA

Caracas
VENEZUELA
Georgetown
Paramaribo
Cayenne
GUYANA
FRENCH GUYANA
SURINAM
Bogotá
COLOMBIA

Quito
ECUADOR

EQUATOR

Belém

PERU

BRAZIL

Recife

Machú Picchú
Lima
Cuzco

BOLIVIA
La Paz

Brasilia

PARAGUAY

Rio de Janeiro
São Paulo

TROPIC OF CAPRICORN

Asunción

Pacific Ocean

C H I L E

ARGENTINA
URUGUAY

Santiago
Buenos Aires
Montevideo

Atlantic Ocean

make travel-guide research hazardous, since hotel and restaurant prices can move up (or down) suddenly.

To our chagrin, this has happened from time to time in Argentina, Brazil, Chile, Colombia, and Peru. Thus, some of the prices we have previously quoted were out of date virtually as soon as our book was published. The cause was an inflationary explosion that catapulted prices up. Although sometimes the dollar increases in value, enabling tourists to purchase more pesos and other currencies, generally price jumps outpace the dollar's purchasing power.

To further complicate things, some countries (for example, Peru) occasionally counterbalance inflation by devaluing their currency. In other words, prices shoot up because of inflation, but a devaluation of the local currency in relation to the dollar more or less corrects the price "deviation" for U.S. visitors.

PARALLEL CURRENCY MARKET An intriguing phenomenon has emerged in recent years—the "parallel market" in currency exchange. This means that for many Latin currencies there are two money-exchange rates, the official one and the unofficial (parallel market) one; the latter offers a better rate of exchange for your dollar.

The official rate is the one you receive in the host country during your stay. The parallel-market rate, which can and does change suddenly, is at times available in South America, in the host country, and in the United States through major international banks or currency dealers. Although a parallel market does not always exist for all countries, it is worth checking before your departure for, as well as on your arrival in, South America. It could make a big difference in your budget. (In early 1989, the official exchange rate in Brazil was 700 cruzados to the U.S. dollar; the parallel-market rate was 950 to the dollar!)

Warning: Some South American countries view the parallel rate as a "black market" and strongly discourage its use. Obviously, this guide does *not* recommend participation in black-market activities, but we believe you have a right to know about practices that are common in some areas.

So, how do travelers to South America guide themselves through this intricate money maze to avoid unpleasant price shocks? Complete protection is impossible, but the following precautions may be helpful:

- Do not accept any currency information as gospel, even the data in this guide. Changes take place too abruptly. Check with a currency dealer or the international section of a large bank for the latest information just before your departure. (In New York, Citibank is particularly knowledgeable, since it has many South American branches.)

- We have noted all prices in U.S. dollars instead of the local currency. Thus, we avoid the confusion that arises if the price in pesos (or any other currency) rises but the real price to you remains the same due to devaluation of that local currency.

- Where appropriate, we have listed the upper range of all budget prices charged by hotels and restaurants. The hope is to reward you occasionally with lower-than-expected bills. In each chapter we have included a currency section that reviews each country's recent money history, including price and exchange-rate fluctuations. Study these carefully, particularly in the chapters on Bogotá, Buenos Aires, Lima, Rio, and Santiago.

A final suggestion: It is advisable to have several dollars' worth of local currency when you arrive in each country to cover tipping and other incidentals.

EXCHANGE RATES Here, country by country, are the exchange rates between the local currencies and the U.S. dollar, as of late 1992. Remember that each exchange rate is *subject to sharp changes.*

Argentina The basic monetary unit is the *peso:* US$1 = 1 peso.
Bolivia The currency unit is the *boliviano:* US$1 = 3.9 bolivianos.

Brazil The currency unit is the *cruzeiro:* US$1 = 4,500 novo cruzeiros. (The Brazilian economy is one of the most inflationary in South America. Be sure to read up on the currency changes detailed under "Currency" in "Fast Facts: Rio de Janeiro" in Chapter 3 as you plan your itinerary in Brazil.)

Chile The currency unit is the Chilean *peso:* US$1 = 356 pesos.

Colombia The basic currency unit is the Colombian *peso:* US$1 = 585 pesos.

Ecuador The primary unit is the *sucre,* composed of 100 centavos: US$1 = 1,600 sucres.

Panama The basic currency unit is the U.S. dollar, called the *balboa;* like the U.S. dollar, it is divided into 100 cents. The coins are different, but the denominations are the same as in the United States, from the penny and quarter to the half dollar and even silver dollar.

Paraguay The basic unit is the *guarani:* US$1 = 1,480 guaranis.

Peru The currency unit is the *nuevo sol,* introduced in 1992: US$1 = 1.19 nuevos soles. (Over the past several years inflation in Peru has been rampant, and there have been several currency changes. For more information, see under "Currency" in "Fast Facts: Lima" in Chapter 13.)

Uruguay The currency unit is the Uruguayan *peso,* which has steadily eroded in value: US$1 = 3,275 pesos. (See under "Currency" in "Fast Facts: Montevideo" in Chapter 4.)

Venezuela: The monetary unit is the *bolívar,* divided into 100 centimos (or centavos): US$1 = 66 bolívars. (For decades a sturdy currency, the bolívar fell in value beginning in the early 1980s because of a drop in world oil prices. Its decline has made Caracas, one of the world's most expensive cities, more attractive to the limited-budget traveler. However, it is not clear how long the situation will last.)

TRAVELER'S CHECKS Traveler's checks are a must, of course; those sold by Barclays Bank are free, as opposed to the standard 1% fee charged by most others.

CREDIT CARDS Credit cards are widely accepted in Latin America, especially VISA, Diners Club, MasterCard, and American Express. However, in Colombia and Peru it is usually better to pay in cash, because credit-card purchases boost prices, often by as much as 10% (if not more) as a hedge against inflation.

2. HEALTH & INSURANCE

MEDICAL AID The **International Association for Medical Assistance to Travelers (IAMAT)** is a nonprofit organization providing travelers in 450 cities in 120 countries with English-speaking doctors who are familiar with North American medical techniques. Membership is free, but members pay a moderate fee to the treating physician abroad. Each member receives the World Climate Chart, a new series of eight publications that provide specific climatic and sanitary conditions for the most popular travel destinations. For example, if you were going to Buenos Aires in January, you could consult the chart and learn that the highest average temperature is 29°C/85°F, the lowest average temperature 12°C/65°F, and the mean relative humidity 71%. January averages about seven rainy days. Also included is information on the quality of drinking water, milk, and dairy products, as well as advice on proper clothing.

IAMAT members also receive the *Directory,* a Traveler's Clinical Record, and a World Immunization and Malaria Risk Chart. The pocket-size *Directory* lists IAMAT centers abroad. Most of the individual English-speaking physicians associated with IAMAT centers have been trained in internal medicine. Each doctor has had some postgraduate training in the United States, Canada, or the United Kingdom and has agreed to a fixed schedule of fees for his or her services. The Traveler's Clinical Record is designed to record the traveler's medical history and any treatment during his or her journey. The World Immunization and Malaria Risk Chart lists the required and recommended inoculations for all countries. Countries with a risk for malaria are noted as well.

Anybody may join IAMAT by writing to 736 Center St., Lewiston, NY 14092, or 123 Edward St., Suite 725, Toronto, Ontario M5G 1E2. All donations to IAMAT are tax deductible in both the United States and Canada. The funds are used for research into the medical aspects of travel.

HEALTH PREPARATIONS Although no immunizations are required for travel in South America, if you plan to be in the jungles of Brazil, Peru, or Bolivia, a yellow fever shot would be advisable.

The recent outbreak of cholera in many South American countries (especially Peru) should not deter you from traveling there. If you stay on the beaten track, there should be no problem. Here are some simple precautions:

- Drink only water that has been boiled or treated with chlorine or iodine. Other safe beverages include tea and coffee made with boiled water; bottled mineral water and carbonated beverages (without ice).

- Eat only foods that have been thoroughly cooked and are still hot or fresh fruit that you have peeled yourself.

- Do not eat undercooked or raw fish or shellfish, including ceviche.

- Make sure that all vegetables are cooked; avoid salads.

- Do not buy foods and beverages from street vendors.

- Do not bring perishable seafood back to the United States.

A simple rule of thumb is this: "Boil it, cook it, peel it—or forget it."

INSURANCE Before leaving on your trip, contact your health insurance company to find out whether your policy will cover you while you are out of the country. If it does not, consult your travel agent regarding travel health insurance policies. Some credit-card companies provide trip insurance when you use their cards to charge an airline ticket, so be sure to check on this. If this insurance is inadequate, ask your travel agent about various types of travel insurance, including insurance against cancellation of a prepaid tour and luggage losses.

3. WHAT TO PACK

LUGGAGE & CLOTHING Here are two vital packing rules to follow: (1) Take a minimum of clothing, and (2) make sure that every item of clothing is crease-resistant or wash-and-wear.

Each person should take only one suitcase, 24 inches or 26 inches wide, plus a small airline bag. This will automatically limit the amount of clothing you can take, freeing you from hours of packing and unpacking, and enabling you to carry your own bags from place to place.

A zippered cloth or canvas-type suitcase is best. A couple traveling together might take one 26-inch case plus a hanging bag, instead of two suitcases. We always travel this way and find that the hanging bag keeps our clothes wrinkle-free. There is no need to unpack it, since it hangs in the closet as is.

The airline totebag or large handbag can be carried personally aboard the plane (it does not count in your luggage weight). These bags are ideal for cameras, books, cosmetics, maps, and odds and ends.

Note: The maximum luggage weight permitted by some airlines is 44 pounds per person; others allow two bags per person, regardless of weight. Expect to pay about $2.25 per pound for any extra weight.

Another reason for taking minimum clothing and gear is to allow room for the gifts, maps, and books you may want to purchase in South America. Your bag will probably get heavier as you travel.

Careful planning will allow you to leave behind some necessary clothing. For example, you may want to buy a good-quality sweater in Buenos Aires at bargain prices, and not bring one from home. You can do this by planning your itinerary so that you visit warm areas (such as Rio) before going on to Buenos Aires and other cooler areas.

One of our travel tips is to compare your packing list with our suggestions under "Savvy Shopping" in each city that you plan to visit. If there are clothing items you definitely plan to buy, reduce your travel wardrobe accordingly.

When we first started traveling in South America, women rarely wore pants in the big cities, especially at night. Now, of course, the dress code has totally changed, and you'd have difficulty distinguishing Americans from "natives." Pants suits and even jeans are acceptable almost everywhere.

Try to coordinate your clothing so that shirts and sweaters can be worn with several pants outfits. Always wear comfortable walking shoes—even at night. Espadrilles and sandals may sound great but aren't for real walkers. Take wools or heavy cottons from May through October and lightweight clothing from November through February. (Check each chapter if you are uncertain about season.) You don't need a heavy winter coat—stick to a heavy sweater and a lined raincoat, except for skiers or those camping out.

The dress codes for men has also changed; where jackets and ties were once required, jackets alone are now acceptable. Turtlenecks are very common, as are ascots. Sport jackets and slacks can be worn in place of suits.

PACKING TIPS To prevent suits and dresses from wrinkling in your suitcase, place tissue paper between garments. Transparent zippered plastic bags, sold at variety stores, are ideal for separating such articles as lingerie, cosmetics, and shoes.

Carry all liquids, such as shampoos and lotions, in plastic bottles only; plastic bottles are available at variety stores.

Remember that since you will be doing your own laundry as you go (laundry service in most South American cities is expensive and slow), you should carry cold-water soap packets. One packet will do several items in your hotel sink. A small clothesline, with suction cups, is handy for hanging up your wet wash-and-wear clothes.

U.S.-manufactured drugs and sundries are widely available in South American cities, so don't load yourself down with assorted pills and remedies; but do bring your own prescription drugs.

Since South American hotels tend to be generous with towels, soap, and toilet tissue, you don't need to bring these along. However, packets of towelettes, which are ideal for a fast freshening-up while touring, are useful.

Some tourists always pack a travel alarm clock and a travel iron. However, most hotels we recommend have wake-up service, and if you stick to wash-and-wear clothes, you shouldn't need an iron.

4. GETTING THERE

BY PLANE

The only practical method of getting to South America—and of traveling about once there—is by air, and the reasons are obvious: South America is a huge continent, roughly the size of the United States and Canada combined. Within that massive area, the principal cities are widely scattered. Rio, for example, is 1,000 miles from Buenos Aires; Lima is 1,500 miles from Santiago. Complicating things even further is the awesome Andes mountain range, which splits the entire continent from north to south—another factor making land travel slow and arduous.

MULTIPLE STOPOVERS An equally important reason for traveling to South America by air is the privilege of multiple stopovers provided by air travel. In effect, air travelers can, without extra charge, make two stops on the way down and two additional stops on the way back. Thus, on a round trip to Buenos Aires (we strongly recommend the Argentine capital as your farthest destination), you can stop free at several other cities at no additional cost.

BUDGET FARES Check with your airline or travel agent on any special money-saving fares. Besides the regular airfares, at this time there is an APEX fare, an individual tour inclusive fare (which includes land arrangements), and a 28-day excursion fare. Charter flights can also help you save money when heading to a particular destination.

THE AIRLINES The major U.S. carriers are **American Airlines** and **United Airlines.** Both offer daily service to many South American cities. **Canadian Airlines International** offers service to South America from Canada.

Many of the South American national airlines fly worldwide and are renowned for their excellent service. **Varig** (Brazil's flag carrier) has long been called the "Swissair of South America" by frequent travelers because of its superb service and reliability. Varig also offers a fabulous cost-saver—the Brazil airpass for travel throughout Brazil.

Other carriers are **VIASA** and **AVENSA** (Venezuela), **Lan Chile** and **LADECO** (Chile), **Aerolíneas Argentinas** (Argentina), **Avianca** (Colombia), **Ecuatoriana** (Ecuador), **Lloyd Boliviano** (Bolivia), and **Aero Perú** (Peru). Their equipment is modern, and each line adds a touch of its homeland to your flight. Like Varig in Brazil, Avianca offers discounted air travel throughout Colombia.

BY SHIP

It is, of course, possible to travel to South America by ship, but only if you have 2 or more weeks to spare on transportation and are willing to pay extra for air transportation within the continent. New York to Rio, for example, is 4,700 sea miles, and the cruise takes 2 weeks; traveling by sea to Chile will take you longer.

BY PACKAGE TOUR

Grand Prix Journeys, 425 Madison Ave., New York, NY 10017 (tel. 212/319-8600 or toll free 800/242-7749) is the premier U.S. tour operator in Brazil. It offers package tours to Rio, including the Club Rio plan, as well as "ecological expeditions" to the Amazon and the Pantanal.

Metropolitan Touring is a major tour operator in Ecuador. It was the first to go to the Galápagos and offer a wide range of services to the islands as well as the rest of Ecuador, including Cuenca and Guayaquil. For information, contact its U.S. representative, Adventure Associates, at 13150 Coit Rd., Suite 110, Dallas, TX 75240 (tel. toll free 800/527-2500).

To arrange tours in Chile, including the Wine Country, the Lake Region, and Glacier Cruises in Patagonia and Tierra del Fuego, call the **Lan Chile Tour Department** (tel. toll free 800/995-4888).

CHAPTER 2

CARACAS, VENEZUELA

1. INTRODUCING CARACAS & VENEZUELA
- WHAT'S SPECIAL ABOUT CARACAS
- WHAT THINGS COST IN CARACAS
2. ORIENTATION
3. GETTING AROUND
- FAST FACTS: CARACAS
4. WHERE TO STAY
5. WHERE TO DINE
6. ATTRACTIONS
- DID YOU KNOW . . . ?
7. SPORTS & RECREATION
8. SAVVY SHOPPING
9. EVENING ENTERTAINMENT
10. EASY EXCURSIONS
11. MARGARITA ISLAND
12. SUGGESTED ITINERARIES

Caracas is an important stop on your itinerary, for its climate (warm and sunny much of the year), sophistication, and exciting nightlife, as well as for the warmth of its residents (called Caraqueños). It's a different side of Latin America.

Only 2½ hours by jet from Miami and 4½ hours from New York, Caracas is a gracious, sophisticated city of more than 4 million people; it has probably the highest standard of living of any Latin American city, including Mexico City. Sprawling, like Los Angeles, for almost 10 miles, Caracas incorporates about a score of separate communities, several of which are popular with North Americans. High-rise office buildings, apartment houses, and residential co-ops speckle the ever changing skyline.

1. INTRODUCING CARACAS & VENEZUELA

When you arrive in the Venezuelan capital, you'll probably be struck by the strong North American influence in the food; the architecture; and the skillful merchandising techniques of the city's shopping centers, specialty shops, and dazzling boutiques. Thousands of U.S. and Canadian citizens are employed here by North American companies originally drawn to Venezuela by the rich oil finds in Maracaibo. Not surprisingly, English is the second language—you'll hear it in hotels, in stores, and even in the streets.

Venezuelans are well dressed, and fashions imported from Italy, France, and the United States are de rigueur in restaurants, discos, and theaters. Only in the most exclusive French restaurants are ties required, although men do wear jackets at night.

Symbolic of Venezuela's wealth is the large number of autos in Caracas. The city is intersected by several modern highways, but the traffic problem rivals what we've seen anywhere, especially since gas is so inexpensive. The metro helps alleviate the problem a bit. Not quite 10 years old, it covers a distance of 40 kilometers, with 35 stations throughout the city.

WHAT'S SPECIAL ABOUT CARACAS

Beaches
☐ Just 45 minutes from downtown Caracas are lovely Caribbean beaches.

Climate
☐ Caracas is warm and sunny all year long.

Museum
☐ The Sofia Imber Museum of Contemporary Art is the home of works by internationally acclaimed modern masters.

Park
☐ Mt. Avila Park offers an expansive view of Caracas and the Caribbean beyond.

Great Town
☐ Colonia Tovar, a German mountain village, is just 40 miles from Caracas.

Zoo
☐ The Parque Zoológico de Caricuao is one of the best in South America.

After Dark
☐ Caracas nightclubs are among the finest in South America.

Natural Spectacle
☐ Angel Falls, the highest waterfall in South America, is just a 2½-hour flight from Caracas.

Venezuela—an independent nation since the early 1800s, when Simón Bolívar, the "George Washington" of South America, helped liberate it from Spanish colonial rule—has an area of about 350,000 square miles; it is more than twice the size of California. In 1990 its population was about 20 million. Venezuelans are mostly of European and Indian ancestry, and they are predominantly Roman Catholic.

Venezuela is a federal republic, with a democratic tradition. Its president is elected every 5 years by direct vote and its bicameral legislature, consists of a senate and a chamber of deputies.

The name *Venezuela* is credited to the Italian explorer Amerigo Vespucci. It is said that when he first saw the natives' abodes along Lake Maracaibo, he was reminded of his own Venezia (Venice): *Venezuela* means "little Venezia."

If there was ever a time for a budget traveler to visit Caracas and to explore this beautiful country, this is it! While Caracas is still among the continent's more expensive cities, you can certainly live quite comfortably and cleanly here for $40 a day. Hotel rates are on a par with those in Buenos Aires and Rio de Janeiro; comfortable double rooms are available in the $30–$50 range. Around town are moderately priced restaurants and many fast-food establishments where you can eat three meals on a budget. Although Caracas's elegant restaurants are above budget level, you can dine in some if you select carefully from the menu and limit your alcohol intake. As for transportation: Cab fares are low; there is the already mentioned metro; and low-cost jitney and bus alternatives are available.

IMPRESSIONS

[Caracas] is one of the most astonishing cities I have ever seen. . . . [It] does not have a center or focal point. It expands like a hand with fingers constantly stretching out and grabbing bits of hill or valley.
—JOHN GUNTHER, *INSIDE SOUTH AMERICA*, 1967

Caracas is brash, bustling, and successful, and doesn't hesitate to let you know it.
—JOHN MANDER, "MEXICO CITY TO BUENOS AIRES," *ENCOUNTER*, SEPTEMBER 1965

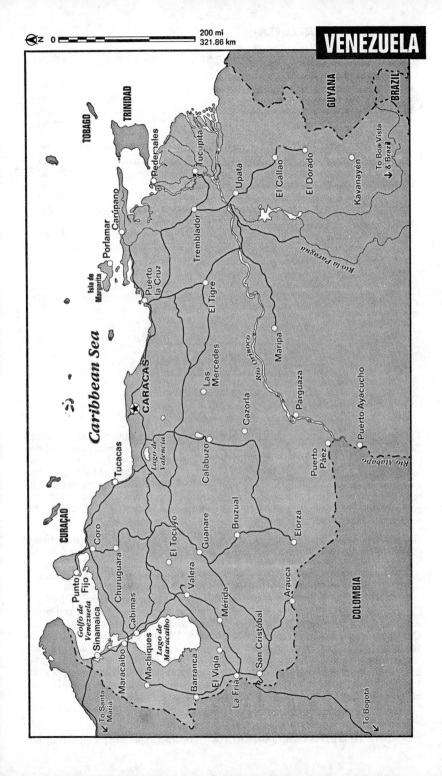

WHAT THINGS COST IN CARACAS — U.S. $

Taxi from the airport to downtown	20.00
Airport bus to downtown	2.00
City bus	.50
Bus to the beach	2.00
Double with bath at the Hotel Odeón (budget)	18.00
Double with bath at the Kursaal Hotel (moderate)	32.00
Double with bath at the Paseo Las Mercedes (deluxe)	65.00
Double with bath at the Hotel Tamanaco (luxury)	130.00
Double with bath at the Royal Atlantic (beach)	38.00
Lunch at La Gaggia (budget)	4.00
Fixed-price dinner at Cervecería Juan Griego (moderate)	8.00
Dinner with wine and coffee at Il Mulino Rosso (moderate)	9.00
Dinner with wine at Il Foro Romano (splurge)	15.00
Cup of coffee	.50
Coca-Cola	.50

2. ORIENTATION

ARRIVING

BY PLANE

The best way to get to Caracas is via **Avensa** (tel. toll free 800/872-3533), **VIASA** (Venezuelan International Airways; tel. toll free 800/468-4272), **American Airlines** (tel. toll free 800/433-7300), or **United** (tel. toll free 800/241-6522). Flying modern jet aircraft and featuring good service, excellent food, and in-flight films, all four airlines offer frequent nonstop flights from New York and Miami. Be sure to check for special fares before finalizing your arrangements. VIASA offers a Saturday-to-Saturday package tour year round, nonstop to Margarita Island. American Airlines also has service to Caracas via Puerto Rico.

AIRPORT When you exit from your plane at **Simón Bolívar International Airport,** the first hot and humid blast of sea-level air will be enough to drive you back into the jet. But cheer up: The airport is in the coastal city of Maiquetía (pronounced Mai-keh-*tee*-ah). The cool breezes of Caracas are only 13 miles, or 30 minutes, away.

In a few moments you will enter the modern, air-conditioned terminal building. Customs and Immigration are mere formalities; the officials are efficient and polite. After a stop at the **Cambio de Moneda** office to exchange your dollars, head to **Corpoturismo,** Venezuela's tourist corporation. You'll recognize it by the orange-and-black sign. The personnel there will provide you with information on hotels, restaurants, trips, prices, crime, and any other subject of interest to you. To the right is a booth for hotel reservations; next to it are several car-rental services. Transportation services are available just outside the Customs area, so that unless you're loaded with baggage you can easily make it without a porter.

The smaller adjacent airport that you pass on your way to Caracas is used for domestic flights.

AIRPORT TO DOWNTOWN CARACAS The least expensive method is by bus, which runs from the airport to the Parque Central, near the Caracas Hilton Hotel but not near most of our inexpensive choices. The cost is $2 for each passenger and 75¢ for each bag. The bus, not air-conditioned, is scheduled to leave every half hour, but its departure time is irregular. The trip takes about 1 hour. You then must take a cab or jitney (*por puesto*) to your hotel. Purchase bus tickets at the terminal. To catch the bus, turn left at the exit and go past the taxis: You'll come straight to the bus stand. Check at the tourist counter to find out whether **por puestos** are available. When available, they charge $5 per person (five in a cab) to downtown; for $1 more, you can ask to be dropped at your hotel.

For a taxi from the airport, go to the orange-and-black sign that says VENTA DE BOLETOS. At this station, you will be given a receipt for a taxi into the city; hand the receipt to your driver. The ride should cost you no more than $20. If you choose to go by taxi, this is your best bet. There are a lot of taxi drivers hawking rides, and although they will get you to your destination without a problem, they will be more expensive.

BY SHIP

If you come by ship, the boat will dock at **La Guaira,** a port adjacent to Maiquetía. A local bus stops at the port entrance, but it does not allow luggage. You can take a taxi to the airport and then the bus into Caracas.

TOURIST INFORMATION

The **Venezuelan Tourist Corporation** (Corpoturismo) has an office downtown on the ground floor of the Centro Capriles (tel. 781-8311) in the Plaza Venezuela.

CITY LAYOUT

Situated in a valley surrounded by the higher reaches of the Andes, Caracas is a long, narrow city that extends for miles east to west. You enter the city from its older, western section, which is dotted with poor homes, markets, shops, and commercial buildings. As you do so, you cannot help noticing the clusters of shacks clinging to the mountainsides, much like the favelas of Rio. These are the homes of squatters who've come to Caracas from other parts of Venezuela and Colombia to eke out a living. The government is building low-income projects for these people but has been unable to keep up with the demand. Moving eastward, you'll see more modern skyscrapers (20 stories), lovely parks, and upper-middle-class homes. As you move vertically from the highways, the neighborhoods increase in wealth. Within this east-west/north-south breakdown are numerous subcommunities called **urbanizaciónes** (quarters). Wide tree-lined boulevards and three major highways cut through the city—the **Autopista del Este, Avenida Libertador,** and the **Cota Mil** (also called Avenida Boyaca).

NEIGHBORHOODS IN BRIEF

Most *urbanizaciónes* are residential and filled with apartment dwellings, shopping centers, and schools. But there are 12 districts that are important for the traveler to know. These are the areas where hotels, restaurants, and nightspots are clustered.

El Silencio and Altagracia   These districts are adjacent to each other in the city's older westside section. El Silencio is highlighted by twin 32-story buildings called the **Centro Simón Bolívar** (Simón Bolívar Center), each housing government offices, shopping arcades, and the city's commercial center. These are the structures most featured in skyline photos. Altagracia, immediately to the north, is near the famous **Plaza Bolívar,** along with the National Congress building and the National Library. Key streets are **Avenida Urdaneta,** which runs west to east, and **Avenida Baralt,** which runs north and south.

Parque Central   This is an expanding modern complex that houses the deluxe Hilton Hotel (and the Residencias Anauco), the Contemporary Art Museum, a trilevel shopping center, the Tereas Carreño Cultural Center, and luxurious condominiums.

San Bernardino Situated in the higher, northern section, San Bernardino is a respectable middle-class section, home of many Jewish families, where several moderately priced hotels, restaurants, and nightclubs are to be found, along with the delightful Hotel Avila. The important thoroughfares are **Avenida Vollmer** and **Avenida La Estrella.**

Sabana Grande and Chacaíto This key area was the heart of Caracas during the 1970s and early '80s. A traffic-clogged street, the Sabana Grande was broken up to allow the subway to be constructed beneath it. When it was rebuilt it was cobblestoned; studded with benches, trees, and tables for shoppers and strollers; and lined with fancy shops and restaurants. By the late '80s, however, Caracas had expanded greatly eastward, and the chic shops and eateries relocated. The Sabana Grande has become a middle-class shopping street, with many fast-food stops.

The traffic that once clogged the Sabana Grande snakes through the two parallel thoroughfares of **Avenida Lincoln** (the main street) and **Avenida Casanova.** Chacaíto, the city's first shopping center at the end of the Sabana, is still a mecca for shoppers and revelers. It has good shops, lots of inexpensive dining options, and several popular nightspots.

El Rosal Adjoining Chacaíto on the east is the small El Rosal section, which is a good place to go to after the sun goes down. Virtually every street in the four-block area has restaurants and nightspots. The major street is **Avenida Tamanaco.**

Las Mercedes In the southeastern area of Caracas is the North American quarter, where employees of U.S. and Canadian companies live in comfortable surroundings. (An estimated 20,000 North Americans reside in Caracas.) Look for the famous Tamanaco Hotel, the city's best-known luxury hotel. Also in this section is the modern **Paseo Las Mercedes** shopping complex.

La Castellana and Altamira Farther east are these two upper-income sections, a few blocks apart, where the night people congregate in late-opening discos, clubs, and after-midnight restaurants. The boulevard that cuts through both of these swank areas is **Avenida Francisco de Miranda.**

Los Palos Grandes Just east of these areas is the Palos Grandes section, where the U.S. Embassy is located. The shopping center in this area is a big singles' meeting place.

Mariperez From this northern working-class section of Caracas, the *teleférico* (cable car) begins its 4,000-foot ascent to Mt. Avila, a sightseeing must. On cloudless days the view of the city is magnificent. At this writing, however, the cable car is being renovated.

FINDING AN ADDRESS For some reason the locals don't bother with street numbers, which can make things *muy difícil* for the traveler. Caraqueños assume that the street and the section (and at times the corner, *esquina*) are enough for anyone. The address for El Carrizo Restaurant, for example, is simply "Avenida Blandin, La Castellana," which tells you only that this recommended steak place is in the Castellana section of Caracas, on Avenida Blandin (this street, however, runs for many blocks). Fortunately, hotels will list the corner as their address along with the street name. Even better, cabbies and jitney (*por puesto*) drivers unerringly know exact locations. So the problem is minimal—unless you're a walker, as we are.

3. GETTING AROUND

BY SUBWAY The metro is efficient, air-conditioned, and clean, with stations marked by the big orange **"M."** Check for your destination on the charts posted at the entrance. Tickets can be purchased from the booth or a ticket machine; the fare is based on distance. Put the ticket in the slot on the turnstile: At the entrance it flips out

CARACAS

N

SEBUCAN

LOS PALOS GRANDES

SANTA EDJVIGIS

ALTAMIRA

Parque Rómulo Betancourt

Autopista del Este

Av. El Ávila

LA CASTELLANA

Av. San Juán

La Castellana

Plaza La Cadelaria

Aeropuerto La Carlota

Av. Libertador

Cota Mil

Parque El Ávila

CAMPO ALEGRE

EL ROSAL

Av. Río de Janeiro

MERCEDES

Av. Orinoco

ALTA FLORIDA

ÁVILA

CHAPELLIN

LOS CEDROS

CHACAITO

BELLO MONTE

COLINAS DE DENO MONTE

Autopista del Este

LA CAMPINA

Bulevar Sabana Grande

LAS LOMAS

Avenida Libertador

LA FLORIDA

Av. Las Acacias

LAS PALMAS

Av. Las Palmas

LOS CAOBOS

Plaza Venezuela

Cota Mil

Parque Aristides R. Ojas

Av. Augusto César

LOS CHAGUARAMOS

Via Valencia

Paseo Los Ilustres

Plaza Andrés Bello

SARRIA

SANTA ROSA

GUAICAIPURO

Av. Andrés Bello

Parque Los Caobos

Jardín Botánico

CIUDAD UNIVERSITARIA

Av. Sucre

SAN BERNARDINO

Av. Vollmer, Av. Alameda

CANDELARIA

Autopista del Este

EL CONDE

Av. Bolívar

SAN AGUSTIN

TERRAZAS DE LAS ACACIAS

LAS ACACIAS

Airport

back to you; at the exit it doesn't. The main line runs from east to west, from Propatria to Parque del Este. It is open from 5am to 11pm.

BY BUS   Buses are the cheapest way to get around town (fare 50¢). They're clean and generally in good condition; enter from the front and exit through the rear. For $2 you can get a bus from Nuevo Circo to the beach. Check with your hotel clerk for exact locations.

BY TAXI   Taxis are plentiful and equipped with meters that start at $1. They can be hailed, but most often you'll spot them at taxi stands.

BY CAR   Because of the fine highway system and the reasonable price of gas, this is one of the few South American countries where you might consider car rentals. **Avis, Budget Rent-a-Car,** and **Hertz** have bustling outlets here (desks are located in hotel lobbies), and rates are comparable at each. Your hotel clerk is your best bet for making arrangements. Advance reservations are usually unnecessary. While a car is a nuisance within the city, day trips nearby are fun and easily accessible. Just as in all of South America, driving is on the right; road signs are in kilometers and international driving symbols are posted.

BY POR PUESTO   The quickest way to get around is by the jitneylike autos called *por puestos*. These group cabs, which are standard sedans, zip along the main thoroughfares, picking up and dropping off passengers constantly. Each passenger pays *por puesto*, "by the seat"—that is, only for the distance during which you're in the cab and occupy a seat, not for the cab's entire trip. Look for the POR PUESTO sign and the destination. Raise your hand to hail a *por puesto;* the driver will respond with his hand.

FAST FACTS   CARACAS

Airlines   In Caracas, American Airlines can be reached at 285-3133; AVENSA at 561-3366; United at 284-4908; and VIASA at 572-1611.

American Express   The American Express Office is on the ninth floor of the Torre California Building on Avenida San Francisco in Macaracuay (tel. 210-522).

Area Code   The area code for Caracas is 02. The country code for Venezuela is 58.

Babysitters   The concierge desks at the larger hotels can usually arrange for an English-speaking babysitter. At smaller hotels one of the staff (Spanish-speaking) will sometimes babysit.

Bookstores   Bookstores in the Eurobuilding and in the Tamanaco and Hilton hotels have English-language books, including best-sellers.

Business Hours   Shops usually open at 9am and close at 7pm or later, with most taking a midday break from noon to three. Most businesses also take a midday break.

Car Rentals   See "Getting Around" earlier in this chapter.

Climate   Nestled in the Andes 3,000 feet above the Caribbean, Caracas has ideal weather almost all year round, with sunny afternoon highs in the 80s and the nights cooling down into the breezy 60s (Fahrenheit). However, in the months between October and February you might expect a light shower on many afternoons. Swimming, of course, is a year-round sport.

There are no beaches in the city, since Caracas is inland. To swim in the ocean, you must take a bus, jitney, or taxi to the beach area, 40 minutes away. There are many public beach areas that rent cabanas for the day.

Currency   When we revisited the city to update this guide, Venezuela's currency, the bolívar, had reached a record 66 bolívares to the dollar. (The earlier exchange rate was 14 bolívars to the dollar.) There was a lot of talk that the government would step in and fix the rate, but that hasn't materialized. Check to see what has happened before you leave. For the purposes of this guide, we have pegged our prices at 66 bolívars to the dollar.

Bolívars, abbreviated Bs (and pronounced "bees"), are now worth about 1½¢ each. There are 100 centimos to the bolívar. Centimo coins come in units of 5 (*apuya*), 25 (*medio*), and 50 (*real*, pronounced "ray-*al*"). There are also 1-, 2-, and 5-bolívar coins. Bills come in denominations of 10, 20, 50, 100, 500, and 1,000 Bs.

If you want to **exchange currency,** try the *cambios* (exchange places), which are scattered throughout the city; they offer the best exchange rate. Banks will offer the official exchange rate for your dollars. Shops, too, will gladly exchange your dollars for Bs with no discount. *Note:* Try to avoid exchanging dollars at your hotel, which will invariably offer less for your money.

Dentists/Doctors   Your hotel may be able to direct you to an English-speaking dentist or doctor. If not, contact the U.S. Embassy for a list of recommended dentists or physicians.

Drugstores   Drugstores are located throughout the city. Your hotel should be able to direct you to one nearby. As in most other South American cities, the pharmacies in Caracas work under the "*de turno*" system, in which pharmacies in every neighborhood take turns being open 24 hours. Should you need a pharmacy late at night, the desk clerk in your hotel should be able to direct you to the *farmacia de turno* in your neighborhood.

Embassies/Consulates   The **U.S. Embassy** is located on Avenida Principal La Floresta (tel. 32-5287). The **Canadian Consulate** is on the seventh floor of the Torre Europa on Avenida Francisco de Miranda in Chacao (tel. 951-6166). The **United Kingdom Consulate** is on the third floor of the Torre Las Mercedes on Avenida La Estancia in Chuao (tel. 751-1022).

Emergencies   In case of a **medical emergency,** call the Centro Móvil de Medicina Permanente at 483-7021 or 412-439, and a doctor will be dispatched to you. The emergency number for the **metropolitan police** is 169 (or call 815-872). To report a **car accident,** call the transit police at 167 or 495-371.

Eyeglasses   You will find opticians located throughout the city. Your hotel should be able to direct you to one nearby.

Hairdressers/Barbers   Hair salons are located throughout the city and in many of the major hotels.

Holidays

New Year's Day	January 1
Carnival	Varies
Easter Week	Varies
Declaration of Independence Day	April 19
May (*Labor*) Day	May 1
Battle of Carabobo Day	June 24
Independence Day	July 5
Bolívar's Birthday	July 24
Columbus Day	October 12
Death of Bolívar	December 17
Christmas Day	December 25

Hospitals   The **Hospital Clínica Caracas** is located on Calle Alameda at the corner of Avenida Panteón in San Bernadino (tel. 57-420). The **Policlínica Santiago de Leon** is on Avenida Libertador in Sabana Grande (tel. 719-151). The **Clínica Cardiológica San Pablo** (cardiology) is at the corner of Calles La Guarita and La Peña in Lomas de Las Mercedes (tel. 922-211).

Laundry/Dry Cleaning   The **Lavandería Automática Bello Monte,** a Laundromat, is in the Piar Building on Avenida Orinoco in Bello Monte (tel. 729-563). The **Tintorería CCCT,** a dry cleaner, is on Avenida Estancia in Chuao (tel. 959-3280). Many of the major hotels offer laundry and dry-cleaning service.

Lost Property   Report lost property to the police (tel. 815-872).

Luggage Storage/Lockers If you're planning a short trip, you may be able to store your things at your hotel.

Newspapers/Magazines The *Daily Journal,* published in Caracas, is the best English-language newspaper in South America. In addition to regional news, it covers sports and stocks and includes theater schedules. U.S. publications are also available. Day-old editions of the *New York Times* are often sold at the Avila, Hilton, and Tamanaco hotels for $3. *Time* magazine's Latin American edition is available on Wednesdays at most newsstands for $2.50. Current issues of the *Herald Tribune* and *Miami Herald* are available every afternoon.

Photographic Needs Film is readily available in Caracas.

Post Office The main branch is on Avenida Urdaneta, at the corner of Carmelitas, diagonally opposite the Central Bank of Venezuela. Branch offices are located in the Centro Ciudad Comercial Tamanaco in Chuao, in the Cediaz Building on Avenida Casanova in Sabana Grande, and in the modulo IPOSTEL on the Avenida Principal of Las Mercedes at Transversal 1.

Radio Radio Libertador broadcasts in English several hours each day. Check the *Daily Journal* for program information.

Religious Services Check the local papers or speak to the concierge in your hotel regarding the times and locations of religious services.

Restrooms There are accessible restrooms in the lobbies of most hotels throughout the city.

Safety Caracas is a big city. Exercise the same caution here as you would in any major city. Keep an eye on your belongings at all times and think twice about bringing valuables with you. Be careful downtown and try to avoid it at night.

Shoe Repairs The concierge at your hotel should be able to direct you to a nearby shoe repair.

Taxes Expect to pay an airport tax of about $15 upon leaving Venezuela.

Taxis See "Getting Around" earlier in this chapter.

Telephones/Telexes/Faxes Telephones are easy to operate: Just wait for a dial tone, deposit a *ficha* (token), and dial. Telex service is available on the first floor of the Centro Comercial Tamanaco in Chuao (tel. 922-489) on Monday through Friday from 7:30am to 7:30pm. AT&T Direct is a great cost saver. For an AT&T direct line, dial 800 11-120.

4. WHERE TO STAY

Caracas has many fine hotels in all categories. They range from deluxe to basic, but the majority are in the middle range. All hotels are rated from one to five stars by the government; hotel prices correlate with the rating. The majority of our hotels are in the three- and four-star range, and most offer private baths. Many of the rooms are carpeted and air-conditioned, and all are well maintained. You'll find the government-authorized rate posted on your door, with no hidden extras. To simplify your hotel search, we have grouped our selections geographically, by city section. A catchall category covers luxury choices, plus selections in other areas. Unless otherwise noted, all multistory hotels have elevators.

SABANA GRANDE

Easily the most desirable area for travelers is this centrally located district. Consider it first.

DOUBLES FOR LESS THAN $30

CRISTAL HOTEL, Calle Real de Sabana Grande, corner of Pasaje Asunción. Tel. 71-9131. 30 rms (all with shower).
$ Rates: $12 double. Major credit cards accepted.
If you don't mind staying in an area known for its ladies of the evening, then look into the six-story Cristal. It features radios in most rooms. We were impressed by the neat, clean, modern furnishings. The entrance to the Cristal is on the bustling Pasaje Asunción.

HOTEL BRUNO, Avenida Las Acacias, Sabana Grande. Tel. 781-8324. 115 rms (all with bath). A/C
$ Rates: $18 single; $20 double. Major credit cards accepted. **Parking:** Free.
The rooms here, on 10 floors, are well worn but also well maintained—and the price is right. The hotel has a piano bar and restaurant.

HOTEL LOS CAOBOS, Avenida Bogotá. Tel. 781-6322. 15 rms (all with bath).
$ Rates: $15 double.
This hotel, between Plaza Venezuela and Avenida Libertador, resembles a Spanish home, with large comfortable rooms. In service and amenities it is basic.

JOLLY INN, Avenida Francisco Solano. Tel. 71-4887. 30 rms (all with bath). A/C TEL
$ Rates: $15 single; $18 double.
The Jolly Inn has been recently refurbished and enlarged. Doubles have private tiled baths, Venetian blinds, and spruced-up furnishings. TVs are available on request.

HOTEL MARI, Avenida Casanova, Bello Monte. Tel. 951-1476. 28 rms (all with shower).
$ Rates: $15 single; $18 double.
The Mari is a relatively new budget choice with rooms on three floors. Units are small and not air-conditioned, but each has a clean bed and a shower.

HOTEL MIRIAM, Avenida Las Acacias between Avenidas Libertador and Francisco Solano. Tel. 71-3311. 39 rms (some with bath).
$ Rates: $15 single; $18 double.
This two-story hotel resembles a private home with a small garden in front. Clean and neat, the rooms are modestly furnished and offer good value. An extra touch is the TV in the tiny lobby.

HOTEL ODEON, Avenida Las Acacias. Tel. 782-1823. 54 rms (all with shower). A/C
$ Rates: $16 single; $18 double. **Parking:** Free.
Try the Odeón, which opened in 1968 and offers rooms on nine floors. Piped-in music in the rooms and good service are bonuses here.

HOTEL SAVA, Avenida Lima. Tel. 781-1718. 33 rms (all with bath).
$ Rates: $12 single; $15 double.
Want something cheap? Try the six-story Sava, near the Teatro del Este. Most of its rooms have terraces with a fine view of the surrounding Andes. Soft leather chairs, modern dressers, and piped-in music make the rooms most comfortable. Doubles, with telephones, are a bargain. The restaurant and bar are very popular at this fine-value hotel.

HOTEL TANASU, Sur Avenida Las Acacias. Tel. 781-1273. 28 rms (all with bath). A/C
$ Rates: $18 single; $20 double. Major credit cards accepted.

The rooms here, spread over four floors, are small but carpeted, and some have tiny balconies overlooking noisy Avenida Casanova. It's a good bargain.

HOTEL TIBURON, Avenida Las Acacias. Tel. 782-8987. 32 rms (all with bath). TEL
$ Rates: $22 single; $24 and up double. Major credit cards accepted.
The six-story white Tiburon offers small doubles (each with shower, bidet, and piped-in music) and singles. Air-conditioning comes with the higher-priced rooms. The best feature is the stunning view of the mountains from the upper floors. Keep this one as a second choice.

VILLA VERDE, 2a Avenida Las Delicias de Sabana Grande. Tel. 72-1092. 40 rms (some with bath). A/C TV TEL
$ Rates: $18 single or double without bath; $22 single or double with bath.
The two-story Villa Verde has recently been enlarged. Its rooms are very comfortable.

DOUBLES FOR LESS THAN $40

HOTEL LAS AMERICAS, Calle Los Cerritos at the end of Avenida Casanova in Bello Monte. Tel. 951-7387. Fax 951-1717. Telex 21-497 AMERH VC. 72 rms (all with bath). A/C TEL
$ Rates: $35 single; $38 double. Major credit cards accepted.
A semiluxury bargain in this area is the jazzy Las Américas, two blocks off the main street. A small outdoor swimming pool (relatively rare in Caracas) on the eighth floor highlights this place, as do the plush rooms. Panoramic windows in the eighth-floor bar offer brilliant views of the city. Further pluses are the restaurant, gift shop, barbershop, and cab service.

HOTEL COLISEO, Avenida Casanova between Calle Coromoto and 1st Calle Bello Monte, Sabana Grande Metro Station. Tel. 72-7916. Fax 71-7333. 42 rms (all with bath). A/C TEL
$ Rates: $30 single; $35 double. Major credit cards accepted.
Open since 1975, the three-star Coliseo offers colorful carpeted and draped rooms. Its Nerone Restaurant offers home-style Italian cooking.

HOTEL EL CONDOR, 3 Avenida Las Delicias Sabana Grande. Tel. 72-9911. Fax 72-8621. 72 rms (all with bath). A/C TEL
$ Rates: $25 single; $30 double. Major credit cards accepted.
Located in a low brick building, El Condor is near Avenida Solano and just a 2-minute stroll from Chacaíto. The rooms are comfortable in size and decor; there is a restaurant in the hotel. Its great location makes this a terrific choice.

HOTEL LUNA, Calle El Colegio. Tel. 72-5851. 67 rms (all with bath). A/C TV TEL
$ Rates: $30 single; $35 double. Major credit cards accepted.
Back at the beginning of Sabana Grande is the slightly more expensive eight-story Luna. This ultramodern hotel, completed in 1964, leans to Scandinavian decor in the large, airy rooms. Doubles have piped-in music and tiled baths (shower only).

HOTEL MONTPARK, Calle Los Cerritos in Bello Monte. Tel. 951-0240. 48 rms (all with bath). A/C TV TEL
$ Rates: $20 single; $25 double. Major credit cards accepted.
The rooms in this yellow hotel, near Las Américas (see above), are carpeted and cheerful; some have small balconies, and all have piped-in music. For $5 you can have a TV in your room. An added bonus here is the rooftop terrace.

HOTEL ROYAL, Calle San Antonio at Boulevar de Sabana Grande. Tel. 72-5494. Fax 72-6459. 33 rms (all with bath).

$ Rates: $30 single; $38 double. Major credit cards accepted.
The Royal is located in the heart of this district, near the Centro Commercial del Este (a major downtown shopping center). Well into its second decade, the Royal, while certainly not luxurious, offers roomy accommodations with draperies and sliding-door closets. Air conditioning is $1 extra. The hotel is a good value, but during the day the area tends to be crowded and full of street noises.

KURSAAL HOTEL, Avenida Casanova, corner of Calle El Colegio. Tel. 72-5714. Fax 72-5715. Telex 27 457. 50 rms (all with bath). A/C TEL
$ Rates: $30 single; $32 double. Major credit cards accepted.

⭐ Without hesitation, we suggest that you head for the modern Kursaal, where two elevators service the eight floors. You will be impressed by the carpeted floors; the private tiled baths (with shower and bidet); and the fairly new desks, chairs, and bureaus in all rooms. There's a TV in the lobby. The hotel has an attractive bar and restaurant. Highly recommended.

KING'S INN, Calle Olimpio. Tel. 782-7033. 53 rms (all with bath). A/C TV TEL
$ Rates: $28 single; $38 double. Major credit cards accepted. **Parking:** Free.
This small informal hotel offers modest carpeted rooms at a reasonable price. Its convenient location makes it an even better value.

SAVOY HOTEL, 2a Avenida Las Delicias de Sabana Grande. Tel. 72-1971. Fax 72-2792. Telex 21031 SAVOY VC. 100 rms (all with bath). A/C TV TEL
$ Rates: $28 double. Major credit cards accepted.
A longtime favorite, one block off the Sabana Grande, is the three-star Savoy. Near the Centro Comercial Chacaíto, it has small carpeted rooms with piped-in music and fine service. Try for a terrace room overlooking this bustling area.

SPLURGE CHOICES

HOTEL CRILLON, Avenida Libertador. Tel. 71-4411. Fax 71-6911. Telex 21203 HOCRI VC. 80 rms (all with bath). A/C MINIBAR TV TEL
$ Rates: $45 single; $55 double. Major credit cards accepted.
If you're on business and have to entertain in your room, try the Hotel Crillon. Each room has a small sitting area, a refrigerator, and a terrace. All are individually appointed with modern furniture and very comfortable.

HOTEL TAMPA, Avenida Solano Lopez. Tel. 72-3772. Fax 72-0112. Telex 24403 TAMPA VC. 140 rms (all with bath). A/C TV TEL
$ Rates: $47 single; $53 double. Major credit cards accepted.
Large, clean, and comfortable is the best way to describe this fine hotel, which almost reminds us of a motel, but much classier. It has its own restaurant and bar.

SAN BERNARDINO

This upper-middle-class residential district in the northern part of Caracas is known to tourists largely because the luxurious Hotel Avila is located here, as are several good restaurants and nightclubs. But it's also a good area for nonluxury hotels.

DOUBLES FOR LESS THAN $30

HOTEL ERASO, Avenida Caracas at Plaza Estrella. Tel. 51-7719. 18 rms (all with bath). TEL
$ Rates: $10 single; $14 double.
The two-story Eraso, in a good location, offers fair doubles (with piped-in music) and singles. The yellow building with a garden out front resembles a private home. The rooms are small, and the furnishings only adequate.

HOTEL LAS MERCEDES, Avenida Vollmer 11. Tel. 52-3148. 15 rms (all with bath).
$ Rates: $9 single; $12 double.
Far older in furnishings and decor than many other hotels is the aging Las Mercedes, in front of the Hospital de Niños (Children's Hospital). The doubles have minimal furnishings.

HOTEL WALDORF, Avenida La Industria across Urdaneta. Tel. 571-4733. (all with bath).
$ Rates: $15 single; $20 double; $30 suite for three.

S We're fond of the pale-white Waldorf, a three-story edifice noted for its large, comfortable, informal rooms and good lobby-level restaurant. Wide, inviting hallways lead to the linoleum-floored rooms. Desks and large closets are standard features.

DOUBLES FOR LESS THAN $45

AVENTURA CARACAS, Avenida Sorocaima at Avenida Francisco Fajardo. Tel. 51-4011. Fax 51-9186. Telex 27359 AVCAR VC. 93 rms (all with bath). A/C MINIBAR TV TEL
$ Rates: $35 single; $45 double. Major credit cards accepted.
Almost strictly for business travelers, this is a great-value four-star hotel, with services that include a pool, a spa, a fine bar and restaurant, and satellite TV. It has a good location near the cable-car terminal.

HOTEL AVILA, Avenida Washington. Tel. 515-155. Fax 523-021. Telex 21637 AVILA VC. 120 rms (all with bath). TV TEL
$ Rates: $45 single or double. Major credit cards accepted.

★ The Avila is known as a home to international celebrities. It was founded by Nelson Rockefeller. Stressing a Spanish motif, the comfortably furnished rooms are a paean to relaxation, with area rugs, plush beds and dressers, and small terraces. It is set in a 14-acre garden park with tropical birds and a pool and houses a first-class restaurant and bar. The prices represent solid value. Even if you don't stay here, stroll through the Avila at least once and note the magnificent vegetation and floral displays throughout the hotel and its grounds. *Note:* The Avila charges the same rates year round and is a perfect spot for a winter vacation.

ALTAMIRA

If you're a night person and like to be in the center of the action, you should consider staying in Altamira. This upper-income area, on the east side, is home to many of Caracas's late-night discos and clubs and after-midnight restaurants.

HOTEL LA FLORESTA, Avenida Avila at the Sur Plaza Altamira. Tel. 284-4111. Fax 262-1243. 83 suites (all with bath). A/C MINIBAR TV TEL
$ Rates: $35 single; $45 double. Major credit cards accepted.
The relatively new La Floresta features suites, each with a small refrigerator. Black-leather couches, draperies, thick carpeting, and upholstered chairs highlight the decor. Most units offer good views of the private La Floresta Park. There's even a telephone in the elevator.

HOTEL RESIDENCIA MONTSERRAT, Sur Plaza Altamira. Tel. 284-3111. (all with bath). A/C MINIBAR TV TEL
$ Rates: $35 double; $40 triple. Major credit cards accepted.
The Residencia Montserrat is a great bargain—with one restriction: You must stay at least 1 week. If you plan a 7-day stay in Caracas, by all means check in here, where you'll find large, well-furnished studio apartments, with full kitchens and baths. A

refrigerator, stove, sink, and glass serving window highlight each modern kitchen; with the abundance of supermarkets all over Caracas, you can cut the cost of your stay substantially by eating in.

SPLURGE CHOICES

CARACAS HILTON, Avenida Sur 25 y Avenida México, El Conde. Tel. 571-3808. Fax 575-0024. Telex 21171. 900 rms (all with bath). A/C MINIBAR TV TEL
$ Rates: $80 single; $90 double. Major credit cards accepted.

⭐ The Hilton, in the Parque Central area near El Silencio, is the city's social center, and virtually every night Caracas's beautiful people gather here at lavish parties. Many professional seminars and government conferences are held here as well. For convenience, a walkway has been built across the highway connecting the Hilton with the Teresa Carreño Cultural Center. The hotel has doubled in size since it was originally built. With tennis courts, a small pool, several restaurants (including the rooftop Cota 880), and a small shopping area, the Hilton is a terrific choice if you're on an expense account or a special trip.

CCCT HOTEL, in the CCCT Shopping Center. Tel. 959-1044. Fax 261-4122. Telex 29815 ACCTV VC. 80 rooms, 122 suites (all with bath). A/C MINIBAR TV TEL
$ Rates: $100 single; $115 double.
Located in the city's finest shopping center, the five-star CCCT is a hub of constant activity. Geared toward traveling executives, it features suites and has an exceptional conference center, private access to its restaurants, soundproof walls, recording equipment, and complete business facilities. It also has a swimming pool and tennis courts.

EUROBUILDING, Calle Amazonas, Chuao. Tel. 907-1111. Fax 92-2069. Telex 27-579 EUROB VC. 473 rms main building, 180 suites (all with bath). A/C MINIBAR TV TEL
$ Rates: $120 single; $130 double. Major credit cards accepted.

⭐ Overlooking Mt. Avila on one side and the skyline of Caracas on the other, the magnificent Eurobuilding offers everything for a complete vacation or business stay. It has two pools, tennis courts, a spa, a gym, panoramic elevators, and two restaurants (the Cassandra features Spanish nouvelle cuisine, and the Verde Lecho serves vegetarian dishes). The hotel also has a cocktail bar, an executive bar, and a poolside bar and barbecue. Thoughtful extra touches include afternoon tea and pastries. The rooms are all tastefully decorated. Although it is just a few steps away from the city's finest shopping, at the Centro Comercial Ciudad Tamanaco, the hotel has its own shopping arcade.

HOTEL PRESIDENT, Avenida Valparaíso, Los Caobos. Tel. 782-6390. Fax 782-6144. Telex 29037 PARDO VC. 165 rms (all with bath). A/C MINIBAR TV TEL
$ Rates: $100 double. Major credit cards accepted.
Beautifully furnished, with wood paneling and Venetian glass, the five-star President has a marvelous Italian restaurant, a cocktail lounge with live music, a gymnasium, a beauty parlor, and a pool with Jacuzzi. The doubles are comfortable and include TVs with parabolic antennas so that you can catch some of your U.S. favorites.

HOTEL TAMANACO, Avenida Principal de Las Mercedes. Tel. 208-7000. Fax 208-7116. Telex 23260. 600 rms (all with bath). A/C MINIBAR TV TEL
$ Rates: $120 single; $135 double. Major credit cards accepted.
Part of the Inter-Continental hotel chain, the Tamanaco sits on a hill overlooking central Caracas. More of a resort hotel than the Hilton, it has a large swimming pool surrounded by a grassy sunning area, as well as tennis courts and a state-of-the-art fitness club. Its shopping arcade has fine shops. The Tamanaco is also home to the celebrated Le Gourmet restaurant, which offers haute cuisine along with a fabulous

view of Caracas; La Brasserie, an American-style coffee shop; several bars, all with phenomenal views of the city; and the renowned Le Boîte nightclub.

PASEO LAS MERCEDES HOTEL, Avenida Principal de Las Mercedes. Tel. 910-444. Fax 921-797. Telex 23127. 198 rms (all with bath). A/C TV TEL
$ Rates: $60 single; $65 double. Major credit cards accepted.
Formerly the Holiday Inn, this four-star choice is part of a small but attractive shopping center. All the rooms are spacious and carpeted. The hotel has its own restaurants, a piano bar, and a pool.

FOR FAMILIES

HOTEL SANTA FE SUITE GARDEN, Avenida José María Vargas, Santa Fe Norte. Tel. 979-8355. Fax 172-312. Telex 27889. 100 suites (all with bath). A/C TV TEL
$ Rates: $60–$75 suite. Major credit cards accepted.
Most of the accommodations are four-room suites with kitchens and two or three baths. There are a pool and a restaurant on the premises. The accommodations go quickly.

RESIDENCIAS ANAUCO HILTON, Parque Central, El Conde. Tel. 573-4111, ext. 304. Fax 573-7724. Telex 21886 ANAHI VC. 317 units (all with bath). A/C TV TEL
$ Rates: $55–$65 studio; $85 two-bedroom suite; $100 three-bedroom suite. Major credit cards accepted.
A new dimension in hotel accommodations in Caracas, the Hilton's first-class offerings range from studios and two-bedroom suites to multibedroom duplexes. They're perfect for families or for the long-staying traveler. Residencias Anauco is part of Parque Central, an urban complex with several hundred shops, fine restaurants, and a theater. Apartments are attractively appointed in contemporary style, and most have balconies overflowing with leafy plants. All apartments have refrigerators; for monthly tenants there are full kitchen facilities, including a clothes washer/dryer. Also, there are a rooftop club with a swimming pool, a gymnasium, and a lobby bar. As an added bonus, guests of the Anauco can also use all the facilities of the Caracas Hilton, which is connected to Parque Central by a bridge and tunnel. With a modern supermarket nearby, you can cut your food costs enormously by occasionally eating in. Highly recommended.

EL LITORAL

If you crave sandy beaches along with the Venezuelan sun, head to El Litoral (The Beach), the Caribbean coastal area. Just 45 minutes from downtown Caracas you'll find calm waters and weather perfect for swimming against a background of mountains reaching toward Caracas. Hotels here tend to be higher priced than our in-town selections, but you pay for resortlike accommodations. Our next selections rival the finest Caribbean hotels anywhere.

DOUBLES FOR LESS THAN $45

HOTEL FIOREMAR, Avenida Principal del Caribe, Caraballeda. Tel. 031/94-1743. 23 rms (all with bath). A/C TEL
$ Rates: $33 single; $44 double.
This hotel is within walking distance of the beaches. Its restaurant, La Gran Paella del Caribe, specializes in seafood and stays open until midnight.

HOTEL LAS QUINCE LETRAS, Avenida La Playa, Macuto. Tel. 031/4-5821. 80 rms (all with bath). A/C TEL
$ Rates: $32 single; $40 double. Major credit cards accepted.
This three-star hotel is renowned for having one of the best seafood restaurants in Venezuela. The hotel was opened in 1974 and immediately became a popular weekend favorite.

HOTEL MACUTO, Avenida La Playa, Macuto. Tel. 031/4-4561. 75 rms (all with bath). A/C TEL
$ Rates: $30 double. Major credit cards accepted.

⑤ Nearest to the airport (10 minutes), this older hotel is noted for its first-rate restaurant and large salt-water pool. The good service more than makes up for the no-frills furnishings. A terrific value.

HOTEL ROYAL ATLANTIC, Boulevard Naiguata Caraballeda. Tel. 031/ 94-1350. 20 rms (all with bath). A/C TEL
$ Rates: $30 single; $38 double. Major credit cards accepted.
Opposite the Macuto Sheraton (see below), this small hostelry has simply furnished rooms. Guests have beach privileges as well as use of the hotel pool (they are also permitted to use the Sheraton's pool and beach for a $2 fee). The Royal Atlantic has a fairly good seafood restaurant and a piano bar.

SPLURGE CHOICES

MACUTO SHERATON, Caraballeda, La Guaira. Tel. 031/944-300. Fax 031/944-318. Telex 395/31165. 492 rms (all with bath). A/C MINIBAR TV TEL
$ Rates: $90 single; $115 double. Major credit cards accepted.

★ The Macuto Sheraton—deluxe in class and cost—has long dominated most tourist brochures. If you can afford it, go right ahead and book a room. It is comparable to the Tamanaco and Hilton hotels in luxury and service. It boasts a private marina, which offers boating, scuba diving, and fishing; two swimming pools; a shopping arcade; a bowling alley; a discotheque; fine restaurants; and, of course, a private beach.

MELIA CARIBE, Caraballeda, La Guaira. Tel. 031/94-5555. Fax 031/941-509. Telex 31192. 300 rms (all with bath). A/C MINIBAR TV TEL
$ Rates: $95 single; $105 double.
The most expensive hotel on the beach is the Melia Caribe, opened in 1978. This ultramodern hotel, only a 45-minute drive from downtown Caracas, is an ideal vacation retreat. All rooms feature terraces with stunning views of the Caribbean. Facilities include both a grill and an excellent seafood restaurant, a beauty salon, a gym and sauna, and a discotheque.

5. WHERE TO DINE

This graceful city justifiably prides itself on its fine international cuisine (including some quite good North American dishes). Caraqueños eat out often, insisting on an imaginative menu and on good service.

Before we offer our dining recommendations, we should describe some of the popular local dishes. **Pabellón criollo** is a tangy main course consisting of shredded beef in a spiced tomato sauce and served with fried *plátanos* (plantains), black beans, and white rice. Equally popular here is **hallaca,** which is usually pieces of beef (sometimes turkey or chicken) mixed with onions, peppers, raisins, and chickpeas and wrapped in banana leaves before being boiled in water—delicious. **Arepas** are tasty, hard-crusted buns made of cornmeal.

Some restaurants feature meats, sausages, and poultry **a la parrilla,** or grilled. Your order is brought to your table in a small charcoal oven, where it stays hot through the entire meal. These restaurants are very popular in Caracas, and there are many good ones.

Before your meal, try the domestic rum, inexpensively made from local sugarcane (our favorite brand is Ron Anejo Colonial Santa Teresa). The two widest-selling Venezuelan beers are Polar and Zulia; both are excellent.

Note: Most restaurants are open from 11am to 3pm and from 6 to 11pm, with the 8–10pm period the most popular. A 10% service charge is added to all bills. Men need to wear jackets and ties only in the very expensive dinner restaurants; women may always wear pants.

Money-saving tip: Avoid eating breakfast in your hotel—the prices generally are high. More important, for maximum-value lunches and dinners, look for multicourse fixed-price meals, identified by the word *cubierto* (cover) on the menu.

ALTAMIRA

CERVECERIA MARACAIBO, in the Sur Plaza Altamira shopping center.
   Cuisine: SEAFOOD. **Reservations:** Recommended.
$ Prices: Appetizers $2–$4; main courses $4.25–$7. Major credit cards accepted.
   Open: Mon–Sat 11am–1:30am.
For superb garlic-flavored shrimp or succulent clams, look no farther than Cervecería Maracaibo. The front is shaped like a huge face; you'll enter the dining room, usually crowded with area workers and shoppers, through its "mouth." The garlic shrimp (*camarones ajillo*), like nearly all the fish here, are flown in daily from Lake Maracaibo. Other recommended choices are the paella for two and the *pargo gratinado al lago* (a red snapper dish).

BELLO CAMPO

EL TIZON, in the Centro Comercial Bello Campo. Tel. 31-6715.
   Cuisine: PERUVIAN/MEXICAN. **Reservations:** Recommended.
$ Prices: Appetizers $1–$3; main courses $4–$8. Major credit cards accepted.
   Open: Noon–3pm and 7–11:30pm. **Closed:** Sun nights.
This rather small restaurant brings a touch of Lima to Caracas. You'll find the likes of *ceviche* (marinated fish) and *anticuchos de corazón* (marinated chunks of heart) interspersed with Mexican fare. We suggest that you stick to the Peruvian food and sip a pisco sour.

BELLO MONTE

PARRILLADA ONASSIS, Avenida Casanova at the corner of Baldo.
   Cuisine: INTERNATIONAL.
$ Prices: Appetizers $1.50–$3; main courses $4–$7.
   Open: Noon–3pm and 7–11pm.
While rather basic and raunchy in decor, this is a fine choice. The Onassis serves two very affordable and tasty specialties, the *parrilla mixta Argentina* ($8 for two) and the *parrilla especial de la casa* ($10 for two). The marisco dishes are popular, too.

CHACAITO

CERVECERIA BERLIN, in the Centro Comercial Unio (Chacaíto).
   Cuisine: GERMAN/INTERNATIONAL.
$ Prices: Fixed-price lunch $2; à la carte $1.45–$4.
   Open: Noon–10pm.
Located on the second level of the Centro, this chalet-style eatery is a delightful stop for either lunch or dinner. Lunch features a hardy soup, a choice of main course from three offered, and a dessert. A la carte dishes include several types of wursts, burgers, and meats.

EL ROSAL

LA BARBA ROJA, Avenida Tamanaco. Tel. 951-1062.
   Cuisine: SEAFOOD. **Reservations:** Recommended.

$ Prices: Appetizers $2–$5; main courses $6–$10. Major credit cards accepted.
Open: Lunch and dinner.
La Barba Roja (the Red Beard) is a combination seafood restaurant and piano bar.
Dining here is a great way to spend an evening. After dinner you can head upstairs to
the bar to enjoy the entertainment and have a nightcap.

BODEGON DEL BOGAVANTE MARISQUERA, Avenida Venezuela. Tel. 952-0146.

Cuisine: SEAFOOD. **Reservations:** Recommended.
$ Prices: Appetizers $3–$6; main courses $7–$14. Major credit cards accepted.
Open: Lunch and dinner.
This highly attractive restaurant resembles a whaler's inn. Naturally, the specialty of
the house is seafood, well prepared and interestingly served. The sauces are light and
delicate. Avoid the shellfish dishes, which are astronomically priced, and you can eat
reasonably. Look for the sail out front.

DON SANCHO, Avenida Pichincha El Rosal. Tel. 711-156.

Cuisine: SPANISH. **Reservations:** Recommended.
$ Prices: Appetizers $2.50–$4; main courses $6–$8.
Open: Lunch and dinner.
Excellent Spanish cuisine, with emphasis on seafood, is on the menu at Don Sancho.
Come with an appetite. You'll enjoy heaping platters of *arroz con mariscos* (rice with
shellfish), grilled shrimp with garlic sauce, and *paella Valenciana*.

FRITZ & FRANZ, Avenida Naiguata. Tel. 31-0702.

Cuisine: GERMAN.
$ Prices: Appetizers $1–$2; main courses $2.75–$5. Major credit cards accepted.
Open: Noon–3pm and 7–11pm; all day Sat and Sun.
For delicious Bratwurst, Eisbein, or goulash soup, head directly to Fritz & Franz. The
restaurant offers both indoor and outdoor eating at attractive wooden tables in a
Bavarian setting. The Bratwurst includes a salad; you might top it off with a fine
Apfelstrudel.

GIRAFE, Avenida Venezuela in the Venezuela Building. Tel. 261-8218.

Cuisine: FRENCH. **Reservations:** Recommended.
$ Prices: Appetizers $4–$6; main courses $8–$14. Major credit cards accepted.
Open: Noon–3pm and 7–10:30pm. **Closed:** Sun.
Girafe has wonderful food (the duck is fabulous), live music, and elegant
surroundings. It's not easy to find, since it is in an apartment house, but tell the driver
to stop in front of the Edificio Venezuela.

LOS PILONES, Avenida Pichincha. Tel. 718-8367.

Cuisine: VENEZUELAN.
$ Prices: Appetizers $1–$3; main courses $2.50–$5.
Open: Lunch and dinner.
Los Pilones is a criolla restaurant with Spanish colonial decor, whitewashed walls, and
wrought-iron grillwork separating the various dining rooms from one another. Ask for
one of the booths, which have high wooden backs. A sliced tomato-and-onion salad
comes with a tangy vinaigrette dressing. For your main course you might choose a
thick steak with a fried egg atop (*a caballo*) or chicken in the basket.

PIZZA HOUSE, Avenida Tamanaco.

$ Prices: Pizza from $5; pasta dishes $2.50–$5.
Open: Lunch and dinner.
This bright, cheerful spot looks like a greenhouse (note the waterfall). The pizzas here
are thick and doughy and are offered with a score of topping choices. Sizes range from
a minipie for one to a large pie with eight slices. Pasta dishes, a large salad bar, and

daily specials are all worth examining further. When your meal is done, you might like to head next door to the Red Parrot, the hottest club in town (see "Evening Entertainment" later in this chapter).

SHOGUN RESTAURANT, Avenida Tamanaco.
Cuisine: JAPANESE.
$ Prices: Appetizers $1–$2; main courses $3–$6. Major credit cards accepted.
Open: Lunch and dinner.

This lovely dining spot has a sushi bar, which will be on your left as you enter. The decor is beautiful, with lots of mats, light woods, and stone floors. The daily menu, which includes soup, a salad, a main course, and coffee, is $4. Teppanyaki, tempura, and sukiyaki are a bit higher.

EL TEJAR, Avenida Tamanaco.
Cuisine: VENEZUELAN.
$ Prices: Appetizers $1–$2; main courses $3–$6.
Open: Lunch and dinner.

El Tejar is well known among Caraqueños for its criolla cooking. It's worth a visit. Sample the *sancocho* or *arroz con mariscos*. Both dishes are delicious.

LA FLORESTA

DA PEPPINO, Avenida José Felix Josa.
Cuisine: PASTA/PIZZA.
$ Prices: Pizzas from $4.50; pasta dishes under $5; meat dishes $4–$8.
Open: Lunch and dinner.

Da Peppino is an informal family restaurant that reminds us of a typical pizzeria back home, but it is quite large and attractively decorated. Crisp pizzas with sausage and olives, fettuccine, spaghetti with a variety of sauces, and lasagne are among the offerings.

LAS MERCEDES

DALLAS: TEXAS CAFE, Avenida Principal de Las Mercedes at New York.
Cuisine: TEX-MEX.
$ Prices: Appetizers $2–$3.50; main courses $3–$5.50.
Open: Noon–2am.

The Dallas: Texas Café features an all-out Tex-Mex menu. Start your meal off with a margarita (what else) and deluxe nachos or tortilla chips and guacamole. Then move on to the San Antonio–style fajitas or maybe the cowboy brisket of beef or an Alamo T-bone Texas steak. Other offerings include Dallas chile, chicken pot pie, and Houston chicken fried steak. Be sure to save room for a slice of Texas cheesecake, peach cobbler, or rich chocolate-chip mousse cake. Don't worry, you can dance the calories off to the live music.

GAZEBO, Avenida Río de Janeiro. Tel. 92-5568.
Cuisine: FRENCH/CONTINENTAL. **Reservations:** Recommended, especially on weekends.
$ Prices: Appetizers $2–$5; main courses $6–$12. Major credit cards accepted.
Open: Lunch and dinner.

Gazebo is probably our favorite French restaurant in Caracas. The fare here is nouvelle cuisine served in elegant surroundings. There's no menu, but the maître d' will explain the offerings to you in English. Silver plates and candles on the tables set the mood. Try any of the fresh fish dishes.

GRAN CHINA, Avenida Principal de Las Mercedes at Calle Orinoco. Tel. 914-023 or 922-042.
Cuisine: CHINESE.
$ Prices: Appetizers $2–$4; main courses $4.50–$7. Major credit cards accepted.
Open: Lunch and dinner.

You can eat in or take out at the Gran China, not far from the Hotel Tamanaco. This spacious Chinese restaurant features an equally expansive menu. The shrimp with vegetable soup is an excellent first course. We followed it with the lemon chicken and the fried rice with duck—both were delicious.

KIBBE, Calle Madrid at the corner of Mucuchíes. Tel. 910-519.
   Cuisine: MIDDLE EASTERN/VEGETARIAN. **Reservations:** Recommended.
$ Prices: Appetizers $1–$2; main courses $3–$6. Major credit cards accepted.
   Open: Lunch and dinner.
For a different dining experience, head to the attractive Kibbe. Its decor resembles a Bedouin tent, with flowing gauze fabrics overhead and mosques and minarets painted on the walls. Undulating music is piped in at lunch but is live at dinner. Lentil soup, baba gannoush, and hummus are on the menu, as are grilled meats. Kibbe has a three-course cubierto at lunch for $2.50.

LA PETIT SUISSE, Calle La Trinidad at the corner of Calle Madrid. Tel. 912-357.
   Cuisine: SWISS. **Reservations:** Recommended.
$ Prices: Appetizers $2.75; main courses $5–$11. Major credit cards accepted.
   Open: Noon–11pm.
Straight out of a Swiss postcard is the best way to describe La Petit Suisse. It's decorated just like a chalet, with red cheesecloths on the tables and bright checkered curtains. The staff are dressed in Swiss costumes, and the menu is no less Swiss. Fondues, beef, and cheese and chocolate for dessert dominate. Appetizers include onion tart, trout mousse, and pea soup. Also recommended: the goulash with spaetzle and the sausage grill with potatoes.

LA STRADA DEL SOLE, Avenida Rio de Janeiro between Caroní and Madrid. Tel. 912-572.
   Cuisine: PASTA/PIZZA. **Reservations:** Recommended.
$ Prices: Pizza $4–$7; pasta dishes $3–$8. Major credit cards accepted.
   Open: Lunch and dinner.
La Strada del Sole, at Calle Caroní, has outdoor tables on a covered atrium, with a large tree in the center. The indoor dining area, which isn't air-conditioned, has walls covered with Chianti bottles and hanging garlic and ceramics. There are fixed-price dinners that change nightly, pasta dishes, and a variety of pizzas.

MAMMA MIA, Avenida Las Mercedes.
   Cuisine: PASTA/PIZZA.
$ Prices: Pizzas $5–$7; pasta dishes $3–$5.
   Open: Lunch and dinner.
The attractive Mamma Mia, between Calle Monterrey and Calle Mucuchíes, draws the locals to both its indoor air-conditioned dining area and terrace tables. Pizza is king here, but the fettuccine and ravioli dishes are popular, too. *Gerente* (manager) Mario advised us that the specialty is *"pasta e pizza."*

PETITE BISTRO DE JACQUES, Avenida Principal de las Mercedes, next to the Banco Venezuela. Tel. 918-108.
   Cuisine: FRENCH. **Reservations:** Recommended.
$ Prices: Appetizers $3.50; main courses $10. Major credit cards accepted.
   Open: Noon–2:30pm and 7:30–11:00pm. Sat dinner only. **Closed:** Sun.
This small French bistro will have you convinced you're in Paris. It's usually packed. The onion soup and crab salad are very good, as are the lamb and fish dishes. House specialties include cassoulet, choucroûte, and blanquette.

EL TINAJERO DE LOS HELECHOS, Avenida Río de Janeiro. Tel. 915-502.
   Cuisine: INTERNATIONAL.
$ Prices: Appetizers $2.50–$5; main courses $7–$10. Major credit cards accepted.
   Open: Lunch and dinner.
Good piano music and dim lighting enhance the superb steak and grilled-chicken platters. You dine here rather than eat.

PLAZA BOLIVAR

GAGGIA, Avenida Urdaneta.
Cuisine: INTERNATIONAL.
$ Prices: Appetizers $1–$3; main courses $2.50–$7.
Open: 11am–11pm.

The clean and cheerful Gaggia, near Avenida Veroes, is replete with recorded music, air conditioning, and possibly the widest choice of dishes in Caracas— served cafeteria-style from 11am to 3pm and with waiter service from 3 to 11pm. For your meal, consider the fixed-price special (about $4), usually featuring a small steak, chicken croquettes, or a generous salad plate. Or try the *pollo en su jugo*, a tasty à la carte chicken dish. This is a fine place to laze over late-afternoon coffee or tea.

SABANA GRANDE

CERVECERIA JUAN GRIEGO, Calle Coromoto.
Cuisine: SPANISH/INTERNATIONAL.
$ Prices: Appetizers $1–$3; main courses $3–$9.
Open: Lunch and dinner.
This restaurant, at Avenida Casanova, has as large a selection as we've seen anywhere, with many fish choices, as well as meats. There is a fixed-price dinner that runs $8.

LA CAZUELA, Avenida Francisco Solano.
Cuisine: INTERNATIONAL.
$ Prices: Full meal (*parrillada* with salad) $5–$8.
Open: Lunch and dinner.
La Cazuela, at Calle Apamate, is air-conditioned. The specialty here is *parrillada* (barbecue), beef and chicken. The fish dishes are also quite good.

DELICATESSES INDU, Calle Villa Flor. Tel. 720-669.
Cuisine: INDIAN.
$ Prices: Lunch buffet $3.
Open: Lunch buffet Mon–Fri noon–2:30pm; à la carte menu 3–10pm. Sat à la carte 3–10pm. **Closed:** Sun.
Delicatesses Indu serves authentic Hindu cuisine, vegetarian only. The lunch buffet features salads, rice dishes, and assorted croquette-type items. The frozen yogurt is especially good.

LA HUERTA, Avenida F. Solano. Tel. 724-413.
Cuisine: SPANISH. **Reservations:** Recommended.
$ Prices: Appetizers $2–$5; main courses $6–$10. Major credit cards accepted.
Open: Lunch and dinner.
La Huerta features highback couches, beamed ceilings, and white stucco walls. Among the dishes are *paella Valenciana* (for two) and *camarones al ajillo* (shrimp with garlic sauce). There's also a fine bar.

PIDA PIZZA, Calle Bello Monte. Tel. 728-069.
Cuisine: PIZZA.
$ Prices: Pizzas $4–$8.
Open: Daily 7pm–4:30am.

Pida Pizza serves great pizza. The large cellarlike setting and the disc jockeys make this a popular hangout with the younger set, who come here to meet their friends and sing along with the music. There's also a Pida Pizza in Altamira.

RESTAURANT NUEVA ESPARTA, Avenida Los Manguitos.
Cuisine: SPANISH.
$ Prices: Appetizers $2–$4.50; main courses $5.50–$10. Major credit cards accepted.
Open: Lunch and dinner.
This attractive Spanish-style restaurant is near Francisco Solano. Its white-stucco walls

and low wooden ceilings create a cozy atmosphere. The menu is varied, with many meat and fish dishes.

TASCA GRUTAS DE SAN ANTONIO, Calle Pascual Navarro.
   Cuisine: SPANISH.
   $ Prices: Three-course meal (daily special) $6. Major credit cards accepted.
   Open: Lunch and dinner.
Stonework dominates the decor, and paella tops the list of specialties, at this fine Spanish restaurant. Music with dinner makes this an even more worthwhile selection.

LA TINAJA, Avenida Sabana Grande. Tel. 723-906.
   Cuisine: VENEZUELAN. **Reservations:** Recommended.
   $ Prices: Appetizers $2-$4; main courses $5-$9.
   Open: Lunch and dinner.
This is the place at which to try such criolla dishes as *pollo deshuesado* (boned chicken), *pabellon criollo,* and *punta trasera.* Daily specials are offered.

AVENIDA FRANCISCO SOLANO

Avenida Francisco Solano may be called Caracas's "Little Italy." For here you'll find one Italian restaurant after another. The selections described below are, we believe, among the finest.

DA SANDRA, Avenida Francisco Solano. Tel. 726-546.
   Cuisine: PASTA/PIZZA.
   $ Prices: Appetizers $1-$3; main courses $4-$8. Major credit cards accepted.
   Open: Noon-3pm and 7-11pm.

S Da Sandra is a new entry. Its casual atmosphere and reasonable prices have made it a fast favorite. The dining area is divided into two rooms, with the rear one doubling as a wine cellar. Among our favorite dishes are steak pimienta, ravioli, and chicken parmigiana.

RESTAURANTE/PIANO BAR FRANCO, Francisco Solano and Avenida Los Jabillos. Tel. 720-996.
   Cuisine: ITALIAN.
   $ Prices: Pizza $3-$4.75; platters $3.25-$6.50.
   Open: Noon-midnight.
Franco doubles as a pizzeria and a fine restaurant. You can choose from assorted pizzas and antipasti to pasta dishes, chicken cacciatore, veal parmigiana, and other Italian favorites. Stained-glass windows against white-washed walls create an almost cloisterlike ambience. There is live music from 7pm on.

IL MULINO ROSSO, Avenida Francisco Solano. Tel. 71-0387.
   Cuisine: ITALIAN.
   $ Prices: Appetizers $1.50-$3; main courses $4-$6.
   Open: 11:30am-2am.
White-washed walls, red-velvet chairs, and Chianti bottles dangling from the ceiling create a very Italian atmosphere at Il Mulino Rosso. Daily specials make up most of the menu. The most frequent of these are fettucine Alfredo, canneloni, and veal scallopine. Also featured are assorted antipasti, which are fine as appetizers or as a meal in themselves.

EL POLLO ITALIANO. Avenida Francisco Solano.
   Cuisine: ITALIAN.
   $ Prices: Full meals $2-$5.
   Open: Daily 11:30am-midnight.
El Pollo Italiano has wooden tables placed in a large rectangular dining area and not much decor, but it has a delicious salad bar and very good barbecued chicken. Half a chicken is $1, as is the spaghetti bolognesa. Pizzas are very popular at lunch; they run $1-$4, depending on the toppings.

SORRENTO, Avenida Francisco Solano.

Cuisine: ITALIAN.
$ Prices: Appetizers $1–$3; main courses $5–$10.
Open: Lunch and dinner.

⭐ This is a top-value, southern Italian-style restaurant. You may dine in any one of three rooms, all comfortably informal. The popular Sorrento attracts a large clientele. You really can't go wrong with any of the main dishes—try the *cotolleta à la Boloñesa* (veal and cheese); the *escalopa de lomito* (steak); or perhaps your best bet, the $6 daily cubierto.

SAN BERNARDINO

EL JARDIN II, Avenida Panteón at Avenida Alameda.
Cuisine: VENEZUELAN.
$ Prices: Appetizers $1–$3; main courses $4.50–$7.
Open: Lunch and dinner.

⭐ Save at least one evening for dinner at the popular El Jardin II, generally acknowledged as having the best local cuisine. Try the *pabellon* (shredded meat, rice, beans, and fried bananas) or the *solomo* (sirloin steak, arepas, and black beans in a spicy sauce). Large and attractive, El Jardin (the Garden) appropriately bedecks its indoor and outdoor tables with fresh flowers.

RINCON DE BAVIERA, Avenida Gamboa at Avenida Panteón. Tel. 518-562.
Cuisine: GERMAN.
$ Prices: Appetizers $1–$3; main courses $4–$8. Major credit cards accepted.
Open: Noon–midnight.

If your palate tingles at the thought of red cabbage and Apfelstrudel, head to the Rincón de Baviera. The sauerbraten is delicious; or you might choose the veal escaloppe à la Vienesa, followed by a splendid strudel or a Liederkranz cheese. The sour pickles are incredibly good.

SPECIALTY DINING

LOCAL BUDGET BETS

Caracas has scores of fast-food stops that are perfect for inexpensive but satisfying breakfasts and lunches. Familiar places such as McDonald's, Burger King, Pizza Hut, Dunkin' Donuts, and Kentucky Fried Chicken are scattered throughout the city. Better still are **fuentes de soda,** which are neighborhood coffee shops; while not uniformly acceptable, they serve wholesome food.

Another choice for breakfast are the **panaderías,** which are bakeries serving hot breads, rolls, pastries, and tea or coffee. Breakfast "continental-style" in a *panadería* can keep this meal under $1.50.

Probably the most colorful and attractive *fuente* in Caracas is the bright **Papagallo,** a large eatery located on the main level (center area) of the Chacaíto Shopping Center on Avenida Lincoln in the Sabana Grande district. Here a king-size cheeseburger, served with french fries and lettuce and tomato, costs $2.50; pizza runs $3–$4. Breakfast, served from 7 to 11am, ranges from $1 to $3.

Doña Arepa, with several locations in town (near the Chacaíto and Capitolo metro stop), is a Venezuelan fast-food chain. It serves arepas, pabellon, batidos, and great coffee. Service is quick and very clean. A quick lunch shouldn't cost more than $2.50.

Probably the best fast-food complex is the **Plaza Broadway,** near Chacaíto and the Sabana Grande. This complex includes a Pizza King, a Tropiburger (local version), and a Lung Fung (for Chinese delights), plus great Wurst at La Alemanita.

Charcutería Tovar on the Sabana Grande serves delicious delicatessen food. Pick up your food at the counter and head to one of the nearby tables. Salami, ham, and pork sandwiches are only $1.25, while a burger platter or Wurst platter will cost $2.50. There are good salads, too.

If you find yourself in the Parque Central at lunchtime, head to the **Fiesta del Parque.** You'll find counters serving burgers, pizza, Wursts, pastry, coffee, and sandwiches. Tables are available.

For inexpensive hamburgers, **Tropiburger** is tops. Two popular locations are Avenida Las Mercedes and the Los Palos Grandes Shopping Center. Try the *guapo*, a whopper of a burger, for $2.50.

If you're feeling homesick, there is a McDonald's in the Chacaíto Shopping Center. **Arturos** is the Venezuelan equivalent of Kentucky Fried Chicken. For chicken that's *crujiente y más sabroso* (crispy and very delicious), it can't be beaten.

FAVORITE MEALS

LA CALETA, Avenida Las Acacias, Sabana Grande. Tel. 782-7243.
   Cuisine: SPANISH.
$ Prices: Full platters $6–$8.
   Open: Lunch and dinner.
A fine neighborhood restaurant (few tourists dine here) is La Caleta. Specialties are the shellfish (*mariscos*) and paella dishes. There is a full à la carte menu, but stick to the Spanish platters.

CASTELLINO, Avenida Francisco Solano.
   Cuisine: ITALIAN.
$ Prices: Appetizers $1–$3; main courses $3.50–$7.
   Open: Lunch and dinner.
Castellino has a bargain cubierto (Monday through Saturday) for $5, which usually includes an Italian main dish. The à la carte menu has pasta dishes for $3.50 to $6, fish dishes for under $4, and meat dishes from $5.50 and up. Head to the main dining room in the rear, beyond the open-sided foyer. We highly recommend this colorful, attractive restaurant.

EL PORTON, 18 Avenida Pichincha. Tel. 71-6071.
   Cuisine: VENEZUELAN. **Reservations:** Recommended on weekends.
$ Prices: Appetizers $2–$5; main courses $7–$10. Major credit cards accepted.
   Open: Lunch and dinner.
For a fun way to spend an evening, stop by El Porton, in the El Rosal district, where a five-piece combo plays folk music on Monday through Saturday. Although the criolla food has won gourmet awards, the prices are surprisingly not astronomical. Try the *hallacas, yucca* (manioc), and *nata* (a sour cream–type spread), which come with all meals.

WEEKENDS, Avenida San Juan Bosco, Altamira. Tel. 262-8339.
   Cuisine: NORTH AMERICAN. **Reservations:** Recommended.
$ Prices: Meals $4–$8. Major credit cards accepted.
   Open: Lunch and dinner.
Weekends, in the Altamira district, is a recommended nightspot and a great place for a burger or sandwich reminiscent of those at home. It's a restaurant-nightspot on three floors, full of young people.

A LATE-NIGHT ESPRESSO

CAFE MEMPHIS, in the Galería Bolívar, Avenida Sabana Grande.
   Open: All day.
For an after-theater dessert, drop by this informal sidewalk café. The sandwiches are also quite good. The Memphis is a big meeting place for single people. On a weekend evening, the party-goers and night people of Caracas congregate here for cappuccino

and music from strolling singers. You can sit for hours and gaze at the pedestrians. The street is closed to traffic, and the tables are placed on the mall.

SPLURGE CHOICES

BELLO CAMPO

IL FORO ROMANO, Avenida Principal. Tel. 33-1164.
   Cuisine: ITALIAN. **Reservations:** Recommended.
$ **Prices:** Appetizers $3–$7; main courses $10–$14. Major credit cards accepted.
   Open: Lunch and dinner.
A big splurge choice among the Italian restaurants is definitely Il Foro Romano. It's worth the trip here just to see the decor, evoking ancient Rome, and the toga-clad (red, no less) waiters. You'll recognize the place by the Roman statues and torches outside; inside, the walls are decorated with bacchanal scenes. Entertainment is provided by a singer, a guitarist, and an organist.

LA CASTELLANA

EL CARRIZO, Avenida Blandin. Tel. 32-9370.
   Cuisine: INTERNATIONAL. **Reservations:** Recommended.
$ **Prices:** Appetizers $2–$4; main courses $6–$9. Major credit cards accepted.
   Open: Mon–Sat noon–2:30pm and 7–11pm; Sun noon–11pm.
⭐ This is a popular Venezuelan dinner choice and a true favorite of ours.
   Portuguese-born David Gomez and his Italian partner, Mario, are usually
   around to tend to your every whim. Try the steaks (*punta trasera* is our favorite)—enough for two. An excellent appetizer is the *cocktail de aguacate* (avocado). A luncheon special of juice, salad, steak, and coffee is $5. The rustic bamboo setting is a delight. Highly recommended.

LA ESTANCIA, Avenida Principal. Tel. 311-937.
   Cuisine: ARGENTINE. **Reservations:** Recommended.
$ **Prices:** Full meals $7–$10.
   Open: Noon–midnight.
Argentines in Caracas flock to La Estancia, named after the famous *estancias,* or ranches, in Argentina. *Parrillada* (mixed grill cooked on individual skewers) is the thing here, served, as per tradition, on a small stove at your table. Also featured are the *bistec de churrasco* (steak) and the *pollo à la parrilla* (chicken that is boned by the waiter and served on a wooden platter). La Tapera, a lovely cocktail lounge, is in front of the restaurant—a nice place for a drink before dinner.

LEE HAMILTON STEAK HOUSE, Avenida San Felipe. Tel. 325-227.
   Cuisine: STEAK. **Reservations:** Recommended.
$ **Prices:** Full meal $8–$10. Major credit cards accepted.
   Open: 11am–11:30pm.
This U.S.-style restaurant is in a converted private home. The Hamilton family sold this landmark to new owners, who have remodeled it, adding scenes from U.S. history and naming each dining area for a state. The food remains first-rate: steaks, roast beef, shish kebab, and a tempting half chicken—with potato and garlic bread included. You get excellent beef (rivaled only by Argentina's), a garden setting, and piano entertainment.

LAS MERCEDES

LA VIA EMILIA RISTORANTE, Avenida Orinoco. Tel. 926-904.
   Cuisine: ITALIAN. **Reservations:** Required.
$ **Prices:** Appetizers $3–$6; main courses $7–$12. Major credit cards accepted.

Open: Mon–Sat lunch and dinner.

The very elegant Via Emilia, once a private home, is one of our more formal selections. Candlelight creates an intimate ambience, as does the live background music. The menu is primarily Italian. *Gnocchi en salsa de hongos* (gnocchi in mushroom sauce) and *penne à la crema* (penne in cream sauce) are both very good, as is the *trucha ahumada* (smoked trout). The dress code is on the formal side.

EL ROSAL

LA MANSION, Avenida Tamanaco. Tel. 331-937.
  Cuisine: INTERNATIONAL. **Reservations:** Recommended.
$ Prices: Appetizers $3–$6; main courses $8–$12. Major credit cards accepted.
  Open: Lunch and dinner.

One of Caracas's more attractive dining spots is La Mansion. Its wood-paneled walls contrast with the central open courtyard, filled with greenery and gently shooting fountains. Meats are featured here. A perfectly grilled filet mignon will cost $4.

READERS RECOMMEND

Checheres, *Local B (upstairs) la Calle, Bello Monte, Sabana Grande. Tel. 723-549.*
"Checheres is a European-style café opened about 20 years ago by Noris Ugueto, a young Caraqueño who is also a professional folk dancer. The menu changes daily, and the "home-style" cooking features criolla (typical) dishes. For $4.75 you get soup, a main dish, bread and butter, and coffee. Extras are natural fruit juices and home-baked pastries. Occasionally wine and cheese nights draw an international crowd. Open Monday through Friday from 11am to 1am.—Judith Blythe, Caracas

EL LITORAL

We've discovered some new and good restaurants on the beach. Avenida Playa, the main street in the Caraballeda district, is lined with many open-air eateries.

THE COOKERY, Avenida Principal, Caraballeda. Tel. 031/91866.
  Cuisine: INTERNATIONAL.
$ Prices: Appetizers $2–$4; main courses $5–$8. Major credit cards accepted.
  Open: 11am–11pm.

This beautiful restaurant is the most attractive and expensive place on the beach. Candlelit tables, with sparkling white cloths and fine service, enhance the meal. Stick to the pasta, chicken, and fish dishes and you won't break the bank.

HONG KONG CHEF, Boulevar Naiguata. Tel. 031/941-656.
  Cuisine: CHINESE.
$ Prices: Appetizers $1–$3; main courses $4–$10. Major credit cards accepted.
  Open: Lunch and dinner.

Hong Kong Chef serves chop suey and chow mein, beef in oyster sauce, and shrimp in curry sauce. Dishes are seasoned to taste.

LA GRAN PAELLA DEL CARIBE, Hotel Fioremar Avenida Principal del Caribe, Caraballeda. Tel. 031/941-743.
  Cuisine: SPANISH.
$ Prices: Appetizers $1.50–$4; main courses $4–$8. Major credit cards accepted.
  Open: 7pm–midnight.

Paella is the specialty of the house. Ultrafresh seafood made it one of the best we've had anywhere. The avocado-and-shrimp salad and the *arroz con pollo* (chicken with rice) are also very good.

LAS QUINCE LETRAS, Avenida La Playa, Macuto. Tel. 031/44226.

Cuisine: SEAFOOD. **Reservations:** Recommended.
$ Prices: Appetizers $1–$4; main courses $4–$8. Major credit cards accepted.
Open: 11am–11pm.

Las Quince Letras is another good choice. It juts out on a peninsula into the Caribbean, with Símon Bolívar Airport in full view. As you dine, you can observe jets taking off and landing; you can also see cruise ships passing by and waves beating against the nearby rock formations.

PORTON DE TIMOTES, Avenida Principal, Caraballeda.
Cuisine: VENEZUELAN.
$ Prices: Three-course meal $10. Major credit cards accepted.
Open: 11am–11pm.

Timotes is one of the beach strip's finest restaurants, located in a Spanish colonial house. There are several dining rooms, all decorated with swords and bullfighting paraphernalia. Specialties here include seafood dishes, with the freshly caught fish prepared in a multitude of fashions. Timotes has another branch in the Cada shopping center in Maiquetía.

6. ATTRACTIONS

Since we're inveterate walkers, we always recommend a strolling tour as the fastest way to get to know a city and its people. You can make a quick visit to most major museums, monuments, and shopping areas while deciding which of the places that you discover along the way are worth a return trip.

CARACAS ON FOOT

Since Caracas is such a sprawling city, we've divided your footwork into one long, leisurely walk and two quick strolls.

EL SILENCIO   This section of Caracas houses the major historical sites of the city. Take the metro to the La Hoyada stop or ask at your hotel for the nearest bus stop, then take the bus marked EL SILENCIO, which will drop you at the **Centro Símon Bolívar** (twin office buildings) on Avenida Baralt. This wide north-south street is the heart of the older (and poorer) Silencio district, easily the city's most teeming and most photographed area.

Once there, poke around the magnificent Centro Símon Bolívar, which houses government and commercial offices as well as shopping arcades. Then head north (left, as you face the 32-story Centro) and turn right on Avenida Universidad, two blocks up; on your right is the impressive **Biblioteca Nacional** (National Library), housing 300,000 volumes, many from as early as the 16th century. Opposite the library is the golden-domed **El Capitol,** the national congress. The exotic vegetation and fountain in the courtyard are worth a look. On your left, the elliptical building decorated with native Venezuelan art is the **Assembly.**

As you leave the congress head right to Esquina Padre Sierra, then right again for one block, and you'll be in the **Plaza Bolívar,** the traditional center of Caracas. This is a restful spot, graced with fountains, lush foliage, trees, benches, and a huge equestrian statue of Símon Bolívar, a copy of which stands on New York's Central Park South. A rich variety of activities will occupy your attention. If it's a Sunday (or a holiday) afternoon, you can join the throngs of Caraqueños listening to the outdoor concerts; or you can browse through the fascinating underground gallery, where you'll see old photos and newspaper clippings of the plaza's history; or, if it's nighttime, you can simply admire the floodlit architecture. Before the revolution of 1821 this was an execution arena.

City dwellers, used to parks with nothing more exotic than a squirrel or two, might be unnerved by the *peresas,* small monkeys that casually swing from the trees here. Don't worry—they're harmless; once you get used to them, they won't distract you

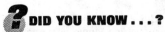

DID YOU KNOW . . . ?

- Caracas is the birthplace of two national heroes, Simón Bolívar and Francisco Miranda.
- The statue of Simón Bolívar in Plaza Bolívar is on the exact spot where patriot José María España was hanged in 1799.
- The oldest bell in Venezuela is in Caracas, in the cathedral in Plaza Bolívar. It was made in Liverpool, England, in 1844.
- In the rural areas of Venezuela dancing is not allowed at weddings because it is believed to bring bad luck to the newlyweds.
- In Venezuela the cowboys are called *llaneros*—"men of the *llanos*," the Venezuelan grasslands.
- The Urdaneta Bridge, which links Maracaibo with Cabimas across Lake Maracaibo, is the longest (more than 5 miles) prestressed concrete bridge in the world.
- The area surrounding Mt. Roraima (2,810 feet) was used by Arthur Conan Doyle, the creator of Sherlock Holmes, as the setting for his novel *The Lost World*.
- Traffic delays are legendary in Caracas. It is estimated that there is a traffic accident every 10 minutes.
- El Salto Angel Falls, on the Cherún Meru River, is the highest waterfall in South America, with a total drop of 3,212 feet. It was named for the U.S. bush pilot Jimmy Angel, who discovered the falls in 1935—two years later, his plane crashlanded on the top of the mountain there.

from the impressive changing-of-the-guard ceremony that takes place every hour on Sunday (and holidays) in front of the Bolívar statue.

The impressive building on the plaza's east side is the late 16th-century **Catedral de Caracas,** the city's oldest church, twice rebuilt after earthquakes. Inside are the vaults of the Bolívar family, as well as several notable works of art, including a Rubens and a Murillo. The large yellow edifice on the south side of the plaza is the **Edificio Municipal** (Municipal Building), an outstanding example of colonial architecture. Ask the guard to let you see the conference room, with its beautiful ceiling frescoes.

Now head east (to the right, if you're facing the plaza) and walk to the intersection of Avenida San Jacinto (one block). Look for the **Museo Bolívar,** dedicated to Bolívar's career, and the nearby **Casa Natal,** a reproduction of the adobe house in which Bolívar was born. Now walk back past the plaza, then five blocks farther along Avenida Veroes to the magnificent **Panteón Nacional,** a former church and now the resting place of Bolívar and many other Venezuelan heroes. Men must wear jackets when visiting the Panteón, which is open daily from 8am to noon and 3 to 6pm.

SABANA GRANDE The Sabana Grande is a mile-long galaxy of boutiques, theaters, and discos running from the Plaza Venezuela along Avenida Lincoln to the **Centro Comercial Chacaíto.** Recently modernized, the Sabana Grande's main street, **Avenida Lincoln,** has been made into a shopping mall—no traffic! You can stroll along the cobblestone street, window-shop, nosh, and rest on benches along the route.

ALTAMIRA & LA CASTELLANA To see how the upper middle class of Caracas lives and plays, save an afternoon to explore the residential sections of Altamira and La Castellana. Any *por puesto* going along Francisco de Miranda will take you there. Start at the Plaza Castellana, surrounded by nightspots and restaurants, and walk two blocks to the Plaza Altamira. This is a pleasant place to pause and admire the apartment houses, restaurants, and clubs. A few blocks off Avenida Miranda (to the north) are the fine mansions of wealthy locals and the Caracas Country Club. The exact streets you choose to walk on are not important; it's the general impression of the area that you get on foot. We think you'll find it interesting.

CARACAS BY SUBWAY

All the major attractions can be reached by subway, or metro, as it's called. The following is a list of the main stops and what is nearby.

CAPITOLIO STATION Located in the center of Caracas, the Capitolio Station is within walking distance of most monuments and historic sites, including the National

Library, the Plaza Bolívar and the cathedral, the Municipal Council, and the Casa Amarilla, office of the Foreign Ministry. Both the National and Municipal theaters are also nearby.

LA HOYADA STATION   From the Hoyada Station you'll step out into colonial Caracas. Nearby are the Casa Natal (birthplace of Símon Bolívar) and the Museo Bolívariano (Bolívar Museum).

PARQUE CARABOBO STATION   Just outside the station is the well-known fountain by Francisco de Narvaez, the design of which was strongly influenced by native art. Parque Carabobo is the traditional meeting place for visitors from the provinces. The Plaza de la Candelaria, home to much of Caracas's Iberian population and, of course, numerous Spanish restaurants and cafés, is within walking distance.

PARQUE BELLAS ARTES STATION   This station is in the midst of what is aptly known as the "Cultural Triangle." Not only is the Fine Arts Museum here, so are the Museum of Contemporary Art, the Audiovisual Museum, the National Art Gallery, the Atenco de Caracas, and the Teresa Carreño Theater.

PLAZA VENEZUELA STATION   The Plaza Venezuela Station is a favorite meeting and studying place among students of the Central University. The Botanical Gardens and Sabana Grande are nearby.

SABANA GRANDE STATION   A great shopping stop, this station is located in the heart of the city's commercial district.

PARQUE DEL ESTE STATION   Away from the noise and traffic of the city, this stop lets you off at the beautiful Rómulo Betancourt Park, better known as Parque del Este.

THE TOP ATTRACTIONS

MT. AVILA PEAK.   The most spectacular sight in Caracas is Mt. Avila, the 7,000-foot peak that rises majestically behind the city. The summit is reached by cable car (carrying 24 people) from the terminal in the northern Mariperez section. Try to avoid a trip on the weekend, when the long line snakes around Mariperez Terminal. Get a rear seat and you'll watch a magnificent panorama unfold as the car starts its ascent up the sheer cliffs of Avila. Houses, churches, and great office and apartment buildings gradually diminish in size; small wispy clouds brush past the car. From time to time the car stops in midpassage, and your heart will probably skip a beat as you dangle thousands of feet above sprawling Caracas.
    The view from the top alone is worth the airfare to Venezuela. You'll peer down between the clouds at the impressive expanse of Caracas, 4,000 feet below. In addition to the breathtaking views, the peak offers an ice-skating rink (it's 10 degrees cooler up here), a children's playground, a snack bar, and an informal restaurant. But, of course, the main thing here is the view. A good suggestion is to schedule an afternoon ascent to the summit so that you can watch the soft approach of the South American evening, have dinner at the restaurant, and then take a leisurely stroll along the parapets to admire the vista of the city by night, transformed into a shimmering multicolored bed of jewels nestled in the dark Andean slopes. When you've lingered with romantic thoughts long enough, catch the *teleférico* (cable car) back to town (the last car descends at midnight). Sit in the front of the car this time and watch the city gradually grow in size until it enfolds you in its noise and lights. *Note:* As of this writing, operation of the cable car has been suspended. Service is, however, expected to resume. Inquire at your hotel.
    Admission: $1.50 round trip.
    Open: Tues–Sun 8am–10pm.

MUSEO DEL ARTE COLONIAL, Quinta Anauco and Avenida Panteón, San Bernardino.
This perfectly preserved colonial estate reflects Venezuelan life of a century ago.

Once owned by a marquis, the estate embraces gardens, stables, a chapel, and a mansion that features a sunken bathtub fed by fresh stream water. It's located in the San Bernardino district, and you can walk there from anywhere in this section. Otherwise, it's better to take a cab (about $2.50).
Admission: 10¢.
Open: Tues–Sat 9–11:30am and 3–5pm; Sun 9am–6pm.

BOLIVAR MUSEUM, Avenida San Jacinto and Avenida Traposos. Tel. 545-9828.

✪ One block east of Plaza Bolívar is the home of military, artistic, and literary remembrances of the life and times of Símon Bolívar. The three-story museum is a fascinating tour through Venezuela's independence era (early 19th century). The main floor contains exhibits of contemporary cannons and armor, as well as copies of the famous newspaper *Correo del Orinoco*, which inspired the revolution against Spanish colonial rule. The second floor is an art gallery; among the works displayed here is an impressive painting that depicts Bolívar signing the Declaration of Independence from Spain. The top floor is devoted to Bolívar's personal papers; it also contains the golden altar on which the great soldier-statesman's body was carried to the Panteón in Caracas.
Admission: Free.
Open: Tues–Fri and Sun 9am–noon and 2–5pm.

CASA NATAL, Avenida San Jacinto and Avenida Traposos.
Adjacent to the Bolívar Museum (see above) is the Casa Natal, a 1920s reproduction of Bolívar's birthplace (the original adobe home was destroyed by an earthquake). Inside you'll see personal belongings, original furniture, and a Tito Salas painting of Bolívar's marriage in Spain.
Open: Tues–Fri 9am–noon and 3–5pm; Sat–Sun 10am–1pm and 3–6pm.

MUSEO DE BELLAS ARTES, Plaza Morelos, Los Caobos. Tel. 571-1819.
The Fine Arts Museum has everything from modern art to old masters, many on loan from private collections. It also has an antique Chinese art collection, a movie theater, a cafeteria, and a charming lily pond.
Open: Tues–Fri 9am–noon and 3–5:30pm; Sat–Sun and hols 10am–5pm.

MUSEO DE CIENCIA NATURAL, Plaza Morelos, Los Caobos.
Located in Los Caobos Park, the Museum of Natural History contains pre-Columbian ceramics and stuffed wildlife and has extensive sections devoted to geology and entomology.
Open: Tues–Fri 9am–noon and 2–4:30pm; Sat–Sun and hols 10am–4pm.

MUSEO DE ARTE CONTEMPORANEO DE CARACAS SOFIA IMBER, Parque Central East Mohedano Building. Tel. 573-4602.

✪ Founded in 1973, this museum is home to a growing collection of works by famous international artists, including Picasso, Botero, Chagall, and Matisse.
Wall sculptures by Jesus Soto, a free-hanging rope sculpture by Gego that spans all three floors, and sculptures by Alejandro Otero and Francisco Narvaez form an intricate part of the museum's architecture and landscape. Temporary exhibits are featured in the museum's eastern and western annexes.
Works by local artists are offered for sale at the museum's artisan shop. A poster and frame shop and a minimall with a restaurant, boutiques, and artshops form part of the museum complex.
Open: Tues–Sun 10am–6pm.

UNIVERSITY CITY.

✪ Located on 400 acres in the heart of Caracas, near Plaza Venezuela, is the University of Venezuela. Originally the site of a colonial sugarcane plantation, the university houses one of Latin America's most extensive libraries, as well as 174 acres of the magnificent **Botanical Gardens**. The gardens—including a miniature rain forest, a waterfall, lily ponds, and cactus plantings—are open daily from 8am to noon and from 2 to 6pm.

PARQUE ZOOLÓGICO DE CARICUAO.
The natural habitats of giraffes, elephants, rhinoceri, deer, and other animals have been re-created in the hills outside Caracas in the Parque Zoológico, or Zoo, of Caricuao. They're joined by peacocks and Cuacamayas, which seem to take pleasure in showing off their plumage.

Flamingoes and other birds add their charms to the park's lakes and ponds, while all kinds of snakes bask in the sun in their private garden. There's also a petting zoo for kids with a variety of goats, ducks, and other small animals. On the weekends, complementary trains offer a complete tour of the park.

You can use the metro to get here. Or, if you're driving, take the *autopista* (highway) Francisco Fajardo west and follow the signs to Caricuao. Once there, follow the signs to the park.

Open: Tues–Sun 9am–4:40pm.

ORGANIZED TOURS The best-value tours in Caracas are offered by **Turismo Internacional Nina,** Torre Lincoln Building, Eighth Floor, Suite F, in Sabana Grande (tel. 781-5188). Trips can be arranged to Colonia Tovar, Margarita, Merida, and Angel Falls. Day and night tours are offered.

---

7. SPORTS & RECREATION

Venezuela's most popular sport is **futbol** (soccer). Major international matches can be seen in Caracas at the 50,000-seat **University City Stadium,** where prices range from $5 to $15 for championship contests. Check the *Daily Journal,* the English-language newspaper, for schedules.

U.S.-style **baseball**—called *béisbol*—has caught on big in Caracas. Helped along by the publicity generated by Venezuelan-born stars, such Luis Aparicio, a former White Sox shortstop, local games draw up to 45,000 fans. Many U.S. major leaguers play winter ball in Caracas. Tickets are $3 to $8. The season is from October to February (never on Monday).

Track aficionados should head to the magnificent **Hipódromo Nacional de la Rinconada,** in the southern suburb of El Valle. Even though off-track betting is legal in Venezuela, the track is packed most Saturday and Sunday afternoons (admission 25¢, minimum bet 50¢). There are 12 races between 1pm and 6pm. The Hipódromo offers several ingenious ways to relieve you of your money, one of the riskier being the *cinco y seis,* or "five-in-six." This means that you must pick at least five of the last six winners.

Scheduled irregularly, **bullfighting** does not have the hold here that it does in Mexico. Depending on the reputation of the matador, prices range from $3 to $20. Check the *Daily Journal* or ask at your hotel for schedules at the Nuevo Circo arena in downtown Caracas. Most events are on Sunday from November to March. Bullfighting also takes place in Maracay.

Prizefighting is big business in Venezuela. A new arena, the **Poliedro,** was inaugurated for the Norton-Foreman fight in 1974. Most events, however, are held in the Nuevo Circo bullring on Saturday night.

BEACHES If you crave sandy beaches along with the Venezuelan sun, head to **El Litoral,** the Caribbean coastal area about three-quarters of an hour from downtown Caracas. You'll find calm waters and weather perfect for swimming, plus a background of mountains reaching toward Caracas.

There are many beaches and towns along the miles-long stretch of El Litoral, but the quality of the beaches varies greatly. **Macuto Beach,** nearest the cable-car terminal, is a popular one, accessible by the "Macuto" bus, which leaves from the terminal. Macuto Beach is jammed on weekends. There are many ultrabasic hotels in this rather raunchy area. Several have open-air restaurants, where you can dine; better still, bring sandwiches. By all means, use the hotels to change clothes.

Most Americans head for the **Playa Sheraton,** next to the Macuto Sheraton Hotel, while most organized tours head for **Marina Grande,** the beach closest to downtown Caracas. Many readers have written about **Los Angeles Beach,** about 3 miles beyond the Macuto Sheraton Hotel; take the bus marked LAS CARACAS. Look for the **Camuri Yacht Club,** which is next to Los Angeles Beach.

Finally, consider the **Camuri Chico Balneario,** about a mile from the cable-car terminal. You can rent lockers and chairs, and there is even a cafeteria on the premises.

Besides buses, *por puestos* ply the main beachfront avenue, so getting around is no problem.

Getting There A delightful excursion combines a trip to Mt. Ávila with a *teleférico* ride 7,000 feet down the other side of the mountain to the warm Caribbean coastal region. The view during the descent to the blue waters of the Caribbean is so stupendous that you probably won't even notice the rising temperatures. The total price is $3 (*reminder:* at present the cable car is not operational). If you have a group of five, split the $15 cab fare. Otherwise, take a *por puesto* to La Guaira. Buses run from behind the Centro Comercial Chacaíto and the OVNI Restaurant and the El Silencio Bus Terminal. The cost is $2.25.

8. SAVVY SHOPPING

The shops of Caracas are as chic as any in North or South America. Few, however, offer the unusual values that we like to recommend. Possible exceptions are those selling pearls from Margarita Island and ladies' shoes. At this writing, many shops have locally made leather shoes in beautiful styles for a fraction of their U.S. price. A good pair of shoes costing $150 and up in the United States could be found for under $50 in Caracas. You may also stumble on a "find" among the rusty swords and other knickknacks touted by local shops.

Most stores are open from 9am to 1pm and from 3 to 7pm, including Saturday.

SHOPPING CENTERS

Caracas is studded with magnificent shopping centers. Among the finest are the Centro Ciudad Comercial Tamanaco, near La Carlota Airport. Others worth at least a browse are Concresa, the city's largest, in Prados del Este; Paseo Las Mercedes; and Chacaíto, near Sabana Grande. **Avenida Lincoln,** the principal avenue of La Sabana Grande, is something of a shopping center itself. This 1-mile stretch holds hundreds of shops, where you'll find samples of all that the city has to offer.

The **Centro Comercial Chacaíto** is crammed with specialty shops whose names are found along New York's fashionable Fifth Avenue—Charles Jourdan, Gucci, Yves St. Laurent, and Pierre Cardin. Styles and prices are much the same as those in New York. You might try **Biki Bou** for bikinis, **King's Row** for ladies' sportswear, and **España** for handbags and belts.

CENTRO CIUDAD COMERCIAL TAMANACO [CCCT], Chuao.
This is the newest and probably the best shopping center. An ultramodern complex, it is home to many of the city's trendiest boutiques. Among them are **Affascimanti,** a great place to look for beachwear; **L'Officiel,** with the latest women's fashions; **Complice,** with an excellent selection of shoes and brightly colored clothing; and **Telas Orbe,** which stocks a fine selection of imported European fabrics. On the second level, you'll find the **Centro de Arte Contemporáneo,** which offers an impressive choice of contemporary art.

CENTRO COMERCIAL CONCRESA, Prados del Este.
The Concresa is a huge trilevel shopping complex, grouping together every type of shop, movie theater, bar, restaurant, and nightclub; there is even a supermarket.

CENTRO COMERCIAL PASEO LAS MERCEDES, Las Mercedes.

The Paseo Las Mercedes is another trilevel shopping center. Some of our favorites are **Elena,** located on the mezzanine, which has magnificent papier-mâché figures, hammocks, masks, and molas; **Selecta,** a purveyor of fine fabrics, specializing in bridal wear; and **El Taller de la Esquina,** which has lovely rugs, ceramics, and hanging plants. For beautiful *típico* items, stop in at **El Artesano.**

SHOPPING A TO Z

ANTIQUES

A. E. LIMES, Calle Gerosal, Prados del Este.

If you'd like to pick up reproductions of Spanish colonial furniture and accessories, take a cab to A. E. Limes. Prices start at $15. Another A. E. Limes outlet is in the Paseo Las Mercedes.

BORIS Y SAMUEL (B y S), Avenida Luis Roche, Local 1, Altamira. Tel. 284-5009.

Among the most knowledgeable and respectable antiques dealers in the city, Boris y Samuel has just opened up this new shop in Altamira. If you don't find what you're looking for here, you can try the main shop in Los Chorros.

GALERIA PRESTIGE, Avenida Principal, La Florida. Tel. 744-365.

Paintings by classical Venezuelan masters, a fine selection of European furniture and silver, and one of the most famous Baccarat lamp collections in the city are among the treasures you'll find here.

ARTESANIAS

Artesanías means "crafts," and in our view the following stores have the best buys in the city. All offer unusual, decorative, and well-made wares.

ARTESANIAS VENEZOLANAS, Calle Real de Sabana Grande.

This is the best place to browse. Vases, ashtrays, carvings, sculptures, hammocks, ponchos, straw bags, religious items, and jewelry are just some of the items to be found.

GUAJIRO INDIAN MARKET, Boulevar Sabana Grande (near the Centro Comercial Chacaíto).

This open-air market is a good choice for authentic Indian handicrafts. The colorful Guajiro tapestries are hard to resist, as are the *mantas,* loose colorful robes worn by the Guajiro women. Prepare to bargain; prices are on the high side.

PRO-VENEZUELA, near the Plaza Venezuela Metro Station.

Here you'll find handicrafts from all over Venezuela, including blankets from the Andes, necklaces, dolls, hats, and ponchos. Basket collectors have a lot to choose from here.

JEWELRY

Jewelry designed with pearls from Margarita Island is sold at every jewelry store in the city. Your best bet is to comparison-shop along Sabana Grande for style and price (18-karat gold pins with a small pearl start at $25).

South America's leading jewelry concern, **H. Stern,** has stores at the airport and in the Tamanaco, the Eurobuilding, and the Hilton hotels. In addition to gemstones, typical Cochano jewelry of gold and natural pearl are for sale. We also recommend the 22-karat gold coins available.

PIÑATAS

Papier-mâché figures, *piñatas* make great gifts for youngsters. Stuff them with small toys and candy—traditionally, the figure is broken at birthday parties. Stop at **La Piñata,** in Chacaíto or at **Piñatas Mary Silvia,** at the Paseo Las Mercedes.

RUGS

For fine rugs, woven by Guajiro Indians, shop at **Tere,** at the CCCT. Prices for small rugs start at about $50. They're original works of art of super quality. We have two rugs displayed in our apartment.

9. EVENING ENTERTAINMENT

Caracas is for night people. The posh restaurants, classy nightclubs, and swinging discos are thronged with late-to-arrive, late-to-exit youngish *couples* (in Caracas, as in much of Latin America, unescorted women and even single men are discouraged from entering most clubs).

THE PERFORMING ARTS

A CONCERT HALL

TEATRO TERESA CARREÑO, Paseo Colón, Los Caobos. Tel. 574-9122.

⭐ The best in opera, ballet, and theater appears here, at a new cultural complex that can rival Lincoln Center in New York. Every seat in the theater affords unobstructed views. Prices are low—$10 is on the high side for an opera or ballet.

THEATERS

The **Teatro Municipal,** Plaza Municipal, still hosts touring companies. Other live theater productions can be seen in the **Teatro Nacional,** Esquina Cipreses in downtown Caracas, and at **Aula Magna,** in University City. There are also occasional English-language performances at the **Caracas Theatre Club,** near Las Mercedes. Check with the local *Daily Journal* for details.

THE CLUB & MUSIC SCENE

NIGHTCLUBS

COTA 880, in the Hilton Hotel, Avenida Libertador, El Conde. Tel. 574-3122.

Cota 880 offers dancing to two orchestras. It also provides a panorama of the city. Open Tuesday to Thursday from 8pm to 2am and Friday to Sunday from 9pm to 4am.

FEDORA, Calle Madrid, Las Mercedes.

Designed like a ship, Fedora offers both live and disc-jockey music nightly. The bar is enormous, and the place is crowded. Open Monday to Saturday from 7pm to 3am.

HIPOCAMPO, in the Centro Comercial Chacaíto. Tel. 725-096.

If you ask any with-it Caragueño where you can find the best nightspot, the answer will invariably be the jumping Hipocampo. Climb to the upper tier, Local 215, where three bands—Latin, mild pop, and mad rock—pound out the beat from 10pm to 5am every night. Tiny tables ring the roomy dance floor, and a red-hued ceiling covers the clinched couples; the lighting is subdued.

The bar, our favorite in Caracas, manages to convey an air of intimacy; it's here that the singles of Caracas gather faithfully. Best of all is the cost—no cover, and one drink can be nursed through most of the evening. *Caution:* Occasionally, on weekends particularly, the Hipocampo offers rather elaborate floor shows. The tab then is a stiff $10 cover charge—so check before entering. Jackets are necessary for men. Open nightly from 10pm to 5am.

Admission: No cover most nights; $10 if there's a weekend floor show.

DISCOS

XANADU, Avenida Blandin, Plaza la Castellana. Tel. 322-336.

Patrons here dance and listen to both live music and recorded disco music in very nicely decorated and comfortable surroundings. Jackets are required for men. Closed on Sunday.

MAGIC, Calle Madrid, Las Mercedes. Tel. 92-8704.

Live music is often on tap at Magic, another of the more popular spots in town. A favorite with singles, the large dance floor is surrounded by comfortable couchettes and tables. You can't miss the waterfall at the entrance. There's no cover charge here. Open Monday to Saturday from 5pm on.

LA MIRAGE, Avenida Principal de las Mercedes, Las Mercedes. Tel. 752-2434.

La Mirage is another good choice for a big night out. Although there is no cover charge, this club attracts a very well dressed and exclusive clientele. The bilevel club has a huge dance floor and excellent videos. Expect a big crowd here.

1900 MY WAY, in the CCCT Shopping Center. Tel. 92-1010.

This is one of the most attractive clubs we've seen anywhere. It's actually a private club. Men need jackets. The place opens at 10pm and has both live and disco music. Mirrored ceilings, hanging plants, and a large bar area make this one special. Drinks are a steep $6—but the atmosphere is worth the price.

PALADIUM, in the CCCT Shopping Center. Tel. 959-3274.

This is another good choice for dancing. It features high ceilings and large video screens; couches on all sides are a welcome sight after an hour or so on the dance floor. The Paladium attracts a young and lively crowd. Open Tuesday to Sunday from 8pm on.

RED PARROT, Avenida Tamanaco, El Rosal.

For a lovely evening of imbibing and dancing, head to the newest spot in town, the Red Parrot. Mirrored walls, comfortable tub chairs, and a sleek chrome bar, plus the raucous music, make this a special spot. When the disco is quiet, the beat is taken up by the piano player. This place is for couples only, and men must wear jackets. Drinks are $3. Open from 9pm to 4am.

WEEKENDS, San Juan Bosco, Altamira. Tel. 262-8339.

Here you'll find booths and tables with huge video screens all over the trilevel establishment. The bar, among the best in town, is a great meeting place. Definitely worth a visit.

THE BAR SCENE

BAR CACIQUE, in the Hotel Tamanaco, Avenida Las Mercedes.

For a marvelously relaxing cocktail hour in intimate alcoves, try the Bar Cacique. Stroll onto the adjoining terrace for a marvelous view of the city below. Most drinks are about $4, but you should try the cóctel Zorba ($3.50), a secret concoction that has won awards, we're told.

EL DECAMERON, Avenida Venezuela, El Rosal.

El Decameron is one of the city's nicest piano bars. The delightful music ranges from pop to show tunes and even a little Latin beat. The seating is comfortable and the lighting dim.

MADISON PUB AND PIANO BAR, Avenida Principal, Bello Campo. Tel. 331-164.

⭐ This elegant club is a very upscale selection; if you plan to come here, you'd better dress up. Despite its large size, it has an intimate atmosphere. The bar is a great place to be if you're hoping to meet someone new. There are couches situated all about, with a large dance floor in the rear. A strategically placed portrait of Winston Churchill overlooks the evening's goings-on. Expect to be here until 5am. Open nightly from 8pm.

EL PALACIO DEL MAR, Avenida San Juan Bosco, Altamira.

The piano bar here is another good spot for a nightcap. It's a little on the formal side, so men will need jackets and women should dress accordingly. Comfortable couches and booths will make you feel at home. For dancers, there's a disco here as well. It is open every night until 3am.

LA RONDA BAR, in the Caracas Hilton Hotel, El Conde.

At this plush cocktail retreat, drinks range from $4 to $5. A stop here should be combined with a nonorganized tour of the hotel, which is almost a city unto itself. Men will need jackets after 7pm.

---

10. EASY EXCURSIONS

MARACAY

Some 70 miles west of Caracas, in what is called the "interior" (Caraqueños call everything outside the capital the "interior") is the state of **Aragua.** You'll spend most of your time here in Maracay (pop. 150,000). The favorite home of former dictator Juan Gómez (1908–35), it is known for its well-stocked zoo and lavish bullring, a replica of the one in Seville, Spain. But what makes the trip particularly worthwhile is the **Hotel Maracay** (tel. 43-62-12)—truly a total resort city. Operated by Conahotu, the 156-room government-owned Maracay offers tennis courts, horseback riding, a free (to guests) golf course, a huge free-form pool, a film theater, a disco/nightclub, and a first-class restaurant and coffee shop. In case you want to stay overnight, doubles are approximately $50 and singles are $40. Another good choice is **El Pipo Internacional,** on Avenida Principal El Castano (tel. 412-022).

There are other things to keep you busy in Maracay. If you are interested in old airplanes, check the **Museo Aeronáutico,** located on the outskirts of the city and open each weekend. Also, one of South America's most beautiful beaches, **Playa Cata,** is a 1½-hour drive over the Andes from Maracay. You must rent a car in town to get there. The drive along the winding road will take you through an exotic rain forest, complete with waterfalls—better not try it at night, though.

Getting to Maracay (via a modern six-lane highway) is an easy matter. Buses ($8 per person) and *por puestos* ($10 per person) leave regularly from the El Silencio district; check with your hotel for precise departure locations.

COLONIA TOVAR

⭐ Anyone for a detour to Bavaria? Just 40 miles and 90 minutes from Caracas is the authentic southern German mountain village of Colonia Tovar, where the architecture, dialect, and food are much like what you would have found in the Black Forest in the mid-19th century. Settled more than a century ago by German immigrants (whose blond, blue-eyed descendants still predominate), the area has retained the customs and culture of old Germany and boasts excellent restaurants and quaint hotels. By all means pick up some delicious homemade jelly. Don't forget to bring a jacket, since the mountain air is chilly.

You can get to Colonia Tovar by bus or *por puesto.* Buses leave from the Nuevo Circo terminal; check for schedules and costs. If traveling by *por puesto,* you have to go from Caracas to Playa Cata and then to Junquita, where you'll change for Colonia Tovar. If you plan to stay overnight, you have two fine hotels to choose from: the **Selva Negra** (tel. 51-415), which charges $40 for a double, and the comparably priced **Alta Baviera** (tel. 51-333). Be sure to arrive early or reserve ahead, as both hotels fill up quickly. There are also several guesthouses in town.

You can also go by organized tour. Every tour operator in the city runs one—the price averages $35 per person.

11. MARGARITA ISLAND

17 miles off the Venezuelan coast

GETTING THERE   By Plane   The best way to get to Margarita Island is by air from Caracas. There are several flights daily by both AVENSA and Aeropostal, Venezuela's domestic carriers. At this writing, the 35-minute nonstop flight runs under $35 round trip. You'll land at Aeropuerto Internacional del Caribe, a 15-minute, $7 cab ride from downtown Porlamar, where most of the island's hotels and restaurants are located.

By Bus and Ferry   You can take a bus from the Nuevo Circo bus terminal (downtown Caracas) to the mainland ports of Cumana and Puerto La Cruz and then ferry across to Margarita's Punta Piedras. Ferries from Puerto La Cruz run six times a day and have both first class and tourist class. Tourist class costs under $7 one way. The ferry from Cumana goes twice daily; the fare is also under $7.

ESSENTIALS   The traditional heart of Porlamar is **Plaza Bolívar.** It's marked by the **Cathedral of St. Nicholas.** The commercial center has two major streets: **Avenida 4 de Mayo** and **Avenida Santiago Mariño.** For maps and information, your first stop should be the **Información Turística Kiosk** in the airport as well as the **Camara Nueva Esparta counter.** There is a **Tourist Information Office** in the Don Ramón Building, on the corner of Avenida Santiago Mariño and Avenida Amador Hernández (tel. 611-954). It's open from 8am to 7pm.

Until 1970, Margarita was a quiet 300-square-mile jewel, a budget traveler's Caribbean paradise—with a terrific climate, endless beaches, inexpensive hotels and restaurants, and a score of picturesque fishing villages to explore. That year, however, the Venezuelan government declared Margarita a duty-free port, and things haven't been the same since. Virtually overnight, chic shops and boutiques stocking imported clothes from France, Italy, and the United States sprang up in Porlamar, the island's capital city. The shops lured Venezuelans in droves on weekends, and it seemed that the island's character would be forever lost. We're happy to report that it isn't so.

WHAT TO SEE & DO

Obviously, as with any resort blessed with magnificent beaches (there are 18 officially listed in Margarita, but we've counted a dozen more), you'll while away many an hour on the warm, thick sands. Not a beer can or candy wrapper pollutes your vision, and the sea is always a clear blue no matter where you swim.

THE BEST BEACHES   In Porlamar, the main swimming area is **Bellavista Beach,** a wide white expanse that extends from the city center beyond the Bella Vista Hotel to Punta El Morro. Rarely crowded, the beach is best for swimming in the morning. By late afternoon, the waters can get choppy.

Heading east, you reach the small but lovely **Playa Moreno,** near Pampatar, a beach distinguished by unusual rock formations and the angel that overlooks the sands and the calm waters.

In Pampatar, a fishing village 7 miles from Porlamar, there is the scenic **Pampatar**

Beach. Boats line the bay, and in the background are the fishermen's hillside homes. A restaurant here caters to swimmers.

Incredibly beautiful is the mile-long **Guacuco Beach,** near the town of Asunción, 3 miles beyond Pampatar. The waves, which are swimmable until late in the day, gently lap against the spotless uncrowded sands. Lockers and a restaurant are available.

Another favorite of ours is the lovely **El Agua** beach, in the section of that name. Despite waves that are truly formidable, snorkelers seem to congregate here. Huge coconut trees lend a tropical look to El Agua. There are lockers and a restaurant here.

In the island's most northerly portion is the quiet **Manzanillo Beach,** where you might like to picnic in seclusion. While calm, the waters are a shade cool in winter.

EXPLORING MARGARITA You should spend a couple of days exploring the island's colonial fortresses, religious shrines, fishing villages, and out-of-the-way unmapped inlets and coves. For this you'll need a car. Roads are generally excellent: Most are asphalt, and road signs are large and easy to read; by following our suggestions, you won't need a guide. You must be 21 to rent a car and must show a valid driver's license (U.S. and Canadian licenses are fine). Rental costs are reasonable. **Volkswagen** and **Mercedes** are located at the airport or on Avenida 4 de Mayo (near the old airport). There is a **Jeep Rental** at Avenida Santiago Marino and Calle Marcano, as well as a **Fiesta Rental** at the airport and on Calle 4 de Mayo. You might want to rent a bike at **Bici-Rent,** on Avenida Santiago Marino. All rentals can be made through your hotel.

Or you might prefer the convenience of a cab, with the driver acting as your guide. The cost runs $40 per day—be sure to establish the fare and trip hours in advance. A bit of bargaining sometimes helps, depending on how busy your cabbie is that morning.

Remember that the Margariteños are invariably friendly to Norte Americanos, so don't hesitate to ask directions from a man astride a donkey or from a woman carrying well water in buckets.

Only 15 minutes northwest of Porlamar, in the village of **El Valle,** is the island's most revered shrine, a pale-blue church housing a statue of the Virgin Mary, reputed to have been found in a nearby cave by a Guaiqueri Indian. Today, the statue is the patron of all fishermen and sailors in Venezuela, and thus many families make pilgrimages here. In the parish house next door is a famous pearl. Legend has it that a pearl diver, stung in the leg by a deadly stingray, offered the next pearl he found to the Virgin if she would save him. He raised himself up and found his leg healed. His next pearl, shaped like a leg and with a mark on it said to resemble a stingray's sting, is now on display.

Some 7 miles from Porlamar is the lovely fishing village of **Pampatar,** the island's main port. Overlooking the harbor is the famous **San Carlos Fortress,** now a museum housing Spanish colonial paintings, as well as armor and weapons dating back to the 17th century. The best site for photos is the drawbridge, where you can look out over the fishing boats in the bay (try to catch the colored balloons affixed to the boats for luck). It is open until 5pm on Thursday to Tuesday. Also, take a look at the colonial-style church opposite the museum; it features a statue called *Christ of the Happy Voyage.* Originally destined for Peru, the statue was unloaded because the ship carrying it from Spain couldn't weigh anchor with the statue on board.

Your trip should include a stop in the state capital of **Asunción** (pop. 6,000), 6 miles from Porlamar; architecturally, it is the most authentically colonial town in Margarita. Look in at the **Santa Rosa Fortress,** which overlooks most of the island. A local heroine of the revolution, Luisa Arismendi, was imprisoned here. A statue of the lady stands in the city's main plaza amid lush tropical plants and flowers. Check the **Museo de Nueva Esparta,** in Plaza Bolívar, for a topographical understanding of Margarita and its two sibling islands. The museum is open daily from 8am to noon and 2 to 5pm.

Couples in love and other hopeless romantics should drive to the opposite end of the island from Porlamar to the village of **Juan Griego,** where sunsets are magnificent. The sky is filled with beautiful colors and blends with the bay and surrounding mountains. A ruined hillside fortress, the **Galera,** outside the town, offers the best panorama.

La Arestinga Lagoon, an inland waterway, is one of the few places we know where you can go to get away from urban pollution and noise. Only the sounds of nature are heard. The area has unusual bird life, a good beach, thick mangrove trees, and water sports. An added plus are the oyster beds—you may even find a pearl. The lagoon is located off the highway to Punta de Piedras, on the narrow strip that connects the two parts of Margarita.

SHOPPING The major shopping streets, Avenida Santiago Mariño and Avenida 4 de Mayo, are lined with boutiques selling clothing imported from Europe, the Far East, and the United States. Items are expensive but less so than in the United States.

Margarita has two excellent handcraft shops. **Galería del Arte Del Bellorin,** on Calle Cedeño, is filled with primitive paintings, lovely wall hangings, and wood carvings. Nearby, **Los Makiritares,** on Calle Igualdad, is more *típico,* with ceramic and wooden masks, straw baskets, and lovely woven hammocks.

EVENING ENTERTAINMENT Margarita is not an island for night folk. There are not many nightclubs, and the ones that do exist are tame in comparison with those in Caracas.

For those who love gambling, there is the **Canódromo** (dog track), on the road from Porlamar to Pampatar. The greyhounds race every Thursday, Friday, and Saturday night in an open-air stadium. Check with your hotel for details and tips.

Of the few discos here, the best are **Doce 34,** on Avenida 4 de Mayo, and **Mosquito Coast,** on Paseo Guaraseo, behind Margarita Plaza. There are also attractive **piano bars** at the Hotels Concorde, Bella Vista, and Guaiqueri.

Bowling is available at the **Margarita Bowling Club,** on Avenida 4 de Mayo, near the airport.

WHERE TO STAY

There are many hotels here. If you don't choose a peak time, such as Christmas or a weekend, you can come without a reservation.

Representative of the accommodations available in the budget category is **Hotel Colibri,** on Avenida Santiago Mariño (tel. 095/78-130). Run by a family, the hotel has 58 small but clean rooms, with bath and air conditioning; singles go for $25 and doubles for $28. Furnishings are minimal, and the atmosphere is homey and informal.

Informality also distinguishes two smaller hostelries that have appealed to us: the 24-room **Hotel Flamingo,** on Avenida 4 de Mayo (tel. 095/61-375), and the 42-room **Hotel María Luisa,** on Avenida Raúl Leoni, Punta El Morro (tel. 095/61-7964). Both offer clean, comfortable rooms, with baths and air conditioning, at comparable rates. The María Luisa is located on a beach and has a bar and gift shop.

A SPLURGE CHOICE

MARGARITA HILTON INTERNATIONAL, Calle Uveros, Playa Moreno. Tel. 615-822; or 574-1122 in Caracas. 291 rms (all with bath). A/C MINIBAR TV TEL

$ Rates: Doubles $100 and up.

You can make reservations for this hotel in the United States or in Caracas at the Caracas Hilton. Amenities include lighted tennis courts, a health club with sauna and steambaths, two restaurants, a lobby bar, a discotheque, a game room, and fine shops. Try for a room facing the Playa Moreno. This is a magnificent place.

WHERE TO DINE

Seafood is very much the thing here, and, of course, the catch of the day is just that. You'll enjoy Caribbean lobster (no claws), shrimp, clams, and crayfish. Prices are very low: A lobster dish, invariably the most costly item on the menu, is $12. The island's specialty is a tiny clam called *chipi-chipi*, usually served in a delicious broth. Popular, too, is a shellfish stew called *zarzuela* or *cazuela*, with a tomato-based sauce.

All restaurants here are informal (nevertheless, most men wear jackets to dinner). Among our choices are **Da Gaspar,** on Avenida 4 de Mayo (tel. 613-486). Da Gaspar features seafood but also serves a smattering of German and Italian dishes. The loud communal atmosphere does not negate the fine service. We heartily recommend the lobster, as well as the German dishes. This moderate-price restaurant is open daily from noon to 3pm and 6pm to midnight **El Chipi,** on Calle Cedeño, is an institution here, noted for its seafood, served at lunch and dinner. The restaurant is ensconced in a lovely new building—look for the flags out front. As a delightful low-calorie meal, try the *chipi-chipi* chowder and the *pargo meunière* or grilled bass.

As a splurge choice, we suggest **El Yate,** on Calle J. M. Patino (tel. 618-708). It's one of the newest and most attractive eateries here. You'll be welcomed aboard by the sounding of a ship's bell and served excellent seafood, especially the lobster dishes. Try the carpaccio to start. Hours are noon to 3pm and 6:30 to 11:30pm; prices are expensive. We recommend that you make reservations.

For classical French cuisine at moderate prices, try **L'Eté,** on Avenida 4 de Mayo (tel. 616-586). The menu at this formal restaurant offers pâtés and mousses as well as such excellent creations as *truite farcie au champagne* (trout dish). Hours are 7pm to midnight; reservations are recommended.

If you like shrimp the place to go to is **Los Tres Delfines,** on Calle Cedeño (tel. 617-757). The shrimp are prepared in several ways, and all are delicious. Our favorite here, however, is the seafood paella—enough for two. Shrimp dishes run about $8; other dishes are less. The restaurant is open all day.

For Italian cuisine we recommend **O Sole Mio,** on Calle Cedeño at Calle Molave (tel. 611-220). This large restaurant has couches scattered throughout and boasts its own piano bar. The seafood dishes are excellent; prices are moderate. Open from 6:30 to 11pm. A self-service eatery that we recommend for all three meals is **Pastissima,** on Avenida 4 de Mayo. It offers an international menu (in English and Spanish) at inexpensive prices. Pastissima is open all day. Tables are inside.

12. SUGGESTED ITINERARIES

MERIDA   This city, as famous for its university as for its fishing, is nestled in the Andes at 5,400 feet. Venezuelans flock here for peace and quiet and the chance to ride the world's highest cable car—to a height of almost 16,000 feet. Locals claim that the trout fishing in the nearby lagoons is the world's best.

The cable-car journey, via four separate cars, will take you to **Pico Espejo,** 16,000 feet above sea level, the highest point of the Venezuelan Andes.

You can get here via AVENSA or Aeropostal in about an hour from Caracas.

There are excellent restaurants and fine hotels, all at bargain rates. Our first accommodation choices would be **Hotel Pedregosa** (tel. 632-505) and the **Park Hotel** (tel. 634-866).

The *teleférico* runs on Wednesday through Sunday. It's an incredible 1-hour trip, which all by itself will make the Merida excursion worthwhile.

CANAIMA & ANGEL FALLS   A visit to **Canaima,** carved out of the jungle to draw tourists to the interior, is an experience to consider. Some 500 miles southeast of Caracas are two camps that will enable you to experience Venezuela's teeming wilderness and natural beauty.

The memorable 2½-hour flight to Canaima passes **Angel Falls,** with its record 3,200-foot drop. If time permits, definitely consider making Canaima a part of your itinerary. Make arrangements through **Turismo Internacional Nina** (tel. 781-5188). It has an office in the Lincoln Building in Sabana Grande.

CHAPTER 3

RIO DE JANEIRO, BRAZIL

1. **INTRODUCING RIO & BRAZIL**
- **WHAT'S SPECIAL ABOUT RIO**
- **WHAT THINGS COST IN RIO**
2. **ORIENTATION**
3. **GETTING AROUND**
- **FAST FACTS: RIO**
4. **WHERE TO STAY**
5. **WHERE TO DINE**
6. **ATTRACTIONS**
- **DID YOU KNOW . . . ?**
7. **SPECIAL & FREE EVENTS**
8. **SPORTS & RECREATION**
9. **SAVVY SHOPPING**
10. **EVENING ENTERTAINMENT**
11. **EASY EXCURSIONS**
12. **SALVADOR**
13. **SUGGESTED ITINERARIES**

Rio is an exciting introduction to Brazil—it has a beat and a beauty all its own. Its breathtaking appearance, which you first glimpse as your plane glides in low over blue Guanabara Bay, is the perfect prelude to this capital of the samba, of nightclubs that never seem to close, and of *futebol* (soccer) matches that rival the World Series in spectator fervor.

From the moment you step off the plane at Galeão International Airport, you'll sense a special tempo in the air. During the 40-minute taxi ride from the airport into Rio, you will be struck by the city's many exotic sights and shapes, ranging from the teeming *favelas* (colorful hillside shanties of the poor) to the sleek ultramodern office buildings, to the jam-packed sidewalks in "center city," where you'll expect to see pedestrians break into a samba. And at carnival time they do. There is no languor here, despite the fact that Rio is a semitropical city whose Copacabana Beach is an attraction in June as well as January. The pace is fast, and the residents have a zest for life. Rio is truly one of the world's great cities.

Get into the habit of referring to Rio de Janeiro simply as Rio. The longer name is never used by Cariocas (the city's residents) and is seldom used in other parts of South America.

To say hello or goodbye in Rio, the standard gesture is thumbs up, which means "All is well," or sometimes thumbs down, which, of course, means the reverse.

---

1. INTRODUCING RIO & BRAZIL

Brazil has a fascinating mix of three very different cultures: African, Indian, and European. It was founded and colonized by the Portuguese in the early 1500s, and the earliest settlers mixed with the Indians, who are believed to have numbered almost one million. Gradually, much of the Indian culture was lost (except for the tribes that still remain deep in the Amazon Basin). In the late 16th and early 17th centuries, large numbers of slaves were brought to Brazil to work on the sugar plantations. They brought with them the culture, religious practices, and mores of Northwest Africa. Their culture blended with that of the Portuguese. Much of what makes Brazil so distinct—its hue and beat—originated with the African slaves.

WHAT'S SPECIAL ABOUT RIO

Beaches
☐ Rio's beaches attract visitors from all over the world.

Climate
☐ Rio is warm and sunny all year long, making any time a great time to visit.

Festival
☐ Rio's pre-Lenten Carnival is one of the most remarkable celebrations anywhere.

Natural Spectacle
☐ Rio enjoys a privileged location like no other South American city, surrounded by a series of hills on one side and beaches on the other.

Religious Shrine
☐ Cristo Redentor (Christ the Redeemer) watches over the city from atop Corcovado.

After Dark
☐ Rio is truly a city that doesn't sleep. Calm sunny days are paired with a frenzied nightlife.

Great Village
☐ Quiet Buzios should be on the itinerary of every traveler to Rio.

Brazil owes its freedom from Portuguese rule to Napoleon. In 1808 he forced Portuguese King Dom João VI and 15,000 nobles to flee Portugal to Brazil. Dom João Europeanized the colony and brought new wealth. When Dom João returned to Portugal, he left his son, Dom Pedro, in charge. A year later Dom Pedro declared Brazil's independence and appointed himself emperor. These acts were not well received by Parliament or by his father. Eventually he was forced to resign and cede his title to his five-year-old son, Dom Pedro II.

In time, Dom Pedro II proved himself a popular leader. He encouraged education and opened Brazil to new immigrants who brought with them important skills that the country needed. Dom Pedro II's rule came to an abrupt halt in 1889 when his daughter declared emancipation for the slaves. However, she neglected to provide compensation to the slave owners, who then led a revolt against the emperor—and Brazil was proclaimed a republic.

Today the Brazilian government is based on the American model; from the mid-1960s until 1985, there had been a military leadership, but in more recent years there has been a civilian president.

Although nominally a Roman Catholic country, millions of Brazilians are inspired by **Macumba** (Rio) or **Candomble** (Salvador). These are African religions, complete with saints (aligned with Christian ones), ceremonies (attended by thousands of devotees), and houses of worship called ***terreiros.*** Some of the mediums through whom the rites are expressed have become so well known that the death of one was reported in an article in the *New York Times*.

WHAT THINGS COST IN RIO	U.S. $
Taxi from the airport to Copacabana	25.00
Inter-city bus	.20
Double with bath at the Hotel Braganca (budget)	15.00
Double with bath at the Guanabara Palace (moderate)	41.00
Double with bath at the Hotel Gloria (deluxe)	100.00

	US$
Double with bath at the Hotel Apa (beach/moderate)	30.00
Double with bath at the Hotel Everest Park (beach/deluxe)	80.00
Dinner at Leiteria Mineira (budget)	8.00
Dinner with wine at Terraco Atlântico (moderate)	12.00
Dinner with wine at Antiquarius (expensive)	22.00

2. ORIENTATION

ARRIVING

BY PLANE   International flights arrive at **Galeão International Airport,** an air-conditioned, well-organized modern facility with a duty-free shop. After you pick up your bags, head to the Customs area. There you'll press a button that randomly turns on either a green or a red light. If it's green, you can just proceed; if it's red, you must stop for a polite spot check of your bags.

Next, step outside, where two rival **taxi** companies (Cootramo and Transcoopass) provide cab service to Copacabana for about $25 and to Leblon or Gavea for about $30. (You purchase taxi tickets at the airport terminal as you exit and give your ticket to the waiting cabbie.) If you're traveling light, you can take **bus** no. 322, 324, or 328 downtown for a fare of about 50¢.

There are two special buses leaving the international airport. One heads to Santos Dumont Airport, where domestic flights usually originate, and the other heads to the Barra area, each for under $1.50. Look for the bus marked AEROPORTO INTERNACIONAL-ALVORADA.

TOURIST INFORMATION

The tourist information booth at the airport, on the first floor of Section C, is open daily from 5am to 11pm (tel. 398-4073). In Copacabana, maps and information are available at the **RioTur** office, Rua Princesa Isabela 183 (tel. 541-7522), open daily from 9am to 9pm. **Embratur,** Rua Maria e Barros 13 (tel. 273-2212), another good source of information, is open daily from 9am to 6pm.

CITY LAYOUT

Dominating the southwest side of the city and guarding the entrance to Guanabara Bay is the famous **Pão de Açúcar** (Sugarloaf), a mountain shaped like a giant brown gumdrop. Look for the 1,230-foot-high peak—at the end of the beach area—as your plane circles before landing. If you're a climber, try scaling it. A British woman was the first to do it—some 150 years ago. You can also reach the top by cable car (see "Attractions," below).

IMPRESSIONS

Rio de Janeiro is the world's most beautiful city and the worst thing that has ever happened to Brazilians.
—HERNANE TAVERS DA SÁ, *THE BRAZILIANS: PEOPLE OF TOMORROW,* 1947

It is hard for man to make any city worthy of such surroundings as Nature has given to Rio.
—JAMES BRYCE, *SOUTH AMERICA,* 1912

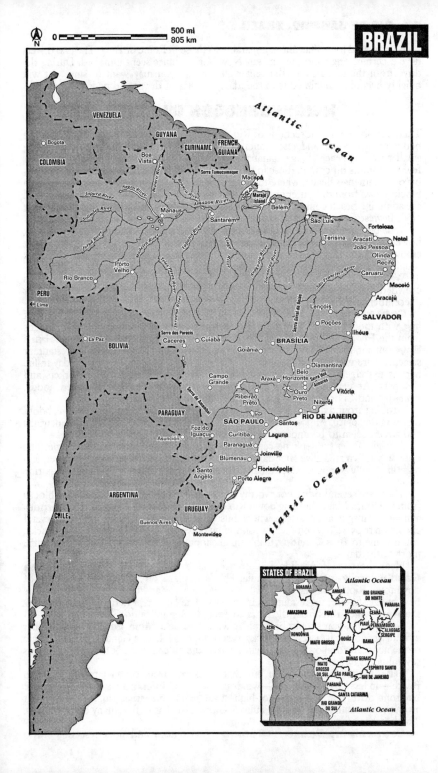

BRAZIL

0 — 500 mi
— 805 km

STATES OF BRAZIL

Be prepared for traffic jams comparable to those in Rome or Paris. The taxi drivers have a certain originality that makes New York cabbies seem inhibited. During the drive from the airport into the center city, where you may want to stay, you will quickly become acquainted with the idiosyncrasies of driver and pedestrian alike.

NEIGHBORHOODS IN BRIEF

There are six important sections of Rio you need to know: **center city,** where the better budget hotels and restaurants are located; **Flamengo Beach,** a charming small stretch of beach along Guanabara Bay, where there are several budget hotels but few restaurants other than those in the hotels; world-famous **Copacabana Beach,** beyond Flamengo Beach, where there are several good-value hotels and restaurants a block or two from the glitter of the beachfront and its $200-a-day establishments; and the adjoining beach communities of **Ipanema, Leblon,** and **Vidigal,** which are the city's newest commercial and residential areas.

Your best bet for movies, theater, shopping, and sightseeing is downtown Rio. If, however, you crave quiet, try a Flamengo hotel; if you like hectic nightlife and rubbing elbows with the wealthy, then stay at one of our beach choices. Budget-hotel rates are roughly the same in all of these sections.

We prefer staying in Ipanema or Copacabana. These sections are somewhat less crowded than downtown, and the restaurants there are generally better. In summer (December to February), it's a shade cooler, too.

Center City   To orient yourself rapidly to downtown Rio, familiarize yourself first with the important **Avenida Rio Branco,** a wide thoroughfare that extends from the **Praça (Plaza) Mauá** (dock area) just over a mile south to **Guanabara Bay,** not far from Flamengo Beach; most of our center-city hotel and restaurant selections are within walking distance of Avenida Rio Branco. During the day traffic here is extremely heavy, and the sidewalks are crowded with office workers and shoppers. At nearly every corner there's a Bahian woman selling baked goods. Everyone moves briskly. The pace is much like that of New York.

Strolling around downtown, you'll be conscious of the tremendous building boom that is taking place. Almost every block has a construction project, and the sidewalks and streets seem to be undergoing endless repair.

At night, quiet suddenly descends as the cars and pedestrians head for home. The only downtown area alive after dark is the movie district, **Cinelandia.** However, Rio nightlife really jumps in Copacabana, Ipanema, and Leblon, a 20-minute bus ride away.

There are several other noteworthy center-city streets and areas. First, five blocks from the Praça Mauá, heading down Rio Branco, is **Avenida Presidente Vargas,** a major transportation artery where buses leave for the beaches and for several excursion trips we'll recommend. Continuing down Rio Branco for four more blocks, you'll come to **Rua Ouvidor,** Rio's main shopping street, which is closed to traffic most of the day.

Near the end of Avenida Rio Branco, off to the right, is **Praça Mahatma Gandhi,** locally known as Cinelandia. This large plaza, often considered the heart of downtown Rio, is the hub of several bus lines. Nearby are the movie district and the best budget hotels and restaurants in the city. The key street here is **Rua Senador Dantas,** which runs from the plaza to Avenida República do Chile.

And, finally, you should be familiar with **Avenida Mem de Sá,** in the higher altitude section of Rio, several blocks west of Praça Mahatma Gandhi, behind the site of the new cathedral of Rio de Janeiro. This is the older section of the city, which has several good budget hotels.

Flamengo Beach   The bus that takes you from center city to Flamengo Beach—in less than 10 minutes—winds its way along **Avenida Beira Mar,** a scenic bayfront drive that has 150-foot-high royal palms on either side. This tiny but attractive community houses the famous Gloria Hotel as well as many budget hotels. The beaches are free and open to the public.

Copacabana Beach and Leme   An exclusive and modern section of Rio is Copacabana Beach, a sightseeing must. If you have time, go for a swim—it's free. The cool water is a deep blue, and as you enjoy the ocean, glancing now and then at the plush beachfront hotels, you'll feel for an instant like one of the millionaires strolling along **Avenida Atlântica.**

Copacabana is less than 20 minutes from downtown Rio by bus, which you can catch at the intersection of Rio Branco and Presidente Vargas or at the Praça Mahatma Gandhi. The fare is about 50¢. It's an enchanting drive: The bus follows the bayfront, in and out of tunnels, with the blue of the Atlantic on the left and the splendor of the royal palms on the right.

For budget hotels, stick to **Avenida Copacabana,** one block from the beach. Many of our restaurant and nightclub selections, as well as the largest stores, are here.

Ipanema and Leblon   Just beyond Copacabana is the modern beach community of Ipanema. The main streets to remember are **Avenida Vieira Souto,** on the beachfront, and **Visconde de Pirajá,** two blocks inland, where some of the city's finest shops are located. Two popular meeting points are the **Praça General Osorio** and **Praça Nossa Senhora de Paz.**

Leblon, the next beach area, is separated from Ipanema by a canal. **Avenida Delfim Moreira** is the beachfront street, while **Ataulfo de Paiva** is the principal commercial thoroughfare.

Vidigal   Just south of Leblon are the beach communities that house three of Rio's most elegant hotels: the Sheraton (closest to Leblon in Vidigal), the Inter-Continental (in São Conrado), and the Nacional (across the street). The beachfront street is **Avenida Niemeyer.** Beyond them lies **Barra da Tijuca,** a lovely beach area rapidly being developed as a residential and commercial hub. The principal avenue in Barra is Sernambetiba.

The Lagoon   The center of Rio houses **Lagoa Rodrigo de Freitas,** which is particularly lovely at night. Located behind Ipanema and Leblon, the Jockey Club Racetrack and Tivoli amusement park are landmarks.

FINDING AN ADDRESS   Streets in downtown Rio—as throughout South America—are named after famous people, events, and dates. The people so honored are not limited to Brazilian heroes. Don't be surprised when you come across streets named after Woodrow Wilson; Franklin D. Roosevelt; and even Medgar Evers, the slain U.S. civil rights leader. Street signs at each corner note both the name of the avenue and the house numbers on that block, with an arrow indicating which way the numbers run.

3. GETTING AROUND

BY BUS   The best way to travel around Rio is by bus—buses are cheap (about 20¢), quick, and plentiful. You enter at the rear, pay, and receive a token, the color varying with your destination. Since the exit door is in front, it is best to gradually work your way forward to avoid a last-minute crush. Incidentally, no matter how hot and crowded the buses are, the even-tempered Carioca is invariably calm and polite. However, on a crowded bus here, as elsewhere, beware of pickpockets.

Important bus stations are at Praça Mauá, on Presidente Vargas just off Rio Branco, along Rio Branco, and at Praça Mahatma Gandhi.

The major bus terminal is the **Rodoviária Novo Rio,** located near the start of Avenida Brasil. Bus no. 123 will get you there. Buses leave hourly from here to São Paulo (seven hours away; the fare is $10.50); to Petropolis ($2.50) every 15 minutes; and even to Brasília.

BY TAXI   Taxis (usually Volkswagens) are easy to come by (just wave your arm), and they are cheap, even though rates jump 20% between 11pm and 6am. A cab from Praça Mahatma Gandhi to Copacabana Beach should cost about $5 during the day and $7 after 11pm. Although taxis are required to post an accurate rate chart, frequently they do not. If you feel you're being overcharged, ask to see the driver's rate chart.

BY CAR If you want to rent a car, try **Hertz,** at Avenida Princesa Isabel 344 (tel. 275-4996), in Copacabana. A VW will cost $50 per day, plus 50¢ per kilometer; a Super VW goes for $60 per day and 80¢ per kilometer. **Budget** has an office down the street, at Avenida Princesa Isabel 350 (tel. 275-3244). Because taxis are so plentiful and Rio has unusual traffic patterns, we don't recommend that you rent a car for driving in the city.

FAST RIO

Airline Offices The American Airlines Office is downtown at Avenida Presidente Wilson 165 (tel. 210-3126). United is also downtown at Avenida Beira Mar 200 (tel. 220-3821). The Brazilian airline Varig has several offices: The downtown office is at Avenida Rio Branco 277 (220-3821); the Copacabana office is at Rua Rodolfo Dantas 16/A (tel. 541-6343); and the Ipanema office is at Rua Visconde de Pirajá 351/D (tel. 287-9440).

American Express The American Express office is at Praia de Botafogo (Botafogo Beach) no. 228, 514 Bl. A. (tel. 552-7299 or 552-2243). Cardholders can call toll free 011/800-5050.

Area Code Rio's telephone area code is 021.

Babysitters Child care is provided at most five-star hotels. The concierge at your hotel may be able to help you arrange for a babysitter.

Bookstores The **Livraria Kosmos,** Rua Rosario 135–137, charges about 50% above U.S. prices for English-language paperbacks. If you're in Rio during carnival season, pick up a copy of *Escolas de Samba* (*The Samba Schools*), a good background study, in English, of this local phenomenon ($3). You can buy English-language books at the airport shop, too, along with copies of *Time* and *Newsweek*.

Business Hours Banks are open Monday through Friday from 10am to 4:30pm. Most **stores** are open Monday through Friday from 9am to 7pm, until 1pm on Saturday.

Car Rentals See "Getting Around," above.

Climate Semitropical Rio is warm enough for swimming all year round. In many respects, the climate resembles Puerto Rico's. The best period for travelers is April through November, which is the dry winter season, when afternoon temperatures hover around 80°F. Evenings then are delightfully cool. The summer rainy season (December to March) is only slightly warmer but far more humid. The mercury seldom rises above the mid-80s. Remember that this latter period is vacation time in South America, and many Brazilians and other nationals flock to Rio—especially during the frenetic carnival season in February.

Currency For the past decade, the Brazilian currency, the *cruzeiro,* tended to decline in value in relation to the U.S. dollar. In a superficial sense, the traveler has benefited by being able to purchase more Brazilian money for his or her dollar. But in reality galloping inflation has eroded the cruzeiro's purchasing power. Prices became totally unpredictable, since one's costs were affected by the swing of the currency devaluation versus inflation rate. Further complicating the situation was the frequent discrepancy between the official rate and the world (parallel-market) rates of exchange. The discrepancy could be as much as 30%, 40%, or even 300%; the average is 12%.

In early 1986 the cruzeiro soared to as much as 17,000 per US$1, with the parallel-market exchange rate exceeding 20,000 to the dollar. Later that year, under Brazil's first democratic government since 1964, a bold new economic policy was inaugurated. The *cruzado* replaced the cruzeiro, with each cruzado worth 1,000 old cruzeiros. By early 1989 the situation had again become reversed. Inflation had hit

RIO ORIENTATION

SANTO CRISTO

Marechal Floriano
Av. Presidente Vargas
Buenos Aires
Pres. Kubitschek
Campo de Santana
CENTRO
Nilo Peçanha
Av. Rio Branco
Av. G. Justo
República
Dantes
Av. do Chile

Av. Mem de Sá

LAPA

Praça Mahatma Gandhi

Av. Beira Mar

Guanabara Bay

TUNNEL

Av. Augusto Severo

Av. Infante don Henrique

GLÓRIA

Praia do Flamengo

CATETE

FLAMENGO

TUNNEL

❶ Praia de Botafogo

Av. João-Luiz Alves

URCA **PÃO DE AÇÚCAR**

✝ TUNNEL

Av. Pasteur

Av. Portugal

CORCOVADO MTN.

Nações Unidas

❷

ⓘ

Jardim Botânico

BOTAFOGO

Praia Vermelha

LEME

Rodrigo de Freitas Lake

Praia do Leme

COPACABANA

Praia de Copacabana

Ocean

Av. Atlântica

IPANEMA

Praça General Osório

Av. Vieira Souto

Praia de Ipanema

Atlantic

Information ⓘ

Church ✝

American Express ❶
Cable Car ❷
Santos Dumont Airport ❸

900%; and Brazil introduced a new monetary unit, the **cruzado novo,** with each cruzado novo worth 1,000 old cruzados. Once again, inflation became rampant, surpassing 1760%. In March 1990 the new president, Fernando Collor de Mello, replaced the cruzado novo with the resurrected **cruzeiro.** At this writing US$1 will purchase 7,700 cruzeiros. Since there are still some old cruzado bills in circulation, be aware that each old 1,000-cruzado note is now equal to 1 cruzeiro.

We recommend that you change only small amounts of dollars into cruzeiros on an as-needed basis, since exchange rates might not be favorable for changing your left-over Brazilian money back into dollars.

Be sure to *check the exchange rate prior to your visit,* so that you'll have a better idea how far your dollars will stretch. By the way, the dollar sign is widely used in South America, but you should not assume it refers to U.S. dollars. More likely it indicates pesos, sucres, or cruzeiros.

Currency Exchange Try **Belle Tours** in the Casino Atlântico at Avenida Atlântica 4240 (tel. 267-2944). **Casa Piano** has several branches throughout the city, including Visconde de Pirajá 365 in Ipanema (tel. 267-4615).

Dentists/Doctors The concierge at your hotel may be able to direct you to an English-speaking dentist; you can also contact the U.S. consulate for a list of English-speaking dentists. For a doctor, call 236-2887, 24 hours a day.

Drugstores U.S. drugs are sold all over Rio. One store popular with North American travelers is **Farmácia Mundial,** Senador Dantas 118D, in Cinelandia, near Praça Mahatma Gandhi. If your feet are tired or hurt, see the good **Doctor Scholl** on Avenida Copacabana, on the corner of Figueiredo Magalhaes (second floor) or downtown on Rua Buenos Aires. The **Farmácia de Leme** at Avenida Prado Junior 237 (tel. 275-3847) in Copacabana is open 24 hours, as is the **Farmácia Piaui** on Rua Barata Ribeiro 646 (tel. 255-7445), also in Copacabana.

Embassies/Consulates The **U.S. Consulate** is at Avenida Presidente Wilson 147 (tel. 292-7117) in center city. The **United Kingdom Consulate** is in Flamengo at Praia do Flamengo 284/2 (tel. 552-1422). The **Australian Consulate** is at Rua Voluntários da Patria 45, 5th floor (tel. 286-7922).

Emergencies In case of fire, dial 193; for the police, dial 190. If you need an ambulance, dial 192 or call the Clinic Savior at 227-5099 or 227-6187.

Entry Requirements In order to visit Brazil, U.S. citizens need a visa, valid for 90 days (you must leave the United States within 90 days after you obtain the visa). You can get your visa the same day upon presenting to the Brazilian consulate a completed form with a passport-size photo and a round-trip airline ticket.

Etiquette Clothes will be no problem in Rio, since the city's residents dress informally day and evening.

Eyeglasses There are opticians located throughout the city. A good one is **Luneierrie** on the second floor of the Galería 550 at Visconde de Piraja 550.

Hairdressers/Barbers Jorge in the **Meridien Hotel** (tel. 275-8295), Beto Rerro in the **Caesar Park** (tel. 287-3122), and Jean Claude in the **Terrasse Center** in Leblon on Rua Conde de Bernadolte 26 (tel. 294-1696) have been recommended to us.

Holidays

New Year's Day	January 1
Founding of Rio Day	January 20
Carnival	varies
Easter	varies
Tiradentes Day	April 21
May *(Labor)* **Day**	May 1
Corpus Christi	June 1
Independence Day	September 7
Nuestra Señora de la Aparecida	October 12
All Souls Day	November 2
Proclamation of Republic Day	November 15
Christmas Day	December 25

Hospitals   **Sousa Aguiar** (tel. 221-2121) is in center city, **Rocha Maia** (tel. 295-1145) is in Botafogo, and **Miguel Couto** (tel. 274-2121) is in Gávea.

Hotlines   In case of a water emergency, call 195; call 196 about electricity or 197 about gas.

Information   See "Tourist Information," above.

Language   Portuguese is the national language of Brazil, with Spanish readily understandable, especially in the south. Many Brazilians understand some English. Most hotels have an English-speaking staff, and many restaurants have menus in English and Portuguese. Carioca Portuguese, spoken in Rio, may be difficult for other Brazilians to understand very well. If you speak some Spanish, use it!

Laundry/Dry Cleaning   There is a self-service laundry in Copacabana at Avenida Nuestra Señora de Copacabana 1226 (tel. 521-2342).

Lost Property   There are lost-property departments at the bus terminal and the airport. You should also contact the police.

Luggage Storage/Lockers   If you're planning a trip from Rio, you may be able to store your luggage at your hotel.

Newspapers/Magazines   The *Daily Post* (60¢), an English-language daily published here, is your best bet for keeping up on U.S. news, local sports, and entertainment events. *Newsweek* is $1.50, and *Time* (Latin American edition) is $1.20. The *Miami Herald* and *Herald Tribune* are available in the afternoon.

Photographic Needs   Film is much more expensive in Rio than at home. If you need to buy some, try **Lutz Ferrando** at Nuestra Señora de Copacabana 426 and Ataulfo de Pavia 725. Film is also available at the **Rio Sul, Barra Shopping,** and **Fashion Mall** shopping centers.

Police   There are police stations in Copacabana at Nuestra Señora de Copacabana 1260 (tel. 247-9345) and on Hiláru de Gouveia (tel. 257-1121). The station in Leblon is at Humberto de Campos 315 (tel. 239-6049).

Post Office   You will find the main building at Rua Primeiro de Marco 64. The Portuguese word for stamp is *selo*. An airmail letter to the United States is $1. In Copacabana the post office is at Nuestra Señora de Copacabana 540, near Rua Siqueira Campos; in Ipanema, it's at Rua Visconde de Pirajá 452. Hours are Monday through Friday from 8am to 6pm, Saturday until noon.

Radio   For popular Brazilian music, tune to 93FM or 102.1FM.

Religious Services   There are a few English-speaking churches in Rio. The **International Baptist Church** is at Rua Alfredo Russel 146 in Leblon (tel. 239-8848); the **Associação Religiosa Israelita** is at Rua General Severiano 170 in Botafogo (tel. 295-6444); the **Christ Church** is at Rua Real Grandeza 99 in Botafogo (tel. 226-2978); and **Our Lady of Mercy** is also in Botafogo at Rua Visconde de Caravelas 28 (tel. 246-8060). Check the local paper or call for information on services.

Restrooms   Hotel lobbies usually have accesible restrooms. Restaurants have restrooms for patrons.

Safety   In recent years, Rio has acquired the reputation of a crime-ridden city, where tourists are preyed upon for their cash and jewelry. We have received letters from several readers who were robbed in Rio, either on the beach or upon leaving a shop or restaurant.

Crime is a serious matter wherever it occurs, but if you use the same common sense abroad that you would use at home, you should be fine. Unless you will be attending a special event, do not take expensive personal items with you. Carry your passport, currency, traveler's checks, and credit cards in a moneybelt (not in your pocket or in a purse). Pay for most of your purchases with traveler's checks or credit cards.

We have been in Rio many times and have never had a problem. Rio is a wonderful combination of resort and big city—but, unfortunately, big city means crime.

Shoe Repairs   The concierge at your hotel should be able to recommend a nearby shoe repair. There is one on the corner of Garcia D'Avila and Nascimento Silva and another in the Galería dos Correio on Rua Visconde de Pirajá. Look for SAPATEIRO.

Taxes   When flying out of Brazil, you'll have to pay an airport tax of about $18 per person; for flights within Brazil, you'll pay $1.50.

Taxis See "Getting Around," above.

Telegrams/Telexes/Faxes You can send telegrams from any post office or can dial 135 (national) or 000222 (international). You can send a telex by dialing 935 or go to the post office at Nuestra Señora de Copacabana 540, in Copacabana, as well as the post offices in the center at Rua da Alfándega 5 and Praça Mauá 7. All post offices have fax machines.

Telephones Many stores and restaurants will allow you to use their phones, at a cost of about 10¢. If the shop has a public phone, buy a *ficha* (token) for 10¢ at the cashier. Newsstand vendors sell tokens for street booths (10¢). By using AT&T Direct you will save significantly on international calls. The AT&T Direct number in Rio is 000-8010.

Television Channels There are seven television stations, all broadcasting in Portuguese, in Rio: TV Globo (4), TV Manchete (6), TV Bandeirantes (7), TV Corcovado/MTV Brasil (9), TVS (11), and TV Rio (13). Channel 3 is usually used as the video channel. Some of the larger hotels have parabolic antenas and offer CNN.

Tipping Since cab drivers do not receive tips from Brazilians, they won't expect to receive tips from tourists. Bellhops should be tipped about 50¢ per bag, and waiters should be tipped about 5% above the 10% service added to your bill (the 10% service charge is for the restaurant, not the waiter).

Useful Telephone Numbers Credit-card emergency numbers: VISA/ Diners Club toll free 011/800-3738; American Express toll free 011/800-5050. If your visa expires and you need it restamped or if you lose your passport and need a new visa, you must contact the police, **Departamento de Policía Marítima E Aérea,** at Avenida Venezuela 2 (tel. 203-2142), not far from Praça Mauá.

---

4. WHERE TO STAY

Because of inflation, there are no more luxury-hotel bargains in Rio. The $10-a-day, air-conditioned double with bath in a five-star hotel is now $150 and up. Nevertheless, we've found a number of acceptable and clean hotels in center city and the nearby beach communities that offer good value at moderate cost. All rates, unless otherwise noted, include a three-course breakfast (fruit, rolls, cheese, and coffee) or a continental breakfast, plus the hotel tax. All prices are based on the *official* exchange rate.

Tip: For variety, you might want to divide your time in Rio between a downtown hotel and one at the beach; this will enable you to experience two distinct aspects of the city.

Hotels are ranked by the Brazilian government on a star basis, from one to five, with five being the top. We have generally omitted the rankings in this chapter.

CENTER CITY

Undoubtedly, the best downtown budget hotels are on or near the mile stretch of Rio Branco, between **Praça Mauá** (dock area) and Praça Mahatma Gandhi, near Guanabara Bay. The **Praça Mahatma Gandhi** area, which is adjacent to a large park and numerous movie theaters (Cinelandia district), is the most attractive section. The streets, wide and generally tree-lined, are bustling with traffic. Yet the tempo picks up even more in the evening, when the area is thronged with moviegoers who jam the sidewalks.

Although somewhat out of the way, the high-altitude **Avenida Mem de Sá** section offers a number of advantages. It is somewhat cooler, and certainly quieter, than other center-city sections. And this district—site of the new cathedral of Rio—has a subdued charm that endears it to many travelers who would not think of staying anywhere else in Rio. To reach the area, walk west from Rio Branco along Avenida do Chile or Avenida Mem de Sá.

DOUBLES FOR LESS THAN $30

HOTEL BELAS ARTES, Rua Visconde do Rio Branco 52. Tel. 021/242-1707. 60 rms (all with bath). A/C
$ Rates: $9 single; $12 double.
Here you'll find tidy but sparsely furnished rooms that are ideal for students and others young in spirit. Ask for Mrs. Carmen.

HOTEL BRAGANCA, Avenida Mem de Sá 117. Tel. 021/242-8116. Fax 021/252-4732. Telex 021/38455. 113 rms (all with bath). A/C TV TEL
$ Rates (including breakfast): $10 single; $15 double.
If not for its slightly out-of-the-way location, not far from Rua dos Invalidos, the Braganca would be a great bargain. As it is, you'll find the rooms spotless and extremely cheerful (many have balconies), with excellent rates. The Braganca's maids, garbed in charming blue uniforms and white aprons and armed with huge featherdusters, are invariably neat and polite.

HOTEL GLOBO, Rua dos Andradas 19. Tel. 021/221-6602. 110 rms (all with bath). A/C TV
$ Rates (including breakfast): $10 single; $12 double. Full board $15 per person double.
Here you'll find a cheap room in the downtown shopping area, with the option of having three meals. Although accommodations here are only a notch above basic, the rates make the Globo an unusually good value. Meals are served in the bright 50-table restaurant located just beyond the lobby. Breakfast consists of fruit, eggs, bread, and coffee. Since this hotel is in the heart of the shopping district, there is a lot of morning traffic, but the nights are quiet.

GRANDE HOTEL O.K., Rua Senador Dantas 24. Tel. 021/292-4114. Fax 021/533-0163. Telex 021/38001. 180 rms (all with bath). A/C TV TEL
$ Rates (including breakfast): $15 single; $20 double. Major credit cards accepted.
$ This outstanding hotel has attractive, spacious rooms, all with radios. Air-conditioning is available for $2 extra. Although the furnishings are somewhat worn, and the hotel is starting to show its age, it is still a good value. There is a bar off the lobby, and a highlight is the top-floor sun deck overlooking the bay.

GRANDE HOTEL PRESIDENTE, Rua Dom Pedro I 19. Tel. 021/297-0110. Fax 021/533-1894. 206 rms (all with bath). A/C MINIBAR TV TEL
$ Rates (including continental breakfast): $15 single; $18 double. Major credit cards accepted.
$ You get to this favorite of ours by walking from bustling Largo da Carioca along Rua Carioca until you come to popular Tiradentes Plaza (the "Greenwich Village" of Rio). Turn left for one block and on your left is the Presidente. There are 2 elevators for the 12 stories, and the handsome lobby is air-conditioned. Most rooms offer splendid views of the hills in and around Rio, including Corcovado; all are highlighted by attractive desks, vanity tables, and highly polished wood floors. A modern bar, writing room, and barbershop are located off the lobby. The management is extremely eager to please.

HOTEL NICE, Rua Riachuelo 201. Tel. 021/297-1155. Telex 021/22539. 120 rms (all with bath). A/C MINIBAR TV TEL
$ Rates (including breakfast): $15 single; $17 double.
Another budget choice is the white-brick Nice, with 2 elevators and 11 floors. The accommodations are light, clean, airy, and quiet, with relatively new furnishings. A top-floor sun deck has attractive shrubbery and benches. One disadvantage: The hotel is six long blocks from the Cinelandia district.

HOTEL PAULISTANO, Rua Visconde do Rio Branco 28. Tel. 021/222-2689. All rooms with bath. A/C TEL
$ Rates (including breakfast): $10 single; $15 double.
The furnishings here are somewhat dated, but the friendly and efficient service more than makes up for it. A terrific value.

MARIALVA, Avenida Gomes Freire 430. Tel. 021/221-1187. 97 rms (all with bath). A/C TV TEL
$ Rates (including breakfast): $10 single; $15 double.

⑤ Marialva is on the corner of Avenida do Chile, a new street built through Morro St. Angelo, a hill that was leveled to provide a site for the new cathedral. The enormous breakfast features bananas, oranges, bread, and coffee. It's a modern hotel, with 2 elevators serving its 11 floors; the rooms are large and bright, with not a speck of dust. Service is excellent, and you'll feel right at home.

HOTEL GRANADA, Avenida Gomes Freire 530. Tel. 021/224-6652. All rooms with bath. A/C MINIBAR TV TEL
$ Rates (including continental breakfast): $15 single; $20 double.
At this three-star hotel, located 10 minutes from downtown, the spacious rooms offer a fine value.

HOTEL NELBA, Rua Senador Dantas 46. Tel. 021/210-3235. Some rooms with bath. A/C TV TEL
$ Rates (including breakfast): $10 single without bath, $18 single with bath; from $15 double without bath, from $20 double with bath.
The attractive eight-story, two-star Nelba, a short walk from the Ambassador (see below), is a modestly priced selection in an ideal location. Here you'll find airy, carpeted rooms, many with terraces. Add $3.50 for air conditioning. One of our top budget restaurants, Mon Jardin, is adjacent to the Nelba.

DOUBLES FOR LESS THAN $40

AMBASSADOR, Rua Senador Dantas 25. Tel. 021/297-7181. Fax 021/220-4783. Telex 021/21796. 173 rms (all with bath). A/C MINIBAR TV TEL
$ Rates: $30 single; $35 double. Major credit cards accepted.

★ The handsome Ambassador is one of Rio's best downtown hotels, half a block from Praça Mahatma Gandhi. Marked by a circular driveway in front and a uniformed doorman, the Ambassador features spotless rooms with radios. Add $5 for air conditioning. Although relatively small, the rooms are comfortable, with attractive draperies. The hotel's bar—Juca's—is packed with locals most evenings. And the second-floor barbershop is highly recommended.

GRANDE HOTEL SÃO FRANCISCO, Rua Visconde de Inhauma 95. Tel. 021/223-1224. Fax 021/233-2364. Telex 021/28422. 300 rms (all with bath). A/C MINIBAR TV TEL
$ Rates (including breakfast): $27 single; $30 double. Major credit cards accepted.
Not far from the Praça Mauá, this clean, 17-story elevator-equipped hotel is a good choice on the corner of Rio Branco. The huge double rooms have throw rugs, radios, and draperies.
There is a first-class restaurant on the premises. The treat here is breakfast in bed. You get a boiled egg with cheese slices; an orange, a banana, and a *mamão* (papaya); rolls and bread with butter and marmalade; and coffee, tea, milk, or hot chocolate. Breakfast is served until 10am; after phoning in your order, you will have it within 10 minutes.

ITAJUBA, Rua Alvaro Alvim 23. Tel. 021/210-3163. Telex 021/34703. 110 rms (all with bath). MINIBAR TV TEL
$ Rates: $31 single; $37 double.
Several hotels are within a few steps of each other on Rua Alvaro Alvim, a small street that runs between Rio Branco and Senador Dantas. Itajuba, the best of the lot,

features cozy rooms with parquet floors. While unimpressive from the outside, the 15-story Itajuba is clean and tidy inside. Plush leather chairs and a TV are available in the second-floor lobby. There's no air conditioning, however.

DOUBLES FOR LESS THAN $45

GUANABARA PALACE, Avenida Presidente Vargas 392. Tel. 021/253-8622. Fax 021/516-1582. Telex 021/35084. 304 rms (all with bath). A/C MINIBAR TV TEL
$ Rates (including breakfast): $30–$37 single; $32–$41 double. Extra bed $8. Major credit cards accepted.

⭐ Walk to the corner of Rio Branco and Presidente Vargas and turn right. Half a block up, on your right, is a truly outstanding 22-story first-class hotel, furnished in old-world style. The Guanabara Palace offers large, airy rooms, all with parquet floors, radios, bureaus, and large closets; some even have anterooms. The breakfast buffet is outstanding. This area, which is within easy walking distance of our recommended shopping streets, is relatively quiet at night and not too populated. Morning traffic, however, can be a problem if your room faces Avenida Vargas. Although meals are available in the rooms, there is no restaurant on the premises.

HOTEL AMBASSADOR SANTOS DUMONT, Rua Santa Luzia 651. Tel. 021/210-2119. Telex 021/32540. 44 rms (all with bath). A/C MINIBAR TV TEL
$ Rates: $38.70 single; $43 double. Major credit cards accepted.
The rooms here are well appointed, and the service is first-rate.

A SPLURGE CHOICE

HOTEL AEROPORTO OTHON, Avenida Beira Mar 280. Tel. 021/210-3253. Fax 021/210-3253. Telex 021/37857. All rooms with bath. A/C MINIBAR TV TEL
$ Rates: $70 single; $75 double. Major credit cards accepted.
The three-star Aeroporto Othon is located close to the downtown Santos Dumont Airport. Dated yet comfortable, it's a member of the Othon group of hotels.

FLAMENGO BEACH

This quiet, elegant beach area, 15 minutes by foot from Praça Mahatma Gandhi, is the home of the world-famous Gloria, a luxury hotel that attracts frequent international conferences. It is also home to several budget hotels, a block or two off the beach. But keep in mind that Flamengo Beach has two minor disadvantages: First, there are few restaurants here, except in the hotels, and most of these are rather expensive; second, for excursions and sightseeing you'll still have to use center city or Copacabana Beach as your departure point.

DOUBLES FOR LESS THAN $40

HOTEL CAXAMBU, Rua Correia Dutra 22. Tel. 021/265-9496. 35 rms (some with bath).
$ Rates: $5 single without bath; $12 single or double with bath.
The Caxambu is a two-story hotel that's clean and well maintained. Adjoining the lobby is an outdoor covered courtyard with several highback chairs. Two parakeets and fish brighten the lobby. Air-conditioning and TVs are available.

HOTEL MENGO, Rua Correia Dutra 31. Tel. 021/285-3343. Some doubles with bath.
$ Rates (including breakfast): $19 single without bath; $20 double without bath; $24 double with bath.
The Mengo is the best of three fine and equally plain choices on this street, even though there's no elevator. The rooms are clean, and those with baths have showers rather than tubs. The floors are bare wood—notice how clean they are.

FLORIDA, Rua Ferreira Viana 69. Tel. 021/245-8160. Telex 021/33400.
267 rms (all with bath). A/C MINIBAR TEL
$ Rates (including breakfast): $25 single; $30 double; $36 triple.
The roomy doubles, with parquet floors, are a good value at this first-class hotel. An intimate bar and TV room are situated off the spacious lobby, where red-jacketed bellhops abound. Four elevators service the seven floors, and the rooms, as you might expect, are modern and bright.

HOTEL INGLES, Rua Silveira Martins 20. Tel. 021/265-9052 or 265-7797.
40 rms (all with bath). A/C
$ Rates (including continental breakfast): $20 single; $30-$35 double. Major credit cards accepted.
The small, comfortable doubles here have polished wood floors and large closets. Most rooms come with circular floor fans and some with private terraces. The more expensive rooms are at the front. It's a good value, especially since off-season rates are a third cheaper.

IMPERIAL HOTEL, Rua do Catete 186. Tel. 021/205-0212. 80 rms (all with bath). TV TEL
$ Rates: $28 single; $32 double. **Parking:** Free.
The rooms here have modern furnishings and piped-in music. Air-conditioning and minibars are available in more expensive rooms.

REGINA HOTEL, Rua Ferreira Viana 29. Tel. 021/225-7280. 130 rms (all with bath). A/C TEL
$ Rates (including breakfast): $20 single; $25 double; $30 triple. Major credit cards accepted.
A cut below the Novo Mundo (see below), but a truer budget buy, is the handsome Regina, with attractive, airy rooms boasting modern furnishings. The singles are small but comfortable. Located less than a block from the beachfront, this six-story hotel is carefully maintained, and service is outstanding. Breakfast is served in the top-floor dining room. TVs are available.

DOUBLES FOR LESS THAN $50

GRANDE HOTEL NOVO MUNDO, Praia do Flamengo 20. Tel. 021/205-3355. Fax 021/265-2369. Telex 021/213-3282. 180 rms (all with bath). A/C MINIBAR TV TEL
$ Rates (including breakfast): From $42 single; from $46 double. Major credit cards accepted.
Apart from the Gloria (see below), this is the best hotel near the beach, facing the sea and not far from the Museum of the Republic. Here you'll find large rooms with modern furnishings. For an enchanting interlude, gaze at Sugarloaf and the surrounding beaches and giant palm trees from in front of the hotel at twilight. After you've forgotten much else about your travels, you'll recall those sights. The 12-story Novo Mundo features a North American–style bar and restaurant, a barbershop, and a beauty salon.

HOTEL FLAMENGO PALACE, Praia do Flamengo 6. Tel. 021/205-1552.
Fax 265-2846. Telex 021/30794. 60 rms (all with bath). A/C MINIBAR TV TEL
$ Rates: $40 single; $45 double. Major credit cards accepted.
If you want a modern hotel, consider the well-regarded 15-story Flamengo Palace, which opened its doors in 1974. A coffee shop is on the premises.

A SPLURGE CHOICE

HOTEL GLORIA, Rua do Russel 632. Tel. 021/205-7272. Fax 021/245-1660. Telex 021/23623. 700 rms (all with bath). A/C MINIBAR TV TEL
$ Rates (including breakfast): From $80 single; from $100 double. Major credit cards accepted.

✪ The Hotel Gloria is one of the best-known hotels in South America. The decor is classic throughout; the lobby and the guest rooms are smartly furnished in traditional style. Many rooms overlook the bay. The kidney-shaped pool is popular year round with guests, who seem to prefer it to the nearby beach. On the premises are a drugstore, a beauty salon, a barbershop, and a sumptuous bar and restaurant. Breakfast is served in your room or in the plush dining room.

Be sure to stroll through the lobby and pick up maps, brochures, and information on car-rentals and excursions. Here you can buy U.S. cigarettes, which are not easy to find in Rio.

COPACABANA BEACH

The hub of Rio, Copacabana Beach is lined with high-priced private homes, apartment buildings, and, of course, luxury hotels. We have been told by several well-traveled Cariocas in downtown Rio not to waste our time in Copacabana Beach: "You will find expensive hotels and unlivable hotels—that's all," one center-city hotel manager told us. However, we've uncovered half a dozen clean, comfortable budget hotels in this community of 400,000, bounded on one side by the mountains, on the other by the ocean. The key rule here is to avoid the beachfront (Avenida Atlântica) and concentrate on streets a block or two from the water.

Note: Copacabana Beach is only 20 minutes from center city by bus, which you can catch at Rio Branco and Presidente Vargas or at Praça Mahatma Gandhi. Remember, too, that Copacabana and Rio's other beach communities are packed in the Brazilian summer (December to February), but only moderately crowded the rest of the year.

DOUBLES FOR LESS THAN $40

HOTEL ANGRENSE, Travessa Angrense 25. Tel. 021/255-0509. 37 rms (some with bath). A/C MINIBAR TEL
$ Rates (including breakfast): $24 single without bath, $31 single with bath; $31 double without bath, $38 double with bath. Major credit cards accepted.
Most maps do not indicate this tiny street, located off Copacabana (heading away from the beach), between Santa Clara and Raimundo Correa, where you'll find the Angrense, a three-story walk-up. While accommodations are only a notch above basic, the Angrense is unusually quiet for Rio, due to its location. Some rooms have terraces.

HOTEL CANADA, Avenida Copacabana 687. Tel. 021/257-1864. Fax 021/255-3705. Telex 021/29371. 72 rms (all with bath). A/C MINIBAR TV TEL
$ Rates (including breakfast): From $25 single; from $30 double. Major credit cards accepted.
⑤ Near Rua Santa Clara, this first-class hotel, with an awning outside, has cheerful rooms brightened by print bedspreads and piped-in music. Two elevators service the 10 floors. If you're a late sleeper, ask for a room that doesn't overlook traffic-jammed Avenida Copacabana. The desk clerks, who speak some English, are eager to suggest dining and nightclub possibilities within budget limits.

HOTEL COPA LINDA, Copacabana 956. Tel. 021/267-3399. 30 rms (some with bath). A/C
$ Rates (including breakfast): $15 single; $17 double.
The Copa Linda, near Rua Bolívar, is probably the best budget bargain here. While the rooms are small, they are relatively tidy, each with a sink and mirror. You can't miss the Copa Linda—it's opposite the Cine Roxi cinema.

HOTEL PRAIA LEME, Avenida Atlântica 866. Tel. 021/275-3322. Fax 021/275-5545. Telex 021/23988. 50 rms (all with bath). A/C MINIBAR TV TEL
$ Rates: $35–$45 double; 10% more for front rooms.

★ The Praia Leme is a true budget beauty and a personal favorite of ours, right on the beach. The rooms are tastefully furnished in jacaranda wood. Because of its modest rates, it tends to attract long-term guests, so make your reservations well in advance. The service is excellent.

HOTEL APA, Rua República do Perú 305. Tel. 021/255-8112. Fax 021/256-8112. Telex 021/307941. 52 rms (all with bath). A/C MINIBAR TV TEL
$ Rates (including breakfast): $30 double; $35 triple. Major credit cards accepted.
The impressive APA (pronounced "*ah*pa"), on the corner of Copacabana, is attractive and well regarded. Handsome inside and out, the seven-story hotel features comfortable rooms with red linoleum floors, rather startling black-tile bathrooms, plus radios, club chairs, and huge closets.

BIARRITZ HOTEL, Rua Aires Saldanha 54. Tel. 021/521-6542. Fax 021/3066. 29 rms (all with bath). A/C MINIBAR TV TEL
$ Rates: $27 single; $30 double. Major credit cards accepted.
Ⓢ Behind the deluxe Othon Palace on Copacabana Beach is the 10-story Biarritz. Accommodations are quite comfortable, making it a great value for the price. The Rio Sul shopping center is nearby.

TOLEDO HOTEL, Rua Domingos Ferreira 71. Tel. 021/257-1990. 95 rms (all with bath). A/C MINIBAR TV TEL
$ Rates (including breakfast): $25 single; $30 double. Major credit cards accepted.
The Toledo is half a block from the beach, near Santa Clara. Manager Antoine Georges Albanakis is of French extraction and speaks seven languages, including English. You'll find him a wonderful host, spilling over with sightseeing tips and restaurant suggestions. The rooms are large and comfortable. *Note:* Rua Domingos Ferreira is a small street—between Avenidas Copacabana and Atlântica.

DOUBLES FOR LESS THAN $55

HOTEL ACAPULCO, Rua Gustavo Sampaio 854. Tel. 021/275-0022. Fax 021/275-3396. Telex 021/32900. 123 rms (all with bath). A/C MINIBAR TV TEL
$ Rates: $35 single; $40 double. Major credit cards accepted.
This is a popular choice with spacious doubles. You will be more than comfortable here.

HOTEL BANDEIRANTE, Rua Barata Ribeiro 548. Tel. 021/255-6252. Telex 021/37854. 90 rms (all with bath). A/C MINIBAR TV TEL.
$ Rates: $47 double. Major credit cards accepted.
A convenient location is just one of the strong points of this fine hotel, just two blocks from the beach and close to movies and good restaurants.

HOTEL COPAMAR, Rua Santa Clara 116. Tel. 021/236-5184. 25 rms (all with bath). A/C MINIBAR TEL
$ Rates (including continental breakfast): $41 single; $46 double. Major credit cards accepted.
This establishment, with an unfortunately gloomy entrance stairway, is half a block from Avenida Copacabana (away from the beach) and just a few steps from Rio's fine budget luncheonette—the Arosa.

PRAIA LIDO, Avenida Copacabana 202. Tel. 021/541-1347. Fax 021/541-1347. 50 rms (all with bath). A/C TV TEL
$ Rates (including breakfast): $45 single; $50 double. Major credit cards accepted.
The rooms in this hotel, one of the best of its category, are distributed over six floors, and each has a radio. Head up one flight to the usually crowded lobby. The American bar is open 24 hours.

SPLURGE CHOICES

HOTEL CASTRO ALVES, Avenida Copacabana 552. Tel. 021/257-8815. Telex 021/38184. 74 rms (all with bath). A/C MINIBAR TV TEL

COPACABANA & LEME

LEME

COPACABANA

A t l a n t i c   O c e a n

Leme Beach

Copacabana Beach

To Pão de Açúcar

To Botafogo

To Lagoa

To Ipanema

Morro da Babilônia

Morro de São João

Morro dos Cabritos

Morro de Cantagalo

Av. Lad. do Leme

Rua F. de Oliveira

Av. B. de Castro Júnior

Av. Princesa Isabel

Av. Gustavo Sampaio

Av. Atlântica

Av. Viveiros de Castro

Av. Prado Júnior

Rua Duvivier

Praça do Lido

Rua Dantes

R. Inhangá

Rua Mendes

Av. Rep. do Perú

Av. Toneleros

Paula Freitas

Rua H. De Gouveia

Praça S. Correia

Rua S. Campos

Rua Lad. Dos Tabajaras

Rua Siqueira

Rua Figueiredo Magalhães

Av. Barata Ribeiro

Av. de Copacabana

Av. Atlântica

Rua Santa Clara

Rua Correia

Rua Cinco de Julho

R. Dias da Rocha

R. Dias da Rocha

Rua C. Ramos

Major Vaz

Túnel

Rua Barão de Ipanema

Rua Bolívar

Rua X. Da Silveira

Miguel Lemos

Av. N. Senhora

Rua D. Ulrich

Av. Atlântica

Dodsworth

Av. Henrique

R. Prof. G. Bahiana

Morro de Cantagalo

Túnel Eng. Marquês Porto

Rua Saint Romain

Rua Sá Ferreira

Rua Souza Lima

$ Rates (including breakfast): $60 single; $70 double. Major credit cards accepted. Bedrooms large enough to serve as sitting rooms can be found at the Castro Alves, on the corner of Rua Sequeira Campos. The Alves has 2 elevators servicing its 12 stories. Accommodations feature large bathrooms with separate shower stalls, wall-to-wall draperies, writing tables, bureaus, and twin beds.

PLAZA COPACABANA HOTEL, Princesa Isabel 263. Tel. 021/275-7722.
Telex 021/31198. 180 rms (all with bath). A/C MINIBAR TV TEL
$ Rates (including breakfast): $55 double. Major credit cards accepted.
As you arrive from center city, the first major street in Copacabana you reach is Princesa Isabel, where you'll find the top-notch Plaza Copacabana. This huge 17-floor hotel has rooms with wall-to-wall carpeting, vanity tables, and club chairs. The mammoth lobby is a showplace, with plush sofas, deep chairs, and pile carpeting in a sunken area. Cocktails are served in a discreet rear bar.

IPANEMA & LEBLON

ARPOADOR INN, Rua Francisco Otaviano 177. Tel. 021/247-6090. Telex
021/22833. 50 rms (all with bath). A/C MINIBAR TEL
$ Rates: $25–$60 singles; $35–$70 doubles. Major credit cards accepted.
Located at the beginning of Ipanema, just off the beach, the quaint Arpoador features a refrigerator and piped-in music in each comfortable room. You'll pay more for a room facing the beach. TVs are available.

HOTEL CARLTON, Rua João Lira 68. Tel. 021/259-1932. Telex 021/2833.
46 rms (all with bath). A/C MINIBAR TV
$ Rates: $30 single; $45 double. Major credit cards accepted.
This very comfortable hotel is in Leblon, just one block from the beach. There is a cinema nearby.

HOTEL VERMONT, Rua Visconde de Pirajá 254. Tel. 021/521-0057. 84
rms (all with bath). A/C MINIBAR TV TEL
$ Rates: $33 single; from $40 double.
Located on the main street of Ipanema, the Vermont is in a prime location, just two blocks from the beach and close to all the finest restaurants. Doubles here are simple yet comfortable.

IPANEMA INN, Rua Maria Quiteria 27. Tel. 021/287-6092. Telex 021/
22833. 56 rms (all with bath). A/C MINIBAR TEL
$ Rates: From $50 double. Major credit cards accepted.
The Ipanema Inn, opened in 1976, boasts a pool. Just two blocks from the beach, its also convenient to area nightspots. TVs are available.

A SPLURGE CHOICE

EVEREST PARK HOTEL, Rua Maria Quiteria 19. Tel. 021/287-8282.
Telex 021/22254. 169 rms (all with bath). A/C MINIBAR TV TEL
$ Rates: $70 single; $80 double. Major credit cards accepted.
⭐ This beautiful three-star hotel offers guests the amenities of a five-star hotel, simply because they have access to all the facilities of the deluxe Everest. Definitely worth a try if your budget allows it.

YOUTH HOSTELS

Youth hostels are far cheaper than hotels and pensions. Those who are planning to stay in hostels would do well to contact the youth hostel organization in their own countries first for membership and information on travel benefits. In the United States, it's the **American Youth Hostels Association,** 733 Fifteenth Street NW,

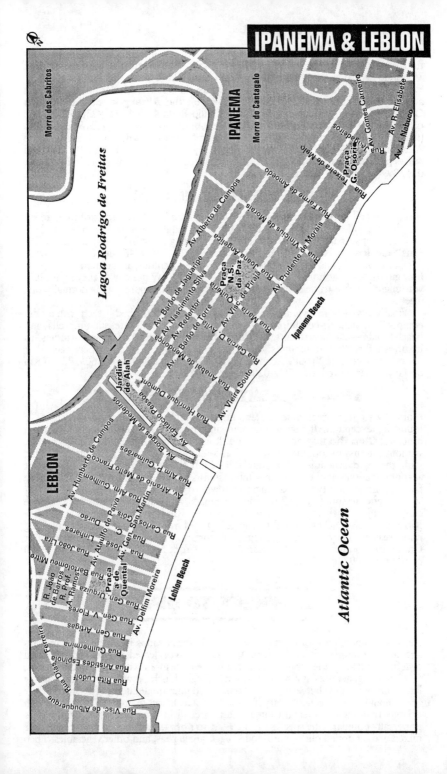

IPANEMA & LEBLON

IPANEMA

LEBLON

Lagoa Rodrigo de Freitas

Atlantic Ocean

Ipanema Beach

Leblon Beach

Morro das Cabritos

Morro do Cantagalo

Jardim de Alah

Praça N.S. da Paz

Praça a de Quental

Av. Gomes Carneiro

Av. R. Elisábete

Av. J. Nabuco

Rua Teixeira de Melo

Praça G. Osório

Rua Farme de Amoedo

Rua Vinícius de Morais

Rua Prudente de Morais

Av. Alberto de Campos

Av. Barão de Jaguaripe

Av. Nascimento Silva

Av. Redentor

Av. Barão de Torre

Rua Joana Angélica

Rua Maria Quitéria

Rua Visc. de Pirajá

Rua Garcia D. Ávila

Rua Anibal de Mendonça

Rua Henrique Dumont

Av. Epitácio Pessoa

Av. Borges de Medeiros

Rua Alm. P. Guimarães

Av. Afranio de Mello Franco

Av. Humberto de Campos

Rua Gen. San Martin

Rua Ataulfo de Paiva

Av. Gen. Urquiza

C. Gois

Rua Carlos Góis

Durão

Linhares

Rua João Lira

Rua Bartolomeu Mitre

Rua Gen. V. Flores

Av. Delfim Moreira

Av. Vieira Souto

Rua Gen. Artigas

Rua Guilhermina

Rua Aristides Espínola

Rua Rita Ludolf

Rua Visc. de Albuquerque

Rua Dias Ferreira

R. João de Barros

R Prof. A. Ramos

Washington DC 20005 (tel. 202/783-6161). Members of the Federation of International Youth Travel Organizations can contact **International House,** at Rua Visconde de Caravales 1, Botafogo (tel. 021/266-0890).

There are five hostels in Rio: The **Albergue da Juventude Bello,** in Gloria, is at Rua Santo Amaro 162 (tel. 021/222-8576); the **Albergue da Juventude Copacabana** in Copacabana, is at Rua Emilio Berla 41 (tel. 021/236-6472). The others are the **Casa do Estudante do Brasil,** on Praça Ana Amelia 9, in Castelo (tel. 021/220-7123 or 220-7223); the **Pousada do Garuda,** at Rua Almirante Alexandrino 2840 in Santa Teresa (tel. 021/225-0393 or 326-1419); and the **Albergue da Juventude Barra Sol,** at Avenida Grande Canal 301 in Barra (tel. 021/399-0659).

RESIDENTIAL HOTELS

Rio has several decent apartment hotels suitable for a family or group of three to six people. A good choice is **Apart-Hotel,** at Rua Barata Ribeiro 370 (tel. 021/256-2633), in Copacabana. All 70 apartments have cooking units. In Leblon, the larger **Rio Flat Service,** at Rua Alm. Guilhen 332 (tel. 021/274-9546; fax 021/239-8792; telex 021/32914), has 103 apartments, with kitchen facilities, accommodating two to four guests. Rates at both are about $350 per week or $57 per day. If they're not full, you might be able to negotiate a daily rate, but the minimum stay is normally one week.

Finally, Swiss-born Yvonne Reiman has bought and furnished—each with a fully equipped kitchen, air-conditioning, telephone, color TV, wall safe, sun umbrella, and beach chairs—20 apartments in Copacabana, ranging from simple studios to luxurious three-bedroom units. Rates start at a little over $300 per week. For reservations, contact Yvonne Reiman, Avenida Atlântica 4066, Apto. 605, 22070 Rio de Janeiro, Brazil (tel. 021/227-0281 or 267-0054).

SPECIAL MENTION: BIG SPLURGE

Normally we don't recommend prearranged, all-inclusive packages; however, we've found an exception. If you want some time out from a hectic South American itinerary, **Club Rio** may be right for you. It will enable you to enjoy Rio worry free, without the fuss of looking for suitable accommodations and restaurants or dealing with the rigid schedules of a tour. The Club Rio package includes beachfront accommodations at the luxurious Inter-Continental Hotel; all meals, including a farewell dinner at a typical Rio night club with dancing; unlimited tennis and water sports; dance lessons (samba, bossa nova, lambada, and other Latin favorites); exercise classes; and sightseeing and shopping tours. Club Rio is a terrific way to experience Rio at your leisure. The six-night package is priced from $999 per person, depending upon season. They can also arrange your airfare. For more information, contact Grand Prix Journeys at 425 Madison Ave., New York NY 10017 (tel. 212/319-8600 or toll free 800/242-7749).

---

5. WHERE TO DINE

Rio has an abundance of inexpensive U.S.-style snack shops ideal for quick lunches and late-afternoon coffee and pastry. At those we have selected, you will find the food tastefully prepared, the service efficient, and the prices well within our budget limits.

Cariocas generally eat a heavy breakfast, a light lunch between noon and 2pm, a late-afternoon tidbit between 4 and 6pm, and dinner quite late by U.S. standards.

Although food specialties vary from state to state in this mammoth country, which is larger than the continental United States, three dishes and one alcoholic drink are universally popular. One specialty is the *frango com arroz,* boned chicken and rice mixed with chopped olives, hard-boiled eggs, green peas, and other vegetables. Then there's *churrasco,* beef steak grilled over an open fire. (A variation of this is *bife de panela,* a thin steak grilled with onions and tomatoes.) A much tangier dish is *feijoada,* black beans and rice cooked with sausage or tongue, bacon, tomatoes, onions, and hot spices. And the ever-popular drink is *batida,* a potent sugarcane extract served in fruit juice. Ultrasweet, this beverage has a kick, so watch it!

Tips: It is perfectly acceptable in Rio for two people to share one order, so if you're not too hungry or are short of cash, tell the waiter to bring one main dish and two settings.

Many restaurants charge a *couvert* (a cover, which might include celery, cucumber, radishes, and even quail eggs). Prices range from $1 to $3 per person. To save this charge, tell the waiter "No *couvert,* please."

CENTER CITY

BAR LUIZ, Rua da Carioca 39. Tel. 262-6900.
   Cuisine: GERMAN. **Reservations:** Recommended.
$ Prices: Appetizers $2; main courses $4–$8.
   Open: Mon–Sat 11am–11:30pm.
If German cuisine sounds appealing, head here. It's not fancy or expensive, but it is good.

CHICKEN HOUSE, Rua Miguel Couto 36.
   Cuisine: INTERNATIONAL.
$ Prices: Full meal $2.75–$5.
   Open: 10am–10pm.
For some of the best chicken in Rio, try the Chicken House, in the shopping district, on a small street between Rio Branco and Gonçalves Dias. The restaurant features in the window a large rôtisserie filled with chicken quarters. If you're on a tight budget, consider the egg platters for $2.75 and up. Brightening the decor here are the pert yellow-uniformed waitresses.

CRUZEIRO DO SUL, Avenida Reporter Nestor Moreira 42. Tel. 295-2347.
   Cuisine: CHURRASCO (BARBECUE). **Reservations:** Recommended.
$ Prices: $10 (all included).
   Open: Lunch and dinner until midnight.
This wonderful *churrascaria* is downtown in Botafogo. It's all-you-can-eat salad and meat for $10.

ESQUINA-SABOR BRASIL, Rua do Ouvidor 14. Tel. 231-2362.
   Cuisine: INTERNATIONAL. **Reservations:** Recommended.
$ Prices: Appetizers $1.50; main courses $4–$6.
   Open: Mon–Fri 11am–5pm; happy hour 5–11pm.
Here in the shopping district, a couple can dine in comfortable surroundings for less than $10. By day it's a favorite of shoppers and people who work in the area; by night it's a popular after-hours hangout.

FICHA, Rua Teofilo Otoni 126. Tel. 233-8496.
   Cuisine: GERMAN. **Reservations:** Recommended.
$ Prices: Appetizers $2; main courses $6. Major credit cards accepted.
   Open: Mon–Fri 11am–4pm.
This restaurant, near Praça Maúa, offers excellent German dishes which have been attracting a steady following since 1917. Check out the daily specials. Because the small dining room could not accommodate Ficha's many devoted patrons at lunchtime, the owners opened a second branch—the Restaurante Maria Schaade, at Rua Teofilo Ottoni 98, named in honor of the original chef and manager of Ficha.

HEALTH'S, Rua Beneditinos 18. Tel. 253-0433.
   Cuisine: VEGETARIAN. **Reservations:** Recommended.
$ Prices: Appetizers $1.50; main courses $4–$5. Major credit cards accepted.

Open: 11am–3pm.

This Health's is located near Praça Mauá, and there's another on Rua Senador Dantas, downtown. A fine health-food restaurant, it's a favorite lunchtime spot of office workers.

LEITERIA MINEIRA, Ruada Ajuda 35A. Tel. 533-2931.
   Cuisine: BRAZILIAN. **Reservations:** Recommended.
$ **Prices:** Appetizers $2; main courses $5.
   Open: Mon–Sat 8am–8pm.

⭐ This small restaurant, a block and a half east of Rio Branco (away from Largo da Carioca), was recommended to us by a former secretary of tourism, who eats lunch here regularly. The restaurant is spotless and the service prompt. The *Sugestoes do Dia* (suggestions of the day) are your best bets—platter prices rarely exceed $5. Or try the *risoto de frango*, an inexpensive chicken dish; the fish stew; or the steak dishes. The chef of this 50-year-old restaurant heartily recommends a Brazilian dish called *tutu à mineira*, made of beans mixed with manioc flour and served with pork chops. Recommended, too, is the *camarao com arroz* (shrimp and rice).

MISTER PIZZA, Rua 13 de Maio. Tel. 224-4477.
   Cuisine: PIZZA.
$ **Prices:** Pizzas and other items $1.50.
   Open: All day.
Here, near the Teatro Municipal, $1.50 will get you a pizza, hot dog, sandwich, or salad. Beer and fruit juices are also available.

NATURAL, Barrao da Torre 171. Tel. 267-7799.
   Cuisine: VEGETARIAN.
$ **Prices:** Appetizers $1.50; main courses $4.50.
   Open: 11:30am–11pm.
Located in Ipanema, this is a good choice for vegetarian cuisine, including whole-grain breads. You can also buy grocery items in the small shop here.

RESTAURANTE VEGETARIANO GREEN, Rua do Carmo 38. Tel. 252-5356.
   Cuisine: VEGETARIAN.
$ **Prices:** Appetizers $1.50; main courses $4. Major credit cards accepted.
   Open: 11am–3pm.
Head up one flight for a self-service delight in the vegetarian tradition. Start with a nonalcoholic drink, then choose a salad, fruit juice, soup, a hot plate (rice, vegetables, and the like), and dessert—the whole meal will probably cost less than $8 total.

CAFE DO TEATRO, in the Teatro Municipal on Avenida Rio Branco. Tel. 212-4164.
   Cuisine: INTERNATIONAL. **Reservations:** Recommended.
$ **Prices:** Appetizers $2–$4; main courses $4–$20. Major credit cards accepted.
   Open: Lunch only, Mon–Fri noon–4pm.
You owe it to yourself to have one lunch at the Café do Teatro, which replaced the theatrical museum previously here. The tiled walls and columns resemble a scene from *Aïda*. The restaurant serves a fixed-price four-course luncheon, including soft drinks or beer, for $15. But come here for the atmosphere, casually elegant and relaxing. Some 200 diners, mostly businesspeople, crowd into this popular luncheon retreat. On Fridays they have a fixed-price *feijoada with caipirinha* for $7.

CHURRASCOLANDIA, Senador Dantas 31. Tel. 220-9534.
   Cuisine: BARBECUE. **Reservations:** Recommended.
$ **Prices:** $7.50 Rodizio (all-you-can-eat salad and barbecue). Major credit cards accepted.
   Open: 11am–11pm.
For superb steaks, roast beef, or *feijoada* at moderate prices, head directly for

Churrascolandia ("Steak Land"), located opposite the Nelba Hotel near Praça Mahatma Gandhi. You'll pass several beer barrels serving as tables in the bar area before entering the attractive dining room. Popular dishes include *feijoada completa,* roast beef with potato and salad, and the *churrasquito* with rice. Chicken dishes are available, too. Many customers use the take-out service.

OXALA, Rua Alvaro Alvim 36A. Tel. 220-3035.
   Cuisine: BAHIAN. **Reservations:** Recommended.
$ Prices: Appetizers $1.50; main courses $4–$10
   Open: 11am–1am.

For the best affordable Bahian food, head for Oxalá, inside the gallery in Cinelandia. Try any of the numerous shrimp dishes. Air-conditioned, usually crowded, and not known for its decor, Oxalá offers true value for your cruzeiro. The *vatapá* is excellent.

FLAMENGO

AURORA, Rua Capitão Salomão 43. Tel. 226-4756.
   Cuisine: BRAZILIAN.
$ Prices: Appetizers $1.50; main courses $5.
   Open: Mon–Sat 11am–1am; Sunday 11am–7pm.
A hangout for artists at the corner of Rua Visconde de Caravelas in Botafogo, this eatery was called to our attention by a Varig executive who eats here regularly. The menu is varied, and the prices are low.

BISMARQUE, Rue São Clemente 24. Tel. 226-1032.
   Cuisine: PORTUGUESE.
$ Prices: Appetizers $1.50; main courses $3–$7.
   Open: Mon–Sat 11am–10pm; Sunday 11am–6pm.
Another popular spot in Botafogo is Bismarque. Enter through the swinging bar, pass the counter stand-up service area, and you will reach the small restaurant in the rear. Daily specials, such as *badejo frito* and liver with onions, are usually generous.

CAFE LAMAS, Rua Marques de Abrantes 18. Tel. 205-0799.
   Cuisine: BRAZILIAN. **Reservations:** Recommended.
$ Prices: Appetizers $1; main courses $3.
   Open: 11am–3am.

A landmark in this area is the usually packed 110-year-old Café Lamas. On our last visit we stopped by on a Wednesday morning at 2am and had to wait for a table. The *carne assado* is a good buy, as is the *peru* (turkey) with rice.

JANINA, Rua Senador Correia 10. Tel. 205-3844.
   Cuisine: BRAZILIAN.
$ Prices: Buffet $6.
   Open: All day.
At Janina, near Praça São Salvador, you can dine for about $6, including dessert. The nonstop buffet is well worth the price.

MAJORICA, Rua Senador Verqueiro 11. Tel. 245-8947.
   Cuisine: BARBECUE. **Reservations:** Recommended.
$ Prices: Appetizers $2; main courses $4–$10.
   Open: 11:30am–midnight.
Fine steaks are available at this churrascaria. The Picanha at $10 is enough for two—a real bargain.

PARQUE RECREIO, Rua Marques de Abrantes 92. Tel. 552-1748.
   Cuisine: BRAZILIAN. **Reservations:** Recommended.
$ Prices: Appetizers $1.50; main courses $4. Major credit cards accepted.
   Open: Daily 11am–1am.
This good churrascaria is usually crowded, especially on weekends. The meat here is tasty, and the prices are reasonable.

A SPLURGE CHOICE

RIO'S, in Parque do Flamengo. Tel. 551-1238.
   Cuisine: INTERNATIONAL. **Reservations:** Recommended.
$ Prices: Appetizers $2.50; main courses $10–$20. Major credit cards accepted.
   Open: Noon–1am.

⭐ Undoubtedly, your best scenic dining spot in this area is Rio's, on the bay. It's part of a complex that includes a disco, a bar/restaurant, and an outdoor snack area. The restaurant offers great views of Sugarloaf, Guanabara Bay, and the yacht club. It's located between Botafogo and Flamengo Park, on the right as you head downtown. Look for the conical pyramid as a landmark.

COPACABANA BEACH

ARATACA, Rua Dias Ferreira, 135-A. Tel. 255-7448.
   Cuisine: BRAZILIAN. **Reservations:** Recommended.
$ Prices: Appetizers $2; main courses $10. Major credit cards accepted.
   Open: Noon–1am.
A reader suggested Arataca, a small restaurant specializing in fish from the Amazon as well as a long list of tropical fruit juices and *batidas*. There's another branch of Arataca in Leblon.

AROSA LANCHONETTE, Santa Clara 110. Tel. 255-4761.
   Cuisine: INTERNATIONAL.
$ Prices: Appetizers $1.50; main courses $4–$6.
   Open: Daily 11am–midnight.

Ⓢ The best-value all-around eatery in the Rio area is this counter-only establishment, near Barata Ribeiro, where you can get a filling fixed-price lunch or dinner for $7.50 and up. The Arosa offers one-price selections from three columns—including one hot dish (such as chicken or beef), three side dishes (vegetables and salads), a dessert, and a beverage (you may even choose an excellent Brazilian beer at no extra cost). Packed with shoppers and office workers at lunchtime, the Arosa also features numerous pizza selections and a lengthy sandwich list. Portions are absurdly large, and the place is immaculate.

CANTINA BELLA ROMA, Avenida Atlântica 928. Tel. 295-3047.
   Cuisine: ITALIAN. **Reservations:** Recommended.
$ Prices: Appetizers $1.50; main courses $3–$6. Major credit cards accepted.
   Open: Daily 11am–4am.
This is a fine restaurant in a private house, with an ocean view as a bonus. Spaghetti is king here. Pizza and *frango* are in the same price category, and a favorite of ours is the *gnocchi a bolonhesa* (meat with tomato sauce).

LA MOLE, Avenida N. S. Copacabana 552. Tel. 235-3366.
   Cuisine: BRAZILIAN. **Reservations:** Recommended.
$ Prices: Appetizers $1.50; main courses $3–$6.
   Open: 11am–2am.
This popular hangout is next to the Castro Alves Hotel. Here, the *massas* (pasta) dishes are in demand, and the steak au poivre is delicious. The branch in Leblon, at Rua Dias Ferreira 147 (tel. 294-0699), is even more crowded and newer. There are additional branches in the Barra Shopping Center (tel. 325-5271) and on Praia de Botafogo 228 (tel. 551-9499).

RESTAURANTE ORIENTO, Rua Bolívar 64. Tel. 257-7798.
   Cuisine: CHINESE.
$ Prices: Appetizers $2; main courses $6.
   Open: Mon–Fri noon–3pm and 6pm–midnight; Sat–Sun noon–2am.
This restaurant, at Rua Bolívar, is recommended highly. Head up one flight. The soups (one portion will serve three) are delicious and cost only $5.

SHIRLEY, Rua Gustavo Sempaio 610. Tel. 275-1398.

Cuisine: SPANISH/SEAFOOD. **Reservations:** Recommended.
$ Prices: Appetizers $2.50–$3; main courses $5–$10.
Open: Noon–2am.

For the finest Spanish seafood dishes in Rio, you'll have to wait for one of the few tables at Shirley. This small, nondescript backstreet restaurant, behind the Meridien Copacabana, features *zarzuela de mariscos,* paellas, calamares, and shrimp dishes that are absolutely out of this world.

CHURRASCARIA COPACABANA, Avenida Copacabana 1144. Tel. 267-1497.
Cuisine: BARBECUE. **Reservations:** Recommended.
$ Prices: Appetizers $1.50–$2; main courses $6–$12. Major credit cards accepted.
Open: 11am–2am.

For fine steaks at bargain prices, try Churrascaria Copacabana. Fine baby beef, filet mignon, and delicious *galeto* (baby chicken) are offered at unbelievably low prices. Attractive mirrors and red-brick walls brighten the surroundings.

CHURRASCARIA JARDIM, Rua República do Perú 225. Tel. 235-3623.
Cuisine: BARBECUE. **Reservations:** Recommended.
$ Prices: Appetizers $2; main courses $9. Major credit cards accepted.
Open: Daily noon–1am.

A favorite of German tourists in Copacabana is this huge—and invariably jammed—*churrascaria.* No fewer than four chefs grill the wonderful steaks and chops on a blazing hearth at the left side of this beef oasis.

Don't be misled by the exterior, which resembles a private home. Part of the dining complex area is outside, covered by a canopy of branches, leaves, and lanterns.

Co-owners Eugene Gudman (Hungarian) and James Brager (German) are justifiably proud of their filet mignon platters and mixed grill. Most tempting, too, are the superb *maminha de alcatra* (baby beef) and *cordeira* (lamb). Incidentally, the mixed grill (*churrasco mixto a Jardim*), a house specialty, is a feast of steak, liver, and sausages—enough for two. Domestic wines are only $4 per bottle.

MARIUS, Avenida Atlântica 290. Tel. 542-2393.
Cuisine: BARBECUE. **Reservations:** Recommended.
$ Prices: All-you-can-eat $10. Major credit cards accepted.
Open: 11am–midnight.

Marius, one of the local *churrascaria* favorites, is in Leme, on the beachfront. Here you can enjoy all-you-can-eat sausage, chicken, turkey, steak, tomato, salad, heart of palm, and potato salad. Empty liquor bottles line one wall of this bilevel eatery. A second Marius has opened at Rua Francisco Otaviano 96 in Ipanema (tel. 287-2552).

LE MAZOT, Rua Paula Freitas 31. Tel. 255-0834.
Cuisine: SWISS/FRENCH. **Reservations:** Recommended.
$ Prices: Appetizers $2.50; main courses $5–$10. Major credit cards accepted.
Open: Noon–1am.

A brother-and-sister team, René and Irene Brulhart, have been the talk of Copacabana for years with their fine cuisine at Le Mazot. It's a classy, though small, dinner club, with both outdoor and indoor dining. Any of the blue-jacketed waiters will tell you that the *fondue bourguignonne* is a superb delicacy. We heartily concur, but we enjoy the *filet de sole meunière* almost as much. Frequently jammed in the evening, Le Mazot would be a good lunch choice. The $1.50 cover and 10% service charge boost the prices somewhat, so if you're on a tight budget, order carefully.

RESTAURANTE A MARISQUEIRA, Barata Ribeiro 232. Tel. 237-3920.
Cuisine: SEAFOOD. **Reservations:** Recommended.
$ Prices: Appetizers $1.50; main courses $5–$10. Major credit cards accepted.
Open: 11am–1am.

Seafood fans should try this restaurant, off Rua República do Perú, near the Uruguay Hotel, where the house specialty is *peixe frito a marisqueira* (fried fish filet).

RIAN, Rua Santa Clara 8A. Tel. 255-4984.
Cuisine: BARBECUE. **Reservations:** Recommended.
$ Prices: Appetizers $1.50; main courses $6–$10. Major credit cards accepted.
Open: 11:30am–1am.

For perhaps the largest T-bone steak served anywhere in Rio, you might try the Rian, located just off the beach. On our last visit, the $7 steak spilled over the plate and was easily enough for two. Also recommended is the shrimp en brochette with Brazilian rice, called *brochettes de camarão com arroz a grega*. Small and cozy, the Rian has a good wine and liquor stock, too.

TERRACO ATLÂNTICO, Avenida Atlântica 3432. Tel. 521-1296.
Cuisine: INTERNATIONAL. **Reservations:** Recommended.
$ Prices: Appetizers $2; main courses $6–$12. Major credit cards accepted.
Open: Daily 11am–3am.

You should try Terraco Atlântico, primarily for the spectacular view of the beach and ocean. Head up to the second floor, next to the Help Discotheque. Vie for one of the outdoor tables. You can also dine indoors in air-conditioned comfort. Choose from an enormous menu and enjoy the pasta, fish, meat, and typical Brazilian dishes.

RESTAURANT MOENDA, Avenida Atlântica 2064. Tel. 257-1834.
Cuisine: BAHIANA. **Reservations:** Recommended.
$ Prices: Appetizers $2; main courses $5–$12. Major credit cards accepted.
Open: Daily noon–midnight.

The *muqueca de peixe,* at $13, is a must. A bonus here is the scenic view. A $2 cover charge puts Moenda in the splurge category. Try it—if you're willing to pay the tab.

IPANEMA & LEBLON

ALVARO'S BAR, Ataulfo de Paiva 500. Tel. 294-2148.
Cuisine: BRAZILIAN.
$ Prices: Appetizers $1.50; main courses $6–$15.
Open: Noon–2am.

Alvaro's, on the corner of Cupertino Durão, is more a "whiskería" than a confeitería. Hot plates, sandwiches, and pizza are available, but beer, wine, and whisky are best-sellers. A second branch has opened in the São Conrado Fashion Mall (tel. 322-2726).

CELEIRO, Rua Dias Ferreira 199. Tel. 274-7843.
Cuisine: HEALTH/NATURAL FOOD.
$ Prices: Appetizers $1.50; main courses $1.50–$6.
Open: 11:30am–5pm.

This is a fairly sophisticated health-food restaurant. Self-service salads are $1.50 per kilogram. Hot dishes average $6.

LE COIN, Ataulfo de Paiva 658. Tel. 294-2599.
Cuisine: BRAZILIAN/INTERNATIONAL. **Reservations:** Recommended.
$ Prices: Appetizers $1.50; main courses $4–$7. Major credit cards accepted.
Open: Noon–2am.

This Argentine-type confeitería, bustling and noisy, is a fine choice in Leblon. Customers sit for hours, enjoying sandwiches, tea, coffee, and whisky. Hot plates (*frango* or steaks) are often enough for two, making the prices hard to beat.

DELICAT'S, Avenida Henrique Dumont 68. Tel. 274-0242.

Cuisine: KOSHER/DELI.
$ Prices: Sandwiches $1.50–$2.
Open: Mon–Sat 10am–6pm.
This is Rio's only "Judaica" restaurant, a small counter-service (or take-out) spot, where you can stuff yourself on such things as a kosher salami or pastrami sandwich, knishes, or gefilte fish. On Friday, chicken soup with kneidlach is the draw. Come early.

GORDON'S, Rua Dias Ferreira. Tel. 255-6246.
Cuisine: SANDWICHES.
$ Prices: Sandwiches $2–$5.
Open: Daily 10am–2am.
Gordon's, near Final do Leblon, specializes in sandwiches. Customers can choose either sidewalk tables or indoor seating. Huge kangaroo toys attract the small fry. Buy tickets at the counter and then pick up your hamburger, egg-salad sandwich, or tuna.

A GRELHA, Rua Garcia D'Avila 73. Tel. 239-6045.
Cuisine: BRAZILIAN.
$ Prices: Appetizers $2; main courses $3–$7. Major credit cards accepted.
Open: 11am–11pm.
A Grelha is a pizza restaurant with an enormous menu half a block from Visconde de Pirajá. The decor is just above plain—the real attractions are the Brazilian-style pizzas with almost any imaginable topping, the *frango,* and the fish platters.

RIO NAPOLIS, Rua Teixeira de Melo 53. Tel. 267-9909.
Cuisine: ITALIAN.
$ Prices: Appetizers $1.50; main courses $3–$7. Major credit cards accepted.
Open: Daily 11:30am–1am.
This is another fine Italian choice, where pizzas, spaghetti *bolonhês,* and cannellone are featured. The menu is fairly extensive. The pizza and pasta dishes are the least expensive.

SABOR SAUDE, Avenida Ataulfo de Paiva 630. Tel. 239-4396.
Cuisine: HEALTH/NATURAL FOOD.
$ Prices: Appetizers $1.50; main courses $3–$5.
Open: Daily 7am–10pm.
This restaurant features eggplant, a salad bar, pure juices, quiche, and vegetable and meat dishes called *carne de soja.* We highly recommend it.

IL CAPO, Rua Visconde de Pirajá 276. Tel. 287-2845.
Cuisine: ITALIAN.
$ Prices: Appetizers $1.50; main courses $5. Major credit cards accepted.
Open: Noon–2am.
Individual pizzas are the featured selection at Il Capo. Seafood dishes are also good here, as is the pasta.

FINAL DO LEBLON, Rua Dias Ferreira 64. Tel. 294-2749.
Cuisine: BRAZILIAN/INTERNATIONAL. **Reservations:** Recommended.
$ Prices: Appetizers $2; main courses $5–$10.
Open: 11am–2am.
The young crowd takes to this bustling Leblon restaurant where sidewalk tables are at a premium. Prices are reasonable for *milanesa, churrasco,* the daily special, and other items on the varied menu. There is also indoor dining for those who prefer a quieter setting.

LAGOA CHARLIES, Maria Quiteria 136 at the corner of Epitácio Pessoa. Tel. 287-0335.
Cuisine: MEXICAN. **Reservations:** Recommended.
$ Prices: Appetizers $2–$3; main courses $5–$10. Major credit cards accepted.

Open: Dinner only, noon–2am.

For the best in Mexican food, try Lagoa Charlies. The three Mexican owners operate three restaurants in their home country. We enjoy dining on the outdoor terrace, particularly on warm nights. Try the guacamole salad and the pollo curry. Humorous Mexican posters adorn the festive indoor dining room, and there are strolling musicians.

SPLURGE CHOICES

ALBACORA, in the Marina da Gloria. Tel. 205-6496 or 265-3997.
   Cuisine: INTERNATIONAL. **Reservations:** Required.
$ **Prices:** Lunch cruise and dinner cruise $50 per person. Major credit cards accepted.
   Open: Mon–Sat noon–1am; Sun noon–6pm.

The view of the city is spectacular from Guanabara Bay aboard the *Albacora,* a yacht that doubles as a restaurant. Friday and Saturday nights it sets sail for a moonlit dinner cruise from 9pm until 1am.

ANTIQUARIUS, Rua Aristides Espínola 19. Tel. 294-1496.
   Cuisine: CONTINENTAL. **Reservations:** Recommended.
$ **Prices:** Appetizers $5–$15; main courses $15–$30. Major credit cards accepted.
   Open: Daily noon–2am.

For the finest in continental cuisine, especially seafood, Antiquarius is a definite must. The attractive interior of this elegant restaurant is worth a look. Both floors are filled with antiques, and from the dining areas you can see the sculptures in the garden. Upstairs, valuable antiques are for sale. Small private alcoves encourage intimate dining.

CHALE, Rua da Matriz 54. Tel. 286-0897.
   Cuisine: BAHIAN. **Reservations:** Recommended.
$ **Prices:** Appetizers $2; main courses $7–$10. Major credit cards accepted.
   Open: Tues–Sun 11:30am on.

Chalé, in Botafogo, is probably Rio's most popular Bahian restaurant. Located in an 1884 home, it has waitresses in traditional Bahian dress. Sample the *xinxim de galinha* and *moqueca de peixe* here.

GROTTAMMARE, Rua Gomes Carneiro 132. Tel. 287-1596.
   Cuisine: SEAFOOD/ITALIAN. **Reservations:** Suggested.
$ **Prices:** Appetizers $1.50–$3; main courses $12. Major credit cards accepted.
   Open: 6:30pm–2am.

Excellent seafood, as well as Italian dishes, is offered at this normally packed restaurant at the beginning of Ipanema. The *peixe ao Grottammare* special is enough for two, and the sauce is spectacular. Ask for a table on the terrace.

MR. ZEE, Avenida General San Martín 1219. Tel. 294-6240.
   Cuisine: CHINESE. **Reservations:** Recommended.
$ **Prices:** Appetizers $2; main courses $10–$15. Major credit cards accepted.
   Open: Noon–1am.

You'll be well taken care of here by owner David Zee, a Hong Kong native educated in the United States who left a banking career to open one of Rio's finest Chinese restaurants. Among the delights on the menu are Beijing duck, sweet-and-sour spareribs, and squid with onions and black-bean sauce. Dessert choices include caramel-fried bananas with ice cream and honeyed pears with crème de menthe sauce.

PORCAO CHURRASCARIA, Rua Barão da Torre 218. Tel. 521-0999.
   Cuisine: BARBECUE. **Reservations:** Recommended.
$ **Prices:** $12 Rodizio (all you can eat). Major credit cards accepted.
   Open: 11:30am–2am.

The Porção Churrascaria's fixed-price, all-inclusive meal is not only extremely generous—you'll find more than you can handle on your plate—but also very delicious. Look for the pig logo on the sign.

SPECIALTY DINING

LOCAL BUDGET BETS

CENTER CITY A chain of 10 stand-up snack bars called **Bob's** are scattered throughout downtown Rio. In the shopping district is one on Rua São José, in Largo da Carioca, a parklike plaza. The branches we've seen are all spotless and tidy, the waiters are polite, and the service is fast. Bob's has good burgers for under $1.50, thick milkshakes for $1.35, and ham and eggs for $2.

In the Praça Mauá area, try the small but clean **Lanches Cerejinha,** on Presidente Vargas and Uruguaiana, near the Guanabara Palace Hotel. Fried shrimp is recommended here; all sandwiches cost under $3.

Nearby is the much larger **Insalate,** on Rio Branco and Rua Inhauma, opposite the São Francisco Hotel. In this eatery, with counter service only, you pay first and order later. We enjoy the ham and eggs at $1.50. Hot dogs (90¢), served with tomato and relish, are also quite tasty. The ice cream is as good as any we've found outside Italy and the United States; try an ice-cream cone (*sorvete*) for 75¢.

COPACABANA BEACH Copacabana has several fast-service stand-up eateries similar to Bob's downtown. Our favorites are **Boninos,** on Avenida Copacabana, near Rua Bolívar, and **Bonis,** on Avenida Copacabana, near Rua Siqueira Campos; purchase a ticket before you order.

For tasty burgers, sandwiches, and inexpensive meat platters, try **Top Top,** on Rua C. Ramos, near Avenida Atlântica. Look for the large orange sign.

Nearby, at the Woolworth-type **Lojas Americanas,** one can enjoy inexpensive dishes at the counter. Sandwiches start at $1.25; beef dishes range from $4.50 to $7.50; and a soft drink is 50¢. Other good choices nearby are **Cervantes,** at Rua Prado Junior 335; and **Cupim Minas,** at Avenida Copacabana 895. All are similar in menu and decor.

IPANEMA & LEBLON Our favorite fast-food stop in this section is **Chaplin,** at Visconde de Pirajá 187, near Farme de Amoedo. Murals of the tramp in Chaplin's classic films line the walls. Purchase tickets at the cashier and enjoy magnificent crêpes (70¢), delicious ice cream, or tasty sandwiches.

Finally, for some of the best freshly squeezed juices south of the equator, try **Polis Sucos,** on Visconde de Pirajá, at Teixeira del Melo, opposite Praça General Osorio.

Several other fine fast-food eateries are located on Rua Visconde de Pirajá in Ipanema. Try **Bob's,** at no. 463, opposite the H. Stern building, and sample a delicious hot dog for 40¢ or a tuna sandwich for 75¢; look for the red-and-white sign. **Bonis,** at no. 595C, is a stand-up fast-food sandwich shop with fine milkshakes (50¢). **Chaika,** at no. 321, has stand-up service in front and booths at the rear (extensive menu). Finally, the ubiquitous **McDonald's** is at no. 206.

A CONFEITARIA

A late-afternoon tradition in Rio is the tea and cocktail hour, a rite celebrated in establishments known as *confeitarías,* (loosely translated as "confectionary shops"). The better ones remind us of old-world European cafés where one sips coffee, nibbles a pastry, and observes what's going on at the next table.

COLOMBO, Rua Gonçalves Dias 36. Tel. 232-2300.
  Cuisine: CONFEITARIA.
$ Prices: Pastries and sandwiches $2–$4; lunch $3.50–$6.
  Open: 11am–6pm.

This huge confeitaría, near Rua 7 de Setembro, is the most elegant in Rio. Large old chandeliers dangle from the high ceilings, and enormous breakfronts, filled with odd-shaped liquor bottles, line the sides. Smartly jacketed waiters scurry about the block-long dining room and the second-floor balcony catering to sophisticated matrons. Well-dressed men who look as if they had just arrived from Madison Avenue comprise another group of customers. You can hear Portuguese, Spanish, French, and English being spoken around you. Within minutes after you're seated, the waiters will bring you a tray loaded with tarts, napoleons, eclairs, and other pastries. Order coffee, tea, or a cocktail and prepare to relax for an hour or two in an atmosphere reminiscent of Vienna. Surprisingly, the prices are quite low—if you avoid the regular menu. We recently paid $4.50 for four pastries and two pots of coffee. (You are charged for what you eat from the pastry tray.) Some hot dishes on the menu are also reasonably priced. If you're in a hurry, try some stand-up empanadas, croquettes, and a soft drink.

Note: There is a sibling confeitaría, with the same name, in Copacabana Beach, Avenida Copacabana 890, at the corner of Barão de Ipanema.

6. ATTRACTIONS

Beach lovers will want to make Rio's beaches their home during the daytime. But remember not to miss the sights of Corcovado and Sugar Loaf (Pão de Açucar) and romantic boat rides to delightful islands in Guanabara Bay. You will also have fun strolling through the historic downtown district, interesting museums, and fabulous shops.

SUGGESTED ITINERARIES

IF YOU HAVE ONE DAY   In the morning, take a quick city tour, which should include Corcovado and Pão de Açucar. In the afternoon, head to Copacabana and Ipanema to people-watch on the beach and at the bars. Spend the evening at a Samba Club (Plataforma or Oba Oba).

IF YOU HAVE TWO DAYS   In addition to the activities for Day 1, add the Botanical Gardens, the Tijuca Forest, and Paquetá.

IF YOU HAVE THREE DAYS   Consider a side trip along the Costa Verde to Parati. Buzios is another delightful place to visit, as is Petropolis.

IF YOU HAVE FIVE DAYS OR MORE   Foz do Iguaçu is a "must see" after Rio. Another recommended destination is Salvador.

THE TOP ATTRACTIONS
BEACHES

Since Flamengo and Botafogo, on Guanabara Bay, are sometimes polluted, we strongly advise you *not* to swim there. Head for Leme and Copacabana Beach, which are the next closest beaches to center city. Beyond Copacabana are **Ipanema** (setting for the song "The Girl from Ipanema"), where some of our top nightclub recommendations are located; **Leblon;** and **Vidigal.** All these beaches are open year round. In general, the waters are calmest early in the day. The waves tend to build up as the day progresses so that by late afternoon it may be rather difficult to swim.

To reach any of these beaches, take bus no. 415, 438, 464, or 472 from Avenida Presidente Vargas and Rio Branco. From Praça Mahatma Gandhi take bus no. 119, 121, 122, 128, 132, 175, or 179. From Praça Mauá, take bus no. 121, 123, 128, or 173. The fare is less than 30¢ to the farthest point.

Vidigal and **Sao Conrado** are quiet beach areas with three of Rio's most lavish hotels located just beyond Leblon. Nearest to Leblon is the **Sheraton,** in Vidigal, with its excellent restaurants, clubs, and pools. A mile or so farther out, and next to each other, are the **Nacional** and the **Inter-Continental,** in Sao Conrado. Don't leave Rio without dropping by. While here, note **Rocinha,** Rio's largest favela, near the Nacional Hotel.

❓DID YOU KNOW . . . ?

- Brazil is the largest Roman Catholic country in the world.
- Brazil commands about 60% of the world market for orange juice.
- About one-fourth of the world's vegetable species are found in Brazil.
- The Spix's Macaw of Brazil—the world's most endangered parrot—has been extinct in the wild since 1988. There are only 10 left in captivity—2 are in Brazil.
- As early as 1625 there was a Jewish community in the state of Pernambuco (Recife is its capital), consisting of 5,000 individuals.
- Brazil was Portugal's only colony in the Americas.
- Carioca refers to a native of Rio de Janeiro. Of Tupi Indian origin, the word originally had negative connotations.
- The largest lagoon in the world is Brazil's Lagoa de Patos; it is 158 miles long and extends over 4,110 square miles.

A beautiful, though somewhat treacherous, way to reach Vidigal is by walking along the coast. The only drawback is the heavy oncoming traffic. *Be warned:* Cars along here often travel at fairly high speeds, and there isn't much room between you and them. Starting in Ipanema, follow Avenida Vieira Soto, which becomes Avenida Delfim Moreira in Leblon and Avenida Niemeyer in Vidigal. You'll enjoy breathtaking views of the mountains, including Sugarloaf, as well as of the islands and Rio itself. You'll also pass fishermen with bamboo rods along the cliffs jutting out from the shore and huts built right into them. A return trip by cab should cost you no more than $5.

MOUNTAINS

SUGARLOAF Vying with Corcovado as Rio's major tourist draw is the ✪ **Paõ de Açúcar** (Sugarloaf), to the southwest of center city in the bayfront community of **Urca**, near Botafogo. This world-famous gumdrop-shaped peak, which overlooks Guanabara Bay, offers a stunning view of Rio.

To reach the top of Sugarloaf, you must take two cable cars—one will take you 700 feet up to Urca, the lower adjacent mountain, while a second car will lift you the additional 500 feet to the 1,230-foot peak. After disembarking at Urca, stroll about and then pick up the second car at the area's far side, beyond the restaurant. At several points during the ascent, the 75-passenger car appears to be rising vertically, and it just about is. Besides the stupendous view, there are lovely winding paths and unusual vegetation at both levels. Bring your camera and a sweater if the day is cool. (Prepare for a wait on weekends, when Brazilians from other cities as well as foreigners throng here.)

Take any **bus** marked "Lins-Urca" and ask to be dropped at **Praia Vermelha** (the end of Avenida Pasteur, near the cable-car entrance), a 25-minute ride from Praça Mahatma Gandhi. (From center city, bus no. 442 is your best bet.) The cable cars leave frequently, beginning at 8am and continuing until 9pm; the round-trip cost is $3.50. If you're going only up to Urca, the cost is still $3.50.

CORCOVADO Fifteen miles from center city is another legendary landmark—the 2,300-foot ✪ **Corcovado** (Hunchback) Mountain. At its peak is the famous 130-foot-high Statue of Christ the Redeemer, built as a peace symbol; the figure's outstretched arms welcome all travelers.

Families live in small *favelas* along Corcovado's hillside, and the 50-passenger train makes several stops during its ascent. At each station, shoeless children throng around the visitors, selling bags of roasted peanuts for 25¢. The vegetation is exotic and worth a picture or two.

Before beginning the fascinating 227-step climb to the peak, refresh yourself with an ice cream (60¢) sold at a stand near the train exit. As a thirst quencher, pick up a fresh orange (30¢), too. You can rest during the climb at a midpoint café that has an outdoor dining area jutting out from the mountain. At the top, stroll along a winding uphill path that carries you to the foot of the Christ statue. The inevitable souvenir stands (prices are high) dot the scene. From the lookout balconies you can spot the famous Maracaña soccer stadium, the Joquei Club racetrack, and the Botanical Garden palm trees. And look for Sugarloaf, which dominates the bay side. At night the statue is floodlit—an awe-inspiring sight.

Directions: From center city, take the metro from Largo da Carioca to Largo do Machado. Then catch bus no. 569 (labeled COSME VELHO) to the Corcovado train station. You'll undoubtedly be approached by numerous taxi drivers offering to take you to the top. Bargain with them; you should be able to get the fare down to about $7.50. The view of the bay and surrounding countryside is unbeatable from the road; you'll miss it if you take the train.

The open-sided train departs every hour beginning at 8am on weekdays and every half hour on weekends. The last train leaves for the top at about dusk. The round-trip fare is $5.

DOWNTOWN WALKING TOUR

We suggest that you begin with a stroll through center city at **Praca Mauá,** the northside dock area of Rio Branco—the city's main thoroughfare. As you walk south on this bustling street, note the enchanting sidewalk mosaics. Some blocks have animal or bird designs imbedded in the concrete. Other sidewalk areas are decorated with undulating lines that resemble abstract paintings.

Four blocks down is **Avenida Presidente Vargas,** a wide thoroughfare used by buses heading to the beaches and to suburban districts. After two more blocks you'll find yourself at **Rua Buenos Aires,** where a wooden sign with an arrow pointing to the right indicates the **Mercado das Flores** (flower market) in the nearby Praça Olavo Bilac. The outdoor shops sell beautiful flowers; orchids are a specialty.

Praça Olavo Bilac is located at the beginning of Rio's shopping district, where traffic is barred much of the day. Alongside is the **Rua Gonçalves Dias,** which is lined with hundreds of shops. Browse through the alligator goods and the native handcrafts. (Some of these shops are listed in our shopping section below.)

The **Largo da Carioca,** a parklike plaza, is your next destination, which you will reach by following Gonçalves Dias. On a small hill is the **Convento de Santo Antonio,** a convent and church that you might like to visit.

A small overhead two-car railway runs from here toward the Corcovado district, where the famous **Statue of Christ the Redeemer** is located. The round-trip fare is only $5.

The new tree-lined thoroughfare here is **República do Chile,** built as part of the reclamation program. Turn left on República do Chile for one block and you'll be back on Rio Branco. Continue along that street for two blocks until you reach Rua Araujo.

On your left, across Rio Branco, is the **National Museum of Fine Art** (open Tuesday through Friday from 1 to 5pm, on Saturday and Sunday from 3 to 6pm; admission is free). Adjacent to the museum is the **National Library,** where browsers are welcome.

To the right is the elegant **Municipal Theater** (see "Evening Entertainment"), which is a small replica of the Paris Opéra. On the theater's lower level is a restaurant. The front of the theater faces **Praça Floriano,** which is the start of **Cinelandia** (movie district). The area is noted for good budget restaurants as well. The street leading from Praça Floriano winds up at **Praça Mahatma Gandhi,** considered the heart of downtown Rio.

From here you can stroll to **Flamengo Beach** (a 15-minute walk) by heading to the bay and making a right on **Avenida Beira Mar,** a wide, winding bayfront drive that leads to Flamengo's center. It's a lovely walk, with the bay and Sugarloaf peak on the left and landscaped gardens on the right.

To reach **Copacabana Beach** from Flamengo, take any bus from Praia Flamengo, the main street, heading in that direction. We recommend this scenic ride. Direct buses will return you to downtown Rio in about 20 minutes.

RIO ORLA

Probably the best way to orient yourself to Rio's sights is via the air-conditioned microbuses labeled RIO ORLA, which run along the beachfront from Praia Vermelho (near Sugarloaf) to São Conrado (near the Inter-Continental Hotel) in about 1½ hours. We suggest you board at Leme for best viewing.

MORE ATTRACTIONS

MUSEUM OF MODERN ART, Avenida Infante D. Henrique 85, Flamengo Park. Tel. 210-2188.

In 1978 a fire destroyed virtually the entire collection of the Museum of Modern Art, one of the most important collections in Brazil. Of the 834 works in the present collection, 500 were obtained after the fire and unfortunately don't measure up to those that were destroyed; however, it is expected that the quality may improve over time. The museum's Cinema Club is worth visiting on a rainy afternoon.
Admission: Free.
Open: Noon–6pm.

MONUMENT TO WORLD WAR II HEROES, Flamengo Park. Tel. 240-1283.

On the bay and visible from Praça Mahatma Gandhi is an awesome monument to Brazilians who served in World War II. This structure has a portico that rests on two 150-foot-high concrete pillars. Three sculptured military figures protect the monument, and an eternal flame burns at the base.

A small museum here houses a collection of World War II weapons (mostly submachine guns and automatic rifles) as well as brilliantly colored war murals. The mausoleum under the monument is moving. Even if you usually avoid monuments, try to visit this one.
Admission: Free.
Open: Mon–Sat (Sun also in Apr).

MUSEUM OF THE REPUBLIC, Praia do Flamengo, Flamengo Beach. Tel. 225-4875.

Ever wear slippers in a museum? Well, to tour the Museum of the Republic, you'll have to don them to protect the century-old wooden floors in this handsome structure, which was once a palace. Every room here, with varying colors and decors, represents a different era of world history.

Equally interesting is the garden, dotted with 120-year-old royal palm trees that soar 150 feet in height. And there are lily ponds here bridged by wooden walks. Enchanting. The entrance is on Rua do Catete, one block from the beachfront, off Silveira Martíns.
Admission: Free.
Open: Tues–Fri 1–6pm; Sat–Sun 3–6pm.

INDIAN MUSEUM, Rua do Palmeiras 56. Tel. 286-0845.

Visit this museum for a look at the primitive Indian tribes of the Amazon River Basin. On exhibit are native ceramics, baskets, religious articles, and clay dolls. There is also an interesting exhibit explaining the art of canoemaking.
Admission: Free.
Open: Noon–6pm.

MUSEUM OF NATIONAL HISTORY, Praça Marechal Ancora. Tel. 220-5908.

This museum has interesting collections of porcelain, crystal, silver, weapons, coaches, and imperial coats-of-arms.
Admission: Free.
Open: Tues–Fri 10am–5pm; Sat–Sun and hols 2:30–5pm.

CARMEN MIRANDA MUSEUM, Rua Barbosa 560, Flamengo. Tel. 551-2597.

 Here you will have a nostalgic look at the life of this 1940s star through photographs and displays of her costumes (including the legendary turbans), jewelry, and high-heeled sandals.

Admission: Free.
Open: Tues–Fri 11am–5pm; Sat–Sun 1–5pm.

OUTDOOR MARKET, Praça General Osorio, Ipanema.
This fair draws thousands of locals every Sunday. Youthful vendors display their wares, and prices range from under $2 to several hundred dollars. The most popular items are paintings, leather goods, inexpensive jewelry, and unique clothes.
Admission: Free.
Open: Sun 11am–6pm.

QUINTA DE BOA VISTA, near Maracana Soccer Stadium.
Just outside center city, near Maracana Soccer Stadium, is this large park, which houses the National Museum, a zoo, and an aquarium. The museum exhibits Indian weapons, clothing, and utensils; a six-ton meteorite (largest ever to hit Earth); and other relics from Brazil's past. Admission is free. A variety of South American animals and birds can be seen at the nearby zoo, along with Asian and African species.
Open: (museum): Tues–Sun 10am–5pm.
Directions: From Avenidas Presidente Vargas and Rio Branco, at Copacabana, take bus no. 472 or 474 and get off at Cancela. From Cinelandia (Praça Mahatma Gandhi), catch bus no. C4, and from Praça Mauá take bus no. 312; the stop is the same.

JOQUEI CLUB, Jardim Botanico 1003, Gavea. Main entrance: Gate 18. Tel. 297-6655.
Fifteen miles from downtown Rio, in the Corcovado district near the Botanical Gardens, is this famous and aristocratic racetrack. Betting windows at this handsome oval track range from 60¢ and up.
Admission: 10¢.
Open: Mon and Thurs 7:30pm; Sat–Sun 2 or 4pm. **Bus:** No. 172 or 178 from Praça Mauá or no. 438, 558, or 592 from Presidente Vargas and Rio Branco. The last three buses also run from Copacabana Beach, along with no. 592.

BOTANICAL GARDENS, Jardim Botanico 1008. Tel. 274-8246.
The Jardim Botanico are located on 120 acres dotted with 7,000 species of trees (including 100-foot-high royal palms) and 600 varieties of orchids. On the grounds also are a museum, a library, and an aquarium. We recently combined a visit here with our trip to the track.
Admission: 35¢.
Open: Daily 8am–5pm.

FAVELAS
Rio's rock-bottom poor—estimated at 1 million—live in shacks clustered in steep hillside communities that are called *favelas* (shantytowns). In all there are 100 *favelas* scattered through the city's hills. The largest is probably **Rocinha** (near Gavea), which houses thousands. *Black Orpheus,* a brilliant movie filmed in the Pasmado *favela* (which no longer exists), beautifully captured the spirit of *favela* life during carnival time.
Note: It makes us uncomfortable to recommend entering a *favela* even with a tour, and it certainly is not advisable to enter one on your own.

SANTA TERESA
For a pleasant afternoon, why not head to Santa Teresa, one of Rio's oldest areas, via one of the few remaining trams in the Western Hemisphere. For 20¢, the *bonde,* a trolley with open sides, will take you up the mountain to Santa Teresa. Be sure to take the one that says DOIS IRMÃOES. The views are spectacular, and getting there is almost an adventure. You can take the same trolley back or stroll around and catch the next one. Along the way you pass **Chacara do Ceu Museum.** The *bonde* station is located downtown near the new cathedral and the foot of the old aqueduct. It's open Tuesday through Friday from 2 to 5pm.
Warning: Do not bring cameras or other valuables with you on the trolley, since thieves have frequented the route.

THE COUNTRYSIDE

Numerous wealthy Cariocas live in the state of Rio de Janeiro, just outside Rio. A popular suburb in the mountains about 40 miles from center city is **Petrópolis,** where Brazil's emperors once lived. The **Imperial Museum** is located here, not far from a venerable old hotel, the **Quitandinha** (now a country club). Buses leave for Petrópolis every 15 minutes, from the Rodoviária Novo Rio. The fare for the two-hour ride is $1 each way.

Closer to Rio is **Tijuca Forest,** a lush tropical area, floodlit at night, where the famous **Cascatinha** (waterfall) can be seen amid grottoes and caves in the area. To reach the forest, take bus no. 233 or 234 (marked RODOVIARIA–B. TIJUCA) from Praça Saenz Pena. The main square (**Praça Saenz Pena**) in the village of Tijuca is where you pick up bus no. 640 (marked SAENZ PENA-BARRA DA TIJUCA), which passes within walking distance of the waterfall. A cab will cost you $12 from center city.

Inexpensive tours to Petrópolis and Tijuca are available.

ORGANIZED TOURS

CRUISES   If you need a few days to catch your breath after the hectic pace in Rio, you may want to take a **Costa Verde** cruise. The weekend cruise, which leaves on Friday and returns on Sunday, will take you to Itacuruca and Ilha Grande. There is also a four-day cruise, from Monday to Thursday, which goes to Itacuruca, Ilha Grande, Ilha Sandri, and Paqueta Island. Both include breakfast and dinner. For more information, including current prices, contact **Camargo Yachting in Rio,** Avenida Prado Junior 160, Copacabana (tel. 275-0643).

The **Bâteau Mouche** cruise was one of Rio's most popular tourist attractions. It suspended operations because of a New Year's Eve tragedy in 1988 in which one of the boats capsized and almost all the revelers on board perished. Many yacht cruises around Guanabara Bay would stop for swimming at Jurujuba, then continue on to Paquetá Island, where first-class passengers would be given a tour in a horse-drawn carriage. (Everyone, however, got a superb look at the Rio skyline and at nearby communities.) The concierge at your hotel should be able to tell you if the Bâteau Mouche cruise is back in operation.

7. SPECIAL & FREE EVENTS

Ever been in New Orleans during Mardi Gras? Multiply the frenzy there by several times and you'll come up with an approximation of what happens in Rio each year during the three days and four nights preceding Ash Wednesday, the beginning of Lent.

This is a period when the life of Rio is devoted only to carnival. Business is suspended; commercial life stops. Hundreds of costume balls are held throughout the city, and the Cariocas talk, walk, and breathe in time to the samba, Brazil's national dance. The streets are filled with dancers, small Latin combos, confetti, strong perfume, and endless parades organized by the many private samba schools in Rio.

Pre-Lent celebrations are traditional in most Latin countries. Each country puts its own special stamp on its carnival or Mardi Gras. In New Orleans the beat is jazz; in Trinidad it's steel bands. In Rio the beat is the samba, and it's everywhere—on the radio, blasting out of record shops, and among improvised groups along the beaches. The frenzy, excitement, and gaiety of Rio's carnival celebration are infectious. You'll find yourself moving with a lighter step, caught up in the beat of the samba bands along the streets. There is dancing the length of Rio Branco, from Presidente Vargas to Cinelandia. Everyone is in costume, and you'll probably want to be in one, too.

Every evening, specific carnival events take place at the Sambódromo, an expanse of Avenida Marquês de Sapucaí that has been blocked off specifically for carnival events. Buy grandstand tickets, around $20, for best viewing, and be sure to be in your seat Sunday and Monday nights for the most famous event—the **Parade of the**

Samba Schools (Escolas de Samba). It lasts until the next morning. There are ten schools, each with its own theme and song (samba, of course). There may be 2,000 to 3,500 costumed people dancing down the street to each band. The people in the stands join in the singing, and it's a thrilling experience.

There are also balls at some hotels and theaters, but they're expensive and not worth the money. Instead, go to Canecão and dance on the tables all night. The carnival season formally begins at midnight on New Year's Eve, when sedate orchestras in the hotels and at private balls give way to the frenetic rhythms of native bands.

8. SPORTS & RECREATION

Brazilians are mad about athletics and athletes. Night after night—there are few daytime events because of the sun—huge crowds flock to basketball, boxing, and horse-racing events in and around Rio.

However, for the South American, and particularly the Carioca, there is one special hero: the *futebol* (soccer) star; *futebol* is the national sport (Brazil has won three of the last nine world cups) and much more a part of life here than even baseball is in the United States. *Futebol* is played everywhere by youngsters and even oldsters—on the beaches, in the streets, in the parks, and (via television) in the living rooms and basements of private homes. This year-round devotion pays off. Every year at least one of Brazil's many teams reaches the international soccer playoffs.

You should not miss seeing a *futebol* match here, whether or not you are a sports fan. You will be roused to a fever pitch of partisanship for one team or the other. On a recent visit to magnificent **✪ Maracaña Stadium**—a mammoth oval amphitheater completed in 1950 that has an official seating capacity of 150,000 but squeezes in 200,000 for major matches—we found ourselves shouting for the Vasco da Gama team as if we were veteran fans (we'd never seen them play before). When the main match started at about 9:15pm, it seemed that every spectator had a small transistor radio pressed to an ear to catch the broadcast of the contest.

Tickets for *futebol* matches at Maracaña Stadium can be purchased in advance at the Municipal Theater box office (see "Evening Entertainment") or at the park. For important weekend matches, plan to reserve ahead. Reserved-seat prices range from $25 for an upper-tier midfield location to $10 for a lower-deck ticket. An unreserved bleacher ticket costs about $3, and you can stand for $1.25.

Unlike the food at many U.S. stadiums, it is cheap here. Sandwiches run about $1.25, a can of beer about 80¢, and soft drinks 40¢.

All teams are owned by private social clubs. There are several matches a week in Rio. For schedules, check the *Daily Post,* an English-language daily, or ask your hotel clerk.

To reach the stadium, take bus no. 234 or 241 from Praça Mauá or bus no. 434 from Copacabana Beach. A cab from center city costs about $2.50.

Near Maracaña Stadium is a 50,000-seat indoor arena, **Maracanazinho Stadium,** which features boxing and basketball.

9. SAVVY SHOPPING

Rio is a bargain-hunter's paradise. It offers superb buys in semiprecious stones and jewelry, woodcarvings, wooden trays, handcrafted native goods, natural stone ashtrays and pendants, and alligator and leather handbags and wallets.

SHOPPING CENTERS

RIO SUL, Lauro Müller 116, Botafogo. Tel. 295-1332.
The largest shopping center in Rio is located in front of the Canecâo Club. This modern trilevel arcade features a Mesbla department store on the mall level, an H. Stern outlet, boutiques, music stores, men's shops, toy stores, and lots more—excellent for browsing. It's centrally air-conditioned, with escalators.

CASINO ATLANTICO, Avenida Atlântica 4240. Tel. 247-8709.
This convenient air-conditioned center adjoins the Rio Palace Hotel in Copacabana and is connected by a passageway.

BARRA SHOPPING CENTER, Avenida das Americas 466. Tel. 325-3233.
This is the newest shopping center, way out beyond Gavea in Barra da Tijuca, a growing community. There are wonderful shops here. The center offers free bus transportation from the beach communities.

SHOPPING A TO Z

CHOCOLATE

CHOCOLATE KOPENHAGEN, Rua Ouvidor 147. Tel. 222-6671.
If you're partial to chocolate, hustle into one of these stores, with branches scattered throughout Rio. Manufactured in São Paulo, this delicious chocolate comes in jars and boxes at prices starting at $1. This branch is between Avenidas Rio Branco and Gonçalves Dias; others are at Rua Visconde de Pirajá 250 in Ipanema; at Senador Dantas 24B; and at Avenida Rio Branco 181.

CRAFTS

CASAS DO FOLCLORE, in the H. Stern Building, Rua Visconde de Pirajá 490. Tel. 259-7442.
This first-floor shop is crammed with woodcarvings, trays, and native handcrafts. Best buys are the Indian figures fashioned from jacaranda wood (rosewood, a hard, dark variety) that sell from $10 to $30. Butterfly trays range from $5 to $50; handsome native dolls are as low as $10. Inexpensive native drums, masks, and headpieces are interesting gift ideas.
We've been happy, too, with our batik and jewelry purchases. Reader's comments confirm our opinion that Folclore is your best-value shop for folkloric items. Other Folclore branches are in the Sheraton, Inter-Continental, Leme Palace, and Gloria hotels.

JEWELRY

H. STERN, Rua Visconde de Pirajá 490. Tel. 259-7442.
⭐ For the best in rings, necklaces, bracelets, and other uniquely designed jewelry with Brazilian gemstones (topaz, tourmaline, aquamarine, emerald, and amethyst), you cannot surpass the H. Stern shops. This naturalized Brazilian has been in business since 1946. Today he has more than 150 retail outlets in Latin America, Western Europe, and the United States. We strongly urge you to visit the company's main office and workshop in its own building for a free plant tour (English-language cassette-tape guides are available). You can see how a stone is chosen, cut, shaped, and placed in a setting. And you don't have to buy anything. Since Brazil is the largest producer of colored gemstones, however, prices are quite reasonable. If you can't make it to the main office, browse through the H. Stern shop at Galeão Airport (open 24 hours); at the Copacabana Beach outlet at Avenida Atlântica 1782, near the Excelsior Hotel; or in many of the major hotels. You will find

additional outlets at the Touring Club do Brasil, in Praça Mauá, and at Santos Dumont Airport, as well as in most South American cities. *Note:* All sales are refundable within one year—regardless of reason for return. The New York store will gladly accept returned merchandise.

LEATHER

COPACABANA COUROS E ARTESANATOS, Rua F. Mendes at Avenida Copacabana.

At this store, you will find fine leather goods such as hassocks, wallets, and belts. All the items for sale are made on the premises, and the prices are reasonable.

LES GRIFFES, Rua Garcia D'Avila 113, Ipanema. Tel. 259-7442.

We recommend this branch (as well as the one at Avenida Atlântica 1702, in Copacabana) for its famous designer-label handbags, wallets, apparel, accessories, and other fine leather goods. Gift items and linens also are offered.

LIDO BAGS, Avenida Copacabana 267.

This fine leather shop features wallets, cigarette cases, travel bags, and other novelty items.

TOYS

CARROUSEL, Rua Garcia D'Avila 69. Tel. 239-1697.

For colorful gifts for the kids back home, stop in here.

SHOES

DATELLI, Rua Visconde de Pirajá 317, Ipanema. Tel. 276-5445.

This exclusive shop features top-quality Italian-style leather shoes and accessories.

ROTSTEIN, Rua Visconde de Pirajá 371. Tel. 521-2540.

This is a fine shop in which to browse for Brazilian shoes.

SPORTING OUTFITS

AMOR PERFEITO, Rua Visconde de Pirajá 371. Tel. 287-8349.

For sporting outfits that are different, try this popular shop.

MASKA, Rua Visconde de Pirajá 371. Tel. 247-1919.

You will find the latest styles here.

VARIETY & HANDCRAFTS

ARTEZANIA, in the Vitrine de Ipanema gallery, Visconde de Pirajá 580, Loja 111, Ipanema.

Here you will find goods from other Latin American countries—puno bulls from Peru, gourds from Ecuador, handcrafts from Guatemala, and many items from Bahia. Great for browsing.

IVIOTICI, in the Cassino Atlântico Shopping Center, Avenida Atlântica 4240.

Here we suggest you look at the ceramics and paintings. All the other traditional items are available as well.

LIANE SOUVENIRS, Rua Santa Clara 27.

At this unusual store, between Avenidas Copacabana and Atlântica, Indian masks of palm and straw are good buys at $8 and up. Wooden art pieces, Bahian dolls, and stone ashtrays are interesting gift items, too. Another branch is located downtown, at Rio Branco 25 (17th floor).

MESBLA, Barra Shopping, Rio Sul, Rua de Passeio 42. Tel. 297-7720.

Mesbla, an 11-story department store located near Praça Mahatma Gandhi, is

Rio's equivalent of Macy's; it offers clothing, records, sports equipment, and even an elegant theater on the top floor.

PE DE BOI, Rua Ipiranga 55.
This excellent choice for gaily colored Brazilian handicrafts is right off Pirajá.

SOUVENIR DE RIO, Rio Branco 25.
For inexpensive alligator belts and wallets, drop in here (located near Praça Mauá), where prices start at $10. Dolls, beads, and keychains are also attractively priced.

THOMPSON, Avenida Copacabana 371A.
Thompson specializes in wooden items, leather bags, dolls, and beads.

10. EVENING ENTERTAINMENT

Cariocas come alive in the wee hours. If you are a night person in this world of day people, waste no time in center city. Head straight for Copacabana or Ipanema, where the later the hour the wilder the beat of the bossa nova and the latest hip-action step.

THE PERFORMING ARTS

MUNICIPAL THEATER, Rio Branco and Praça Floriano. Tel. 297-4411.
The cultural center of Rio is the Teatro Municipal, a regal 2,200-seat structure located at Praça Floriano. At carnival time this is the site of exclusive masked balls. In other seasons you can see domestic opera, ballet, concerts, and Portuguese-language theater—at prices ranging from $7 to $15. International companies often appear here but at somewhat higher prices.

In the theater's basement, there is a fine restaurant that's open for lunch.

LIVE ROCK SHOWS

CANECAO, Rua Lauro Muller 1, Botafogo. Tel. 295-3044.
The rage of Rio's younger set is the mammoth (600-table) Canacão, the wildest—and least intimate—nightspot we've seen anywhere. Opened in early 1967, the bayfront Canecão caught on instantly. On weekends, there may be 2,400 young people here from 7pm until the last music fades away in the early morning. The ear-shattering music—emanating from two rock-and-roll quartets and one bossa nova combo—nearly shakes the murals (by Ziraldo) from the walls. There is a $10 (more on weekends) cover, but the cost is only $1.50 for a stein of good domestic beer, $3 for Brazilian whisky, and $3.50 for gin and tonic. You enter through a courtyard, which serves as an area to screen out minors and doubles as a waiting area on weekends, when tables are at a premium. Inside, there is a large reception area where a hostess will lead you to a table on a lower level. The elevated bandstand—in the center of the oval-shaped room—is surrounded by the dance floor, which in turn is encircled by tables. Each combo emerges from below on a moving platform and when finished departs the same way. The use of colored lights helps create a pleasingly theatrical effect. For a quick look at Canecão from the highway, look to the left when heading out to the beach area from center city. Just past Flamengo, and immediately before your bus passes through the Botafogo tunnel, you'll see the huge club. This is a must. Open Tuesday to Sunday from 7pm.
Admission: $10–$15.

THE CLUB & MUSIC SCENE
NIGHTCLUBS & CABARETS

Check with your hotel to make sure which clubs are open. Remember—dress informally.

SCALA, Avenida Afaranio de Melo Franco 296, Leblon. Tel. 239-4448.
This new club features a two-hour show, with samba performances of singing and dancing. The show, starting at 11pm, has been compared to that at the Lido in Paris.
Admission: $15.

OBA-OBA, Rua Humaita 110, Botafogo. Tel. 286-9848.
A popular—and, we think, touristy—show that attracts people, particularly those on package tours, is Oba-Oba. Visitors are drawn by the stunning dancers and the variety show.
Admission: $20.

PLATAFORMA, Rua Adalberto Ferreira 32. Tel. 274-4022.
The lower level has a restaurant (high-priced *churrascaria*). Upstairs, starting at 11pm, is a carnival-dancing show.
Admission: $20.

ASA BRANCA, Avenida Mem de Sá 17. Tel. 252-4428.
At this popular downtown club, there are two shows nightly. You can drink or eat here.
Admission: $10 minimum.

CAFE NICE, Rio Branco 277. Tel. 240-0490.
Popular local singers and dancers perform at this downtown club nightly.
Admission: Varies according to entertainment.

CARINHOSO, Visconde Pirajá 22, Ipanema. Tel. 287-0302.
This is a popular restaurant with dancing and live music. For an additional $3 cover, you can be entertained while you dine.
Admission: $3.

PEOPLE, Avenida Bartolomeu Mitre 370, Leblon. Tel. 294-0547.
⭐ People, one of our favorite spots in Rio, is a bar and restaurant with live music ranging from pop and jazz to Dixieland and old movie favorites. The show starts at 11pm, but we particularly enjoy the pianist who precedes it at 9pm. You can eat or drink here. The bar is crowded with sing-along patrons, whose requests are always honored.
Admission: $3.

DISCOTHEQUES

Rio abounds with dance clubs where the emphasis is on one thing, dancing. Most are usually crowded and feature popular Latin and North American music. Admission is generally $3 to $5. These clubs go in and out of favor rather quickly. At the time of this writing, the following clubs were in vogue: **Caligola,** Praça General Osorio, Ipanema (tel. 287-1369); **Columbus,** Raul Pompéia 94, Copacabana (tel. 521-0279); **Kitschnet,** Barato Ribeiro 543, Copacabana (tel. 235-2045); **New York New York,** Ministro Ivan Lins 80, Barra (tel. 399-0105); and **Vogue,** Cupertino Durão 173, Leblon (tel. 274-8142).

BARS & PUBS

BARRIL 1800, Avenida Vieira Souto, 110 Ipanema. Tel. 287-0085.
Barril 1800 can hold close to 500 guests. For informal dining, choose an outdoor patio table, where you can have pizza ($4 per pie) or any of two dozen platters ($3 to $6). Open daily from 9pm to 3am.

A GAROTA DE IPANEMA, Rua Vinicius de Moraes 49A, Ipanema. Tel. 267-8787.
This popular meeting place inspired the song of the same name ("The Girl from Ipanema").

VARANDA DE IPANEMA, Rua Vinicius de Moraes 39, Ipanema. Tel. 267-5757.

This establishment near the beach attracts young people who stop by for a late snack and a chance to watch the passing scene. The *Vinicius* piano bar upstairs has often been called the "Temple of Bossa Nova."

GAY & LESBIAN CLUBS

Rio has a sizable gay and lesbian population. One of the most popular hangouts is in the **Galeria Alaska**, in Copacabana, where certain clubs and shows feature transvestite male strippers. There is usually a minimum, but no cover for entering. Other clubs include **La Cueva**, in Copacabana, at Rua Miguel Lemos 51, and **Zig-Zag**, Avenida Bartolomeu Mitre 662, in Leblon.

THE CAFE SCENE

CAFE DO TEATRO, Avenida Rio Branco, Center City. Tel. 220-1998.
This place is perfect for an early cocktail from 3 to 6pm, with drinks at only $2 to $3. You can enjoy the opulent decor of this former museum in the Teatro Municipal (the city's cultural center). Enjoy your drink along with the Cariocas who are waiting for the evening's performance. Note the tiled walls and columns. Open Monday to Friday from 3 to 6pm.

PIANO BARS

CAFE UN DEUX TROIS, Avenida Bartolomeu Mitre 123, Leblon. Tel. 239-0198.
This wine-and-cheese restaurant has a fantastic piano bar upstairs. Fernando Gallo, a worldly pianist, heads a three-piece combo. Stop by and let him know your favorites; no request will be denied. You can drink and dine at this friendly oasis, where there's a $5 minimum. Open daily until 5am.

FOR SINGLES

BIBLOS, Epitácio Pessoa 1484. Tel. 521-2645.
A good meeting place is Biblos, which faces the lagoon above the Rive Gauche restaurant. There is live music, usually jazz, and the drinks are under $3. The clientele are usually well-dressed businesspeople out for fun.

CHIKO'S BAR, Epitácio Pessoa 1560. Tel. 287-3512.
Chiko's nearby is another popular nightspot in Rio for singles. The place is similar to Biblos (above) in price, clientele, and ambience. If one is too crowded, you can easily hop over to the other.

LORD JIM, Rua Paul Redfern 63, Ipanema. Tel. 259-3047.
Since this is one of the most popular clubs around, frequently there is standing-room only downstairs, where singles congregate to drink and play darts. If you're hungry, head upstairs, where fish and chips ($5), shepherd's pie ($4), and steak-and-kidney pie ($6) are popular. Open Tuesday to Sunday from 4pm to 2am.

MORE ENTERTAINMENT

MOVIES The movie district—**Cinelandia**—is on Rua Senador Dantas, off Avenida Rio Branco, not far from Praça Mahatma Gandhi. Tickets, all unreserved, are much in demand: For popular films, be sure to pick up your ducats the morning of the day you plan to go. Prices at the best theaters run no higher than $2, while at others the admission may be as low as $1. Before performances, queue up early, because there's a mad scramble for seats when the doors open.

Other good cinemas are in Copacabana, Ipanema, Flamengo, Leblon, the Barra Shopping Center, and São Conrado Shopping Mall. Most English-language films are not dubbed into Portuguese. X-rated films are shown at certain cinemas that are advertised as such.

FOR MEN ONLY Two clubs that offer erotic shows, nude go-go dancers, and an attractive setting are **Assyrius,** downtown at Avenida Rio Branco 277, and **Erotika,** in Copacabana, at Avenida Prado Júnior 63. Both have a $10 minimum, and drinks are about $3 to $5. Many couples come for the show. An expensive Copacabana club is **Holiday,** at Avenida Atlântica and Rua Ronaldo Carvalho.

At **Help,** Avenida Atlântica 3432, in Copacabana, attractions include a fantastic light show; loud, pulsing music; and a large dance floor with go-go platforms at each corner. There's a $5 cover charge.

11. EASY EXCURSIONS

PAQUETA ISLAND ✪ In Guanabara Bay, just off Rio, are dozens of lovely islands that are used as weekend retreats and as stations for thousands of yachtsmen and sailors here. Many Cariocas consider Paqueta Island the most enchanting of these for swimming and boating. Horse-drawn carriage tours around the island are recommended, and there are cabins for changing at the beaches.

The cheapest way ($1 round trip) to reach the island is on an aged ferry that takes 90 minutes. Departure times vary with the season, but the first boat invariably leaves at 5:30am from Estação 1 in Praça 15 de Novembro ("Praça Quinze"), and there is usually a boat at about 7 and 10:15am and 1:30, 3, 5:30, and 7pm. The final boat back to the mainland leaves at 8:30pm. To reach Praça 15 de Novembro, walk four blocks east from Rio Branco and 7 de Setembro toward the Imperial Palace. You can also reach the island by hydrofoil. One leaves on the hour from 10am to 4pm on weekdays and from 8am to 5pm on the weekend. The cost is $1 each way.

If you prefer to travel in greater style, you can get a tour package for about $25 (tourist class) that includes a 30-minute yacht cruise to the island, an island tour, and swimming. For an additional $3.50 you'll be picked up at your hotel by limousine and you travel first class. Make arrangements through your hotel.

On the way you'll pass the **Costa da Silva Bridge,** the longest bridge in South America, which joins Rio with Niteroi.

BUZIOS ✪ A lovely day trip from Rio is the exclusive seaside resort village of Buzio in the district of Cabo Frio—a 2½-hour drive from Rio.

Originally discovered by Portuguese settlers, Armação de Buzios was used as an outpost to protect the land from marauding pirates. For centuries fishing was the village's primary industry, until tourism arrived.

Brigitte Bardot discovered Buzios nearly 30 years ago, and it quickly became a chic alternative to Cabo Frio, a larger resort nearby.

Although Buzios is more crowded today than formerly, it still retains its quaintness and tranquility. The wealthy who first came here have kept their homes hidden. The roads are unpaved, but you will find 27 sandy coves and 17 beaches. The water is not polluted. Ferradurinha is a hidden cove beach. Several beaches are private, but the more popular public beaches are Ossos and João Fernandes.

Getting There One way is to take a bus from Rio to Cabo Frio, then another bus to Buzios. The concierge at your hotel should be able to direct you. Driving is fairly simple. Cross the Niteroi bridge and follow the signs to São Goncalo and Rio Bonito; then go past Campos and Manilha until you get to BR-101, which you'll take to the outskirts of Cabo Frio. From there take Rj-106 into Buzios.

COSTA VERDE A lovely drive is the 280 kilometers along the Rio-Santos Highway known as the Costa Verde (Green Coast). As the name implies, the area is lush and dense with greenery and rolling hills. Buildings along the route date back to the colonial days.

About 100 miles from Rio you'll come to the Italia National Park, a preserved forest with many waterfalls. Angra dos Reis looks over the Ilha Grande Bay and has many beaches, islands, and marinas. Its colonial buildings are still intact.

At the end of the route, at the border of the states of Rio de Janeiro and São Paulo, is the historic town of **Parati,** which dates back to 1650. It played a key role for gold shipped from Minas Gerais and destined for Portugal. With the completion of the Rio–São Paulo road, the town lost its importance and was virtually forgotten. Even though it was rediscovered in the 20th century, Parati still remains just as it was during colonial times.

In the Indian language of Tupi-Guarnani, *Parati* means "Home of the Gods." It was the setting of John Doorman's film *The Emerald Forest.*

12. SALVADOR

1,000 miles NE of Rio

GETTING THERE   By Plane   You'll probably arrive by plane at the modern **Dois de Julho Airport** after a 1¾-hour flight from Rio via a modern jet. Your best bet is to take a cab ($20) to the center city 20 miles away. Use the buddy system, since cabs hold four to five passengers for the same fare.

By Bus   You can travel by bus from Rio. The trip may take up to 30 hours, with stops.

By Car   It is a 20-hour drive from Rio to Salvador.

SPECIAL EVENTS   Special events include two important religious festivals. On January 1 the **Festival of Our Lord of the Seafarers** begins with a procession of boats crossing All Saints Bay. What follows is a frenetic festival of music and dancing that lasts until the wee hours. On February 2 the **Ceremony of Iemanjá** is held in Rio Vermelho. Small fishing boats head out to the beautiful goddess, who lives under the sea and "steals" fishermen. Each wife throws gifts (flowers, perfume, or makeup) to the vain goddess, praying that Iemanjá will not steal her husband. (When a fisherman drowns, it is commonly said that he has gone to Iemanjá).

Perched on the Atlantic about 1,000 miles northeast of Rio, exotic Salvador is a year-round tourist mecca. What draws over half a million visitors to this capital of the state of Bahía? For openers, it has 40 miles of magnificent beaches in year-round use and a bay that rivals Guanabara for sheer hypnotic beauty. Next, it has a colonial history (it was founded more than 400 years ago and was Brazil's first capital and the center of Portugal's New World colonies) and boasts some of South America's finest colonial architecture and museums. Add a population of African origin, which retains the folklore of Candomblé (a mystic form of voodoo) in its everyday culture, plus local Bahian dishes that make dining here a delight, and you can understand why we strongly recommend (time permitting) that you visit Salvador.

Like Rio, Salvador has year-round swimming and warm temperatures. Salvador can get even warmer than Rio, which is understandable since it's nearer to the Equator. The hottest months are during our winter season (December to March). From May through September there are occasional rainy days, with mild afternoons.

A LITTLE BACKGROUND

The African influence is still strong in Bahía's religion, music, food, and customs. Some 300 years ago slaves were brought in from Africa to work the plantations. Their culture strongly influenced the indigenous Indians and the Portuguese settlers, so that today Bahía, unlike the rest of Brazil, retains a mixed culture.

Since the religion of the slaves was originally suppressed by the Portuguese, the slaves surreptitiously conducted their ceremonies in out-of-the-way places. When the Roman Catholic Church tried to convert them and destroy their religion, the Africans shrewdly renamed their gods with equivalent Christian and biblical names. Slowly but surely, however, the ceremonies and traditions of the Africans mingled with those of the native Indians and Christians; today, they differ significantly from the original. In Bahía, a form of voodoo called Candomblé is practiced in certain houses of worship called *terreiros*. Catholic saints have become an integral part of the religious ceremonies. The worshipers, attired in bright costumes, hypnotically move to the beat of drums until they seem to become lost in a trance. The altars and statues somewhat resemble those normally seen in Catholic churches, but there are differences. If you would like to attend services at a *terreiro*, check with your hotel clerk to make arrangements. Few *terreiros* have precisely scheduled services.

WHAT TO SEE & DO

Salvador is a large city of more than one million people, bounded on the south by the Atlantic Ocean and on the west by the scenic All Saints Bay. It is a bilevel city—its center area is separated into a "lower city" and an "upper city."

Let's start at **Rio Vermelho,** on the south (Atlantic Ocean) side. This beach area, which is the site of the Meridien Bahía Hotel, has several charming inlet bays that are ideal for swimming. West along the Atlantic from here is the main oceanfront avenue, Avenida Presidente Vargas. After passing the zoological park, we come to the **Ondina** area. Ondina Beach is here—an excellent place to swim. Back on Vargas again, we pass **Morro do Cristo,** a fort jutting out into the ocean, and continue until we reach **Farol da Barra,** marked by the lighthouse at the entrance to All Saints Bay **(Bais de Todos os Santos)** on Salvador's west side. Here the Atlantic Ocean meets the bay. Nearby is the 17th-century fortress (Brazil's oldest) of **Santo António,** which extends into this ocean-bay area. From here the main bayfront thoroughfare is **Avenida 7 de Setembro;** we are now heading north toward center city, with the magnificent bay on our left. Just ahead is the **Santa Maria Fortress** (also 17th century), and just beyond is **Porto da Barra**—a beach area offering spectacular views of the bay as well as elegant boutiques and shops. A top hotel, the Praiamar, is located here too. Locally, this area is called the **Barra** section.

Continuing toward center city (north), we pass the **Costa Pinto Museum,** at Avenida 7 de Setembro 2490. Originally the home of Carlos Costa Pinto, this museum is known for its fine collections of silver, china, jewel, furniture, and art. Just beyond, on the bay, is the **Vitoria** section. At this point, Avenida 7 de Setembro continues downtown through the heart of Salvador. A parallel street downtown is **Rua Carlos Gomes,** the main shopping thoroughfare, where you will find such department stores as **Mesbla** and **Casa Sloper.**

From here the bayfront avenue is **Avenida do Contorno,** which continues downtown toward the lower city, passing near the famous **Museum of Sacred Art,** at Rua do Sodre 24. This classic structure houses religious treasures, including paintings, murals, and sculpture. It's definitely worth a visit.

We are now in the heart of the downtown area in the "lower city." To reach the "upper city," you can drive, walk, or take the **Elevador Lacerda,** a century-old elevator (originally built to tote whale oil), which will take you there in about a minute.

In **Cidade Baixa** (lower city) you'll find the fascinating outdoor market **Mercado Modelo,** with its endless stalls, shops, and cafés jam-packed with Bahians and merchandise. A must stop is **Largo do Pelourinho** (Torture Square); its streets and buildings provide the best example of colonial (18th-century) architecture in Brazil and perhaps in all of South America. In this square Africans and political prisoners were tortured. Historians note that "proper" ladies in their finest clothes would peer down from their elegant balconies to observe the whippings. Visit the **Igreja do Rosário dos Pretos,** a church in the square that houses a black order. Note the rococo architecture. On the third floor, in a room on the right, you can see images of the Candomblé saints, all bearing Christian names.

You might want to head to the upper city via **Santo António,** one of the oldest residential sections of Salvador, with steep hills and charming cobblestone streets, offering memorable views of the bay.

SALVADOR, BAHIA

0 | 5 mi / 8 km

Terminal Turístico Maritimo

CENTRO
Mercado Modelo ❿

Capitania dos Portos

Baía de Todos os Santos

PELOURINHO

Praça dos Arcos

Praça Anchieta

Praça da Sé ❽

Praça Tomé de Sousse

Praça dos Veteranos

Santa Teresa

GARCIA

TORORÓ

❶ ❺ ❸ ❾ ❹ ❻ ❼ ❷ ❿ ❽

Streets and labels: Av. Franca, da Argentina, Polónia, Conde D'Eu, Caminho Novo, do Tabuão, Ribeiro Santos, Luta Viana, Eduardo Carta, A. Gomez, Av. Estados Unidos, da Grécia, Av. Miguel Calmon, Av. Portugal, Conselheiro Dantas, Gonçalves, Av. Prito, J.C. Rabelo, de Mass, Av. Pinto Martins, Senador Dumont, Corpo Santo, da Bélgica, Rosário de Misericórdia, Monte Alegre, Gregório de Mattos, Frei Vicente, Av. de Bastos, Av. Francisco M. Barreto, 12 de Outubro, Lad. da Prata, do Desterro, Lad. da Montanha, Lad. da Misericórdia, 3 de Maio, Queda de Brito, São Francisco, 28 de Setembro, do Tira, Chile, Lad. da Praça, Viara do Tesouro, R. Barbosa, Rua Silva, Chapla, Dr. José Joaquim Seabra, da Gravela da Fonte, do Gravatá, do Desterro, Lad. de Santana, da Palma, da Barroquinha, da da Lama, Eng. Afion, Rocha Galvão, do Banga, da Independencia, Junqueira Freire, do Tingui, do Chaco, Blvd. Suíço, Dr. Vitorino, Macedo Costa, D. Martins, Av. do Contorno, Visconde de Mauá, Areal de Cima, Rue do Sodré, Carlos Gomes, do Paraíso, Silva Lima, Américo Simas, F. Ferraro, Marquês do Brasil, José Duarte, da Manguiera, Democrata, Soares, Av. Franca, Av. Joana Angélica, Conquero da Piedade, Senador Costa Pinto, Av. 7 de Setembro, do Rosário, Alegria dos Barris

Legend

Catedral Basílica ❶
Mercado Modelo ❿
Museu de Arte da Bahia ❷
Museu de Arte Sacre ❸
Museu de Arte Moderno ❹

Museu da Cidade ❺
Museu do Instituto Geográfico e Histórico ❻
Igreja e Convento de São Francisco ❼
Praça da Sé ❽
Tempostal ❾

Information ⓘ

Before leaving Salvador, be sure to visit the **São Francisco Church,** located in Praça Terreiro de Jesus, often called the "Golden Church." It was built from chipped stone. Also, the **Bonfim Church** is visually stunning, both externally and internally. Completed some 200 years ago, the imported-marble construction is truly magnificent.

WHERE TO STAY

Salvador has in the $60-to-$90 range several deluxe hotels that rival the finest in Rio. Among the best are the **Meridien Bahía Hotel** (tel. 248-8011), in the Rio Vermelho Beach area; the **Bahia Othon Palace** (tel. 247-1044) and the **Salvador Praia Hotel** (tel. 245-5033), both in the nearby Ondina Beach area; and the **Hotel da Bahía** (tel. 237-3699) downtown. Each has its own pool and first-class amenities. The Meridien even has tennis courts and a sauna.

There are, however, several fine hotels in the $30-to-$50 range (doubles). Typically, they offer comfortable rooms with baths, telephones, and piped-in music; air conditioning is available, either as a standard amenity or an option. Unfortunately, none of these hotels has a pool.

DOUBLES FOR LESS THAN $40

BARRA TURISMO HOTEL, Avenida 7 de Setembro 3691. Tel. 071/245-7433. Telex 071/2964. 60 rms (all with bath). A/C MINIBAR TV TEL
$ Rates: $14 single; from $25 double. Major credit cards accepted.
This should be your first choice. The hotel is located on one of the main streets leading to the downtown area.

HOTEL PELOURINHO, Rua Alfredo Brito 20. Tel. 071/321-9022. All rooms with bath. A/C MINIBAR TV TEL
$ Rates: $29 single; $35 double.
This charming renovated colonial house near Pelourinho Square retains much of its former character.

HOTEL SOLAR DA BARRA, Avenida 7 de Setembro 2998. Tel. 071/247-4917. 18 rms (all with bath). A/C MINIBAR TV TEL
$ Rates: $26 single; $31 double. Major credit cards accepted.
This small hotel offers good value. Air conditioning is $2 extra.

VILA ROMANA HOTEL, Rua Lemos de Brito 14. Tel. 071/245-4303. Fax 071/247-6748. Telex 071/2879. 56 rms (all with bath). A/C MINIBAR TV TEL
$ Rates: $33 single; from $38 double. Extra bed $3. Major credit cards accepted.
This hotel in the Barra section is worth the money.

DOUBLES FOR LESS THAN $60

HOTEL BAHIA DO SOL, Avenida 7 de Setembro 2009. Tel. 071/336-7211. Fax 071/336-7776. Telex 071/184. 91 rms (all with bath). A/C MINIBAR TV TEL
$ Rates: $39 single; from $48 double; $52 triple. Major credit cards accepted.
This hotel is downtown in the Vitoria section.

HOTEL MARAZUL, Avenida 7 de Setembro 3937. Tel. 071/336-2110. Fax (071)235-2121. Telex 071/229. 124 rms (all with bath). A/C MINIBAR TV TEL
$ Rates: $50–$60 double. Major credit cards accepted.
This hotel is in the Barra section, facing the water near Porto da Barra.

A SPLURGE CHOICE

HOTEL QUATRO RODAS, Rua da Passagarda, Praia Farol de Itapao. Tel. 071/249-5533. Fax 071/249-6949. Telex 071/2449. 195 apts (all with bath). A/C MINIBAR TV TEL

$ Rates: $82 single; $90 double. Major credit cards accepted.
This deluxe hotel is situated in a large area and has a pool, a tennis court, and sauna.
It's 200 yards from the beach and close to the airport.

LONG-TERM STAYS

If you're planning to stay for a few weeks and would feel more at home in an apartment, consider staying in an apart-hotel. We recommend either **Farol Barra flat,** Avenida Oceanica 409, Barra (tel. 071/336-6722; fax 071/336-4250; telex 071/4267) or **Ondina Apart,** Avenida Oceanica 2402, Ondina (tel. 071/203-8000; fax 071/203-8382; telex 071/4285).

WHERE TO DINE

Bahian cuisine includes such typical Brazilian dishes as *vatapa* (a combination of fish, nuts, onions, pepper, and coconut milk), *xinxim de galinha* (chicken stew in a mild sauce), and *frigideira* (shrimp or crab boiled with eggs, coconut, and oil). In Salvador these dishes are truly special. Try to have at least one Bahian meal here.

Although Salvador offers a variety of international restaurants, we have confined our recommendations to those specializing in Brazilian dishes. They are: **Agda,** Avenida Otavio Mangabeira, Boca do Rio (tel. 231-2851); **Bargaço,** Rua A.S. Coelho 18, Boca do Rio (tel. 231-5141), for excellent seafood; **Casa da Gamboa,** Rua da Gamboa de Cima 51 (tel. 321-9776), for a good choice of Bahian dishes; and **Iemanjá,** Avenida Otavio Mangabeira, Praia da Armacao (tel. 231-5770). In all of them the setting is attractive, the atmosphere inviting, and the service attentive. Reservations are recommended.

For an enjoyable evening out, dine buffet-style on a wide assortment of Bahian dishes at **Senac,** Largo Pelourinho 7 (in the Teatro Senac), for about $7 per person—all you can eat. The restaurant is located in a colonial house that typifies the architecture of this area (perhaps the most intriguing in Brazil). There is a nightly open-air samba show, starting at 8:30pm on the second floor. The restaurant is one flight up. Dress informally.

SAVVY SHOPPING

Since Bahía is famous for its artists and their works, you'll find many shops specializing in handcrafts. If you're here on Sunday, be sure to visit the **Hippie Fair,** in the upper city, at Praça Terreiro de Jesus (near Praça da Sé). You'll find a great assortment of bracelets, jewelry, leather goods, carvings, paintings, tapestries, and pottery.

For the finest in gemstones, **H. Stern** has several shops in Salvador (at the Meridien Hotel, the Othon Palace Hotel, the Hotel da Bahia, the Barra Shopping Center, and the airport).

EVENING ENTERTAINMENT

Salvador's nightlife ranges from the earthy to the elegant. At the latter end you have **Le Zodiaque** disco in the Meridien Hotel. This plush, expensive private club admits tourists, but the tab is high—$5 to $8 per drink. **Hippopotamus,** at the Bahia Othon Palace Hotel, is also a first-rate disco. The Salvador **Praia Hotel Champagne Bar** features live music and dancing.

For a pleasant evening, take a cab to **Bual'Amour** in Praia do Corsario (tel. 231-9775), where nostalgic music alternates with rock. It's usually crowded with local young people.

CAPOEIRA

The African slaves brought with them not only their dance but a self-defense technique called *capoeira*, which is actually a system of body movements often done in pantomime style. On holidays, a musical instrument (*berimbau*) sets the rhythmic beat. Ask your hotel clerk where you can see a *capoeira* show; you'll long remember it.

AN EASY EXCURSION

Itaparica, a lovely island that's visible from the bay, is a 45-minute ferry ride from Salvador. Time permitting, you might enjoy spending a day visiting this island and roaming its beaches. Ferries leave all day, and you can even go by car. The boat ride offers incredible views of Salvador and its bay. Check with your hotel clerk for current schedules.

While there is much to see on the island (for example, the São Lourenco Church and Fortress), come for the beaches and tropical fruits. The island has several acceptable hotels and pensions if you should wish to stay overnight. The **Grande Hotel de Itaparica** has 60 rooms and charges $50 for singles and $60 for doubles.

CLUB MED   In 1979 the club's first Brazilian village opened on Itaparica, at the entrance to All Saints Bay. Built in an 86-acre lush palm grove facing the Atlantic Ocean, the village enjoys fresh sea breezes year-round. A fine white-sand beach and reef-protected waters invite swimmers and beachcombers alike. For more information, call toll free in the United States 800/CLUBMED.

---

13. SUGGESTED ITINERARIES

BRASILIA

More than 30 years ago, in a bold plan to develop Brazil's interior, President Juscelino Kubitschek (1956–61) implemented a 200-year-old idea to carve a new city out of the wilderness. A site 575 miles west of Rio was chosen because of its low humidity and relative coolness and because of its accessibility from Rio (1½ hours by air).

Kubitschek insisted that the city become the official capital of Brazil in order to attract international attention, not to mention commerce and industry. Thus, in 1960, Brasília became Brazil's seat of government. Today, it's a sleek modern city, with a population of well over 1.5 million.

The architecture of Brasília is truly dazzling. Lucio Costa designed the city along two main highways that intersect at the city's center. Along the east-west axis are the government buildings, designed by the internationally famous architect Oscar Niemeyer (he designed the United Nations in New York).

At the end of this axis **(Eixo Monumental)** is the most famous Brasília landmark, the spacious Plaza of Three Powers **(Praça dos Três Poderes)**, where the executive, legislative, and judicial branches occupy separate buildings. Note the center **Congress** building, with its twin towers set in a "bowl" and "saucer." The House of Representatives meets in the bowl, while the saucer structure is home to the Senate. To the left is the **Planalto Palace,** the executive office building; to the right is the **Palace of Justice,** where the Supreme Court meets.

An artificial lake was created inside the city; on its far bank is the **Palácio da Alvorada** (Palace of Dawn)—the residence of the president. Nearby is "Embassy Row," also worth a visit for its architectural diversity.

Note: Most of Brasília's hotels are in the southern and northern sections, near one another and not far from Eixo Monumental. Their rates are modest.

Tours can be arranged through Rio travel agencies. In addition, there are frequent flights from Galeão Airport for $180 round trip.

Tip: Some airlines allow you to include Brasília in your United States–to–South America airfare at no extra cost. One way is to fly from New York to Brasília and then on to Rio. Check your airline for multiple-stopover itineraries.

WHERE TO STAY

There are five hotels in the budget category: **Hotel Aristus** (tel. 061/223-8675); **Brasília Imperial Hotel** (tel. 061/321-7337); **Byblos Hotel** (tel. 061/223-1570); **Itamaratí Parque Hotel** (tel. 061/225-6050); and **Mirage Hotel** (tel. 061/225-7150). All cost less than $25 for a double.

The most popular hotels are probably the **Carlton** (tel. 061/224-8819), **St. Paul Park** (tel. 061/321-6688), and **Nacional** (tel. 061/321-7575). Each charges less than $80 for a double.

A five-star hotel has opened recently, the **Naoum Plaza Hotel,** at Setor Hoteleiro sul Quadra 05 (tel. 061/226-6494). If you're looking for a more reasonably priced, although still expensive, place to stay, consider the **San Marco Hotel,** at Setor Hoteleiro sul Quadra 05 (tel. 061/321-8484).

BELO HORIZONTE

About halfway between Rio and Brasília is Belo Horizonte, capital of the state of **Minas Gerais.** It's an industrial city located near some of Brazil's most important historic areas. The city of **Ouro Preto** has been preserved as it was centuries ago. It can be reached in about 2 hours by bus from Belo. Since Ouro Preto is a mining center, unset gemstones can be purchased at excellent prices.

A planned city, Belo Horizonte was established in 1897; it's a good base from which to visit Ouro Preto, as well as Mariana, 70 miles away, and Congonhas, which is closer.

WHERE TO STAY

HOTEL BOULEVARD PLAZA, Avenida Getulio Vargas 1640. Tel. 031/ 223-9000. Fax 031/225-8438. Telex 031/5029. All rooms with bath. MINIBAR TV TEL
$ Rates: $77 double. Major credit cards accepted.
In the same neighborhood as the Hotel Savassi (below), this establishment is close to some very sophisticated shops and restaurants.

REAL PALACE, Rua Espirito Santo 901. Tel. 031/213-1211. Fax 031/273-2643. Telex 031/313733. 256 rms. MINIBAR TV TEL
$ Rates: $85 standard; $117 deluxe. Major credit cards accepted.
You'll be assured of a pleasant stay here, although the rooms are rather expensive. Advantages include its central location, pool, and health club.

HOTEL SAVASSI, Rua Sergipe 939. Tel. 031/212-3266. Fax 031/212-3628. Telex 031/393073. All rooms with bath. MINIBAR TV TEL
$ Rates: $68 single; $78 double. Major credit cards accepted.
This new hotel is located near the government ministries in Praça da Liberdade. It boasts a swimming pool, a sauna, and a pleasant bar.

OTHON PALACE, Avenida Alfonso Pena 1050. Tel. 031/273-3844. Fax 031/212-2318. Telex 031/2052. All rooms with bath. MINIBAR TV TEL
$ Rates: $121 single; $135 double. Major credit cards accepted.
The Othon is a splurge choice. Located in the center of town, it offers, for its higher rates, a more luxurious decor, with service to match.

WHERE TO DINE

As the national capital, Brasília boasts many fine restaurants, appealing to its political and diplomatic residents, as well as to ordinary visitors of varying budgets. Our choices include **Buona Tavola,** Rua Santa Rita Durao 309 (tel. 227-6155), where dinner (featuring Italian dishes) runs about $5 sans alcoholic beverages; **Dragon**

Palace, Avenida Contorno 6557, Savassi (tel. 225-2568), and **Yun Ton,** Rua Santa Catarina 946 (tel. 337-6371), for delicious selections in Chinese cuisine at comparable prices; and **Pier 32,** Avenida Alfonso Pena 3328 (tel. 225-0782), a self-service restaurant offering an excellent buffet of salads, meats, and fish. Reservations are recommended for each restaurant.

SAO PAULO

One hour from Rio via air shuttle—**Ponte Aerea** (and a free stopover on most flights in and out of Rio)—is the booming modern metropolis of São Paulo, Brazil's largest city. The combination of skyscrapers, luxury apartment houses, and super-highways exemplifies South America's industrial potential. A popular expression here is: "We work hard, so we can play in Rio."

Whenever heading to São Paulo, we like to visit the world-famous **Butantan Institute and Snake Farm** (where antitoxin research is being carried out) and the Sunday **Hippie Fair** in Praça da República. It is also worthwhile to spend a few days at the magnificent resort of **Guaruja,** just off Santos.

Getting around São Paulo is very easy: Taxis are abundant and there is a clean, efficient subway.

WHERE TO STAY

Many hotels in São Paulo are above our budget, since they cater primarily to the business traveler on an expense account. However, when you arrive at the airport, go to the **hotel reservation desk.** The English-speaking staff will help you find a hotel within your budget.

A budget hotel we've tried and can recommend is the **Bourbon,** Avenida Vieiro de Carvalho 99 (tel. 011/223-2244). Rates here are $40 per double, and all rooms have a bath. In the higher-price category two fine hotels are the Augusta Palace and the Bristol. The **Augusta Palace,** Rua Agusta 467 (tel. 011/256-1277, fax 011/259-9637, telex 011/87956), has 152 rooms (all with bath, air conditioning, minibar, TV, and telephone). Rates, including breakfast, are $85 single, $97 double. The hotel, which is conveniently located near the business and shopping district, has a pool and exercise facilities, as well as a restaurant. Similar facilities can be found at the **Bristol,** Rua Martins Fontes 277 (tel. 011/258-0011, fax 011/231-1256, telex 011/24734). Its 90 rooms (all with bath, air conditioning, minibar, TV, and telephone) go for $105 single and $115 double. For further recommendations, see *Frommer's Brazil '93–'94.*

WHERE TO DINE

A city as large and cosmopolitan as São Paulo has, of course, many fine restaurants in a variety of price categories. In the brief compass of this section, however, we can mention only a few (for further recommendations, see *Frommer's Brazil '93–'94*).

For excellent steak, consider the three branches of **Dinho's Place,** Largo de Arouche 246, Alameda Santos 45, and Avenida Morumbi 7976; and **Bassy,** at Rua 13 de Maio 334 and Avenida Cidade Jardin 389. Naturally in a city this size, with so many ethnic groups, there are many ethnic eateries. For a romantic view of the city, dine and dance at **Terraço Itália,** at Avenida Ipiranga 344 (tel. 257-6566). Head for the 41st floor.

We heartily recommend two nightclubs: **Clydes,** at Rua Mata 70, and **House,** at Rua Manoel Guedes 110 in Itaim. Both are singles watering holes.

IGUAÇU FALLS

When listing "must" places to visit in South America, many people would put Iguaçu Falls near the top. The waterfalls on the Iguaçu River mark the border between Brazil and Argentina; 18 miles farther downstream, at the confluence of the Iguaçu and Parana rivers, Argentina, Brazil, and Paraguay meet. You can visit the falls on the Brazilian or Argentinean side, but the Brazilian side offers more amenities for tourists.

Getting there entails a 2-hour flight from Rio via São Paulo. Varig offers daily flights to Iguaçu; the airport is located midway between the falls and the town of **Foz do Iguaçu.** Buses will take you from the airport to Foz, which has a population of about 200,000, more than 50 hotels, and not much else. If you visit in December, January, February, or July, *you must have a reservation.*

WHAT TO SEE & DO

There is bus service between Foz and **Iguaçu Falls** every 2 hours, and the 14-mile trip takes 45 minutes. The falls here are not continuous, nor are they uniform in size or water volume. Still, the average drop into the river is about 1½ miles, and the sheer amount of water spilling over is truly astonishing. You walk along a path and can stop at various lookout points, each at a different height and with its own magnificent view.

The most spectacular fall is the U-shaped Devil's Throat, **(Garganta do Diablo)** on the Argentinean side. Don the slicker you'll be offered and walk right into the center of the U. The roar is deafening and the spray drenching—it's slightly scary (but not dangerous). For excellent photos, take the elevator over Iguaçu Falls.

Since 85% of the falls are on the Argentinean side of the river, they are best viewed from the national park on the Brazilian side. The park provides lots of good scenery, making it a fine place for a picnic.

You can easily visit Argentina or Paraguay from here. There are small towns nearby, and many people go to Paraguay at night to gamble at the casino. Since the falls are closer to Buenos Aires and Asunción, it is cheaper to come from there; however, since the bordering towns have nothing to offer, we suggest staying on the Brazilian side.

To cross over to Argentina, use the Tancredo Neves Bridge. It spans the Iguaçu River after the falls, leading to the Argentinean city of Puerto Iguassu.

It was not until 1973—with the signing of a treaty between Brazil and Paraguay—that an effort was begun to harness the water power of these falls. Construction began on the **Itaipú Dam** (20 miles from the falls) in 1975, with the artificial diversion of the Parana River. The length of the dam is almost 5 miles, and it's as tall as a 62-story building. The project was such a massive undertaking that a company town was established nearby. It accommodates 9,000 people and has schools and a hospital. At peak periods during the construction process more than 40,000 workers were employed here. The hydroelectric plant has 18 generators, and you'll be amazed to learn that one-third of the energy produced by just one of these generators supplies all of Paraguay's electrical needs.

Monday through Saturday there are four daily tours of the dam, each preceded by a film explaining the construction and operation of Itaipú. Don't miss it!

WHERE TO STAY

Since this is a resort area, you might want to splurge a little bit in order to enjoy a pool and other resortlike facilities. There are several hotels offering such facilities on the 14-mile stretch between Foz and the falls.

BOGARI, Avenida Brasil. Tel. 0455/23-2243. Fax 0455/231125. Telex 455/ 250. All rooms with bath. A/C MINIBAR TEL
$ Rates: $57 single; $64 double. Major credit cards accepted.
The rooms here are comfortable and have piped-in music. There is a bar on the premises.

HOTEL SAN MARTIN, Avenida das Cataratas, Km 17. Tel. 0455/74-3207. Fax 0455/74-3207. Telex 0455/113. All rooms with bath. A/C MINIBAR TV TEL
$ Rates: $65 single; $75 double. Major credit cards accepted.
This hotel has a restaurant, a lounge area, and a bar, as well as a pool and tennis facilities.

Two other good budget choices, offering comparable amenities and service but at somewhat lower rates, are Hotel Foz do Iguaçu and Hotel Salvatti. At the 140-room

Hotel Foz do Iguaçu, Avenida Brasil 97 (tel. 0455/74-4455, fax 0455/74-1775, telex 0455/171), singles are $45 and doubles $60; at the 100-room **Hotel Salvatti,** Rua Rio Branco 577 (tel. 0455/23-1121, fax 0455/74-3674, telex 0455/100), singles are $50 and doubles $60. All rooms at both hotels come with bath, air conditioning, minibar, TV, and telephone.

Splurge Choices

HOTEL BOURBON, Avenida Das Cataratas, km 002. Tel. 0455/23-1313. Fax 0455/74-1110. Telex 0455/247. 150 rms (all with bath). A/C MINIBAR TV TEL
$ Rates (including breakfast and dinner): $104 single; $120 double.
This lovely five-star hotel may be the best in town.

HOTEL DAS CATARATAS, Rod das Cataratas Km 28, Parque Nacional. Tel. 0455/23-2266. Fax 0455/74-1688. Telex 0455/113. All rooms with bath. A/C MINIBAR TV TEL
$ Rates: $90 single; $100 double. Major credit cards accepted.
This hotel is directly across the road from the falls, in the national park of Iguaçu. An E-shaped pink building with lovely grounds, it has plush sitting rooms with fireplaces, pool tables, good food, a pool, and even a menagerie.

HOTEL INTERNACIONAL, Rua Almirante Barroso 345. Tel. 0455/23-1414. Fax 0455/74-5201. Telex 0455/167. 214 rms (all with bath). A/C MINIBAR TV TEL
$ Rates: $110 single; $125 double. Major credit cards accepted.
This five-star hotel, in the center of the city, features a pool and a *churrascaria* restaurant.

WHERE TO DINE

Eat at least one meal in the dining room of the **Hotel Das Cataratas,** where fixed-price dinners are about $13. The first-course smörgåsbord could be an entire meal by itself. **Restaurant China,** on the highway, features Chinese and Brazilian food and an English menu. The **Restaurant Rafaian,** Avenida das Cataratas, Kilometer 6.5, and **Cabeça de Boi,** Avenida Brasil 1325, are good choices for beef and grilled meats. We also recommend **La Mamma** on Avenida das Cataratas, which specializes in Italian fare.

OFF THE BEATEN TRACK

Grand Prix Journeys has introduced a series of "ecological expeditions" to Brazil's seldom-visited Amazon and Pantanal regions. Great for family vacations, both the Amazon and the Pantanal are living classrooms for young people. The excursions include stays at Amazon jungle lodges and at a buffalo ranch on the Isla de Marajo; visits to a large island in the Amazon estuary near Belém; a riverboat cruise; and a Jeep safari in the Pantanal.

The 13-day "ecological wonders" excursion covers the Amazon, starting in Manaus and ending in Belém, Brazil's major Amazonian ports. The itinerary includes jungle treks, fishing for piranha, nighttime alligator watching, visits to boat-building and pottery-making villages, and a lecture on Amazonian ecosystems by a scientist from Belém's famed Goeldi Museum.

For more information on these and other exciting Amazon trips, contact Grand Prix Journeys at 425 Madison Ave., New York, NY 10017 (tel. 212/319-8600 or toll free 800/242-7749).

CHAPTER 4

MONTEVIDEO, URUGUAY

1. INTRODUCING MONTEVIDEO & URUGUAY
- WHAT'S SPECIAL ABOUT MONTEVIDEO
- WHAT THINGS COST IN MONTEVIDEO
2. ORIENTATION
3. GETTING AROUND
- FAST FACTS: MONTEVIDEO
4. WHERE TO STAY
5. WHERE TO DINE
6. ATTRACTIONS
- DID YOU KNOW . . .?
7. SPORTS & RECREATION
8. SAVVY SHOPPING
9. EVENING ENTERTAINMENT
10. PUNTA DEL ESTE
11. EN ROUTE TO BUENOS AIRES

About the size of Nebraska, Uruguay is a seacoast nation with some of the finest beaches anywhere. Within two hours from Montevideo by bus is the great playground of the rich, **Punta del Este,** the Riviera of eastern South America, where the high-stakes casino never closes.

The authentic folk hero in Uruguay—as in Argentina—is the fabled **gaucho,** who can be seen on horseback roaming the huge ranches outside Montevideo.

Montevideo, with 1,300,000 residents (45% of the population of Uruguay), is an aging city with wide, tree-lined thoroughfares and enormous parks. Eight beach communities lie within 45 minutes of downtown, on the Río de la Plata; the two closest—**Ramírez** and **Pocitos**—can be reached by bus in 15 minutes.

Located between Rio and Buenos Aires, Montevideo makes a good midtrip stop on your journey to those cities—in much the same way that Switzerland offers a change of pace on a trip between Italy and France. And the comparison, we think, is apt, because the welfare state of Uruguay resembles Switzerland in its well-ordered and quiet life.

South American tourists flock to Uruguay by the tens of thousands from December through April (summer in South America), when the weather is far more temperate than that in tropical Rio. (Understandably, accommodations are difficult to get at that time, so make your reservations well ahead.) Amazingly, few North Americans come to this cosmopolitan city, which is surrounded by beautiful beaches; it's a superb tourist find!

1. INTRODUCING MONTEVIDEO & URUGUAY

Uruguay, officially called *República Oriental del Uruguay,* proclaimed its independence in 1828. It is the smallest independent state in South America, with an area of about 69,000 square miles and a population of some 3 million, more than a third of

WHAT'S SPECIAL ABOUT MONTEVIDEO

Beaches
- [ ] The famous resort of Punta del Este—site of international conferences—only 2 hours away.

Parks/Gardens
- [ ] Parque José Batlle y Ordóñez, with its national *fútbol* stadium, Estadio Centenario, site of the first World Cup Soccer Championship in 1930.
- [ ] The lovely El Prado with more than 800 varieties of roses.

For the Kids
- [ ] Montevideo's planetarium, one of the finest in South America.

Museum
- [ ] The Museo del Gaucho y de la Moneda, which offers an interesting look at the famed gaucho.

Ace Attraction
- [ ] The Mercado del Puerto, a favorite gathering place among residents and visitors to Montevideo.

After Dark
- [ ] Unknown to most, Uruguay has its own dance, the candombe. Similar to the tango, it is as much fun to watch as it is to dance.

whom are concentrated in Montevideo, the capital. The people of Uruguay are predominantly of European descent, chiefly Spanish and Italian. The majority are Roman Catholic.

The country has had an uneven political history, alternating between democratic governments and dictatorships. The most recent dictatorship lasted from 1973 to 1985. Political power has been traditionally shared between the Colorados and the Blancos. One of the leading figures of the Blanco party was José Batlle y Ordóñez (1856–1929), for whom the popular park in Montevideo was named.

Today, Uruguay is a functioning democracy, with a freely elected president and Congress. The country has been the site of several international conferences; in 1961 the Alliance for Progress, a U.S.-inspired program for inter-American economic and social development, was officially adopted in Punta del Este.

WHAT THINGS COST IN MONTEVIDEO	U.S. $
Taxi from airport to the city center	20.00
Airport bus to the city center	5.00
Double with bath at the Hotel Cervantes (budget)	25.00
Double with bath at the California Hotel (moderate)	40.00
Double with bath at the Hotel Lafayette (deluxe)	85.00
Lunch at El Chivito de Oro (budget)	3.00
Lunch at Club de Golf de Uruguay (expensive)	20.00
Dinner for one at Bungalow Suizo (moderate)	9.00
Dinner at Doña Flor (deluxe)	20.00
Average museum admission	.50
Coca-Cola	.45
Cup of coffee	.50

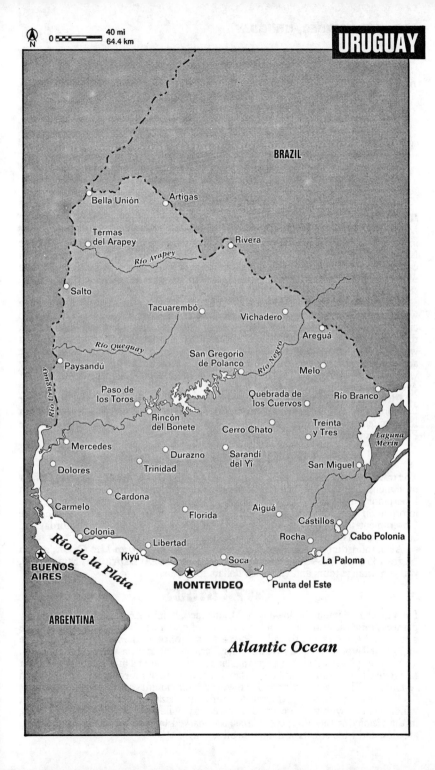

URUGUAY

0   40 mi
    64.4 km

BRAZIL

Bella Unión   Artigas
Termas
del Arapey   Rivera
          Río Arapey
Salto
      Tacuarembó   Vichadero
                                    Areguá
          Río Queguay
                  San Gregorio
Paysandú   de Polanco   Río Negro
                                  Melo
        Paso de   Quebrada de
        los Toros   los Cuervos   Río Branco
        Rincón
        del Bonete   Cerro Chato   Treinta
                                        y Tres   Laguna
Mercedes   Merín
            Durazno   Sarandí
Dolores   Trinidad   del Yi
                                        San Miguel
        Cardona
Carmelo   Aiguá
            Florida   Castillos
Colonia   Rocha   Cabo Polonia
        Libertad
    Kiyú   Soca   La Paloma
BUENOS
AIRES   MONTEVIDEO   Punta del Este

Río de la Plata

ARGENTINA
                    Atlantic Ocean

IMPRESSIONS

Montevideo . . . is much like cities in the United States, with broad boulevards, neat suburban houses, and an informal social life. "Emotionally and spiritually," a friend told me, "it is the Left Bank of Buenos Aires."
—JOHN GUNTHER, *INSIDE LATIN AMERICA*, 1941

2. ORIENTATION

ARRIVING

BY PLANE   The modern **Carrasco Airport,** about 13 miles from the center of Montevideo, is equipped to assist the arriving traveler. The Government Tourist Office in the arrivals area will gladly confirm or make hotel reservations for you. Head for the NINGUN BIEN A DECLARAR ("Nothing to Declare") exit sign; on your way you can change money at the Banco de la República del Uruguay, which offers a fair rate of exchange. Nearby are several auto-rental agencies; rates are extremely low by U.S. standards.

Airlines maintain shuttle-bus service from downtown to the airport to coordinate with your international flight. An airline bus costs $5, while a taxi costs $20 into the city. The route into town passes along the attractive beachfront and then inland a bit, through the rolling ranch-and-dairy farmland that surrounds the capital city. (If you want to take a taxi, try to assemble a group of five to keep your cab cost down.) There are also regular city buses from the airport to the city (ticket price: 50¢)—but they will not accept luggage. The bus terminal is located on Calle Yaguaron, just off Avenida 18 de Julio.

Pluna, the national airline of Uruguay, maintains an office at Colonia 1021, near La Torre (tel. 921-414). The **American Airlines** ticket office is on the Plaza Independencia at the corner of Sarandí. Most other airline offices are located in the Plaza Entrevero, off 18 de Julio, at Río Negro.

TOURIST INFORMATION

The traveler who does not speak Spanish will find the **Government Tourist Office** of immense help. One branch is near the Hotel Lancaster in Plaza Libertad at Avenida Libertador Lavalleja 1409, 6th floor (tel. 914-340). There you can obtain general information (the personnel are multilingual) as well as street maps in English. The Government Tourist Office is open Monday to Friday from 8am to 8pm, Saturday and Sunday from 8am to 2pm.

Also, tourist information is offered at the **Office of Wagon-Lits Cook,** at Río Negro 1356 (tel. 911-426), on the corner of 18 de Julio. At **Exprinter,** Sarandi 700, you can arrange tours and exchange dollars for pesos.

CITY LAYOUT

For a quick orientation in downtown Montevideo, familiarize yourself with three key plazas: **Constitución,** in the older, west side of center city; **Independencia,** in the center; and **Libertad** (also called **Plaza Cagancha**), in the newer, east side. The important **Avenida 18 de Julio** links Plaza Independencia with Plaza Libertad. These three plazas fall within a rectangular area that's about a mile long and a quarter of a mile wide. In and around the rectangle are most of our recommended hotels and restaurants. The others are located in the beach communities a mile or so to the south.

The older section of Montevideo, around Plaza Constitución, has narrow, winding streets with well-preserved 18th-century buildings. The more modern areas, in the vicinity of the other two plazas, are marked by large parks, smart shopping arcades, and wide streets with statues all about.

Plaza de la Independencia is the city's social hub and the center of government buildings, theaters, shops, and luxury as well as budget hotels. Heading away from this plaza is Avenida 18 de Julio, which is lined with restaurants, hotels, shopping arcades, and motion-picture theaters. At the end of it—beyond Plaza Libertad—is beautiful **Batlle y Ordóñez Park.**

Playa Ramírez, a 15-minute bus ride from 18 de Julio, is the nearest beach area. In one of our listed budget hotels here—the Parque—is a famous casino. Nearby is **Parque Rodo,** a huge park that houses an open-air theater, an amusement center, and a lake.

The newer **Playa Pocitos,** our other nearby recommended beach community, is an additional mile from the center city; it has several fine restaurants and hotels that are within our budget range only because of the peso's declining value in relation to the dollar. The main avenue in Pocitos is Boulevard España.

Continuing from Pocitos, along the **Rambla** (beachfront avenue), and heading toward the airport, you pass the beach communities of **Puerto del Buceo** and **Playa Buceo** before reaching **Malvin.** Then come **Playa Honda; Playa Carlos Gardel;** and, approximately 6 miles from downtown, **Punta Gorda,** the home of the fine Oceania Hotel. Three miles farther out, near the airport, is the attractive beach area of **Playa Carrasco.** There are two fine hotels in this area, the Hotel Bristol and the renowned Carrasco Hotel, which has a government-run casino. The area has lovely beaches and is surrounded by a thick forest. However, this is not a convenient area for budget travelers, who will be using public transportation. Still, readers who don't mind the distance have written that they enjoyed staying in Carrasco.

FINDING AN ADDRESS   Many streets have changed their names, so that looking at a map or for an old address can be annoying. Notably, Convención was changed to **La Torre,** and the diagonal street leading to the Capitol, Avenida Agraciada, is now **Avenida Libertador.** The main beachfront avenue, **Rambla,** changes its name as it heads toward the airport. Rambla Presidente Wilson suddenly emerges as Rambla Mahatma Gandhi, then as Rambla del Perú, followed by Rambla República de Chile, Rambla O'Higgins, and finally, near the airport, Rambla República de México.

STREET MAPS   Street maps are available at the Government Tourist Office in the Plaza Libertad.

---

3. GETTING AROUND

BY BUS   The bus system in Montevideo is quite efficient, and there is frequent service to all parts of the city. All you need to know is the bus route number, which you can obtain from your hotel management.

However, since buses go by zone, you'll be asked your destination when you enter. For beach areas, such as Pocitos and Carrasco, this is no problem. If necessary, hold in your hand more carfare than is needed and be sure to keep the ticket you receive. An inspector frequently strides through, checking to see if everybody has paid. You will not be thrown off, but it can be embarrassing if you have not paid the proper fare. Also, do not pull the cord that runs from the front to the rear: The conductor uses it to signal the driver to start and stop the bus. As in any city, avoid the rush hour and crowded buses (there are occasional pickpockets).

Key Local Bus Routes

To Playa Ramírez and Playa Pocitos: Bus no. 116, 117, 121, or 300
To Parque Batlle y Ordóñez: Bus no. 121
To Parque Rodo: Bus no. 117

To the zoo and planetarium: Bus no. 141 or 142
To the stadium: Bus no. 121
To the Parque Casino Hotel (for gambling): Bus no. 116, 117, or 300
To the airport: Bus no. 209 or 214
To the Golf Club: Bus no. 117 or 300

BY TAXI   Taxis are plentiful and astonishingly cheap here. The meter starts at 75¢ and jumps 15¢ every quarter of a mile. Therefore, a 2-mile trip will cost you under $2. Be sure to look for the chart showing cost of metered travel. Although most drivers are honest, you may find an occasional one who will overcharge.

BY COCHES   The word *coche* means "car," but a *coche* is always an unmetered car whose driver can charge whatever he wishes. If you must take one, ask the fare in advance. Although not so prevalent in Montevideo as in Buenos Aires, *coches* can be found at boat landings or wherever there is a temporary shortage of taxis.

BY CAR   If you insist on driving, for a rental try **Sudamcar** at Piedras 533 (tel. 958-150), **Snappy Car** at Andes 1363 (tel. 958-150), or **Avis** at Rambla R. Mexico (tel. 605-060). All charge $30 per day, plus 30¢ per kilometer for a small car. A deposit of $1,000 is required unless you use a credit card. Your hotel clerk will make all the arrangements.

FAST   MONTEVIDEO

Airport   Carrasco Airport information is 602-261.

American Express   The American Express office is at Mercedes 942 (tel. 920-829).

Area Code   The country code for Uruguay is 598. The city code for Montevideo is 02.

Babysitters   Ask the concierge at your hotel about the availability of child care.

Bookstores   **Libros Libros** in the Montevideo Shopping Center at Avenida Luis de Herrera 1290 is a good source for English books.

Business Hours   **Shops** are usually open daily from 9am to 7pm. **Banks** are open Monday to Friday from 1 to 5pm.

Car Rentals   See "Getting Around" above.

Climate   Montevideo has an almost ideal climate—temperate and dry. Remember that the seasons are reversed here, so that the period June through September is winter. Nevertheless, even July and August are mild, with afternoon highs in the 60s and evening lows in the mid-40s. Snow is unknown.

In summer (December to February), highs are in the low 80s, and the evenings are a delightful 60° to 65°F.

Crime   See "Safety" below.

Currency   Exchange rates for the Uruguayan **peso** shift so rapidly that it is vital for you to check carefully before you leave on your trip. For example, in late 1980 the U.S. dollar was worth about 9 pesos. By 1986 the exchange rate had risen to 180 pesos per U.S. dollar, and by 1988 it had risen to 400 pesos.

At this writing, you can purchase 3,000 pesos for each U.S. dollar, and prices, while adjusted, are consequently quite low. Because of frequent changes in the peso's value, however, it's impossible to know what the situation will be at the time of your trip.

Currency Exchange   A branch of the **First National City Bank** is located at 18 de Julio, on the corner of Paraguay (tel. 901-981 or 986-848). **Exprinter** maintains an office at Sarandi 700, where you can arrange tours and exchange dollars for pesos. **Gales: Casa de Cambiaria** is at Avenida 18 de Julio 1906 (tel. 920-229).

Dentists/Doctors   The concierge at your hotel should be able to recom-

MONTEVIDEO

Atlantic Ocean

N

Parque F. Rivera

Av. Italia
Av. Rivera
Rambla Rep. de México
Rambla O'Higgins
Rambla Rep. de Chile

Playa Verde
Punta Gorda
Playa Honda
Playa de los Ingleses

Punta del Descanso

Playa de Malvin

Playa del Buceo

Av. Italia
Rambla Armenia
Av. Rivera
Rambla Rep. de Pa

Av. de Octubre
Bul. Batlle y Ordóñez
Av. Dr. L.A. de Herrera

Parque Zoológico

Parque José Batlle y Ordóñez

Av. Dr. Soca
Av. J. Ponce
Av. Brasil
Bul. España

Playa de los Pocitos
Punta Trouville
Playa La Estacada

Rambla M. Gandhi

Parque Rodó
Rambla Pres. Wilson

Punta Brava

Av. Garibaldi
Av. 18 de Julio
Av. F. Crespo

Plaza Cagancha

Constituyente

Av. Gen. Flores
Av. G. San Martín
Bul. Gen. Artigas

Av. L. Lavalleja
Plaza J.P. Fabini

Plaza Independencia

Rambla Rep. Argentina

Playa Ramirez
Punta Ramirez

Parque El Prado

Av. Uruguayana
Bul. Gen. Artigas
Av. Agradacia
Rambla Dr. B.B. Mendoza

Rambla Sud América

Plaza Constitución
Rambla Sur

Rambla F.D. Roosevelt

Plaza Zabala

Port of Montevideo

Punta Santa Teresa

mend an English-speaking dentist or doctor. Or you can contact the embassy for a list of English-speaking dentists or doctors.

Drugstores   Ask the concierge at your hotel to direct you to the nearest drugstore. Dial 124 to find out which drugstore is open 24 hours.

Electricity   The electrical current is 220 volts at 50 cycles. You may find sockets for 110 volts in major hotels.

Embassies/Consulates   The **Canadian Embassy** is at Juan Carlos Gómez 1348 (tel. 958-234). The **U.S. Embassy** is at Lauro Muller 1776 (tel. 236-276) and is open from 8:45am to 4:30pm. The **United Kingdom Embassy** is at Marco Bruto 1073 (tel. 623-625) and is open from 8am to 2pm.

Emergencies   In case of medical emergency, call Primeros Auxilios (first aid) at 401-111. The mobile coronary unit can be reached at 800-000. For diabetic emergencies, call the Diabetic Institute of Uruguay at 916-214. The number for the Automobile Club of Uruguay is 982-020.

Entry Requirements   You will need a valid passport to enter the country.

Eyeglasses   The concierge at your hotel should be able to recommend a nearby optician.

Hairdressers/Barbers   The concierge at your hotel should be able to help you locate a hairdresser or barber.

Holidays

New Year's Day	January 1
Carnival	Varies
Easter	Varies
Landing of the *Orientales* Day	April 19
May *(Labor)* Day	May 1
Battle of Las Piedras Day	May 18
Don José Gervacio Artiga's Birthday	June 19
Constitution Day	July 18
Independence Day	August 25
Columbus Day	October 12
Christmas Day	December 25

Hospital   The **Pereryra Rosser Hospital** is at Bulevar Artigas 1550 (tel. 787-741).

Information   See "Tourist Information" above.

Language   Spanish is the official language of Uruguay. English is spoken at the larger hotels.

Laundry/Dry Cleaning   Most hotels offer laundry and dry-cleaning services.

Lost Property   Call **Perdidos y Hallazgos** (lost and found) at 297-187.

Newspapers/Magazines   The *International Herald Tribune, Time,* and *Newsweek* are available at the **Heber, Berriel and Nery Martínez** newsstand at Paraná 750 and also in most larger hotels.

Photographic Needs   Film is readily available throughout the city. Prices will be significantly higher than those in the United States.

Police   The chief of police can be reached at 989-101.

Post Office   The concierge at your hotel will direct you to the post office nearest your hotel.

Religious Services   The concierge at your hotel should be able to inform you of the schedule and location of religious services.

Restrooms   Bars and restaurants have restrooms for patrons only. Restrooms are also available in most museums and in the lobbies of most hotels.

Safety   By modern standards, Montevideo is a safe city. Nevertheless, you should exercise the same caution here as you would anywhere else.

Shoe Repairs   The concierge at your hotel should be able to direct you to the nearest shoe repair.

Taxes   Expect to pay a tax of about $10 when leaving Uruguay.

Taxis See "Getting Around," above.

Telegrams/Telexes/Faxes The main telegraph office is at Treinta y Tres 1418 (tel. 951-150). Ask the concierge at your hotel if there is an office closer to your hotel.

Telephone To get a dial tone, deposit a *ficha* (token), currently costing 5 pesos. If you are calling from a private home and would like to repay the owner, give him 10 pesos. AT&T Direct is a great cost saver. To get an AT&T Direct line dial 001-410.

Tipping Service is not included in restaurant bills, so leave a tip.

Transit Info See bus routes listed earlier in this chapter.

4. WHERE TO STAY

The best budget hotels are conveniently located on Avenida Mercedes, between Plaza Constitución and Plaza Libertad. In general, the basic hotels in Montevideo are less grim and generally cleaner than their counterparts in other South American cities. One can live on a budget here without sacrificing comfort. These small hotels often carry the word *pension,* since many have been converted from private homes. Accommodations, however, are very basic; a room may be equipped with only a bed, sink, table, and chair. Private baths usually consist of a toilet and a sink; for a shower, there is simply a showerhead, with a drain in the floor. Bring a pair of rubber thongs if you're squeamish about stepping onto a cold, bare floor to shower. On the bright side: Owners often take personal pride in keeping their hotels clean and tidy.

Note: The rates we quote exclude breakfast (unless otherwise noted), include tax and service, and are based on an exchange rate of 3,000 pesos to the dollar. All prices noted here are in-season rates (December to February); they may be lower in other months. All prices include a 20% value-added tax (VAT—known as IVA in South America).

THE PLAZA DE LA INDEPENDENCIA AREA
DOUBLES FOR LESS THAN $30

THE ATENEO, Colonia 1147, halfway between Plaza Independencia and Plaza Libertad. Tel. 922-496. Some rooms with bath. TV
$ Rates: $7 single without bath, $12 single with bath; $14 double without bath, $18 double with bath.

Although most of our starvation choices are located near the Plaza Libertad, this good, basic hotel is near Plaza de la Independencia. Several rooms here have private baths (a basic shower with no stall). The bedspreads are a bit thin, and the mattresses have a slouch. On the other hand, the hallways have nice tile floors, and many rooms have French windows and high ceilings.

HOTEL CERVANTES, Soriano 868. Tel. 907-991. 66 rms (some with bath). TEL
$ Rates (including breakfast): $15 single with bath; $25 double with bath.

The high-quality Cervantes can be reached by strolling along Andes an additional block from 18 de Julio. This three-floor hotel (with elevator) has clean, bright doubles. The management is friendly and helpful, and your stay here should be pleasant. Take the elevator to the reception office on the first floor.

HOTEL KINGS, Andes 1491. Tel. 920-927. 35 rms (all with bath). TV TEL
$ Rates (including breakfast): $20 single; $25 double.

Ⓢ Just 200 yards from the Plaza Independencia is a smart hostelry that opened in 1980. The seven-story Kings has comfortably furnished rooms, all with carpeting. Breakfast is served in your room.

HOTEL CRILLON, Andes 1316. Tel. 920195. Fax 920-849. Telex 22532. 80 rms (all with bath). A/C MINIBAR TV TEL
$ Rates (including breakfast): $34 single; $42 double. Major credit cards accepted.

✪ The first-class Hotel Crillon, located between 18 de Julio and San José, is a great choice. Here you can stay in a large, modern, carpeted double with a double bed, a night table with lamp, and comfortable chair; some rooms even have terraces. The Crillon has a bar and the impressive Restaurante Marini.

HOTEL ESPAÑOL, at La Torre (Convencion) 1317. Tel. 904-772 or 903-816. 45 rms (all with bath). TEL
$ Rates (including breakfast): $30 per person.
You might also try this two-story hotel located at the corner of San José. The rooms are well cared for, and the owners are exceptionally friendly.

HOTEL LOS ANGELES, Avenida 18 de Julio 974. Tel. 920-439. Fax 921-072. Telex ANGELES UY 23249. 102 rms (all with bath). A/C TV TEL
$ Rates (including breakfast): $32 single; $40 double. Discounts available for families of four or more. Major credit cards accepted.
On the main thoroughfare, just beyond Rio Branco, is this renovated hotel that's ideal for families—its manager has assured us he gives special rates to families of four or more. This five-story elevator hotel is extremely well maintained; the high-ceilinged rooms are spotless and airy. You enter through a gate, and the reception desk is on the second floor. Also, 24-hour medical assistance is available.

A SPLURGE CHOICE

VICTORIA PLAZA, Plaza de la Independencia 759. Tel. 914-201. Fax 921-628. Telex 22037 VICPLAZ UY. 358 rms (all with bath). A/C MINIBAR TV TEL
$ Rates: $70 single; $90 double. Major credit cards accepted.

✪ This 21-story palace is the city's prestige hostelry. Although starting to show its age a bit, the Victoria Plaza is still a comfortable place. Remodeling, as well as construction of a new tower, is currently underway as part of a plan to convert the hotel into a world-class five-star hotel with modern conference facilities.

THE PLAZA LIBERTAD [CAGANCHA] AREA

CALIFORNIA HOTEL, San José 1237. Tel. 920-408. Fax 920-412. Telex 23808 HOCALIF UY. 84 rms (all with bath). A/C MINIBAR TEL
$ Rates (including breakfast): $32 single; $40 double. Major credit cards accepted.
Nine stories high, the California has large, airy doubles with comfortable furnishings. A bar, a TV room, and writing rooms are off the handsome lobby.

HOTEL ARAMAYA, 18 de Julio 1103, at the corner of Paraguay. Tel. 983-354. Fax 986-192. 80 rms (some with bath).
$ Rates: $12 single without bath, $15 single with bath; $16 double without bath, $20 double with bath.
This hotel is a few steps from the Plaza Libertad. It has large rooms, with drapes and basic furniture. An elevator services the six floors. Walk up a short flight of stairs to reach the reception desk.

HOTEL BALFER, Zelmar Michelini 1328, at the corner of 18 de Julio. Tel. 920-073. Fax 920-009. Telex 22152 HOTEMBA UY. 74 rms (all with bath). A/C TEL
$ Rates: $28 single; $30 double. Major credit cards accepted.
Located a few blocks from the Plaza Cagancha, this three-story hotel is a less expensive choice for this area. The ONDA bus depot is only a few steps away. TVs are available.

GRAN HOTEL AMERICA, Río Negro 1330, at the corner of Avenida 18 de Julio. Tel. 920-392. Fax 920-485. Telex 22515 AMERICA UY. 80 rms (all with bath). A/C MINIBAR TV TEL
$ Rates (including breakfast): $40 single; $58 double. Major credit cards accepted.
The added attractions here include a garage, a bar, a barbershop, a beauty parlor, and 24-hour room service.

HOTEL KLEE, San José 1306, at the corner of Yaguarón. Tel. 910671. Fax 987-365. Telex 222-59 INTER UY. 108 rms (all with bath). A/C MINIBAR TV TEL
$ Rates (including continental breakfast): $36 single; $48 double. Major credit cards accepted.
⭐ We learned of this eight-story hostelry from a reader. The management tries to ensure that every guest feels at home. The hotel is located in the heart of the city, close to many restaurants and bus routes; there is a fine restaurant in the hotel.

LANCASTER, in the Plaza Libertad, at No. 1334. Tel. 920-480. 80 rms (all with bath). TV TEL
$ Rates (including continental breakfast): $38 single; $48 double; $70 triple. Major credit cards accepted.
⭐ Modern and roomy, this 12-story hotel offers large doubles, with radios, lamps, and writing desks. The breakfast consists of juice, coffee, a variety of breads, and cheese. A uniformed doorman greets you outside, and red-suited bellhops whisk your luggage up to your room. A bar and *confitería* (snack shop) are located off the lobby. Guests can enjoy free use of the nearby golf course at Playa Ramírez.

HOTEL PRESIDENTE, 18 de Julio 1038. Tel. 920-003. Fax 984-856. Telex UY 26988. 80 rms (all with bath). A/C MINIBAR TV TEL
$ Rates: $45 single; $55 double. Major credit cards accepted.
The rather new, 14-story Presidente is situated over the Galería Madrileña shopping arcade near Río Negro. The rooms are appropriately modern, and there are two elevators for the building. The on-premises lounge and bar are popular, and the management is most anxious to please. Services include dry cleaning, babysitting, and 24-hour medical and dental assistance.

OXFORD HOTEL, República de Paraguay 1286. Tel. 920046. Telex UY 23935. 70 rms (all with bath). A/C MINIBAR TV TEL
$ Rates (including continental breakfast): $26 single; $32–$43 double; $60 triple; $70 quadruple. Major credit cards accepted.
Half a block from the plaza, just off San José, is an outstanding nine-story hotel. The Oxford borders on the regal, with a winding stairway that leads from the flag-bedecked, mirrored lobby to the top floor. (Fear not, there's an elevator.) The large rooms have parquet floors and modern furnishings. For triples and quadruples, the management normally brings extra beds into a double room. Although the hotel is beginning to show some signs of age, it still is an excellent bargain.

A SPLURGE CHOICE

HOTEL LAFAYETTE, Soriano 1170. Tel. 922-351. Fax 921-301. All rooms with bath. A/C MINIBAR TV TEL
$ Rates: $60 single; $85 double. Major credit cards accepted.
The four-star Lafayette is the newest addition to Montevideo's list of world-class hotels. It offers comfortable, fully equipped rooms conveniently located in center city, as well as a fine restaurant, a health club (with fitness room), a pool and sauna, a snack bar, two conference centers (one with facilities for simultaneous translation), and plenty of parking.

ALONG AVENIDA MERCEDES

CLARIDGE, Mercedes 924. Tel. 915-746. Some rooms with bath.
$ Rates: $10 single with bath; $15 double with bath.

S Although many of the hotels on Avenida Mercedes tend to look alike, we have singled this one out because it offers exceptional value. (You have to climb a staircase to reach this hotel.) The large rooms come equipped with small heaters. There are only a few singles.

THE PLAZA CONSTITUCIÓN AREA

DOUBLES FOR LESS THAN $20

ARTIGAS HOTEL, Bartolome Mitre 1361, at the corner of Sarandi. Tel. 959-569. 35 rms (some with bath).
$ Rates: $9 single with bath; $10 double with bath.
The four-story Artigas is situated next to a popular nightclub, the Bonanza, which may make it attractive for those who like night life. The large, bare doubles with bathrooms have showers.

REINA HOTEL, Bartolome Mitre 1343. Tel. 959461. 40 rms (all with bath). TEL
$ Rates: $15 single; $18 double.
The elevator-equipped six-story Reina, located on the corner of Sarandi and a block from the plaza, has recently been renovated. The rooms are pleasant and airy, if somewhat small. The fifth-floor cafeteria is bright and cheerful, with an excellent view over the rooftops of the city. Continental breakfast is about $2.50.

A SPLURGE CHOICE

COLUMBIA PALACE HOTEL, Rambla República de Francia 473. Tel. 960001. Fax 960-192. Telex 22524 COLUTEL UY. 150 rms (all with bath). A/C MINIBAR TEL
$ Rates: $42 single; $65 double. Major credit cards accepted.

★ This is the "class" hotel in this section of Montevideo. The Columbia Palace faces the river south of the plaza. After a doorman opens the front door for you, you'll stroll through the plush lobby, past the beauty salon, barbershop, bar, and restaurant, to the front desk. You'll get a carpeted room with large bath, modern twin or double beds, a dresser, a vanity table, enormous closets, and a radio; a uniformed bellhop is at your disposal within minutes after you summon him by telephone. Some rooms come with sitting rooms and front rooms offer splendid views of the Plata River. To reach the Columbia Palace, go to the Plaza Matriz, then walk down (south) along Ituzaingo and make a right on Brecha to the hotel.

THE SEASIDE

If you prefer seaside to city, you might consider a budget hotel in one of the eight beach communities at the edge of Montevideo. Remember that in winter (June through September) these areas can be damp and chilly; we recommend this area primarily for summer stays. Nevertheless, since winter temperatures rarely dip below 40°F, staying here in August may not be a hardship.

ALONG PLAYA RAMIREZ

Closest to downtown Montevideo, this community is a 15-minute ride from any of the main plazas via bus no. 116, 117, 121, or 300. Near the Municipal Golf Club (where golf is free) and the lovely Rodo Park, Playa Ramírez is less than 2 miles south of Plaza Libertad and faces the mouth of the Río de la Plata.

PARQUE HOTEL CASINO, Rambla Presidente Wilson 1991. Tel. 488-372. Fax 488-380. Telex 23220 PARQHOT UY. 60 rms (all with bath). A/C TEL
$ Rates: $30 single; $40 double. Major credit cards accepted.
Probably your best choice here is the old and courtly three-story Parque, which houses the government-owned casino. Facing the beach, the aging—but still popular—hotel offers comfortable rooms, which are priced according to location.

Although the furnishings are quite old, they are well maintained. Guests have free admission to the casino.

ALONG PLAYA POCITOS

Five minutes (by bus) beyond Playa Ramírez is a second beach community, Playa Pocitos, which is larger and somewhat newer than its neighbor.

GRAN HOTEL ERMITAGE, Juan Benito Blanco 783. Tel. 704-021. Telex 266649 ЕRMITE UY. 100 rms (all with bath). A/C TV TEL
$ Rates: $38 single; $48 double. Major credit cards accepted.
This outstanding modern hotel has bright and airy doubles. Situated on a rise 50 yards from the beach and two blocks from Bulevar España, the main thoroughfare, the nine-story Ermitage offers a fine view of the city from its upper stories. With an elevator, a bar, and a restaurant, it is an excellent value. Look for the green-and-white awning (there may be no sign).

PUNTA GORDA

THE OCEANIA, Mar Artico 1227. Tel. 600-444. Fax 602-273. Telex 26589 UY. All rooms with bath. A/C TV TEL
$ Rates: $40–$50 single; $50–$68 double. Rooms with ocean view are higher priced. Major credit cards accepted.
⭐ This fine hotel offers all the advantages of a beach resort even though it's just a 15-minute ride from center city. Rocky shores, scuba diving, tennis, casinos, sandy beaches, and shady parks make Punta Gorda a popular weekend and holiday retreat. One of Montevideo's finest hotels, the Oceania, rounds out the attractions at Punta Gorda with seaside restaurants, boîtes, and excellent accommodations.

CARRASCO
Doubles for Less than $50

CASINO CARRASCO HOTEL, Rambla República de México. Tel. 610-511. Fax 570-405. All rooms with bath. A/C TEL
$ Rates: $20 single; $32 double.
The Casino Carrasco, which sports one of Montevideo's two casinos, offers spacious rooms at reasonable prices. It ranks with the Ermitage in decor and service.

HOTEL COTTAGE, Miraflores 1360, at the corner of Rambla República de México. Tel. 600-867. Telex 26928 COTTAGE UY. Most rooms with bath.
$ Rates (including breakfast): $28 single with bath; $45 double with bath.
This hotel is a comfortable choice located across from Carrasco beach.

A Splurge Choice

HOSTERIA DEL LAGO, Arizona 9637, Lago de Carrasco. Tel. 612-210. All rooms with bath. A/C MINIBAR TV TEL
$ Rates: $95 single; $110 double. Major credit cards accepted.
This is a beautiful colonial-style hotel in a long and low building. Most of the rooms face the lovely lake; all have stereo music systems.

5. WHERE TO DINE

Uruguay raises some of the best beef in the world. A popular restaurant dish in Montevideo, therefore, is the **parrillada,** a combination of beef chunks with organ meats, chicken, and sausage cooked over an open fire on a *parrilla,* or grill.
Other Uruguayan specialties are **carbonada,** stewed meat, rice, peaches, raisins,

and pears; *carne asado*, a grilled steak; *churrasco*, a thin steak; and *puchero*, beef stew served with vegetables and beans. The steak sauces, particularly the tangy *salsa criolla*, are noteworthy. And be sure to try a *chivito*, a typical Uruguayan sandwich made with steak, ham, egg, tomato, bacon, melted cheese, olives, and lettuce. This treat can be ordered at any cafeteria.

Dinner here is served late—well after 9pm. Therefore, you'll find the late-afternoon tea hour a must; it also gives you an opportunity to sample Uruguayan pastries, which are exceptional. The locals wash them down with a strong tea, *mate*, made of yerba leaves.

Since many Uruguayans are of Italian descent, you'll also find many good Italian restaurants here.

Note: Service is not included in the price of your meal, so be sure to leave a tip.

CENTER OF TOWN

You'll probably want to have breakfast or lunch at one of the many downtown cafeterias. There are one or two on every block. Most are Swisslike in their cleanliness and are ideal for light meals. They cater to crowds of shoppers and office workers.

CERVECERIA LA PASIVA, on the Plaza Independencia.
 Cuisine: SANDWICHES/LIGHT MEALS.
 $ Prices: Less than $3.

We are quite fond of the Cervecería La Pasiva—one of the few budget choices west of the Plaza de la Independencia. Located on the main floor of the Alhambra Hotel, it has a Spanish colonial decor, with enormous chandeliers that dominate the dining room. There are booths, tables, and even counter service. We've enjoyed the ham-and-cheese sandwiches, the franks, and the delicious beer. There are six other Cervecería La Pasiva restaurants in town.

EL CHIVITO DE ORO, 18 de Julio 1251. Tel. 905-160.
 Cuisine: LIGHT MEALS.
 $ Prices: $3–$4.
 Open: Until 3am.
This cafeteria serves a great steak sandwich called *chivito*. Other sandwiches, both hot and cold, are made to order.

CONAPROLE, Calle Eduardo Couture.
 Cuisine: URUGUAYAN/INTERNATIONAL.
 $ Prices: Full meal $2–$5.
 Open: Breakfast, lunch, and dinner.
Conaprole, set in a large park, will be your second home if you're staying at a hotel in Carrasco. It serves breakfast, *chivito* sandwiches, and omelets and gears up for dinner with huge steak platters.

EL GATTO ROSSO, Juan Benito Blanco between España Boulevard and Avenida Brasil. Tel. 771-122.
 Cuisine: PIZZA/PASTA. **Reservations:** Not accepted.
 $ Prices: Pizzas $3–$8. Pasta dishes $2.50–$5.
 Open: Noon–midnight.
For pizza with a taste of the *exótico*, stop in here and order a Pizza Tropical. It's a pizza topped with pineapple, apple, lettuce, hard-boiled egg, and cucumber.

HISPANO BAR, San José 1050 at Río Negro. Tel. 980-045.
 Cuisine: PIZZA/SANDWICHES/SNACKS.
 $ Prices: $2–$5 pizza; full meals $2–$6.
 Open: Mon–Fri 7am–2am; Sat–Sun until 4am.
The pizzas here are doughy, with a generous helping of cheese and a choice of toppings.

LOKOTAS, at the corner of Ellauri and 21 de Setiembre.
 Cuisine: URUGUAYAN.

$ Prices: 50¢–$1.50.
Open: Daily 10am–1am.
Montevideo's best *empanadas* (meat or cheese pies with many variations) are at Lokotas. What makes them so good? They're baked very slowly instead of fried. Other locations include Juan B. Blanco 986 and Avenida 18 de Julio 898.

THE MANCHESTER, 18 de Julio 899. Tel. 904-383.
Cuisine: SNACKS/PASTRIES/SANDWICHES.
$ Prices: Light meal $2–$5.
Open: All day.
The Manchester is a good stop for a quick breakfast (*café con leche*—coffee with steamed milk—and a small croissant) or lunch (ham-and-cheese sandwich). The place is crowded at teatime.

PUMPERNIC, Avenida 18 de Julio, between La Torre and Río Negro.
Cuisine: HAMBURGERS/SANDWICHES/PIZZA.
$ Prices: Full meal $3–$5.

Montevideo has two branches of this popular Buenos Aires fast-food chain (the second is in the Montevideo shopping center). Photos of the available dishes on the menu make ordering easy. Burger selections range from the plain to a deluxe hamburguesa gigante.

TITOS, at the top of Coimbra and General Paz, almost at the Plaza Verde.
Cuisine: URUGUAYAN.
$ Prices: $2–$3.
For the best *chivito* in Montevideo, try Titos. Your mouth is guaranteed to water as you watch the chef build your *chivito*.

LAS BRASAS, San José 909, at La Torre. Tel. 902-285.
Cuisine: URUGUAYAN. **Reservations:** Recommended.
$ Prices: Appetizers $3; main courses $6. Major credit cards accepted.
Open: Sun–Fri 11:30am–3:30pm and 8pm–1am; Sat until 2am.
Las Brasas, part of a chain, is a fine restaurant for *parrillada*. Or you might choose a steak or a chicken platter. A bottle of good domestic wine will run you $3. Add 50¢ for cover (bread and butter).

BUNGALOW SUIZO, Sol 150. Tel. 611-073.
Cuisine: SWISS. **Reservations:** Recommended.
$ Prices: Appetizers $2–$5; main courses $6–$9. Major credit cards accepted.
Open: Mon–Sat 8pm–12:30am.
Attractive and offering live music nightly, the Bungalow Suizo may be the finest downtown restaurant. It serves delicious cheese fondue. Also recommended are the Swiss potatoes.

EL DAVID, Rivera 2000. Tel. 484-862.
Cuisine: URUGUAYAN. **Reservations:** Recommended.
$ Prices: Appetizers $1–$3; main courses $4–$9. Major credit cards accepted.
Open: 11:30am–4pm and 8pm–1am.

A Luxembourg businessman told us about this excellent but far from fancy steak restaurant—*churrascaría*—downtown. It serves the best *parrillada* (mixed meat grill) in Montevideo. Also recommended are the entrecôte and the *cordero* (lamb). One whiff of the meat cooking as you enter will make your mouth water. El David has a second restaurant in Punta Del Este.

BAR ANTICUARIO, Maldonado 1602. Tel. 438-500.
Cuisine: INTERNATIONAL. **Reservations:** Recommended.
$ Prices: Appetizers $3–$5; main courses $6–$9. Major credit cards accepted.
Open: Tues–Sun 11am–4pm and 6pm–2am.
This bilevel restaurant is a nostalgically decorated old house with antique street signs along the walls. The house specialty is *pollo al ajillo* (chicken cooked in garlic). Other

entrées include chateaubriand, *lomo antiquario* (filet of beef) and *pollo apio* (baked chicken).

EL FOGON, San José 1080, between Río Negro and Paraguay. Tel. 900-900.
Cuisine: URUGUAYAN. **Reservations:** Recommended.
$ **Prices:** Appetizers $2–$4; main courses $5–$8. Major credit cards accepted.
Open: Mon–Fri Noon–4pm and 7pm–1am; Sat until 2am.

Another typical Uruguayan restaurant is the comfortable El Fogon, which manages to keep two *parrillas* going at the same time. We like the lower-level dining area, which we have labeled the "Old West Room" because it reminds us of the living room of an old ranch house. It's quieter and more intimate than the main dining room above. Again, the *parrillada* is the specialty, but you might also try the entrecôte Fogon.

LA GENOVESA, San José 1242. Tel. 908-729.
Cuisine: SPANISH. **Reservations:** Recommended.
$ **Prices:** Appetizers $3–$5; main courses $6–$10. Major credit cards accepted.
Open: Mon–Fri noon–3:30pm and 8pm–12:30am; Sat until 1am.

Paella and all types of seafood are tops on the menu at one of Montevideo's finest Spanish restaurants. The gazpacho is famous citywide.

OTTO, Río Negro 1301, at the corner of San José. Tel. 901-994.
Cuisine: GERMAN.
$ **Prices:** Appetizers $3–$5; main courses $4–$9. Major credit cards accepted.
Open: Mon–Fri 11:30am–12:40am; Sat–Sun noon–midnight.

For a taste of Bavaria, try Otto. Highly recommended are the Leberwurst (liver pâté) and the *salchichas de Viena*. You'll find excellent beer and German wines. Wooden tables and red-jacketed waiters brighten the decor.

DEL AGUILA, Buenos Aires 694 in the Plaza Independencia. Tel. 959-905.
Cuisine: INTERNATIONAL. **Reservations:** Recommended.
$ **Prices:** Appetizers $1–$3; main courses $4–$6. Major credit cards accepted.
Open: Mon–Fri noon–3pm and 8pm–2:30am; Sat 8pm–2:30am; Sun noon–3pm.

Stone archways lead to this popular local favorite. The white-jacketed waiters will no doubt suggest the *brochette de lomo,* the *entrecôte parrilla,* the *chicken cazadora,* or the *arroz aguila.* For dessert, try the peaches Chantilly or the guayaba fruit.

RESTAURANT MORINI, Ciudadela 1229. Tel. 959-733.
Cuisine: INTERNATIONAL. **Reservations:** Recommended.
$ **Prices:** Appetizers $2–$4; main courses $5–$8. Major credit cards accepted.
Open: Lunch noon–3pm; dinner 8pm–1am.

This restaurant is two blocks down from the Plaza de la Independencia, in the Mercado Central. It is decorated like a ship's dining room. Try the *cazuela de mariscos*, a delicious sea stew, or the *suprema de pollo.*

RESTAURANTE LA VEGETARIANA, Yi 1344. Tel. 907-661.
Cuisine: VEGETARIAN.
$ **Prices:** Appetizers $1–$3; main courses $3–$6.
Open: Lunch 11:30am–3pm; dinner 7:30–11:30pm.

At La Vegetariana, located near the Plaza Libertad, you can feast on a huge variety of vegetable dishes and excellent juice combinations. The restaurant also has take-out service. Other branches of La Vegetariana are located at San José 1056 (tel. 910-558) and Brasil 3086 (tel. 787-357).

LA VASCONGADA, Yaguaron 1386, between 18 de Julio and Colonia. Tel. 983-980.
Cuisine: INTERNATIONAL. **Reservations:** Recommended.
$ **Prices:** Appetizers $2–$4; main courses $4–$8.

Open: 11am–4pm and 6:30pm–1am.

⑤ The meat and fish dishes here are excellent, but the prices are well below those found at the fancier restaurants a block away. Another advantage: This is one of the few restaurants that opens for dinner at 6:30pm. Specialties here include *abadejo à la marinera,* prepared with fresh mussels, and *suprema de pollo al cognac,* chicken prepared in a cognac sauce. There is a large TV, and waiters often get absorbed in the 8 o'clock news or the Spanish programs that follow.

AT THE BEACH

LA AZOTEA, Mercado del Puerto, Local 028-027. Tel. 951-425.
   Cuisine: URUGUAYAN/SEAFOOD.
 $ Prices: Appetizers $2–$5; main courses under $8. Major credit cards accepted.
   Open: Mon–Sat 10am–5pm.
In the Pocitos area, we're fond of this modern restaurant facing the beach. The T-bone steak here is nothing short of magnificent. We have also enjoyed *riñones* (barbecued steer kidneys) as an appetizer, as well as barbecued lamb.

LE RENDEZVOUS, in the Hotel Ermitage, J. Blanco 783. Tel. 704-021.
   Cuisine: INTERNATIONAL. **Reservations:** Recommended.
 $ Prices: Appetizers $2–$4; main courses $4–$9; three-course special $8.50.
   Major credit cards accepted.
   Open: Daily lunch and dinner.
This attractive restaurant serves a daily three-course special—soup, meat, and dessert, plus a beverage.

RODO PARK, Gonzalo Ramírez, next to the Rodo Park Hotel.
   Cuisine: PARRILLADA/SEAFOOD.
 $ Prices: Appetizers $1–$3; main courses $4–$8.
   Open: Lunch and dinner.

⑤ The better seaside restaurants are in Playa Pocitos, but this is one acceptable budget choice in Playa Ramírez. The *parrillada* dishes are only one highlight of the extensive menu. Try the plate of the day (from a list of 10 entrées) for about $5.

SEA GARDEN RESTAURANT, Rambla República de Peru 1402, in Pocitos.
   Cuisine: SEAFOOD.
 $ Prices: Appetizers $2–$5; main courses $4–$9. Major credit cards accepted.
   Open: Evenings.
Sporting a lovely bar and music at night, the Sea Garden serves fine seafood in a romantic setting. We highly recommended this place, especially if you're staying at the Ermitage.

SPECIALTY DINING

CONFITERIAS

Since dinner is served late, Montevideans typically have late-afternoon tea (or, more often, a cocktail) to tide them over. There are many informal tearooms (*confiterías*) located in the 18 de Julio vicinity.

   A particularly attractive confitería with marvelous pastries is **Horniman's Tea Room,** 18 de Julio 907 (upstairs). The superb strawberry tarts are $1 (5¢ extra for whipped cream). The pastries are so good you may want to take some back to your hotel. The tearoom is invariably crowded.

   Other fine pastry shops include **Oro Del Rhin** (Convención 1403/09 at the corner of Colonia), and **Confitería Francesca** (San José 923, near Las Brasas restaurant). You will also find many take-out eateries, for example, on Yaguaron between 18 de Julio and San José, or around the corner on San José between Yaguaron and Cuareim.

In Pocitos, **Giorgio's** (Rambla Republica de Peru 871) offers a view of the ocean through its glass windows; try the nut pastry called *plancha de almendrez* ($1.25) or the sandwiches ($1.50 and up). A block farther along Peru, at no. 893, on the corner of Espana, is **Las Palmas,** another good-value confitería. The **Café de la Paix** (Bulevar España 3000) offers a delightful oceanfront location in addition to hard-to-resist pastries; credit cards are accepted here, and it stays open until 4:30am on the weekends.

L'ETOILE, in the Victoria Plaza Hotel, Plaza de la Independencia 759. Tel. 914-201.
  Cuisine: FRENCH. **Reservations:** Recommended.
$ Prices: Appetizers $2–$6; main courses $5–$10; full dinner $10; five-course fixed-price lunch $7. Major credit cards accepted.
  Open: Lunch and dinner.
At the elegant Victoria Plaza grill room, diners are entertained by a strolling violinist and an orchestra.
  Yet prices are moderate. For $7 you can have an excellent inch-thick steak; with an appetizer, vegetables, a special *criolla* meat sauce, dessert, coffee, service, and tax, your bill will still be under $8. A special treat? Try the *canard à l'orange* (wild duckling with orange sauce) or the superb boneless chicken with whiskey or champagne. And if you're hungry at noontime, be sure to sample the five-course fixed-price lunch, which includes soup, steak, almond cake, and coffee.

SHORT HORN GRILL, in the Columbia Palace, Rambla República de Francia 473. Tel. 960-001.
  Cuisine: INTERNATIONAL. **Reservations:** Recommended.
$ Prices: Appetizers $4–$8; main courses $6–$12. Major credit cards accepted.
  Open: Daily 11:30am–11pm.
North American Colonial in motif, this inviting restaurant has wood paneling throughout. The imaginative hors d'oeuvres are an immediate attraction, since they are wheeled from table to table (as are the desserts). Our favorite entrées are the chateaubriand with béarnaise sauce and the boiled fish served Spanish-style. For an extra treat, try the apple pancake dessert.

MAKAO, in the Oceania Hotel, Mar Artico 1227 (Punta Gorda). Tel. 600-444.
  Cuisine: INTERNATIONAL. **Reservations:** Recommended.
$ Prices: Appetizers $4–$8; main courses $6–$12. Major credit cards accepted.
  Open: Dinner only, Mon–Fri from 9pm; lunch and dinner, Sat–Sun.
Makao offers elegant oceanside dining. Salmon canapés and crab pâté top the list of appetizers. Entrées include *brochette de lomo* (beef brochette), *lenguado Stroganoff* (sole Stroganoff), and *filet moscovita* (flambé in vodka). The prices are steep, but the impeccable service and elegant surroundings (not to mention the view) are well worth the extra cost. Jackets and ties are appropriate. Makao is located 6 miles outside center city in Punta Gorda, so you may need a cab to get here.

CLUB DE GOLF DEL URUGUAY, Br. Artigas 379. Tel. 701-721.
  Cuisine: FRENCH/ITALIAN. **Reservations:** Recommended.
$ Prices: Appetizer, main course, and coffee $20.
  Open: Lunch only, Mon–Fri 12:30–3:30pm.
To see the upper echelon of Montevideo, splurge for lunch at the Club de Golf. This private golf club is open to the general public for lunch during the week. *Tournedo gratinado a la mostaza de Dijón* (tournedos in a dijon-mustard sauce) is the chef's specialty. Entrecôte and *conejo cazador* (rabbit hunter style) are also on the menu.

DONA FLOR, Bulevar Artigas 1034. Tel. 785-751.
  Cuisine: FRENCH. **Reservations:** Recommended.
$ Prices: Appetizers $4–$7; main courses $8–$12; full meal $22. Major credit cards accepted.
  Open: Dinner only.

⭐ Doña Flor, about 10 minutes by taxi from the center of town, is our favorite dinner restaurant in Montevideo. At the top of a flight of stairs in this white stucco house are three small dining rooms, with stained-glass windows and skylights. Each room has only three or four tables. Circular, arched columns add a Roman touch to the decor. Surprisingly, the prices are not out of sight. Try the *champignons à la provençale*, the *escalope de veau à la compôte d'orange* (veal in orange sauce), or the *steak au poivre*. For dessert, the soufflé with oranges or cherries is fantastic. Doña Flor has another branch in Punta del Este.

RESTAURANT DEL FERROCARRIL, Estación Central General Artigas, Río Negro 1746. Tel. 905-786.
   Cuisine: INTERNATIONAL. **Reservations:** Recommended.
$ **Prices:** Appetizers $3–$6; main courses $6–$12. Major credit cards accepted.
   Open: Mon–Thurs and Sun noon–3pm and 8pm–midnight; Fri–Sat until 1am.

⭐ The Restaurant del Ferrocarril is the perfect choice for a sample of Montevideo's past and present. Built at the turn of the century as the city's central rail station, it has recently been converted to a fine restaurant. Its international menu includes *escalopes marsala* (scallops marsala), *suprema Maryland*, *pâté de mariscos* (shellfish pâté), *atún fresca à la plancha à la Vasca* (fresh grilled tuna basque style), and *cazuela de mariscos* (traditional shellfish stew). Dining here is really lovely. Be sure to get a close look at the model train station as you enter. A must for history and architecture buffs.

LE GAVROCHE, Rivera 1989. Tel. 497-371.
   Cuisine: FRENCH. **Reservations:** Recommended.
$ **Prices:** Appetizers $5–$7; main courses $10–$15. Major credit cards suggested.
   Open: Mon–Thurs 12:15–3pm and 8pm–midnight; Fri–Sat until 1am; Sun 12:15–3pm.
Here is another good choice if you're in the mood for traditional French cooking. Try the crêpes Suzette.

RESTAURANT PANORAMICO, Soriano 1375. Tel. 920-666.
   Cuisine: INTERNATIONAL. **Reservations:** Recommended.
$ **Prices:** Appetizers $4–$8; main courses $7–$14. Major credit cards accepted.
   Open: Lunch and dinner.
On the 24th floor of the Palacio Municipal atop the lookout tower, this restaurant offers an extensive menu and its prices are in the big-splurge category. The views are spectacular, though, and worth the extra cost.

6. ATTRACTIONS

PARKS

Montevideo enjoys an abundance of well-manicured parks. One of the loveliest, a popular weekend gathering spot, is the 60-hectare **Parque José Batlle y Ordóñez** (named after a president of Uruguay who introduced far-reaching social and political reforms earlier in the century). Located at the end of 18 de Julio, it's about 2 miles from Plaza Libertad. You can reach it by taking any bus along 18 de Julio. The park has some of the country's most important monuments, such as José Belloni's **La Carreta** (dedicated to the pioneers of Uruguay) and the **Obelisk** (dedicated to the constituents J. L. Zorilla de San Martín in 1928). Remarkably clean, the park offers a bicycle path, a running track, and a stadium, the **Estadio Centenario,** where *fútbol* matches are held.

Actually, the city's most popular park is the huge **Parque Rodó,** at Playa Ramírez, near Rambla Presidente Wilson. You can rent a rowboat, canoe, or paddleboat and have a remarkably idyllic time on the beautiful island-dotted lake in the center of the park. Or you can stroll over the footbridge leading to some of the

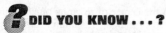

DID YOU KNOW . . . ?

- Montevideo's main street, Avenida 18 de Julio, commemorates the date in 1830 when Uruguay's first constitution took effect.
- In 1603 the Spanish conquistador Hernando Arias shipped cattle and horses to Uruguay. By 1726, the number of cattle reached 25 million.
- Montevideo was settled in 1726 by families from Buenos Aires, Spain, and the Canary Islands.
- In 1885, Uruguay passed a progressive divorce law, allowing a woman to divorce her husband on grounds of cruelty.
- An atmosphere of religious and political freedom in the 1930s inspired Jews to emigrate from Germany to Uruguay.
- Montevideo was the first city in Latin America to install an adequate electric-light plant.
- Forty-five varieties of marble were used in the mosaic floors and walls of the Legislative Palace in Montevideo, constructed at a cost of $12 million.

islands and watch the swans and ducks in the water. Near the lake is the **Teatro Municipal del Verano,** where open-air concerts are often held. And the park has a major amusement center, one of the reasons for its popularity. Be sure to stop at the **National Museum of Fine Arts,** which displays the works of contemporary Uruguayan artists. Admission is free, and it is open Tuesday through Sunday from 4 to 8pm (tel. 416-317). To reach the park, take bus no. 116, 117, or 121.

Flower lovers would enjoy another park, **El Prado,** off Avenida La Torre, a diagonal street leading off 18 de Julio, between Plaza Independencia and Plaza Libertad. Designed at the turn of the century by Lasseaux, the park's impeccably maintained gardens showcase 800 varieties of roses. Be sure to visit the **Botanical Garden and Museum,** where Charles Racine has assembled more than 800 species of trees and plants.

Finally, the **Parque Zoológico Municipal** houses both a planetarium and a zoo (zoo admission is 50¢, which includes free admission to the planetarium). The elaborately equipped planetarium (one of South America's finest) has shows at 5, 6, and 7pm on Saturday, Sunday, and holidays (6pm and 7pm on Tuesday and Thursday). The zoo, which has unusual camel species as well as vicuñas, llamas, guanos, and varieties of snakes, is open until sundown every day. To reach this park, take bus no. 141, 142, 144, or 191 from Plaza Independencia or Plaza Libertad. Trolleys 63, 67, and 68 also head here. A cab should cost no more than $2.

MUSEUMS

MUSEO DEL GAUCHO Y DE LA MONEDA, 18 de Julio 998. Tel. 908-764.

Located downtown at the corner of Julio Herrera y Obes, this museum combines gaucho artifacts and history with antique money and coins. Formerly a palace, the museum has interesting gaucho bolos, cooking utensils, horse equipment, and other items associated with Uruguay's cowboys.
Admission: 50¢.
Open: Tues–Fri 9:30am–12:30pm and 3:30–7:30pm; Sat–Sun 3:30–7:30pm.

MUSEO DE BELLAS ARTES "JUAN M. BLANES," Avenida Millan 4014. Tel. 385-420.

This museum is located at the corner of Mauá. It is dedicated to the works of Juan Manuel Blanes, the official painter of the Uruguayan republic.
Admission: 50¢.
Open: Tues–Sun 2–6pm.

MERCADO DEL PUERTO

No visit to Montevideo would be complete without a stroll through the Mercado del Puerto. It's located in the **Ciudad Vieja** across from the **Customs Building (Aduana).**

Since opening in 1867, this has been a meeting place for both visitors and immigrants alike. While big business was conducted at the Customs House across the street, sailors would wander into the Mercado to trade with the local merchants. As the years passed small restaurants, wine shops, and *parrilladas* have replaced the original greengrocers, butchershops, and small markets.

A WALKING TOUR

Depending on where you're staying, you can begin a walking tour either at the Plaza de la Constitución or at the Plaza de la Independencia.

If you begin at the centrally located Independencia, you'll be near important government and office buildings as well as the famous **Teatro Solis** (for ballet and drama) and the **Museum of Natural History** (open on Tuesday, Thursday, and Sunday from 2–5pm; admission free). At the museum you'll see stuffed snakes, tortoises, and alligators, as well as shrunken heads and mummies.

At the west end of the plaza is the tall, colonial-style **Puerto de la Ciudadela,** which is the starting point for a tour of the city's older section. Walk under the archway onto **Calle Sarandi** and in two blocks you'll reach the **Plaza de la Constitución,** Montevideo's oldest square. The **Cathedral of Montevideo** is here, along with the old **Cabildo,** the former town hall and current home of the municipal museum. Cross the plaza to Calle Rincón. Stroll along Rincón for three blocks until you reach the **Plaza Zabala,** the city's commercial center. Nearby are the stock exchange, the National Bank, and the Customs House. All of the buildings on these narrow, winding streets are of 18th-century design and construction.

Return now to Plaza de la Independencia on Rincón and find **Avenida 18 de Julio.** Walk along this lovely tree-lined street (heading east) to the **Plaza Libertad (Cagancha),** site of arcades, department stores, restaurants, and hotels. Continuing on 18 de Julio four blocks beyond Plaza Libertad, you'll come to the **Municipal Palace,** which houses municipal offices. On the 20th floor is an observation deck, **Mirador Panorámico,** where you can enjoy a breathtaking view of the city.

Note the two elevators outside the building. Pay 10¢ and ascend. You'll glide rapidly upward as a view of the ocean expands in front of your eyes. Getting out, you can walk around all sides and enjoy a panoramic view of the harbor, some of the beaches, and a large part of the city. We like it best at sunset, when the sun slowly dips into the sea and the upper arc degenerates into a straight line and then goes out. There is a confitería where you can get drinks and light refreshments. Not so visible is the charming restaurant on top, whose prices are slightly higher than elsewhere in the city.

Be sure to note the replica of Michelangelo's *David* that stands in front of the Municipal Palace. On a nearby corner is a well-known equestrian statue of a gaucho, Uruguay's folk hero.

ORGANIZED TOURS

Day bus tours of the city, including the planetarium, can be arranged through the **Cot Agency,** Plaza de la Cagancha 1124 (tel. 921-605). The cost is about $18. Cot also offers a $35 night tour of the city, including a casino visit and dinner at a good restaurant; and there are organized tours to Punta del Este as well.

Another reliable tour agency is **Tudet,** Julio Herrera y Obes 1338 (tel. 987-921), near 18 de Julio, two blocks from Plaza Libertad. Tudet runs tours to Punta del Este ($30 with lunch), city tours ($18), nightclub tours ($38), and inexpensive scenic tours of the coast and highlands.

Viajes Cynsa, at 18 de Julio 1120, in Plaza Libertad, is also highly recommended. Stop by and pick up their brochure, which lists departure times and precise costs.

7. SPORTS & RECREATION

ESTADIO CENTENARIO, in the Parque Batlle y Ordóñez, at the end of Avenida 18 de Julio. Tel. 784-270.

As elsewhere in South America, soccer is the national sport in Uruguay. Major matches are held at this 70,000-seat stadium. Tickets can be purchased directly at the stadium. Bus no. 121 will take you to the stadium from Plaza de la Independencia, but a taxi is quicker.

Admission: Nonchampionship matches $2; important contests, including international events, $3–$10.

HIPODROMO DE MARONAS, José M. Guerra.

Uruguayans are also fond of the turf, and on racing afternoons they flock here. This is an exciting Montevideo activity.

Admission: 85¢; minimum bet $1.

Times: Sat–Sun (sometimes Thurs) first race 1pm. **Trolley:** From Plaza de la Independencia, nos. 4 and 5 will drop you at the Hipodromo. **Bus:** From Plaza de la Independencia, take no. 102; from Plaza Matriz, take no. 5. **Taxi:** $6.

8. SAVVY SHOPPING

Not far off the Rambla, near Playa Buceo, is the **Montevideo Shopping Center,** a large, two-story, modern red-brick shopping mall. Virtually a self-contained outlet, it's open daily from 10am to 10pm (restaurants open until midnight). You might want to browse around to get a general idea of the prices. Or you might want to check out specific boutiques, such as **Yves St. Laurent, Pierre Cardin,** or **Daniel Hechter.** In addition, you'll find several fine restaurants and snack shops like **Mister Pizza, Bier Hot, Pumpernic,** and **McDonald's,** as well as a supermarket, music shops, and pubs.

SHOPPING A TO Z

Downtown shops are generally clustered in small arcades called *galerías*. The modern shopping arcades off Avenida 18 de Julio house some of our favorite shops.

ACCESSORIES

GUCCI, Avenida 18 de Julio 989. Tel. 900-577.

Gucci has come to Montevideo. It has a fine selection of shoes, wallets, and everything else for which Gucci is world famous. Open Monday to Friday from 9am to 7:30pm and Saturday from 9am to 1:30pm.

TABORELLI'S, in Galería Madrileña.

This elegant shop has a large selection of handbags in leather ($40 and up), alligator ($125 and up), and leather with suede trim ($40 and up). A second branch is at 18 de Julio 1184, in Plaza Libertad.

CLOTHING

CASA MARIO, Piedras 641. Tel. 962-356.

Casa Mario offers suede and antelope clothing for men and women, sheepskin and cowskin rugs, and leather handbags—all at bargain (factory) prices.

GENERAL STORE, Sarandi 582.

This is Uruguay's answer to Banana Republic, though the clothes here are better suited to the pampas than to the jungle.

LA OPERA, Calle Sarandi near Plaza Matriz.
In this large department store, you can get sweaters made of a cashmerelike wool called burma for $25 and up. Handbags trimmed with nonato, suede, or pony skin start at the same price.

RACHEL BOUTIQUE, Río Negro 1320, near San José.
For women's clothing, we're particularly fond of this boutique. (We're pleased to report that a wool sweater and slacks purchased here are wearing well.) Rachel is in an arcade that houses other good value, high-fashion shops.

GIFTS & ANTIQUES

Near Plaza Matriz are several shops that offer fine antiques; gifts such as ashtrays, clocks, and paperweights; and interesting items made from agates, amethysts, and other minerals.
Antique lovers should head for the Feria de Antiguedades (antiques fair) on Saturdays at Plaza Zabala, behind Zabala and Colón.

AMATISTAS DE BENITO SITYA, Sarandi 650.
In this shop, you'll find an excellent selection of Uruguayan gemstones, including amethysts, topaz, agates, and quartz, as well as fine jewelry.

ANTIGUEDADES 584. Esmeralda 584. Tel. 393-5618.
Owners Enrique E. Nuñez and José M. Galdeano are deservedly proud of the fine collection of antique artwork, firearms, jewelry, and watches they've collected. This shop is an antique lover's paradise.

JEWELRY

CUARZOS DEL URUGUAY, Sarandi 604, at the corner of J. C. Gomez. Tel. 959-210.
This fine shop, offering Uruguayan gems such as amethysts, topaz, and agates, is well stocked and conveniently located in front of the Plaza de la Constitución.

TOPAZ INTERNATIONAL JEWELRY, in the Victoria Plaza Hotel.
For the best in jewelry—including the local specialty, topaz—try this gemstone outlet. Other excellent values are the amethysts and the top-quality agates.

LEATHER

KING'S, Plaza de la Independencia 729.
Montevideo has several leather factories where you can get good buys on ready-to-wear garments or have them made to order. A typical one is King's, which maintains a large showroom for customers. Suede coats for women start at $350; vests and unusual sport tops are only $50. Men's suede or leather jackets are also available.

MONTEVIDEO LEATHER FACTORY, upstairs at Plaza de la Independencia 832. Tel. 916-226.
Opposite the Victoria Plaza Hotel, this is another excellent shop for leather goods. Women can find custom-made nutria coats, handbags, jackets, or stoles, as well as nonato bags and gloves; men can find antelope and suede jackets. There are also clothing for children, plus alligator and ostrich bags.

PIELES VICTORIA, at the Victoria Plaza Hotel. Tel. 914-201.
One of our favorite shops is owned by two English-speaking women, Alba and Marta, who offer excellent buys in coats, belts, and handbags. You can charge your purchases with American Express or Diners Club.

PLAZA LEATHER, Plaza de la Independencia 707.
This shop is ideal for gifts. There are wallets from $12, purses made of calf and pony skin for $50, and gloves for $5 and up.

SWEATERS

MAGDALENA, in the Montevideo Shopping Center. Tel. 620-794.
You'll discover a fine selection of sweaters at hard-to-beat prices at Magdalena. The store has styles for all ages, plus good buys in angora and cashmere. Name brands include Burma, Barroco, Fernand Pierre, and Calvin Klein. Another branch is located at Soriano 989, just off Plaza Independencia.

MANOS DE URUGUAY, in the Montevideo Shopping Center. Tel. 620-650.
This store specializes in sweaters that exemplify Uruguayan folk art. Manos has several convenient branches: at Reconquista 602 and at San José 1111. There are also branches in Carrasco (at Arocena 1552) and in Punta del Este (on Gorlero, across from the casino).

URUGUAYAN PRODUCTS

EL EMPORIO DEL TURISTA, Colonia 804, at the corner of Florida.
Located a few blocks from the Victoria Plaza Hotel, El Emporio offers an extensive selection of typical handicrafts, including copper items, pottery, rugs, and wood carvings, as well as amethysts, topazes, and T-shirts.

LA PUERTA DEL TURISTA S.A., Plaza Independencia 1374.
Here you'll find a wide variety of handicrafts, wool and fur rugs, regional weavings, leather items, and amethysts and agates.

9. EVENING ENTERTAINMENT

THEATERS & CONCERTS

Touring international shows, including some from the United States and Great Britain, appear regularly at the **Solis Theater** (Buenos Aires 678, at Plaza de la Independencia). Performances are generally at 8pm (the early, or "vermouth," show) and at 10pm. Although prices vary with the event, they are seldom higher than $8. In some cases, you may be required to buy tickets for two different events (a common practice in certain South American cities), so check first at the box office.

Free, open-air concerts in the summer (December to February) are a delight in the **Rodo Theater,** in Parque Rodo (Playa Ramírez).

THE CLUB & MUSIC SCENE

DISCOTHEQUES

CHANTCLAIRE, Soriano 1338 (upstairs), at the corner of Ejido. Tel. 921-953.
Chantclaire's convenient downtown location and free entrance make it a favorite for those aged 18 to 25. It's not as fancy as our other selections, but it's a lot of fun. Things don't really heat up until late.

NEW YORK, in the Oceania Hotel, Mar Artico 1227 (Punta Gorda). Tel. 600-444.
Tourists and well-heeled residents are the primary patrons here. DJ Henry Mullens

plays favorites from north and south of the equator. Open Saturday and Sunday from 10pm to 2am.

PORTOFINO, Belastiqui 1325 (Punta Gorda).
This is another top club, in a country setting. The club faces Playa Verde. The daily show, at 1am, features three groups and attracts a large crowd. If you're staying downtown, you'll need a cab to get here—the trip will be about $6.

TAROT, Motivos de Proteo, at the corner of Rambla O'Higgins (Punta Gorda). Tel. 616-405.
Tarot is great for late nights and early mornings. A combination discotheque and small boîte, it has a couples-only policy. In addition to great music, it boasts a beautiful location—on top of a hill overlooking the ocean. If you do dance until dawn, be sure to stick around for sunrise over the Atlantic.

ZUM ZUM, Rambla Armenia 1647 (Buceos). Tel. 721-007.
Housed in what was formerly a large warehouse, Zum Zum is one of Montevideo's hottest nightspots for couples only. Red predominates—from the flashing lights at the entrance, to the dance floor, to the decor throughout the club. Though large, the dance floor is always crowded; if it's too packed, retire to the comfortable lounge. Open Monday to Saturday from 10:30pm on.

FOLK & ROCK

A BAIUCA, Francisco Vidal 755 (Playa Pocitos). Tel. 704-516.
This jumping place, on the corner of Juan Mara Perez, jams in couples on weekends. It is a dark and intimate disco, where rock is very much the thing. You can get here very easily by taxi for about $6 or via bus no. 116 (get off at Juan Blanco and Juan María Perez). Open daily from 10pm to 6am.

CANDOMBE

Uruguay's contribution to the world of dance is *candombe,* which is somewhat similar to the tango. Its tempo can get quite feverish.

LA VIEJA CUMPARSITA, Carlo Gardel 1181. Tel. 916-245.
For the best in candombe and the tango, head to this couples-only club located on Carlo Gardel. (Incidentally, Carlos Gardel, the Argentinean singer who died in 1935, was the greatest interpreter of the tango.) Located on a quiet street not far from downtown, this club quickly gets crowded. Open Friday and Saturday from 11:30pm to 5am.

FOR MEN ONLY

BAIRES DISCOSHOW, San José 872. Tel. 903-304.
Baires is probably the most popular club. Striptease is the lure, and when the live music stops, blasting disco music sets in. Open daily from 9pm to 4am.

CLUB DE PARIS, San José 876. Tel. 917-177.
Club de París is a warm, inviting nightspot for single guys. It's open from 9pm on.

WILLY'S, San José 1077.
Willy's offers a large attractive bar, an ample dance floor, and a congenial environment. The strip shows blast off after midnight.

VILLAGE, Río Negro 1283.
Village also offers a large attractive bar, an ample dance floor, and a congenial environment. The strip shows start after midnight.

THE BAR SCENE
PUBS

CLAVE DE FU, 26 de Marzo 1125. Tel. 781-418.

Here you'll find one of the best *feijoadas* in Montevideo (during the winter months only) as well as live music nightly. Open Wednesday to Sunday from 10pm on.

LA MUESTRA DEL BOLICHE, at the corner of Gonzalo Ramírez and Santiago de Chile.
The music here is live every weekend. Open Saturday and Sunday from 10pm to 2am.

SPLURGE CHOICES

HOTEL COLUMBIA PALACE BAR, in the Hotel Columbia Palace, Rambla República de Francia 473. Tel. 960-001.
Our favorite place to relax in Montevideo is the elegant bar in this hotel. Here you get a feeling of pleasant seclusion as well as a fine view of the Río de la Plata and the shore. Surprisingly, drinks are not expensive. Domestic brandy is as little as $2.50, cocktails are about $3.50, and imported scotch can cost $4.50.

VICTORIA PUB, in the Victoria Plaza Hotel, Plaza de la Independencia. Tel. 914-201.
You might enjoy at least one drink at this plush cocktail lounge, where the decor is Gay '90s, complete with gaslights. The best scotch runs about $5 per drink, but manhattans are $4 and martinis only $3.50. The pub opens just before noon and closes at 1am.

MORE ENTERTAINMENT
MOVIES

Montevideans are great moviegoers, and U.S. and British films are enormously popular. Admission is about $3. Spanish subtitles are used; there is no dubbing.

CASINOS

HOTEL CARRASCO CASINO, near the Carrasco International Airport, Rambla República de México. Tel. 610-511.
Roulette, punto y banca, blackjack, and bingo are on the tables at the Hotel Carrasco Casino.
Admission: You must purchase $8 worth of chips, which are redeemable if not used. Minimum bet 80¢; maximum bet $6. All tables open at 10pm, except roulette, which opens at 5pm.

HOTEL PARQUE CASINO, Rambla Presidente Wilson (Playa Ramírez). Tel. 415-953.
Stakes aren't quite as high at the unpretentious Parque Hotel Casino. There are about 30 separate tables (baccarat, roulette only, blackjack, and bingo), with smartly jacketed waiters circulating among the well-dressed gamblers. *Note:* Don't cash your traveler's checks here; the rate is not nearly as favorable as you could get at a bank or *cambio*. Bus no. 117, in Plaza de la Independencia, will take you right to the casino; or you can get there by cab (about $1.25). Open daily from 6pm to 3am.
Admission: Nonguests $2; minimum bet 80¢, except for blackjack, which has a $7 minimum.

BILLIARDS & POOL

The newest craze here is the proliferation of pool halls, but they're quite different from the smoke-filled halls of a Minnesota Fats/Jackie Gleason movie setting. Located all around the city, these halls have only a few tables and are generally quiet, homelike places serving food and drink. In most, you don't have to play; you can order simply a drink or some food (many of these halls have extensive menus). Do not expect to find many pool sharks. Most of the players are rank amateurs; you can play poorly without drawing attention. One of the most popular is **Flanagans** at Cavio 3082 (tel. 789-827); open 8pm to midnight. The restaurant offers standard pub fare, including pizza, sandwiches, *chivitos,* and omelettes. The pool tables in the rear provide the opportunity to meet and mingle with the regulars.

10. PUNTA DEL ESTE

80 miles E of Montevideo

South America's Riviera is a series of beach communities about 80 miles east of Montevideo, where the Río de la Plata and the Atlantic meet at the peninsula called Punta del Este. On the side of the point facing Brazil is the ocean, with huge waves that challenge the most rugged swimmers and surfers. The beach here is called **Playa Brava.** On the inner side—the side facing Montevideo—are the gentle waters of the bay, where waterskiers and sailors are visible from dawn to dusk. The bayside beach is the **Playa Mansa.** Sea breezes keep the temperature moderate during summer, when it is quite crowded. About 70% of the summer visitors are from Argentina and Paraguay.

Of the many beaches in the area, the most popular is Playa Brava on the oceanside. Condominiums and mansions abound here. As you would imagine, watersports are very popular, followed by fishing, golf, tennis, and horseback riding.

GETTING THERE

The COT bus company in Montevideo operates several buses a day to Punta del Este (the trip is about 2 hours) for a round-trip fare of around $10. COT is located at Plaza de Cagancha 1124 (tel. 921-605). In addition to regular buses, COT runs tour buses to Punta del Este that travel leisurely along the coast and stop at various beach communities en route. Going north from Montevideo, you'll get the impression that Uruguay is a land of beaches and more beaches. The cost of the day trip is $17.50; lunch is $9.

WHERE TO STAY

Hotel rates here are generally a bit higher than those in Montevideo but still lower than one would generally expect at such a well-known resort. Make sure to reserve in advance if you plan to come in season.

AJAX, Parada 2. Tel. 84-550. 69 rms (all with bath). TV TEL
$ Rates: $45 double. Major credit cards accepted.

Conveniently located just two blocks from Playa Mansa, Ajax is a comfortable basic choice. Since large rooms (with space for additional beds) and suites are available, this hotel is a good choice for families.

HOTEL EMBAJADOR, Risso Parada 1. Tel. 81-008. Fax 86-750. Telex 28-146 EMBATEL UY. 27 rms (all with bath). TV TEL
$ Rates: $50 double.
The Embajador is very well located, especially if you arrive in Punta by bus (it's just across from the bus terminal and halfway between Playas Mansa and Brava). A game room, 24-hour room service, and spacious doubles should ensure you a pleasant stay.

SHELTON HOTEL, Calle 31 with Gorlero. Tel. 82-543. 40 rms (all with bath). TV TEL
$ Rates: $50 double.
The Shelton is conveniently located downtown, not far from the casino and the bus terminal.

SPLURGE CHOICES

HOTEL ALHAMBRA, Calle 28 no. 573. Tel. 40-094 or 41-422. Fax 40-094. 40 rms (all with bath). A/C TEL

$ Rates: $74 double.

The Alhambra is conveniently located in the center of town, half a block from Avenida Gorlero and three blocks from the Playa Brava. The rooms are comfortably furnished, and the hotel has its own bar and restaurant.

L'AUBERGE, Barrio Parque del Golf. Tel. 82-601. 27 rms (all with bath). A/C MINIBAR TV TEL

$ Rates (including breakfast): $150 double.

⭐ Tucked away in the Barrio Parque del Golf, L'Auberge offers its guests European luxury and comfort in a lovely setting. It's hard to believe that this beautifully furnished, fully equipped five-star hotel was originally a water tower. Guests come here year round to enjoy tennis; golf; horseback riding; cocktails by the fireplace; and, of course, La Draga beach, which is just two blocks away.

WHERE TO DINE

BUNGALOW SUIZO, Avenida Roosevelt Parada 8. Tel. 82-358.
   Cuisine: SWISS.
$ Prices: Appetizers $2–$5; main courses $6–$9. DC.
   Open: Lunch and dinner.
This restaurant, located not far from the Playa Mansa, serves delicious Swiss-style food, heavy on cutlets and wursts.

CLUB CICLISTA, Calle 20.
   Cuisine: SEAFOOD/ITALIAN. **Reservations:** Recommended.
$ Prices: Appetizers $3–$6; main courses $6–$12.
   Open: Dinner only.
⭐ Try Club Ciclista for shrimp, mussels, clams, and a variety of freshly caught fish prepared in countless ways—all delicious. The Italian dishes are also exceptional. You may have to go above your budget a bit here.

DI PAPPO, Avenida Gorlero at the corner of Calle 28. Tel. 42-869.
   Cuisine: ITALIAN.
$ Prices: Appetizers $2–$4; main courses $4–$8.
   Open: Lunch and dinner.
Di Pappo specializes in Italian cuisine, but the *chivitos* and *paella* are also hard to beat.

SPAGUETTI-NOTTI, on Costanera at Parada 12. Tel. 87-776.
   Cuisine: ITALIAN.
$ Prices: Appetizers $2–$4; main courses $4–$8. Major credit cards accepted.
   Open: Lunch and dinner.
Italian cuisine is the specialty here, including homemade pastas and sauces.

A SPLURGE CHOICE

DONA FLOR, the Plaza París in San Rafael. Tel. 84-720.
   Cuisine: FRENCH. **Reservations:** Recommended.
$ Prices: Appetizers $4–$8; main courses $8–$14. Major credit cards accepted.
   Open: Dinner only.
Montevideo's finest French restaurant also has a dining room in Punta del Este, on the Plaza Paris. The windows all around take full advantage of a spectacular garden setting. The menu is similar to the one in Montevideo.

EVENING ENTERTAINMENT

Most visitors while away the evening hours here at the two gambling casinos, both open year round. The **Hotel San Rafael** casino, in a chic beach area just east of town (Rambla L. B. Pacheco), attracts elegantly clad high rollers. Jackets are required. The in-town **Casino Nogáro** draws a younger, less affluent, but livelier group. It's open Monday through Thursday from 8pm to 4 or 5am, Friday until 6am, and Saturday and Sunday from 5pm to 6am. Both casinos have roulette, blackjack, baccarrat, and slot machines.

If gambling doesn't appeal to you, you might enjoy dancing at several discos in town. Try the stunning nightclub at the San Rafael Hotel or **Le Club,** a discotheque across the street. Another good choice is **Rainbow,** at La Drega Beach. Clubs with shows include **Casas and Cartas,** at the port, and the **Mozart Piano Bar.**

11. EN ROUTE TO BUENOS AIRES

If your next stop is Argentina, you may want to go by plane (**Aerolineas Argentinas** and **Pluba** have regular 30-minute flights from Montevideo to Buenos Aires that cost $60 one way) or by a combination of either bus and ferryboat or bus and prop plane. If you choose to go by **bus and prop plane,** make arrangements with Arco, which operates a daily service that costs $35 one way. First, you'll have a 3½-hour bus trip through farmland to an airstrip in Colonia. There you'll board a small prop plane for the 15-minute flight to Buenos Aires's Aeroparque. *Budget tip:* The taxi fare from the Aeroparque to most of our hotel recommendations is around $20, but many of these hotels can be reached by subway. Take a taxi to Plaza Italia ($5); from there take the subway line "D" to Catedral (30¢) and get off at Florida. (The "D" line connects at 9 de Julio Pelligrini with both the "B" and the "C" lines.)

You can also travel to Buenos Aires by taking a **bus** to Colonia (a 3½-hour trip) and catching the **ferryboat** (a 3-hour ride) to Buenos Aires. This far more scenic trip costs about the same: $35. Cars can also be transported via ferry from Colonia, a service offered by **Aliscafos.** You can purchase tickets through **COT** in the Plaza de Cagancha 1124 (tel. 92-404).

Another option is to take the **Buquebus Bus Hydrofoil Service.** Operating via Colonia, this entire trip takes about 4½ hours, and costs about $40. You can make direct reservations by calling Buquebus at 920-670.

CHAPTER 5

BUENOS AIRES, ARGENTINA

1. **INTRODUCING BUENOS AIRES & ARGENTINA**
- **WHAT'S SPECIAL ABOUT BUENOS AIRES**
- **WHAT THINGS COST IN BUENOS AIRES**
2. **ORIENTATION**
3. **GETTING AROUND**
- **FAST FACTS: BUENOS AIRES**
4. **WHERE TO STAY**
5. **WHERE TO DINE**
6. **ATTRACTIONS**
- **DID YOU KNOW . . . ?**
7. **SPORTS & RECREATION**
8. **SAVVY SHOPPING**
9. **EVENING ENTERTAINMENT**
10. **SUGGESTED ITINERARIES**

The travel brochures describe Buenos Aires as the "Paris of the Americas." We'd go even further and say that this enchanting city combines the sophistication of the French capital, the cultural variety of New York City, and the gemütlichkeit of Vienna.

Buenos Aires is one of the largest cities in the world, with approximately 12.5 million residents in its metropolitan area. In atmosphere, attitudes, architecture, and contemporary awareness, this pulsating metropolis more closely resembles a European capital than any other South American city. The Porteños (as residents are called) dine late, generally after 10pm, in fine restaurants that dot the city; browse in boutiques and specialty shops that would be perfectly at home on the rue de la Paix; and revel in the joys of wine, sports, and politics.

Yet basic to the fascinating magnetism of Buenos Aires is the startling hold exercised on the civilized urban community by the rural world of the gaucho, the pampas, and the *estancias* (ranches)—unchanged for a century or more—that can be found within 12 miles of the center of the city. We shall suggest one-day excursions to gaucho country—don't pass them up.

Still, Buenos Aires has never attained the fame it deserves, not even with the jet set. Perhaps its unpredictable economy has confused travelers. At times inflation has run rampant in this fabulous city. In an earlier edition of our guide, for example, prices had skyrocketed, tripling and quadrupling over those quoted in the prior edition. Buenos Aires was, for a period of almost two years, the world's most expensive city.

Buenos Aires, with its sultry climate, pulsating beat, and combination of sophistication and local color, is a city that you would not want to miss.

1. INTRODUCING BUENOS AIRES & ARGENTINA

GEOGRAPHY Argentina, the second-largest country in South America after Brazil, covers an area of over 1 million square miles. More than 2,000 miles long and

WHAT'S SPECIAL ABOUT BUENOS AIRES

Streets/Buildings
- ☐ Avenida 9 de Julio, the widest boulevard in the world.
- ☐ The gaily colored houses of La Boca.
- ☐ The Casa Rosada, or "Pink House," the official residence of the president of the republic.
- ☐ The majestic Teatro Colón, considered by many to be South America's foremost opera house.

Plazas
- ☐ The Plaza de los dos Congresos (Plaza of the Two Congresses), actually a series of small plazas, each with a monument in its center.

Monuments
- ☐ The Monument of the Two Congresses, whose fountains come alive at night with lights and music.

- ☐ The Recoleta Cemetery, final resting ground of Buenos Aires's most elite residents, including Eva Perón. The artistry of the mausoleums here is without equal.

Parks/Gardens
- ☐ Bosques de Palermo (Palermo Park), a favorite weekend retreat.
- ☐ The *Rosaleda* and Japanese Gardens are lovely for strolling.

Zoo
- ☐ Young and old alike will delight in the unusual fin-de-siècle residences at the Jardín Zoológico across the street from Palermo Park.

Tango Bars
- ☐ Tango is the traditional dance of Buenos Aires. Tango bars are still going strong in San Telmo, especially on Calle Balcarse.

only 870 miles wide, it offers dramatic contrasts in topography and climate. The country is home to tropical jungles and rain forests, deserts, and perenially snow-capped Andes peaks, plus an ever-expanding glacier. Climates range from tropical in the north to subAntarctic in the south, although temperatures here are moderated by the proximity of the ocean on both sides. Buenos Aires lies in the temperate zone on the shores of the Río de la Plata and surrounded by the beautiful pampas, home of the gaucho and the basis of the country's economic wealth.

HISTORY Argentina and Chile were the last regions of modern-day South America to be inhabited by early humans. Unlike the other South American countries, Argentina had no advanced cultures such as the Maya, Aztec, or Inca. The most developed area was the northwest because of its proximity to Bolivia and Peru. In 1480, the Inca invaded this area and incorporated it into their empire.

The city of Buenos Aires was founded in 1536 by Pedro de Mendoza, then more definitively by Juan de Garay in 1580. Unfortunately, as decreed by the king of Spain in 1554, all trade from Spain was required to come through Peru and Panama. Buenos Aires was cut off from commercial traffic for the next 200 years and remained a small town, inhabited primarily by "Criollos," a mixture of Spanish and natives. Eventually the Spanish opened the Río Plata for transatlantic trade, and Buenos Aires became its administrative center. The population exploded and the city flourished. In 1816, after years of conflict, Argentina declared its independence from Spain. Buenos Aires became the capital in 1880.

Falklands War While in Argentina, you may still feel the repercussions of the 1982 clash between Argentina and Great Britain over the Falkland Islands, which the Argentineans call **Las Malvinas.** The war left behind scars that one hopes will fade

IMPRESSIONS

Buenos Aires must be the most truly international city in the world. Its banks and offices . . . recall the solid solvent grandeur of Victorian London. Many of its restaurants . . . have the well-stocked gemütlichkeit of pre-1914 Munich and Berlin. Its boulevards and private mansions belong to the Paris of forty years ago. But . . . these foreign elements have been blended and transformed into something indigenous, immediately recognizable, unique.
—CHRISTOPHER ISHERWOOD, THE CONDOR AND THE COWS, 1949

[Buenos Aires] has all the elegance of the old world in its buildings and streets, and in its people all the vulgarity and frank good health of the new world.
—PAUL THEROUX, THE OLD PATAGONIAN EXPRESS, 1979

with the passage of time. The question of which country has a rightful claim to the islands, which lie about 250 miles east of Argentina, is an extremely emotional issue to Argentineans, and a word of tact to the wise should be sufficient.

THE PEOPLE Argentina's national constitution contains a paragraph identifying an Argentinean as "anybody in the world who wishes to reside in Argentina." And, indeed, the nation's over 30 million inhabitants all have their roots in faraway places. The majority are Europeans, especially Spanish and Italians, but also Germans, British, and French. Many immigrants to Argentina have come fleeing wars or persecution in their homelands. You'll find a surprising number of Southeast Asians in Argentina nowadays.

MONEY Historically, the Argentine exchange rate has fluctuated sharply and suddenly—sometimes even overnight. This means that you must check the rate *immediately prior to* your visit to Argentina, as prices may be dramatically affected.

In 1980, for example, when inflation soared out of sight, a cup of coffee cost as much as $5 and a cab to Ezeiza Airport was over $50.

In 1986 the peso was replaced by the **austral** as the unit of currency at approximate par with the U.S. dollar. In the years following, however, the dollar soared, and so did inflation in Argentina. In 1989, the country's new president, Perónist Carlos Menem, enforced strict austerity measures. Eventually, and not without hardship, the Argetine economy began to improve.

In 1992 a **new peso** replaced the austral at a rate of 10,000 to 1. The new peso has remained at par with the U.S. dollar, with 1 new peso equal to $1.

WHAT THINGS COST IN BUENOS AIRES	U.S. $
Taxi from the airport to center city	45.00
Subway ticket	.50
Local telephone call	.10
Double with bath at the Camino Real Hotel (budget)	35.00
Double with bath at the Hotel Victory (moderate)	50.00
Double with bath at the Gran Hotel Buenos Aires (expensive)	90.00
Lunch for two at Café la Barra (budget)	8.00
Dinner for two, without wine, at Las Deliciosa Papas Fritas (moderate)	20.00
Dinner for two, with wine, at Harper's (moderate)	40.00
Dinner for two, with wine, at Gato Dumas (deluxe)	60.00
Cup of coffee	1.25

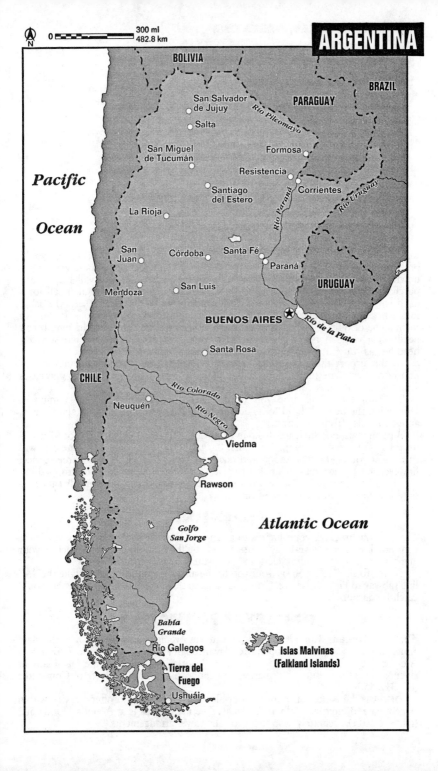

	U.S.$
Coca-Cola	1.25
Museum admission	1.50

CAVEAT: Look out for the austral, which is still in circulation. Remember that 10,000 australes are equal to 1 new peso.

2. ORIENTATION

ARRIVING

Reaching center city from modern **Ezeiza International Airport,** where you'll probably land, is simple. The Customs check is perfunctory. Your best way to get downtown is by the **Manuel Tienda León Buses,** which meet every flight. You can purchase tickets at the TRANSPORTES sign. The fare is $14. You can also call for a fixed-fare or REMIS cab here. You'll find the price to be around $50. At the same location, government clerks will call ahead and confirm hotel reservations. If you give them some of our selections, you'll get a sheet listing your hotel and the rate. If you need to exchange money, a *cambio* (exchange office) is nearby. For all these services, head left as you exit from Customs and look for the bus and taxi sign.

At the airport there is a **duty-free shop** where you can pick up inexpensive liquor, cigarettes, perfumes, and the like. You are permitted to take these purchases with you into Buenos Aires.

The airline bus will drop you at your downtown hotel in about 45 minutes. Otherwise, the bus will head to its downtown office at Carlos Pelligrini and Lavalle, about 21 miles from the airport.

A public bus, no. 86, leaves from in front of the International Hotel. For $1 it will drop you downtown in about 1½ hours. Baggage can be a problem. Private cars will then meet you at the bus station and take you to your hotel. This is a free service; however, hang onto your bus ticket to give to the driver when you are dropped off.

The other airport, **Aeroparque** (or **Jorge Newberry** as it is officially called), is only 2½ miles from the center of the city. A taxi is best.

DEPARTING

The best way to catch your flight is to arrange to have the special bus pick you up at your hotel. You must give 1 day's notice, and you'll be picked up 3 hours before your flight. Call or ask your desk clerk to assist you. The bus is $14.

Note: To slice $5 or $6 off your trip to the airport, instead of a taxi take the "A" line subway to Plaza Miserere. Cross the plaza to the Once bus terminal, where you'll catch the airport bus.

TOURIST INFORMATION

The **Government Tourist Office** is located at Avenida Santa Fe 883, near the main American Airlines office. It is open Monday through Friday from 10am to 7:30pm. On Avenida Florida there are also two tourist booths, which offer free city maps of Buenos Aires. For visitor information you can also call the Chamber of Commerce (tel. 312-550).

ONDA is the American Express equivalent in Argentina and offers service within Argentina and internationally to Uruguay. The main office is at Avenida Florida 502 (tel. 392-5011). Definitely stop there for any travel arrangements.

Exprinter is located on Avenida Sante Fe on the corner of Suipacha, next door to the American Airlines office.

CITY LAYOUT

Downtown Buenos Aires—which amounts only to a 16- by 10-block rectangular area—is the true hub of the city. The best budget hotels and restaurants are located here. It is the center of commerce, shopping, and nightlife.

While a few Porteños live downtown, most come here to work, eat, and play. The only major aspects of life not found downtown are the soccer stadiums and racetracks, which are within 20 minutes by commuter railroad.

MAIN ARTERIES The major streets you'll need to know for orientation purposes are **Avenida de Mayo, Avenida 9 de Julio, Avenida Corrientes,** and **Calle Lavalle**—plus **Avenida Florida,** a bustling shopping thoroughfare that runs from Plaza San Martín to Avenida de Mayo, near Plaza de Mayo. Florida and Lavalle are closed to vehicles.

Note: Avenida 9 de Julio is so wide that each side has its own name—**Carlos Pellegrini** on the near (east) side and **Cerrito** on the far (west) side.

Buenos Aires's newest "in" area is **Recoleta,** home of the poshest restaurants and clubs and a popular meeting place. **San Telmo** is the oldest part of town, located near the dock area, and Avenida Necochea is the main street of **La Boca,** an old Italian section where at night you can join in some of the wildest tarantella while dining on home-cooked Italian food.

FINDING AN ADDRESS Street signs are very helpful in Buenos Aires. Each names the block and street numbers, with an arrow indicating which way the numbers run.

NEIGHBORHOODS IN BRIEF

DOWNTOWN There are four major center-city areas, each with its particular attractions and share of budget hotels.

Plaza de la República Marked by a 220-foot-high obelisk that commemorates the 400th anniversary of the city's original founding in 1536, the plaza is on Avenida 9 de Julio. It fringes the entertainment-and-theater district that thrives particularly on two parallel streets—Calle Lavalle and Avenida Corrientes. These are the "Broadway" of Buenos Aires, and you'll find good budget hotels and restaurants in the vicinity. But don't look for relaxation: This area swings day and night.

Plaza de Mayo Considered the true center of the city, Plaza de Mayo houses government and office buildings; the many parades that help keep this city constantly alive often start here.

Plaza San Martín Adjoining an exquisitely manicured park and several luxury hotels and shops is the third major downtown section. Be sure to see the replica of London's Big Ben that decorates the park in the nearby **Plaza Fuerza Aerea** (formerly Britania). This area, located near one of the important suburban train stations, has fine hotels and restaurants well within our limits. The deluxe Sheraton and Plaza Hotels are here, too.

Plaza del Congreso This impressive plaza, a quarter of a mile beyond the far side of Avenida 9 de Julio on Avenida de Mayo, is where you'll find the Roman-style National Congress building. A short walk from the plaza is one of the world's great restaurants by any standard, La Cabaña (see "Where to Dine"). The deluxe Bauen Hotel is near the plaza.

LA BOCA La Boca is Buenos Aires's most colorful neighborhood, noted both for the gay colors of its homes there and for the lively spirit of its residents. It was named for its location at the mouth (or *boca* in Spanish) of the **Riachuelo,** a small river that flows into the Río de la Plata.

La Boca is also known for its **cantinas,** informal Italian eateries with a lively atmosphere that usually feature a nightly show in which both patrons and management participate.

PALERMO   Palermo, a large neighborhood to the north of the city, is known for its famous park, **Los Bosques de Palermo,** as well as for the zoo and botanical gardens across the street. The track and polo fields are also here. Palermo takes its name from its founder, Juan Domínguez de Palermo, who arrived in Buenos Aires in 1836 and dedicated himself to the improvement of the marshlands through the construction of drainage systems.

RECOLETA   Palermo Chico and Recoleta form the Barrio Norte, or the northern district, of Buenos Aires. After the city's second founding in 1580, the land that is now Recoleta was donated to the Recoleto Friars, who built the convent and Church of Pilar there in 1706. During a yellow fever epidemic in 1871, many of Buenos Aires's wealthiest residents fled to Recoleta, where they built the French-style homes and gardens that are so characteristic of the neighborhood. Today Recoleta is the city's most fashionable and exclusive residential district. Many trendy restaurants and nightspots, as well as numerous art galleries and cafés, are here.

SAN TELMO   The southern neighborhood of San Telmo is the city's historic district. Narrow sidewalks, cobblestoned streets, and one-story buildings with wrought-iron railings around their windows characterize this area, which is borded by Calle Chile to the north, Parque Lezama to the south, Avenida Paseo Colón to the east, and Bernardo de Irígoyen to the west. Home to artists and intellectuals, San Telmo has many museums, restaurants, and nightclubs. The main square is **Plaza Dorrego,** where popular street fairs are held.

3. GETTING AROUND

You should have little trouble finding your way around Buenos Aires if you use a map, available free at most hotels. Much of the center of the city is easily accessible on foot; but if you should need transportation, you'll find taxis cheap and plentiful and subways simple to use.

BY SUBWAY   Five lines of subways (*subterráneos*), link the center of the city with the terminus stations of the two suburban railroads. One station is **Retiro,** near Plaza San Martín; the other is **Constitución,** outside the city center. The five subway lines are designated "A," "B," "C," "D," and "E." The "C" line, which connects the Retiro and Constitución stations, intersects the other four lines. Transfers are free. Subway maps are available, and the fare is a modest 30¢. Buy a token (*ficha*) before entering. *Note:* To identify a subway, look for the sign that reads SUBTE; the same sign will list the line and the station.

BY BUS   The city's numerous buses are often individually owned and operated. To attract attention, the owner-drivers decorate their vehicles in brilliant colors. Bear in mind, however, that color is no guide to destination. Fares are usually 30¢. Bus numbers and destinations are listed on the front.

BY TAXI   Cab fares are reasonable. Meters start at 25¢. A short "in-city" trip can cost under $1. You enter taxis from the right, and a chart will adjust the meter to the current exchange rate.

BY CAR   If you must rent a car—*we advise against it*—try **Hertz,** Calle Ricardo Rojas (tel. 312-1317); **Budget,** Carlos Pellegrini 977; or **Avis,** Maipu 942 (tel. 311-1000). A Fiat or Renault will cost you about $60 to $70 per day, including

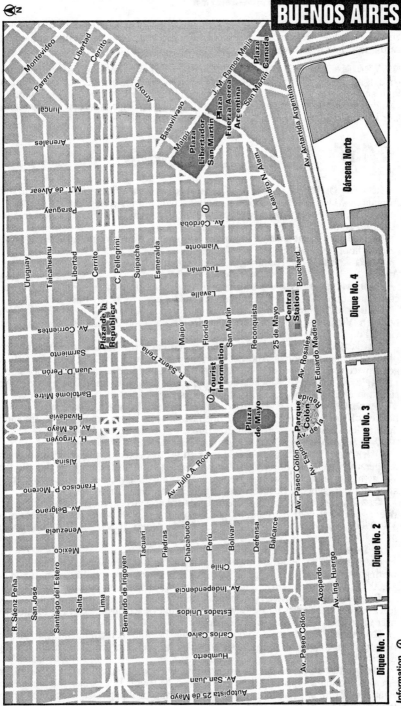

BUENOS AIRES

Información ⓘ

insurance, plus 50¢ per kilometer. To rent a car, you must be at least 25 years of age and have a valid U.S. license; a deposit of $200 is required (plus a passport and credit card). Your hotel clerk will gladly make all the arrangements.

BY TRAIN The main office of the **Ferrocariles Argentinos** (Argentine Railroad) is at Florida 753 (tel. 311-6411); it's open Monday through Friday from 7am to 9pm and Saturday from 7am to 1pm. You should definitely stop here if you intend to visit the interior of Argentina. The efficient railroad links Buenos Aires with Mendoza, Córdoba, and Mar del Plata, among other interesting places.

FAST FACTS **BUENOS AIRES**

Airline Offices The **Aerolíneas Argentinas** office is at Calle Perú and Avenida de Mayo. (*Note:* Perú is the name Avenida Florida changes to at Avenida de Mayo.) A large **Varig Airlines** office is located at Avenida Florida 630. **American Airlines** is located at Santa Fe 881.

American Express The American Express office is located at Arenales 707, seventh floor (tel. 312-0900).

Area Code The country code for Argentina is 54; the city code for Buenos Aires is 1.

Babysitters Ask the concierge at your hotel or inquire at your embassy or consulate about making arrangements for child care.

Banks A branch office of the First National City Bank is at Florida 744, between Viamente and Córdoba. The Royal Bank of Canada is on Florida at Congallo.

Bookstores At Avenida Florida 937, **Librería del Turista** carries a full line of English-language books. Another good shop is **Librería ABC,** at Cordoba 685. A good place to browse at is the bookshop at **Harrods.** A fine antiquarian bookstore, **Libreria de Antaño,** Sanchez de Bustamante 1876, first floor, has an extensive selection of antique books in many languages.

Business Hours Banks and **exchange houses** can change money between 10am and 3pm. **Shops** are open Monday to Friday from 10am to 1pm and 4pm to 8pm, Saturday from 10am to 2pm.

Car Rentals See "Getting Around" earlier in this chapter.

Climate The Buenos Aires winter (June to September) is quite mild, with temperatures generally hovering in the 50s and 60s Fahrenheit during the day and the 40s at night. Summer readings average in the mid-70s, with occasional sweltering afternoons. In general, Buenos Aires is milder than New York City.

Credit Cards All major credit cards are accepted in most establishments in Buenos Aires. If your card should get lost or stolen, call **American Express** at 312-0900, **Diners Club** at 322-4545, **MasterCard** at 331-1022, and **VISA** at 313-2804.

Crime See "Safety" below.

Currency The basic unit of currency is the **peso,** which at the time of this writing is at par with the dollar (1 peso = US $1). It replaced the austral at a rate of 10,000 to 1. *Be forewarned:* There are still some australes in circulation.

Currency Exchange Cook's, on Avenida Córdoba, is a convenient place to cash your traveler's checks. *Cambios,* or money-exchange places, are located all over town and offer fair rates of exchange.

Dentists/Doctors Your hotel should be able to recommend a dentist or doctor. If not, call your embassy or consulate to request a list of English-speaking dentists or physicians.

Drugstores The largest drugstore in Buenos Aires is **Franco Inglesa,** at Avenida Florida 323, near Sarmiento; it's stocked with U.S. drugs and open late. Pharmacy 2100, at Libertador 2101, on the corner of Bilinghurst, is open 24 hours (tel. 802-9318).

Electricity   The local voltage is 220.

Embassies/Consulates   The **U.S. Consulate** is located at Colombia 4300 (tel. 774-8811). The **Canadian Consulate** is at Suipacha 1111, on the 25th floor (tel. 312-9081). The **United Kingdom Consulate** is at Avenida Santa Fe 846 (tel. 803-7070), as is the **Australian Consulate** (tel. 312-6841). All are open Monday through Friday from 8:30 to 11:15am.

Emergencies   CIPEC, the Health Emergencies and Catastrophe Center, can be reached by phone at 34-4001 or 923-1051.

Eyeglasses   Alemana Schinitzler y Eder is at Avenida Santa Fe 2076. There are three branches of **Lutz Ferrando,** at Avenida Florida 971, Avenida Santa Fe 1561, and Avenida Callao 134.

Film   See "Photographic Needs" below.

Hairdressers/Barbers   Alberto y Luis at Montevideo 1683 and Roberto Giordano Guemes 3553 (tel. 826-6192) are two good options. For kids, try **Reynaldo** at Libertad 984.

Holidays

New Year's Day	January 1
Easter	varies
May (Labor) **Day**	May 1
Anniversary of the First Argentine Government	May 25
Malvinas Day	June 10
Flag Day	June 20
Independence Day	July 9
Anniversary of the death of San Martín	August 17
Columbus Day	October 12
Christmas Day	December 25

Hospitals   The **British Hospital** is at 74 Pedviel (tel. 23-1081). The **Israelite Hospital** is at Terrada 1164 (tel. 581-0070). To reach the **Ricardo Gutierrez Children's Hospital,** phone 86-5500.

Hotlines   The **AIDS** hotline is 334-6018 or 334-6019; **Alcoholics Anonymous** is 97-6666; **S.O.S** (an anonymous friend) is 738-8888; **Suicide Prevention** is 962-0303; and **Dial-a-Priest** is 84-2000.

Information   See "Tourist Information" earlier in this chapter.

Laundry/Dry Cleaning   Most hotels offer laundry and dry-cleaning service.

Libraries   A U.S. Information Agency library is maintained on the second floor of Lincoln Center at Avenida Florida 935. It is open Monday, Tuesday, Thursday, and Friday from 9am to 7pm. You must be at least 18 years old and have a valid passport to be admitted.

Luggage Storage/Lockers   Many hotels will store luggage for you while you travel around the country.

Newspapers/Magazines   An excellent daily in English is the *Buenos Aires Herald,* available at many downtown newsstands. Also available are the *Miami Herald* and the *Herald Tribune.* A local version of *Cue* magazine is called *Que Hacemos,* (in Spanish only) a weekly sold at most newsstands, listing movies, theater performances, restaurants, and TV programs. *Lumi,* a fine magazine, is sold at kiosks all over town and lists streets and other useful information.

Photographic Needs   Most types of films are available, but they're expensive.

Police   In the case of a lost or stolen passport, contact the **Federal Police Bureau** (tel. 37-7469). For other emergencies, a police station is located at Sarmiento 151 (tel. 101-37-111).

Post Office   The main post office is at Sarmiento 151.

Radio/Television   There are more than a dozen radio stations in Buenos Aires and seven television stations. CNN is available at the deluxe hotels.

Religious Services   Buenos Aires has a diverse selection of faiths. Speak to the concierge in your hotel regarding religious services or check the schedule in the local paper.

Restrooms   Hotel lobbies usually have accessible restrooms. Restaurants and bars have their own restrooms, as do most of the museums.

Safety   The same rule of thumb applies in Buenos Aires as in any big city. Always keep an eye on your belongings, especially in crowded areas. Valuables, including airline tickets and passports, should be left in a safe-deposit box in your hotel.

Shoe Repairs/Shoeshines   An office of **Dr. Scholl,** the foot-care specialist, is located at Esmeralda between Florida and Corrientes. Numerous shoeshine "boys" (usually over 50 years of age) will gladly put a sparkle on your shoes.

Taxes   You will pay a departure tax of $13 when flying from Argentina to any foreign country.

Taxis   See "Getting Around" earlier in this chapter.

Telegrams/Telexes/Faxes   The telegraph office, which also offers telex and fax services, is at Avenida Corrientes 707. It's open Monday to Friday from 9am to 7:30pm.

Telephone   To make a local telephone call, deposit 10¢-token (*ficha*) and then dial your number. For international calls, AT&T Direct is a great cost-saver. To get an AT&T Direct line, dial 001-800-200-1111.

4. WHERE TO STAY

We can flatly state that we found fewer *un*acceptable hotels in Buenos Aires than in any other city to which we have traveled, be it in Europe, or South America. Unlike budget hotels in Europe, most of the less expensive Buenos Aires establishments are large, often with 100 or more rooms. Only a few (deluxe) hotels have pools.

Be aware, however, that hotel prices occasionally rise drastically and that now many of the centrally located luxury hotels are on a cost scale with deluxe hotels in major American cities. Hotel prices are currently affected by the 18% surcharge added to the normal 13% tax and service charges. *Note:* Prices do *not* include breakfast, unless otherwise indicated, but generally do include a private bath, a telephone, and the tax and service charges.

ON OR NEAR AVENIDA FLORIDA

Many of the best budget hotels in Buenos Aires are found along Avenida Florida and the blocks adjoining it. We personally prefer staying in this area, since it is in the heart of things.

DOUBLES FOR LESS THAN $40

CAMINO REAL HOTEL, Maipu 572. Tel. 322-3162, 322-1744, or 322-3512. Fax 325-9756. 75 rms (all with bath). TV TEL

$ Rates (including breakfast): $25 single; $35 double. Major credit cards accepted.

The Camino Real, which offers rooms spread over 10 floors, is a bargain. There's a fine confitería in front of the hotel, and the location makes this a convenient, quiet stop.

DOUBLES FOR LESS THAN $60

EIBAR HOTEL, Avenida Florida 334, between Corrientes and Sarmiento.

Tel. 325-6661 or 325-0969. Telex 12-17109 EIBAR AR. 100 rms (all with bath). TEL
$ Rates (including tax): $44 single; $55 double; $60 triple. Breakfast $3.50 extra.
While not plush, the Eibar makes you feel right at home. The friendly staff are helpful and can offer good tips on shopping and sights. Two high-speed elevators serve the seven carpeted floors. Rooms are modern, and several doubles have comfortable sitting areas. Request units away from the street, as those facing Avenida Florida can be noisy, especially on weekends.

Breakfast consists of luscious croissants (*medias lunas*) and coffee, served in the adjacent cafetería. This is an excellent place to meet friends or just linger over a pot of tea.

A SPLURGE CHOICE

HOTEL CARSSON, Viamonte 650, between Avenida Florida and Calle Maipu. Tel. 322-3551. Fax 322-3551. Telex 23511 HOCARAR. 108 rms (all with bath). A/C MINIBAR TV TEL
$ Rates (including service and tax): $67 single; $77 double. Major credit cards accepted.
This wondrous old-world hotel is an excellent choice. It offers spotless, roomy doubles with twin beds and radios. The single rates are high, but you get a double-size room. A four-story building with a bar, a coffee room, and an elevator, the Carsson will enchant you with its handsome lobby bedecked with soft leather chairs and deep-red carpeting. Manager Adriano Lopez aims to please. Rooms here are highly desired by Argentineans and tourists alike.

THE "BROADWAY" AREA

We recommend these hotels, along Calle Corrientes and Calle Lavalle, for night people. If you retire early, skip this noisy area.

DOUBLES FOR LESS THAN $40

KING'S HOTEL, Calle Corrientes 623, near Avenida Florida. Tel. 322-8161. 50 rms (most with bath). TEL
$ Rates (including continental breakfast): $37 double with bath.
King's is an excellent choice and is somewhat unusual in that it includes a continental breakfast (croissants and coffee) in the price. Rooms are clean and furnished simply but adequately.

DOUBLES FOR LESS THAN $60

LIBERTY HOTEL, Calle Corrientes 632, near Avenida Florida. Tel. 325-0261. Fax 325-0265. Telex 18442 LIBTY-AR. 100 rms (most with bath).
$ Rates (including breakfast): $35 single with bath; from $55 double with bath. Major credit cards accepted.
The Liberty has high-speed elevators for its 12 stories. The doubles are beautifully furnished, with piped-in music.

REGIS, Calle Lavalle 813, on the corner of Calle Esmeralda. Tel. 393-5181. 100 rms (all with bath). A/C TEL
$ Rates: $40 single; $50 double.
At the top-notch Regis you can stay in an air-conditioned double. A bar and cafeteria are on the premises.

GRAND HOTEL, Calle Tucuman 570, at the corner of Avenida Florida. Tel. 393-4073. Fax 393-4786. Telex 23966 GRAND AR. 110 rms (all with bath). A/C MINIBAR TV TEL
$ Rates: $50 single; $55 double. Major credit cards accepted.
A recent renovation has transformed this four-star classic (formerly Sussex Hotel) into an almost deluxe hosterly. Its amenities include a pool, a sauna, and a solarium.

NEAR PLAZA SAN MARTIN

This area—in the northern section of downtown Buenos Aires—is ideal for travelers who have a passion for spectator sports. The commuter railway, Bartolome Mitre, begins its run from Plaza San Martín (Retiro railroad station) and will carry you in less than 30 minutes to the 120,000-seat River Plate soccer stadium or to the two major racetracks just outside the city. *Note:* An important street in this vicinity is **Marcel T. de Alvear,** which locals prefer to call **Charcas,** its former name.

DOUBLES FOR LESS THAN $40

GRAN HOTEL ORLY, Calle Paraguay 474. Tel. 312-5244. 170 rms (all with bath). TV TEL
$ Rates: $26 single; $35 double.
This is a fairly new 10-story hotel that has clean doubles; those in front are more expensive than those in back. The Orly also offers a novel option—for an extra 10¢ per day you'll be covered for all medical expenses incurred while a guest at the hotel!

HOTEL CENTRAL CORDOBA, Calle San Martín 1021/23. Tel. 311-1175 or 312-8523. All rooms with bath. A/C TEL
$ Rates: $22 single; $28 double.
This is a small hotel with an authentic stone facade and overhanging balconies, located four blocks from the bus terminal and the Retiro railroad station. The neat rooms have showers only.

HOTEL TRES SARGENTOS, Calle Tres Sargentos 345. Tel. 312-6081. 60 rms (most with bath). TEL
$ Rates: $22 single; $30 double with bath. Major credit cards accepted.
On Tres Sargentos—a short two-block street that connects San Martín and 25 de Mayo (between Calle Paraguay and Calle Córdoba)—is this outstanding hotel. It's a spotless modern selection with superior service. Look for the three soldier figures on the marquee. This place, by the way, is a favorite with visiting athletic teams.

PROMENADE, Avenida de Alvear (Charcas) 444. Tel. 312-5681. Fax 311-5761. 70 rms (all with bath). TEL
$ Rates (including continental breakfast): $28 single; $38 double.
This fine 10-story hotel, situated a block from Plaza San Martín, offers airy, comfortable doubles with twin beds.

DOUBLES FOR LESS THAN $70

HOTEL PRINCIPADO, Calle Paraguay 481. Tel. 313-3022. 88 rms (all with bath). TV TEL
$ Rates: $58 single; $65 double. Major credit cards accepted.
The Principado opened in 1978. It has 11 floors and a colonial Spanish decor. The rooms are clean and comfortable.

HOTEL REGIDOR, Tucuman 451. Tel. 392-9939 or 392-9589. All rooms with bath. TV TEL
$ Rates: $42 single; $65 double. Major credit cards accepted.
Another fine choice, the posh Regidor is located between Calle Reconquista and Calle San Martín.

HOTEL VICTORY, Calle Maipu 880, near Calle Paraguay. Tel. 322-8415 or 322-3440. All rooms with bath. A/C TV TEL
$ Rates (including tax and service): $40 single; $50 double. Major credit cards accepted.

The carpeted 10-story Victory is one of the city's best values. Each spotless room has blue drapes and blue sheets. The desk clerks will provide you with city maps and helpful restaurant and nightspot hints.

SAN ANTONIO, Calle Paraguay 372. Tel. 312-5381. All rooms with bath. TEL
$ Rates: $42 single; $52 double. Major credit cards accepted.
The cheerful San Antonio is located in a quiet area. All rooms are heated when necessary and have radios. Manager Luís Laurent speaks five languages. We have found nothing lacking here.

WALDORF, Calle Paraguay 450. Tel. 312-2071. Telex 27733. 90 rms (all with bath). A/C TEL
$ Rates: $32 single; $60 double. Major credit cards accepted.
Each room in the Waldorf is attractively decorated and equipped with all modern conveniences. An American bar is located in the lobby. The impressive Waldorf is fairly priced.

SPLURGE CHOICES

GRAN HOTEL BUENOS AIRES, Alvear (Charcas) 767. Tel. 311-6220 or 311-6228. Fax 111-347. Telex 22594 HOTBAR. 100 rms (all with bath). A/C MINIBAR TV TEL
$ Rates (including tax and service): $80 single; $90 double. Major credit cards accepted.
You'll be hard-pressed to match the luxury of the Buenos Aires for the same price. Rooms are spacious and comfortably furnished. Every morning a newspaper in your native language is delivered to your room.

GRAN HOTEL DORA, Maipu 963, near Paraguay. Tel. 312-7391. Fax 313-8134. Telex 21406. 100 rms (all with bath). A/C TV TEL
$ Rates (including tax and service): $66 single; $74 double. Major credit cards accepted.
An aristocrat among our Buenos Aires selections is the Dora. This magnificent hostelry, which rivals splurge hotels we've seen in Europe, is always crowded, so make reservations in advance.

ROCHESTER HOTEL, Calle Esmeralda 542. Tel. 393-9712 or 393-9939. Fax 322-4689. Telex 24127 ROBVE AR. 160 rms (all with bath). A/C MINIBAR TV TEL
$ Rates: From $59 single; from $89 double. Major credit cards accepted.
The four-star Rochester offers an excellent location in the heart of the city, plus all the comforts of home. All rooms are carpeted and comfortably furnished; service is courteous and efficient. The Rochester offers special suites for newlyweds and celebrants of silver and golden anniversaries. It has 24-hour room service, as well as laundry and dry-cleaning service.

NEAR AVENIDA DE MAYO

This last area has many budget choices, especially between Plaza de Mayo and Avenida 9 de Julio, but it's the least desirable location in terms of good restaurants, nightlife, and sightseeing. We've listed what we think are the best.

DOUBLES FOR LESS THAN $20

GRAN HOTEL SAN CARLOS, Calle Suipacha 39. Tel. 40-7021. Fax 45-9224. Telex 801-7844. All rooms with bath.

$ Rates: $8 single; $11 double.

⭐ The San Carlos is off Rivadavia. We'd give this above-average hostelry a higher recommendation if it were more centrally located. Still, it's on a quiet street, two blocks from Avenida de Mayo.

DOUBLES FOR LESS THAN $40

DU HELDER, Rivadavia 857. Tel. 40-3404. Some rooms with bath.
$ Rates: $23 single with bath; $25 double with bath.

Ⓢ The above-average Du Helder is on a quiet street, two blocks from Avenida de Mayo. We'd give this a higher recommendation if it were more centrally located. Bathless rooms cost less.

NOVEL, Avenida de Mayo 915. Tel. 381-0214 or 383-4993. 80 rms (all with bath). A/C
$ Rates: $25 single; $35 double.
The owner of the very simple Novel is a retired merchant seaman who speaks English and loves to talk of his adventures in the United States and Europe. Breakfast in bed is a plus here.

NUEVO MUNDIAL HOTEL, Avenida de Mayo 1298. Tel. 383-0011 or 383-0012. Fax 383-6318. Telex 18660 DELPHI AR. All rooms with bath. A/C TV TEL
$ Rates (including breakfast): $32 double.
Located near the obelisk in the center of the city, the Nuevo Mudial is a good value. Not opulent, it has basic yet comfortable furnishings. As for amenities, it has its own coffee shop, hairdresser, boutique, and conference hall.

RITZ, Avenida de Mayo 1111. Tel. 383-9001. No rooms with bath.
$ Rates: $14 single; $20 double.
Rooms are large and plainly furnished in this small hotel. Lights in the large public bathrooms turn on automatically as the door is closed.

SUIPACHA PALACE, Calle Suipacha 18. Tel. 35-5001. 50 rms (some with bath).
$ Rates: $20 single with bath; $28 double with bath; $32 triple.
The small three-story Suipacha Palace offers basic but quite acceptable accommodations, considering the price. Bathless rooms cost even less.

DOUBLES FOR LESS THAN $60

GRAN HOTEL ARGENTINO, Carlos Pellegrini 37, at Rivadavia. Tel. 35-3071. Fax 325-9591. Telex 28347 GRATEL AR. 150 rms (all with bath). A/C TV TEL
$ Rates: $46 single; $58 double. Major credit cards accepted.

⭐ The best choice in this price category is the modern Argentino, on Carlos Pellegrini (as mentioned, Pellegrini is the east side of Avenida 9 de Julio). A large neon sign quickly identifies it. In addition to offering outstanding rooms (some with separate sitting areas), the hotel has top-notch service.

GRAN HOTEL HISPANO, Avenida de Mayo 861. Tel. 342-4431. Fax 331-5266. 160 rms (most with bath). TEL
$ Rates: $30 single; $40 double.
The Hispano is a converted older home with an ample lounge and TV area and an indoor court on each floor. The friendly manager will proudly show you to a spotless room that is spacious and cheerful. The baths have been fully modernized.

CASTELAR, Avenida de Mayo 1152. Tel. 38-7873. Fax 325-6964. 200 rms (all with bath). A/C TV TEL

$ Rates (including breakfast): $50 single; $57 double. Major credit cards accepted.

⭐ A great choice in this neighborhood is the huge Castelar, on the Cerrito (west) side of Avenida 9 de Julio. The Castelar once was an old-world deluxe hotel, with a marble lobby and plush leather furnishings. The rooms are large and luxurious. Off the spacious lobby is a popular cafeteria that is usually crowded. A fitness center (complete with Jacuzzi, sauna, and tanning bed) and a beauty salon are recent additions to the facilities.

5. WHERE TO DINE

Beef is a major natural resource in Argentina. As a result, the locals have developed a gourmet's eye for meat—and for food in general. Accordingly, Buenos Aires houses more first-class restaurants than any other city in South America. The world-famous national dish is *parrillada*, a delectable mixed grill of prime steak bits, chicken sections, small sausages, animal organs, and lamb and pork slices—all barbecued on small stoves (*parrillas*) at your table. When you have dined on *parrillada*, you'll appreciate why we consider Buenos Aires a city that rivals Paris in culinary pleasures.

The local mineral water (carbonated) is the best we've ever tasted. Also, Argentine wines vie with the Chilean as South America's best, and they're quite inexpensive.

Keep in mind that Porteños traditionally enjoy a late dinner, eaten anywhere from 10pm to midnight. Restaurants usually remain open until 2am. *Note:* Service is not included in the bill. It's customary to tip 10%.

THE "BROADWAY" AREA

Many of our choice restaurant selections are located in the Buenos Aires nightlife district, along Calle Corrientes and Calle Lavalle.

ARTURITO, Corrientes 1124. Tel. 35-0227.
Cuisine: INTERNATIONAL. **Reservations:** Recommended.
$ Prices: Appetizers $3–$5; main courses $4–$8. Major credit cards accepted.
Open: Lunch and dinner.
At Arturito, across 9 de Julio, the *cazuela de mariscos* and the *paella valenciana* will make your mouth water. Hanging wine bottles brighten the rather plain atmosphere.

LA CHURRASQUITA, Corrientes 1220.
Cuisine: ARGENTINE/ITALIAN. **Reservations:** Recommended.
$ Prices: Appetizers $1–$3; main courses $4–$6.
Open: Lunch and dinner.
Ⓢ Somewhat out of the way is this good-value restaurant, where the specialties are beef and veal dishes and the friendly atmosphere makes you feel right at home. The baby beef steak is a delicious bargain.

LAS DELICIOSAS PAPAS FRITAS, Maipu 529, between Lavalle and Tucuman. Tel. 322-9865.
Cuisine: ARGENTINE. **Reservations:** Recommended.
$ Prices: Appetizers $1–$4; main courses $5–$8. Major credit cards accepted.
Open: Lunch and dinner.
⭐ During our first visit to this restaurant, we ordered a platter of chicken and a *bife de lomo* (small steak). Delicious! In addition, we had a tasty tomato-and-onion salad, red wine, mineral water, and coffee. Standard with all platters is an enormous serving of potatoes—the best in town—plus a basket of fresh rolls; the puffed fried potatoes, a house specialty, are light, round, and crisp. Our total bill for

two was $15, with tax and service. And this is no dive—the tables are decked with spotless white cloths, and the waiters are white-jacketed.

LA ESTANCIA, Lavalle 941, near Avenida 9 de Julio. Tel. 35-0336.
   Cuisine: ARGENTINE. **Reservations:** Recommended.
$ **Prices:** Appetizers: $1–$3 main courses $5–$8. Major credit cards accepted.
   Open: Daily noon–2:30am.

⭐ At this atmospheric restaurant, we recently savored a magnificent *parrillada* (beef chunks, chicken sections, sausages, and giblets grilled on charcoal-burning stove at your table), a generous tomato salad garnished with red onion, and half a bottle of domestic red wine, for about $12 for two, including cover and service (10%). The quality of the dishes and fine service have made this a much-sought-out restaurant. Huge, comfortable, and scrupulously clean, it's always crowded.

The most popular dish here, where steaks are the house specialty, is the *parrillada,* enough for two. Try the succulent *bife de lomo* or the *bife la estancia.* If you prefer chicken, order the grilled *medio pollo al spiedo*—superb and virtually enough for two. Vegetables, salads, and beverages are modestly priced.

Note: The most expensive item on the menu is the *parrillada.* There are additional rooms next door; head upstairs.

EL MUNDO, Maipu 550 between Lavalle and Tucuman. Tel. 394-7060.
   Cuisine: ARGENTINE. **Reservations:** Recommended.
$ **Prices:** Appetizers $1–$3; main courses $5–$8. Major credit cards accepted.
   Open: Lunch and dinner.
El Mundo serves prime steaks, *parrillada,* lamb, and chicken dishes. The crowds at this large restaurant attest to the quality of the food. The *bife de lomo* is the best in Buenos Aires.

LA NAZARENAS, Reconquista 1126, in front of the Sheraton Hotel. Tel. 312-5559.
   Cuisine: ARGENTINE. **Reservations:** Recommended.
$ **Prices:** Appetizers $1–$3; main courses $5–$8. Major credit cards accepted.
   Open: Lunch and dinner.
This attractive bilevel eatery offers as a bonus a fine view of this bustling area. By all means try the entrecôte or baby *bife.*

EL PALACIO DE LA PAPA FRITA, Lavalle 954 and 735. Tel. 394-7060 or 393-5849.
   Cuisine: ARGENTINE. **Reservations:** Not required.
$ **Prices:** Appetizers $1–$3; main courses $2–$6.
   Open: Lunch and dinner.
Two "The Palace of the Fried Potato" restaurants are located within a few steps of each other. They offer excellent beef and chicken values for under $6, plus outstanding potatoes. The menu features half a baked chicken (*pollito al horno*) and a baby beef platter. The colonial decor is quite handsome.

LA POSTA DEL GAUCHO, Carlos Pellegrini 625, between Viamonte and Tucuman.
   Cuisine: ARGENTINE.
$ **Prices:** Appetizers $1–$3; main courses $5–$8.
   Open: Lunch and dinner.
This fine restaurant features outstanding meat platters and local wines. The decor is that of a gaucho ranch. The service is rather good, considering the usually crowded conditions.

SORRENTO, Corrientes 668, near Florida. Tel. 325-3787.
   Cuisine: ARGENTINE/ITALIAN. **Reservations:** Recommended.
$ **Prices:** Appetizers $2–$6; main courses $5–$10. Major credit cards accepted.
   Open: Lunch and dinner.
The Sorrento is noted for its unusual assortment of dishes. We especially enjoyed the

chicken Portuguesa, which resembled sectioned chicken cacciatore; it was cooked in a tomato, pepper, and onion sauce enhanced by local spices. Served with either vegetables or potatoes, this proved a superb treat. With wine, ice cream, and coffee, the total bill for two amounted to about $12, including cover and service. For approximately the same tab you can choose instead a grilled steak or veal cutlet.

OTHER DOWNTOWN CHOICES

CAFE LA BARRA, on Córdoba.
  Cuisine: INTERNATIONAL. **Reservations:** Not required.
$ Prices: Appetizers $1–$3; main courses $4–$8.
  Open: Lunch and dinner.
This is a great spot, especially if you're on a tight budget. A bonus here is the outdoor dining. The restaurant is open late, even on Sunday. It is clean and has good service.

CHINO CENTRAL, Avenida Rivadavia 658. Tel. 331-3670.
  Cuisine: CHINESE. **Reservations:** Not accepted.
$ Prices: Appetizers 75¢–$2; main courses $2.50–$6.
  Open: Lunch and dinner.
A friend of ours, a resident of Buenos Aires, considers Chino Central the best Chinese restaurant in town. There is a daily four-course special for about $4. The restaurant is just off Avenida Florida.

FRIDAYS, San Martín 965. Tel. 311-5433.
  Cuisine: INTERNATIONAL.
$ Prices: Appetizers $2–$5; main courses $4–$12.
  Open: Mon–Sat lunch and dinner.
The bilevel Fridays has a fixed-price four-course lunch for $8, plus daily specials. The meat dishes are good, and the decor has a British flavor. House specialties include tenderloin scallops with salmon sauce and salmon in capers.

OTTO CERVECERIA, Sarmiento 1679. Tel. 35-1143.
  Cuisine: GERMAN.
$ Prices: Appetizers $3–$6; main courses $5–$12.
  Open: Lunch and dinner.
At Otto the veal is juicy and tender and the breading just right. Other favorites here are the *Schweinbraten mit Sauerkraut* and the *gefüllte Tomaten mit Thunfisch.* Inexpensive, this ski lodge–type eatery is not fancy but boasts an extensive menu.

PARILLA LAS TEJAS, Arenales 1934. Tel. 814-1142.
  Cuisine: ARGENTINE. **Reservations:** Recommended.
$ Prices: Appetizers $2–$4; main courses $4–$8.
  Open: Lunch and dinner.
This restaurant boasts of having the best executive lunch menu in Buenos Aires. At only $6 for a complete *parrillada,* lunch here is a true bargain. Another branch is at Córdoba 4083.

RISTORANTE SUBITO, Paraguay 640. Tel. 313-6125.
  Cuisine: ITALIAN. **Reservations:** Recommended.
$ Prices: Appetizers $2–$5; main courses $6–$10.
  Open: Lunch and dinner.
This modern, slick Italian restaurant specializes in pasta. In fact, the noodles are made in front of your eyes in the center of the restaurant. Besides the pasta we heartily recommend the antipasta parmigiana and the stuffed pimentos *alla Subito.*

RECOLETA

Recoleta is Buenos Aires's trendiest area, 10 minutes by cab from downtown. It's where Porteños go to be seen. There are many excellent restaurants and lively clubs open until the wee hours; the restaurants abound with outdoor tables. A great meeting place is **Café de la Paix,** at Avenida Quinana 595, offering coffee and snacks. Popular, too, are **Café Gran Victoria,** at H. Yrigoyen, and **New Park Lane,** at Avenida Quintana 570. One of the trendiest spots right now is **Open Plaza,** a 24-hour coffee shop on Avenida del Libertador in Barrio Norte. Across from Café de la Paix is another favorite of ours, **La Biela,** at Quintana 600.

For dining, you have several excellent places from which to choose.

CLARKS, Junín 1777. Tel. 801-9502.
Cuisine: INTERNATIONAL. **Reservations:** Recommended.
$ **Prices:** Appetizers $3–$6; main courses $8–$15. Major credit cards accepted.
Open: Lunch and dinner.

Both cuisine and decor make Clarks one of Buenos Aires's finest restaurants. Tops on the menu are the salmon blinis, vichyssoise, grilled salads, prawn-and-pineapple brochettes, filet mignon, and suckling pig.

HARPERS, Junín 7763. Tel. 801-7140.
Cuisine: INTERNATIONAL. **Reservations:** Recommended.
$ **Prices:** Appetizers $3–$6; main courses $8–$15. Major credit cards accepted.

Harper's is very similar to Clarks (above), in both decor and cuisine. A glass-enclosed garden and well-dressed clientele add to the decor. Recommended are the *lomo champignones; entrecôte Bordalese;* and a fine fish dish, the *gran paraná Harper.*

LOLA, Roberto M. Ortíz 1805. Tel. 804-3410.
Cuisine: INTERNATIONAL. **Reservations:** Recommended.
$ **Prices:** Appetizers $3–$6; main courses $8–$15. Major credit cards accepted.
Open: Lunch and dinner.

Lola offers an excellent international menu for lunch or dinner. You'll linger over coffee as you relax and enjoy the beautiful surroundings, highlighted by well-tended plants and sketches by local artists.

RISTORANTE TOMMASO, Junín 1735.
Cuisine: ITALIAN. **Reservations:** Recommended.
$ **Prices:** Appetizers $3–$6; main courses $4–$10. Major credit cards accepted.
Open: Lunch and dinner.

Tommaso is highly recommended for its fine Italian dishes. The upper level is a popular nightspot; the restaurant is down a winding staircase. The tortellini, canneloni, and saltimbocca are excellent.

DON JUAN, Dr. Roberto Ortiz 1827 off Guido.
Cuisine: INTERNATIONAL/SPANISH.
$ **Prices:** Appetizers $2–$5; main courses $6–$12. Major credit cards accepted.
Open: Lunch and dinner.

At this fine Spanish restaurant, the Spanish decor invites you to some of Buenos Aires's finest *arroz valenciana* and paella. One serving is usually enough for two.

HAPPENINGS, Guido 631.
Cuisine: INTERNATIONAL. **Reservations:** Recommended.
$ **Prices:** Appetizers $3–$6; main courses $8–$15. Major credit cards accepted.

This is a trendy little bistro. The dining room is bilevel, with wood paneling and a high ceiling. A large glass panel in front of the kitchen lets you watch the chefs as they prepare the excellent trout and salmon dishes, as well as the highly recommended baby bife and *supremo de pollo Maryland.*

GATO DUMAS, Roberto M. Ortiz 1809. Tel. 804-5858.
Cuisine: NOUVELLE CUISINE. **Reservations:** Recommended.
$ **Prices:** Appetizers $4–$8; main courses $6–$14.
Open: Dinner only.

Owned by one of Argentina's finest and most innovative chefs, Gato Dumas, this is a great choice for celebrating a special occasion. Among the exquisite menu selections are *cartacci,* tenderloin with caviar, stuffed trout, and stuffed chicken breast. Many dishes and salads are prepared with produce straight from Gato's garden. Prices are on the expensive side.

NUÑEZ

If, after attending a *futból* match or a horserace, you decide to tour the suburbs, consider dining at either of two first-rate restaurants in the suburb of Nuñéz, 20 minutes by cab from center city. Remember, too, **Los Años Locos** and **A' Nonna Immacolata,** on Avenida Costanera, for late night dining by the sea.

EL AGUILA, Avenida D. Alvarez 1999. Tel. 581-1344.
    Cuisine: INTERNATIONAL. **Reservations:** Recommended.
$ Prices: Appetizers $3–$5; main courses $4–$8. Major credit cards accepted.
    Open: Lunch and dinner.
Near the River Plate Stadium, El Aguila has a complete international menu featuring beef and chicken *a la parilla.*

LA TRANQUERA, Avenida Fugueroa Alcorta 6466. Tel. 784-6199.
    Cuisine: ARGENTINE. **Reservations:** Recommended. **Bus:** No. 130 from Avenida de Mayo.
$ Prices: Appetizers $3–$5; main courses $4–$8. Major credit cards accepted.
    Open: Lunch and dinner.
La Tranquera can seat almost 1,000 customers. It offers an excellent *parrillada;* perhaps, however, you'll be tempted by the half a chicken. Patrons dine in comfortable wicker chairs.

SPLURGE CHOICES AROUND TOWN

ABC, Lavalle 545. Tel. 322-3992.
    Cuisine: GERMAN. **Reservations:** Recommended.
$ Prices: Appetizers $4–$8; main courses $8–$14.
    Open: Lunch and dinner.
If you have a craving for German cuisine, head for ABC. The patois and fare are authenticly German, with delicious wurst and daily specials.

AU BEC FIN, Vicente López 1827, just off Callao (Recoleta). Tel. 801-6894.
    Cuisine: FRENCH/INTERNATIONAL. **Reservations:** Recommended.
$ Prices: Appetizers $4–$9; main courses $10–$16. Major credit cards accepted.
    Open: Dinner only 8pm–2am.
This elegant restaurant is in an old house, with only three or four tables per room, creating an intimate atmosphere. Menu highlights include prawn mousse, filet mignon, picquant champagne, and plum Bavarois. Men will feel out of place without coats and ties.

LA CABANA, Entre Ríos 436 (in Belgrano). Tel. 38-2373.
    Cuisine: ARGENTINE. **Reservations:** Required.
$ Prices: Appetizers $3–$6; main courses $6–$12. Major credit cards accepted.
    Open: Lunch daily noon–3pm; dinner daily 8pm–3am.
Porteños insist that La Cabaña is probably the world's best beef restaurant. After several visits, we agree. Located about 10 minutes from the center of the city, La Cabaña offers excellently prepared food amid elegant surroundings, with service to match.

We ordered soup, baby beef steak, tomato-and-onion salad with sardines, ice cream, coffee, a flask of wine, and a bottle of mineral water. The total (for two), including tax and service, was an unbelievable $40! We failed to finish nearly a quarter of the steak—that's how large it was. A spectacular steak dish is the double T-bone cooked in a tangy wine sauce. It could be cut with a fork. Vegetables, salad, and rolls are extra. Most steak platters are under $8. Exotic soups enrich the menu. Look for the mammoth stuffed steer in the entranceway.

EL COMITE, Carlos Calvo 375 (San Telmo). Tel. 361-6201.
  Cuisine: CONTINENTAL. **Reservations:** Recommended.
$ Prices: Appetizers $4–$8; main courses $6–$12. Major credit cards suggested.
  Open: Sun–Fri lunch and dinner; Sat dinner only.
El Comite is the gathering place for Buenos Aires's elite. Housed in a very old building, the fin-de-siècle setting fits right in with the cobblestoned streets of San Telmo, the city's historic neighborhood. The menu is continental, with a political twist; don't be surprised if your main course is preceded by a "perestroika" salad. Piano and violin music make dining here memorable.

LONDON GRILL, Reconquista 455. Tel. 311-2223.
  Cuisine: ENGLISH. **Reservations:** Recommended.
$ Prices: Appetizers $3–$6; main courses $6–$14. Major credit cards accepted.
  Open: Daily noon–midnight.
For classic British fare, try the very popular London Grill. The atmosphere is authentic, and the Yorkshire pudding, kidney pies, and roast beef will convince you that you're in London.

SPECIALTY DINING

CAFETERIAS

The cafeterias offer excellent meals at only a fraction of the prices charged by fancier dining spots. The ones we've listed are on or near Avenida Florida and Avenida de Mayo.

At Bernardo Irigoyen and Carlos Pelligrini your best bet is **Oriente,** where you can choose self-service, if in a hurry. Dishes range from sandwiches and coffee to egg platters or even pretty good *parrillada.*

At **Las Brases,** Viamonte 683, eggs are a bargain at $1.10; for lunch you may choose lasagne, *bife de chorizo,* or lomo, among other dishes. Local wine or cognac is $1. Another good spot is **Mimo's Bar,** at San Martín 954, in the Galería Larretta. A filling breakfast of juice or fruit, ham and eggs, toast, butter, and coffee is not much over $2.50. Homemade soup is featured for lunch here.

One of our favorite places is **Florida Garden,** at Avenida Florida 899, which shares its premises with Harrods department store. It serves sweet, buttery croissants (*medias lunas*) with steaming coffee, plus eggs done just the way you like them. *Desayuno americano* (American breakfast, consisting of eggs, bacon, toast, and coffee) costs about $3. Consider Florida Garden for a late-afternoon cocktail (*cóctel* or *aperitivo*). Order domestic rather than imported liquor; local Scotch, for example, is 90¢ to $1.50 per drink, whereas the imported variety is $3. By the way, the Florida Garden is best known for its chocolate mousse.

An excellent grill with relatively inexpensive prices is **Via Florida,** at Avenida Florida 261. Here you can enjoy ham sandwiches at $1.25 or salami sandwiches at 90¢ (add 25¢ for tomato).

Finally, a few blocks away, at Lavalle 999 (at Carlos Pellegrini), is **Café Parisien,** a stand-up cafeteria where businesspeople pop in for a quick lunch or snack between appointments.

Two sit-down or stand-up restaurants frequented by government workers are the low-priced **Grill Oriente,** at the intersection of Avenida de Mayo and Avenida 9 de Julio, and the **Auto Service Grill,** at Mayo and Suipacha. Typical dishes are *bife de lomo* and mixed *parrillada.*

CONFITERIAS

When the day is done, at around 5pm, friends congregate in Viennese-like cafés called *confiterías.* Found throughout the city, these pleasant places serve magnificent pastries and tiny sandwiches that Porteños usually devour with a pot of tea. Cocktails are served but are not as popular in the *confiterías.*

Ask for the pastry and sandwich plates (*platos variados*) and the waiter will quickly put before you half a dozen or more samples of each. The two plates cost about $5, but the waiter deducts from the bill any pastries or sandwiches that remain.

Our favorite *confitería* is the **Richmond Tea Room,** at Avenida Florida 648 between Lavalle and Corrientes. Extremely popular with young executive types and chic matrons, it offers an elegant decor combined with courtly service. If tea is not your kind of preprandial drink, try a cocktail for $3. If you'd like to brush up against an Argentine congressman or two, then you'll definitely enjoy a pastry-and-tea respite at **Confitería del Molino,** at Callao and Rivadavia, near Plaza del Congreso. Prices are a shade over those at the Richmond, but the quality and atmosphere are equivalent. The *medias lunas* are particularly good.

One of the most famous *confiterías* is **Queen Bess,** at Avenida Santa Fe 868, a popular stop for shoppers. Take your choice between the small tables or the bar. Photos of Queen Elizabeth adorn the establishment. A good snack is the ham-and-tomato sandwich and tea for $3.

Does Victor Herbert–type music help your disposition? Try the **Confitería Ideal,** at Suipacha 384, where a piano, accordion, and singer entertain most afternoons and evenings from 5 to 9pm. The Ideal is best known for its light sandwiches and pastries. The music from the bandstand will remind you of what Vienna must have been like in the 1890s. It's Buenos Aires at its campiest.

The **Gran Café Tortoni,** at Avenida de Mayo 825, has been popular for over a hundred years. Founded in 1858, the huge café resembles an old-fashioned U.S. ice-cream parlor—sans soda jerks. It supports the arts by encouraging talented young groups to perform evenings. The food is reasonable. Ham sandwiches are $2; coffee with milk and three croissants is $1.50. If you choose to go during show hours, expect a cover charge.

The **Confitería My House,** at Córdoba 616, has won a place in our hearts by being open as late as we have ever been out. It's attractive and features fine service, sandwiches, pastry, and drinks until 3am. The 1920s-style **Café Petit Colón,** at Libertad 523, across from the law courts and just a block from the Teatro Colón, is popular with lawyers and theatergoers. Finally, we cannot omit the first-rate **St. James,** at Córdoba 770; it was our favorite stop in Buenos Aires when we first stayed at the nearby Victory Hotel.

OUTDOOR CAFES

From September to May, Porteños enjoy sipping cocktails and nibbling on sandwiches at the city's many outdoor cafés. One of our favorite places is the **Confitería Obelisco,** on the Carlos Pellegrini side of Avenida 9 de Julio, at no. 329. Two other recommended spots are **Confitería Jockey Club,** at Sarmiento 1101, and **Lord Gin,** at Córdoba 628. And in Recoleta people-watchers head to the outdoor tables of **La Biela,** at Quintana 600.

VEGETARIAN RESTAURANTS

Vegetarian fans should head for lunch to **Granix Restaurant Vegetariano,** opposite the Richmond Tea Room, at Avenida Florida 467. It offers a self-service lunch from 11am to 3:30pm.

Another convenient choice is **Yin Yang,** at Paraguay 858 (tel. 311-7798). The menu is similar to Granix's and features macrobiotic, vegetarian, and naturist cuisine. The restaurant is open Monday to Friday for lunch and dinner, Saturday for lunch only. Try also **La Huertan** at Paraguay 445 (tel. 311-0470).

Also in this category are the **La Lecherisima** dairy chain outlets, where you can feast on yogurt, cereals, and the like. They are scattered all over town, with two convenient locations at Corrientes 839 and Santa Fe 726.

WHISKERIAS

Good conversation and free-flowing liquor dominate the numerous informal cocktail lounges called *whiskerías,* common to Buenos Aires. One of our favorites is **Park**

Lane, at Avenida Florida 719. Its panoramic windows overlook Avenida Florida: the antique lampposts are a nice touch. On the near side of Avenida 9 de Julio you'll find **Exedra,** at Carlos Pellegrini 801. We enjoy the French decor at **Café Paris,** on Carlos Pellegrini at Rivadavia (next to the Buenos Aires Hotel). Also try **La Barra,** a popular meeting place after work at Córdoba and San Martín.

PIZZERIAS

The pizza at **Los Inmortales,** at Lavalle 746 in the movie district, is the best we've ever eaten. At this near-elegant pizzeria the service, decor, and wines are all worthy of first-class continental restaurants. The menu, which also offers steak and chicken platters, lists 50 different pizza choices. The pizzaiola is a tantalizing blend of spices, tomato, and garlic on a crisp crust. The empanadas, another house specialty, are large and crusty. Considered one of the city's best eateries, Los Inmortales has branches elsewhere in the city.

The ubiquitous **Pizza Hut** has made its appearance in Buenos Aires, at Lavalle 876. A pizza slice or spaghetti with a soft drink and coffee costs $1.50. **Pizza Roma,** on the same block, is another good choice.

FAST FOOD

For a change of pace, you might try the North American–style **Chéburger,** on Avenida Florida at Sarmiento, a bilevel eatery where the gran chéburger (with cheese) is $1.25. Fried fish is popular, too, as is the fried chicken (*pollo frito*). You might also enjoy stopping at **Pumpernic,** at Avenida Florida 532 and on Suipacha between Corrientes and Lavalle. Hamburgers run $1 and up. There are several Pumpernics in the city.

McDonald's has found a niche in Buenos Aires with several outlets. The most convenient is at Lavalle 964. Another is at Florida 568.

Another popular hamburger hangout is **Di Pappo,** on Corrientes at Carlos Pellegrini. The low prices and fast service are the draws here. Open from 11am to 5am, it has sandwiches, ice cream, hamburgers, a salad bar, and pizza. Another branch, **Di Pappo d'Or,** is at Santa Fe 1937.

For a quick hot dog, stop off at **Frankfurt,** located in an alley between Corrientes and Jarelli, close to the Multicine. With more than the usual number of relishes to choose from, you won't be disappointed.

SNACK SHOPS

These individually owned eateries, found on virtually every busy street, serve varied light snacks, including pizza. Most of them, however, specialize in a wonderful Argentine delicacy—*empanadas,* soft-crusted pies stuffed with beef, chicken, sausage, tuna, cheese, or sardines. For a memorable introduction, try the **Roma Pizzería,** on Lavalle between Suipacha and Esmeralda.

Another popular snack in Buenos Aires is *churros*—thin, hot, crispy, elongated crullers, sold plain or cream-filled. Try Roma's annex around the corner, on Suipacha, for these.

Finally, that familiar standby, the hot dog, hasn't been overlooked in Buenos Aires. You're sure to spot vendors throughout the city selling **panchos,** as hot dogs are called here, for $1 each. *Reminder:* As we noted earlier, however, you should avoid buying foods and beverages from street vendors (see the list of health precautions in Chapter 1, section 2).

6. ATTRACTIONS

Buenos Aires is endlessly varied. To get a feel of the city and its many attractions—not least its exuberant and friendly inhabitants—take a leisurely stroll during your first

DID YOU KNOW . . . ?

- Argentina received the largest proportion of immigrants to Latin America. By 1914 half of the population of Buenos Aires was foreign-born.
- Of the 4 million immigrants who came to Argentina between 1885 and 1965, about 46% were Italian and 33% Spanish.
- Many Jews have settled in Argentina. In the early days they lived in a neighborhood known as Once, where Yiddish dailies are still on sale.
- About 150 years ago Welsh immigrants settled in Patagonia. Some Protestant churches there still conduct services in ancient Welsh.
- Southern Patagonia is where the legendary Butch Cassidy and the Sundance Kid, accompanied by Miss Eta Place, hid from the law in the early 1900s.
- The deepest natural lake in the world is Argentina's Natuel Huapi—1,437 feet at its greatest depth.
- Mt. Cerro Fitz Roy is named after the commander of H.M.S. *Beagle*, Capt. Robert Fitz Roy. The *Beagle* carried Charles Darwin on his explorations of southern South America.
- At 23,081 feet, Argentina's Mt. Aconcagua is the highest peak in the western hemisphere.

day here. You'll be charmed and at the same time gain a fast orientation to some of the places we describe.

SUGGESTED ITINERARIES

IF YOU HAVE ONE DAY If you have just 1 day in Buenos Aires, spend it strolling about the city, taking in a museum or two. Enjoy the evening in Recoleta.

IF YOU HAVE TWO DAYS To Day 1 add La Costanera Norte and San Telmo.

IF YOU HAVE THREE DAYS Plan a day trip to the Tigre River Delta.

IF YOU HAVE FIVE DAYS OR MORE After visiting Buenos Aires and the suburbs, consider a quick trip to Mar del Plata or Bariloche.

THE TOP ATTRACTIONS
NATIONAL CONGRESS

Argentina's legislature is located in **Plaza del Congreso,** on Avenida de Mayo about half a mile beyond Avenida 9 de Julio. In front of the huge edifice is a monument dedicated to the Congress of 1816, which was instrumental in Argentina's fight for independence. Stop at the nearby park and relax with the Porteños. If you don't feel like walking here, take the "A" train to the Congreso station. Before heading home, make sure you stop for tea at the nearby Confitería del Molino.

LA BOCA

The original heart of Buenos Aires, ✪ La Boca ("The Mouth") is a small area populated by working-class Italians. It is located at the mouth of the Riachuelo River, a small arm of the Río de la Plata. The section still retains the color and air of a village in southern Italy.

Plan a trip to the old city, where the cobblestone streets are clogged with *futból*-playing children. The houses, many unchanged for a century, are colorfully painted. To reach La Boca, head for the back of Plaza de Mayo, where, at the foot of a steep hill directly behind the Casa Rosada, is Avenida Paseo Colón. From the near side of Paseo Colón, take bus no. 33 or 64 and tell the driver to drop you at La Boca, a 15-minute ride. On the way you pass the University of Buenos Aires. The driver will drop you near La Boca's main street, **Necochea,** which is lined with neighborhood bars and restaurants. Late at night these are crowded with area residents and other Porteños who dance and sing until 4 and 5am.

A daytime sight not to be missed is the view from the **Avellaneda Bridge,** which spans the Riachuelo. To get there, head for Pedro de Mendoza, the street that runs along the dock. Look for the bridge and enter the building at the near end of the span. There, an escalator will carry you onto the bridge itself for a full view of La Boca and the surrounding industrial area.

SUBURBIA

Five fashionable suburbs lie northwest of the Plaza San Martín area. All can be reached via the same commuter railway system, the **Bartolomé Mitre Railway,** which has its terminus at **Retiro station,** behind Plaza San Martín. Buy a round-trip ticket (about 60¢) to the farthest and largest suburb, **San Isidro.** This will enable you to stop at the four nearer communities—Palermo, Belgrano, Nuñéz, and **Olivos.**

Palermo, only 10 minutes from Retiro station, is noted for its huge government-owned racetrack called the **Hipódromo,** high-rent apartments, a large zoo, and a magnificent botanical garden and lovely park.

After 10 minutes on the train you'll be in plush Olivos, located on the Río de la Plata; here many U.S. Embassy employees live. The large suburb (with some 160,000 residents) is a popular fishing, swimming, and golfing resort.

San Isidro, the next important train stop, is another beautiful suburb, known for the finest racetrack in Argentina—the **Jockey Club**—and for its colonial homes. It is also a summer resort area and very picturesque. If you should be hungry by this time, try the **Mi Casa,** near the train station.

MUSEUMS

MUSEO NACIONAL DE BELLAS ARTES, Avenida del Libertador 1473. Tel. 803-8817.

⭐ The Museo Nacional de Bellas Artes (National Museum of Fine Arts), founded in 1895, is one of the finest museums in South America, comparable to the best in Europe and North America. Its more than 40 rooms overflow with masterpieces from every epoch and culture. European art from the 16th to the 20th century is aptly represented by, among others, Rembrandt, Goya, and El Greco; Rodin, Manet, and Degas; van Gogh, Daumier, and Pisarro; and Kandinski, Klee, and Picasso.

The museum's largest collection is dedicated to Argentine art, both historic and contemporary. Key artists to look for are Emilio Pettorutti, Ernesto de la Cácova, Pueryrredón, Morel, Pellegrini, Butler, and Panozzi. The museum is also host to numerous temporary exhibits.

Admission: $1.50 (50% discount for students).
Open: Tues–Sun 9am–12:45pm and 3–6pm.

MUSEO HISTORICO NACIONAL, Defensa 1600 (San Telmo). Tel. 274-767.

Housed in an Italianate villa, the National Historical Museum is the most visited museum in San Telmo. Exhibits cover the stages of Argentine history. Highlights include a display of bolts from Columbus's ship *Santa Maria,* an original map of the city drawn by the Spanish conquistador Juan de Garay, and a fascinating sundial made by the Indians in the 16th century.

Admission: $1.50.
Open: Thurs–Sun 2–6pm.

MUSEO DE ARTE HISPANO-AMERICANO, Suipacha 1422. Tel. 393-6318.

The artistry of the exhibits at the Museum of Hispanic American Art is breathtaking and intensely Spanish. Among the items on display are *peinetones,* large tiaralike tortoise-shell hairpieces worn by wealthy señoras. There is a large collection of gold and silver artifacts from the Río de la Plata, as well as an outstanding collection of old pottery and *mates,* the silver vessels used to hold the tea of the same name. All are masterpieces.

In the Peruvian room you'll find religious art from the Cuzco school. The museum also contains Flemish works as well as art from the Philippines and Goa, a former Portuguese colony on the western coast of India.

Admission: $1.50.
Open: Tues–Sun 3–8pm.

MUSEO MUNICIPAL DE MOTIVOS ARGENTINOS "JOSÉ HERNANDEZ," Avenida del Libertador 2373. Tel. 802-9967.

The José Hernandez Municipal Museum of Argentine Motifs was donated to the city in 1984 by Don Felix Bunge in order to preserve the folklore and legends of the Argentine pampas. It contains the largest collection of folkloric art in Argentina, among them *mates*, firearms, knives, silverware, leatherworks, musical instruments, paintings, lithographs, and pottery.
Admission: $1.50.
Open: Mon–Fri 10am–4pm; Sat–Sun 4–8pm.

INSTITUTO NACIONAL SANMARTINIANO, corner of Mariscal Ramón Castilla and Aguado (Palermo Chico).

The two-story building housing the National San Martín Institute is a faithful reproduction of the home that independence hero José de San Martín lived in during his exile in Boulogne-Sur-Mer, France, from 1834 to 1848. It contains an interesting collection of paraphernalia either belonging or relating to the general, including documents, portraits, personal articles, and writings on his life.
Admission: $1.50.
Open: Mon–Fri 9am–noon and 2–5pm; Sat–Sun 2–5pm.

MUSEO NACIONAL HISTORICO DEL CABILDO DE LA CIUDAD DE BUENOS AIRES Y DE LA REVOLUCION DE MAYO, Calle Bolívar 65.

The full name of this museum is the National Historical Museum of the Council of the City of Buenos Aires and of the May Revolution, ensconced in a white-washed colonial building, on the corner of the Plaza de Mayo, that was the home of the original council, or junta. Erected in 1725, the clock tower and arched porticoes have become symbols of the city. The numerous salons display exhibits from the era of the Wars of Independence, including collections of arms, medals, and furniture. The main room, the **Sala Capitular** faithfully reproduces the original decoration of the **Cabildante** Period, when the meetings leading to the nation's independence were held. Also on display is religious art from the Jesuit Missions.
Admission: $1.50.
Open: Thurs–Sun 2–6pm. For guided tours in English, call 30-1782.

MUSEO MITRE, San Martín 336. Tel. 394-8670.

This is the former home of Bartolomé Mitre, the celebrated general who began his career as a soldier and later became the President of the Republic and founder of the intellectual daily *La Nación*. The museum is best known for its coin and map collection and historical archives. The general's quarters are just as they were at the time of his death.
Admission: $1.50.
Open: Tues–Fri 1–6pm.

MORE ATTRACTIONS

PALERMO PARK (BOSQUES DE PALERMO).

Until 1836 Palermo had been nothing more than uninhabited marshland. Then the iron-fisted ruler Juan Manuel de Rosas ordered the marshes drained to make way for his palatial estate, complete with groves of orange and magnolia trees as well as various exotic plants. When he was deposed in 1852 the property was abandoned until nearly two decades later, when President Sarmiento decided to turn it into a public park. The park was later redesigned by Jule Dormals, the landscape artist who designed the Bois de Boulogne in Paris.

Today Palermo Park is a favorite retreat of Buenos Aires residents. Five lakes, some large enough for speedboating, and lots of grassy fields make the park ideal for boating, jogging, bicycling, soccer, picnics, and just relaxing. Highlights include the Patio Andaluz, the Rosaleda, El Puente Blanco, the Jardín de los Poetas, and the Japanese Garden.

PALERMO ZOO (JARDÍN ZOOLÓGICO), Avenida Las Heras and Sarmiento.

✪ Just over 100 years old, the Palermo Zoo maintains its fin-de-siècle ambience. Young and old will delight in the unusual homes of the residents here: the bears' gothic palace; the lions' French palace; the buffaloes Indostan temple; the condors' Eiffel Tower-shaped cage; and, best of all, the Bombayian temple that the elephants call home. Lovely sculptures are placed throughout. Don't miss the Byzantine Ruins, a seven-column portico at the rear of Darwin Lake. The columns are authentic, brought to Buenos Aires from Trieste, where they had formed part of a Byzantine palace.

To reach the zoo, located in the nearby suburb of Palermo, take the "D" line subway to Plaza Italia. While there, you can fill up on hot dogs and enjoy the interesting arrangements of animals (set on islands). Across the road from the zoo are the Botanical Gardens (below).

Open: Winter, daily 8am–6pm; summer, daily 8am–8pm.

BOTANICAL GARDENS (JARDÍN BOTÁNICO), Avenida Las Heras and Santa Fe.

Across Las Heras from the zoo (above), this 150-acre retreat was designed by naturalist Carlos Thays at the end of the 19th century. It is home to over 6,000 species from around the world and is a favorite destination of Porteños looking for a quiet spot to relax, read a book, or take a nap. There are lovely fountains, sculptures, and greenhouses throughout. One of our favorite spots is the Pond of the Water Lilies by the entrance.

Open: Thurs–Tues 8am–noon and 2–6pm.

RECOLETA CEMETERY, corner of Junin and Quintana.

As you pass through the neoclassical portico at the entrance to the ✪ **Cementerio del Norte,** or Recoleta Cemetery as it is more commonly known, you enter a silent world of majestic splendor. The cemetery opened in 1822 on the site of the Recoleta Convent's orchard. Spanning over 10 acres, it is the final resting place of 6,400 of Buenos Aires's most illustrious citizens and courageous heroes. Many of the tombs and mausoleums are the works of famous artists. Over 70 have been declared national monuments. One of the most visited is that of Eva Perón.

CENTRO CULTURAL LAS MALVINAS.

This magnificent museum at Avenida Florida 750 has a rotating exhibition of Argentine history, current events, and art. On our last visit, the museum's theme was the Malvinas (Falkland Islands) War, with exhibits used and connected with the war. Helpful guides will take you to the main points of interest.

A WALKING TOUR

Begin at the city's oldest plaza, the **Plaza de Mayo.** It dates back to the second founding of Buenos Aires in 1580 when Don Juan de Garay designated it as the city's principal square. It's still considered the heart of Buenos Aires and is where the important government buildings are located. The **Cabildo,** now a historical museum, is the site of the former town hall; from here began the movement to gain independence from Spain 300 years ago. Also in the plaza is the pink-hued **Casa Rosada,** which serves as the president's office. The 17th-century **San Martín Cathedral** nearby is where José San Martín, the famous liberator, is buried. Also here are the regimental flags Argentine troops have captured in wars and battles and numerous works of art, both lay and religious.

Once you've circled the plaza, walk six blocks west up Avenida de Mayo to **Avenida 9 de Julio,** said to be the widest avenue in the world. Broader even than a

100-yard football field, this major thoroughfare has been subdivided into three streets: 9 de Julio, the central portion; Calle Carlos Pellegrini, the eastern segment; and Calle Cerrito, on the western side. In general, however, refer to this 13-block-long expanse as 9 de Julio.

Stroll down the tree-lined street for five blocks until you reach the 220-foot-high **obelisk** at the intersection of Corrientes (Plaza de la República). As previously mentioned, the obelisk, constructed in 1936, marks the 400th anniversary of the founding of Buenos Aires. Instantly identifiable, the most famous landmark in Buenos Aires, this spot is a good meeting place.

Turn right on Corrientes and in a few minutes you'll find yourself in the movie-and-nightlife center of the city.

Corrientes and the neighboring street, **Lavalle,** are the "Broadway" of Buenos Aires. Stroll two blocks and turn left at Esmeralda. At the next block, Lavalle, veer right. Here are even more film houses, as well as some of the best restaurants, nightclubs, and *whiskerías.* Look for the Ocean movie theater on Lavalle, between Esmeralda and Maipu. Opposite is a small alley, comparable to Shubert Alley in Manhattan, which is the headquarters for ticket brokers. But more useful for planning the evening ahead is the multiplicity of posters listing all the week's major film, sport, opera, and variety-show attractions. Bear in mind that first-run films are usually on a reserved-seat basis. (See "Evening Entertainment" later in this chapter for more information.)

To continue your stroll, keep walking down Lavalle for another block and you'll reach **Avenida Florida**—the city's main shopping street. Turn left and admire the shops on either side of you. One of our favorite sections of Buenos Aires, Florida is closed to traffic all day, when the pedestrian becomes king. The 10-block shopper's paradise is described in detail in our shopping section later in this chapter. Five blocks down Florida is the beautiful **Plaza San Martín,** nestled in a stunningly landscaped park. Two luxury hotels—the Sheraton and the Plaza, both beyond our budget— border the park. Look down Florida beyond the plaza and you'll see a replica of London's Big Ben. There's no need to walk there, though.

Tip: If you're pressed for time, you can cut five blocks from your walk by using the **Saenz Peña** diagonal as you leave the Plaza de Mayo. This will lead you directly to the obelisk, bypassing much of 9 de Julio.

ORGANIZED TOURS

A number of center-city bus tours are available through the many travel agencies in Buenos Aires for about $8. Your hotel clerk will gladly make all arrangements for no extra charge. A 3½-hour night tour through **La Boca** (the colorful Italian section) will cost you $25, including dinner, transportation, and a show. Arrangements can be made through **Buenos Aires Turs,** Lavalle 1444 (tel. 40-2304 or 40-2390).

Two excursions outside Buenos Aires should definitely be considered: One is an all-day visit to an Argentine ranch (*estancia*) for about $45, including meals (see "Suggested Itineraries" later in this chapter); the other is an afternoon river cruise on the **Río de la Plata** for $18.

7. SPORTS & RECREATION

SPORTS

In case we haven't gotten the point across, South Americans are passionate about many things, but there are two areas in which their feelings take on a special frenzy: *futból* and horse racing.

FÚTBOL   The supreme national sports craze in Argentina is what we call soccer and South Americans call *fútbol.* Without exaggeration, it's World Series time every weekend in Buenos Aires, which has 18 first-division (major-league) teams, each owned by a different social-athletic club. And each club has its own huge stadium. This is big business, and no respectable Argentinian would be caught with his club membership dues in arrears. There is great prestige in belonging to the "right" club, with the prestigious Jockey Club in San Isidro ranking highest in status.

First-division games (which draw up to 120,000 fans for ordinary nonchampionship contests) are played usually on Sunday, beginning at 2pm in the summer. For complete schedules, check the Sunday *Buenos Aires Herald*, an English-language daily. Your hotel clerks will be delighted to display their knowledge by rattling off data as to whom is playing where and when.

A must is a visit to the beautiful 80,000-seat **River Plate Stadium,** owned by the River Plate Club. Take the Bartolomé Mitre commuter railway from Retiro station to Belgrano station (60¢ for a round-trip ticket). Buses will then take you to the stadium. Or you can stay on the train to Nuñéz station and walk the short distance.

General-admission tickets, available at the stadium or in advance at the club's office in center city, run about $3. The best seats are $10 to $30, and tickets are usually available the day of the contest—except during the national playoffs or for international games, which take place in the summer and fall (December through April). Minor-league contests are held on Saturday at 2pm at most stadiums.

THE TURF Second only to *futból* is the track, which raises huge sums for social-welfare projects. There are two major tracks in Buenos Aires—the huge government-owned **Hipódromo de Palermo** (tel. 744-6807), a dirt raceway in the suburb of Palermo, whose proceeds go to charity; and the swank grass-turfed **Jockey Club** (tel. 743-4011) in San Isidro, owned by the exclusive Jockey Club. Remember the **Tabac** *confitería,* at Libertador and Colonel Diaz, if you're hungry in Palermo.

The two tracks are open weekends and holidays most of the year. However, the Hipódromo de Palermo is closed in summer. Check the *Buenos Aires Herald* to find out which track is operating when you plan to go or ask your hotel clerk.

The best seat (padded at that) at the Hipódromo will cost $12 to $24. But to get a truer feel of the excitement this sport generates among Argentines, stand at the rail for $1.50. Between races you can sit on stone bleachers and warm your hands (in winter) over potbelly stoves. Programs in either location are free, and the inevitable tout sheet, "guaranteeing" at least three winners, sells for 50¢.

Minimum bet at the Hipódromo is $2. To reach this track, take the Bartolomé Mitre commuter rail line from Retiro station one stop to Lisandro de la Torre station. You will see the track from the train just before arriving at the station. Round-trip fare is 60¢ and trains run every 10 minutes.

LIVE SPORTING EVENTS The Madison Square Garden of Buenos Aires is **Luna Park** (tel. 311-5100), a 26,000-seat arena at Corrientes and Bouchard, six long blocks downhill from the intersection of Corrientes and Florida. The "B" line subway, L. N. Alem station, drops you at the door. Prices for the Saturday- and Wednesday-evening fights are $6 to $15. Ice shows, basketball contests, and the circus usually book the arena. Check the *Herald* for schedules.

RECREATION

BOWLING Enthusiasts head toward **Bola Loca,** on Maipu between Córdoba and Paraguay, a combination restaurant and bowling alley that's open until midnight. Cost is $3 per game. Another option is the **Bowling Bar** at Libertador 13054 (tel. 792-8009).

GOLF The English brought golf to Argentina at the end of the last century. Today there are over 100 golf courses in the province of Buenos Aires alone. The municipal golf course is in Palermo Woods at the intersection of Tomquist and Olleros (tel. 772-7576). Some of the larger hotels, including the Sheraton, can arrange for guest passes to private clubs. For more information on golf in Argentina, contact the **Argentine Golf Association** at Avenida Corrientes 538 (tel. 394-3743).

HEALTH SPA A fine place to keep fit while in Buenos Aires is **Lavalle Stadium**

on the first floor at Lavalle 835. Available here are aerobics classes, gymnastic equipment, exercise machines, and the like for both men and women.

8. SAVVY SHOPPING

Buenos Aires is one of the best bargain shopping cities in South America. Its top values are alligator and lizard handbags, belts, and wallets. Other good buys are sweaters, suede jackets, and handbags. (Incidentally, suede is known here as "antelope.")

SHOPPING ARCADES

Avenida Florida has an abundance of new shopping malls located in arcades on both sides of the street. They contain several levels of stores and every variety of item. Among our favorites are the **Galería Jardín, Galería Via Florencia,** and the **Galería del Sol.**

SHOPPING CENTERS

In addition to the arcades, large upscale shopping malls are opening around Buenos Aires. First on the scene was **Patio Bullrich** at Avenida Libertador 750. Since it opened its doors in 1867, the Patio Bullrich has been a center of commerce as well as a gathering place for Argentina's wealthy livestock breeders and patrons of the arts. Recently converted to a modern shopping mall, it is now home to numerous restaurants, cinemas, and snack bars, plus some of Buenos Aires's most elegant boutiques. Shops are open daily from 10am to 9pm, restaurants and cinemas until 12:30am.

The ultramodern **Alto Palermo** shopping center on the corner of Coronel Diaz and Beruti is home to 180 shops spread out over three levels. Calvin Klein, Benetton, Sergio Tacchini, Christian Dior, Pierre Cardin, Yves St. Laurent, and a score of others are here. An architectural wonder complete with an atrium and glass elevators, the $45-million Alto Palermo opened in October 1990. Take the "D" line on the metro to Palermo's Bulnes station. This shopping center is open daily from 10am to 10pm. Restaurants and cinemas are open until midnight during the week and until 2am on weekends.

A local hang-out, but out of the way for tourists, is the city's largest shopping center, **Unicentro,** located in the suburb of Martinéz.

SHOPPING A TO Z
CANDY

For the best in chocolates, try **Corcega,** with shops all over town. A convenient outlet is at Avenidas Florida and Lavalle. Their boxed candies make excellent gifts.

DESIGNER BOUTIQUES

Licensed boutiques featuring France's top designers are flourishing in Buenos Aires. Prices are generally high, but the quality and style are Paris at half the price. Examples include **Yves St. Laurent** at Florida 925; **Monsieur Pierre Cardin** at Florida 915; **Cacharel** at Florida 849; **Christian Dior** at Florida 832; **Ted Lapidus** at Florida 623; and **Cerruti** and **Calvin Klein** nearby.

If you'd like to investigate local designs, try **Adriana Costantini** at Alvear 1891; **Beatriz Jordán** at Rodríguez Peña 1047; and **Elsa Serrano** with three stores— Mansilla 3045, M. T. Alvear 1602, and the Patio Bullrich shopping center.

An Argentine doctor tipped us off to her favorite boutique, **Dede,** at Maipu and Paraguay, where they sell unique designer items at prices substantially lower than those in most of the other shops. A personal inspection confirmed her opinion.

Drugstore, at Florida 902, on the corner of Paraguay, carries a large selection of Cacharel and Gloria Vanderbilt attire. It has several locations, but the others are a bit out of the way.

For fine men's clothing, you shouldn't overlook **Peter Kent,** with two locations—at Arenales 1210 and Paraguay 654. It's a family-run business owned by Berta and Hector Neer. Another excellent men's shop with an especially beautiful selection of sweaters is **Rhoder's.** It has three locations: Florida 471, Avenida Alvear 1920, and M. T. de Alvear 1175.

FURS

CHARLES CALFUN, Avenida Florida 918. Tel. 311-1147 or 311-4185.
The selection is overwhelming at this fine shop, open since 1953, across from the Plaza Hotel. You'll find excellent values in mink, sable, chinchilla, nutria, guanaco, and a wide variety of foxes. Charles Calfun also stocks fur blankets, rugs, and skins.

DENNIS FURS, Avenida Florida 989.
Here you'll get incredible values in all types of furs, from mink to fox to nutria, many with Yves St. Laurent labels. There is a branch of Dennis Furs in Paris.

FRANÇOIS SABER PIELES, Avenida Florida 963.
Originally from France, François is known all over the world for his original fur designs. He's even done some work with Fendi.

JEWELRY

H. STERN, in the Sheraton, Alvear Palace, and Park Hyatt hotels.
With branches throughout South America and major cities throughout the world, this Rio-based jeweler is known for high-quality gemstones. At his stores in Buenos Aires you'll find an unbeatable selection of aquamarines, topaz, tourmalines, and the like. You can also get Inca Rose (rhodochrosite), a beautiful red stone mined in Argentina. Prices range from $20 to $300. By all means check the H. Stern outlets at the International Airport as well.

LEATHER

LE FAUNE, Santa Fe 925. Tel. 393-9537.
We recommend this shop for fine ladies' handbags in high-fashion leather. On a recent trip here, we purchased a superb blue leather bag. Quality and style here are tops.

LEBON, Avenida Florida 1055 (near the Plaza San Martín). Tel. 311-2300.
This is one of our favorite shops for leather goods. On our last five visits, we haven't been able to resist purchasing leather and suede jackets for ourselves and for gifts. You get attentive service, rock-bottom prices, and high quality here.

MICHELE'S, Avenida Florida 681 (near Viamonte).
Head here for quality wallets, belts, and handbags. Michele's manager, Viviana, will attend to your purchases without high-pressure tactics. Another Michele branch, headed by Michele himself, is at Avenida Florida 537, between Tucuman and Lavalle, next to the Galería Jardín.

PULLMAN, Avenidas Florida 350, Florida 985, and Esmeralda 321.
This is the place to shop for excellent leather attaché cases, briefcases, and men's and women's bags.

CELINE, Avenida Florida 977.
Here you'll find the finest leathers with exclusive French fashions. Owner John Manguel regularly visits Paris and gets the latest designs.

FRENKELS LEATHER WORLD, Avenida Florida 1075 and 1085. Tel. 312-4523.

This family-run shop specializes in shoes for both men and women in alligator, lizard, ostrich, and kidskin. They also design and manufacture fashionable handbags, belts, and wallets, as well as high-fashion clothing in kidskin, suede, and sheepskin.

BERNES, San Martín 1145, on the side of the Plaza Hotel, facing Plaza San Martín.

Prices and quality here are hard to beat, with alligator bags running as low as $100 (and up to $500), while lizard bags range from $125.

LOPEZ, Alvear 640 (near the Plaza Hotel).

While prices here may be slightly higher than at the other shops in town, this is a great shop for browsing. Here you'll find exotic goods. López has wallets ranging in price from $30 down to $20. Somewhat unusual are the sealskin jackets for $30 and up and the snake bags for $90 and up. You can buy an entire hide here if you know what to do with it once you have it.

CIUDAD DEL CUERO, Avenida Florida 940.

This is an unbeatable center for browsing. Here a multitude of shops featuring leather are housed under one roof, making it a good place to check and compare prices of various leather items in the separate alcoves. A few good choices are **Pedro Hidalgo** for an excellent selection of leather jackets at hard-to-beat prices; **Guido Gabrielli's** booth for jackets and furs; and **Camolana** for all-around selections.

PELLICE, Avenida Florida 953.

On each of our last visits here we picked up leather jackets that would have cost triple in the United States. They have held up well, and "mavens" back home have attested to the fine quality of the leather.

AGUE, Cerrito 1128. Tel. 393-3066.

This a popular shop with local ladies. Leather bags and purses here are of the highest quality, with equally high prices.

WILLY KENI & MAYORANO, Alvear 1907.

Not far from the Alvear Palace, this is a good choice for designer leather clothing and handbags (at designer prices).

ROSSI Y CARUSO, Avenida Santa Fe 1601.

Very popular with the horsey set, this store sells everything for the horse and rider. The king and queen of Spain are among the most loyal customers.

MUSIC

Two excellent shops feature the best of Argentinian music, boleros, folklore, and the like. Try **Supermercado del Disco,** at Carlos Pellegrini 481, near Lavalle. This is an enormous shop, featuring records, tapes, and so on of every type of music. The **Broadway Microfono,** at Avenida Florida 463, is a funky shop, with records, cassettes, sunglasses, and the like.

ONCE

The area of Buenos Aires known for its bargain shops selling just about anything is known as Once (pronounced "ohn-say")—New Yorkers might be tempted to call it Orchard Street. If you get hungry, stop for a knish at a nearby snack shop. To get here, take the "B" line subway to the **Pasteur** stop, 10 minutes from downtown.

There are probably as many shops here as on Avenida Florida. If you like to browse, look in at **Salome,** Pasteur 366, where quality sweaters are sold. For fine suede, try the arcade shops at Corrientes 2450; or **Selección,** Corrientes 2300 at Pasteur, and note the factory in the rear where the jackets are made. For handbags, stop at **El Jabali** at Azcuenaga 365. There are many shopping galleries, and many new shops are opening.

Finally, if your sweet tooth needs soothing, try **Confectionary Bombonera Abel,** at the corner of Suipacha and Saenz Peña.

SWEATERS

LOS CUATRO ASES (The Four Aces), Avenida Florida 519.
The best place for sweaters of wool and cashmere, this shop offers handsome men's and women's wool sweaters for $40 to $50, children's slipovers for $35, and warm wool ski sweaters for $45 and up (a wise purchase if you're heading to chilly La Paz), alpaca sweaters for $85, and magnificent cashmere sweaters for $80. There's no bargaining here. We've purchased sweaters here on each trip to Buenos Aires and can't seem to wear them out.

ALEFA S. A., Doblas 164. Tel. 99-1570.
Actually part of an Uruguayan chain, this fine shop specializes in top-quality sweaters at very affordable prices. Take time to browse through their fine selection of blouses, stockings and accessories.

TIPICOS

The stores below carry a variety of Argentinean arts and crafts at reasonable prices. They are, of course, only a selection of the many stores where such *típico* (typical) handmade products are sold in Buenos Aires.

ARTESANIA TROPICAL, Avenida Florida 681 (store no. 23 inside).
Here you'll find intricately carved gaucho heads ($15 and up); bolos ($15); ponchos ($50); and *mate* (tea) sets ($35), consisting of a gourd and a thin tube (called a *bombilla*) through which gauchos drink a dark, strong, bitter tea made of yerba leaves.

MANOS DE AMERICA, Paraguay 769, near Esmeralda.
You'll find a lovely selection of hammocks and woven fabrics. Novelty items include shrunken heads, masks, and Bolivian musical instruments.

EL ALTILLO DE SUSANA, M. T. de Alvear, 515. Tel. 311-1138.
El Altillo specializes in ornamental stones, ponchos, mates, gaucho knives and belts, *boleadores,* woodcarvings, and antiques. Of particular interest are the colorful hammocks and costume jewelry, along with the usual artifacts found in this type of shop.

FRANKEL'S GIFT SHOP, San Martín 1088.
This gift shop specializes in Argentinean handcrafts, yet also carries items from other South American countries, primarily Peru. Throughout the shop's two levels you'll find a fine selection of handmade musical instruments, *boleadores,* woodcarvings, ceramics, *mate* cups, and rhodochrosite jewelry. Leather jackets, alpaca sweaters, bedspreads, and guanaco and cowhide rugs are also for sale here.

TOYS

If you're looking for a gift for a youngster back home, try **Juguetería Avenida,** at Rivadavia 846 near Suipacha. You might also look in on **Juguetería Lito,** nearby at Rivadavia and Suipacha. There are many other toy stores along Avenida Florida recognizable by their children's displays. Another shop offering creative and unusual toys is **Un Mundo de Ensueño,** on Avenida Florida off Lavalle.

9. EVENING ENTERTAINMENT

This is a city of night people. The Porteños delight in dining late (after 10pm) and dancing and drinking even later. The pace here will most certainly do you in unless you nap between 6 and 8pm—an almost necessary respite for the long evenings ahead in some of the best clubs we've seen anywhere. In fact, Buenos Aires ranks with London and Paris in the abundance and variety of its nightlife.

Tip: Most clubs now charge at least $5 for cocktails (although the entrance fee, in most places, does include the first drink). If you're traveling on a limited budget, it might be wise to save your nightclubbing for cities where it is not quite so expensive. A pleasant (and much less costly) form of nightly entertainment is to drop into a local restaurant or cafeteria, take a window seat, and order a bottle of wine to put you in a mellow mood as you observe the city's active nightlife—especially in the "Broadway" section of town (Avenida Florida and Calle Lavalle).

Note: Before stepping out, check the "On Stage and Screen" section of the *Buenos Aires Herald* and the magazine *Salimos* (available at newstands). The *Herald* lists movies, theater, and opera daily.

THE PERFORMING ARTS
OPERA

Buenos Aires boasts a world-famous opera company and opera house—the ✪ **Teatro Colón**—which has been called by Metropolitan Opera soprano Phyllis Curtin "the most exciting opera house in the world"; internationally famous opera singers regularly appear here. During one visit we saw an excellent performance of *Il Trovatore* that cost us $2 per ticket. The best seat was under $10, with standing room (paradero) available for about $1. Tickets, as you can well imagine, are very much in demand—particularly for Wagnerian operas, traditionally presented at the end of the season in September and October. Italian and French operas predominate until then. The box office, located in the Arturo Toscanini side of the opera house, is open from 10am to 8pm, with tickets going on sale at the box office one day in advance. Due to a strong mail-order and advance subscription sale, the only sure tickets available at curtain time may be standing room on the sixth and highest tier—from which you can see and hear perfectly.

Tip: If you stand, arrive about 8:30pm, 30 minutes before curtain time, to get the best position. Drape your program on the iron railing in the standee area. Then wait on nearby benches for the opera to start and your place will be reserved. You can repeat this procedure between acts.

The entrance to the magnificent oval hall, completed in 1908, is red-carpeted, and imposing marble columns support the lobby. On the far side of Avenida 9 de Julio at Tucuman 1161 (tel. 35-1430), the opera house is open from May to October and holds almost 4,000 operagoers. Ballets and symphonies are presented on nonopera evenings. There are no performances on Monday.

THE CLUB & MUSIC SCENE
NIGHTCLUBS & CABARETS

CASA BLANCA, Balcarce 668. Tel. 331-3633.

A spectacular two-hour show at 9:30 and 11:15pm is the lure at Casa Blanca. Set in an attractive colonial home in historic San Telmo, Casa Blanca offers a series of shows featuring the tango with scores of dancers and singers. On our last visit, the artists were forced (by applause) to perform four encores.

Admission: Call ahead for reservations and cover charge.

CASA ROSADA, Chile 318, in San Telmo. Tel. 361-3633.

Casa Rosada competes for patrons with Casa Blanca. The show and beat are similar—but Casa Blanca seems to draw a consistently larger crowd.

Admission: Call ahead for reservations and cover charge.

MICHELANGELO, Balcarce 433. Tel. 343-6542.

If your senses are quickened by the sight of professionals flawlessly executing the bolero and tango, then the historic Michelangelo is for you. It's located upstairs in a 250-year-old cloister, and patrons make it a point to visit the various rooms displaying memorabilia. The dancers and live music are a ritual on Monday to Saturday at 10:30 and 11:45pm. Drinks run about $7.50. The lower floor houses a magnificent international restaurant where a memorable dinner will cost about $15 to $20.

Definitely drop by at least once for a taste of traditional Argentina. Take a taxi (about $4 from the center of town).
Admission: Two-drink minimum. Call ahead to make reservations and check the program.

PERCAL, Entre Ríos 1055. Tel. 27-6178.
Near the Congress Building, this is the city's first adults-only disco. Music here favors old favorites. Open Friday and Saturday from midnight on.
Admission: Two-drink minimum.

TANGO OPEANDO, Balcarce 605.
Although the atmosphere may appear subdued at first glance, tango frenzy is the norm. Everybody joins in at this piano bar.
Admission: $8 minimum.

EL VIEJO ALMACÉN, Balcarce and Independencia. Tel. 362-3702.
This club packs in 250 cheering patrons for its nightly shows (10:30pm and 1:15am). Customers aren't allowed to dance but often sing along. You can nurse your two drinks all night. Don't let the first negative impression of the area deter you. To get here, head eight blocks along Paseo Colón from the Casa Rosada to the corner of Calle Independencia.
Admission: Two-drink minimum (about $10).

DISCOS & DANCE CLUBS

AFRICA, in the Hotel Alvear Palace, Avenida Alvear 1885. Tel. 804-4031.
Africa is one of the city's most popular night spots. Intimate nooks are the attraction, as are the two orchestras that start playing at 11pm. A cab (about $3) is your best bet to get here. Head downstairs.
Admission (including one drink): $13.

HIPPOPOTAMUS, Junín 1787, in Recoleta. Tel. 804-8310.
This is a huge club with a mirrored dance floor and flashing ticker-tape lights. Several levels create a romantic effect, and the dance floor is usually packed until 4am. Hippopotamus attracts a mixed crowd, from late teens and up. Dress here is fairly formal. Open nightly until 4am.
Admission: Prices here are on the high side.

MAU MAU, Arroyo 866. Tel. 393-6883.
The Mau Mau is a must, if only to see the most imaginative decor this side of MGM Studios. Housed in its own building, between Esmeralda and Suipacha, the Mau Mau has high beamed ceilings that overlook individual love seats and barrel-like chairs in the dimly lit main room. This spacious, plushly carpeted club manages to maintain an air of intimacy despite its size (600 patrons squeeze in on weekends). There's North American music, and a samba band takes the stage four times nightly to pound out a frenetic Brazilian beat. While there is no minimum, drinks are high: $10 to $15 on weekends and $10 on weekdays. The Mau Mau has established itself as the city's leading watering hole for the with-it set; many a celebrity has spent an evening here. The intricately carved African-style totem poles, conversation pieces, were replaced after a fire gutted the club in early 1966. Open Monday to Saturday from 11pm to 4am.
Admission: $15.

NEW YORK CITY, Alvarez Thomas 1391, in Belgrano. Tel. 552-4141.
A very informal atmosphere and a lively crowd make New York City tops with the younger set. Special parties are on tap most weekends. It's a bit out of the way; a cab from downtown should cost $5.
Admission: Prices here are reasonable.

PALADIUM, Reconquista 945. Tel. 312-9819.

Probably the most popular rock club (weekends only), the Paladium is in an old structure that was home for an electric utility company. This is a huge club with high ceilings and psychedelic effects that on Friday and Saturday nights draws a with-it young crowd. It's dark, noisy, and fun.

SHAMPOO, Quintana 362 (Recoleta). Tel. 42-4427.

Elegant decor makes this hot new club number one with the "in" crowd. Mirrors and plants complement the large video dance floor where patrons move to the latest releases. There are couchettes arranged throughout the club and a large bar area, perfect for enjoying the two international shows performed nightly at 1 and 3am. Prices here are steep. Drinks run $20. Open nightly from 11pm to 6am.

CLUBS WITH LIVE MUSIC

KARIM, Carlos Pellegrini 1143. Tel. 393-1884.

The 28-and-over crowd seems to congregate at this attractive rectangular club. Three variety shows nightly amuse the customers, who gladly fork over $12 to $15 per drink. Shows are on Monday to Saturday at 11:45pm and 1:30 and 3am. A bonus here for unattached men are the two dozen sexy hostesses who are available as dance partners.

Admission: $15 minimum.

SATCHMO, Aguero 2279 in Palermo Viejo.

Satchmo is one of Buenos Aires's top jazz clubs. Besides great jazz, you can catch an occasional play or stand-up comedian here as well. The drinks come highly recommended.

Admission: Cover charge varies based on the entertainment.

SHAMS, Federico Lacroze 2121 in Belgrano. Tel. 773-0721.

Argentina's best rock and pop stars perform weekends at this large pub.

Admission: Cover charge varies based on the entertainment.

CAFE CONCERTS

Popular with Porteños are concerts held in cafés around town. Check with your newspaper to find the particulars. One such place is the **Café Petit Colón,** near the opera house, at Libertad 523 (across 9 de Julio). This "arty" *confitería* features music and attracts singles as well as couples. Opera posters abound. If you don't like the scene, head downstairs. The **Café Vienés Mozart,** at Esmeralda 754 (tel. 322-3273), is also recommended, for both the excellent Viennese pastries and the exceptional entertainment.

FOR STUDENTS

The whole area around Reconquista is lined with raunchy bars and street hawkers, promising anything if you will only buy the bar girls a drink. However, within this area are exciting clubs popular with students and others young at heart.

Barbaro, on Tres Sargentos off Reconquista, is a noisy student hangout, where the beer and soda flow like wine and peanut shells are ubiquitous. Resembling more an old-fashioned ice-cream parlor (ice cream is served) than a club, the place is jammed, particularly on Wednesday nights, when a combo usually entertains.

FOR GAY MEN & LESBIANS

Buenos Aires's most popular spot for gay men is **Contramano,** at Rodriquez Pena 1082, half a block off Sante Fe. Look for the canopy and head downstairs to the dance floor packed with couples. The bar is a popular pickup area.

FOR MEN ONLY

There are a few clubs that cater to men, who flock here primarily for the female "entrepreneurs" who congregate here nightly. Each club offers live shows.

The fanciest of the lot is **Karina,** at Corrientes 636, between Maipu and Florida. The club, featuring tango music and striptease, is open nightly from 10pm to 4am. There is a $15 minimum. The **Maison Dorée,** on Viamonte between Florida and Avenida San Martín, offers similar talent, musical and otherwise.

Lovely ladies abound at **Black** at Ayacuco 1981, a disco not far from the Alvear Palace. Finally, you might enjoy the regulars at **Mon Bijou,** at Charcas 965, next to La Cuesta. Drinks are $7–$9, and you needn't drink alone.

NIGHTLIFE IN LA BOCA

This jumping, older section of Buenos Aires, known as Little Italy, houses the least inhibited nightspots in the city. A dozen clubs line La Boca's main street, **Avenida Necochea,** which is thronged with Porteños until 5 every morning.

Known as *cantinas,* the clubs are small informal restaurants that offer a fixed-price menu along with a "show." The show usually consists of lively entertainment performed by the owner, singing waiters, and the patrons themselves.

A recommended first stop is a favorite of ours, **La Cueva de Zingarella,** at Necochea 2384, where the owner tries to see that every guest is "king for a moment." Toward that laudable goal, he encourages patrons to take the microphone and do their bit, whatever it is. Magnificent Neapolitan songs flood the club. A four-piece band picks up the tempo and decibels as the evening wears on. By closing time (5am on weekends) the dance floor is packed. Come about 10pm, shortly after La Cueva opens, and savor a five-course Italian dinner (antipasto, ravioli, fish or chicken, salad, dessert, and wine) for about $20.

The same festive atmosphere is found at most of the other clubs we recommend. Among them are **Spadavecchia,** Necochea 1178, large and lavish, and **Il Piccolo Navio,** next to Spadavecchia, where the family owners keep the customers happy and full. Dancers should head for **Rimini,** at Necochea 1234, where a skillful use of drums powerfully accentuates the pulsating music. If you don't want to take a cab, take the "A" train to Plaza de Mayo station. Walk downhill to Avenida Paseo Colón and take bus no. 33 or 64 on the near side of the street. Ask the driver to let you off near Avenida Necochea.

MORE ENTERTAINMENT

MOVIES Porteños apparently believe that Hollywood movies are better than ever, for the city is dotted with attractive film houses featuring the latest U.S. imports. Evening performances, generally with reserved seats, are crowded, so buy your tickets in advance (the afternoon of the evening you wish to go).

Try the **Multicine,** a five-theater complex, each showing a double feature for about $4. As you might expect, Multicine is in the theater district, on Lavalle under the Hong Kong Restaurant.

The "Radio City" of Buenos Aires is the **Metro,** at Cerrito 570, near the opera house. The best seats are $1.50; the price includes (for some performances) a live stage show. Other leading theaters are the **Opera,** Corrientes 860 (tel. 396-1335), which usually has an art display on one of its three levels; and the **Atlas,** Lavalle 869. The **Rex,** across from the Opera, often features live shows.

Another popular area for movie theaters is in and around Avenidas Santa Fe and Callao. The **Cine America,** at Callao 1057 (tel. 410-3818), is modern and shows the latest flicks without dubbing.

Note: On many theater schedules you'll see the word *Vermouth.* This denotes a special cocktail-hour showing at about 5pm, in addition to the usual matinee and evening shows. Most of the first-run movie theaters are on Corrientes and Lavalle.

LATE-NIGHT DINING BY THE SEA The "fisherman's wharf" area of Buenos Aires, where the seafare is fresh and first-rate, is **Los Carritos,** located north of center city along the Río de La Plata on the Costanera Norte, next to the Airport Aeroparque. It has dozens of inexpensive restaurants, most of them open 24 hours. We particularly like **Los Años Locos** (tel. 784-8681; open noon to 6am), on the main street, where most of the *parrilla* platters are about $7 and you can get a small steak (*bife de lomo*) for $5. Wines, cocktails, and beer are equally cheap. Major credit cards are accepted.

There's a terrific Italian restaurant on Costanera Norte, **A'Nonna Immacolata** (tel. 782-1757; closed Monday). Specialties here include homemade pasta, scalope Sorrentina, and chicken alla cacciatore; of course, the seafood dishes are nothing short of divine. Major credit cards are accepted.

To get here by taxi from center city will cost you about $5; or you can pick up bus no. 226 at Retiro station. If you're heading to Los Carritos from the suburbs, take bus no. 407 from Palermo. Tell the driver to drop you off at Los Carritos de la Costanera.

10. SUGGESTED ITINERARIES

LIFE ON AN ESTANCIA In the late 16th century, Juan de Garay, the second founder of Buenos Aires, distributed land grants to his men in order to foster cattle breeding. The region's temperate climate and abundant pastureland favored cattle breeding.

As time went on and earnings increased, the colonial *estancias* became more sophisticated; buildings were constructed with high standards of beauty and comfort in mind. But the men who worked on the plains, the **gauchos,** remained virtually unchanged.

The life of the gaucho is steeped in tradition. Dressed today as he was hundreds of years ago, he wears a broad-brimmed black hat, a tight-fitting shirt, a bolero jacket, baggy trousers, a silver-decorated belt, and leather boots. If it's cold, he also wears a *ruana* (poncho). He carries a gourd and *bombilla* (straw) for sipping *mate* (a type of strong, bitter tea). Finally, he carries on his saddle his *boleadoras,* used to fell stray cattle. These tools of the gaucho are demonstrated and exhibited on the tours. After savoring the urban scene, we're sure you'll be surprised to find this rural excitement so close to Buenos Aires.

Today *estancias* are a favorite destination of visitors to Argentina who are eager to get a firsthand look, combined with more modern pleasures, at the life of the Argentine gaucho. Within a 2-hour drive from Buenos Aires are a few *estancias* that have opened themselves to the public, making for an ideal day trip. We suggest that you go on an organized tour—and we don't recommend such a thing often! These can be arranged directly through the *estancia* or by various travel agencies that arrange tours in conjunction with hotels.

There are three working *estancias* within an hour's drive from Buenos Aires. Most offer overnight accommodations. The **Estancia San José** is a 19th-century Spanish-colonial home located on 400 acres of forest, pampas, and marshland just 50 miles outside the city on the banks of the Paraná river. For information call Claudia at 89-0644. The **Estancia San Ceferino,** 42 miles outside Buenos Aires, combines your visit with a tour of nearby San Antonio de Areco, a traditional Gaucho pueblo with "gaucho" museums and colonial-style buildings as well as handicraft shops. For information call 855-2014.

Las Talas, located 12 miles outside Buenos Aires, was the hiding place of one of Argentina's best-known writers, Juan Bautista Alberdi. Las Talas was his place of refuge from Juan Manuel de Rosas back in 1840. Today the main house is home to a library of 40,000 volumes, many of which are the only ones left in existence, along with the writers personal files. For information contact Etelvina Furt de Rodríguez at 0323-24063 or 783-5720.

MAR DEL PLATA From December through Easter the population of Mar del Plata swells to more than three times its size as visitors from Buenos Aires, other cities across South America, and even Europe throng here to soak up the sun and ambience of this chic summer resort on the Atlantic coast, 250 miles south of Buenos Aires.

Violent surf crashing against rocky shores contrasts sharply with the calm waters of bathing beaches along the city's 40-kilometer shoreline. Garden plazas dot the city, which doubles as a commercial port. Modern buildings surrounding the port neighbor the more rustic chalets of the city's summer residents.

There's plenty to do in town when you're not on the beach, such as strolling through the city's numerous garden plazas and shopping along the pedestrian-only San Martín and Leandro N. Alem. The best buys are the sweaters that are made here and sold throughout Buenos Aires. Museumgoers should head for the **Museo Municipal de Ciencias Naturales "Lorenza Scaglia"** (Natural Science Museum), on the Plaza España at Avenida Libertad 2999, and the **Museo Municipal de Arte "Juan Carlos Castagnino"** (Municipal Art Museum), in the Villa Ortiz Basualdo on the corner of Avenida Colón and Alvear.

Besides the beach, the city is known for its nightlife, specifically for its casinos. Mar del Plata boasts one of the largest in the world, the Bristol Beach Casino. There is another casino next door in the Provincial Hotel. As if the casinos weren't enough, after dark Avenida Constitucíon, fondly referred to as "Avenida del Ruido" (Noise Avenue), comes alive with partygoers out for a night of music and dance. For those who prefer more quiet evenings, there are the oceanfront restaurants and bars along Avenida Martínez de Hoz. The city's finest restaurants are along Calle Alem, as are numerous pubs, many with live music.

Until recently Mar del Plata catered almost exclusively to the elite. Today you'll find hotels and *residencias* in all price ranges. **Hostal del Bosque** at Diagonal Norte 29 (tel. 84-0001), **Bell Mar** at B. Mitre 1966 (tel. 32-287), and **El Cortijo** at Tucuman 2912 (tel. 35-092) offer basic one-star accommodations with doubles near $30. Two-star hotels average $40 and include **Aguila Blanca** at Sarmiento 2455 (tel. 515-172), **Biarritz** at Avenida Luro 2964 (tel. 20-526), and **Torremolinos** at Martínez de Hoz 1805 (tel. 84-1006). Moving upward, the **Rivoli** at Avenida Luro 2260 (tel. 30-051) and the **Gran Hotel Conti** at Cordoba 1929 (tel. 48-433) are three-star hotels with doubles averaging $55. If you're planning a trip to Mar del Plata during high season, it is advisable to make hotel reservations far in advance.

For more information, visit the **regional tourist office** in Buenos Aires at Avenida Callao 237 (tel. 40-7045).

SAN CARLOS DE BARILOCHE   This is a year-round tourist resort offering fantastic skiing (July to September) and trout fishing (December to March). For information, including facilities and where to stay, stop in at the **Río Negro Tourist Office,** Tucumàn 1920 (tel. 45-9931).

Often called the "Switzerland of South America," Bariloche is a 2-hour flight from Buenos Aires. There are numerous hotels to chose from. One of our favorites is the four-star **El Casco.** We urge you to take a city tour. Both full and half-day tours are available, as well as lake tours. Prices range from $11 to $25. Travel arrangements can also be made through American Express at Arenales 707 (Plaza San Martín) (tel. 312-0900, ext. 6015).

VALLE DE LAS LEÑAS   Opened in 1983, Las Leñas has catapulted into one of Latin America's finest ski resorts, featuring 20 miles of ski runs, magnificent slopes, modern hotels, and apartments. Las Leñas is located approximately 700 miles west of Buenos Aires, near Mendoza. The ski areas range from beginner, intermediate, and difficult to expert. Hotel facilities include color TVs, a shopping center, and fine restaurants. Remember, the ski season runs from June to November. For further information and reservations, check the **office of Las Leñas** at Marcelo T. Alvear 540 or the **provincial tourist office** for Mendoza at Avenida Callao 445 (tel. 40-6683).

IGUASU FALLS   One of the world's great natural wonders is located on the borders of Argentina and Brazil near Paraguay. Travelers from the world over are attracted to the mammoth falls (also spelled Iguassu, Iguazu, Yguasu or Iguaçu, depending on which side of the border you're standing on), 50 feet higher than Niagara Falls. (See our excursion to Iguaçu in Chapter 3 since we prefer the hotels on the Brazilian side.)

The most convenient way to visit the falls from Buenos Aires is by bus. Tickets for about $100 can be purchased from **Expreso Singer,** at Reconquista 866 (tel. 31-5894), or from **Tigre Iguazu** (tel. 31-6850). (Prices change monthly, so call to check.) The bus leaves from the terminal at Plaza Once (Bartolomé Mitre and Ecuador) twice daily at 11:30am and 3:30pm. The bus travels steadily, with rest and lunch stops, and the trip takes approximately 24 hours. This is a long, rugged trip, even though the buses have comfortable reclining seats.

You can also reach the falls by train. The trains depart for **Pasados** from Buenos Aires on Wednesday, Thursday, Friday, and Sunday at 8:15 or 10am, arriving the next day. The 8:15 train on Wednesday and Sunday has Pullman coaches with sleeping accommodations. The cost is $100 one way for a private room with twin beds, $105 in the Pullman car with sleeping berths. From Pasados you can take a bus to Iguaçu for $20 one way.

MOVING ON TO MONTEVIDEO If your next stop is Montevideo, consider heading there by boat or plane. **Aerolineas Argentinas** and **Pluna** have daily flights to Montevideo for $75 one way. The flight is half an hour long. Purchase your ticket a day in advance from their office at Calle Perú and Avenida de Mayo.

For a more scenic trip, check out the ferry, leaving daily at 8am from Darsena Sud (South Dock) and arriving in Colonia, Uruguay, 3 hours later. An ONDA bus connects with the ferry for a 3-hour ride into Montevideo, arriving at around 3pm. Take a taxi ($7) to the dock and buy your ticket aboard ship an hour or so before departure, or in advance (preferable!) from **Buquebus** at Córdoba 867 (tel. 313-9861) or **Aliscafos** at Córdoba 787 (tel. 332-2473). One-way fare for the ferry-and-bus trip is $35. You can also transport a car on the ferry for an additional charge. It is also possible to travel to Montevideo exclusively by bus. ONDA buses depart for Montevideo at 10am and arrive at 10pm. The cost is $20 one way or $40 round trip. *Note:* The bus connection from Colonia to Montevideo is somewhat irregular on Sunday. Check the schedule before leaving.

For a quicker trip, try the high-speed hydrofoils run by **Alimar** and **Belt,** at Córdoba 780. These depart daily at 8 and 11am, on Monday to Saturday also at 4:30pm and on Sunday also at 5:30pm. The 1-hour crossing connects with a bus for the 3-hour trip into Montevideo. One-way fare is $80. Again, purchase your tickets in advance at ONDA or Alimar's offices at Avenida Córdoba 1801.

The luxurious way to make the trip is via ships operated by **Flota Fluvial** (offices at Corrientes 389). For a few dollars more you will board a ship that accommodates 700 passengers, with Pullman seating, a comfortable lounge, and café service. The ships leave twice daily for Colonia, at 8am and 2pm, with bus service from Colonia to Montevideo. The trip lasts approximately 6 hours.

If you're pressed for time, consider taking a prop plane to Colonia (the service is run by **Arco**). The 15-minute flight leaves Buenos Aires's Aeroparque daily at 10am and 7pm, with additional flights on Monday and Sunday at noon and 2pm and on Tuesday, Friday, and Sunday at 4:15pm. Once again, the plane is met by an ONDA bus for the 3-hour journey into Montevideo. One-way fare is $35.

If you'd rather travel leisurely, try the overnight ferry leaving from the Darsena Sud at 8pm and arriving in Montevideo 12 hours later. Check with ONDA (see above) for schedules and rates.

CHAPTER 6
SANTIAGO, CHILE

1. INTRODUCING SANTIAGO & CHILE
● WHAT'S SPECIAL ABOUT SANTIAGO
● WHAT THINGS COST IN SANTIAGO
2. ORIENTATION
3. GETTING AROUND
● FAST FACTS: SANTIAGO
4. WHERE TO STAY
5. WHERE TO DINE
6. ATTRACTIONS
● DID YOU KNOW . . .?
7. SPORTS & RECREATION
8. SAVVY SHOPPING
9. EVENING ENTERTAINMENT
10. EASTER ISLAND
11. SUGGESTED ITINERARIES

How magnificent the moment when first you view the awesome Andes on the 2-hour flight between Buenos Aires and Santiago! Not even the Alps compare in beauty to the jagged snow-covered peaks that seem close enough to touch. And if you fly here from Lima or Buenos Aires, you'll see the highest peak in the Western hemisphere—Aconcagua, rising 23,000 feet.

After landing at Santiago's modern Comodoro Arturo Merino Benitez Airport, you'll be struck by the air—cool, clean, crisp, much like a windless Vermont day during ski season—and by the physical beauty of the area. Unfortunately, the modern age has impacted Santiago. There's often a haze of smog similar to that in Los Angeles or New York hovering just above the mountains around the city. However, on a clear day, if you look east, you'll see the Andes, 30 miles away, snow-tipped 9 months of the year. And just about wherever you are in Santiago, you'll find yourself in or near parklike plazas, oases in a busy urban center.

Santiago is a city of paradoxes. Although large (with a population of 5 million), it retains many charming small-town qualities. The pace is leisurely, and the residents appear to be somewhat less worldly than the Porteños of Buenos Aires or the Cariocas of Rio. Yet, the city suppports 12 legitimate theaters, 2 symphony orchestras, 2 ballet companies, and 3 respected universities.

Contrary to popular North American belief, the name *Chile* has nothing to do with the climate, which is really quite mild in winter, but rather is an Indian word meaning "end of the earth." In fact, Chile is called the country of the "three Ws"—wine, women, and weather.

1. INTRODUCING SANTIAGO & CHILE

GEOGRAPHY Chile is directly west of Argentina over the Andes, south of Peru, and south of almost everywhere else. It is, in fact, one of the world's most southerly capitals. The nation itself, shaped like a long, thin pretzel with several bulges, is 2,700 miles long and has an average width of 110 miles.

PEOPLE The population bears a strong northern European resemblance. There is virtually no Inca influence apparent in the faces or culture of its residents, as there is in Peru or Ecuador. There was little intermarriage of the settlers (Europeans) with the Indians.

Today the people are easygoing and unhurried. Many are avid skiers, almost all are rabid *fútbol* and racing fans, and national and international politics are a constant

WHAT'S SPECIAL ABOUT SANTIAGO

Beaches
- [ ] The seaside resort of Viña del Mar, just 2 hours from the city.

Buildings
- [ ] The Estación Mapaocho, an excellent work of fin-de-siècle architecture.
- [ ] The Palacio Cousiño, a glowing tribute to Chile's splendid past.

Museum
- [ ] The pre-Columbian Museum, with its more than 2,000 exemplary pieces of art from Central and South America.

For the Kids
- [ ] Mundo Mágico and Fantasilándia, which are fun for kids of all ages.

Great Tours
- [ ] A tour of one of the vineyards outside Santiago, which is a wonderful way to spend an afternoon.

Great Neighborhoods
- [ ] Bellavista, the city's bohemian quarter, home to artists and intellectuals.
- [ ] Providencia, with its art galleries, cinemas, and theatres.

conversational topic. By the way, the Chilean equivalent of the Argentine gaucho is called a *huaso*. He dominates the rural scene and lives on his *fundo* (ranch).

WHAT THINGS COST IN SANTIAGO	U.S. $
Taxi from the airport to the city center	22.00
Subway ticket	.35
Local telephone call	.15
Double with bath at the Hotel Calicanto (budget)	40.00
Double with bath at the Hotel Santa Lucia (moderate)	60.00
Double with bath at the Hotel Fundador (expensive)	120.00
Lunch for two at Chez Henry (moderate)	10.00
Dinner for two at El Carillon (budget)	8.00
Dinner for two, with wine, at Eladio (moderate)	22.00
One-way *teleférico* ticket at San Cristobal	2.00
Average museum admission	.50
Cup of coffee	1.00
Coca-Cola	1.00

2. ORIENTATION

ARRIVING

BY PLANE Santiago has recently installed in its **Comodoro Arturo Merino Benítez Airport** the same type of system that is used in Rio. When you enter the Customs area, you'll be instructed to press a button that randomly activates either a

IMPRESSIONS

Chile is the pleasantest country in Latin America, bar none.
—JOHN GUNTHER, *INSIDE LATIN AMERICA*, 1941

Everyone is more European here than in Europe.
—GEORGE MIKES, *TANGO! A SOLO ACROSS SOUTH AMERICA*, 1961

---

green or a red light. If it's green, you may continue on your way; if it's red, you must wait for a polite search of your bags.

The best budget way to travel the 13 miles to downtown Santiago, where you'll probably want to stay, is by bus. The comfortable **Tour Express buses** leave from the airport every half hour and head downtown for the corner of Moneda and San Martín. The $1 fare is an absolute bargain. Tickets are purchased on the bus. Another bus line—**Flota Lac**—offers service for only 80¢. You can also take the **metro** to center city for 25¢. The metro stops at 10:30pm.

A **taxi,** which will cost about $22, is the most convenient way to travel. The taxi fare is fixed at $22—per cabful, not per person. Use the buddy system with other travelers.

Note: Santiago has another airport, **Los Cerrillos,** 15 kilometers from downtown. This used to be the principal airport, but now all international flights arrive at and depart from the newer Aeropuerto; Los Cerrillos is currently in military use.

BY TRAIN Trains arrive at the **Estación Central de Ferrocariles** (Central Railway Station) at Avenida Libertador B. O'Higgins 3170. You can take the subway to many of our hotel selections.

TOURIST INFORMATION

The **Government Tourist Bureau (Dirección de Turismo),** whose office is at Avenida Providencia 1150 in center city, will provide free maps and advice; it's open Monday to Friday from 8:30am to 5:15pm. **Wagons Lit** is at Agustinas 1058; **Exprinter** is nearby at Agustinas 1074.

CITY LAYOUT

MAIN ARTERIES Your hotel probably will not be too distant from the main boulevard in Santiago—the 2-mile-long **Avenida Bernardo O'Higgins,** known here as the **Alameda.** This bustling street, which cuts through the heart of the city, is the site of the Biblioteca Nacional (National Library, largest on the continent), the University of Chile, and the Catholic University. A major promenade in Santiago, the Alameda is an unusually beautiful tree-lined street with pedestrian walks running down its center.

To orient yourself quickly to Santiago, keep in mind that downtown—where travelers spend most of their time and money—is shaped like a rectangle. The four avenues and landmarks that shape it are the important **Plaza de Armas** on the north, near which you'll find many hotels and restaurants; **Bernardo O'Higgins** (the **Alameda**), the promenade to the south that draws as many visitors and natives as does the Champs Elysées; the stunning **Cerro Santa Lucía** on the east, a large elevated park that attracts flocks of photographers to its stone stairways and landscaped terraces, with a 230-foot-high summit overlooking all of center city; and the **Plaza de la Constitución** on the west, site of the Palacio de la Moneda, the president's former residence.

The Alameda runs into the **Plaza Italia** and then becomes **Avenida Providencia.** Avenida Providencia stretches for miles (the numbers going up as you head away from the center), and on it are several of our recommended restaurants. At the 2000 block, Avenida Providencia is intersected by the important **Avenida Pedro de**

CHILE

N 0 ▭▭▭▭ 300 mi
482.8 km

Pacific

Ocean

BOLIVIA

ARGENTINA

Atlantic
Ocean

1 Portillo (ski area)
2 Viña del Mar
3 Chilean Lake Region
4 Patagonia (Magallenes)
5 Tierra del Fuego
6 Easter Island

Tacna
Arica
Iquique
Olligüe
Tocopilla
Calama
Mejillones
Antofagastoes
Taltal
Chañaral
Copiapó
← 6
Huasco
La Serena
Coquimbo
Illapel
Viña del Mar 1
Valparaíso 2
★ SANTIAGO
Rancagua
Cuncó
Talca
Concepción
Chillán
Los Angeles
Temuco
Villarrica
Valdivia
3
Osorno
Puerto Montt
Chaitén
Puerto
Aisen
Coyhaique
Puerto
Ibáñez
Puerto
Natales
Punta Arenas 4
Porvenir
5
Tierra del
Fuego
Puerto Williams

Valdivia. Avenida Vitacura also crosses Providencia and houses several of our recommended nightspots.

Continuing out from center city, Providencia successively changes its name to **Avenida Apoquindo,** then to **Avenida Las Condes.** The latter avenues are in the attractive modern sections of Santiago. The "Providencia" bus heads out here from the Alameda, downtown. Better still is the new subway that runs the length of the Alameda and Avenida Providencia. North of center city is the **Mapocho River.**

Remember that from virtually any point in downtown Santiago you can walk to any other center-city sector. Follow our recommended walking tour (later in this chapter) for the quickest orientation.

FINDING AN ADDRESS Three streets undergo a name change at the Plaza de Armas: Ahumada becomes Puente, Estado turns into 21 de Mayo, and Catedral changes to Monjitas. And most streets change as they cross the Alameda. To avoid confusion, check your map carefully. Free **street maps** are available free from the Government Tourist Bureau (see "Tourist Information" above).

NEIGHBORHOODS IN BRIEF

Downtown Over 400 years old, downtown Santiago is home to much of the city's history. The city of Santiago was founded by Pedro de Valdivia, who followed the model established by the city of Lima. The location of the **Royal Audiencia** (Government Palace), opposite the Plaza de Armas and near the river, is similar in both cities, as is the location of the San Cristobal Hill. Just as in many South American cities, the Plaza de Armas has long been the centerpoint of Santiago, host to public ceremonies including celebrations, bullfights, executions, and military drills, as well as commerce.

Since its founding, the downtown area has received several facelifts. The first was at the hands of Italian architect Joaquin Toesca at the end of the 18th century. His contributions include the **Casa de La Moneda,** current seat of the government; the original **Courts of Justice,** now home to the **Chilean Museum of Pre-Columbian art;** and the **Cathedral.**

The city lost its provincial character at the end of the 19th century, when Benjamín Vicuña Mackenna modernized Santiago to prepare it for the new industrial age. His contributions include the remodeling of the **Santa Lucia Hill** and the addition of tramways and horse-drawn carriages to the transportation system.

Modern-day highlights include the hustle and bustle of the Paseo Ahumada, a pedestrian mall dotted with shops, cafés, and street vendors, and the numerous arcades and small streets reminiscent of the commercial galleries in Europe in the late 19th century.

Providencia Past and present meet in Providencia, one of Santiago's busiest neighborhoods. It was first created late in the 19th century to the east of Santiago proper by members of the middle class—civil servants, carabineers, and foreigners, all planning to take up residence there. The neighborhood was named after the **Divina Providencia Church,** located opposite Calle Padre Mariano on Avenida Providencia.

However, it was in the 1920s that the suburb really got its start. The Chilean upper-crust decided to leave their downtown mansions and join the middle class in Providencia. There they set up house in the English style, detached homes surrounded by parks and gardens.

Today, Providencia is home to many of Santiago's cultural attractions, including art galleries, cinemas, and theaters, as well as chic boutiques, restaurants, and pubs. Many of the city's most popular pubs are located on Avenida El Bosque.

Major thoroughfares in Providencia include Avenida Providencia; Avenida Pedro de Valdivia, which runs as far as the National Stadium on Nuñoa to the San Cristóbal Hill; and the tree-lined Avenida Ricardo Lyon, home of some of the city's most lavish mansions. The best way to get to Providencia is by metro. The M. Montt, P. de Valdivia, Los Leones, and Tobalaba stops are in Providencia.

Bellavista Home to artists and intellectuals, Bellavista is best described as Santiago's bohemian quarter, bordered by Calle Loreto on the west and Calle Arzobispo on the east. The San Cristóbal Hill and Mapocho River form natural borders on the north and south.

Bellavista residents include craftspeople and artists who have set up workshops, galleries, photographic studios, and design centers. The neighborhood is also home to theaters, restaurants, bars, bookshops, record stores, and lapis lazuli shops.

Bellavista's bohemian bend is most evident at night, when the quarter comes alive with folk singers, wine and-cheese pubs, coffeehouses, and numerous restaurants serving exotic foods.

3. GETTING AROUND

BY METRO Santiago's new metro has two lines (Line 1 runs east to west, and Line 2 runs north to south) and an extensive network of stops, running all the way from La Alameda to Las Condes. There are maps posted in each station. Buy a ticket (**boleto**) for 35¢ and insert it in a machine to enter. Service stops at 10:30pm every night. Incidentally, the metro here is one of the cleanest we've ever seen.

Subway stations are designated with lighted red signs marked METRO. The station in the center of Santiago is **Universidad de Chile.**

BY BUS Fares are about 35¢. You enter from the front and pay the driver. Buses are usually quite crowded, and a common sight is passengers hanging out the front or back during the rush hour.

In addition to regular buses, there are smaller vehicles called *liebres* (literally, "hares"), which cost 35¢ a ride. These do not run as frequently as the large buses, and standing room is not permitted. Microbuses run during rush hours only.

BY TAXI The simplest way to move about in Santiago is by cabs, which are quite cheap and easy to come by. All taxis are black with yellow tops and are metered. The first kilometer will cost you about 90¢, with an additional amount clocked for every 200 meters. Cost comes out to about $1.50 per mile, with an additional 50% charge after 9pm and on Sunday. It is not necessary to tip the driver.

BY COLECTIVO Jitneylike taxis (*colectivos*) holding up to five passengers zip along the Alameda picking up and discharging passengers. Fare is under $1.

BY CAR You will find car rentals quite expensive; but if you feel you must have a car, you do have a few choices. **Hertz** has an office at Avenida Costanera 1469 (tel. 225-9328). A Daihatsu Giro costs $18.80 daily, plus 22¢ per kilometer; additional costs for insurance and tax apply. There is a branch of **Budget Rent-a-Car** in the Omnium Shopping Center, as well as in the Hotel Carrera. Rentals here run between $36 and $104 daily. Finally, there is an **Avis** in the Hotel Sheraton San Cristobal and another at Eliodoro Yanez 869 (tel. 49-5757). You can rent a Daihatsu Giro for $13.50 per day, plus insurance and tax.

If you're planning a motor trip, the **AAA (Affiliated Automobile Club)**, at Avenida Pedro de Valdivia 195 (tel. 74-9516), will map it out for you and give you helpful hints.

 SANTIAGO

Airline Offices The **American Airlines** office is at Moneda 1160, 9th floor (tel. 671-0919). **Lan Chile's** office is at Estado 10 on the 12th floor (tel. 632-3211). **Varig** has an office at Miraflores 156 (tel. 395-261).

American Express There is an American Express office located at

Agustinas 1360 (tel. 672-2156). The branch in the Hotel Carrera is the authorized American Express agent in Santiago; it's open weekdays from 9am to noon and from 4 to 6pm.

Area Code   The country code for Chile is 56; the city code for Santiago is 2.

Babysitters   The concierge at your hotel may be able to arrange child care.

Bookstores   The **Librera Studio,** at Huerfanos 1178, has a large selection of books in English. There is also a branch at Andres de Fuenzalida 36 (the Los Leones underground station).

Business Hours   Shops are open Monday to Friday from 10am to 1pm and Saturday from 10am to 2pm. **Banks** are open Monday to Friday from 9am to 2pm. **Money-exchange offices** are open from 9am to 2pm and 4 to 6pm.

Car Rentals   See "Getting Around" earlier in this chapter.

Cigarettes   U.S.-made cigarettes are hard to come across. However, Lucky Strike and Viceroy are produced here under license and sold under those brand names. Many local brands are sold, of course.

Climate   Santiago summers (December to February) are much like those of New England, while the fall and spring are much like those of southern California—warm. Winters (June to September) are cool and brisk, but temperatures never dip below freezing. Snow is a rarity.

Crime   See "Safety" below.

Currency   We cannot emphasize too forcibly that the Chilean **peso** is subject to wide fluctuation on the world market, often suddenly and without warning. Adding to the traveler's confusion is that at times there have been enormous variations between the international exchange rate and the "official" rate fixed by the Chilean government. Contact a foreign-currency dealer or international bank to receive up-to-date information and advice *before you leave.* In the event that there is a fixed exchange in Chile below the world rate, you had best purchase your pesos in the United States before departure.

There is no legal limit on the amount of pesos you can bring into Chile, and you should be able to estimate the approximate amount you'll need by perusing this chapter. We are happy to advise that as of this writing there are approximately 350 Chilean pesos per US $1, whether purchased in Chile or internationally.

Currency Exchange   There are two legitimate dollar-peso exchange rates in Chile. The "formal" rate is a commercial rate, primarily used in export/import transactions. Should you change money in a bank, this is the rate you would get. We recommend that you change money at *a casa de cambio,* where you would get the slightly more favorable informal rate. This rate is used for actual currency transactions. For example, try **Casa de Cambio Andino Ocho** at Agustinas 1062 (tel. 699-0842).

Dentists/Doctors   The concierge at your hotel can recommend a local dentist or doctor if necessary. Contact your embassy or consulate for a list of English-speaking dentists and doctors.

Drugstores   U.S.-manufactured drugs are widely available at pharmacies. Two well-stocked, clean establishments are **Farmacia Petrizzio,** at Estado 93, near Moneda (tel. 38-1096), and **Farmacia Franco-Inglesa,** Plaza de Armas at Merced and Estado. The **Farmacia Ahumada,** at Avenida da Portugal 155, and the **Farmacia Reunidas,** Providencia 2012 (tel. 21-0831), are at your disposal 24 hours.

Electricity   U.S. appliances need a converter to be operated on the 220-volt Chilean current.

Embassies/Consulates   The **U.S. Consulate** is at Merced 230 (tel. 71-0133); the **U.S. Embassy** is next to the Hotel Carrera, on Agustinas. The **Australian Embassy** is at Gertrudis Echeñique 420 (tel. 228-5065) in Las Condes. The **United Kingdom Embassy** is at La Concepción 177 (tel. 223-9166) in Las Condes. The **Canadian Embassy** is at Paseo Ahumada 11, 10th floor (tel. 696-2256).

Emergencies   Day and night medical service is available through the **Emergency Clinic** at Estoril 480 (tel. 211-1002). Your hotel clerk will call for you if necessary.

N

Providencia ↑

Plaza
Ibaquedano

Avenida Vicuña Mackenna

Cerro San Cristóbal

Avenida Portugal

Lira

Via Subercaseaux

Cerro
Santa
Lucia

Carmen

J.M. de la Barra

San Isidro

Miraflores

Santa Rosa

MacIver

San Francisco

Monjitas

Merced

San Antonio

Estado

Serrano

21 de Mayo

Arturo Prat

Bernard O'Higgins

Ahumada

San Diego

Puente

Huérfanos

Agustinas

Moneda

Bandera

Plaza
Libertad

Plaza
Bulnes

Rosas

Santo Domingo

Morandé

Plaza de la
Constitución

Catedral

Compañia

Teatinos

Alameda

Amunategui

San Martín

Eyeglasses Opticians are conveniently located all over town. **Optica Moneda Rotter** is a major chain with branches at Huérfanos 1029 (tel. 698-0465), Moneda 1152 (tel. 698-0714), and the Mall Panorámico at Avenida 11 de Septiembre 2155.

Hairdressers/Barbers **Salones Joaquin** at Avenida Apoquindo 4925 (tel. 228-5231) and **Atelier Ricardo Y Nestor** at Avenida Victoria 5816 (tel. 229-8168) are two good choices.

Holidays

New Year's Day	January 1
Epiphany	January 6
San Bernardo's Day *(Festival of Chilean Folklore)*	January 10
Founder's Day *(Santiago founded by Pedro de Valdivia in 1541)*	February 12
May *(Labor)* **Day**	May 1
Battle of Iquique Day *(Commemorating a battle in 1879 between Chile and Peru)*	May 21
Corpus Christi	June 2
Day of the Fisherman	June 29
Assumption Day	August 15
National Day	September 11
Independence Day	September 18
Armed Forces Day	September 19
Columbus Day	October 12
Christmas Day	December 25

Hospitals For the emergency hospital call 222-4422; the heart attack unit is at Luis Thayer Ojed 85 (tel. 251-4444).

Information See "Tourist Information" earlier in this chapter.

Laundry/Dry Cleaning There's a dry-cleaner (*lavaseco*) on the corner of Compañia and Bandera.

Luggage Storage/Lockers If you're planning a short trip you may be able to store your things at your hotel while you're away.

Newspapers/Magazines The *Wall Street Journal, Miami Herald,* and *The Herald Tribune* are available. The Hotel Carrera publishes its own English-language daily and distributes it free to guests and visitors. You can also purchase *Newsweek, Time,* and *Vogue,* as well as English-language books, at the Carrera Hotel.

Photographic Needs Film is readily available in Santiago. Prices, however, are high.

Police If you need to reach the police in the case of an emergency, dial 133 or 131. Otherwise, the switchboard number is 696-4764.

Post Office The main one is near the Plaza de Armas. Look for the CORREO CENTRAL.

Religious Services Check with the concierge at your hotel for additional services. Catholic services in the cathedral are Sunday at 10 and 11am and noon and 1pm. Jewish services are held Sunday at 7:30pm at the Comunidad Israelita de Santiago, Tarapaca 870. Presbyterian services are held Sunday at 11am and 7pm at the Iglesia Presbiteriana Central, Santo Domingo 639 (tel. 33-6987).

Restrooms Restaurants and bars have restrooms for patrons. There are restrooms in most museums. Restrooms in hotel lobbies are usually very accessible.

Safety Santiago is a big city. The same precautions taken in other cities apply here. Watch out for pickpockets and keep close watch over your personal belongings, especially cameras.

Shoe Repairs The concierge in your hotel should be able to direct you to a nearby shoe-repair shop.

Taxes You pay an airport tax of $13.00, in U.S. dollars or in pesos, when you fly from Santiago to a foreign destination.

Taxis See "Getting Around" earlier in this chapter.
Telegrams/Telexes/Faxes Most larger hotels offer fax and telex services. You should be able to send telexes from the Entel-Chile office.
Telephone For local calls, deposit 5 pesos and dial. The best way to make international calls is from the Centro de Llamadas Internacionales Entel-Chile, at Huérfanos 1137. It is open Monday through Friday from 8:30am to 10pm and Saturday from 9am to 2pm. The AT&T Direct program is a great cost-saver. To get an AT&T Direct line, dial 00312.
Television CNN is available in many of the larger hotels.

4. WHERE TO STAY

Santiago, unfortunately, has too few hotels. By our own personal tally, there are fewer than 60 "real" hotels in the entire city, and many of these fail to meet acceptable standards. After careful screening, though, we've come up with a number of recommendations in the moderate price range.

Many good budget hotels, including several of our first-rate choices, are on the upper floors of high-rent office buildings. Government regulations require that hotel rates be posted in every room, and all the hotels listed observe this rule.

Note: Hotels add 18% tax and service charge to your bill. The rates quoted include those costs. However, if you pay cash, you won't be charged the tax.

THE PLAZA DE ARMAS AREA
DOUBLES FOR LESS THAN $50

HOTEL CALICANTO, Santo Domingo 444 (Cal Y Canto metro station).
Tel. 33-3001 or 33-3002. Fax 33-3003. 19 rms (all with bath). A/C TV
$ Rates (breakfast included): $40 double.
The Calicanto is a fairly basic and comfortable hotel not far from the Parque Forestal. Your needs will be personally attended to by owner Juan Carlos Bravo Ponce de Leon.

HOTEL ESPAÑA, Morande 510. Tel. 696-6066. Most rooms with bath.
$ Rates: $27 double with bath. Major credit cards accepted.
This very basic hotel, two blocks from the Plaza de Armas, offers very basic accommodations, plus a TV lounge and dining room. Single rooms generally run about 20% less than doubles.

CITY HOTEL, Compañía 1063. Tel. 695-4526. Fax 695-6775. 72 rms (all with bath). TEL
$ Rates: $45 single; $47 double. Major credit cards accepted.
This outstanding hotel, just off the Plaza de Armas, is entered through an archway leading to a courtyard. On the left is the hotel and on the right is the elegant hotel restaurant (beyond our budget). The atmosphere and furnishings are old-world European. Be sure to reserve ahead.

HOTEL RITZ, Estado 248. Tel. 39-3401. Fax 39-3403. Telex 24-8042 HUSACL. 65 rms (all with bath). A/C MINIBAR TV TEL
$ Rates (including breakfast): $38 single; $45 double.
The Ritz extends from the second to the sixth floor of an eight-story elevator building. The doubles are large and comfortable, and you can rent even lower-priced

singles that have baths with showers only. This is a modern hotel with all the comforts you'll need, plus excellent service.

PANAMERICANO HOTEL, Rosa Rodriques 1314, near the corner of Teatinos and Huerfanos (Moneda Metro Station). Tel. 672-3060. 120 rms (all with bath). MINIBAR TV TEL
$ Rates (including breakfast): $36 single; $40 double. Major credit cards accepted.
This hotel has carpeting, smartly groomed bellhops, and new furnishings. All rooms are spacious and comfortable. There are also a large dining room and conference facilities for 150.

A SPLURGE CHOICE

SANTA LUCIA, Huérfanos 779. Tel. 39-8201. Fax 330-1844. Telex 24-2292CL. 80 rms (all with bath). A/C MINIBAR TV TEL
$ Rates: $50 single; $60 double. Major credit cards accepted. **Parking:** Free.

The keynote in the Santa Lucia is superb service. This hotel occupies the third and fourth floors of an office building; the reception desk is on the fourth floor.
All the rooms are large and airy, and meals are served in a cozy glass-enclosed terrace, which is particularly fetching in warm weather. The restaurant has been redecorated and faces a charming garden.

THE BERNARDO O'HIGGINS (ALAMEDA) AREA

HOTEL RIVIERA, Miraflores 106. Tel. 33-1176. Fax 33-5988. 39 rms (all with bath). TV TEL
$ Rates: $42 single; $48 double. Breakfast $2 extra.
The Riviera, one block from the Alameda, is easily the best choice in this vicinity. The eight-story hotel boasts attractive Spanish-style accommodations and excellent service.

LIBERTADOR HOTEL, Alameda 853, between Estado and San Antonio (Universidad metro stop). Tel. 39-4211. Fax 33-7128. 110 rms (all with bath). MINIBAR TV TEL
$ Rates: $33 single; $40 double. Breakfast $1.80 extra. Major credit cards accepted.

With 11 floors, the Libertador is one of the larger low-priced hotels in town. All the rooms are comfortable in both size and decor.

EDIFICIO SAN RAFAEL, Miraflores 264 (Santa Lucia metro stop). Tel. 330-289 or 396-865. Fax 222-5629. All rooms/apartments with bath. TV TEL
$ Rates: $28 studio, $49 double. Major credit cards accepted.
If you're planning to spend more than a few days in Santiago, the San Rafael may be a good choice. Featured here are studio and double efficiency apartments, comfortably furnished and complete with fully equipped kitchenettes.

NEAR IGLESIA DE SAN FRANCISCO

HOTEL VEGAS STAR, Londres 49. Tel. 38-3225. Fax 38-3225. 40 rms (all with bath). TEL TV
$ Rates: $29 single, double $42. Major credit cards accepted.
Housed in a classic-style colonial building, the Vegas Star is a very good basic hotel.

RESIDENCIAL LONDRES, Londres 54. Tel. 38-2215. 30 rms (some with bath).

$ Rates: $12 single without bath, $14 single with bath; $15 double without bath, $18 double with bath. Cash only.

The best of the budget hotels in the area, this was once a private home and is now primarily a residential hotel. But some transients are accepted. The doubles with baths are unusually large. Be sure to reserve ahead.

NEAR SANTA LUCIA HILL

FORESTA HOTEL, Victoria Subercaseaux 353 (Santa Lucia metro station). Tel. 39-6261. Fax 39-6261. 26 rms (all with bath). A/C MINIBAR TV TEL
$ Rates: $48 single; $66 double; $75 triple. Major credit cards accepted.

A delightful find is the Foresta, behind Santa Lucia Hill near Forestal Park. It's so well known to businesspeople that tourists are the exception here. The Foresta has colonial decor, a panoramic bar and restaurant (on the seventh floor), and fine service.

HOTEL DE DON TITO, Huérfanos 578. Tel. 39-1987. Fax 39-8175. 24 rms (all with bath). A/C TV TEL
$ Rates (including breakfast): $55 single; $68 double. Major credit cards accepted. **Parking:** Available.

This very homey hotel is an excellent choice, with rooms distributed over four floors; TV is available upon request. The friendly management here guarantees a pleasant stay.

NEAR AVENIDA PROVIDENCIA

HOTEL MONTE BIANCO, Isidora Goyenechea 2911. Tel. 233-0427. Fax 233-0420. 35 rms (all with bath). A/C. TV. TEL.
$ Rates (including continental breakfast): $35 single; $40 and up double. Major credit cards accepted.

This very lovely hotel opened in 1990 in Las Condes and is conveniently located near the city's finest restaurants and shops. A multilingual staff, fax machine, private parking, and 24-hour room service make the Montebianco a favorite with business travelers.

HOTEL ORLY, Avenida Pedro de Valdivia 27, just off Avenida Providencia. Tel. 231-8947. 15 rms (all with bath). A/C. TV TEL
$ Rates: $65 single; $72 double.

In the heart of Providencia, the Orly resembles a private house. Note the carved-wood door as you enter. Most rooms are carpeted.

HOTEL PRESIDENTE, Eliodoro Yanez 867 (Salvador Metro Stop). Tel. 225-5019. Fax. 49-1393 (all rooms have a private bath). A/C. MINIBAR. TV. TEL.
$ Rates: $60 single; $70 double. Continental breakfast $2.50 extra. Major credit cards accepted.

The Hotel Presidente is another top notch hotel, Although located on a quiet street, Santiago's finest shopping district, Avenida Providencia, is close by as is the financial district and many cultural attractions. Rooms are attractively furnished and the hotel has its own restaurant and bar.

DOWNTOWN

HOSTAL DEL PARQUE, Merced 294. Tel. 39-2694. Fax 39-2754. Telex 24-2758 HOPAR CL. 14 rms, 13 suites, 2 penthouses (all with bath). A/C TV TEL
$ Rates (including breakfast): $94 double. Major credit cards accepted.

Located across from the Parque Forestal, a wonderful place for strolling or just relaxing after a busy day of sightseeing, this hotel is charming. Rooms are spacious, each with a kitchenette. There are a small bar and a restaurant on the premises.

HOTEL CONQUISTADOR, Miguel Cruchaga 920. Tel. 696-5599. Fax 696-5599. Telex 24088 KONKICL. 120 rms (all with bath). A/C MINIBAR TV TEL
$ Rates: $92 single; $108 double. Major credit cards accepted.
This world-class hotel has attractive rooms on 12 floors. The entrance is off an alley on Estado (between Alameda and Moneda). Top-notch service and conference facilities make the El Conquistador a favorite with visiting businesspeople.

HOTEL FUNDADOR, Paseo Serrano 34 (Universidad de Chile and Santa Lucia Metro Stops) Tel. 632-2566. Fax 632-2566. Telex 341214 HOFUND CK. 105 rooms (all with bath) A/C MINIBAR TV TEL
$ Rates: $105 single; $120 double.
One of the newest five-star hotels in the city, the European-style "El Fundador" is appropriately located in the historic "Paris Londres" district, not far from the city's business-and-commercial center. All rooms have been decorated with comfort in mind, and the personalized service provided by the cordial staff ensures that no guest's needs will go unfilled.

TUPAHUE HOTEL, San Antonio 447. Tel. 38-3810. Fax 39-5240. Telex 24-0842 HUSACL. 209 rms (all with bath). A/C MINIBAR TV TEL
$ Rates (including breakfast): $85 single; $95 double. Major credit cards accepted.
The elegant Tupahue is in an excellent location for business travelers and for those exploring downtown. It has its own pool and piano bar, and all the rooms are carpeted.

PROVIDENCIA

ALOHA HOTEL, Francisco Noguera 146 (Pedro de Valdivia metro stop). Tel. 233-2230 or 233-2352. Fax 233-2494 or 233-2838. 52 rooms, 13 suites (all with bath). A/C MINIBAR TV TEL
$ Rates: $118 single; $130 double. Major credit cards accepted.
The Aloha offers modern comfort in lovely surroundings, with carpeted and tastefully furnished rooms. Among the amenities here are a restaurant, a cafeteria for light meals, a bar, a fitness center with sauna, and a pool.

SAN SEBASTIAN II, Nueva de Lyon 105. Tel. 231-2903 or 231-0393. Fax 232-6564. One- and two-bedroom apts (all with bath). A/C TV TEL
$ Rates: $85 one bedroom; $112 two bedrooms.
The San Sebastian II is the perfect choice if you're looking for a "home away from home"; it offers fully furnished one- and two-bedroom apartments, each complete with a living room, dining area, and fully equipped kitchen. The Providencia is close to restaurants, nightlife, and shopping.

5. WHERE TO DINE

While Argentina and Uruguay are steak countries, Chile is decidedly seafood land, although excellent beef is nevertheless served in most restaurants. Since the Chilean coast is almost as long as the United States is wide, fishing is a major industry in these parts—and shellfish eating is a major pastime. Highly seasoned oysters, lobsters, clams, crabs, and shrimp, widely served in Santiago, are among the finest seafood we've ever eaten.

Typical Chilean dishes include *cazuela de ave* (chicken soup with onions, corn, potatoes, and spices), *pastel de choclo* (pie made with corn and meat), *chupe de mariscos* (shellfish), *humitas* (ground corn with seasoning), and *caldillo de congrio* (eel broth). The world-famous Chilean wines are, of course, consumed in great quantities here, and we recommend that you include them in your dining.

Chileans traditionally eat four meals a day—a light breakfast (coffee and rolls); a heavy lunch, served from 1 to 3:30pm; *once* (pronounced "*ohn*-say"), a sandwich-and-tea snack served from 5 to 7pm; and a late dinner usually eaten after 9pm.

DOWNTOWN

LES ASSASSINS, Merced 297B. Tel. 38-4280.
   Cuisine: FRENCH/CONTINENTAL. **Metro:** Baquedano.
$ Prices: Appetizers $1–$2; main courses $4–$6.
   Open: Mon–Sat 12:30–5pm and 7pm–midnight.
This French restaurant near Forestal Park serves excellent food and is popular with the locals. Try the *steak au poivre*, served with rice, or *lenguado stragon* (fish). An inexpensive lunch might be *omelette de champignon*. The bar is always crowded, so there is often a wait for tables.

CANTON, Santa Rosa 83. Tel. 39-4024.
   Cuisine: CHINESE. **Metro:** Sta. Lucia.
$ Prices: Appetizers $1–$3; main courses $4–$8.
   Open: Lunch and dinner.
For delicious Chinese fare, look no farther than the usually crowded Canton with its three large rooms. Particular favorites of ours are the chicken with almonds, fish with shrimps (*corvina con camarones*), and sweet-and-sour chicken.

CASA SUIZA, Huerfanos 640, at the corner of Ricardo Velázquez. Tel. 38-3113.
   Cuisine: SWISS.
$ Prices: Appetizers $1–$3; main courses $4–$8.
   Open: Noon–midnight.
Casa Suiza is a good choice if you want to linger over lunch on a sunny afternoon. Tables are available outside, and the interior is just as charming. The fondue for two is delicious, as are the meat, chicken, and fish dishes.

DA CARLA, MacIver 577. Tel. 33-3739.
   Cuisine: ITALIAN.
$ Prices: Appetizers $1–$3; main courses $4–$7.
   Open: Lunch and dinner.
This quaint Italian restaurant was recommended to us by an airline employee who lives in Santiago. We tried it one evening and returned the next day for lunch.

CHEZ HENRY, Portal Fernandez Concha 962 in the Plaza de Armas, Tel. 696-6612 or 698-5183.
   Cuisine: CHILEAN/ITALIAN. **Reservations:** Recommended.
$ Prices: Appetizers $1–$4; main courses $3–$10. Major credit cards accepted.
   Open: Daily 10am–midnight.
This is one of our favorites. Chilean and Italian dishes are featured here. Highly recommended is the *pastel de choclo* (chicken and corn) or any of the fish or poultry dishes. To cut your bill, select from the *menu económico,* on which you'll find the likes of noodles Italian style, fruit, and a beverage for just under $3. Of the three large dining rooms, we find the middle one most comfortable.

ELADIO, Avenida 11 de Septiembre 2250, 5th floor, in Providencia. Tel. 231-4244.
   Cuisine: CHILEAN. **Reservations:** Recommended.
$ Prices: Appetizers $2–$4; main courses $4–$10; full meal (with wine) $12. Major credit cards accepted.
   Open: Lunch and dinner.

Eladio has a selection of grilled meats (*carnes a la parrilla*). Other Eladios are at Avenida Ossa 2234 (tel. 227-0661) and at Pio Nono 241 (tel. 77-3337).

STEAK HOUSE, Huérfanos 1052. Tel. 38-0079.
Cuisine: INTERNATIONAL.
$ Prices: Appetizers $1–$3; main courses: $4–$8.
Open: Daily 11:30am–midnight.

The Steak House is near Ahumada, downstairs in a shopping arcade (there's a sign on the street). It's huge, with several dining areas. At the central counter you pick up your main course—grilled fish, steak, or chicken. Salads, potatoes, and other side dishes cost extra. There is another branch at Huérfanos, on the corner of MacIver.

LOS ADOBES DE ARGOMEDO, Argomedo 411. Tel. 222-2104.
Cuisine: CHILEAN. **Reservations:** Required.
$ Prices: Appetizers $3–$5; main courses $8–$14; dinner from $16.50. Major credit cards accepted.
Open: Mon–Sat lunch and dinner.

★ For a night of sheer fun, plan to have one meal at this huge restaurant with three dining rooms, located in one of the oldest sections of Santiago. The decor resembles that of a typical Chilean ranch, and the waiters dress like *huasos* (Chilean cowboys). Dinner prices here are not cheap as they cover nightly entertainment—live shows feature singers, dancers, and stand-up comedians. Try the lemon chicken (delicious!) or the succulent grilled steak; seafood dishes are even less expensive. Expect to spend the entire evening. Show time is 10:30pm.

EL CARILLON, Huérfanos 757. Tel. 39-2213.
Cuisine: INTERNATIONAL. **Reservations:** Not required.
$ Prices: Appetizers $1–$3; main courses $3.50–$7.
Open: Daily 10am–midnight.

⑤ El Carillon, which is inside an arcade, is a budget traveler's dream. It has a cafeteria for self-service and several levels of tables. There is a grill in one area where meats, fish, and poultry are sizzling, and there are fresh salads. The selection is huge. At night the lights dim and the music starts.

LA JACARANDA, Huerfanos 640. Tel. 39-3754.
Cuisine: SEAFOOD/FRENCH/AUSTRIAN. **Reservations:** Recommended.
$ Prices: Appetizers $2–$5; main courses $7.50–$11. Major credit cards accepted.
Open: Noon–4pm and 7–11pm.

★ Another favorite is La Jacaranda, located beyond the Lido Theater through a narrow walkway. The Yugoslavian proprietor, Ivan Kamberg, speaks seven languages fluently. Ask him to show you the framed autographs of Robert and Ethel Kennedy, who dined here in 1966. You can sit in either of the two neatly maintained rooms. Service is first class. Try the *corvina jacaranda;* coq au vin; cannelloni; or *el candelon,* a seafood crêpe. Homemade strudel is a terrific dessert.

SAN MARCO TRATTORIA, Huerfanos 618. Tel. 333-6880.
Cuisine: ITALIAN. **Reservations:** Recommended.
$ Prices: Appetizers $1–$4; main courses $5–$12. Major credit cards accepted.
Open: Lunch and dinner.

Our vote for best Italian food goes to this festive restaurant a block from Santa Lucia Hill. Checkered tablecloths brighten the room, and travel posters of Italy adorn the walls. The specialty here is the mixed pasta plate, which combines cannelloni, lasagne, and ravioli. It's enough for two, and with a salad and glass of wine it makes a great supper. The veal scaloppine and the dessert flan are wonderful, as is a bottle of excellent domestic white wine. Remo Zoffoli (born in Rimini) takes great pride in his restaurant and is always available for assistance.

DON CARLOS, Avenida Agustinas 1022. Tel. 698-1499.
Cuisine: ARGENTINE. **Reservations:** Required.
$ Prices: Appetizers $2–$4; main courses $7–$10. Major credit cards accepted.

Open: Lunch and dinner.

If you prefer your meat grilled on an Argentine *parrilla,* this is the place for you. We recommend the *bife chorizo,* the baby *bife,* and the roasted half chicken. There are also some fine seafood dishes on the menu. Don Carlos has a folkloric show nightly.

A SPLURGE CHOICE

LE DUE TORRI, San Antonio 258. Tel. 33-3799.
   Cuisine: ITALIAN. **Reservations:** Recommended.
   $ Prices: Appetizers $4–$8; main courses $12–$18.50; *menu económico* $22. Major credit cards accepted.
   Open: 12:30–3pm and 8:30–11pm.
This elegant restaurant has a strictly Italian motif and decor. The waiters, dressed in starchy white, provide first-class service. Most main dishes are $12, with steak running as high as $18.50. The *menu económico* includes an appetizer, a main dish, fruit, and coffee (no real bargain by our standards). Wines run from $8.75 to $13.

PROVIDENCIA & BEYOND

LA PAVITA, Avenida Pedro de Valdivia 047. Tel. 231-9812.
   Cuisine: FAST FOOD. **Reservations:** Not required.
   $ Prices: Full meal $4–$6.
   Open: Lunch and dinner.
This one is one of our favorites. A substantial meal, consisting of salad, turkey with rice, dessert, and beverage, is less than $6. It is also a good place to stop for a quick sandwich or light meal.

SALVAJE, Providencia 1177. Tel. 231-9853.
   Cuisine: INTERNATIONAL. **Reservations:** Not required.
   $ Prices: Full meal $3–$6.
   Open: Lunch and dinner.
Salvaje is a great stop for a quick lunch. Sandwiches average $2.50, while a steak with salad is $3.00. Don't bypass the natural juices.

LOS BUENOS MUCHACHOS, Calle Ricardo Cumming 1031. Tel. 698-0112.
   Cuisine: CHILEAN. **Reservations:** Not required.
   $ Prices: Appetizers $1–$3; main courses $4–$9. Major credit cards.
   Open: Lunch and dinner.
Having celebrated its 50th anniversary in 1989, Los Buenos Muchachos is something of an institution. It's a terrific spot to savor typical Chilean foods. *Empanadas, pastel del choclo, parrilladas,* and all types of seafood are served. There's typical Chilean music with dinner nightly.

LA PIZZA NOSTRA, Providencia 1975. Tel. 231-9853.
   Cuisine: PIZZA. **Reservations:** Not required.
   $ Prices: Complete meal $5–$10.
   Open: Lunch and dinner.
Near Pedro de Valdivia is this colorful trilevel place, where photos of famous Cosa Nostra figures adorn the walls. Almost two dozen pizzas vie with the daily specials for customer interest. The lower lunch-bar area is a popular meeting place. One-person pies, served on wooden planks, are $4.50, with a variety of ingredients, while large pies can hit $7.

PALACIO DANUBIO AZUL, Reyes Lavalle 3240. Tel. 231-3588.
   Cuisine: CHINESE. **Reservations:** Recommended. **Metro:** Line 1 to Golf Station.
   $ Prices: Appetizers $1–$3.50; main courses $3–$9. Major credit cards accepted.
   Open: Lunch and dinner.
This excellent Chinese restaurant is large and attractively decorated. Some of the most

exquisite and exotic Chinese food is served here. We recommend the *sopa de aletos de tiburón* (a soup made with shark meat), the *pato piña* (sweet-and-sour duck), the *congrio futon* (eel), and the *filete con champiñones* (filet with mushrooms).

AQUI ESTA COCO, Concepcion 236A. Tel. 46-5985.
   Cuisine: SEAFOOD. **Reservations:** Required.
   $ Prices: Appetizers $5–$8; main courses $7.50–$12. Major credit cards accepted.
   Open: Lunch and dinner.
A block from Avenida Providencia is this superior seafood restaurant. Set in a private house decorated with anchors and diving bells, it has several small dining rooms. The *ceviche* is superb, as is the *jardín de mariscos,* a cold seafood plate. The large bilingual menu is confusing to read, but virtually everything is well prepared.

COCO LOCO, Avenida El Bosque Norte. Tel. 23-1308.
   Cuisine: SEAFOOD. **Reservations:** Required.
   $ Prices: Appetizers $4–$7; main courses $7.50–$15. Major credit cards accepted.
   Open: Lunch and dinner.
The suburbs boast one of the best seafood restaurants in Santiago. Coco Loco offers the perfect combination of fine food served in the delightful surroundings of an old colonial home that's been tastefully converted. It has abundant special touches: soft candlelight, strolling musicians, and courteous service. The house wine is excellent at $3.50 a bottle. Try the *chirimoya,* a delicate fruit native to Chile. *Note:* Since many dishes are à la carte, it is easy to spend $20 per person without batting an eyelash.

EL GIRATORIO, Avenida 11 de Setiembre 2250, 16th floor. Tel. 251-5789.
   Cuisine: INTERNATIONAL. **Reservations:** Required. **Metro:** Los Leones.
   $ Prices: Appetizers $4–$7; main courses $8–$15. Major credit cards accepted.
   Open: Lunch and dinner.
El Giratorio offers fine international cuisine served in elegant candlelit surroundings with an unbeatable view of Santiago. As the restaurant revolves, you'll enjoy a different view of the city with each course.

EL PARRON, Providencia 1188. Tel. 223-9821.
   Cuisine: ARGENTINE. **Reservations:** Recommended.
   $ Prices: Appetizers $2–$5; main courses $6–$12. Major credit cards accepted.
   Open: Lunch and dinner.
At El Parrón Argentine-style *parrilladas* are featured. You can choose from a large selection of dishes on the bilingual menu. The steaks run from $7.25 to $10.50. Also popular are less expensive fish and poultry dishes. A fireplace adds to your enjoyment, as will the service and decor. Head beyond the entrance to the rear.

A SPLURGE CHOICE

EL CLUB GRAN AVENIDA, Gran Avenida 5067. Tel. 522-65131.
   Cuisine: INTERNATIONAL. **Reservations:** Required. **Metro:** Departamental.
   $ Prices: Appetizers $4–$7; main courses $8–$12. Major credit cards accepted.
   Open: Dinner only.
This Spanish-owned restaurant is a "must." Located in the southern part of town, it has been serving excellent food for over 30 years. The specialties here are beef and seafood. Plus, there's music as well as dancing every night.

LAS CONDES

HOSTERIA LAS DELICIAS, Raul Labbe 340, corner of El Arrayan. Tel. 47-1386.
   Cuisine: CHILEAN. **Reservations:** Recommended.
   $ Prices: Appetizers $5–$8; main courses $8–$14. All major credit cards accepted.
   Open: Dinner only.

This restaurant offers an excellent selection of typical Chilean dishes, accompanied by folkloric music.

HEREFORD GRILL, Avenida El Bosque 0355. Tel. 231-9177.
  Cuisine: STEAKS. **Reservations:** Recommended.
  $ Prices: Appetizers $3–$8; main courses $7–$12. Major credit cards accepted.
  Open: Lunch and dinner.
The Hereford Grill is usually crowded with businesspeople at lunchtime. Fairly upscale, it is best known for its steaks and the fine sauces served with them.

CHEZ LOUIS, Avenida Las Condes 9177. Tel. 229-4175.
  Cuisine: FRENCH. **Reservations:** Recommended.
  $ Prices: Appetizers $4–$8; main courses $8–$15. Major credit cards accepted.
  Open: Mon–Sat 8–11:30pm.
Here *ancienne cuisine* is served in a lovely setting that was originally a private residence. There are an antique carriage at the entrance and tropical birds throughout.

THE BALI HAI, Avenida Colón. Tel. 228-8273.
  Cuisine: POLYNESIAN. **Reservations:** Recommended.
  $ Prices: Five-course dinner $28. Major credit cards accepted.
  Open: Dinner only.
The Bali Hai offers a pleasant, typical Polynesian–Easter Island show, complete with a singer, dancers, and a comic. There are 25 entrées to choose from. The only drawback is that it has become a bit of a tourist trap in recent years.

SPECIALTY DINING

LIGHT FARE For your first morning meal in Santiago, try **La Merced,** one block from the Plaza de Armas, at the corner of San Antonio and Merced. Breakfast here—eggs, toast, and coffee—should be around $3. A good choice at lunchtime is the *menu ejecutivo* or a pizza. Other good choices on the same block include **Cafe Danté,** across the street; **Papa Pollo,** where a complete meal, including a quarter chicken, french fries, bread, a dessert, and a beverage, is less than $2.25; and **Centro Pizza.** Two new self-service restaurants have opened nearby: **Paparazzi,** on the corner of Huerfanos and San Antonio, and **Silvestre,** on Huerfanos between Estado and Ahumada.

  Mermoz, Huérfanos 1046, near Ahumada, is a popular eatery with pizzas, from $2.50 to $4.75, that are filling. Seafood dishes are $3.50 and up, and most entrées are under $5.50. The four-course lunch of the day for $4 is popular.

  Santiago's version of New York's Zum-Zum, and a favorite for lunch, is **Fritz,** on Huérfanos across from the Teatro Opera. Amid Bavarian scenes, you can order fabulous hot dogs (*vienesas*) with side orders of potato salad and other goodies. A small steak sandwich (*lomito*) is $2.25 and beer is 85¢. Counter service only. Look for the large sign outside.

  Similar is the usually crowded **Fuente Alemana,** on the Alameda, near the Plaza Italia, known for its excellent huge sandwiches. Prices are about the same as at Fritz.

  Next to Fritz on Huérfanos is the colorful **Savory,** where you can have a tasty steak (*churrasco*) sandwich for $2.50. Also recommended is the ham (or chicken) sandwich ($1.75) and the hamburgers ($1). There is a tearoom in the rear, and you can take the pastries out. Another Savory is at Ahumada 327, between Huérfanos and Compañía.

  For dessert, try one of the more than 30 different flavors being scooped out at **Bravíssimo,** an ice-cream parlor on the same block.

  Another favorite of ours is **La Naranja,** on Teatinos near Huérfanos, next to the Panaméricano Hotel. Look for the bright-orange sign and ready yourself for delicious breaded chicken (*pollo apanado*), burgers, pizzas, and roast-beef sandwich, with either table or rapid counter service. Another outlet is on the Alameda near Calle Nueva York.

  El Naturista, serving natural food with a vegetarian menu, is at Moneda 846. It opens for breakfast Monday to Friday at 8am and stays open until 9pm (on Saturday until 4pm). A breakfast of juice, fruit salad, bread, and beverage is $1.50. Main dishes range from $2.75 to $6.25. Another vegetarian restaurant, **El Vegetariano,** is located at Huérfanos 827, in the Galería Victoria. A three-course lunch here will run slightly over $3. You can stop by late in the afternoon after shopping and sightseeing for an *once* of cookies, ice cream, and coffee for $2.75.

Café do Brasil, on Huérfanos, at Bandera, has a counter and a few tables. It serves hot dogs, sandwiches, burgers, and ice cream—all inexpensive and good for take-out. Its next-door neighbor, **Bar Nacional,** offers five-course lunches for $4. These are listed in the window, so check to see if anything strikes your palate before you enter.

The **Domus Quick Lunch,** on Bandera between Agustinas and Huérfanos, serves a marvelous *bife lomo* (steak), with rice or potato, for $3.90. There is also a daily *plato diario* consisting of a hot plate for $4.50. Sandwiches range from $1.50 to $3.75. You have your choice of table or counter service. **El 27 de Nueva York,** a small eatery, is open for breakfast, lunch, and *once* only. Nueva York is a tiny one-block street that runs from La Bolsa (the Stock Exchange) to the Alameda. There is a daily three-course lunch, plus sandwiches, pastry, and drinks.

For a fuller lunch, head to Agustinas and MacIver, two blocks from Santa Lucia Hill, where you'll find the clean **Nuria Quick Lunch,** not to be confused with the more expensive Nuria restaurant/nightclub next door. The Quick Lunch has a grocery store in front and offers counter service only. A steak-and-noodle casserole (*tallarines con lomito*), with fresh-fruit salad and coffee, runs about $4.75; more popular with the office workers who crowd the Nuria is a type of hot dog, *bien essas,* served with a tomato-onion relish, for $2.00. The usual lack of seats attests to the quality of the food.

Burger Inn, a Burger King lookalike, has several branches, with large ones at Estado 326 and Ahumada 167. Hamburgers with all the trimmings are $1.85, and fried chicken is $2.25. Soft drinks and fries are also served. It's open from breakfast to dinner. **Charlie's,** on Agustinas, is an air-conditioned three-level restaurant. Continental breakfast here is only $1.50, and a three-course lunch of a quarter chicken, a salad, and a drink is only $2.75. Most other entrées are under $3.50.

Pizza Inn, on Huérfanos at MacIver, is a counter-only stop for lunch on the go. If you're in Providencia, a good spot for a fast bite is **Gatsby,** at Avenida Providencia 1984. In Las Condes there is a **McDonald's** not far from the Hyatt at Avenida Presidente Kennedy 5313, with a **Pizza Hut** at Avenida Apoquindo 5489. There's even a **Kentucky Fried Chicken** at Avenida Vitacura 6345.

ONCE   From 5 to 7pm in Santiago is not the time for cocktails as much as it is the time for tea or coffee and sandwiches. This snack time, called *once* (meaning "11"), is a relaxing prelude to the late dinner hour and is a very civilized habit that we North Americans would do well to pick up.

Once is a custom that local historians trace back to the time when the man of the house would secretly refer to his favorite 5pm drink, *aguardiente*—a potent alcoholic beverage—as *las onces* (the 11-letter drink). In this manner, theoretically, his wife was unaware of his imbibing.

Café Paula has virtually cornered the *once* market with five tearooms. All are open from 7:30am to 9:30pm. Danish pastries, strudel, cookies, and beverages are served at small tables or stand-up counters. Shoppers should head to the Paula at Ahumada 343, across from the Gobelinos department store, while theatergoers will find the branch at San Antonia 218, opposite the Municipal Theater, the most convenient. Two others are in the Pasaje Matte, at 302 and 960, and the last is at Moneda 915. Breakfast is served at all of them.

Café Colonia, at MacIver 161, is a comfortable spot with good service. Try their delicious cakes, pastries, small sandwiches, and hot chocolate. Ice cream is served, too.

One of our favorite stops for *once* is the **Café Santos,** downstairs at Ahumada 312, where the delicious goodies—trays of pastries and sandwiches, served with pots of tea, coffee, or hot chocolate—will tempt you to linger. Generally, you can have a sandwich, pastry, and beverage for $3.50, and the pastries are good enough to take home—as many patrons do.

ESPRESSO Dotting Santiago are small espresso and coffee shops that open early and close well after midnight. We like to stop at an espresso place late in the evening for a nightcap on the way back to the hotel. Many are stand-up establishments, but some have tables. They are leisurely spots where conversation is endless. You'll find that many of your friendships with Chileans begin in espresso places.

Two of our favorites are the **Haiti** and the **Café de Brasil**, both inexpensive and always crowded. The stand-up Haiti, a popular businessperson's meeting place, is on Ahumada, between Agustinas and Moneda. Try the house specialty—*leche con fruta,* a refreshing fruit milkshake—and the unusual varieties of coffee. The Brasil, conveniently located on Morande, near Huérfanos, has tables, but the service is quite leisurely. At either you can stay as long as you like with only a cup of coffee. **Café Caribe,** next to the Haiti, is popular with stockbrokers who work in the area.

6. ATTRACTIONS

SUGGESTED ITINERARIES

If You Have One Day Walk around downtown Santiago, taking in some of the attractions. Also visit Bellavista and Cerro San Cristobal.

If You Have Two Days Day 1: Same as above. Day 2: Shop in Providencia and take a winery tour; or take a day trip to Valparaíso/Viña del Mar or local ski areas, depending on the season.

If You Have Three Days Day 1 same as above. Days 2 and 3: Overnight trip to local ski area or combine winery tour with overnight trip to Valparaíso and Viña del Mar.

If You Have Five Days or More Depending on the season, how much time you have, and your interests, we recommend that you begin your stay with a tour of downtown Santiago. If time and your budget allow, we urge you to go to Easter Island, Patagonia, or the Lake Region.

THE TOP ATTRACTIONS

PARQUE METROPOLITANO and Cerro San Cristobal.

⭐ Comprising the hills known as San Cristóbal, Chacrillas, Piramide, and Cerro Blanco and covering an area of 712 hectares, the Parque Metropolitano is one of Santiago's major natural attractions. The park has a zoo, two pools, picnic areas, restaurants, playgrounds, a chapel, and botanical gardens, making it a favorite with residents on the weekends. It also draws visitors because of the wine tastings offered here.

A quaint funicular railway, which makes an almost vertical ascent starting from Calle Pio Nono, will carry you to the most striking vantage point in Santiago, the 1,115-foot-high Cerro San Cristóbal, located across the Mapocho River a mile from center city.

The railway takes you to the top, stopping en route at the first level, where a zoo—complete with dromedaries—is a must visit. The second level is where several passengers disembark, because they live here! (Homes dot the side of this small mountain, and to reach them the residents use this elevatorlike railroad.) The third and final level is close to the top of San Cristóbal—the highest point in Santiago. Trees, shrubbery, and fountains make this one of the most beautiful sights we've ever seen. And above this level is a path leading to the actual summit, where there is a huge statue of the Immaculate Conception—it's partially the work of Frédéric Bartholdi,

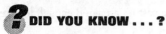
DID YOU KNOW . . . ?

- If a map of Chile were superimposed on a map of North America, the country would stretch from the Yukon Territories in Alaska to Baja California in Mexico.
- The *cueca*, the national dance so commonly performed in Chile, simulates the courtship between a rooster and a hen.
- Scotch sailor Alexander Selkirk spent 5 years shipwrecked on the Juan Fernandez Islands, about 400 miles west of Valparaíso. His experiences inspired Daniel Defoe to write *Robinson Crusoe.*
- The name *Chile* is a corruption of the Aymara Indian word meaning "where the land ends."
- Chile's first European settlers were groups of government-sponsored German immigrants who settled near Puerto Montt in the 1850s. Today this area is still distinctly German.
- The driest spot in the world is Chile's Desierto de Atacama (Atacama Desert) near Calama. The average rainfall there is 0 inches, and up until 1972 it experienced a 400-year drought.

the famous sculptor who did the Statue of Liberty. San Cristóbal is stunning in the evening, when the statue is illuminated and the Santiago lights are clearly visible. But if you plan a late visit, bring a heavy sweater: Temperatures drop sharply at sundown.

In winter, the funicular leaves every 15 minutes on Saturday and Sunday from 9am until 7:30pm; during Summer it operates daily until 9:30pm. The fare is $1.50 round trip.

For an incomparable panoramic view of the city, take the **teleférico** (cable car) to the top of San Cristóbal. You can catch it at the Oasis station on Pedro de Valdivia. The first stop is the Tupahue station. The final stop is **La Cumbre,** just 150 meters from the statue of the Virgin. It runs on the same schedule as the funicular and takes about 20 minutes. The fare is $2.

To reach San Cristóbal, take a taxi ($3), a bus marked LA GRANJA PIRAMIDE or LA GRANJA ZOOLOGICO, or the metro to the Plaza Baquedano stop and walk up Pio Nono toward the park. Your taxi can drive you to the top for an extra $1, but you can easily walk to the funicular (our preference). Walk along Merced to the end of the street; take the bridge over the Mapocho River and walk along Pio IX (Pio Nono). In a few minutes you'll be at San Cristóbal. There are plenty of stores along the way to pick up snacks.

Alternatives to the funicular and the *teleférico* up to San Cristóbal are the open-sided buses affectionately called *tortugas* (turtles). Fare is $1 each way. They are your best bet to take you to the pools, open to the public in the summer ($4).

We like to combine the funicular and the *teleférico,* taking the funicular up to the top and then, to enjoy the spectacular view of Santiago, taking the *teleférico* on the way down.

Open: 8am–10pm.

MUSEO NACIONAL DE HISTORIA NATURAL, in Quinta Normal Park. Tel. 90-011.

There's a 500-year-old—at least—boy here, almost perfectly preserved. The Mummy of Cerro El Plomo, is the major attraction of this museum. Its body was found in 1954, frozen in a mound of snow at the 16,000-foot-high summit of El Plomo Mountain near Lake Titicaca. Anthropologists speculate that the boy was of a pre-Inca civilization, judging from the ceremonial objects found on his person. Apparently, he was a sacrificial victim to the sun god, a conclusion drawn from the kneeling, crossed-leg position of the body.

Admission: 50¢.

Open: Tues–Fri 10am–12:30pm and 2–5:30pm; Sat–Sun and holidays 10am–5:30pm. **Taxi:** $3 from downtown. **Bus:** Take no. 5, marked QUINTA NORMAL.

PALACIO DE BELLAS ARTES (Palace of Fine Arts), Forestal Park and Calle Jose Miguel de la Barra. Tel. 33-0655.

Opposite the U.S. Consulate, three blocks north of the Cerro Santa Lucia near the Mapocho River, is the Parque Forestal, a small park that houses the Palacio de Bellas Artes, home to the **Museo Nacional de Bellas Artes,** the

Museo de Arte Contemporaneo, and the **Museo de Arte Popular Americano.** Built in 1910, this neoclassical palace is a copy of the Petit Palais at Versailles. Art lovers from all over the world come here to see the work of Chilean sculptress Rebecca Matte, a student of Rodin.
Admission: 50¢.
Open: Tues–Sat 10am–6pm; Sun 10am–1pm. **Metro:** Baquedono.

MUSEO HISTORICO NACIONAL (National History Museum), Plaza de Armas 951. Tel. 38-1411.

★ Even if you have no interest in Chilean history, you'll enjoy this historical museum. As you enter, you pass a military display and approach the rooms dedicated to the colonial and conquistador eras. Collections of flags, cannons, carriages, armor, and furniture are featured. Upstairs the emphasis is on the era of independence, with a model of Santiago in 1820 as well as the printing press of Camilo Henriquez, who published the famous *Aurora de Chile* in 1812. The model of the 1850 Plaza de Armas will be of interest when you contrast it to the present plaza. Downstairs are relics of the pre-Columbian period.
Admission: Tues–Sat 30¢; Sun free.
Open: Tues–Sun 10am–5:30pm; holidays 10am–1:30pm.

MUSEO DE ARTE COLONIAL (Colonial Art Museum), Calle Londres 4. Tel. 39-8737.

Located next to the San Francisco Church, this museum houses an excellent collection of religious paintings, including a valuable collection from the Cuzco School representing the life of St. Francis of Assisi. This is probably the largest and best-preserved example of 17th-century American art in South America. Also here is the Gold Medal and Pergamin awarded to the Nobel Prize–winning Chilean poetess Gabriela Mistral.
Admission: 25¢.
Open: Tues–Sat 10am–1pm and 3–6pm; Sun 10am–2:30pm. **Metro:** La Moneda.

MUSEO PRE-COLOMBINO, Calle Bandera 361. Tel. 695-3627.

This fabulous museum features pre-Columbian art and artifacts and is located downtown at Bandera, at the corner of Compania, in the building that once housed the royal customshouse. The once-private collection contains over 2,000 exemplary pieces of artwork from Mexico and Central and South America spanning 4,500 years. The setting is very modern, with subdued lighting, well-placed spotlights, and benches. A written description of the artworks in English may be borrowed from the reception desk.
Admission: 30¢.
Open: Tues–Sat 11am–2pm and 4–8pm; Sun 11am–2pm.

MUNDO MAGICO, 6100 General Bonilla. Tel. 790-0150.

At this museum located in a park near the airport, you can spend a pleasant afternoon learning about Chile and viewing it in miniature, illustrated by region, with emphasis on its historical, economic, and physical aspects. This is a good way to get an idea of the parts of Chile you may wish to visit.
Admission: $2.
Open: Jan–Mar, Tues–Fri 3–9pm; Sat–Sun 11am–9pm. Apr–Dec, Sat 3–9pm; Sun 11am–9pm. **Metro:** Estación Pajaritos.

EL PALACIO COUSIÑO, Diechiocho 438. Tel. 85-063.

Fashioned after Versailles, the Cousiño Palace is proof of the splendor of Chile's past. This elegant mansion was built in 1871 by the wealthy Cousiño Goyenchea family, whose fortune, like most other fortunes during this period, was made in mining. It was decorated by European artists and craftsmen. The mansion was acquired by the municipality of Santiago in 1941 and has been host to many important dignitaries, including Belgian King Balduino; Presidents Joao Figueiredo of Brazil, Gregorio Alvarez, and Charles de Gaulle of France; and Israeli Prime Minister

Golda Meir. Sumptuous chandeliers, exquisitely carved and painted ceilings, and lovely artwork and furniture, as well as beautiful parquet floors, make this home a showplace. The guide speaks English.
Admission: Free, but guide appreciates tip.
Open: Winter, Tues–Sun 10am–1pm; summer, Tues–Fri 10am–1pm.

LA CASA COLORADA, Merced 860. Tel. 33-0723.
La Casa Colorada is Santiago's best-preserved example of colonial architecture. Built in 1769, it gets its name from the red color of its stone-and-stucco exterior. Once the home of Count Don Mateo de Toro y Zambrano, president of the First Junta of the Chilean government in 1810, it now houses the Museum of Santiago, which chronicles the history and development of Santiago.
Admission: 25¢.
Open: Tues–Sat 10am–6pm; Sun 10am–2pm.

ESTACION MAPOCHO (MAPACHO RAILROAD STATION). Between Calles Bandera and Balmaceda and the River Mapocho at the end of Forestal Park.
No longer a working railroad station, the Estación Mapocho is now host to temporary art exhibitions as well as flea markets and antiques shows. A national landmark, it was designed by Chilean architect Emilio Jecquier and inaugurated in 1913. **Metro:** Baquedano.

A WALKING TOUR

Santiago can be appreciated best by walking its streets for a couple of hours. The best place to begin is at the most important plaza in the city, the **Plaza de Armas,** which has been considered the heart of Santiago since its origin in 1541. Designed by the conquistador Pedro de Valdivia, it was used for military exercises. Today, it's used as the reference point from which all distances in Chile are measured. Ringing the square are the main post office, city hall, and the cathedral of Santiago.

Stroll around the handsome shrub-filled plaza and wind up on **Avenida Compañía** on the south side. Facing the plaza, now walk left for two blocks to **Morande,** where you should again make a left. Ambling up Morande, you'll pass Santiago's three main shopping streets, **Huérfanos, Agustinas,** and **Moneda.** Huérfanos has become a wide shopping mall, closed to traffic until MacIver. Ahumada is also a promenade from the Plaza de Armas to the Alameda.

Continuing along Morande, you'll come to the **Plaza de la Constitución,** at Agustinas and the Avenida Bernardo O'Higgins (the Alameda). Adjoining the plaza is the **Palacio de la Moneda,** the government palace. It served as the mint in its early days. It is one of the new Spanish colonial-style structures in Santiago. The changing of the guard takes place at 10am every other day.

Back on Morande, stroll to the **Alameda,** where two plazas—**Libertad** and **Bulnes**—face each other across the wide boulevard. Several federal buildings are located here, and civil servants throng the area's restaurants. Originally, the Alameda was the riverbed of the Mapocho River, until the river was diverted. Now it is a wide, 2-mile-long promenade lined with trees and statuary that Sunday strollers find irresistible. Turn left on the Alameda and try the center promenade walk. After 1½ blocks, cross to the far side of the street, where you'll see the **University of Chile,** one of the city's finest examples of 19th-century architecture. The present university was founded by Andres Bello in 1842 to succeed the Universidad Real de San Felipe. The University of Chile, University of Santiago, and Catholic University are the three major universities in Santiago.

Two blocks farther down you'll pass the 400-year-old **Church of San Francisco,** with its colonial-style red tower. The meticulously etched sacristy doors date from 1700. Next to the church is the **Museo de Arte Colonial–San Francisco,** which features colonial religious paintings in a cloister setting; it's open Tuesday to Sunday from 10am to 1pm. Admission is 50¢.

Now cross back to the near side of the Alameda and continue on for another block, until you come to the largest library in South America, the **Biblioteca Nacional,** which houses Chile's national archives. The adjacent structure, around the corner on Miraflores, is the **Museo Histórico,** home of Indian relics, colonial costumes, folk art, and paintings by Chilean artists.

Two blocks ahead is the **Cerro Santa Lucia,** a park on the hill where Santiago was founded by Pedro de Valdivia. The 230-foot summit is reached via numerous paths and stone stairways. Ready your camera for shots of the Andes above and the city below. A popular folk art museum is located at the summit, where there are also a number of quiet nooks in which you might like to partake of a sandwich.

The final stop is the **Teatro Municipal,** Santiago's major theater, which you reach by heading back to center city along Agustinas until you arrive at San Antonio. The theater is the site of every important musical, theatrical, and dance event in Santiago.

ORGANIZED TOURS

Companies offering tours of Santiago and the nearby countryside include the **Gray Line,** which you can contact by calling 696-0518 or by speaking to the concierge of your hotel; and **SportsTour,** at Teatinos 333, Suite 1001 (tel. 696-8832). Companies specializing in adventure tourism include **Altue Expeditions,** at Encomenderos 83 (Providencia) (tel. 232-1103); **Atacama Desert Expeditions,** P.O. Box 1020, Antofagasta; **Explorandes S. A.,** Matias Cousino, 150 Office 254; **Pablo Sepulveda Expediciones,** Mateo de Toro y Zembrano 1453 (La Reina); and **SportsTour** (see above).

VINEYARD TOURS

At the end of the 16th century, the cultivation of grapes and wine production was introduced in Chile by Spanish settlers. By 1840 Chile had become the largest wine producer in South America. Shortly thereafter, with the introduction of French vines—including Cabernet Sauvignon, Pinot Noir, Sauvignon Blanc, Sémillon, and Merlot—exports of Chilean wine began to increase considerably. A winery tour is a delightful way to spend an afternoon. Many of Chile's most important vineyards are less than an hours' drive from Santiago and are open to the public. If you'd like to go with a prearranged tour, both **Gray Line** (tel. 696-0518) and **SportsTour** (tel. 696-8832) offer winery tours.

VIÑA CANEPA This family-run winery was founded in 1939 by José Canepa Vaccarezza. Sauvignon Blanc, Sémillon, Cabernet Sauvignon, and Cot Rouge are produced here. Visitors are welcome at any time of the year if they call (tel. 557-9121) at least 48 hours in advance to arrange a tour. The free tours are given in French, English, or Spanish.

Getting There The vineyard is located in Maipu at Camino Lo Sierra 1500, just 15 kilometers from the center of Santiago. Take the Pan American Highway to exit 28 and turn right on Camino Lo Sierra.

VIÑA CONCHA Y TORO Concha Y Toro is one of the best known Chilean wines in the United States. The vineyard was founded by the Marques de Casa Concha Melchor de Concha Y Toro and Ramón Subercaseaux in 1883. Tours are given daily from 10am to 1pm and 3 to 6pm (except New Year's Day, Good Friday, May 1, September 11, and Christmas Day. You don't need to call (tel. 850-3123) in advance.

Getting There The vineyard is located in Pirque, 25 kilometers from the Plaza Baquedano. Take a *colectivo* from the Plaza Baquedano or a bus from Avenida B. O'Higgins to Puente Alto and then a *colectivo* to Pirque. If you drive, take Avenida Vicuña Mackenna past Puente Alto to Pirque. At the end of the road turn right.

VIÑA UNDURRAGA Undurraga is another well-known Chilean wine in the

United States. The winery was founded in 1885 by Francisco Undurraga Vicuna, who brought back the finest wine stocks from Europe, including German Riesling and French Sauvignon, Cabernet, Merlot, and Pinot Noir. The winery is open to the public Monday to Friday from 9:30am to 12:30pm and 2 to 5pm. Free tours are given in Spanish, English, or French. Groups should contact Mr. Pedro Undurraga (tel. 817-2346) to make arrangements.

Getting There   Take the Santa Ana road to Melipilla Km. 34. You can also travel by bus (*liebres Talagante*).

7. SPORTS & RECREATION

SPECTATOR SPORTS

THE TRACK   Santiago has two tracks—the fashionable **Club Hípico** and the lower-betting-scale **Hipódromo Chile.** The Hípico, open Sunday, Wednesday, and holiday afternoons, is situated near the Parque O'Higgins, the largest park in the city and site of many parades and festivals. While a taxi (about $2.50) is recommended for reaching the Hípico, you can also get here via bus no. 55 (marked AVENIDA ESPANA), which runs along the Alameda, or by Microbus no. 35, which leaves from Agustinas and San Antonio.

The Hipódromo Chile, open Saturday, every other Wednesday, and holiday mornings beginning at 8am, is reached by bus no. 60 (marked OVALLE-NEGRETE), which you get at the Plaza de Armas; it will drop you at the track in a few minutes.

Note: The horses run clockwise at the Hípico and counterclockwise (as in the United States) at the Hipódromo.

FUTBOL   Like all large South American cities, Santiago has dozens of soccer teams and 8 to 10 major matches every weekend. You can see a first-class match every weekend between February and December at the 80,000-seat **Estadio Nacional;** in January, international matches are scheduled. General admission is $2 to $4. Take bus no. 3 (marked IRARRAZAVAL). A taxi ($2.50) is simplest. *Fútbol* fever is usually highest here in mid-August and early December, when the University of Chile and its traditional rival, Catholic University, play their semiannual matches.

RECREATION

GOLF   Chile is home to many fine golf courses; the best are private. Some of the better-known clubs around Santiago are **Club de Golf los Leones,** Avenida Presidente Riesco 3700 (tel. 231-3406); **Prince of Wales Country Club,** Las Aranas 1901 (tel. 227-2025); and **Club de Polo San Cristóbal,** Mons. Escriva de Belaguer 5501 (tel. 228-4743).

GYM CLUBS & AEROBICS   Even when you're away from home you shouldn't have to give up your fitness regimen. A few of the gyms in town are **Rancho Hans Gildemeister,** Mons. Escriva de Belaguer (tel. 233-1204); **Alicia Francke,** Los Militares 6010 (tel. 246-0562; call for the addresses of downtown branches); and **Gimnasio Gustavo Flores,** Alameda 624A in Santa Lucia (tel. 38-3904). We recommend that you phone ahead to check on the policy concerning visitors.

HORSE TREKKING   **Altue Expeditions** offers one- to five-day horseback treks from Cajon de Maipo to visit the waterfalls, lakes, and hot springs in the high mountain area. A similar trek can also be done on mountain bikes through Altue or Pablo Sepulveda.

If you prefer to limit your riding to the ring, try the **Club de Equitación La Reina** at Talinay 11040 in Reina Alta (tel. 273-1136). Classes are taught in English and Spanish. Another option is the **Club de Polo** at Monseñor Escriva de Belaguer 5502 (tel. 228-4743).

SKIING   Skiing is the most popular participation sport in Chile (see "Easy Excursions" later in this chapter).

TENNIS   Stop at the **Club de Tenis Jaime Fillol** (tel. 224-1147), at Camino de Asis 630, San Francisco de Las Condes, which has fine facilities and is owned by Chile's most famous tennis player. You can rent equipment; the staff will try to set up a game for you. Also, the **Sheraton San Cristóbal** has some courts, but they're only for guests.

8. SAVVY SHOPPING

The major shops in Santiago are located on the streets between the Plaza de Armas and Alameda O'Higgins. Store hours are Monday to Friday from 10am to 7:30pm; Saturday 10am to 2pm.

DEPARTMENT STORES

Your best bets are **Almacenes Paris** with two branches—Avenida Libertador Bernardo O'Higgins 815 (tel. 38-0771) and Avenida 11 de Septiembre 2221 (tel. 232-5045; **Falabella** in the Parque Arauco Shopping Center (tel. 242-0889); and **Ripley** with two branches—San Diego 200 (tel. 696-8013) and Avenida Libertador Bernardo O'Higgins 3031 (tel. 92-245).

SHOPPING ARCADES

Center city has several shopping arcades that house a variety of specialty shops offering exclusive lines at reasonable prices. For good arcade browsing, head for the modern **Galería España,** on Huerfanos, between Estado and San Antonio. A favorite shop of ours is located in the rear of the arcade—**Gundert,** which sells unusual copper and gift items at rock-bottom prices and has a regular nontourist clientele. While you're there, take a peek inside **Casa Chile,** just a few doors down.

   The **Pasaje Matte** is a huge arcade with entrances on all four sides on Huérfanos, Estado, Ahumada, and Merced. Always busy, it's dominated by large stalls selling jewelry and handicrafts. There are also some very nice restaurants here if you're looking for a good place to take a break. The **Galería Imperio,** nearby on Huérfanos, between Estado and San Antonio, is another good choice for window shopping.

SHOPPING MALLS

The **Parque Arauco,** on Avenida Kennedy 5413 in Providencia (take Metro Line 1 to the Escuela Miliar and then the metrobus to Parque Arauco), is home to two department stores and more than 215 specialty shops, restaurants, and boutiques. It's open daily from 10am to 9pm. The even larger **Cosmocentro Apumanaque,** on the corner of Avenida Manquehue Sur and Apoquindo, offers a special service to tourists—transportation from the hotel to the mall. (Or take the metro to Escuela Militar and the metrobus on Avenida Apoquindo.) It has over 300 shops and restaurants, as well as special exhibitions and games for children. Our favorite place for a break here is **Helado Pavaroti.**

   The **Mall Panorámico,** at 11 de Septiembre 215, in Providencia, between Avenidas Leon and Guardia Vieja, has over 130 lovely boutiques. To get there, take Metro Line 1 to the **Los Leones** station. A new shopping center is under construction, the **Alto Las Condes.** It promises to be the largest in Santiago.

SHOPPING FROM A TO Z

CANDY

The huge **Confitería Serrano,** near the Conquistador Hotel, sells delicious candy (loose or in boxes).

CHILEAN CRAFTS

GALERÍA ARTESANAL DE CHILE (CEMA), Avenida Portugal 351.

Located a little out-of-the-way, several blocks on the far side of the Alameda, this should be your first shop to browse. Here you'll find a complete array of Chilean art filling each of the rooms of this attractive house. On exhibit (and for sale) are mobiles, ashtrays, jewelry, ponchos, tapestries, and a complete assortment of copper products. This is a good place to get a feel for prices and variety. Other outlets of CEMA are at Avenida Providencia 1642 and at the airport. CEMA is a cooperative of Chilean artists run by the president's wife.

UIMPALAY, Huérfanos 1162 (Local 3). Tel. 672-1395.

Here you'll find a beautiful selection of genuine Chilean handicrafts, including lapis-lazuli jewelry, silver and copperware, pottery, weavings, *mantas* (cloaks), and wood carvings from Easter Island. One of our most treasured finds here was a copper mask inlaid with lapis lazuli and malachite. Uimpalay is run by the Chilean Society for the Promotion and Commercialization of National Handicrafts.

CHINCHILLA

To identify with the wealthy for a time, skip over to **La Super Furs,** at MacIver 230, 2½ blocks from Huerfanos, where you can gaze at chinchilla—as well as mink, fox, nutria, and beaver—at your leisure. Owners Jacobo Mazor and Raul Ojeda speak English.

COPPER & WOODCUTS

CASA BRISTAL, Portal F. Concha, Plaza de Armas.

This excellent shop features high-quality copper items, as well as fine woodcuts from Easter Island. The English-speaking proprietor will be glad to explain how you can distinguish Easter Island woodcuts from local efforts.

CHILEAN ART, at the San Cristobal Hotel.

One of our favorite shops, it has the largest copper-products selection in the city. Ashtrays and tea kettles start at $8; attractive candlestick holders are $15 a pair. Also, you can pick up wood statues imported from Easter Island for $6 to $30.

CHILE LINDO, Agustinas near Ahumada.

This popular shop features handcrafted copper items. Note the fantastic copper mobiles.

RAUL CELERY, Refugios del Arrayan 1572.

This very talented artist specializes in copper. You'll find a wonderful assortment of his works here, ranging from pencil holders to copper wallhangings. Raul also has a showroom in the Holiday Inne Crowne Plaza.

DUTY-FREE SHOPS

The airport has a series of duty-free shops. You can purchase fine *típicos* and Chilean wines.

FASHION

GUCCI, at the corner of Agustinas and Ahumada and at the Parque Arauco Shopping Center.
This well-known Italian boutique has found its way to Santiago. Prices and quality here are equivalent to those in New York City.

LEO SCHANZ, Merced 535.
High-quality custom-made stretch slacks or ski pants for men and women can be ordered from this upscale boutique near Miraflores, for $40 and up. Women's orders are delivered within 24 hours. Regular slacks are similar in price.

JEWELRY

H. Stern has showrooms at the Carrera, San Cristóbal, and Hyatt hotels. Not only do they sell Brazilian gemstones, all in 18-karat gold settings, but they also feature lovely pieces using two of Chile's natural gems. Deep-blue lapis lazuli, which has become very popular here, and brilliant green malachite are set in rings, pendants, and neckpieces; set in silver, they're so inexpensive that you can stock up on them for gifts. Stern products come with a one-year international guarantee.

Along Bellavista are numerous workshops and showrooms that specialize in jewelry featuring stunning blue lapis lazuli as well as other semiprecious stones, including turquoise, malachite, and obsidian. However, there's not much variation from store to store in price or design. A few that merit some attention are **Chungara,** at Bellavista 0299; **Lapislazuli Cordillera,** at the corner of Bellavista and Salvador Donoso; and **Rofor,** at Bellavista 0284. A noteworthy exception, **Lapislazuli Hector Cespedes,** at Bellavista 0430, features beautiful original pieces, many of which are designed by Hector's lovely wife, Ema Lazcano.

PRE-COLUMBIAN ART

GALERIA ERRAZURIZ, Suecia 84, Providencia. Tel. 231-4993.
For years Chile native Jaime Errazuriz has been one of the foremost authorities of pre-Columbian art in Columbia. He has two galleries there: one in the Hotel Tequendama in Bogotá and the other in Cartagena.

SKI EQUIPMENT

Try **Casandina,** on Merced, a half block beyond Leo Schanz. Here you can get parkas ($30 to $70), gloves ($9 and up), and hats ($5 and up).

---

9. EVENING ENTERTAINMENT

THE PERFORMING ARTS

Santiago is a city of theaters, all open year-round and all featuring plays, concerts, and ballet. The major theater is the old **Teatro Municipal** (built in 1857), on the corner of Agustinas and San Antonio, which offers opera in September and October and ballet and concerts during the other 10 months. Seats range from $2.50 to $10 for most events. A special event could cost more.

THE CLUB & MUSIC SCENE
DISCOS & DANCE CLUBS

LAS BRUJAS, Avenida Príncipe de Gales 9040, in La Reina. Tel. 273-1072.
Las Brujas has a circular disco alongside its restaurant in an exotic setting, on a quiet lagoon, complete with swans, surrounded by weeping willows and old gnarled

trees. When the moon is out, romance is in the air. Look for the twin witches on their broomsticks at the entrance.

Admission: Two-drink ($8) minimum per couple.

CASSAMILA, Alvaro Casanova 298A. Tel. 273-2782.

We're partial to this club, located in a large private house, where the inside has at least three levels, reached by slides and firepoles as well as stairs. Its round dance floor, on the lower level, is illuminated by colorful spinning lights, and the music never stops. Tables at all levels overlook the lights of the city. Open Monday to Saturday from 7pm.

Admission: $10 minimum per couple.

DISCOTHEQUE EVE, Avenida Vitacura 5480. Tel. 218-1323.

This is perhaps the city's most elegant disco. Eve's, which draws equally from the mod and the mink crowds, is a large club with carpeted floors, glass walls, and a fireplace. From downtown, a cab ($5) is your best bet to get here. Drinks are a high $7. Open Tuesday to Sunday to 5am.

Admission: $8 minimum per couple.

KASBBA, Suecia 081, in Providencia. Tel. 231-7419.

Kasbba is a unique club in town. Its Middle Eastern theme and elegant decor combine to create a special ambience that is hard to forget. Open daily.

Admission (including two drinks): $12 per couple.

LA SCALA DISCOTHEQUE, Americo Vespuccio, in La Pirmamide. Tel. 242-6930.

For one of the most unforgettable views of Santiago, drop in at this very exclusive club. Occasionally, La Scala opens during the week for special parties and promotions. Drinks are $7. Open Friday and Saturday from 9pm.

CLUBS & PIANO BARS

CHE BANDONEON TANGO BAR, Apoquindo 4976, Tel. 206-1322.

If you think the tango is exclusive to Argentina, you're wrong. It's alive and going strong at Che Bandoneon. This small yet pretty club is located in Las Condes. Count on taking a cab to get here and home. Open Monday to Saturday from 8:30pm to 2:30am.

Admission (including one drink): $8 (cash only).

CONFETTI'S, Avenida Apoquindo 5002. Tel. 208-7053.

This very elegant piano bar, reminiscent of clubs on the East Side of Manhattan, is a popular spot for a nightcap. The very intimate setting is complemented by candles on the tables and a beautiful bar. Open Monday to Thursday from 5pm to 3am and Friday and Saturday from 7pm to 3am. Drinks run from $2 to $8.

GRINGO'S BAR, Pedro de Valdivia 2153. Tel. 223-0877

If you don't care about the music but want a comfortable place to have a drink and quiet conversation, stop in here. It's popular with locals and tourists.

MISSISSIPPI PUB & BAR, Parque Arauco—Building 2, local 43

Decorated à la old Mississippi with antique photos and posters, this is a favorite stop for a light night supper before heading home. Tops on the menu are club sandwiches, omelettes, crepes, quiche, mini pizzas and grilled chicken. There's live music weekends. This is a great place to mingle with the locals.

1800 PUB, San Pascual 72. Tel. 208-7550.

Designed to look like an old castle, this is a favorite of ours. It's a great place to have a steak and a beer and relax.

EL RELOJ, Avenida Kennedy 4387. Tel. 208-0815.

An equally good choice where you can come and unwind over dinner or drinks is El Pub Reloj. European-style antique furnishings and a Swiss-style fireplace give El Pub Reloj an especially homey feeling.

ROMEO, in the Barrio Alto, Avenida Vitacura 6764. Tel. 212-7117.
For comedy, try this club. A few different acts are featured nightly. You'll need to take a cab here, around $5 from downtown.

FOR MEN ONLY

NIGHT AND DAY, Agustinas 1022.
Night and Day is a downtown spot offering a show and privacy. Enter the arcade and head downstairs. The show features striptease "artists." The doormen are a source of information for unattached male travelers. Drinks are a steep $13 to $15.

PROVIDENCIA 1100 (that's also the address).
This is a cabaret with a strip and simulated-sex show. There are lots of single women around to help you spend your pesos.
Admission: First drink is $15.

SPLURGE CHOICES

Scattered throughout the city are dozens of clubs called *boîtes*, which feature live music and late suppers.

ENOTECA, on San Cristobal Hill. Tel. 232-1758.
Enoteca is new, attractive, and expensive. The well-prepared specialties are seafood and Chilean foods, and the service is impeccable. Several dining rooms are available, with typical Chilean folksingers and dancers moving between them. Make sure to visit the fabulous wine cellar here—it's open for tasting and buying. Expect to spend at least $15 per person for dinner with wine.

EL GIRATORO, Avenida 11 de Septiembre 2250, 16th floor (in Providencia). Tel. 232-1827.
This is a great place to stop for a drink and enjoy the changing panoramic view of the city. It spins once an hour, and you'll see all parts of the city. The restaurant's special dinner is worth sampling, if it's something you like.

10. EASTER ISLAND

On each Wednesday and Sunday at noon, a Lan Chile jet lifts off from Benítez Airport, Santiago, and soars off over the South Pacific. Three and a half hours, and 2,300 miles, later, it sets down on a tiny 45-square-mile triangle—Easter Island—the most sparsely inhabited island in the world. It has several names: Easter Island, the English translation of the Spanish *Isla de Pascua,* was given to it by a Dutch sailor who landed there on Easter Sunday; *Rapa Nui* is the name used by the 1,200 native islanders, who use it to refer to their language and themselves—Rapa Nuians. Some 800 Chileans make up the rest of the population. All 2,000 of the island's residents live in the town of **Hanga Roa.**

Most visitors arrive on Rapa Nui on package tours that include transfers, sightseeing, and accommodations. As prices are high on the island, a packaged tour may be your best bet. If you've come on your own, stop at the Tourist Office kiosk at the airport. They have a list of the hotels (only three) and pensions available; most have no phones. And there are no buses, taxis, or even cars on the island. Local tour operators will meet the plane and while driving you to your accommodation will try to sell you a tour. It's the only way to get around, so listen carefully and compare. **Iorana Tours** (tel. 82) has modern minivans and friendly guides. English is a hit-or-miss thing, so you'll need a guidebook. You may do better with tours offered by the **Hotel Matua** (tel. 242). Tours can be individual or in groups. Excursions on horseback are also available. Guides speak English, German, French, and Spanish.

Tours booked through **SportsTour** in Santiago will be guided by Carlos Wilkens, whose English is impeccable and knowledge of the island is first-rate. SportsTour's head office is in Santiago at Teatinos 333, Suite 1001 (tel. 696-8832; fax 698-3058). In Santiago, you can also book tours through **Tour Kia-Koe** at Moneda 772, Office 402-B (tel. 33-2650; fax same; telex 64-5211 IORANA CT). They offer tours lasting four to seven days, as well as day-long excursions on horseback.

GETTING THERE

At this writing, Lan Chile flies to Easter Island on Wednesday and Sunday leaving at noon and arriving at 3:30pm. Return flights to Santiago leave on Monday and Thursday at 7am, arriving at Santiago's Marino Benítez Airport at 12:45pm. Round-trip airfare is $812. To confirm schedules and rates while in the United States, contact Lan Chile toll free at 800/735-5526.

WHAT TO SEE & DO

You need at least 2 days to see the major sites. Distances are small, but there are no paved roads. You'll be aware immediately of the constant wind that blows across the island. The island is barren, with few people and even fewer animals.

Rano Kau is the largest of the three volcanoes from which the island was formed (*rano* means "volcano"). Plants originally sown in its crater have continued to grow wild. They include pineapple, tobacco, coffee, and sugarcane.

High above Rano Kau is **Orongo,** a ceremonial site where the important annual contest to choose the "Birdman of the Year" was held. (Be sure to get an informative guide, in English, when you pay the $2 entrance fee.) Here the island's chiefs and their manservants gathered each September and stood watch for the first sooty tern to lay an egg on the tiny islands offshore. The servants then swam across the shark-infested waters, and the first to return with an egg won. But it was his master who was proclaimed "Birdman of the Year." This was a religious post that included the power to assign the island's virgins in marriage. (The last such contest was held in 1864.)

Rana Raraku, called *la fábrica* (the factory), is indeed that. It was here that the more than 600 giant statues on the island were carved. Climb inside the volcano crater to see the smaller statues there, which are not as perfectly done.

Ahu Akivi, in midisland, is the most photographed site here. A lineup of seven huge stone giants with long ears and tight lips gaze off to the sea, restored to their *ahu* by a team of archeologists in 1960.

We can't urge you too strongly to consider making this once-in-a-lifetime trip, even though it will make quite a dent in your budget. Check with **Lan Chile** (offices in New York and Miami, tel. toll free 800/735-5526) for package tours. Some are available only in Chile, while others must be purchased here. **SportsTours,** mentioned previously, is another excellent source of package-tour information.

Note: There are several excellent books you might want to read before taking this trip. *Easter Island: Land of Mysteries,* by Peggy Mann, is sold on the island. *Aku Aku,* by Thor Heyerdahl, can be found in bookstores. *Island at the Center of the World,* by Fr. Sebastian Englert, is full of wonderful photos.

Important tip: Bring very comfortable shoes. Also, a flashlight will be useful for night walking.

WHERE TO STAY & DINE

There are three hotels and a few pensions on the island. Most include breakfast in their rates and have their own dining rooms. For the most part, *residenciales* include all three meals in their rates, but check before you book a room. The best restaurant in town is near the church, but most visitors eat in their hotels.

HANGA ROA, Avenida Pont. Tel. 299. 60 rms (all with bath).
$ Rates: $42 single; $50 double. Major credit cards accepted.
The Hanga Roa is one of the finest choices on the island. Although it resembles a

motel from the outside, the accommodations here are first rate. On the grounds are a pool and a disco. A modified American plan (two meals) is available. You can make reservations with their Santiago representative at San Antonio 486, Suite 182 (tel. 39-5334 or 39-6834; telex 24-0118).

IORANA KORNA, Ana Magaro. Tel. 312. 22 rooms (all with bath).
$ Rates: $40 single; $50 double. Major credit cards accepted.
Amenities here include an outdoor pool and a fantastic view of the ocean. The hotel also has a very good tour operator. In Santiago, reservations can be made through Tour Kia-Koe at Moneda 772, Office 402-B (tel. 33-2650; fax 33-2650; telex 64-5211 IORANA CT).

HOTEL HOTU MATUA, Avenida Pont. Tel. 242. 50 rooms (all with bath).
MINIBAR TEL
$ Rates: Contact Tour Kia-Koe or a travel agency in Santiago for up-to-date rate information.
Owner/Manager Orlando Paoa personally ensures that his guests are well cared for at this lovely hotel with comfortably furnished rooms. Additional facilities include an outdoor pool with poolside bar, beautifully landscaped tropical gardens, a dining room, and a bar. Transportation is provided to and from the airport. The Hotel Matua has its own tour operator.

11. SUGGESTED ITINERARIES

SKI COUNTRY

Only 3½ hours by bus or 5 hours by train from Santiago is the most fabulous ski area in South America—**Portillo.** Local skiers argue that Portillo has trails as challenging as any in the Alps. Site of the 1966 World Alpine Ski Championships, Portillo draws thousands of skiers from North and South America between June and October.
   Located 9,400 feet above sea level in the Chilean Andes, Portillo is an overnight trip and definitely worth it. Nowhere else can you ski to the **Christ of the Andes** statue, perched atop a 12,000-foot-high peak on the border between Argentina and Chile. The ski area has instruction for beginners as well as twisting expert trails.
   Only an hour's drive from Santiago, Chile's newest ski area, **Valle Nevado,** promises to become one of the ski capitals of the Southern Hemisphere. It opened in 1988, with eight lifts and 21 trails in operation. More are slated for the future. Its peaks rise to over 16,500 feet above sea level. Three other ski areas, **El Colorado, Farrellones,** and **La Parva** are also nearby.

GETTING THERE

The most practical way to reach either Portillo or Farrellones is to use a travel service that specializes in ski excursions, like **Tour Service,** on the tenth floor of Teatinos 333 (tel. 696-0415). Another good agency is **Grez,** at Ahumada 312, between Agustinas and Huérfanos (Office 315).
   The round-trip bus fare to Portillo is about $35 per person, as arranged through Tour Service. A sister travel agency, **SportsTour** (tel. 698-3058), offers various ski packages.
   A good choice if you're planning to go to nearby Farellones and La Parva is the **Centro de Ski El Colorado,** Avenida Apoquindo 4900 Nos. 47 and 48 (tel. 246-3344). They offer bus service from your hotel and equipment rental. You can also travel by bus on your own via **Gray Line,** Agustinas 1161 (tel. 696-0518 or 698-3341).
   Like to head to ski country via car? Make your arrangements through **Nuevo**

O'Higgins San Martín, a travel agency at San Francisco 24, across the Alameda and near the San Francisco church. The round-trip cost to Farellones is $30 per person (five to a car), while the Portillo journey is $45 per head. Service is on an irregular basis. A private car runs $100 for up to four people.

WHERE TO STAY

In Portillo, your choice is limited to the magnificent Hotel Portillo. If you plan to ski at El Colorado, the Colorado Apart Hotel is in a breathtaking location. And if you plan an overnight trip to Farellones, ask SportsTour to book you in one of the lodges owned by the University of Chile or Catholic University; these budget accommodations are located in La Parva, about 3 miles from Farellones.

COLORADO APART HOTEL, El Colorado. Tel. 246-3344. Fax 220-7738.
Make arrangements in Santiago at Avenida Apoquindo 4900, Office 47 and 48.
$ Rates: Mid-July to early Sept, $800 double per week; mid-June to mid-July, $400 double per week. Major credit cards accepted.
Right in the midst of the ski area, this hotel offers panoramic views of the surrounding mountains. Guests can take advantage of the convenience of going directly from their doorway to the slopes, virtually on skis.

HOTEL PORTILLO, Camino Internacional. Tel. 24-3007. 200 rms. In Santiago reservations can be made at Roger de Flor 2911. Tel. 231-3411 or 231-6305. Fax 231-7164. Telex 44-0370 PORTI CZ.
$ Rates (including four meals a day and taxes): $50 bunk without bath; $105 single with bath; $200 double with bath. Major credit cards accepted.
Hotel Portillo is nestled high in the Andes. Share-the-bath bunks are in the seven-story main building and at the nearby Inca Lodge. Inca Lodge guests dine in a self-service dining room. When not skiing, you can swim in the heated outdoor pool, skate on a nearby pond, loll in a sauna, or relax at a film in the hotel theater. Transportation, accommodations, and lift tickets can be arranged by SportsTour.

VIÑA DEL MAR

When Chileans crave sun, sand, and a resort atmosphere, they head 85 miles to Viña del Mar, a year-round community that's crowded from September 15 to March 15. The jet-setters congregate at the famous **casino** here for roulette, blackjack, baccarat, and the nightclub and cocktail lounge. The racetrack is open on Sunday from December to March.

Every February the city is host to the famed **Viña del Mar Song Festival,** held in the amphitheater at the Quinta Vergara. This international festival attracts aspiring singers from all over the world.

There are more than six beaches (all public) within Viña, and the Pacific beaches extend outside the city for miles in both directions, from Papudo Beach on the north to San Antonio Beach on the south. You'll need to check water conditions because pollution has become a problem in recent years. The water is frigid. The most popular beaches are **Papudo, Renaca,** and **Mirador.**

GETTING THERE

Take any of the buses that leave from the Mapocho Station vicinity. The 1½-hour ride will cost you only $5. Organized bus tours including a visit to Valparaíso cost around $28. A popular stop is a visit to the sundial in Viña del Mar, which is made entirely from flowers.

WHERE TO STAY

HOTEL CASTELLON, Viana 135. Tel. 97-7019. Fax. 66-0510. 20 rms (all with bath).
$ Rates (including breakfast): $42 single; $48 double. Major credit cards accepted.
Located in the center of town just a few blocks from the beach, the two-star Castellón

is a very good basic hotel. Services offered include bus service, car rentals, babysitting, and tour guides. The Castellón has its own restaurant and bar.

SAN MARTIN, Avenida San Martín 667. Tel. 97-2548. Fax 97-2727. Telex 23-4562 SAMAR CL. 180 rms (all with bath). MINIBAR TV TEL
$ Rates (including breakfast): $90 double. Major credit cards accepted.
Conveniently located just off the beach and only a few blocks from shops and nightspots, the four-star San Martín is a fine choice. Amenities include 24-hour room service, a beauty salon, a gymnasium with sauna, a restaurant and piano bar, and a jewelry shop.

O'HIGGINS, Plaza Vergara. Tel. 88-2016. Fax 88-3537. Telex 63-0479 HOH CT. 265 rms (all with bath). MINIBAR TV TEL
$ Rates (including breakfast): $90 double. Major credit cards accepted.
In the heart of Viña del Mar on the Plaza Vergara, this stately hotel stands among the palms as a tribute to the city's past and present. Hospitality is a tradition here. You'll be pleased by the comfortable accommodations and the quality of the service here. A bright, spacious dining room, an old-world bar, conference facilities, and an outdoor pool round out the list of services here.

WHERE TO DINE

There are several excellent and reasonably priced restaurants in Viña del Mar. Some of our favorites are **Armandita Parrillada Argentina,** Avenida San Martín, a good choice for steak lovers; **San Marcos,** Avenida San Martín just off the corner of Calle Siete Norte, a fine Italian place; **Gypsy,** Avenida San Martín at the corner of Calle 8 Norte, a fine choice for French cuisine; and **Rincon Marino,** Avenida Borgoño 17130, a great place for seafood.

There are also a number of *confiterías.* The **Samoiedo** on Avenida Valparaíso is invariably crowded every afternoon at 5pm with natives and tourists alike.

WHAT TO SEE & DO

THE PALACIO RIOJA, Calle Quilota 214.
This French Neoclassic–style mansion, built in 1908, is host to many local events and is home to a lovely historical museum. Hours: Tuesday through Sunday from 10am to 2pm and 3 to 6pm.

THE PALACIO CARRASCO, Avenida Libertad 250.
Built between 1912 and 1923, this two-story mansion houses the Viña del Mar Cultural Center, library, historical archives, and exhibition galleries. Hours: Monday through Friday from 9am to 1pm and 2 to 6pm; Saturday 9am to 1pm only. On the grounds of the palace is a sculpture by August Rodin and a giant Chessboard with meter-high chessmen in the back garden.

ARCHAEOLOGICAL MUSEUM, Calle 4 Norte 784.
Exhibits include Mapuche Indian silver ornaments. A "Moai" from Easter Island is in the garden. Hours: Tuesday through Friday from 10am to 6pm; Saturday and Sunday mornings only.

PALACIO VERGARA MUSEUM OF FINE ARTS, Quinta Vergara.
This Venetian-style mansion was built to replace the original home of the founders of Viña del Mar, the Vergara family, which was destroyed in the earthquake of 1906. Today it is home to the **School and Museum of Fine Arts.** Hours: Tuesday through Sunday from 10am to 2pm and 3 to 6pm.

CASTILLO WULFF (Naval Museum), Avenida Marina opposite the Cerro Castillo.
Originally the private residence of a Valparaíso businessman, today the Castillo Wulff houses the art and rare-book collections of Salvador Reyes (1899–1970), a famed writer of nautical tales. Hours: Tuesday through Saturday from 10am to 1pm and 2:30 to 6pm; Sunday and holidays 10am to 1pm only.

EVENING ENTERTAINMENT

Viña del Mar offers visitors several entertainment choices when the sun goes down. Strollers can venture into the various restaurants and discotheques along the **Muelle Vergara** (Vergara Pier).

Anastasia, at Avenida Borgoño 1500, hosts an excellent dinner and international show nightly. **Topsy** is the hottest disco in town. Perched on a hill above Renaca beach (hence the name), it has rooms with spectacular views.

The **Municipal Casino** is one of the city's best-known attractions, located at the end of Avenida San Martín just off Von Schroeder. Crap, roulette, and cards are in the main game room. Stakes may seem high for amateurs; the minimum bet for blackjack and bacarrat is $10. There is also a room full of the infamous one-armed bandits, *tragamonedas.* The casino has restaurants, bars, a theater, art exhibitions, and convention facilities. Gamblers must be over 21 to enter, and there is a $5 admission charge. Men must wear a jacket and tie.

A STOP IN VALPARAISO

On the way to Viña del Mar, you may want to stop at Valparaíso, a city built in tiers on the hills (there are over 40 of them) rising from the bay adjoining Viña del Mar (your fare to Viña includes this stop). This is Chile's second-largest city, and it bears a striking resemblance to San Francisco—with cobblestone streets and electric cable cars. It is the chief port of the west coast of South America and a beautiful city for walking. Key sights include **Muelle Prat,** the city's main pier—where you'll find a replica of the *Santiaguillo,* the first ship to bring Spaniards to Valparaíso—and, nearby, **Fuerte Esmeralda,** a century-old fortress. Another sight is **Palacio Lyon,** Condell 1546. Built in 1881, it was one of the few buildings to survive the 1906 earthquake. Today it is home to the Valparaíso Museum of Natural History (hours: Tuesday through Saturday 10am to 1pm and 2pm to 6pm; mornings only on Sundays and holidays).

For a breathtaking view of the harbor, take the funicular at Cerro Concepción to the Paseo Gervasoni. On the next hill, Cerro Alegre, is the art nouveau-style **Palacio Baburizza.** A national monument, it is home to the Municipal Museum of Fine Arts (hours: Tuesday through Sunday 10am to 6pm).

If you want to stay in Valparaíso, the Hotel Lancaster at Chacabuco 2362 (tel. 21-7391) is a good choice.

TERMAS DE CHILLAN

About 250 miles south of Santiago, in the foothills of the Andes, is the stunning four-season resort of **Chillan.** The area is known for its fabulous skiing facilities and its mineral baths. The ski facilities and the hotel underwent a costly facelift and are now first-rate. There are five ski lifts in operation, and one is the longest in Latin America. The ski runs vary from expert to novice, but all are covered with a fine powder and a few moguls. The ski season here is longer than that at Portillo. The mineral springs and mud baths are relaxing yet invigorating after a day on the slopes. When there's no snow you can play tennis, ride horseback, and hike. Fine restaurants and lively discotheques round out the facilities. Rates vary depending on the season and class of accommodations requested. Write for details and rates to **Termas de Chillan,** Arauco 600, Chillan, Chile (tel. 223-664).

CHILEAN LAKE REGION

The Chilean Lake Region is often compared to Switzerland, and the natural features—snow-capped mountains; cold, crystal-clear lakes; clean air; wooded hillsides; and attractive towns inhabited by friendly rosy-cheeked people—are similar. The best months to visit are November through March (summer), although skiing is great in Chile's winter. The food is superb: The trout caught in local lakes and the shellfish caught offshore are fresh and prepared in Chilean fashion. There are many

German eateries as well, due to the large German population that emigrated here in the mid-19th century.

Temuco, 450 miles from Santiago, is the northernmost city of the region, and Puerto Montt, 200 miles farther south, is the southernmost point. Lan Chile has several flights daily from Santiago, and for those with unlimited time there are excellent rail connections as well.

Temuco has 170,000 people, many of whom are Arancanian Indians, Chile's only indigenous group. They sell their silver jewelry, ponchos, and handcrafts in the market here. **Villarrica,** a small town nearby (50 miles away), is beside one of the area's loveliest lakes. Its volcano is used for skiing.

Valdivia, on the coast, and **Osorno,** inland, are the centers of Chile's German community. There are hot mineral springs in **Puyehue National Park** near here.

Puerto Montt, a picturesque city of 100,000, is the jumping-off point for treks across the Andes to Bariloche (Argentinean side) and to Patagonia, Chile's southernmost point. Make sure to visit the Angelmo district, where the fishing boats are often left stranded ashore when the tide changes. You'll find excellent handcrafts in the area, too.

If you visit in their summer (our winter), trout fishing in the lakes is big business; in their winter (our summer) the skiing is first-rate. Contact Lan Chile for flight information and SportsTour, Teatinos 333, Suite 1001 (tel. 696-8832), or Box 3300, Santiago, for package tours.

PATAGONIA [MAGALLENES]

Punta Arenas is the southernmost city in the world and capital of the province of Magallenes. The temperature is surprisingly mild, with an average of 36°F in winter and 68°F in summer. Days in summer have 20 hours of daylight, which makes it rough in winter, when the sun shines only 4 hours a day. Visitors use this city as a jumping-off point for visits to Paine National Park, South America's largest. The rugged landscape with jagged hills, lakes, and forests looks like a moonscape. The herds of animals are interesting to see. Contact SportsTour for more information (see above).

GLACIER CRUISES

Patagonia and Tierra del Fuego are the gateways to Antarctica and the world's last great frontiers. One of the most magnificent ways to tour this untamed wilderness of forests, volcanoes, glaciers, icy channels, and fjords is aboard a cruise ship.

The **M/V Terra Australis,** one of the most luxurious vessels in the region, sails south from Punta Arenas on a six-day/seven-night cruise through Patagonia and Tierra del Fuego. You'll pass through fields of glaciers as you travel through the Straits of Magellan, the Magdelena Channel and the Beagle Channel. Ports of call include Puerto Williams, the southernmost city in the world; Ushuaia; Argentina; and Tierra del Fuego, where you'll visit a typical Argentine farm. You'll also stop at Magdelena Island, where you'll visit with the penguin colony and tour the local lighthouse before returning to Punta Arenas.

The M/V *Terra Australis* sails from September to March (high season, December through March). For more information and reservations, contact the Lan Chile Tour Department (in the United States call toll free 800/995-4888).

The **M/S Skorpios** sails from Puerto Montt on a six-night/seven-day cruise through the fjords of Chile. You'll visit the fishing villages of Puerto Aguirre and Melinka, one of the oldest settlements in the Chonos Archipelago; tour a handicrafts fair in Castro; and swim in the indoor spa waters of Quitralco as you travel the Chilean sea to the San Rafael Glacier. The M/S *Skorpios* sails from September through April. For more information contact the Lan Chile Tour Department (in the United States call toll free 800/995-4888) or SportsTour in Santiago (tel. 696-8832).

CHAPTER 7

ASUNCION, PARAGUAY

1. INTRODUCING
   ASUNCION &
   PARAGUAY
   • WHAT'S SPECIAL
     ABOUT ASUNCION
   • WHAT THINGS COST
     IN ASUNCION
2. ORIENTATION
3. GETTING AROUND
   • FAST FACTS:
     ASUNCION
4. WHERE TO STAY
5. WHERE TO DINE
6. ATTRACTIONS
   • DID YOU KNOW . . . ?
7. SAVVY SHOPPING
8. EVENING
   ENTERTAINMENT
9. SUGGESTED
   ITINERARIES

Even at the end of the 20th century, Asunción, the capital of Paraguay—a landlocked nation in the heart of South America—still retains its colonial charm. It's hard to believe that this tiny provincial city, with a population of just under 1 million, was once the capital of the entire Spanish Empire in South America. Life in Asunción today moves at a much slower pace than it does elsewhere on the Continent. It's probably one of the few urban centers in the world where you can still walk the streets safely after dark and where you can generally trust a cab driver.

Asunción will charm you with its lovely plazas and riverside parks, lined with flowering trees and beautifully manicured flower beds; with its turn-of-the-century trolley, installed some years ago as a tourist attraction, which runs through the town; and with the mild manners and cheerfulness of its people. And you'll be no less surprised to find that Asunción is also home to a booming port (and a thriving black market).

1. INTRODUCING ASUNCION & PARAGUAY

BACKGROUND Before the first European explorers arrived, Paraguay was inhabited by the seminomadic Guaraní Indians. In 1524 the Portuguese explorer Alejo García became the first white man to set foot in Paraguay, followed shortly thereafter by the English navigator Sebastian Cabot, who sailed up the Río de La Plata to explore the Paraná River. Then, in 1537, Domingo Martínez de Irala established the first colonial settlement at Asunción, which served as the center of Spanish power in South America until 1776, when Buenos Aires was made capital of the viceroyalty of the Río de La Plata. Paraguay eventually declared its independence from Spain in 1811.

Since that time, two major wars have disrupted life in Paraguay and greatly reduced the male population. In 1870, Paraguay suffered devastating losses in the war of the Triple Alliance against Brazil, Argentina, and Uruguay, followed by 6 years of foreign occupation, political clashes, coups d'état, and civil war until the end of the century.

Border disputes with Bolivia led to the Chaco War, from 1932 to 1935. In 1938 a peace treaty awarded most of the disputed territory to Paraguay, while Bolivia won an outlet to the Paraná River.

From 1954 to early 1989, Paraguay was ruled by Gen. Alfredo Stroessner, whose

WHAT'S SPECIAL ABOUT ASUNCION

Monument
- [ ] The Monumento de la Paz is a fitting tribute to the native Paraguayan.

Monument/Museum
- [ ] The Panteón de los Héroes is the final resting place of Paraguay's greatest heroes.
- [ ] The Center of Visual Arts displays both contemporary and past Paraguayan art.

Shopping
- [ ] Las Recovas de Colón offers unique Paraguayan handicrafts.

Religious Shrine
- [ ] Caacupé is home to Paraguay's holiest shrine, La Virgen de Los Milagros.

Offbeat Oddity
- [ ] Paraguay's national dance is the **bottle dance,** which requires considerable dexterity and concentration.

---

dictatorship was marked by political repression, censorship, human-rights violations, and mistreatment of the Indian minority. However, under Stroessner, Paraguay did make significant economic progress, due in part to aid from the United States and Brazil. On February 3, 1989, Stroessner was removed from power in a bloody coup, led by his son's father-in-law, Gen. Andrés Rodríguez. Three months later, on May 1, Rodríguez was chosen president in democratic elections.

Paraguay continues to be ruled by a democratic government modeled after that of the United States. Executive power is exercised by a president, who is elected by popular vote to a term of 5 years. Legislative power is vested in a two-chamber Congress—a Senate and a House of Representatives. The nation's 30 senators and 60 representatives are also elected by popular vote. Finally, judicial power rests in a Supreme Court and the Courts of Justice.

GEOGRAPHY The warmth of the climate in Paraguay is matched only by the warmth of its people, who are probably the most hospitable in South America.

Although landlocked, Paraguay is surrounded by water on three sides: the Paraguay River to the north, the Alto Paraná River to the east and south, and the Pulcomayo River to the southwest. The Paraguay River flows from north to south, dividing the country into two entirely different regions: The dry, barren plains of the Gran Chaco which cover the western three-fifths contrast sharply with the fertile plains of the east.

Similar contrasts can be seen in the landscape of Paraguay's three borders. Lush, humid primary forest is found at the Paraguayan border with Brazil; the border with Argentina is one of river parkland and wood savannah; while Paraguay's border with Bolivia is typically the semiarid plains and lowland brush of the Gran Chaco.

LANGUAGE The national language is Spanish. However, most Paraguayans are fluent in both Spanish and Guaraní, the delightfully melodic language of the original

---

IMPRESSIONS

Asunción . . is both a mudhole and a charming small metropolis. . . . The people of Asunción represent typical elements in the national character. They are violently chauvinist, but not xenophobic. . . . Almost all are decent, frugal, humble, honest, clean. . . . No racial problem exists at all; nobody thinks anybody is inferior because his skin is dark.
—JOHN GUNTHER, *INSIDE LATIN AMERICA,* 1967

inhabitants—the Guaraní Indians. While Spanish predominates in formal settings, Guaraní is more popular in everyday life. Rich in emotional nuances, it is the language of love, friendship, intimacy, and the home. In Asunción you'll also hear Korean being spoken, as well as German, especially among the Mennonite settlers in the Chaco.

WHAT THINGS COST IN ASUNCION	U.S. $
Taxi from the airport to the city center	15.00
Fare for a city bus	.20
Double with bath at the Ñandutí Hotel (budget)	13.00
Double with bath at the Zaphir Hotel (moderate)	32.00
Double with bath at the Hotel Guaraní (deluxe)	105.00
Lunch at the Lido Bar (budget)	3.00
Lunch at La Pergola di Bolsi (moderate)	9.00
Fixed-price meal at Le Gran Café (moderate)	7.00
Cup of coffee	.35
Coca-Cola	.35

2. ORIENTATION

Asunción is the largest city in Paraguay, with a population just under 1 million. It is the center of the country's political and commercial activity.

ARRIVING

Upon arrival, you'll be issued a tourist card, which costs $3.

The modern **Silvio Pettirossi International Airport** lies several miles outside the city. As you enter the orange-and-green Customs area, you'll see a sign, "BIENVENIDOS AL PARAGUAY, TIERRA DE PAZ Y PROGRESSO (Welcome to Paraguay, Land of Peace and Progress), reflecting the pride that Paraguayans take in their country. Unfortunately, however, the fear of drug smuggling has spread to Paraguay. Nowadays it is not uncommon for Customs officials to search luggage.

As you approach the main area, you'll undoubtedly encounter porters who will offer to help you with your luggage and lead you to an information booth. One word of advice: Stick to our hotel selections and don't let anyone at the information booth persuade you to accept another hotel—unless he can swear that it is what you want. The only way to get to Asunción from the airport is by taxi. You'll do just as well if you hail a cab on your own. The 15-minute drive should cost around $15.

TOURIST INFORMATION

The **Dirección General de Turismo** (National Tourist Office) is located at Palma 468, between 14 de Mayo and Alberdi (tel. 44-1530). They will provide you with a map of Asunción but little else.

CITY LAYOUT

En route to Asunción, notice that there are no shantytowns, roadside litter, or rundown industrial areas. You'll pass through fertile pastures, where you'll see billboards (for French perfumes and imported fashions), grazing horses and livestock, picturesque homes with well-tended gardens, and occasional open-air restaurants.

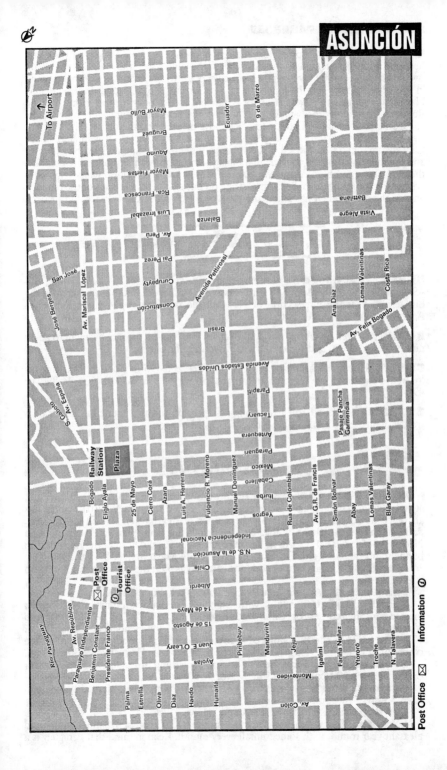

ASUNCIÓN

Post Office ⊠   Information ⓘ

MAIN ARTERIES Approaching the center of the city, you'll find that the route becomes more residential as you drive past the embassies and palatial homes on Avenida España and finally Avenida Mariscal Lopez, which becomes Coronel Bogado in the city center. At the intersection of Coronel Bogado and Independencia Nacional, you are at the very heart of Asunción. Two blocks to your right, Avenida República runs along the bay. Among the lovely gardens and promenades here are the Palacio del Gobierno, El Cabildo (the legislative palace), and the cathedral, as well as Asunción's busy port. The main plaza is two blocks to your left. It is intersected by Calles Palma, Estrella, and Oliva, Asunción's three main commercial thoroughfares and the three symbols on the Paraguayan flag—the palm, star, and olive. Incidentally, the red, white, and blue Paraguayan flag is the only one in the world whose two sides are not identical (the white horizontal stripe on one side bears the arms of the republic and on the other side it has a lion and the words PAZ Y JUSTICIA—Peace and Justice).

3. GETTING AROUND

BY BUS At 20¢, you can't beat buses for the price. Bus nos. 2, 4, 5, 7, 21, 27, and 45 will take you to the Mercado Petti Rossi. Bus nos. 8, 31, and 38 run between the bus terminal (at the intersection of Fernando de la Mora and Avenida República Argentina) and the center of town.

BY TAXI To get anywhere outside the center, you'll find it most convenient to go by taxi, which is cheap and metered; most drivers are honest.

BY CAR **Hertz** has an office at the airport (tel. 206-195 or 22-012). **National** is located downtown, at Yegros 501, on the corner of Cerro Cora (tel. 44-890 or 491-379).

BY TROLLEY If you feel like taking a step back in time, Asunción has its own trolley, which runs along Calle España to Las Mercedes.

FAST FACTS *ASUNCIÓN*

Airline Offices **American Airlines** is located close to the Hotel Guaraní, at Independencia Nacional 557 (tel. reservations, 43-331; sales, 90-201). **Iberia** has an office at 25 de Mayo 161, on the corner of Yegros (tel. 93-351 or 93-352). **Aerolineas Argentinas** is located just below the main plaza at Independencia Nacional 365 (tel. 91-011). **Varig** has an office on the second floor of the Encarnación building, on the corner of General Díaz and 14 de Mayo (tel. 44-8777).

Area Code The country code for Paraguay is 595; the city code for Asunción is 21.

Babysitters Ask the concierge at your hotel about child care.

Banks Major U.S. banks with branches in Asunción include **Citibank,** located on the corner of Chile and Estrella (tel. 94-951 or 94-952); **Chase Manhattan,** at E. V. Haedo 103, on the corner of Independencia Nacional (tel. 92-241 or 92-242); and the **Bank of Boston,** located on Presidente Franco, on the corner of O'Leary (tel. 97-311). Banks are open Monday to Friday from 7:30 to 11am.

Bookstores You may be able to find something in English at **Expolibros,** on the corner of México and 25 de Mayo.

Business Hours Most **shops** open at 8 or 9am, close at noon, then reopen from 3 until 7 or 8pm.

Car Rentals See "Getting Around" above.

Climate The weather in Paraguay is similar to that of Miami—sunny and pleasant year round, with some rainfall every month. Keep in mind that Paraguay is a subtropical country, and so it can get quite hot, with temperatures soaring well past 90°F in summer (December through March). Bring your bathing suit and try to stay in a hotel with a pool, if your budget allows.

Currency Paraguay's currency, the **guaraní,** is one of the most stable in South America. The exchange rate at the time of this writing was 1,480 guaraní to U.S.$1.

Currency Exchange There are exchange houses (*casas de cambio*) on Calle Palma just off Alberdi. Cambios Guaraní, at Palma 449, is a good bet, although all of these houses offer about the same rate. Exchange houses are open from 7am to noon and 3 to 7pm.

Dentists/Doctors Ask the concierge at your hotel to recommend a dentist or doctor in the area or contact the embassy for a list of English-speaking dentists and doctors.

Drugstores The concierge at your hotel should be able to recommend a nearby pharmacy. **Farmacia Madrigal** has branches at Pettirossi 784 and Estrella 452.

Embassies/Consulates The **U.S. Embassy** is located at Avenida Mariscal Lopez 1776. Most embassies are concentrated in this area.

Emergencies There is a special emergency phone number for visitors to Asunción: 441-606. The police can be reached at 449-116; the fire department at 98-777; and the Red Cross at 204-900. To call an ambulance, dial 204-800.

Eyeglasses Ask the concierge in your hotel to recommend an optician.

Hairdressers/Barbers **José Coiffure Unisex** is at Berlín 1035, at the corner of Colón (tel. 82-991).

Holidays

New Year's Day	January 1
Carnival	Varies
Easter	Varies
Feast of St. Blaise (*Patron Saint of Paraguay*)	February 3
Anniversary of Death of Mariscal López	March 1
May (*Labor*) **Day**	May 1
National Independence Day	May 15
Peace of Chaco Day	June 12
Founding of Asunción Day	August 15
Victory of Boquerón Day	September 20
Blessed Virgin's Day	December 8
Christmas Day	December 25

Information See "Tourist Information" above.

Laundry/Dry Cleaning Most hotels offer laundry service.

Luggage Storage/Lockers Most hotels will hold your bags if you plan to go on a short trip.

Newspapers/Magazines You can pick up day-old copies of the English-language *Buenos Aires Herald* at many newsstands scattered around the city.

Photographic Needs Most film is available here; however, prices will be higher than they are at home.

Post Office The post office is located a few blocks from El Cabildo (the legislative palace), on the corner of Alberdi and Benjamin Constant.

Religious Services The concierge at your hotel should be able to find out if there are religious services for your faith. Paraguay is primarily Catholic.

Restrooms Most bars, restaurants, and museums have public restrooms. Hotel lobbies are also a good option.

Safety Asunción is probably one of the safest capital cities. Nevertheless, exercise caution and always keep an eye on your belongings. Valuables, such as airline tickets and passports, belong in the hotel safe.

Shoe Repairs The concierge in your hotel should be able to direct you to a shoe-repair shop.

Taxes Expect to pay a $15 airport tax when leaving the country.
Taxis See "Getting Around" above.
Telephone The telephone office on the corner of Nuestra Señora de la Asunción and Presidente Franco is open 24 hours a day. Buy *fichas* (tokens) to use in public phones. The telephone office also has a telex and fax service.
Tipping Plan on tipping waiters and cab drivers about 10%. Porters should get 50 guaraní per bag.

4. WHERE TO STAY

Despite the city's small size, there is a good selection of hotels in all price categories. Because of its central location on the Continent, Asunción is a popular meeting place for Latin American businesspeople.

In the early 1970s, President Stroessner permitted about 17,000 Koreans to enter the country to work in agriculture. With the passage of time, some of the Koreans have become actively involved in the contraband market (together with their counterparts in Brazil), while others now run electronics shops, small restaurants (or *copetines*), and various garment factories (some of which copy the creations of such famous designers as Pierre Cardin).

A number of Koreans now run small, inexpensive hotels, or **hospedajes/ residencias,** throughout Asunción. *Beware:* Although most of these hotels are clean and quite legitimate, there are a few that charge by the hour. Stay away from those close to the port.

IN TOWN

DOUBLES FOR LESS THAN $20

HOTEL ADELIA, Avenida Fdo. de la Mora, at the corner of Repùblica Argentina. Tel. 533-083. Some rooms with bath. MINIBAR TEL
$ Rates: $8 single; $12.50 double.
Although far from the center of town, the Hotel Adelia is a good choice if you need to be near the bus station. Rooms with ceiling fans are slightly less expensive than those with air conditioning.

HOTEL EMBAJADOR, Presidente Franco 514. Tel. 493-393. All rooms with bath.
$ Rates (including breakfast): $6 single; $10 double.
Located on the corner of Presidente Franco and 14 de Mayo, the Embajador offers sparsely furnished rooms, all with ceiling fans. Although relatively clean, the hotel itself is drab and rundown.

HOTEL LA ESPAÑOLA, L. A. Herrera 142. Tel. 449-280. All rooms with bath.
$ Rates: $10 single; $13 double.
Although sparsely furnished, the rooms here are spotless and are situated around a charming Spanish-style patio. The small family-run hotel is set back from the street, ensuring greater privacy. Coral Turismo, located at the entrance to the hotel, can help you with your travel arrangements to other cities.

NANDUTI HOTEL, Presidente Franco 551. Tel. 446-780.
$ Rates (including breakfast): $6 single; $11 double. All rooms with bath.

Here you'll find clean rooms, most with air conditioning; rooms with ceiling fans are $2 less. You won't beat the price.

DOUBLES FOR LESS THAN $40

ASUNCIÓN PALACE HOTEL, Avenida Colón 415. Tel. 492-151, 492-152, or 492-153. 44 rms (all with bath). TEL
$ Rates (including breakfast): $16 single; $25 double; $35 triple
On the corner of Estrella, the Asunción Palace is one of the city's oldest hotels, and it's starting to show its age. Yet its high ceilings and old-fashioned decor still retain a certain charm, and the rooms are spacious. Be sure to make your reservations in advance, since this hotel is popular with tour groups.

GRAN HOTEL ARMELE, at the corner of Palma and Colón. Tel. 491-061 or 491-064. Fax 445-903. Telex 209 PY. 225 rms, 9 suites (all with bath). A/C MINIBAR TV TEL
$ Rates: $25 single; $30 double. Major credit cards accepted.
Each room here has piped-in music. The Salon Cristal restaurant on the 11th floor offers a great view of the city. The Armele also has its own bar and coffee shop.

HOTEL CONTINENTAL, 15 de Agosto 420. Tel. 493-760 or 491-861. 40 rms (all with bath). A/C MINIBAR TEL
$ Rates (including breakfast): $30 single; $35 double. Major credit cards accepted.
Popular with Brazilian and Argentinean businesspeople (and one of our favorites) is the conveniently located Continental, just off Estrella. TVs are available on request. The hotel has its own bar and restaurant, which offers a complete menu (including a reasonably priced executive lunch). The generous breakfast buffet (included in room price) consists of juices, fruit, cold meats and cheeses, rolls, and coffee. The hotel also has a small pool and terrace on the roof, with a great view of the bay and government buildings.

ZAPHIR HOTEL, Estrella 955. Tel. 490-025 or 490-258. Fax 447-278. Telex 862 PY ZAPHIR. 69 rms (all with bath). A/C MINIBAR TV TEL
$ Rates (including breakfast): $25 single; $32 double. Major credit cards accepted.
The Zaphir is popular among Brazilian and Argentinean businesspeople. Rooms are attractively furnished. Be sure to ask for a room in the front since the other rooms don't have windows. The hotel also has a small bar and restaurant.

SPLURGE CHOICES

EXCELSIOR HOTEL PARAGUAY, Chile 980. Tel. 495-632. Fax 496-748. Telex 44286 PY HOTELEX. 110 rms (all with bath). A/C MINIBAR TV TEL
$ Rates: $95 single; $105 double. Major credit cards accepted.
A big splurge downtown is the English-style Excelsior Hotel Paraguay. Frequent host of international conventions, the relatively new Excelsior has state-of-the-art meeting facilities, with simultaneous wireless translation systems, as well as a beautiful outdoor pool, with a poolside barbecue and cocktail bar. It also boasts a spectacular 500-seat theater, and several first-class restaurants. The rooms are immaculately furnished and the service is impeccable. The Thunder Discotheque is a popular night spot.
The Excelsior has an apart-hotel in a separate building beyond the outdoor pool. The annex features fairly large apartments with fully equipped kitchens for the unbelievable price of $90 per night—ideal for families.

GUARANI, at the corner of Independencia Nacional and Oliva. Tel.

491-131 to 491-139. Fax 443-647. Telex 277 PY. 168 rms (all with bath). A/C MINIBAR TV TEL
$ Rates (including breakfast): $85 single; $105 double.

The triangular-shaped Guaraní has played host to visiting heads of state and dignitaries for more than 25 years. Formerly run by the government, the Guaraní is now privately managed. Among its amenities are a large outdoor pool and terrace; a sauna; a shopping arcade; a lobby bar; and fine restaurants, including the spectacular Guaraní Supper Club, which boasts an unmatched panoramic view of Asunción. Even if you don't stay here, try to visit the 13th floor.

NEARBY

GRAN HOTEL DEL PARAGUAY, at the corner of Calle de La Residenta and Padre Pucheu. Tel. 203-981. 60 rms (all with bath). A/C MINIBAR TV TEL
$ Rates: $40 double. Major credit cards accepted.

The Gran Hotel is located 10 minutes from downtown by trolley or taxi. Once a private estate, it now boasts all the amenities of a modern hotel, including tennis courts and an outdoor pool. Even if you don't stay here, you might enjoy visiting it. The gardens are lovely; and on Wednesday evenings in the Colonial Dining Room there's entertainment as well as dancing.

HOTEL ITA ENRAMADA, Cacique Lambaré and Rivera del Río Paraguay. Tel. 333-049. Fax 333-041. Telex 309 PY ITAHTI. 150 rms (all with bath). A/C MINIBAR TV TEL
$ Rates (including breakfast): $90 single; $110 double. Major credit cards accepted.

Situated at the foot of the Cerro Lambare National Park, the Ita Enramada offers a magnificent view. This 15-acre complex boasts two excellent restaurants, three bars, a poolside barbecue, two pools, tennis courts, water-skiing and fishing facilities, a sauna and health club, and a casino and nightclub. Free shuttle-bus service is provided to and from downtown.

5. WHERE TO DINE

Nearly all restaurants in Asunción offer extensive international menus, featuring pasta dishes, omelets, beef (including *parrilladas*), chicken, and *empanadas*. You'll also find Brazilian dishes, such as *feijoada* and the Argentinean *bife de chorizo*. Paraguayan favorites worth trying are **so-yosopy,** a filling soup of ground beef and soybeans, and **sopa Paraguaya,** a delicious cornbread soufflé, made with mashed corn, cheese, milk, and eggs. The national fish, **surubi,** which is mild in flavor, is available everywhere, prepared in many different ways.

The restaurants are also quite similar, in price. A complete meal with appetizer, dessert, and coffee (but excluding wine and tip) can cost as little as $7 per person. Restaurants tend to cater to businesspeople at lunchtime.

Paraguay's national drink, **yerba maté** (or **tere-re,** as it is called in Guaraní), is a thirst-quenching cold tea made from the dried leaves and shoots of the holly tree. It is sipped from a gourd or gourd-shaped bowl called a **bombilla,** using a small silver straw (available at souvenir stands). *Bombillas* of *yerba mate* are passed from person to person as a ritual of friendship.

IL CAPO, Avenida Peru 29. Tel. 213-022.
Cuisine: ITALIAN. **Reservations:** Recommended.
$ Prices: Appetizers $1–$3; main courses $3–$5.

Open: Lunch and dinner.

One of the city's finest Italian restaurants, Il Capo offers a fine selection of homemade pasta dishes.

DON QUIXOTE RESTAURANT, in the Hotel Continental, 15 de Agosto 420.
   Cuisine: INTERNATIONAL.
$ Prices: Executive lunch $6.
   Open: Lunch and dinner.

Just off Estrella, this restaurant offers an attractively priced executive menu: You can start with either soup or salad, followed by a main course, and then dessert. We found the following main course choices: stuffed tomato with tuna, *surubí* grilled with natural potatoes, and *churrasco*. Selections change daily. You can also order à la carte.

EXEDRA, Alberdi 618, at the corner of General Díaz. Tel. 498-584.
   Cuisine: PARAGUAYAN.
$ Prices: Appetizers 50¢–$1; main courses $2–$5.
   Open: Lunch and dinner.

Exedra is on the lower end of the price scale. Homestyle cooking and daily specials make this unpretentious spot a good choice for lunch or a simple dinner.

LE GRAN CAFÉ, Oliva 476, between 14 de Mayo and Estrella.
   Cuisine: FRENCH/PARAGUAYAN.
$ Prices: Appetizers $1–$3; main courses $4–$8; fixed-price meal $7.
   Open: Lunch and dinner.

In this delightful setting you can dine in an air-conditioned room, in a room cooled by ceiling fans, or, for a little romance, under the stars in Le Gran Café's garden. The French expatriate owners and the restaurant's ambience reminded us of *Casablanca*. Although not haute cuisine, the imaginative menu features traditional French favorites with a Paraguayan twist, such as coq au vin, pork curry, chateaubriand, and *surubí al Roquefort*. Assorted pâtés are the featured appetizers.

LA PERGOLA DI BOLSI, at the corner of Estrella and Alberdi. Tel. 491-841.
   Cuisine: PARAGUAYAN. **Reservations:** Recommended.
$ Prices: Appetizers $1–$3; main courses $3–$6. Major credit cards accepted.
   Open: Lunch and dinner.

The Pergola del Bolsi boasts one of the city's most popular lunch counters (see below) as well as a fine moderately priced dining room. They offer typical Paraguayan cuisine, as well as various pasta dishes. The *surubí* dishes are especially good.

LA PREFERIDA, Calle 25 de Mayo 1005. Tel. 210-641.
   Cuisine: PARAGUAYAN. **Reservations:** Recommended.
$ Prices: Appetizers $1–$3; main courses $4–$8.
   Open: Lunch and dinner.

In contrast to most of Asunción's restaurants, this one specializes in Paraguayan cuisine, with an emphasis on *surubí* and beef dishes.

RESTAURANT-CHOPERIA LA MANIJA, on the balcony of the Galeria Central Shopping Center, Palma 645. Tel. 491-102.
   Cuisine: BRAZILIAN/ARGENTINEAN.
$ Prices: Appetizers 50¢–$3; main courses $3–$6.
   Open: Lunch and dinner.

A *manija* is a large clay mug used specifically for drinking *chopp,* a drink resembling beer but not as fermented. La Manija offers much more than *chopp.* For a little stronger drink, try *caipirinha,* a Brazilian favorite made with *cachaça* (a kind of white rum). *Feijoada* (for Brazilians) and *bife de chorizo* (for Argentineans) are the specialties here. Also recommended are *locro,* a soup made with corn and other vegetables, and the *guiso,* a delicious meat stew served with rice.

SPECIALTY DINING

GERMAN RESTAURANTS

Since Asunción has a large German population, there are many German restaurants.
The chalet-style **Restaurante Westfalia,** at the corner of Avenida General Santos and José F. Bogado (tel. 31-772), features both Paraguayan and German cooking. The **Restaurante El Caballito Blanco** at Alberdi 631 (tel. 444-560) offers both fine German cooking and *chopp.* Slightly more expensive, but just as good, is the plant-filled **Bistro** on Estrella, at the corner of 15 de Agosto (tel. 447-910). **San Marcos,** on the corner of Alberdi and Oliva (tel. 447-302), is another good choice.

LIGHT MEALS FOR UNDER $5

Unique to Asunción are the many lunch counters that serve everything from a quick snack to a complete meal. The most popular of these, especially with students, is the **Lido Bar,** across from the Panteón de los Heroes, on the corner of Palma. It's nearly always crowded.
The **Pergola di Bolsi,** at the corner of Estrella and Alberdi, has an excellent coutner that fills up quickly with businesspeople at noontime. The "Bolsi" is clean and modern and offers an extensive menu. Basic sandwiches start at less than $1.00; a more extravagant one, such as the Beirut (cheese, roast beef, ham, and tomato) is $3.00. Bolsi also offers cold platters, including tuna and ham, and a long list of *surubí* dishes for up to $4.00. Be sure to save room for a sinful dessert. **Restaurant Mundo,** at the corner of Alberdi and Palma, also has a popular lunch counter.
Similar fare is offered at the **Bar Restaurant Asunción,** at the corner of Estrella and 14 de Mayo. The *sopa Paraguaya* (*chicha-mua* in Guaraní) is very good here, as are the *empanadas.* The similar **Café Metro,** two blocks away, at the corner of 15 de Agosto, offers virtually the same menu. Both are popular with the younger crowd.
If you enjoy the ambience of an open-air café, try the **Confitería Alemana,** on the terrace of the Santa Catalina Shopping Center. Here you will find triple-decker sandwiches and such tempting ice-cream concoctions as *sueño de Califas* (Califat's dream), *naranja Sicilia* (Sicilian orange) and *Eiscup Lubeck.* Also on the menu are omelets, a variety of hamburgers, and assorted cold plates. If you're staying at a hotel that doesn't provide breakfast, come here for the $3 breakfast of coffee, tea, juice, eggs, ham, cheese, and rolls.
La Recova, just opposite the artisan shops in Las Recovas de Colon, offers a tempting selection of cakes, cookies, and ice creams. Sandwiches and pizza are served at the lunch counter. Finally, if you find yourself with a craving for Southern-fried chicken, try **American Fried Chicken Paraguay,** across from the Plaza de los Heroes, at Oliva 263.

CONFITERIAS

As is typical in South America, Paraguayans dine about 9 or 10pm. Thus they, too, have adopted the delightful Spanish custom of *merienda* (afternoon tea) for sustenance until dinner time. Right after work, between 5 and 7pm, people flock to the numerous *confiterías* for coffee and pastries, sandwiches, or even a cocktail (though cocktails are not as popular).

Di Trevi, at Calle Palma 591, with its austerely elegant woodwork and bar, reminds us of the *Konditorei* of Austria and Germany. Ceiling fans will keep you cool if you choose a table in the front. The back section is air-conditioned, but you can also choose a table outdoors. Di Trevi offers a wonderful selection of fresh-fruit juices and sandwiches.

The **Confitería Ventura,** next door at Calle Palma 593, is Asunción's oldest *confitería*, which is famous for its homemade ice creams and cakes. Seating is limited, but you can order an ice cream or cake to go.

Another European-style choice is **Da Vinci,** on Estrella, at the corner of Juan O'Leary. People come here primarily for cocktails, but coffee is also available. The cushy seating arrangements will make you feel as if you're in a living room. There's an upstairs room as well, with an ambience best suited for couples.

Also recommended is the **Confitería Imagen,** at Presidente Franco and 15 de Agosto, as well as the Salon de Te at the **San Marcos** restaurant on the corner of Alberdi and Oliva. The *confitería* at the top of the **Vendôme Shopping Center,** offers an excellent view of the bay, plus a full list of cocktails, including those of an exotic variety.

ICE CREAM

Ice-cream lovers will want to stop by **Helados Pucavy,** at 15 de Agosto 235, between Presidente Franco and Palma, for a delicious assortment of homemade ice creams and *granizados* (iced drinks). You can also visit their factory (actually a lovely ice-cream parlor) in a more residential area—on Santa Cruz de la Sierra, between Teniente Farina and Manuel Dominguez. Take bus no. 39 or 40 from the center of town and ask the driver to let you off at Helados Pucavy. It stays open until 9 or 10pm; the garden is delightful in the evening.

DINING WITH A SHOW

The music of Paraguay is lively and delightful. Much of it is derived from the sounds of nature, such as falling rain or singing birds; and much of it is sung in Guaraní, making it even lovelier. The chief instrument is the Paraguayan harp.

No visit to Asunción would be complete without an evening of traditional Paraguayan music and folkloric dances, including the **bottle dance.** One of the most fascinating dances we've ever seen, it requires an incredible combination of balance and skill. Traditionally it is performed by a female dancer, who, while balancing a bottle—or perhaps a vase of flowers—on her head, undertakes a series of elaborate gymnastic moves including dropping a handkerchief to the floor and picking it up with her teeth. You won't want to miss this one.

Although the food at **El Jardín de la Cerveza** isn't quite as good as what can be found elsewhere in Asunción, the excellent folkloric show—featuring traditional Paraguayan music and dancing—makes the evening worthwhile. Since El Jardín is located outside the center of town, at the corner of Avenida Argentina and Castillo (tel. 601-757), you'll probably need to take a taxi.

At **Yguazu** you can dine under the stars (weather permitting) while enjoying one of Asunción's finest folkloric shows. Chief among the attractions is the bottle dance. The international menu features local specialties, including *sopa Paraguaya* and *lomito al Yguazu* (beef stuffed with ham, cheese, and egg and served with a red sauce and mushrooms). Yguazu is 10 minutes by taxi from the center of town, at Calle Choferes del Chaco 1334 (tel. 600-560).

The higher priced **Tayi Poty,** in the casino of the Ita Enramada, offers typical Paraguayan music every Monday to Saturday evening. There's music for dancing as well. Again, you'll probably need a taxi to get here, at Cacique Lambare and Ribera del Rio Paraguay (tel. 333-049).

If you're in Asunción on a Wednesday night, try the show at the **Gran Hotel del Paraguay,** at the intersection of Calle de la Residenta and Calle Triunvirata. Typical

Paraguayan music, as well as music for dancing, is featured. Curry is the Wednesday night special. Since Wednesday is a popular night, it is advisable to make reservations (tel. 200-051).

6. ATTRACTIONS

THE TOP ATTRACTIONS

LA CASA DE LA INDEPENDENCIA, Calle 14 de Mayo, at the corner of Presidente Franco.

⭐ Built in 1772, this house was the secret meeting place of those who conspired against the Spanish government when Paraguay was fighting for its independence. In fact, it was here, that the patriots, led by Capt. Pedro Juan Caballero, declared their independence before taking control of La Casa de los Gobernadores.

Today this small house honors the heroes of Paraguay's independence. Especially noteworthy are two murals of colonial Asunción by Paraguayan artist José Lateraza Parodi and the actual room, located off the back patio, where independence was declared. Spanish-speaking guides are available, but English-speaking guides are scarce.

Admission: Free.
Open: Mon–Fri 7:30–11:30am and 3:30–6:30pm; Sat 7:30–11:30am.

DR. ANDRES BARBERO MUSEUM, Calle Espana, 217. Tel. 200-575.

⭐ This museum houses Paraguay's most important archeological and ethnographic collections. Come here to learn about the Guaraní Indians and life in Paraguay before the Europeans arrived.

Admission: Free.
Open: Mon–Sat 8–11am and Wed 3–6pm. **Trolley:** Mercedes Line.

MUSEO HISTORICO MILITAR [MUSEUM OF MILITARY HISTORY], in the Ministry of Defense building, at the corner of Avenida Mariscal Lopez and Calle Santos.

Paraguay's trophies from the Triple Alliance and Chaco wars, pieces of military equipment, and the uniforms of the two most honored heroes—Francisco Solano López and José Felix Estigarribia—are on display here.

Admission: Free.
Open: Mon–Fri 7:30–11:30am and 2:45–5:30pm; Sat 7–9am.

MUSEO DE BELLAS ARTES, at the corner of Mariscal Estigarribia and Iturbe. Tel. 491-208.

Founded in the 1890s by Juan Silvano Godoy, this museum has paintings and sculptures by both international artists (Murillo, Carbonero, and Tintoreto) and Paraguayan artists (Samudo, Alborno, Colombo, and Hector Da Ponte).

Admission: Free.
Open: Mon–Fri 7:30–11:30am and 3–7pm; Sat 7:30–10am.

MONSEÑOR JUAN SOFORIANO BOGARIN MUSEUM, at the corner of Independencia Nacional and Coronel Bogado. Tel. 200-703.

This small but interesting museum in the seminary, next to the cathedral, houses an interesting collection of religious art, historical pieces, and mineral and coin collections. It was founded by the first archbishop of Paraguay, Juan Soforiano Bogarín (1863–1949).

Admission: Free.
Open: Mon–Sat 8–11am.

BOTANICAL GARDENS, at the corner of Avenida General Artigas and Avenida Santísimo Sacramento. Tel. 446-789.

You might enjoy visiting the botanical gardens and zoo, which are located just outside the center of town in the Barrio Santísima Trinidad. The Museum of Natural History, in the same area, provides a firsthand look at Paraguay's past.
Admission: $1. **Train:** Take the 12:15pm from the Central Train Station. **Taxi:** Less than $3.

CENTER OF VISUAL ARTS, on Isla de Francia, off Avenida de los Aviadores del Chaco.

⭐ The center is home to Asunción's **Museum of Contemporary Art** and **Museo del Barro (Clay Museum).** Here you'll find beautiful Guaraní ceramic pieces dating back to precolonial days, a selection of native ceremonial masks, religious sculptures from the 17th and 18th centuries, and exhibits of modern Paraguayan art. The museum also has a workshop for aspiring young artists.
Admission: Free.
Open: Mon 4–8pm; Tues–Sat 9am–noon and 4–8pm. **Taxi:** Either ask the driver to wait for you or to return for you at a specific time; otherwise, you might have difficulty getting a ride back.

MORE ATTRACTIONS

If you have access to a car or can hire a cab for a couple hours, you might enjoy visiting a few interesting places in the outlying residential areas. **Villa Mora** is one of the wealthiest neighborhoods in Asunción. To get there, follow Avenida Mariscal López out of the city. The U.S. Embassy is on the corner with Avenida Kubitschek; Stroessner's former residence is in the next block. Continuing a little farther outside town, you'll come to the **Recoleta Cemetery,** where many of Asunción's wealthiest are buried. Take a few moments to stroll past some of the mausoleums. The sheer size and opulence will amaze you. To the left of the church is the memorial to Madame Lynch, the Irish mistress of Paraguay's national hero, Francisco Solano López. She died by her husband's side in the War of the Triple Alliance.

You might want to head toward the Itá Enramada along Avenida Felix Bogado, which links up with Avenida General Máximo Santos. Make sure to visit the **Monumento de la Paz** (Monument to Peace), located on a tall hill overlooking the Cerro Lambare National Park and the Paraguay River. Continue on to the Hotel Casino Yacht and Golf Club nearby. The homes along the Avenida del Yacht are actually small estates. Head back toward town through the neighborhood of Las Carmelitas in order to get a good look at the imposing **Banco Nacional del Paraguay,** the Paraguayan counterpart to the Federal Reserve. Avenida Republica Argentina will bring you back into town.

A WALKING TOUR

A great way to start any stroll is with a bird's-eye view of the city you'll be exploring. Thus, you'll want to go up to the 13th floor of the Hotel Guaraní, which offers one of the best views of Asunción and the bay. Be sure to check with the concierge at the reception desk before going up.

Directly in front of the Guaraní is the main (double) plaza. Covering four square blocks, it is bordered by Calle Palma on the side near the bay, Calle Oliva opposite the Hotel Guaraní, Calle Chile, and Calle Independencia Nacional. Estrella runs through the center, dividing it into the **Plaza de la Independencia** (closest to the Hotel Guaraní) and the **Plaza de los Héroes** opposite. The imposing Roman-style building opposite the Plaza on Independencia Nacional is the **Banco de Fomento** (National Development Bank).

Across the Plaza, on the corner of Palma and Chile, is the **Panteón de los Héroes.** It was designed by the Italian architect Rapizzia as a small replica of Hôtel des Invalides in Paris (site of Napoleon's tomb); it is the final resting place of Paraguay's national heroes, including Francisco Solano López, whose death led to the surrender of the Paraguayan forces in the Triple Alliance War, and José Felix Estigarribia, hero of the Chaco War. Soldiers in dress uniform stand watch at the

❓ DID YOU KNOW . . . ?

- Landlocked Paraguay has 1,865 miles of navigable waterways and access to the Atlantic via the Paraguay and Paraná rivers.
- Dried and roasted yerba leaves are used to make a tealike drink called *maté*, which is popular in many South American countries, particularly Argentina and Uruguay.
- Among Paraguay's indigenous people, there are 17 tribal groups, comprising 6 language families.
- During the 17th and 18th centuries as many as 100,000 Indians lived on Paraguay's Jesuit *reducciones* (missions).
- In the late 1970s researchers estimated that more than one-half the nation's Indians lived under the auspices of various missionary organizations.
- When José Gaspar Rodriguez de Francia was named Dictator for Life in 1816, he demanded that Asunción be rebuilt to his specifications. He barred foreigners from entering the country, and tried to eliminate the Catholic Church.
- In the late 1800s Japanese immigrants established agricultural colonies in Paraguay. In the late 1970s many Koreans and ethnic Chinese settled in Paraguay's urban areas.
- By the late 1980s only 20% of Paraguay's roads had been paved.
- Shortly after Gen. Andrés Rodríguez overthrew the government of his father-in-law, Gen. Alfredo Stroessner, Paraguay's border city with Brazil, Ciudad Puerto Stroessner, was renamed Ciudad del Este.

entrance. At the center of the Rotunda, below ground level, is the Tomb of the Unknown Soldier, which commemorates the thousands of Paraguayans who died in battle. The Panteón is also an oratory (place of prayer) for the Virgin Mary, patron saint of the city and marshal in the Paraguayan army. You'll see her statue above the altar; it is carried in a procession through the streets every August 15, the Day of Assumption (Asunción), to celebrate the city's birthday.

After leaving the Panteón, continue west along Calle Palma. This street and Calle Estrella, which run parallel to Calle Oliva, are Asunción's major commercial thoroughfares. Each has chic boutiques (displaying French perfumes and cosmetics) and electronics stores. Three blocks later, just off Palma, on 14 de Mayo, you'll come to **La Casa de la Independencia,** where Paraguay's revolutionaries planned for their independence from Spain in 1811. Fully restored, today it houses a small museum.

Keep heading west, along Presidente Franco, then turn toward the bay at Colón. Walk through the Customs Building at the end of Colón and you'll be in the midst of the hustle and bustle of Asunción's busy port. Freighters dock here to load their cargo of tobacco, soybeans, meat products, and wood. You might enjoy browsing in the various shops that sell Paraguayan handicrafts across the street in **Las Recovas de Colón.**

As you continue east, along Avenida República, notice the buildings. Many go back to the colonial period. A few blocks down Avenida República is Paraguay's government palace, **El Palacio de Gobierno.** Although smaller than most presidential palaces, it still has a majestic air. It was built by Carlos Antonio López in the mid-19th century in the hope that his son, Francisco Solano López, would take up residence there. Unfortunately, the elder López's plans were disrupted by the Triple Alliance War, in which he lost his son in a decisive battle near the Brazilian border before the building was completed. Today, the building houses the offices of the president and the Ministry of Foreign Affairs. It is open Monday to Friday from 8am to noon and 3 to 6pm and Saturday from 8 to 10am.

Continuing through the gardens along the way, you'll pass through the **Plaza Mariscal,** with its large equestrian statue of Paraguay's greatest hero, Francisco Solano López. Benches along the paths make it especially lovely to come here at the end of the day. Many young couples will attest to this. Just a little farther are the **Plaza de la Constitución** and **El Cabildo** (the legislative palace). The small tank in the center of the plaza was captured from the Bolivian forces by the Paraguayan army during the Chaco War. El Cabildo occupies the site of Asunción's original Town Hall. The 19th-century **cathedral,** very basic in design, is at the end of the plaza. A small museum to the left of the main altar houses a fine collection of religious paintings and sculptures dating back to the colonial period, as well as arms from the Triple Alliance and Chaco wars.

ORGANIZED TOURS

The largest tour operator in Asunción is **Inter-Express,** at Yegros 690 (tel. 90-111, 90-112, 90-113, or 90-114). It offers tours throughout Asunción and Paraguay, as well as to the Iguasu Falls (Brazilian and Argentinean sides).

---

7. SAVVY SHOPPING

DEPARTMENT STORES

Most department stores in Asunción offer a lot of "imported" merchandise, especially cosmetics, perfumes, liquors, and designer fashions. They accept all major credit cards and foreign currencies, especially dollars. **Shopping Vendôme,** at the corner of Estrella and O'Leary, and **Galerías Guaraní,** Palma 931, cater to a fairly upscale clientele. They are exclusive representatives of Pierre Cardin, Cartier, Piaget, Guy Laroche, Estée Lauder, Elizabeth Arden, Calvin Klein, and Samsonite. Other lines of fine cosmetics and designer apparel are available at **Magazine Unicentro,** on the corner of Palma and 15 de Agosto, and **Centro de Compras Martel,** at Palma 473.

BEST BUYS

It would be a pity to leave Paraguay without buying a few doilies or placemats made of *nandutí* lace. These colorful items are unique to Paraguay. *Nandutí* combines lace-making as introduced by the Spanish and embellishments added by the Paraguayans.

According to legend, several centuries ago the fiancé of a young Paraguayan woman failed to appear on their wedding day. The distraught young woman searched for him in the woods, only to find his dead body at dusk. She kept vigil beside him all night long. At sunrise, seeing his body covered by a shimmering mantle of spider webs, she rushed home and returned with a needle and thread and copied the patterns of the spider webs in a beautiful shroud for her lover. Thus was born the first piece of *nandutí.*

Today, there are more than 100 basic patterns of *nandutí,* and designers are always creating new ones. Remember that the best *nandutí* is tightly woven; the more intricate the design, the greater its value.

Paraguay also offers good values in leather goods (mostly bags and luggage), as well as in ceramics, straw and rattan products, and *ahó-po-í* (embroidered cotton cloth). An interesting gift idea might be the unique gold and silver rings sold in Asunción; they resemble wedding bands, but once placed on the wearer's finger, they cannot be removed unless you know the ring's secret. For what appears to be one wide band is actually 12 very narrow rings intertwined.

When walking along Estrella and Palma, you may be surprised by the large number of small Korean-run electronics shops. *Beware:* What may seem like a bargain product could actually be a cheap imitation, which will work only briefly before breaking down.

WHERE TO SHOP

The best shopping area is near the port in Las Recovas de Colón. Here you'll find many stores offering an assortment of leather goods, as well as dresses, blouses, and other items made of *ahò-po-í* and *nandutí.* Good choices include **El Pampero, Galería Colón, La Recova,** and **Artesanías el Cacique.** Many straw products, including hats, mats, and baskets, are sold outside by vendors who set up shop under the arches.

Right around the corner, on Presidente Franco, are a number of little shops, typically run by women, selling *ahó-po-í* goods—tablecloths, dresses, blouses, men's shirts, and children's clothing. We especially recommend **Artesanias Nabene, Artesanias Tía Anita,** and **Artesanias Sra. Teresa.**

Victoria, at Iturbe 187, on the corner of Eligio Ayalas, offers a wonderful selection of ceramic items, as well as leather, *ñandutí,* and *ahó-po-í.* It is designed as a small gift shop, and its prices are on the high side.

The best place for leather goods is **Casa Vera,** on Mariscal Estigarribia. For fancier leather items, such as women's handbags and attaché cases, stop by **La Casa del Portofolio,** on the corner of Palma and Montevideo.

Leathers International specializes in high-fashion leather clothing: jackets, skirts, trousers, blazers, and boots (some of original design). One shop is in the Galería Palma Shopping Center; another is in the Yennifer Center Arcad; and the third is on the corner of Palma and 14 de Mayo.

Behage, at Ayolas 222, on the corner of Palma, offers beautifully carved wooden figurines, ranging from peasants in typical dress to more modern designs; as well as more practical items, such as trays and coasters. Prices start at $6.

You can experience the hustle and bustle of an outdoor market at **Mercado Cuatro** or **Mercado Petti Rossi.** Here, you'll find hundreds of stalls, many run by Koreans, selling just about anything. The four-block market is bordered by the Avenida Petti Rossi, Avenida Peru, and Rua de Colombia. From the center of town, take bus no. 2, 5, 7, 14, 15, 21, 27, 38, or 45; ask the driver to let you off at the Mercado Cuatro.

8. EVENING ENTERTAINMENT

Compared with other South American capitals, Asunción has little nightlife. Few people are out on the streets after dark, except for those at outdoor restaurant tables. This may explain why Asunción is one of the safest cities.

DISCOS The largest and hottest dance club in Asunción is **Discotheque Thunder** in the Hotel Excelsior. State-of-the-art special effects and light show, plus great dance music, draw crowds here on Wednesday through Saturday nights from 10pm to 4am.

The next most popular club is **El Caracol** ("The Snail"), 10 minutes away by taxi from the center of town, on Avenida Felix Bogado. Shaped like a huge white snail, it's impossible to miss. The club attracts loyal patrons every weekend. The music really gets going at midnight and doesn't stop until dawn. The club has a couples-only policy, and there's a $5 cover charge.

Two less-trendy choices are **Musap,** on the corner of Avenida San Martín and Del Maestra, and **Tabasco,** on the corner of Avenida Primero de Mayo and Felicidad.

There is also a small disco at the **Casino Yacht and Golf Club Paraguayo.** The patrons here tend to be in their late teens or early 20s, mostly the children of wealthy Paraguayans who are members. The **Boîte Yasy** nearby, in the gambling casino of the Ita Enramada, is also a popular spot for dancing and entertainment.

PUBS There are few pubs in Asunción. Most socializing occurs in restaurants with outdoor tables such as **San Marcos Pepone de Fernando Velázquez y Vezzet** and **Le Gran Café.** Other popular meeting places include some of the confiterías: **Da Vinci,** on Calle Estrella, and the **Café Sibelius Pub,** on Presidente Franco. For a romantic setting, try the piano bar on the 15th floor of the **Hotel Internacional,** at Ayolas 520.

CASINOS Casinogoers have their choice of three. The newest is at the **Hotel**

Casino Yacht y Golf Club Paraguayo, which is managed by Casino Entertainment Ltd. The **Itá Enramada,** open nightly, features 30 roulette wheels, blackjack, and one-armed bandits. In the downtown area, the **Hotel Guaraní** also has a casino.

FOR MEN ONLY Although nightlife here is relatively subdued, such is not the case at a couple of spots that cater only to a male audience: **Le Carousel,** just up the street from the Hotel Guaraní, at Calle Independencia Nacional 659, offers an international cabaret with a striptease. The show at the **Playboy Club,** on the corner of Calle Cinco de Mayo and Calle Oliva, is somewhat less respectable.

9. SUGGESTED ITINERARIES

GOLDEN OR CENTRAL CIRCUIT

A great way to see the countryside is to rent a car and follow the 120-mile Golden or Central Circuit (*Circuito de Oro* or *Circuito Central*). We recommend that you travel the Central Circuit on your own. Driving is safe in Paraguay, and you can rent a car from **Hertz** either at the airport (tel. 206-195) or at the company's office on Avenida Eusebio Ayala (tel. 605-708), just outside the center of town. **National** (tel. 44-890) also has an office in Asunción, at Yegros 501, on the corner of Cerro Cora. If you'd rather take a guided tour, **Inter-Tours** (tel. 211-747) can make arrangements for you.

Leave Asunción on the highway that runs east toward Brazil. Follow it for 5 miles until you reach the highway that runs southeast toward Encarnación. Here the Golden Circuit actually begins. Your first stop should be **Itá,** 20 miles outside Asunción. Founded in 1539 by Dominguez Martínez de Irala, Itá is best known for its pottery, especially the black-and-white ceramic hens that symbolize good luck. Itá's artisans display their wares right on the street.

Seven miles beyond Itá you'll come to **Yguarón,** founded the same year by the same man. During the Conquest, Yguarón served as the seat of the Franciscan missions. Its baroque-style church is Paraguay's most treasured colonial-period work by the Guaraní Indians. The altar pulpit and the confessionals are carved in wood, painted gold, and decorated with inlaid work.

Next along the route you'll come to **Paraguarí,** at the apex of a triangle. You should now begin heading northeast toward the highway linking Asunción and Brazil. The road will become noticeably hillier as you enter the Cordillera. Take time to enjoy the views of the surrounding countryside. Paraguarí was founded in 1775 by Fernando de Pinedo.

Continuing through the Cordillera for another 14 miles, you'll reach picturesque **Chololo.** If you packed a picnic lunch, you'll want to enjoy it here, next to the falls. Otherwise, stop in at the Chololo Restaurant. The dining room is uniquely situated above a small stream, with tables set among tropical shrubbery; the view of the falls is fantastic. If you want to swim, there are changing facilities and showers at the falls. A mile and a half beyond Chololo, you'll see a sign for **Pireta Falls.** Although 6 miles off the route, the falls and the pools are bigger than those at Chololo and worth a detour.

The next stop is historic **Piribebuy.** This tranquil village was the site of a battle on August 11, 1869, during the War of the Triple Alliance. War buffs will want to stop in at the **Pedro Pablo Caballero Museum** to see the collection of trophies and memorabilia from the Triple Alliance and Chaco wars.

Nine miles beyond Piribebuy, you'll come to a junction with the Asunción-Brazil highway. From here, you should head west toward Asunción. Six miles down the road you'll come to **Caacupé,** site of Paraguay's holiest shrine—the Virgen de los Milagros (Virgin of Miracles). Thousands of pilgrims come here each year for the feast of the Immaculate Conception on December 8; after work the previous evening, many people leave on foot in order to arrive in Caacupé for the sunrise mass. The Virgin, best known for her blue eyes, stands looking down upon the altar.

As you head toward Asunción, you'll drive through a beautiful eucalyptus grove. Where the fields become quite orderly, you'll be passing the National Institute of Agronomy, a center of agricultural research run by the Ministry of Agriculture and Cattle Ranching. Shortly afterward, **Lake Ypacaraí,** one of Paraguay's large summer retreats, will appear. To get a good look, take the turnoff to San Bernadino. Once a German colony founded during the presidency of Gen. Bernadino Caballero (1880 to 1884), it is now a popular weekend getaway. Unfortunately, the lake has become rather polluted, but water skiing and sailing are relatively safe. For swimming, however, use the pool at the Hotel Casino San Bernadino or other resort.

Back on the highway heading toward Asunción, you'll pass the town of **Ypacaraí,** founded in 1889, during Caballero's presidency. Our next stop is **Itaguá,** home of ñandutí lace. Here, you'll see brilliantly colored tablecloths displayed along the road. Prices vary from shop to shop, so check prices and be prepared to bargain. Itaguá was founded by Governor Martín de Barua in 1728.

Six miles past Itaguá, at **Capiatá,** the church boasts a beautiful wooden altar, designed and carved by the Guaraní under the direction of the Franciscan fathers. Next, take a quick detour to **Areguá** on the shores of Lake Ypacaraí. Founded by Dominguez Martínez de Irala, Areguá is a popular summer retreat (as well as home of Paraguay's Satellite Communications Station).

San Lorenzo, site of the University of Paraguay, is our final destination before returning to Asunción. The city was founded in 1775 by Governor Fernando de Pinedo. Another major attraction is San Lorenzo's Gothic church.

JESUIT RUINS

At the beginning of the 17th century, the Jesuits began coming to Paraguay to establish missions and evangelize the Guaraní Indians, whom they tried to save from Portuguese slave traders in Brazil. Unlike some South American Indians, the Guaraní were, and still are, a friendly and peaceful people. They welcomed the Jesuits and helped them establish their *reducciónes* (settlements) for the Indians (commonly called *missiones*).

The *reducciónes* were so successful—economically, politically, and culturally—that Voltaire described them as a "triumph of humanity." The reasons for their success are obvious. Unlike Spanish colonists elsewhere in South America, the Jesuits preserved the Guaraní's social system; besides educating them and teaching them Spanish, the Jesuits encouraged the Guaraní to use their own language. Over a period of 150 years, the Jesuits established more than 30 missions (mostly in southern Paraguay but also in Argentina and Brazil) and converted more than 140,000 Indians. They also established the first printing press in South America, introduced the harp and other musical instruments, trained choirs, improved cattle breeding and agriculture, advanced medicine, and established an observatory at **San Cosme.** The Guaraní themselves performed much of the construction and stonework in the missions. Much of this work was left unfinished in 1767, when the Jesuits were expelled from Paraguay by Spain's King Carlos III because they had challenged the monarch's "divine right" to rule over the colony. You can see the ruins of the missions by driving from Asunción to Encarnación. It would be best to drive there one day, spend the night in Encarnación, and return the following day.

To reach the missions, take the road heading south out of Asunción toward Encarnación. The most famous ruins are at Jesús and Trinidad, just outside Encarnación.

San Miguel, some 70 miles beyond Paraguarí, marks the beginning of Jesuit mission territory. Here you'll find excellent buys in woolens, ponchos, and cloaks. From San Miguel onward, the towns were named by their Jesuit founders.

Pass through San Juan Bautista to **Santa María.** A Jesuit *reducción* was founded here in 1674. Most noteworthy are the wooden statues—more than 50 of them, and some nearly 7 feet tall.

The first Jesuit mission was founded in **San Ignacio** in 1610 (not to be confused with the more famous San Ignacio Mini in Argentina). The village itself was founded by the Fathers of the Company of Jesus in 1608. Be sure to visit the Museum of Religious Art, (located in a restored home) with its interesting collection of wooden figures. Most impressive is the 7-foot figure of the Archangel San Raphael. Another *reducción* is in **Santa Rosa,** about 14 miles from San Ignacio.

The ruins at **Santos Cosme y Damian** are especially noteworthy. Founded in 1634 as a Jesuit mission and Guaraní *reducción*, there is an observatory here. Traces of it are visible among the ruins, which include a sundial, an altar chair, and a statue of Jesus. Be sure to study the Mudejar-style church facade.

The best ruins of all, **Trinidad** and **Jesús,** are on the 150-mile Encarnación Highway which connects Encarnación with Ciudad del Este on Paraguay's border with Brazil. About 12 miles outside Encarnación, you'll come to a turnoff for the Tirol Hotel. Follow it for about 6 miles to reach the area's first major Jesuit mission, the village of Trinidad.

The best-preserved mission in Paraguay, it was founded in 1742 and abandoned a few years after the Jesuits were expelled. Most of the original walls are still standing. Serious restoration work began in 1981 with a number of archeological investigations. Some of the statuary has already been restored. The church, built in 1745, contains excellent examples of the Guaraní carvings completed under the direction of the Jesuits. Be sure to look at the friezes depicting Guaraní angels playing harpsichords, pipe organs, and other baroque instruments.

WHERE TO STAY

CRISTAL, Mariscal Estigarribia 1157, at the corner of Calle Cora, Encarnación. Tel. 071-2371. 48 rms (all with bath).
This downtown hotel is first class.

NOVOTEL, Villa Quiteria CC18, Encarnación. Tel. 071-4220. 102 rms, 4 suites (all with bath). A/C MINIBAR TV TEL
All of the accommodations in this first-class hotel have piped-in music. The hotel also has a restaurant, barbecue facilities, a pool, tennis courts, horseback riding, and convention facilities.

TIROL HOTEL, Ruta VI Capitan Miranda. Tel. 071-2388.
A more rustic choice is the Tirol, 12 miles outside the city. Quiet and completely isolated, it offers the choice of a room with private bath or a private bungalow. There are four pools on the grounds, each carved into the rocks and surrounded by subtropical forest. In keeping with the hotel's name, the cuisine is German.

THE CHACO

The northwestern three-fifths of Paraguay are covered by the flat, semiarid, and largely featureless plains of the Gran Chaco, which also extends into Argentina and Bolivia. Barren and desolate for the most part, the Chaco is home to the Quebrancho tree, the world's only source of tannin. It is also the site of Paraguay's **Mennonite colonies.**

The Mennonites—most of whom are Germans—first arrived in Paraguay in 1926. They came to escape the persecution experienced in their homeland due to their religious beliefs, which forbid military service. The Paraguayan government gave them a legal guarantee that they would not be called to military service even during war time and allowed them to establish self-governing communities in the most isolated part of the country, the Chaco. The Mennonites established modern farms, milk-processing centers, cattle ranches, schools, hospitals, and even their own electric-power stations. Most business is conducted in German, although the Mennonites also speak Spanish.

Most Mennonite settlements are in the area of **Filadelfia.** This small city in the Chaco was founded in 1931 as the center of the Mennonite colony **Fernheim** ("Distant Home"). It should be your base for seeing the Chaco.

GETTING THERE

You can either book a tour—through Inter-Express in Asunción—or travel there on your own. The Inter-Express tour will include transportation; hotel accommodations in Filadelfia; a tour of the city (including a visit to the **Jacob Unger Museum,** with its collection of farm tools, exotic stuffed animals, and handicrafts); visits to agricultural and industrial plants; and a farm tour (weather permitting).

WHERE TO STAY

If you decide to visit the Chaco on your own, be sure to book a room in advance at the Chaco's only hotel.

HOTEL FLORIDA, Filadelfia. Tel. 91-354.
Take the Trans-Chaco road out of Asunción; it's about a 7-hour trip. Inquire at the hotel about a guide to take you to the farms.

IGUASU FALLS

If you want to visit Iguasu Falls (see Chapter 3) but don't plan to go to Argentina or Brazil, an excellent and inexpensive way to get there is by bus from Asunción.

The **Nuestra Señora de la Asunción** line has executive buses leaving from the main terminal every day at 12:15am. The large reclining seats make it easy to sleep. The fare is $10 each way. You'll get to Foz do Iguacú about 7am. In Foz, ask directions to the bus station for buses to the falls. You should have no trouble finding it. The bus to the falls costs about $2 and includes admission to the falls. You can spend the entire day there, then catch a bus back to town, and return to Asunción that evening. Be sure to reserve your return-trip ticket either when you buy your ticket in Asunción or before you leave for the falls in the morning.

Although it is more expensive, you can arrange a complete tour, including **Itaipú Dam** and the falls, at a local travel agency, such as Caribe Travel, or through Inter-Express in Asunción.

HISTORICAL TOUR

An interesting way to experience Asunción's colonial past is to take the train from Asunción to the nearby village of **Luque.**

The Paraguayan railway, established by English settlers in 1861, was among the first in South America. The original station and the first wood-burning locomotive are still in operation, just as they were over a century ago. The central train station in Asunción is an excellent example of colonial Paraguayan architecture. While here, be sure to look at the locomotive **Sapucai,** one of the first used along the Río de la Plata, and the "Presidential Wagon," originally reserved for the nation's president.

The train leaves Asunción at 12:15pm and arrives at Luque, 12 miles away at 12:55. Founded in 1636, Luque was the original capital of Paraguay and is today extremely picturesque, since it still retains colonial charm. You will find many small artisan shops that make small guitars and the famous Paraguayan harp, as well as gold filigree jewelry. The train to Luque continues on to **Lake Ypacaraí** and **Itaguá.** Unless you plan to spend the night somewhere en route, be sure to make arrangements for the return trip to Asunción; there may not be a return train until the next day (trains do not run on Sundays). Inter-Express offers guided tours to Luque as well as special chartered train excursions to other towns.

CHAPTER 8
LA PAZ, BOLIVIA

1. **INTRODUCING LA PAZ & BOLIVIA**
- **WHAT'S SPECIAL ABOUT LA PAZ**
- **WHAT THINGS COST IN LA PAZ**
2. **ORIENTATION**
3. **GETTING AROUND**
- **FAST FACTS: LA PAZ**
4. **WHERE TO STAY**
5. **WHERE TO DINE**
6. **ATTRACTIONS**
- **DID YOU KNOW . . . ?**
7. **SPORTS & RECREATION**
8. **SAVVY SHOPPING**
9. **EVENING ENTERTAINMENT**
10. **SUGGESTED ITINERARIES**
11. **MOVING ON**

La Paz is up so high in the Andes that until recently there was no fire department—fires simply don't have much luck in the city's thin, low-oxygen atmosphere. The city leaders, deciding a few years ago that a city without a fire department really couldn't consider itself part of the 20th century, purchased one—but it doesn't get much of a workout.

Change is thus coming to La Paz. There are lovely new hotels and several surprisingly good restaurants, but La Paz is a city where an ancient Indian customs are practiced. The clothing of the Indians, their markets, and their traditions are not a show; they are an integral part of everyday life.

The staggering physical beauty of La Paz surrounds the Indian culture. Deep, tropical jungles only a short distance away provide a startling contrast between the city of La Paz and nearby nature.

1. INTRODUCING LA PAZ & BOLIVIA

La Paz's Indian population (called Paceños, pronounced "Pa-*say*-nyos") makes up about half of the more than 700,000 residents. Many of the Indians trace their lineage back to the proud and wealthy Incas of the 15th and 16th centuries. Ironically, today the Indian quarter, located in the highest reaches of La Paz, is the poorest section of the city. Unlike the upper-income groups of many other cities, the wealthy of La Paz live in the lower-altitude areas where the climate is more moderate, and requires less effort in getting about.

Indian houses cling to the mountainsides on the road which winds its way down from the airport to La Paz. Made of sun-dried mud brick, the houses have metal roofs, sometimes held in place by large rocks. Few have heat or plumbing.

According to Indian custom, women wear several brightly colored skirts

IMPRESSIONS

To be enclosed between two lofty ranges and two deserts, to live at the bottom of a hole and yet be nearly as high above sea level as the top of the Rocky Mountains or the Jungfrau are strange conditions for a dwelling place.
—JAMES BRYCE, SOUTH AMERICA, 1912

[La Paz] was a city of cement and stale bread, of ice storms that produced a Bulgarian aroma of wet tweeds, built above the timber line in a high pass in the Andes . . . it was hard to believe I was not in eastern Europe.
—PAUL THEROUX, THE OLD PATAGONIAN EXPRESS, 1979

WHAT'S SPECIAL ABOUT LA PAZ

Athletic Challenges
☐ Mt. Chacaltaya, an hour's drive from La Paz, features the world's most challenging skiing.

Climate
☐ Although usually quite pleasant, temperatures in La Paz can drop several degrees in a matter of minutes.

Festival
☐ Carnival in Oruro, 100 miles south of La Paz, is one of the most magnificent festivals in South America.

Museum
☐ The Gold Museum (Museo del Oro) contains an excellent collection of over 30,000 Tiwanacu artifacts.

Natural Spectacle
☐ The unusual land formations of the Valley of the Moon never cease to amaze visitors.

Nightlife
☐ At a Peña Folklórica visitors and residents lose their inhibitions as they dance together to the music of the Andes.

People
☐ Over half of La Paz's residents are Aymara Indians. Descendants of the Inca, they still practice their traditional way of dress and language.

Shopping
☐ At the witches market on Calle Linares, you'll find items that will challenge your imagination.

(*polleras*), with knitted shawls or blankets over their shoulders. Their braided jet-black hair is topped off by hard brown or black bowler hats. A common street sight is an Indian mother breast-feeding one child while her other tots play on the rock-strewn roadside. Often women carry babies on their backs in slings made of blankets.

WHAT THINGS COST IN LA PAZ	U.S. $
Cab from the airport into the city	6.00
Downtown bus fare	.25
Double with bath at the Hotel Austria (budget)	10.00
Double with bath at the Hotel España (moderate)	20.00
Double with bath at the Sucre Palace Hotel (deluxe)	45.00
Lunch at Eli's (budget)	3.00
Dinner at the Restaurant de la Paz (budget)	5.00
Dinner with wine at El Tropero (moderate)	8.00
Dinner with wine at Alaya (splurge)	20.00

2. ORIENTATION

About 2½ miles above sea level—higher than Denver and Mexico City—La Paz is the world's highest capital. At almost 13,000 feet, the air is rarified, and you'll undoubtedly feel lightheaded and headachy. *Soroche* (light headedness) is a normal condition for visitors unaccustomed to the altitude and will pass within a day.

ARRIVING

During your flight into **El Alto Airport,** you'll pass over Lake Titicaca, the world's highest navigable lake. It's an incredible and memorable sight. The deep-blue texture of the water blends with the snow covered mountains to create an almost mystic effect.

After your plane lands and you head downwards toward the city, you'll peer down into the bowl-shaped valley containing La Paz. At night the whole scene looks like a bowl of stars. Ever present is the snow-capped Illimani Mountain—an awesome and breathtaking backdrop to the city.

After passing through Customs at the airport, if you don't already have hotel reservations you should stop at the information desk, operated by the Dirección Nacional de Turismo, and give the clerk some of our recommendations. The clerk will gladly call and make a reservation for you, as well as give you a quick orientation to La Paz. Since there isn't an actual exchange office in the airport, you can also change enough money here to pay for a cab into town (around $6).

Until just recently, the best—and virtually the only—way to reach La Paz from El Alto Airport was by taxi. Fortunately, **Cotranstur** now offers minibus service to and from the airport. The fare is $1, and buses operate every five minutes from 7am to 9pm. You can be dropped off anywhere along the route, which passes through Perez Velasco, the Plaza San Francisco, Avenida Camacho, and El Prado, past the university, and ends at the Plaza Isabel La Católica.

TOURIST INFORMATION

The **Centro de Información Turística** is on the 18th floor of the Mariscal Ballivián building on Mercado, between Loayza and Colón (tel. 367-463). A large tour service is **Crillon Tours,** at Avenida Camacho 1223 (tel. 374-566). Make arrangements here for in-city, jungle, and Lake Titicaca tours. Tours come complete with a late-model car, a driver, and an English-speaking guide. A half-day city tour for two, with Moon Valley included, is $20, while a one-day jungle trip will cost a couple $150. Equally good is **Balsa Tours,** at Calle Capitán Ravelo 2077 (tel. 3-57-817), which charges $20 per person for a city tour. Consider, too, **Exprinter,** at Plaza Venezuela 1440 (tel. 355-926), and **Magri Tours,** at Avenida 16 de Julio 1490, 5th floor (tel. 341-201). Be sure to shop for the best prices.

CITY LAYOUT

MAIN ARTERIES   The main artery of La Paz is the Prado, which also has several different names. The most important stretch of the Prado is **16 de Julio,** which runs six blocks from the statue of Simón Bolívar, at **Plaza Venezuela,** to the **Plaza Franz Tamayo** (better known as the **Plaza del Estudiante** because of its proximity to the University of La Paz).

From the Plaza Venezuela to the Plaza San Francisco, the Prado is known as **Santa Cruz** (uphill from 16 de Julio). From the Plaza Roma, downhill toward the university, it is called **Avenida Villazón** and then **6 de Agosto.**

Another orientation point is the **Plaza Murillo,** three blocks above the Prado from the obelisk on Camacho. This large square contains the president's palace and an enormous cathedral. The streets that intersect the Prado run at sharp angles up the hillside, which makes for fatiguing uphill walking when you veer off the main boulevard. Remember that the thin air can cause discomfort when you exert yourself.

Sharply contrasting with bustling downtown La Paz is the higher-in-altitude **Indian quarter,** which extends from the **Plaza San Francisco,** about four blocks from the obelisk, up a fairly steep hillside or, more accurately, a small mountainside. This quarter embraces about two-thirds of the land area in La Paz. A typical Indian street, leading up from the Plaza San Francisco, is the cobblestoned **Calle Sagárnaga,** lined with Indian-owned shops. Other Indian centers are **Avenida Manco Kapac** (named after the legendary first Inca) and the tumultuous **Calle Buenos Aires,** a teeming shopping area high in the Indian quarter.

3. GETTING AROUND

BY BUS Small modern buses called *micros* (pronounced "*mee*kros") charge only 25¢ within the downtown area and 50¢ for distances farther out. There are also large buses called *colectivos,* which charge 20¢, but these are very crowded. Avoid buses called INTERURBANO TRANSPORTATION. They are more like trucks and are jam-packed with people who stand in the rear.

BY TAXI Cabs are so cheap—about 75¢ and up for two passengers to most parts of the city—that we strongly recommend them. But hard-core budgeteers can do even better: there are taxis called *trufis* that operate as jitneys along fixed routes on main streets, such as the Prado, with fares of only 50¢ to 60¢.

La Paz has various radio taxi companies including, **COTRANSTUR** which specializes in airport service. Call 3-78-428 and a taxi will get to you soon after. The fare is $3 for the metropolitan area, $5 to residential sections, and $8 to the airport, plus $1 for each piece of luggage. For about $5 an hour, you can hire a taxi an English-speaking driver to help you see the sights. One reliable driver is Gerhard Arnsdorff (tel. 3-27-078), who also speaks German.

BY CAR You won't need a car if you're planning to visit La Paz only. However, if you're planning to visit Lake Titicaca and the surrounding countryside, a car is the best way to do so. **National Car Rental** is at Calle Federico Zuazo 1935 (tel. 376-581); **International Car Rental** is just a few doors down at Calle Federico Zuazo 1942 (tel. 357-061).

FAST LA PAZ

Airline Offices **American Airlines** has an office in the 16 de Julio Building at 16 de Julio 1566, Office 104 (tel. 351-360). The **United Airlines** office is at Avenida Arce 2355, Office 104 (tel. 366-887). **Lloyd Boliviano** is at Avenida Camacho 1456–60 (tel. 353-054).

American Express **Magri Turismo,** located at Avenida 16 de Julio 1490, fifth floor (tel. 32-3954), is the American Express representative in La Paz.

Area Code The country code for Bolivia is 591; the city code for La Paz is 2.

Babysitters The concierge at your hotel may be able to help you arrange for child care.

Bookstores **Amigos del Libro,** on Calle Mercado and Avenida 6 de Agosto, has some books in English.

Business Hours **Banks** are open Monday through Friday from 8:30 to 11:30am and 2:30 to 5pm. Most **stores** are open weekdays from 9am to 12:30pm and 2:30 to 7pm. Stores are also open Saturday mornings.

Car Rentals See "Getting Around" earlier in this chapter.

Climate The atmosphere is so thin at this altitude that the effects of the sun are quickly felt. Therefore, you'll sunburn easily if you're fair-skinned. But the temperature can change quickly when clouds mask the sun or in late afternoon, and they can drop 10 or more degrees in a few minutes. So, we advise you carry a heavy sweater

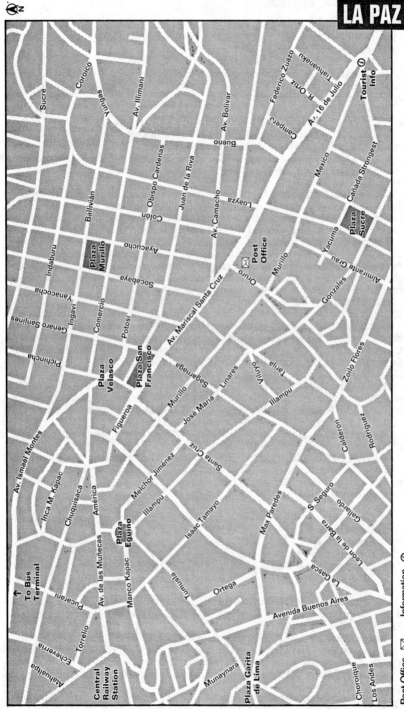

LA PAZ

N

Tourist Info ⓘ

Trahuanaku
R. Ortiz
Federico Zuazo
Campero
Av. 16 de Julio
Mexico
Cañada Strongest
Coroico
Sucre
Yungas
Av. Illimani
Av. Bolívar
Bueno
ouang
Obispo Cardenas
Juan de la Riva
Av. Camacho
Loayza
Plaza Sucre
Balliván
Colón
Ayacucho
Socabaya
Av. Mariscal Santa Cruz
Oruro
Post Office ⊠
Murillo
Yacuma
Almirante Grau
Plaza Murillo
Indaburu
Yanacocha
Genaro Sanjines
Ingavi
Comercio
Potosí
Gonzales
Pichincha
Plaza Velasco
Plaza San Francisco
Sagárnaga
Murillo
José María
Linares
Tarija
Viluyo
Illampu
Zoilo Flores
Figueroa
Rodríguez
Av. Ismael Montes
Santa Cruz
Calderón
Inca M. Kapac
Chuquisaca
América
Melchor Jiménez
Illampu
Max Paredes
S. Seguro
Gallardo
To Bus Terminal
Pucarani
Av. de las Munecas
Manco Kapac
Isaac Tamayo
Tumusla
León de la Barra
La Gasca
Torrelio
Plaza Eguino
Ortega
Avenida Buenos Aires
Atahualpa
Echeverria
Central Railway Station
Munaynara
Plaza Garita de Lima
Choroique
Los Andes

Post Office ⊠   Information ⓘ

with you. While the temperatures can drop quickly, they seldom dip below freezing. The mercury averages about 50°F most of the year. Snow is rare in La Paz. Summer (December to February) is the rainy season.

Crime   See "Safety" below.

Currency   Since a democratically elected government established economic measures to stop the rampant inflation that plagued the country in 1985, the money situation has become more stable.

Currency Exchange   As of summer 1992, 3.9 bolivianos are worth US$1. This rate is just about the same in the exchange houses, the Central Bank, and the hotels, as well as on the parallel market, where it is perfectly legal to change. We usually change at the **Casa de Cambios Caceres,** in the Hotel Gloria on Calle Potosí 909 (tel. 3-41-457); **Casa de Cambios Sudamer,** at Calle Colón 253 (tel. 3-27-341); and **Casa de Cambios América,** at Avenida Camacho 1233 (tel. 3-40-920).

Dentists/Doctors   Contact the embassy for a list of English-speaking dentists or doctors. The concierge in your hotel may be able to recommend one. Dental and medical assistance are available at **SERMEDE** at Avenida Ecuador 2297, at the corner with R. Gutiérrez (tel. 327-421); they accept VISA.

Drugstores   Pharmacies are plentiful here, and most are stocked with U.S.-made goods. Just as in most of South America, pharmacies in La Paz use the **Farmacia de Turno** system, in which one pharmacy in every neighborhood is open 24 hours. To find out which pharmacies are open call 366-823. Also, the concierge in your hotel can direct you to the nearest open pharmacy.

Electricity   Buildings in La Paz are supplied with both 110 and 220 volts, but 220 volts is more common. Other cities in Bolivia are supplied with 220 volts only.

Embassies/Consulates   The **United States Embassy** is located in the Banco Popular building on the corner of Colón and Mercado (tel. 350-251). The **U.S. Consulate** is at Calle Potosí 1285 and is open mornings. The **United Kingdom Embassy** and **Consulate** are at Avenida Arce 2732 (tel. 329-401). The **Canadian Consulate** is a few blocks away at Arce 2342 (tel. 375-224).

Emergencies   The Tourist Police can be reached at 361-138 or 367-441. If you're robbed, contact the Tourist Information Office in the Mariscal Ballivián building (18th floor) on Mercado, between Colón and Loayza (Centro de Información Turística) at 367-463.

Eyeglasses   There are opticians throughout the city. The concierge at your hotel should be able to direct you to one nearby.

Hairdressers/Barbers   If you're in need of a haircut, try **Capelli** (tel. 328-047), on the lower level of the Mariscal de Ayacucho Gallery, or **Roxana Estilista Unisex,** on Avenida Ballivián between Calles 9 and 10 (tel. 785-890).

Holidays

Carnival	Monday and Tuesday before Ash Wednesday
Good Friday	Varies
Labor Day	May 1
Corpus Chrisiti	60 days after Good Friday
Independence Day	August 6
All Saints Day	November 1 or 2

Hospitals   The **Clínica del Sur** (tel. 784-001 or 784-002), at Avenida H. Siles 3539, is equipped for emergencies. It has an office on the second floor of the La Paz Hotel (tel. 390-711 or 390-712).

Information   See "Tourist Information" earlier in this chapter.

Language   The official language is Spanish, but the Indians speak Aymara and Quechua, derivations of Inca and pre-Inca tongues.

Laundry/Dry Cleaning   Most of the large hotels offer laundry and dry-cleaning service.

Luggage Storage/Lockers   If you're planning a short trip, you may be able to store your things at your hotel.

Newspapers/Magazines Los Amigos del Libro on Calle Mercado carries *Time, Newsweek,* the *Miami Herald,* and the *International Herald Tribune.* You can also pick these up at the Plaza Hotel, Paseo del Prado 1789.

Photographic Needs Film is readily available in La Paz, although prices will be considerably higher than those in the United States. Check the expiration date before buying.

Post Office/Mail An airmail letter to the United States costs the equivalent of 75¢. Purchase stamps at any major hotel or at the main post office, on Calle Ayacucho, near the Plaza Murillo; hours are 8am to 7pm. *Tip:* Upon request, and at twice the normal rate, the post office will immediately deliver outgoing mail to the airport to make a flight.

Religious Services The concierge in your hotel should be able to inform you of the availability and schedule of services in your faith. Bolivia is predominantly Catholic.

Restrooms Your best option is hotel lobbies. Most restaurants and museums have restrooms for patrons.

Safety La Paz is relatively safe. However, like anywhere else, keep an eye on your belongings at all times; be careful in crowds; avoid walking alone at night; and leave your valuables at home.

Shoe Repairs Ask the concierge in your hotel to direct you to a nearby shoe-repair shop.

Taxes You pay a $15 airport tax when leaving the country, plus a $2 municipal tax.

Taxis See "Getting Around" earlier in this chapter.

Telegrams/Telexes/Faxes The five-star La Paz and Plaza hotels offer fax and telex services.

Telephone Most pay phones are in stores or hotels. Give the owner or desk clerk about 5¢ and dial your number. When calling the United States, dialing AT&T Direct (tel. toll free 0800/1111) will reduce the cost substantially.

Useful Telephone Numbers For the airport, call 810-122; for the bus station, call 367-274; for the local time, call 117.

4. WHERE TO STAY

As elsewhere in booming South America, prices have been increasing in La Paz. And, naturally, this is reflected in hotel costs. Still, we have found a number of good-value hotels and pensions. Remember, all prices include a hefty 28% tax and service bite.

ON THE PRADO

The most convenient area for travelers to bed down is in the vicinity of La Paz's main street—Avenida 16 de Julio (the center portion of the Prado).

HOSTERIA CLAUDIA, Avenida Villazón 1965. Tel. 3-72-917. 68 rms. (some with bath). A/C

$ Rates: $12 single with bath; $12 double without bath, $21 double with bath. This basic hotel has clean carpeted rooms with drapes and bare furnishings. Avenida Villazón is the extension of the main Avenida 16 de Julio.

HOTEL ESPAÑA, Avenida 6 de Agosto 2074. Tel. 3-54-643. All rooms with bath. TEL

$ Rates (including breakfast): $20 double.

The España is a lovely hotel with comfortable rooms half a block from the University. It has its own restaurant and a small shopping arcade with a gift shop and travel agency. Parking is available.

RESIDENCIAL 6 DE AGOSTO, Avenida 6 de Agosto 2548. Tel. 3-55-122.
Most rooms with bath.
$ Rates: $12 single with bath; $19 double with bath; $25 triple with bath.
In this modest two-story hotel, you'll find comfortable, although basic, accommodations. There are several bathless singles that cost less. The rooms are carpetless, with old furniture, but they're clean.

NEAR PLAZA MURILLO

Paceños consider the Plaza Murillo the true heart of the city. This grassy square, whose benches are usually occupied by office workers, housewives, and couples, is about the highest-altitude non-Indian area of La Paz.

HOSTAL AUSTRIA, Yanacocha 531. Tel. 3-35-1140.
$ Rates (including tax and service): $6 single; $10 double.
This top budget choice is located one block from Plaza Murillo, on a steep street. Recently refurbished and surprisingly colorful, the Austria offers solid value, even if you select the higher-priced front rooms. A heater is included in the more expensive accommodations. The front-windowed doubles are comfortable and sunny. The management provides bulky blankets for heatless rooms (remember there is hot water in the morning and evenings only).

HOTEL AVENIDA, Montes 690. Tel. 3-76-017. 47 rms (some with bath).
$ Rates: $8–$10 single without bath, $14 single with bath; $11–$14 double without bath, $19 double with bath.
The Avenida is near Calle Boso, on the outer fringe of the Indian quarter. Popular with students, it's an aging four-story walkup that has been refurbished just enough to make it a good value. An intercom system connecting all rooms with the front desk assures you of getting towels and messages promptly. We recommend staying in a front double with bath; you'll find it well lit and casually livable, with twin beds, a desk, a bureau, and a sink. Rear bathless doubles are far gloomier. There is no elevator, so try to get a lower-floor room. And be sure to ask for a heater if your room lacks one. (Keep in mind that Avenida Montes, a continuation of 16 de Julio, is in the city's higher, and poorer, reaches.)

HOTEL CALACOTO, Calle 13 8009. Tel. 7-92-524. Some rooms with bath.
$ Rates: $8 single without bath, $15 single with bath; $11 double without bath, $18 double with bath.
The Calacoto, with rooms in all categories, has its own restaurant, which serves all meals—breakfast for $1.25 and lunch and dinner for about $5.

HOTEL LATINO, Junín 857. Tel. 3-70-947. 25 rms (some with bath).
$ Rates: $6 single without bath, $9 single with bath; $9 double without bath, $11 double with bath.
The newer Latino, at the corner of Sucre and only two blocks from the Plaza Murillo, is an excellent budget selection. The rooms are carpeted. There is a cafeteria on the premises, as well as laundry service.

THE SAN FRANCISCO CHURCH AREA

The following establishments are a short walk from the 16 de Julio area and right on the outer fringe of the Indian quarter. Many backpackers stay here purposely; no matter what your intention, these are for the young in spirit only.

GRAND HOTEL, Ev. Valle 127. Tel. 3-23-732. 60 rms (some with bath).
$ Rates: $6 single without bath, $8.50 single with bath; $6 double without bath per person, $14 double with bath.
This hotel has no elevator for its three floors, no heat, and no sign outside; but its

rooms are airy and clean and overlook the Indian market below. Photos of John F. Kennedy, who is remembered fondly in much of South America, are prominently displayed throughout the hotel.

HOSTAL CRIS, Tel. 3-67-919. 15 rms (some with bath).
$ Rates: $6 single with bath, $11 double with bath.

The rooms at this three-story establishment are sparsely furnished but nothing short of immaculate, with fresh paint, shining floors, and comfortable large beds. Bathless rooms cost slightly less. The Cris also has a locked baggage room and security boxes.

HOTEL PLAZA, Plaza Perez Velasco 785. Tel. 3-22-157. 14 rms (none with bath).
$ Rates: $6 single; $10 double.
You'll find Plaza Perez Velasco at the intersection of Montes and Santa Cruz. The Plaza has rooms spread over the first two floors—the owner's large family occupies the top floor. The rooms are quite clean; while sinkless, they do have basins. All the rooms are off an open-air courtyard.

THE INDIAN QUARTER

The Indian section in the mountain area, above the city center, offers some selections that are truly "last resort" only. All are centered near Avenida Manco Kapac and cater primarily to students and backpackers. Of course, some of our choices are more comfortable, but they cost a little more.

HOTEL ALEM, Sagárnaga 334. Tel. 3-67-400. 42 rms (some with bath). TEL
$ Rates: $10 double without bath, $12 double with bath.

Opened in 1982, the Alem is a fairly comfortable choice, with furnishings that are a touch above basic. If you came to study the Indian cultures, the location will be perfect.

HOTEL CONTINENTAL, Avenida Illampu 626. Tel. 3-78-226. Some rooms with bath.
$ Rates: $9.50 single without bath, $11 single with bath; $13 double without bath, $14.50 double with bath.
The Hotel Continental is more expensive than our other choices in this section, but it's also more comfortable, with its own restaurant and also a doctor in residence. The bus company Colectur, which offers daily service to Puno and Cuzco (8 hours), has an office in the lobby; tickets are $8.

HOTEL MILTON, on Illampu 1124, at the corner of Calderón. Tel. 3-53-511. 60 rms (some with bath).
$ Rates: $16 single with bath; $20 double with bath.

The Milton has rooms on five floors. Laundry service and piped-in music are bonuses, as are huge comfortable beds. Ask for a room in the front on an upper floor: The view of the mountains is worth the climb. This is very popular with backpackers.

HOTEL PANAMERICANO, Avenida Manco Kapac 454. Tel. 3-40-810. All rooms with bath.
$ Rates: $15 single; $18 double.
The Panamericano, a good value, has moved up a notch in both comfort and price since private baths were installed. The prices include hot water at all times, piped-in music, and wall-to-wall carpeting. There's a cafeteria on the premises, too. One drawback is the noisy market right outside.

HOTEL SAGARNAGA, Sagárnaga 326. Tel. 3-50-252. Telex 3605 HOTSA BV. 32 rms (all with bath). TEL

$ Rates (including breakfast): $12 single; $15 double. Major credit cards accepted.

⭐ A fine hotel in the Indian quarter, this is on the hilly street next to the Indian market, with rooms distributed over three floors. Bonuses are laundry service and a restaurant.

NEAR THE MIRAFLORES *FUTBOL* STADIUM

To reach this area, walk along Comercio until it becomes Avenida Illimani, some seven long blocks beyond the Plaza Murillo.

HOTEL ELDORADO, Avenida Villazón (no number). Tel. 3-63-403. Fax 3-91-438. Telex 3625 DORADO BV. All rooms with bath. TV TEL
$ Rates: $29 single; $35 double. Major credit cards accepted.
Farther down the Prado, where it becomes Avenida Villazon, you'll find the Eldorado. A few steps away from the Plaza del Estudiante and the National Tourist Center, this hotel offers carpeted, curtained rooms and a restaurant, a coffee shop, and a skyroom.

HOTEL GLORIA, Potosí 909, at the corner of Jenaro Sanjines. Tel. 3-70-010. Telex 2414 BV. 90 rms (all with bath). TV TEL
$ Rates: $76 single; $51 double. Major credit cards accepted.

⭐ The Gloria, owned by the Caceres family, offers the luxury of a first-class modern hotel, along with the small, friendly touches that make for a pleasant stay. Both father and son are on hand to make sure that service is the best. The cozy rooms are nicely furnished. The hotel also has two excellent, moderately priced restaurants (one is vegetarian the other international), and a lovely lobby with a color TV. The Gloria is located a few short blocks from Plaza San Francisco and Plaza Murillo.

HOTEL LIBERTADOR, Calle Obispo Cárdenas 1421. Tel. 3-43-363. Telex HOTELIB 2552 BV. 70 rms (all with bath). TV TEL
$ Rates: $26 single; $30 double. Major credit cards accepted.
This 14-story four-star Libertador, among the city's finer hotels, has lovely doubles. It also boasts an impressive dining room and skyroom, where you can look out at the tile roofs of La Paz's older colonial homes and churches.

RESIDENCIAL LA HOSTERIA, Calle Bueno 138. Tel. 3-22-925. All rooms with bath.
$ Rates: $25 single; $29 double. Major credit cards accepted.
The Residencial La Hostería is just 50 yards from the National Tourist Office. The hotel, a converted office building, has a restaurant, where guests can have a full American breakfast for $3.50 and international dishes for $6.

SUCRE PALACE HOTEL, Avenida 16 de Julio 1636. Tel. 3-63-390. Fax 3-92-052. Telex 2445 BV. 120 rms (all with bath). TV TEL
$ Rates: $35 single; $45 double. Extra bed $8. Major credit cards accepted.
Rooms here are tastefully furnished, all with heaters. A light-gray building, the six-story Sucre offers a fine dining room and a snack shop. It also has a mini shopping arcade with a hairdresser, a jeweler, a gift shop, and an art gallery.

SPLURGE CHOICES

LA PAZ HOTEL, on Avenida Arce (no number). Tel. 3-56-966. Fax 3-91-593. Telex 3241 SHERTON BV. 384 rms (all with bath). MINIBAR TV TEL
$ Rates: $75 single; $95–$105 double. Major credit cards accepted.
In the late 1970s, the owners of the Crillon opened the beautiful 14-story La Paz Sheraton. It is now run by the government and has changed its name to the La Paz Hotel. The lobby is impressive, the service is excellent; there are numerous gift shops, an antique shop, a florist shop, a beauty shop, a barbershop, babysitting services, a travel bureau, and a Lloyd's Airline bureau. The rooms are fully carpeted, many with breathtaking views of the city and Illimani Mountain. The hotel also has a first-class supper club, a disco, a bar, rooftop dining, and a brand new pool and sauna.

PLAZA, Paseo el Prado. Tel. 3-78-311. Fax 3-43-391. Telex 2674 or 2675 PLAZA BV. 200 rms (all with bath). MINIBAR TV TEL
$ Rates: $85 single; $100 double. Major credit cards accepted.

The five-star Plaza, located across from the Copacabana, is everything a luxury hotel should be. Large, with over 200 guest rooms, it has modern furnishings, with native touches that make it very attractive. The hotel's restaurants, El Arcón de Oro and La Fontana, serve international food and are highly regarded. There is also a 24-hour coffee shop. Amenities here include a heated pool with a Jacuzzi and sauna and a lovely shopping arcade including a travel agency. The Plaza is soon to be the home of the city's finest casino.

HOTEL PRESIDENTE, Calle Potosí 920. Tel. 3-68-601. Fax 3-54-013. Telex 2669 PRESIDT BV. 101 rooms (all with bath). MINIBAR TV TEL
$ Rates (including breakfast): $80 single; $95 double.
The Presidente is the city's newest and most luxurious five-star hotel. Rooms are spacious and comfortable, all with magnificent views of the city. One of the highlights of staying here is the Oasis Club, a full-service health spa featuring the services of a masseuse and cosmetologist; a fitness center with aerobics classes; a Jacuzzi and sauna; and a glass-enclosed pool with a poolside restaurant serving spa cuisine.

The Presidente boasts the city's only rooftop gourmet restaurant, **La Bella Vista.** A fine selection of international dishes is featured here, including the house specialty, rainbow trout, along with a breathtaking view of Illimani Mountain. The more informal **La Kantuta,** popular with the business crowd, is a lovely spot for lunch, light supper, or afternoon tea. For after-hours entertainment, there's live entertainment at the **Pub. L'Exclusive** discotheque is a popular nightspot.

---

5. WHERE TO DINE

Corn, potatoes, **quinua** (a high-protein grain), and similar foodstuffs form the basis of the Bolivian diet. But don't leave La Paz without trying two spicy national dishes: **picantes,** chicken or shrimp served in a tangy red sauce, and **chuño,** potatoes mixed with meat, fish, or eggs. And you should definitely try the **salteñas.** You'll see these delicious chicken- or beef-filled turnovers all over the city, in small shops called *salteñerías,* as well as on the streets being hawked by vendors. (See our warning, however, in Chapter 1, under "Health Preparations," against buying food from street vendors.)

Other delicious regional dishes include: **Chairo Paceño,** a soup made with meat broth, dried lamb, minced meat, grain, and dehydrated potatoes, and **Fricase,** a spicy stew made with meat (usually goat or pork), dehydrated potatoes, and corn, which is most commonly served on the weekends. Then there are **mechado de cordero,** stuffed lamb; **lechod,** pork served with sweet potatoes and *plátano;* and **sajta de pollo,** chicken prepared with dehydrated potatoes and onions in a hot spicy sauce.

In general, most restaurants are on or near Avenida 16 de Julio. Remember that the locals seldom dine much before 8pm. Remember, too, to add 22% tax and service to all prices. The better restaurants accept credit cards.

IN TOWN
ON OR NEAR THE PRADO

CAFE CIUDAD, Calle Batallón Colorados 1, at the corner of 6 de Agosto.
Cuisine: INTERNATIONAL.
$ Prices: Light meals $2–$5; full meals $5–$8.
This bilevel café is fine for lunch or dinner. The menu ranges from sandwiches to generous servings of *churrasco,* barbecued chicken and beef. The dining room is lovely, with white-clothed tables that give it a formal air.

CIRCULO ITALIANO, 6 de Agosto 2563.
  Cuisine: ITALIAN.
  $ Prices: Appetizers $1; main courses $4.50.
  Open: Tues–Sun noon–midnight.
At Circulo Italiano you can have any number of spaghetti and lasagne dishes. Large yet homey, the Italiano is owned by Dusan Lauric, a Yugoslav who prides himself on hospitality. Enjoy a drink in the garden before your meal.

ELI'S, 16 de Julio 1497, at the corner of Bueno.
  Cuisine: INTERNATIONAL.
  $ Prices: Appetizers $1; main courses $2.50–$5; breakfast $2–$4.
  Open: Daily 8am–10:30pm.
Possibly the best moderately priced restaurant in the city for any meal, especially breakfast, is Eli's, open since 1942. It has speedy service and offers a Spanish/English menu, on which a U.S.-style breakfast—juice, eggs with ham or bacon, and coffee—runs about $4. A continental breakfast of coffee, toast, butter, and jelly is $2, including tax and service. We also like the french toast served with coffee and jam. Eli's also serves German/American pastries and lunch/dinner specialty.

HONG KONG, Plaza Franz Tamayo 1920.
  Cuisine: CHINESE.
  $ Prices: Appetizers 50¢–$1.50; main courses $3–$5.
  Open: Lunch and dinner.
The small and cozy Hong Kong, located several blocks down the Prado from the Sucre Palace Hotel, was opened by the Kwan family in 1967. (La Paz is now home to over a hundred people of Chinese descent.) Grace Kwan, the manager, recommends No. 15 on the menu, *chicharrón de pollo* (fried chicken pieces); No. 38, shredded beef and peppers; and No. 58, sweet-and-sour pork.

LOS ESCUDOS DE LA PAZ, Avenida Mariscal Santa Cruz 1201. Tel. 3-22-028.
  Cuisine: ECUADORIAN. **Reservations:** Recommended.
  $ Prices: Appetizers $1–$3; main courses $4.50–$7.
  Open: Lunch and dinner.
Rock music blasts out here most evenings, and on Friday and Saturday there are live shows with a Bolivian beat, starting at 9:30pm. Los Escudos calls itself a rathskeller, and it does resemble a German beerhall. Heavy wooden tables and beamed ceilings dominate the look. But the food is strictly Ecuadorian, as is the entertainment. Try the *parrillada Los Escudos* or any of the beef dishes. Locals lean to the *pacumtu*, a long roll of chicken, ham, beef, and pork, served with potatoes.

GARGANTUA, near the Plaza Hotel, on the Prado.
  Cuisine: INTERNATIONAL.
  $ Prices: Appetizers $1–$2; main courses $3–$6.
  Open: Lunch and dinner.
Ordering at Gargantua is easy: The waiter gives you a slip of paper listing all the many selections and you mark your order. We recommend the hamburgers, pancakes, and chicken in the basket. At $4, the chateaubriand is an especially good choice. Furnishings are rather plain; the tables and chairs are wooden.

GIORGGISIMO, Avenida Camacho 1367, at the corner of Loayza. Tel. 3-24-456.
  Cuisine: BOLIVIAN/CONTINENTAL. **Reservations:** Recommended.
  $ Prices: Appetizers $2–$3; main courses $3–$6.
  Open: Noon–3pm and 6–10:30pm.
In this attractive downtown restaurant, you dine in red-leather booths with photos of regulars on the wall. You can choose from omelets, sandwiches, lasagne, and ravioli, as well as Bolivian specialties. Head downstairs to this cellarlike restaurant.

MONACO RESTAURANT, Avenida Villazón 1958. Tel. 3-65-014.

Cuisine: INTERNATIONAL.
$ Prices: Appetizers $1–$3; main courses $3–$7.
Open: Lunch and dinner.

Up a flight of stairs and around a bend is a lovely, carpeted, wood-paneled restaurant offering a fine view of Villazón. The mixed grill and the spaghetti with pesto are fine selections, and the numerous trout dishes are excellent.

PEÑA ANDINA, Avenida 16 de Julio 1473. Tel. 3-22-108.
Cuisine: BOLIVIAN.
$ Prices: Full meal $5.
Open: Lunch and dinner.

The atmosphere here is pure Bolivian, with native musical instruments decorating the walls. Folklorico shows are presented on Friday and Saturday nights. The Andina specializes in *típico* dishes, many priced at $2.75.

PRONTO RISTORANTE, Calle Jauregui 2248. Tel. 3-55-869.
Cuisine: ITALIAN.
$ Prices: Appetizers $1–$2; main courses $4–$7.
Open: Lunch and dinner.

Pronto is just two steps from the 6 de Agosto Cinema. Your first choice here should be the homemade pasta. The antipasto is also recommended. The wine list features a wide variety.

AROUND THE PLAZA MURILLO

CHURRASQUERIA EL TROPERO, Calle Murillo 993.
Cuisine: ARGENTINE.
$ Prices: Full meals $4–$7 (all you can eat).
Open: Lunch and dinner.

Resembling an Argentine *parrillada,* this restaurant serves all courses on wooden boards. "All you can eat" succulent cuts of beef, sausage, or chicken are available.

EL INTERNACIONAL, Ayacucho 206. Tel. 3-42-942.
Cuisine: INTERNATIONAL.
$ Prices: Fixed menu $5.
Open: Lunch and dinner.

The talented organist Oscar Grajeda is on hand weekdays to entertain dinner guests. Saturday night's offering is a colorful "Bolivian Spectacle"— folksinging, music, and dance—which goes on at 9:30pm. The house specialty is El Internacional, a filet *flambeado.* Drinks are $2 and up.

MARILYN'S, at the corner of Potosí and Socabaya.
Cuisine: INTERNATIONAL.
$ Prices: Lunch $3–$5; dinner $7–$9.
Open: Lunch and dinner.

Marilyn's is a very large restaurant. Lunch includes tasty burgers and hot dogs, plus sandwiches and light platters. Dinner includes steaks and fish platters, served with potatoes and corn.

THE SAN FRANCISCO CHURCH AREA

LA CASA DEL CORREGIDOR, Calle Murillo 1040. Tel. 3-63-633.
Cuisine: BOLIVIAN. **Reservations:** Recommended.
$ Prices: Appetizers $1–$3; main courses $4–$8. Major credit cards accepted.
Open: Lunch and dinner.

Walking through the courtyard at this sophisticated and low-key choice is like being transported back to the colonial period. Candlelight, colonial furnishings, folkloric music on Friday and Saturday evenings, and typical Bolivian cuisine make this an excellent place to spend an evening.

NEAR THE PLAZA ISABEL LA CATÓLICA

CHIFA EMY, Calle Cordero 257. Tel. 3-23-725.
  Cuisine: CHINESE. **Reservations:** Recommended.
$ **Prices:** Appetizers 75¢–$2; main courses $2–$6.
  Open: Daily noon–3pm and 6–11pm.
Probably your best bet for Chinese food is in this private house with several dining rooms, hanging lanterns, and a bilingual menu. Recommended are wonton frito, deep-fried spiced chicken, fried noodles with beef, and roast duck Peking style.

CHURRASQUERIA EL ARRIERO, 2523 Avenida 16 de Agosto.
  Cuisine: ARGENTINE.
$ **Prices:** Full meals $5–$8.
  Open: Lunch and dinner.
This restaurant is located in the Casa Argentina, one block above Plaza Isabel la Católica. Locals consider the meat here to be among the finest served in the city.

GRINGO LIMON, Plaza Avaroa, at the corner of Avenida 20 de Octubre and Pedro Salazar. Tel. 3-28-892.
  Cuisine: ARGENTINE/BOLIVIAN.
  Open: Lunch and dinner.
The Gringo Limón is the yellow building on the Plaza Abaroa. The regional dress worn by the waitresses combined with the local art displayed among the restaurant's five dining rooms make this a very colorful place to dine.

EL REFUGIO, Avenida 20 de Octubre 2453. Tel. 3-55-651.
  Cuisine: BOLIVIAN.
$ **Prices:** Appetizers $1–$3; main courses $4–$7.
  Open: Tues–Sat lunch and dinner.
You'll find this restaurant on Plaza Abaroa. Specialties include a variety of dishes made with trout from Lake Titicaca, *pacumatu,* suckling pig, and filet mignon.

IN THE COUNTRYSIDE

LOS LOBOS BALNEARIOS RESTAURANT, Calle Tupac-Katari 15, in the Aranjuez zone. Tel. 7-94-539.
  Cuisine: INTERNATIONAL. **Reservations:** Recommended. **Taxi:** Just 15 minutes from La Paz ($4).
$ **Prices:** Appetizers $2–$5; main courses $7–$12. Major credit cards accepted.
  Open: Lunch and dinner.
This marvelous little restaurant blends in nicely with its lush surroundings, as it is constructed of natural tropical woods. The decor reflects the indigenous folk art of Bolivia—hand-designed and hand-painted fabrics, tropical birds, leather, and leopard and boa skins—all creating a colorful environment. The menu includes a very good *medallones à la Provençal;* our favorites are the *parrillada mixta* and the *picante surtido.* Don't forget that there will be a hefty 22% surcharge for taxes. You can make a day of it by combining this restaurant with trips to nearby sights—Cactus Park, Aniceto Arce, and the Valley of the Moon.

SPLURGE CHOICES

ALAYA, in the La Paz Hotel, Avenida Arce. Tel. 3-56-950.
  Cuisine: INTERNATIONAL. **Reservations:** Recommended.
$ **Prices:** Appetizers $4–$9; main courses $8–$12. Major credit cards accepted.
  Open: Lunch and dinner.
There's deluxe dining at the rooftop Alaya, an Indian name meaning "the best of the best." You'll get the best here but at prices that are definitely high. The La Paz Hotel also offers a daily luncheon buffet at its Tiwanaku Restaurant. It's all you can eat for $8, including dessert and beverage. Fill up at lunch and then dine lightly at night.

LA SUISSE, Avenida Arce 2164. Tel. 3-53-150.

Cuisine: SWISS. **Reservations:** Recommended.
$ Prices: Appetizers $3–$5; main courses $6–$10.
Open: Lunch and dinner.

La Suisse is two restaurants in one. Elegant European cuisine is served in the cozy Swiss-style dining room on the first floor, a favorite meeting place for foreigners living in La Paz. The fondue and the veal are excellent. On the high-tech second floor, you can enjoy a great selection of meats—beef, pork, sausage, and liver—served grilled or cold, to which you add condiments and choose from a great variety of onions, cheeses, sauces, and whatever else they may have to offer. You can also order Argentinean *churrasco*, Swiss *raclette*, or trout.

UTAMA, in the Hotel Plaza, Avenida 6 de Julio 1789. Tel. 3-78-311.
Cuisine: INTERNATIONAL. **Reservations:** Recommended.
$ Prices: Appetizers $2–$5; main courses $5–$10. Major credit cards accepted.
Open: Lunch and dinner.

Here you can have an open salad bar and excellent consommé, along with excellent entrées. The *entrecôte au vert* (steak), *truite Bonne Femme* with wine, *parrilladas* (mixed grill), and *sajat de pollo* are delicious. The large windows offer panoramic views of La Paz.

SPECIALTY DINING

CONFITERIAS La Paz has several tearooms, called *confiterías,* where you can enjoy a light lunch or a late-afternoon bite. Our favorite, owned by a Japanese family, is the **Confitería Tokio,** at 16 de Julio 1832, near Plaza del Estudiante; the owner's son will probably serve you. The aroma of freshly baked pastries fills the small but cheerful room. The coconut pie, a house specialty, is superb and made with strips of coconut and orange rather than custard. Equally tasty is the ham or cheese sandwiches. Coffee, tea, and cocoa run 50¢. Open until 9pm.

Across from Crillon Tours on Avenida Camacho, at the corner of Ayacucho, in the building belonging to the Club de La Paz, you'll find the very popular **Confitería Club de La Paz.** The Club de La Paz is one of the few confiterías where you can amble in and order tea without purchasing anything else. You might also try the **Confitería Rayito del Sol,** at Comercio 1072, near Plaza Murillo, which makes its own bread and pastries. The sweetrolls are superb.

La Paz also has several confitería/restaurants that offer meals at very low prices and are open for both tea and dinner. An excellent one is located just a few blocks from the Rayito del Sol, at Comercio 1266. **Confitería La Florida** features native and international dishes, with prices ranging from $2 to $6 for most plates.

Kremrik, at Plaza Murillo 542 and also on 16 de Agosto, offers a tempting selection of cakes and pastries, not to mention delicious ice creams and a full selection of sandwiches. The ice-cream window at the **Il Fiore** restaurant offers an outrageous selection, including the U.S. favorites After Eight, Chocolate Moca, and Oreo.

Next door to the Eldorado Hotel is the elegant **Monaco** confitería/restaurant. Prices here are on the high side.

ICE CREAM A block off 6 de Agosto, near the university, is **Max Bieber's,** at 20 de Octubre 2020, which resembles an old-fashioned 1920's ice-cream parlor. With three dining rooms, a take-out ice-cream counter, and reasonable prices, this place is always crowded with students, who also order from among the large menu's two dozen hot plates, ranging in price from $1.75 to $2. For $2.50 you can get an excellent small steak served with salad and french fries. Closed Tuesday.

FAST FOOD **Denny's** on Avenida 16 de Julio at the corner of Campero, is a Burger King lookalike. "Whoppers," with lettuce and tomatoes and tangy sauce, run under $2. Fried chicken and potatoes in the basket are a good buy as well. Another good choice is **California Donuts and Burgers,** a new chain of fast-food eateries. There are branches at 1248 Camacho, on Plaza Isabel la Catolica, and just a few blocks down from Denny's, on Avenida 16 de Julio.

Sancho Panza and **Tops,** next door at 2002 6 de Agosto, just below the plaza, are two little snack shops that are very popular with university students. Also a favorite with students, **Tutti Fruti,** on 6 de Agosto, offers a great selection of fresh-fruit shakes for about $1 each. Sandwiches are also on the menu here. The shakes, plus the view of the mountains, make this a great place to take a breather and rest your feet after sightseeing.

If you're looking for pizza, try **Luigi's Pub & Pizzeria,** just up from Max Bieber's, on 20 de Octubre; **Quickes Pizza,** on Plaza Isabel la Catolica; or **Venezia Pizza a la Piedra,** on Loayaza, between Camacho and 16 de Julio. You should also try **Naira Crêperie,** on Sagarnaga, a simple, bare-floored place overlooking San Francisco Church, where sandwiches are $1 to $1.50, pizzas run $1 to $2, and excellent crêpes with fruit and marmalade are available. It's a small restaurant with a capacity of 22.

6. ATTRACTIONS

This is an exciting city for sightseeing—particularly in the hilly Indian section, where some 400,000 residents carry on traditions unchanged for centuries. Three posh residential districts are Obrajes, Calacoto, and La Florida, all located 2,000 feet below the center of the city. Fashionable homes and exclusive clubs dominate these sections.

SUGGESTED ITINERARIES

IF YOU HAVE ONE DAY   Visitors with only one day should wander through the Indian Quarter and markets in the morning. The afternoon should be spent touring the museums and making a trip to the Valley of the Moon. A Peña Folklórica is a good choice for the evening.

IF YOU HAVE TWO DAYS   Follow the itinerary for Day 1. On Day 2, make a day trip to Lake Titicaca and Huatajata.

IF YOU HAVE THREE DAYS   Follow the itinerary for Day 1. Days 2 and 3 can be spent numerous ways, depending on your interests. Adventure travelers should opt to hike along the Inca trail to Chulumani in the Yungas. This tour combines a hike through the Andes with the Yungas below. Another option is the overnight trip to Copacabana, including the hydrofoil cruise on Lake Titicaca.

THE TOP ATTRACTIONS
THE INDIAN QUARTER

⭐ This neighborhood contains a mix of religions. The Indians are devout Catholics; yet Inca and Aymara religious symbols and rituals are basic to their religious observance. The men farm the rugged terrain as they have for centuries, while the women either tend their many children or operate stalls in the Indian markets in La Paz. Most of the markets are outdoors, and the Indian women customarily spread their goods on the ground on straw mats. Typically, you'll see huge *manons* (melons), bananas, oranges, grain, rice, fish, beef, and pastries. Indoor markets usually feature home-fashioned utensils, noodles, and canned foods.

THE BEST MARKETS   Most markets operate daily, but the largest and liveliest are open weekends only. The **Mercado Camacho,** the outdoor market closest to our center-city hotel selections, begins on Camacho and Bueno and on weekdays extends for only one block. But on weekends this market is called **Feria Franca** as it mushrooms out for half of a mile along Camacho, which becomes Liberator Simón Bolívar.

As you thread your way through the maze of stalls, you'll be approached by the operators, who will insist that they have the freshest fruits at the lowest prices. Al-

❓DID YOU KNOW . . . ?

- The technical capital of Bolivia is Sucre, but the de facto capital is La Paz.
- The pre-Inca languages of Uru and Puquina are still spoken in Bolivia.
- Evidence of village agriculture can be traced back to 2500 B.C.
- The Andean region of Bolivia makes up less than one-half of the nation, yet it contains 70% of its population.
- The highest railroad station in the world is Bolivia's Candor Station at 15,705 feet.
- Tin magnate Simón Patiño paid the highest dowry on record when his daughter, Elena, was married.
- According to the *Guinness Book of World Records*, statisticians contend that since 1825, Bolivia has had the most coups of any nation in the world.
- At 12,506 feet above sea level, Lake Titicaca is the highest navigable lake in the world.

though most are actually speaking in their native Aymara tongue (not Spanish), you'll be well aware of what they're saying.

The **Mercado de las Brujas** ("Witches Market"), on Calle Linares, uphill from Calle Santa Cruz, is probably the most interesting in town. For sale are herbs, spirits, elixirs of love, and other items used by witch doctors in special circumstances. They might prescribe crushed lizard cream to cure an aching back. There's a figurine of an embracing couple that will assure a spouse in no time; or if that doesn't work, there's an amulet to wear that's infallible. If you're building a new house, a llama fetus should be mixed into the foundation. If you want a child, a must is a fertility stone (a carving of a mother and child). There are vendor Indians sitting against the wall. Occasionally, a witch doctor will appear to purchase items for the Saumerio ceremony he will perform to put the spirits to work for ailing clients.

Beyond the Witches Market is the **Galería Artesanal las Brujas,** a gallery of shops selling sweaters, ponchos, carpets, and the like. Fine shops in the gallery include Inca Wasi, Winay Inti, and Kory Inti.

Near the San Francisco Church, up the hill on Calle Figueroa, is an open-air market, the **Mercado Artesanal.** There are lines of booths, each owned by a different family, selling jewelry, silver, handcrafts, dolls, and sweaters. Bargaining is a must. Hats, food, and artesanal items are available. Health buffs should try *quinua,* a local cereal grain, used in soup and cereals, that grows only in the Altiplano.

Mercado Lanza, also on Figueroa (you can enter from Montes), is a narrow winding street full of vendors. It's sort of a black market where whisky, cosmetics, perfumes, gloves, and shoes are sold. Try *api,* a drink made from corn, for breakfast. Rows and rows of beautiful flowers are for sale, and there are shoeshine boys galore, plus fruits, breads, chicken, and meat. If you're hungry, try the **Mercado Popular Restaurant.** Here *api* is 15¢ (purple) and coffee 15¢; you can also get pastry, tea, or cocoa. The $1 lunch typically includes steak with rice and salad. You sit on benches around tables. Even if you decide not to eat here, head upstairs to take a look at the unusual Indian-style restaurant.

CALLE BUENOS AIRES, high in the Indian quarter, is the most frenzied street you'll come across in South America. A cacophony of traffic noise, women vendors selling their goods, children playing and laughing and dogs howling and yelping greets you, along with odors so exotic it will take you some time and effort to forget them. Stroll through it and see the Indians furiously bartering and trading their goods.

Traffic moves through these streets at a snail's pace. Open trucks filled with Indians crawl by. Wares are arrayed on rugs, blankets, straw mats, or the cobblestones. You'll have to weave your way through the crowds. There are no scales in the market. Instead, your purchase is measured by the basketful and slapped into a newspaper or brown paper if you're lucky. Most Paceños come prepared with their own large straw baskets. Don't miss this street.

INDIAN SHOPS Head to **Calle Sagárnaga,** a narrow winding cobblestone street lined with Indian shops, which begin at the Church of San Francisco and continue uphill from there. These shops cater to the needs of the Indians in the city. Two blocks up Sagárnaga from the church is a primary school, at no. 228, on the right side. Enter the courtyard and ask to look into the classrooms and see the students in their white jackets at work. The rooms are dark and the furniture old, but the teachers have decorated them attractively. This is an interesting sidelight, especially for teachers.

You should head back down the hill at this point, because the street becomes quite steep beyond here.

PARKS & OUTDOOR SIGHTS

MONTICULO PARK   This is a beautiful park with an exciting view of the city and Illimani Mountain, in the residential district of Sopocachi, which is a mile downhill from center city. Take a cab ($1) and bring your camera. Your taxi ride will introduce you to some of the wealthier residential sections of the city. The contrast between these modern dwellings and those of the Indian Quarter is astonishing. The park itself is small but scenically set with the city below it and the magnificent mountains in the distance.

VALLEY OF THE MOON   To view incredible natural clay formations caused by erosion, which form row after row of praying white figures across a red mountain panorama, head for the Valley of the Moon. It is 3 miles away if you take the no. 11 bus and 20 minutes away if you take a cab from San Francisco Church. The trip here is half the fun of going, for you see La Paz nestled in the mountains and Chacaltaya's snow-covered peaks as a backdrop.

When you arrive in the Valley of the Moon, you'll find it's like being amid millions of sand castles with an incredibly gorgeous red mountain backdrop called "Devil's Tooth" (Muela del Diablo). The world's highest golf course is nearby, and a lovely park is about one block beyond the valley. The winding road leading to the valley is a bit scary, but all the drivers are experts in its navigation.

If you continue onward, after passing through the Valley of the Moon, you'll come to the farming zone of Río Abajo, where the Indians cultivate their land as they did a thousand years ago.

MUSEUMS

OPEN-AIR MUSEUM, in front of Miraflores Stadium.

If you haven't the time to visit Tiahuanaco near Lake Titicaca, you'll greatly enjoy a visit to this museum. Many pre-Inca statues and heads, some weighing a hundred tons or more, have been brought to La Paz from the Aymaran ruins near the great lake. These are surprisingly well preserved, with impressive artistry by the native Indians who lived a thousand years ago. Most interesting are the huge monoliths that guarded the entrance to the Temple of the Sun.

Directions: You can easily walk to this square. From Plaza Murillo, follow Comercio, which later becomes Illimani, for about 10 blocks, all downhill. Take a cab back.

MUSEO ARQUEOLOGICO TIWANAKU, Calle Tiwanaku, at the corner of Fédérico Zuazo.

This archeological museum, located behind the Plaza Hotel on the corner of Tihuanaco and Fédérico Zuazo, is home to an excellent collection of over 30,000 Tiwanaco artifacts, including pottery, textiles, and mummies.

Open: Mon–Fri 9am–noon and 2:30–6:30pm; Sat–Sun 10am–noon.

MUSEO DE METALES PRECIOSOS Y PRECOLOMBINOS, Calle Jaen 777.

★ The Precious and Pre-Columbian Metal Museum features an excellent collection of pre-Columbian pieces from the Tiwanaco cultures, including the treasure of San Sebastian, as well as textiles and ceramics. Be sure to take a close look at the building itself. Dating back to the 14th century, it is an excellent example of colonial architecture.

Open: Tues–Fri 9am–noon and 2:30–6:30pm; Sat–Sun 10am–12:30pm.

MUSEO NACIONAL DE ETNOGRAFIA Y FOLKLORE, Calle Ingavi 916.
The National Ethnography and Folklore Museum, near Plaza Murillo, explores the different ethnic groups that inhabit Bolivia. Two separate exhibits compare the Ayoreo and the Uru Chipaya cultures.
Open: Mon–Fri 8:30am–12:30pm and 2:30–6pm.

CASA DE LA CULTURA, at the corner of Potosí and Jenaro Sanjinés.
This government-sponsored arts center, located a few steps from the Church of San Francisco in Plaza San Francisco, features a theater, a library, and a studio where painters may work.

CASA DE MURILLO, Calle Jaen 790.
The Casa de Murillo, dedicated to preserving the memory of hero Pedro Domingo Murillo, is located in an 18th-century house that once belonged to that martyr of Bolivian independence. Among its exhibits are colonial paintings, Murillo's study, the conspiracy room, Murillo's bedroom, and an exhibit of ethnography and folklore of the Charazani.
Open: Tues–Fri 9am–noon and 2–6pm; Sat–Sun 10am–1pm.

MUSEO HISTORICO LITORAL, Calle Jaen 789.
The Litoral Historical Museum illustrates Bolivia's dramatic loss of its Pacific coast territory during the 1879 Pacific War. Mannequins represent scenes from the battles fought between Chile and Bolivia.
Open: Tues–Fri 9:30am–noon and 2:30–6:30pm; Sat–Sun 10am–12:30pm.

MUSEO COSTUMBRISTA JUAN DE VARGAS, Calle Sucre, at the corner of Calle Jaen.
The Juan de Vargas Museum explores the events and people coloring La Paz's past.
Open: Mon–Fri 9:30am–noon and 2:30–6:30pm; Sat–Sun 10am–12:30pm.

NATIONAL ART MUSEUM, at the corner of Comercio with Socayaba.
This museum is home to a priceless collection of colonial paintings, from masterpieces by the Italian mannerist Vitti to the greatest painters of the Potosi and Cuzqueno schools, including Gamarra, Holguin, Berriost, and Leonardo Flores.
Open: Tues–Sat 9:30am–12:30pm and 4–7pm.

THE PERFORMING ARTS

Free band concerts are held on the Prado in front of the Sucre Hotel and in Plaza Murillo at noon every Sunday.

TEATRO AL AIRE LIBRE, Avenida del Ejército.
For traditional music and dance folklore, spend a Sunday afternoon (from 2 to 6pm) at this open-air theater directly behind the university. More than a thousand devotees throng the open-air theater to see a continuous succession of bands, dance groups, and singers, all dressed in colorful Bolivian folk costumes. The aficionados, many Indian, sit on stone bleachers, and when the seats are all gone, hundreds more stand in back. The involvement of the audience is contagious, and you'll be applauding along. Cash prizes are awarded to the best groups, who perform in teams of 20 to 30 dancers and musicians. The groups consist of tuba, trumpet, drum, cymbal playing, and vocalists. Our favorite dance is the cueca, which you'll recognize by the handkerchiefs held at shoulder level.
Prices: Tickets 80¢.

7. SPORTS & RECREATION

SKIING Good skiing can be found in the middle of the Andes, at Chacaltaya, 29 miles from La Paz, where peaks reach heights of 17,318 feet—1½ miles higher than any U.S. peak and half a mile above the highest European peak. The resort offers skiing on weekends from August to March, with cabins serving snacks, sandwiches, and beverages. The views of La Paz are fantastic. To rent equipment and arrange for bus tours, go to **Club Andino Boliviano** (tel. 3-24-682) or Calle Mexico 1638 (tel. 3-65-065). *Warning:* This is for advanced skiers only.

FUTBOL   Here, as throughout South America, *futból* is a major sport. Every weekend at 2pm, at **Olímpico Stadium** in Miraflores, there is a big game, and for good seats you'll need to reserve well in advance. Reserved seats (in the *tribuna,* or grandstand) are $3.50. A middle category, called *preferencia,* runs $2. General admission is about $1.50. Seating capacity at the Olímpico is 50,000. As we mentioned earlier, visiting teams have a hard time adjusting to the low-oxygen atmosphere and generally lose. Bet on the home team. To reach the stadium, walk via Avenida Illimani from Plaza Murillo or take any yellow bus. A taxi will cost you about 50¢.

The Club Bolivia Stadium is in Tembladerani. Club Bolivia is an old and popular sporting organization. The **Estadio Bolívar** seats 20,000 and is equipped with lights for night games. You can catch the M or B microbus to get there, and fares are on a sliding scale: $1.50 for local games, $2 for national, and $3 for international.

8. SAVVY SHOPPING

ARTESANIAS TITICACA LTD.

Artesanías Titicaca Ltd. resembles a *típico* shop, although it is actually the showroom for one of Bolivia's primary exporters of hand-knitted alpaca sweaters, other apparel, and crafts. It's located in what was once a private home, at Avenida Sanchez Lima 2320, on the corner of Rosendo Gutierrez.

The shop was founded in 1962, by Mrs. Daisy de Wende, with the objective of raising the Bolivian standard of living by organizing small family craft production. The owner hopes to improve Bolivia's image by exporting the fine quality of their goods. Mrs. de Wende creates the clothing and rug designs, supervises quality control, and acts as a goodwill ambassador for Bolivia to fashion and trade shows in North America and Europe.

For you this means you can pick up first-class gifts at about 25% of the U.S. price and far less than the European one.

The de Wendes' son, Kenny, is the proprietor of the equally fine **Alpaca Titicaca Shop,** at Sagarnaga 274 (tel. 7-92-426), offering a wide selection of high-quality items—alpaca knits in traditional or contemporary designs, a truly unique collection of authentic Bolivian fashions (from $15 to $40). The sweaters represent 80% of his business, but he also stocks weavings, local art, ceramics, and jewelry.

BEST BUYS

The two-level showroom and shop, which has opened a special section to exhibit and sell textiles from highland Bolivia, offers high-quality bedspreads starting at $50; a beautiful line of typical, modern, and fashionable alpaca sweaters from $20 to $35; vests at $15 and gloves at $4, plus caps, scarves, and other apparel, all in an assortment of natural pure alpaca; and hand-knitted children's alpaca sweaters, vests, and ponchos from $7 to $14.

Silver jewelry is much in demand—earrings, medallions, and bracelets begin at $6. Pewter ornaments start at $8. The hand-woven wallhangings ($13) and pillow coverings ($5) with appliqué designs make excellent gifts.

On a lower scale, we're partial to the intricately etched wood flutes called *pinkillos* ($1 and up) and a larger version known as a *tarka.* Four flutes joined together, called a *zampona,* is an unusual gift item, too. Ceramics, pottery, ashtrays, and such start at $3; straw toys begin at $1. For children there are delicate llamas; knitted dolls; and a

7-inch-tall god of good luck called Ekeko, made of stucco and dressed in *típico* apparel ($5 and up).

Moving up in price once more, there is the marvelous native *charango,* a stringed instrument resembling a mandolin but covered with tough armadillo skin ($75 and worth it). Be sure to check out the boutique for the couture collection. There's a full line of fashions in alpaca, including shirts for $18 and vests for $15 to $80. The colorful collection of dresses, tunics, and long skirts in cotton, all designed by Mrs. de Wende and all with Bolivian themes, start at $100.

Shop hours are Monday to Friday from 9:30am to 6:30pm and Saturday from 2 to 6pm. However, Mr. de Wende will open on Sunday by appointment. Phone him at the showroom (tel. 3-72-102) or at home (tel. 7-92-426). Ask for a catalog. Mail orders are accepted.

SHOPPING A TO Z
CRAFTS

ARTBOL, Calle Sagárnaga 233. Tel. 3-68-261.
A husband-and-wife team, Sr. and Sra. Javier Ortuño run Artbol. As its name suggests, Artbol specializes in Bolivian *artesanías,* or handicrafts and has a fine selection of alpaca and fur rugs, leather clothing and accesories, pewter pieces, and wood carvings.

CASA GLADYS, Calle Sagárnaga 237. Tel. 3-42-684.
Gladys features an outstanding selection of items crafted of the metals Bolivia is best known for: tin, copper, and pewter. This bilevel store also features weavings, including rugs and wallhangings.

KING'S, in the Sucre Palace Hotel, Avenida 16 de Julio 1636. Tel. 3-28-178.
Magnificent monoliths are the featured items here. For $50 we purchased a 24-inch-high, 7-pound replica of the monolith that guarded the temple in Tiahuanaco. The crown is removable, and we've converted it to a lamp that's the showpiece of our apartment. King's has good prices on authentic silver and pewter items. They also sell silver figurines of the Inca good-luck god, Ekeko, who is an Indian Santa Claus bringing prosperity and good fortune wherever he is: Tiny pots and pans hang from his back. These sell for about $3 and go up according to size.

MADERMA, on the ground floor of the Petrolero Building, Avenida 16 de Julio 1616. Tel. 3-53-385.
The colorful hand-knit 100% alpaca sweaters, cardigans, jackets, and ponchos at Maderma is sure to catch your eye. Ceramic items from Tiahuanaco and guidebooks are also for sale here.

ARTESANIAS SOROTA, Sagárnaga 311.
This small shop offers a beautiful selection of weavings, sweaters, and handmade dolls. We were especially impressed by the unusual colors, very unlike those we had seen anywhere else. Everything is handmade by members of a women's cooperative, who were given an award by the Association of La Paz in 1988.

DIVERSE SHOPS

There are numerous small **tourist shops** in La Paz, but one that we liked is at Loayza 263. Here, you'll find gold and silver bracelets and native woodcarvings that are moderately priced. Also check out the shops at Casilla 2885 and in the La Paz Hotel.

Remember Calle Sagárnaga, in the Indian Quarter, if you want a bowler hat or *pollera* souvenir or if you feel like just browsing. Stop in at **Casa de Flora** here for Indian crafts and other handmade gifts. Many handicrafts shops have opened along the street.

There is the **Galería de las Brujas** (close to Calle Linares), established in an old house, where many handicraft shops have opened, offering a variety of traditional products, such as alpaca knitwear, fur rugs, and silver jewelry. Nearby is the **Galería Artesanal Chuguiagu,** a bilevel gallery off a patio with fountains. **Chaskanawi** is a fine handcrafts shop. Other shops offer high-quality furs and ski clothing.

Two fine shops are located in the Plaza Hotel. **Crisan** has gorgeous handcrafts, pewter, and ceramics, as well as leather and carpet items. Fine alpaca and textiles are for sale at **Milma.** Both shops are elegant and will ship your purchases home upon request. There is another branch of Milma on Calle Sagárnaga.

FURS & LEATHER

CASTILLO DE CUERO, Sagárnaga 270.

You'll find a great selection of leather clothing here at reasonable prices. While the quality is generally good, be sure to check the seams before purchasing.

JOART, Sagárnaga 280. Tel. 3-52-506.

Joart features an outstanding selection of chinchilla, alpaca, and fleece coats, as well as fine leather clothing. They also carry antique coins for collectors, beautiful wood carvings, and pewter items.

JEWELRY

JOYERIA SCHOHAUS, Colón 260. Tel. 2-62-410.

Here you'll find 18-karat gold nuggets set in earrings, pendants, bracelets, and rings at prices ranging from $150 to $2,500, depending on weight and size. According to Mrs. Schohaus, who is extremely knowledgeable and helpful, the natural shape of the nugget is not touched or altered in any way. A nugget weighing 14 grams costs $250 and one at 28 grams costs $500; 18-karat gold rings run $700 to $800. An assortment of silver rings is available at $10, $15, and $18. The Joyería Schohaus also has an excellent selection of pewter goblets, flowerpots, picture frames, and tea and coffee sets.

Mrs. Schohaus fashions rings and pendants with Brazilian stones—these are exclusive designs. And if that's not enough, the Joyería Schohaus has a factory address for quantity purchases: Jacinto Benavente 2230 (tel. 3-24-666).

MUSICAL INSTRUMENTS

CASA CARCAMAVI, Avenida Manco Kapac 368.

This small shop specializes in traditional musical instruments of the Andes, such as those played in *peñas*. So, if you have your heart set on bringing home a *charango, quena,* or *sampina,* you'll find it here. The store does its best to handle special requests.

9. EVENING ENTERTAINMENT

Most travel guides emphasize that La Paz is not much of a night town, since the altitude and chilly evenings call for an early-to-bed routine. But that's not true. This city happens to have some of the liveliest nightclubs in Latin America. Moreover, La Paz is home to the **Peña Folklórica,** a far-out showbiz phenomenon that blends music, dance, audience involvement, and history in one entertaining show. By all means go to bed early—but only for an hour or two, so that you'll be refreshed for the late-evening action ahead.

Tip: The effect of alcohol can be potent here, because of the altitude. Reduce your intake by 50%.

THEATER

TEATRO MUNICIPAL, at Plaza Wenceslao Monroy.

The Teatro Municipal, which is not far from Plaza Murillo, is an attractive, white building constructed in the 1850s. It is the home of the ballet company and symphony orchestra of La Paz. Tickets are, of course, higher for special events and for internationally known performers or companies. While seats for ordinary performances are not hard to get, they should be bought in advance at the box office.
Prices: Tickets 80¢–$3.50.

THE CLUB & MUSIC SCENE
PEÑA FOLKLORICA

The talk of La Paz night people is a mixed-media entertainment that has appeared on the midnight scene, and is now popular among the locals. Labeled *Peña Folklórica* (literally "place of folklore"), this entertainment brings together Indian dancers, singers, and musicians, who perform around and among the audience who are crowded on benches in matchbox-size nightclubs. The audience usually joins in the dancing and singing, which continues throughout the night. The material, representing authentic Indian folklore, is performed with such intensity that every visitor, South and North American alike, is caught up in the *Folklórica* fever. The performers, dressed in traditional clothing, weave through the audience to the accompaniment of *charangos* (guitars made of armadillo skins). Spectators clap or sing in unison, pausing occasionally to reach out to touch a dancer skipping past.

There are several *Peña Folklórica* clubs in La Paz. Almost all are in dilapidated quarters—usually in a converted apartment or basement cellar in the city's poorer sections—and most adhere to a standard $1 admission policy, with the understanding that you'll buy a flask of Bolivian wine (quite good) or a soft drink for another $1.50. Nothing else is served except free popcorn. Fun and games start at 10pm and end at about 5am—Friday and Saturday evenings only. Last time we were in La Paz, there was talk of extending the days of operation, so check with your hotel clerk.

A few of the selections in our restaurant section also double as *peñas*. Chief among them are the **Peña Andina,** at Avenida 16 de Julio 1473; **Los Escudos de La Paz,** on the corner of Avenida Mariscal Santa Cruz and Avacucho; and **La Casa del Corregidor,** at Calle Murillo 1040.

MARCA TAMBO, Calle Jaen 710. Tel. 3-40-416.

⭐ One of the best and least spoiled by the tourist trade, Marca Tambo is invariably packed with 150 suddenly intimate guests who don't seem to mind either the decibels or the crush. It's very popular with young Paceños. We're partial to the "devil dance" (*la diablada*), which is just what you'd imagine, with Lucifer-like costumes. A touching change of pace is the *cueca,* the handkerchief dance that you see not only in Bolivia but in Peru and Paraguay as well. One performer eerily creates the voice of Yma Sumac via manipulation of an ordinary crosscut saw.

BOÎTES

Pub-crawlers in La Paz must come alive in the dark. Why else would they jam into clubs where the brightness illumination comes from their eyeballs? The locals love the intimacy of darkness—but watch yourself when strolling from table to dance floor. *Note:* Most clubs admit couples only, and the music starts late—usually after 10pm. Minimum drinking age is 20.

CLUB NARANJA, in the Hotel Gloria, Potosí 909. Tel. 3-55-080.

On weekends, the Hotel Gloria's dining room becomes the lively Club Naranja, where a *folklórica* show gets underway at 10:30pm and continues well past midnight. When we were there, the place was packed, with the crowd enthusiastically clapping and cheering along with the performers. Reservations must be made in advance.

EL LORO EN SU SALSA, Calle Goitia 553. Tel. 3-20-162.

If you like to dance to a salsa beat, then this club should be your first choice. Even if you're not a salsa aficionado, the unusual decor is worth seeing. The club resembles the courtyard of a colonial home or a Spanish *cantina*. Antique lanterns provide the lighting. There are hanging plants and parrots (*loros*) everywhere.

PACHA, Azpazu 100. Tel. 3-69-107.
Pacha is an excellent private club. Videos on a screen near the dance floor and dark flashing lights add to the decor. There are private couches along the side. Open 10am to 5am.

DISCOTHEQUES

All three of La Paz's five-star hotels have discotheques on their top floors. Each features a fantastic view of the lights of the city. There is **L'Exclusive** in the new Hotel Presidente, Calle Potosí 920 (tel. 3-67-193); the **Penthouse** in the Plaza Hotel, Paseo del Prado 1789 (tel. 3-78-311); and the **Salon Illimani** on the 15th floor of the La Paz Hotel, Avenida Arce (tel. 3-56-950).

THE BAR SCENE

A new phenomenon in the city is the pub. They are scattered around the Plaza Avaroa on Balisario Salinas and 20 de Octubre and near the larger hotels. Drinks run $1 and up, with beer the least expensive.

AMADEUS, Avenida Villasón 1974. Tel. 3-27-498.
Roving guitarists provide the entertainment at this popular bilevel nightspot that's always crowded. Patrons gather at small tables and admire the temporary exhibits of photography and works by local artists.

GRAMMOFON, Belisario Salinas 536. Tel. 3-67-069.
Grammofon has quickly become a favorite in La Paz, even though it's been open only a little over a year. The decor is original: antique gramophones, many of which still work, plus many posters of Europe along the walls.

MATHEUS PIANO BAR, on Calle F. Guachalla, at the corner of 6 de Agosto. Tel. 3-24-376.
Dark wood adds to the British pub look of this fine bar. The bar has hanging glasses, and a booth effect is created by leather seats around tables. The jazz is hot.

NUEVO HAMLET, Belisario Salinas 355. Tel. 3-56-856.
Nuevo Hamlet, spread out over two floors, is a good choice if you're in the mood for a quiet evening. There's live music on the lower level Thursday, Friday, and Saturday nights; the upper level is quieter, with soft piped-in music and no dancing.

EL SOCAVON: LA TABERNA DEL ARTE, Avenida 20 de Octubre 2172. Tel. 3-53-998.
El Socavón attracts the more bohemian residents of La Paz, mostly local artists whose works are displayed here. The small dance floor is usually quite crowded; the music varies.

MORE ENTERTAINMENT

MOVIES The best movie houses in town are on the Prado and favor U.S. films. Admission is $1.50. They're usually jammed on weekends.

FESTIVAL OF SEÑOR DEL GRAN PODER Thousands of Bolivians flock to La Paz in June for this festival, one of the most important of the country's celebrations. A statue of the saint, arrayed with flowers and religious adornments, is carried through the streets, followed by a procession of dignitaries from all over the country, including the president of the republic and the mayor of La Paz. A Folklore Queen reigns over the day's activities, which include performances by 50 folk-singing groups and dancers galore—some 9,000 participants in all!—who dance and sing in the streets from sunup to sundown. The performers are drawn from different parts of the city and nearby countryside, and their dances reflect the cultural heritage of their region. If you are going to be in La Paz during this month, it's well worth checking on the date of the festival (the exact date is not fixed) and making arrangements to catch this colorful fête.

10. SUGGESTED ITINERARIES

TIWANACU [TIAHUANACO]

⭐ The center of the impressive pre-Inca Aymara civilization—which flourished between 600 B.C. and A.D. 900—is in Tiwanacu, not far from Lake Titicaca. This civilization, the ruins of which were founded by the Incas about A.D. 1200, is believed to be the oldest in the Western Hemisphere.

Located on the Bolivian Altiplano at 13,000 feet, this find ranks among the world's great archeological sites. Little is known of the people who built the impressive monuments and monoliths, which were rebuilt on several occasions. But the remains of huge aqueducts, temples, and sun gates bear witness to an advanced civilization of engineers, architects, astronomers, and artisans.

Experts believe that Tiwanaku started around 1200 B.C. as a village nestled between two small mountain ranges not far from Lake Titicaca. The village supported itself through agriculture (primarily potatoes and *quinoa*) and fishing on Lake Titicaca. Pottery has been found that has been attributed to this period; and evidence suggests that metalworking, primarily with copper, was introduced at the end of the period.

With the development of new and better metal tools, Tiwanaku progressed from village to city and eventually became a major center. Irrigation systems were developed, and with them came surplus agricultural production. This in turn allowed for a diversification of labor. Artisans who originally could practice their craft only when not in the fields were now free to develop new skills and technology. A class system emerged, made up of the landowners or ruling class, the artisans, and finally the peasants who worked the fields. Surplus agricultural production paid for architectural and engineering projects. Pottery, sculpture, weaving, metallurgy, and other arts flourished.

With the expansion of agriculture came the need for more land. This led to often-violent clashes with neighbors and the creation of better weapons and armies. The Tiwanaku sculptures known as **chachapumas** (puma men) are representations of the Tiwanaku warriors. Just as in the sculptures, each warrior covered all or part of his face with the head and skin of a puma, in order to acquire the strength, ferocity, and agility of the cat.

The Tiwanaku Empire flourished. Some experts estimate that by the seventh century A.D. it covered an area of 600,000 square miles, extending to the Pacific coast in the west, crossing the sierra and the altiplano until it reached the Andean valleys in the east. Yet, suddenly and for no apparent reasons, the empire collapsed around 1150.

Today Tiwanaku is a desolate spot surrounded by mountains and seemingly in the middle of nowhere. All that remains are the ruins of the civic and ceremonial centers.

The Akapana Pyramid: It is believed that the Tiwanaku, like all Andean peoples, worshiped the mountains. The largest and most important temple of the ruins, the Akapana Pyramid, represents the worship of the mountains through the re-creation of their form in the center of the city.

The Semiunderground Temple: Along the walls of this temple are dozens of club-heads. Many believe that the Tiwanacu warriors used to collect the heads of their enemies and display them in the temple. Eventually, sculpted heads replaced the real things.

Kalassasaya: Experts believe that Kalassasaya was used as an observatory. This open temple was built above ground following strict astronomical lines. Three important monuments are inside the immense temple: the Ponce Monolith, the Priest Monolith, and the **Puerta del Sol** (Gate of the Sun). Experts believe that etchings on the surface of the Puerta del Sol represent an ancient farming calendar.

Putuni This is also called the Palace of the Sarcophagus: stones big enough to hold a human body were discovered in this temple.

Kantat Hallita: This small temple is decorated with figures from mythology. It is believed that originally these figures had been adorned with thin gold engravings encrusted in the stone. Many of the engravings were destroyed by the Spanish conquistadors in their desire to steal the gold.

Pumapunko: Recent excavations of this pyramid have revealed a drainage channel that from the top of the pyramid is divided in two directions, north and south, each with perfectly formed inclines.

The Regional Museum of Tiwanaku: This small museum, located just beyond Akapana, is home to an important collection of Tiwanaku art that spans from the village period to the final years of the empire. There are also some pieces from the Inca period. Almost everything on display was excavated locally.

MODERN-DAY TIWANACU

The village of Tiwanacu is home to one of the oldest churches on the Bolivian altiplano. The Renaissance-style church was constructed from 1580 to 1612 using materials taken from the pre-Columbian city. An excellent example of the merging of the Catholic and Aymaran cultures, the entrance is flanked by two monoliths taken from Tiwanaku, while images of Saints Peter and Paul adorn the facade. The interior is decorated with 17th- and 18th-century paintings. As you stroll through the village, look closely at the buildings. Many of the houses have been built with stones from the Tiwanaku ruins.

The least expensive way to reach Tiwanacu is by bus—a 2-hour journey that will cost less than $5 round trip. **Autolíneas Ingavi** buses leave at 7 and 10:30am and 1:30 and 4pm from the corner of Calle José María Azín and Eyzaguirre (tel. 3-28-991), just above the cemetery, and return according to the same schedule.

Balsa Tours, at Capitán Ravelo 2077 (tel. 3-57-817), offers daily half-day tours to Tiwanacu. Buses leave daily at 8am. The round-trip price per person is $20; advance reservations are mandatory. **Turisbus,** located in the Residencial Rosario, also offers tours to Tiwanacu.

Private cars, which carry up to four passengers, can be hired, with a bilingual guide and chauffeur, for $35 per person if two people are going. If the car is filled (four people), then the rates descend to $21.50 per person. These can be obtained from **Crillon Tours** main office, at Avenida Camacho 1223 (tel. 3-50-363), near the La Paz Hotel.

COPACABANA & LAKE TITICACA

⭐ Copacabana, the famous Indian shrine on Lake Titicaca, is a wonderful excursion if you have the time. In fact, if you're heading to Cuzco from La Paz, this shrine is a convenient detour. **Crillon Tours** has an unusual package arrangement that you might investigate. The first leg is a motorcoach trip from La Paz to **Huatajata,** a village on the southern tip of Lake Titicaca. From there you pick up a 22-seat hydrofoil boat, which deposits you at Copacabana, after a stop at the sacred **Sun Island,** legendary home of the first Inca, Manco Kapac, who is said to have been born from the waters of Lake Titicaca a thousand years ago. You continue by hydrofoil to Juli, on the Peruvian side of the border. During the trip to Juli you'll see the famous Titicaca reed boats; pass through the Strait of Tiquina; and the Island of the Moon and its gorgeous panorama of the Royal Ranges. From Juli you'll travel by car to Puno. After an overnight stop in Puno, you pick up the regular train to Cuzco. The total cost, including hotel, train, taxes, and insurance, is $190 per person, on a double-room basis. If you prefer, you can do the La Paz–Copacabana portion as a round trip for $105. **Exprinter,** at Plaza Venezuela 1440, first floor (tel. 3-55-926), offers comparable tours.

An alternative is to take an **Autolineas Ingávi** bus from the corner of Calle José María Azín and Eyzaguirre to Guaqui and then pick up another bus to Copacabana. But schedules are erratic from Guaqui, so check at the bus station in La Paz first (tel. 3-28-981).

According to legend, the Inca Empire began on the islands of the Sun and the Moon when a golden rod was brought to earth by Manco Kapac and Mama Ocllo and buried there. Supporting this legend are the remains of a large temple; an Inca fortress; and the Inca Water Spring, a course of eternal life.

An Aymara name known throughout the world, Copacabana is an important religious shrine some 30 miles past the straits of Tiquina. It attracts many pilgrims, who make the trip, often from great distances, on foot to visit the famous cathedral and "Virgen Morena." The town is located on gorgeous Titicaca Bay, which, combined with exciting local color, provides a lovely panorama.

HUATAJATA

If you don't plan to go all the way to Copacabana, we recommend a one-day trip to Huatajata and nearby Suriqui Island. This trip enables you to view Lake Titicaca and the Indian life of the Altiplano. On the way you pass Huayma Potos and Condoriri Mountains and a checkpoint leading to the El Alto section. Here is an area near the airport of La Paz that is flat and where many Indians own private land.

You may want to see the **Hotel Titikaka,** a 22-room hotel with a basic but excellent restaurant, where we suggest you stop for lunch. At Huatajata, a small town on the lake, you can glimpse and get a feeling for the life on the lake. Tours to **Suriqui Island** leave from Huatajata on cabin cruisers operated by Crillon Tours, or you can rent a private boat and a sailor to take you there. On Suriqui Island you'll see Indians building reed boats by the same methods employed centuries ago. There is a reproduction of Thor Heyerdahl's *Ra II.* Be sure to visit the small museum owned by Señor Paulino, who was part of the expedition of the *Ra II.* Crillon Tours has just opened its own museum here at the Inca Utama Hotel.

THE INCA TRAIL

Just 3 hours outside La Paz is the San Francisco mine, the starting point of the Inca Trail. From San Francisco, you'll hike the Inca trail past Inca ruins to the Taquesi Pass, where the climate dramatically changes from cold to tropical. From here there is a magnificent view of Mt. Muruata. The trail then descends along a path of stone slabs and steps to the village of Taquesi and continues onward to the Chojilla mine and the Yungas.

Plaza Tours in the Hotel Plaza, at Avenida 16 de Julio 1789 (tel. 3-78-322) offers two- and three-day treks along the Inca Trail, including transportation, meals, camping equipment, mules, a porter, and a guide.

THE JUNGLE BELOW
CHULUMANI

In the north jungle zone, 80 miles from La Paz, is a small town called Chulumani. A trip to this jungle village is a not-to-be-missed experience. You'll be overwhelmed at the beauty and lushness of the jungle flora, coming as it does just a short time after a ride through high mountain ranges.

For the first leg of the trip, you'll be on a circular road ascending 16,500 feet, surrounded by the snowcapped Cordillera Mountains, with a marvelous view of the majestic peaks. There is a chill in the air at this altitude, which will change as you descend the mountain—coming upon verdant plantations ripe with bananas and coffee beans and thick forest growth—to become a balmy 75°F when you reach Chulumani at 2,700 feet above sea level.

The **Flota Yungueña** bus line (tel. 3-12-344) has buses to Chulumani departing from the corner of Yanacochi and Avenida de las Americas at 9am with a 7pm return. **Crillon Tours** offers a two-day tour to Chulumani by private car for $95 per person for two, including lodging and meals.

Where to Stay

Stop overnight or plan to spend a weekend at the **Motel San Bartolomé,** an attractive motel that offers all the comforts of home in the midst of the tropics. The small native huts come equipped with modern conveniences. You can enjoy the silence of a tropical night in cozy privacy in your own little hut, or you can play billiards and Ping-Pong in the recreation hall. There is an international bar on the premises, as well as an excellent restaurant. For daytime activities, the motel has a mini-golf course and a pool. Inquire at the **Hotel La Paz** about the special bus that leaves on Friday at 9am, returning to La Paz on Sunday afternoon. The price of a bungalow for two is $45 per day; for six it's $95 per day. The restaurant offers a fixed-price menu for $4, with $5.50 to $10 for à la carte dishes.

COROICO

Or you can take a tour of the south jungle to the town of Coroico. Along the way you'll pass dazzling waterfalls and breathtaking precipices. This area is inhabited by the descendents of the African slaves who were brought to Bolivia by the Spanish to work in the mines. Interestingly, their native language is Aymara. Make your arrangements through any tour agency and choose between a day trip (about $90 for two for a guided tour in a private car) or an overnight trip, which will probably mean a stay at the government-owned **Hotel Prefectural** for $25 per person per day, including meals. If you'd like to make the trip in a private taxi, it will cost $28.50 per person. You may want to make arrangements to stay overnight in the brand-new **El Viejo Molino Hotel** (in La Paz call 3-61-076; the main office is at Edificio Alborada, Juan de la Riva 1406, first floor, room no. 105). This 20-room hotel offers lovely doubles with bath for $75. It has a pool with sauna, a bar and restaurant, and a discotheque. Buses to Coroico depart Tuesday, Thursday, Friday, and Saturday at 9am and return Wednesday at 7am and Sunday at 1pm.

THE CARNIVAL OF ORURO

The city of Oruro, 100 miles south of La Paz on the Altiplano, is one of Bolivia's principal industrial centers. Since its founding in 1601, it has been a mining city, primarily tin, silver, and tungsten. Virtually all of its 176,000 Indian inhabitants are miners. Oruro is also an important center of transportation and communication. Its railway station links the Bolivian cities of La Paz, Cochabamba, and Potosí to one another, as well as major cities in Chile and Argentina.

The Carnival of Oruro is the best in Bolivia and one of the most spectacular events in Latin America. Every effort should be made to schedule your trip to Bolivia during the end of February or beginning of March so that it coincides with this colorful celebration. The tradition of Carnival dates back to colonial times and combines Catholic and folk elements.

Carnival starts on the Saturday before Ash Wednesday with the **Diablada,** a frenzied procession of masked dancers in colorful costumes. Through dance, they tell the story of the battle between good and evil. Diabladas are performed throughout the 8 days of Carnival by a cast of thousands, including Spanish conquistadors; Inca warriors; Catholic saints and Indian gods; devils, include Lucifer himself; and, of course, the heroine of the festival, the Virgen of Socavón, the patron saint of miners.

WHERE TO STAY

If you're going to be in Oruro for Carnival, be sure to make your hotel arrangements a few months ahead. The moderately priced **Hotel Terminal** (tel. 53-209) is one of the finest in the city and one of the few hotels whose kitchen is open during Carnival. The government-run **Hotel Prefectural,** on Calle Aldana Pagador (tel. 60-588), is also moderately priced. Prices are lower at the **Repostero,** at Sucre 370 (tel. 50505), which offers rooms with and without a bath.

SANTA CRUZ

Santa Cruz is Bolivia's boom town. What was virtually a ghost town 20 years ago is now a prosperous metropolis of over 529,000 and the frontrunner of Bolivia's economic expansion. It's hard to believe that just over 20 years ago donkey carts dominated the dirt roads of Santa Cruz and that only the Principal Plaza was paved. The discovery of oil and natural gas is to be credited for this quick change.

Just 1,250 feet above sea level, Santa Cruz is hot and tropical all year long. As befits such a climate, the **Cruceños** are very happy-go-lucky. Dress is casual, with outdoor restaurants and clubs the rule. Since Santa Cruz is on the border of Brazil, a strong Brazilian influence is felt here, especially during Carnival, when the women dress in costumes similar to those worn in Rio.

TOURIST INFORMATION

The **Centro de Información Turística** is at Calle René Moreno 215, on the corner of Suárez de Figueroa.

WHERE TO STAY

Some of Bolivia's finest hotels are in Santa Cruz. The **Hotel Las Palmas,** on the corner of Avenidas Trompillo and Chaco (tel. 3-30-366), offers moderately priced rooms and a pool, a definite plus in this balmy climate. The slightly higher priced **Hotel La Quinta,** 10 minutes from downtown on Urbarí Perimetral Sur (tel. 3-42-244), is ideal for families planning to spend a few days in Santa Cruz. It has 76 private apartments, 3 pools, and a restaurant.

Many consider the five-star **Hotel Los Tajibos,** 10 minutes from the center of town on Avenida San Martín (tel. 3-30-022; in La Paz 3-72-121), Bolivia's finest hotel. It features comfortable large rooms, a beautiful pool, racquetball courts, lovely gardens, a nightclub, and the Casino Coliseum, one of the key nightspots in Santa Cruz.

WHERE TO DINE

Santa Cruz offers a varied selection of moderately priced restaurants. The **Crêperie El Boliche,** at Calle Beni 22 (tel. 3-90-553), serves crêpes, sandwiches, and full meals in a very elegant setting. **Frances Le Palmier,** Avenida Banzer 87 (tel. 3-31-261), is a moderately priced French restaurant. If you're in the mood for Italian, you have your choice of pasta and Italian specialties at **Michelangelo,** Calle Chuquisaca 502 (tel. 3-48-403), or pizza at **Los Inmortales,** across from the Hotel Tajibo (tel. 333455). **Surubí,** Avenida Irala 515 (tel. 3-21-858), specializes in dishes prepared with the fish caught in the nearby rivers.

There are a number of fine beef restaurants in Santa Cruz, including **El Arriero,** Calle Mendoza 929 (tel. 3-49-315); **El Fogón,** Avenida Viedma 436 (tel. 3-29-675); and **Carcajada del Chulupi,** Calle Horacio Ríos in El Paraíso.

For light meals, there is a branch of **California Doughnuts** at Calle Independencia 481.

WHAT TO SEE & DO

Other than the city itself, there are not a lot of tourist attractions in Santa Cruz. You should visit the **Basílica Menor de San Lorenzo** on the Plaza 24 de Septiembre, the city's principal plaza. It was built between 1845 and 1915 on the ruins of the original cathedral built in 1605. The museum of religious artifacts inside the cathedral is open Tuesday through Thursday from 9am to noon and 3 to 6pm. The **Natural History Museum** and the **Casa de la Cultura Raúl Otero Reich** are also on the main plaza. The latter exhibits the works of local artists. The **Santa Cruz Zoo** is the finest in Bolivia. It features animals native to the Altiplano and to the tropics; some are quite rare. To get here take the no. 8 bus. Admission is free for kids under 12, $1.50 for adults.

NIGHTLIFE

As mentioned earlier, nightlife here can be pretty lively. For dancing try **Sacramuch,** Cristóbal de Mendoza 178, or **Mermelada Discoteque,** Avenida Uruguay 30. **Yesterday Discoteque,** on the road to Cochabamba, and the **Carly Discoteque,** on Calle Pirit in Ramafa, are also very good but slightly out of the way; you'll need a cab to get to both of these. **Mauna Loa,** Avenida Banzer (tel. 3-26-116), features live entertainment. One of the most popular nightspots is the **Coliseum Casino,** in the Los Tajibos Hotel.

11. MOVING ON

TO CHILE An interesting way to make the trip between La Paz and Santiago is by train from the Estación Central (Plaza Kennedy) to Arica, Chile. From there you can catch a LAN Chile flight to Santiago.

A high-speed modern train called a Ferrobus leaves La Paz every Wednesday at 8:40am and drops you in Arica 9 hours later. The fare is $35, first class only. Slower, overnight trains leave on Monday and Friday morning from the station ($15 for first class, $10 for second class) and arrive in Arica the next morning.

There are several direct flights to Santiago from La Paz. Lufthansa also flies to Santiago on Wednesday and Saturday.

CHAPTER 9
QUITO, ECUADOR

1. **INTRODUCING QUITO & ECUADOR**
- **WHAT'S SPECIAL ABOUT QUITO**
- **WHAT THINGS COST IN QUITO**
2. **ORIENTATION**
3. **GETTING AROUND**
- **FAST FACTS: QUITO**
4. **WHERE TO STAY**
5. **WHERE TO DINE**
6. **ATTRACTIONS**
- **DID YOU KNOW . . . ?**
7. **SPORTS & RECREATION**
8. **SAVVY SHOPPING**
9. **EVENING ENTERTAINMENT**
10. **THE GALAPAGOS ISLANDS**
11. **SUGGESTED ITINERARIES**

Despite the fact that *quito* is a pre-Inca word meaning "terrible," the capital is a physically enchanting city with an ideal climate. Because of its 2-mile-high elevation (the second-highest world capital), Quito's year round temperatures are like those of May in New England. And the breezes are just brisk enough to require a light sweater in the evening. (On the coast, the days are much warmer and the air doesn't cool off at night.)

Quito's towering beauty—the city is nestled in a valley between the two Andean mountain ranges—the Cordillera Occidental (Western Range) and the Cordillera Oriental (Eastern Range). Quito is at the base of **Pichincha**, a 4,747-foot dormant volcano, where the Ecuadorian hero General Sucre defeated the Spanish, thereby securing Ecuador's independence. Be sure to see Pichincha at sunset from the Plaza de la Independencia. Also visible from the plaza is the beautiful statue of the Virgin of Quito atop the **Cerro Panecillo** ("Little Breadloaf Hill"). Crafted in Spain after a 18th-century sculpture by Bernardo de Legarda, the statue was unveiled in 1976. The people of Quito are proud of their Virgin, and rightly so—it adds both beauty and drama to the Cerro Panecillo.

Another exciting aspect of Quito is that a 2- or 3-hour bus or train trip will take you to a primitive Indian village that virtually hasn't changed for centuries. And the equator is only 15 miles (30 minutes) away. In the spring and fall, the sun rises promptly at 6am and sets 12 hours later.

1. INTRODUCING QUITO & ECUADOR

BACKGROUND Originally settled by Indian tribes a thousand years ago, Quito was the **Tiangueaz** or **market center** for all Indian communities throughout Ecuador because of its strategic location between the coast, the sierra, and the rain forest. The area was conquered by the Incas during their expansion into the northern Andes in the 13th century and then razed by them when Pizarro's troops approached the city in 1533. After it was rebuilt by the Spanish conquistadors, Quito became the artistic and cultural center of Spanish America.

WHAT'S SPECIAL ABOUT QUITO

Monuments

☐ The monument to the heroes of the August 10, 1809, uprising is an emotional tribute to the nation's fight for independence from Spain.

☐ The monument to the equator, just 15 miles outside the city, is an obligatory part of any visit to Quito.

☐ The Virgen of Quito keeps watch over the city from atop the Panecillo.

Buildings

☐ The La Compañía de Jesús and San Francisco churches are two excellent examples of colonial architecture.

Museum

☐ The Fundación Guayasamín is a loving tribute to Ecuador's cultural legacy.

Park/Garden

☐ Ejido Park boasts a diverse selection of trees (many of which are more than 100 years old) and open-air art exhibits on the weekends.

☐ The Plaza de la Independencia in Old Quito is one of the loveliest in South America.

Great Villages

☐ A tour of Indian villages to the north and south of Quito provide great insight into the soul of Ecuador. Market day is the best time to visit.

City Spectacle

☐ Calle Morales (known as Calle La Ronda) provides a glimpse into Quito's colonial past.

Ecuador has a population of approximately 10 million. Most of the inhabitants of Quito and the Andean villages are Indian, while those on the coast in and near Guayaquil are mestizo.

WHAT THINGS COST IN QUITO	U.S. $
Taxi from the airport to the city center	5.00
Local telephone call	.05
Double with bath at the Hostal Los Maderos (budget)	18.00
Double at the Hotel Chalet Suisse (moderate)	50.00
Lunch or dinner at the Café Niza (budget)	6.00
Lunch or dinner at Las Cuevas de Luis Candelas (moderate)	12.00
Lunch or dinner at Rincón de Francia (splurge)	15.00
Cup of coffee	.15
Coca-Cola	.15

2. ORIENTATION

If this is your first high-altitude stop, you may experience some light-headedness and may feel your heart pounding. A short stroll will seem like a hike and a small hill like

IMPRESSIONS

Quito, the oldest city in the New World, is seemingly built over a sunken roller coaster. Up and down in wide curves and sudden drops go its streets and white houses; the base of one monument is above the spray of the fountain in the next plaza.
—LUDWIG BEMELMANS, *THE DONKEY INSIDE*, 1947

Mount Everest. Don't be overconcerned. *Soroche,* a mild case of altitude sickness, is common and will usually pass in a day.

ARRIVING

BY PLANE   You'll arrive during the day (there are few night flights into Quito), so you'll be able to see the beauty of the city from the air as your plane glides through the northern Andes mountain ranges into modern **Mariscal-Sucre Airport.** The airport has a *cambio* where you can exchange dollars for sucres, as well as a National Car Rental and an office of **CETUR,** a government tourist service that will be glad to assist you by supplying maps and making arrangements.
   After the usual Customs check, which is extremely efficient, you'll want to head into town. You can either take a cab ($5) for the 20-minute ride, or take a bus (no. 1, 7, 15, 21, or 26). Buses marked INAQUITO VILLA FLORA, which leave from Avenida de La Prensa, go to downtown Quito for 20¢.

BY TRAIN   The central railroad station, from which trains depart for Guayaquil and elsewhere, is in the section of Quito called Chimbacalle, south of the Old City. Both standard trains and *autoferros* (small coaches with reclining seats) operate from here. The ticket office is at Calle Bolívar 443 (tel. 26-6144).

BY BUS   Buses traveling to and from Quito from locations throughout Ecuador arrive and depart from the **El Cumanda Bus Terminal,** located 5 minutes' walking distance from the Plaza de Santo Domingo in Old Quito at Maldonado 577 (tel. 57-1163). Tickets cannot be reserved, nor can they be purchased through a travel agency. They can be purchased only at the terminal.

BY CAR   As elsewhere in South America, taxis are fairly inexpensive in Quito. Be sure to get into a "numbered" cab because these belong to the municipal cooperative. Pirate cabs may not be as safe. A car will not be necessary in Old Quito. However, if you plan to explore new Quito and the surrounding countryside, you should consider renting a car. Remember that traffic tends to be chaotic and the streets are not always clearly marked.

TOURIST INFORMATION

A new **Government Tourist Office** is located at Reina Victoria 514 and Roca, directly behind the former Soviet Embassy (tel. 52-7074 or 52-7002); it's open Monday to Friday from 8am to 4pm. They'll gladly provide you with tourist information as well as maps and posters.

CITY LAYOUT

To orient yourself to Quito quickly, remember that there are two important sections: the **Old City,** which centers around **Plaza de la Independencia,** and the **New City,** which extends north from **Ejido Park** to **Avenida Colón** and then into the suburbs. The Old City bustles with workers during the day but then becomes quiet at night. The New City is growing by leaps and bounds; it's hard to keep up with it from one visit to the next. The liveliest street in the New City is **Avenida Amazonas,** which is filled with cafés, shops, and restaurants. This is where you'll want to be at night. So we have sought out new hotels, restaurants, and nightspots within the oddly shaped rectangle of Ejido Park (south) to Avenida Colón (north), **Avenida 12 de Octubre** (12th of October) on the east and **Avenida 10 de Agosto** (10th of August) on the west.

Note: The terms *old* and *new* are ours, to make identification simpler for you. We are always struck by the contrast between these two areas—one is overflowing with a Spanish-colonial tradition that seems not to have changed for centuries, while the other is brimming over with new private homes, shopping centers, and wide thoroughfares. You can easily walk from one area to the other.

MAIN ARTERIES The lovely tree-dotted Plaza de la Independencia—center of the city—is particularly beautiful at dusk, when from the Avenida Chile side you can gaze at the nearby mountains, which seem to be closing in on the city. Office buildings and shops surround the plaza; the famous **cathedral,** which houses many valuable Ecuadorian paintings, is on the south side. Two key thoroughfares that run alongside the plaza are **Venezuela** and **Guayaquil,** which are the main shopping streets. Guayaquil becomes **10 de Agosto** as the street heads north into the New City.

The oldest section of the Old City lies south of the plaza at **Avenida Morales,** popularly called the **Calle de la Ronda.** Here all the streets are steep, narrow, and cobblestoned, and the tiny brightly colored residences are packed solid for block after block.

The New City, in sharp contrast, has large homes built on huge lots. **Ejido Park** is large enough to house a soccer stadium, and it once did. It is also the site of the Legislative Palace. The major street cutting through the New City is **10 de Agosto** (an extention of Guayaquil). Many of our recommended hotels are near 10 de Agosto as far north as Avenida Colón.

The street that probably commands greatest attention from locals and visitors alike is **Calle Vincente Ramón Roca** (not far from Colón), where many houses resemble castles, fortresses, or mosques.

3. GETTING AROUND

BY BUS Buses in Quito are called *colectivos;* they are small, fast, and most convenient, and cost about 20¢. The names on the front indicate the first and last stops. The most important line is the Colón-Camal, which leaves every five minutes from Avenida Guayaquil, one block from the Plaza de la Independencia, and heads to almost all our recommended hotels in the New City for 10¢.

Bus nos. 1 and 7 will take you to the airport. Other major bus terminals are at Plaza T. Cumanda and El Recreo, 45 minutes out of town. Double-decker buses, imported from England, can be found on major streets in the New City. The fare is 20¢.

BY TAXI Cabs are reasonably priced, but be sure to get into a numbered cab with a meter. Within the city, the price for a 15-minute ride should run about $2.50. To New City from the Plaza de la Independencia, the cost could be $4. The fare to (or from) the airport is about $5 (up to five passengers). The base fare starts at $1.20.

BY CAR Rates for an aging Volkswagen are high—$16 per day plus 14¢ per kilometer. A $200 deposit is required, too. The usual weekly rental rate is $93, plus 14¢ per kilometer. The monthly rate is $374.50 (14¢ per kilometer). Gasoline is

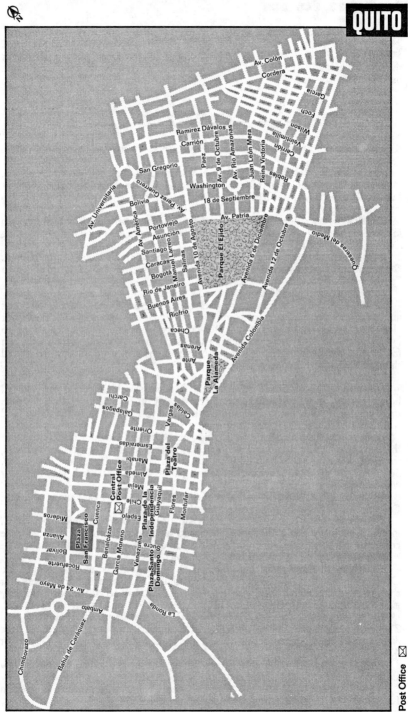

QUITO

Post Office ⊠

included in the rates. **Hertz** is at Santa Maria 517, at the corner of Amazonas (tel. 24-6381). **Budget** is located at Colon 1140, at the corner of Juan Leon Mera (tel. 54-8237 or 23-7026), as well as in the Hotel Colón Internacional (tel. 52-5328) and at the airport (tel. 24-0763). If you want a car for just a few hours, rent a cab—the per-hour rate is about $5.

FAST QUITO

American Express The American Express Office is at Amazonas 339 (tel. 56-0488).

Area Code The country code for Ecuador is 593; the city code for Quito is 2.

Babysitters Contact the **Social Services Assistance** office (SAS) at Lugo 890, at the corner of Vizcaya (tel. 56-0318.) The concierge at your hotel may also be able to help you arrange for child care.

Bookstores Books in English are available at **LibriMundi,** which has two locations in Quito: Juan Leon Mera 851 (tel. 23-4791) and the Hotel Colon Shopping Center (tel. 55-0455).

Business Hours **Banks** are open Monday to Friday from 9am to 1:30pm. **Commercial centers and stores** are open Monday to Saturday from 9am to 7pm.

Car Rentals See "Getting Around," above.

Climate Quito enjoys a nearly perfect climate year round—sunny, mild days and cool, clear evenings. Its proximity to the equator is offset by the 9,400-foot elevation (2,000 feet higher than Mexico City). But the altitude can lead to light-headedness or even a headache on your first day here; therefore, walk slowly, rest frequently, and breathe deeply to absorb maximum oxygen upon your arrival. All should be well after a good night's rest.

Crime See "Safety" below.

Currency North American budget travelers should find that virtually all hotels (except deluxe) and restaurants are reasonably priced. Ecuador's currency used to be stable, but now the exchange rate has soared to 1400 sucres to the dollar (and still rising) from the 150 it was just six years ago.

Currency Exchange Dollars can be exchanged either at banks or one of the currency exchanges (*casas de cambio*) located around the city; for example, the **Casa Paz** in the Proinco Building, at the corner of Amazonas and Robles (tel. 563-900), or **M. M. Jaramillo Arteaga** at Mejia 401 (tel. 210-881), or **Multicambio** at Colon 919 (tel. 549-207).

Dentists/Doctors Ask the concierge at your hotel or contact the U.S. Embassy for a list of English-speaking dentists and doctors.

Drugstores As elsewhere in South America, Quito's pharmacies use a system in which one pharmacy in every neighborhood stays open 24 hours. Check with the concierge at your hotel to find out which neighborhood pharmacy will be open.

Electricity The current here is 110 volts.

Embassies/Consulates The **U.S. Embassy** is at Avenida 12 de Octubre and Patria (tel. 54-800), near Ejido Stadium. The **Canadian Embassy** is at the corner of Colón and Amazonas (tel. 542-205); the **United Kingdom Embassy** is at the corner of Gonzalez Suarez (111) and Avenida 12 de Octubre (tel. 560-309).

Emergencies To reach the **Red Cross Emergency Hospital,** call 214-977 (ambulance tel. 214-966). One English-speaking hospital is the **Metropolitano** at the corner of Mariana de Jesus and Occidental (tel. 431-457 or 431-521).

Eyeglasses You'll find opticians throughout the city, especially in the New City. If necessary, the concierge should be able to direct you to one nearby.

Hairdressers/Barbers **Hair's Unisex** is located downtown at Avenida La Prensa 3230, between Avenidas Florida and J. Piedra.

Holidays

New Year's Day	January 1
Anniversary of the Discovery of the Amazon River	February 12
International Fruit and Flower Fair in Ambato	February/March
Carnival	3 days before Ash Wednesday
Holy Week	Easter Week
Riobamba Fair	April 19–21
Labor Day	May 1
Battle of Pichincha	May 24
Símon Bolívar's Birthday	July 24
Anniversary of the founding of Santiago de Guayaquil	July 23–25
National Independence Day	August 10
Yamor Festival in Otavalo	September 2–15
Our Lady of Mercy Festival in Latacunga	September 23–24
Guayaquil Independence Day	October 9
Cuenca Independence Day	November 3
Founding of Quito	December 6
Christmas	December 25

Information   See "Tourist Information," above.

Laundry/Dry Cleaning   Martinizing at Republica 386 (tel. 238-832) has branches located throughout the city; call for the one nearest you. Another choice is **Junior's Dry Cleaning and Laundry** at San Javier 232, at the corner of Orellana (tel. 527-551).

Luggage Storage/Lockers   If you're planning a short trip, you may be able to store your things at the hotel while you're away.

Newspapers/Magazines   English-language newspapers and magazines— including the *Miami Herald, International Herald Tribune,* and *Time* and *Newsweek*—can be purchased at the major hotels.

Photographic Needs   Because of the altitude, it is a good idea to use a UV filter. Both black-and-white and color film is available in Quito, but be sure to check the expiration date before you buy.

Police   Call 653-780 or 432-263.

Post Office/Mail   Open until 8pm, the post office is located at Benalcazar 688, between Chile and Espejo, a block from Plaza de la Independencia, near the Cueva Restaurant. There is also one in the Centro Comercial InaQuito, near the airport. Airmail postage to the United States is about 40¢.

Religious Services   Catholic: Santa Teresita, at the corner of Robles and 19 de Octubre (tel. 230-502); **Protestant:** Inaquito, at the corner of Villalengua and 10 de Agosto (tel. 247-981); **Jewish:** 18 de Septiembre 954, between Versalles and Manuel Larrea (tel. 233-765).

Restrooms   They're called *servicios* (*damas* is "ladies" and *caballeros* is "men"); it is best to go to a hotel lobby while in Old Quito. In the modern city all public places, including galleries, cinemas, theaters and parks, have them. Hotel lobbies are your best bet here as well.

Safety   Quito is relatively safe for tourists. However, you should exercise the same caution that you would in any city. Watch your belongings when boarding a city bus and in crowded plazas and fairs. Do not walk alone in Old Quito at night.

Shoe Repairs   The concierge in your hotel should be able to direct you to a nearby shoe repair shop.

Taxes   There is a departure tax of $25.

Taxis   See "Getting Around," above.

Telegrams/Telexes/Faxes   These services are available at the large hotels or at IETEL (the telephone office), located at the corner of 6 de Diciembre and Colon, as well as at the corner of Benalcazar and Mejia. Hours are Monday to Sunday 8am to 9:30pm.

Telephone   To make a call, deposit a *ficha* worth 70 sucres and dial. Long-distance calls can be made through the switchboard of your hotel or at an IETEL office. The AT&T Direct Program is a great cost-saver. It is available at the AT&T Calling Centers located throughout the city.

Useful Telephone Numbers   The **fire department** can be reached by dialing 102; the **radio patrol** is at 101. The **Red Cross** is at 214-977. To call an **ambulance** phone 214-966. To call the **police** phone 653-780 or 432-263.

4. WHERE TO STAY

Relative to its population of 1.3 million, Quito probably has more good moderately priced hotels than any other city in South America, with the possible exception of Buenos Aires. In general, the Old City offers the best budget hotels, while the New City has the best pensions (rooms with three meals). Our prices include the 20% tax and service charge.

NEW CITY
DOUBLES FOR LESS THAN $30

HOSTAL FLORENCIA, Wilson 660, at the corner of Juan Leon Mera. Tel. 237-819. 17 rms (some with bath).
$ Rates: $5 per person without bath; $7 with bath. **Parking:** Available.

The Florencia, ideal for those on a tight budget, has basic rooms. Baths consist of showers only, no tubs. There's a small TV lounge off the lobby. The management is friendly and the location is convenient, one block from Amazonas.

HOSTAL LOS MADEROS, Pedro Bazan 7, at the corner of Manosca. Tel. 241-893. 7 rms (all with bath). **Transportation:** Mitad del Mundo bus, Altamira bus, Canal 4.
$ Rates (including breakfast): $18 double.

Owner Carlota de Falani will personally ensure that your stay here is pleasant. This was once a private home, and all seven rooms are comfortably furnished and located on the second floor. There's a dining room, library, and lounge with TV and stereo on the first floor.

HOSTAL RESIDENCIAL SANTA CLARA, Gustavo Darquea 1578. Tel. 54-1472. Some rooms with bath.
$ Rates (including breakfast): $6 per person without bath; $8 room with bath.
This large, well-recommended pension has rooms with private baths (including hot water), which are often hard to get at this price. The manager speaks English.

HOTEL MAJESTIC, Mercadillo 366, at the corner of Versalles. Tel. 54-3182 or 546-388. All rooms with bath.
$ Rates: $20 double.

Another good budget choice is the Majestic. This spotlessly clean hostelry offers bright, well-furnished rooms, with the front rooms facing Panecillo. The hotel is near most bus routes and the main Avenida 10 de Agosto, and within walking distance of Avenida Amazonas.

LOS ANDES HOSTAL RESIDENCIAL, Calle Muros 146 and Avenida 12 de Octubre. Tel. 55-0839. Some rooms with bath.
$ Rates: $23 double with bath.
Originally a large home, this was converted into a family-owned modern hostel. Your host, Alvaro Naranjo, who speaks flawless English, will go all out to make your visit pleasant. Rooms are modern, large, and clean. There are two apartments on the upper floor.

HOSTAL LOS ALPES, Tamayo 233. Tel. 56-1110. Most rooms with bath.
$ Rates: $30 single; $35 double.

★ Los Alpes is like a home away from home. Set in a comfortable private house on a quiet street, rooms look lived in and comfortable. Screened porches for sunning and relaxing, a fine restaurant that serves all meals and specializes in Italian food, and very friendly owners make this a special stop.

HOTEL SANTA MARIA, Calle Ingleterra 933. Tel. 52-9929. Fax 562-429.
36 rms (all with bath). TEL
$ Rates: $19 single; $29 double. Major credit cards accepted.

This seven-story hotel, one block off 10 de Agosto, has nicely furnished rooms. The Santa María boasts a sauna, bar, and restaurant where guests can take all three meals. A 20% discount is offered to guests who opt for full board (room and three meals).

TAMBO REAL, 12 de Octubre and Avenida Patria. Tel. 52-4260. Fax
554-964. Telex 22751 DEPHTL-ED. All rooms with bath. TEL
$ Rates: $20 single; $25 double. Major credit cards accepted.

The Tambo Real, across from the American Embassy, is a bit out of our rectangle but is within easy walking distance. Rooms here are quite large and furnished nicely. The coffee shop downstairs is open 24 hours; breakfast costs $1. There's also a casino.

DOUBLES FOR LESS THAN $50

**HOTEL CHALET SUISSE, Calama 312, at the corner of Reina Victoria.
Tel. 54-8766.** Fax 563-966. Telex 22766 CHASUI ED. 50 rms (all with bath). TV
TEL
$ Rates: $50 double. Major credit cards accepted.

An almost deluxe choice, the six-story Châlet Suisse is built around a fine restaurant. The rooms are plush, and the hotel offers a piano bar, casino, beauty shop, and sauna.

HOTEL REPUBLICA, Avenida República. Tel. 436-553. Fax 437-667. Telex
21033 HOREP-ED. 40 rms (all with bath). TEL
$ Rates: $25 single; $30 double. Major credit cards accepted.

This excellent four-star hotel has rooms on four floors. They're all carpeted and have piped-in music. There's a restaurant and bar on the premises, as well as a popular disco, Zion. The location is great, since Avenida República runs diagonally between Avenida Amazonas and Avenida 10 de Agosto.

SPLURGE CHOICES

ALAMEDA REAL, Calle Roca 653, Amazonas. Tel. 56-2345. Fax 565-759.
Telex 22224 ALAMEDA-ED. 150 rms (all with bath). TV TEL
$ Rates: $72 single; $84 double. Major credit cards accepted.

Among the newer hotels, this one has modern and elegantly furnished rooms. You'll like the comfortable lobby and fine restaurant and coffee shop. There are other branches elsewhere in Ecuador. State-of-the-art conference facilities and business services make this a favorite choice of business travelers. To make reservations from the United States, call toll free 800/223-5652.

HOTEL AMBASSADOR, 9 de Octubre 1052. Tel. 561-777 or 561-993. Fax
503-712. 60 rms (all with bath). TV TEL
$ Rates (including breakfast): $50 single; $65 double. Discounts available for long stays. Major credit cards accepted.

The Ambassador resembles an aged, sprawling private home; it has a bar, restaurant, and pastry shop on the premises; laundry service is available.

HOTEL QUITO BEST WESTERN, Gonzalez Suarez 2500. Tel. 23-0300.
Fax 567-284. Telex 22223 INCUIO-ED. 231 rooms (all with bath). TV TEL
$ Rates: $88 single; $98 double. Major credit cards accepted.

One of the city's first five-star hotels, the Quito boasts a quiet location. Superb Ecuadorian rugs and wood carvings decorate the lobby, making it worthwhile to visit even if you're not staying here. Amenities include a heated outdoor pool, a sauna and steamroom, bars and a nightclub, and a restaurant and casino. A drink at the nightclub costs $3.50.

OLD CITY
DOUBLES FOR LESS THAN $10

Five blocks south of Plaza de la Independencia is the oldest section of Quito, whose center is Avenida Morales, popularly known as the Calle de la Ronda. We cannot emphasize strongly enough that these hotels are rock-bottom basic and *only* for the young in heart and penny-conscious. *Beware:* This section of the city is known for pickpockets.

GRAN CASINO, Garcia Moreno 330. Tel. 51-6368. 60 rms (none with bath).
$ Rates: $4 per person.
An old hotel catering mainly to international students and backpackers is the four-story Gran Casino, which has sparsely furnished rooms. A large doorway opens onto a foyer and reception room with TV. The main hallway leads to a patio with a scattering of tables. There is a restaurant on the premises serving substantial fare at bargain-basement prices.

GRAN CASINO II, at the corner of Avenida 24 de Mayo and Bahia de Cacique. Tel. 514-905. All rooms with bath.
$ Rates: $8 per person.
The owners of the Gran Casino have opened a more comfortable hotel just two blocks away. Prices are about double those at the Gran Casino, but the rooms are much nicer.

HOTEL COLONIAL, Maldonado 3035. Tel. 51-0338. 40 rms (all with bath).
$ Rates: $4 per person.
The Colonial offers small rooms that are neat and adequately furnished. The dining room serves low-priced meals (optional). You enter through a narrow courtyard that has an outdoor prayer altar carved into one wall. Follow the winding stone courtyard path for almost a block to reach the entrance.

DOUBLES FOR LESS THAN $30

HOSTAL CUMANDA, Calle Morales 449. Tel. 51-6984. All rooms with bath.
TEL
$ Rates: $9 single; $14 double.
A good choice is the family-owned Cumanda, opposite the bus terminal and just down the block from the stairs leading to Old Quito. The hotel is immaculate, the management is friendly, and the rooms are quite comfortable; all are carpeted, and the beds are fairly new. The rooms go quickly, so you may want to make an advance reservation and request a room in the back. The front rooms tend to be noisier due to the bus terminal. The hotel has its own restaurant, which serves delicious home-style Ecuadorian meals at super-economical prices. A complete dinner can cost less than $3.50.

HOTEL PLAZA, Espejo 818. Tel. 51-4860. All rooms with bath.
$ Rates (including breakfast): $15 single; $18 double; $22 triple.
Near Avenida Flores, the Hotel Plaza opened in 1972. The blue-and-red-checkered bedspreads are cheery, the bathrooms are large, and the rooms are clean. The reception desk is on the second floor. The dining room on the left attracts a large lunchtime crowd.

HOTEL CASINO REAL AUDIENCIA, Bolívar 220. Tel. 51-2711. 36 rms (all with bath).
$ Rates: $25 double.
Another good choice, this hotel is on the corner of Guayaquil. It's a fine establishment, almost meriting four stars. There's a busy casino downstairs and a restaurant on

the fourth floor with great views of bustling Santo Domingo Church and square, filled with busy shoeshine boys (actually old men). There's no elevator, so you have to hike up to the restaurant.

LA CASONA, Manabi 255, between Flores and Montufar. Tel. 514-764. Fax 563-271. 23 rooms (all with bath). TV TEL
$ Rates: $11–$15 double.

⭐ La Casona is a delightful addition to our list of hotels in Old Quito. Unlike most of the others, which have been showing their age in recent years, La Casona is a restored colonial home which opened in 1991. The rooms are clean and comfortably furnished. If you can, ask for a room with a balcony overlooking the center courtyard and its lovely fountain and garden. La Casona should be high on your list if you decide to stay in Old Quito.

HOTEL VIENA INTERNACIONAL, Flores 610, at the corner of Chile. Tel. 211-329. All rooms with bath.
$ Rates: $7 per person.
The Viena Internacional should not to be confused with the dingy Hotel Viena at Flores 562. This hotel has small but clean rooms, all leading off a small inner courtyard. (The one at no. 562 is for those on a rock-bottom budget.)

APART-HOTELS

APART-HOTEL AMARANTA INTERNACIONAL, Leonidas Plaza 194 and Jorge Washington. Tel. 23-8385 or 52-7191. Fax 56-0586.
$ Rates: $18 single; $20 double.
The Amaranta offers comfortably furnished suites of up to four bedrooms. Facilities include a restaurant and conference center. Laundry service is available. This is an especially good choice for families and small groups as well as travelers planning to spend a week or more in Quito and the surrounding countryside.

HOTEL EMBASSY, Calle Presidente Wilson 441. Tel. 561-990. Fax 563-192. Telex 21181 TRAHOT ED. 14 suites (all with bath). TV TEL
$ Rates: $20 single; $45 suite. Major credit cards accepted.
Near 6 de Diciembre, the Embassy is uniquely set up to handle families. And that's what you find here—particularly U.S. Embassy families. There are two-bedroom suites, complete with a kitchen, living room, and fireplace. There is a full-service restaurant on the premises. Since the motel is 10 blocks from Avenida 10 de Agosto, a car is helpful.

GALAXIE HOTEL SUITES, Avenida Villalengua 748, Urbanizacion Grande Centro. Tel. 243-101 or 243110. Fax 445-700. All suites with bath. TV TEL
$ Rates: $50 apartments; $65 suites.
The Galaxie is an ideal choice for families with young children. Featured here are suites and apartments, with fully equipped kitchenettes, which can accommodate up to six. There is a small deli in the hotel (although it would be better to shop at a nearby grocery store), as well as a restaurant serving international and regional favorites. The Galaxie has its own pool; the spacious Carolina Park is only a few blocks away on Avenida Amazonas.

5. WHERE TO DINE

Ecuadorian cuisine, while not really distinctive, includes several special dishes that are well worth trying. The diversity of the nation's geography is aptly reflected in several regional cuisines—ranging from *cebiche de corvina* (whitefish marinated in lemon sauce), typical of the coastal areas, to *sazonado de mote cuencano,* a corn dish typical of Cuenca, to *tapado esmeraldeño,* dry beef covered with plantain leaves that originated in Esmeraldas, a northeastern province of Ecuador.

Locro, a potato soup made with cheese, vegetables, or meat and avocado is one of our favorites. Other typical dishes we would recommend are the *humitas* (corn tamales), *llapingachos* (a cheese-and-potato dish served with a fried egg on top), *sancocho costeno* (a soup made from plantains, beef, and yuca), and the *chupe de pescado* (fish cooked with potatoes and peanuts). *Chorizos* (sausage), smoked fish, roasted rabbit or guinea pig, and assorted seafood also comprise part of Ecuadorian cuisine.

Be sure to sample the native fruits, many of which are unique to Ecuador. The most popular include the *naranjilla,* a delicious cross between an orange and a peach; *babaco,* a bittersweet and aromatic fruit that resembles a melon; *chamburo,* a member of the papaya family; and *capuli,* a small cherrylike fruit.

As for drinks, the *pisco sour,* made with *pisco* (a local *aguardiente*) and lemon juice is a national, as well as a Peruvian, favorite. Remember that it's quite potent, especially at this altitude.

ON CALAMA IN NEW CITY

The "Restaurant Row" of Quito is a small street—Avenida Calama—tucked between Amazonas and 6 de Diciembre. On the "strip" are some of the finest big-splurge restaurants of Quito—eateries that would be well received in Paris, Rome, or New York. Each restaurant is in its own private house.

In addition to the following, the steakhouse **Pims** and several ice-cream parlors round out the four-block area where you can eat virtually every type of food served in Quito. Calama is the street adjacent to Avenida Colón.

Two more restaurants on Calama Street we would recommend are the **Hereford Grill Steak House,** near Juan Sebastian, and **Dickens,** next door. Hereford Grill is a steakhouse comparable to the Shorthorn (see below); head downstairs. Dickens is a typical English pub with a menu that alternates between Yorkshire pudding and local fare.

EL CEBICHE, Juan León Mera 232. Tel. 526-380.
   Cuisine: CEBICHE/SEAFOOD. **Reservations:** Not accepted. Major credit cards accepted.
   Open: Daily.
Near Calama, this restaurant serves the largest and best *cebiche* in Quito. Raw shrimp, mussels, assorted fish, and a mixture of all of the above are served in a tangy lime juice with garlic and onions and peppers. The juice "cooks" the fish. It's a fabulous dish and tastes great with a margarita.

LE CHALET SUISSE, Avenida Calama at Reina Victoria. Tel. 562-700.
   Cuisine: SWISS. **Reservations:** Recommended.
 $ Prices: Appetizers $3–$5; main courses $8–$15. Major credit cards accepted.
   Open: Daily lunch and dinner.
The roaring fireplace, beamed ceiling, and white stone walls make this excellent restaurant exceptionally appealing. Definitely try the fondues—either cheese or meat (each is $15 for two). The chef is justifiably proud of his chateaubriand Chalet Suisse. You'll enjoy soft piano music as you dine. Growing in popularity and size, the Chalet Suisse recently opened a gambling casino that is packed on weekends, plus a modern new hotel under the same name and management.

LA CREPERIE, Avenida Calama 362. Tel. 233-780.
   Cuisine: FRENCH. **Reservations:** Not accepted.
 $ Prices: Crêpes $3 and up.
   Open: Tues–Sun noon–11pm.
There are 34 different varieties from which to choose, including dessert crêpes. If you can't resist the temptation of a chocolate crêpe with vanilla ice cream and don't mind the slightly high prices, drop in.

EXCALIBUR, Calama 380. Tel. 54-1272.
Cuisine: INTERNATIONAL. **Reservations:** Recommended.
$ Prices: Appetizers $3–$6; main courses $8–$15. Major credit cards accepted.
Open: Lunch and dinner.

★ This cozy restaurant sports carpeted floors and attractive wood-paneled walls. Try the *lomo al jerez* or *corvina al jerez.*

JUAN SEBASTIAN BAR, Avenida Calama. Tel. 54-6955.
Cuisine: INTERNATIONAL. **Reservations:** Recommended.
$ Prices: Appetizers $2–$5; main courses $5–$10. Major credit cards accepted.
Open: Lunch and dinner.

This particularly delightful choice is known for its excellent variety of *marisco* dishes. Try the mussels appetizer or the *tortilla langostinos*—delicious! Head downstairs to the main dining room: There are two large rooms with a wooden bar and pool table. The atmosphere is dark and intimate, somewhat like that of a disco.

SHORTHORN GRILL, Calama 216. Tel. 523-645.
Cuisine: ARGENTINEAN. **Reservations:** Recommended.
$ Prices: Appetizers $2–$5; main courses $4–$8. Major credit cards accepted.
Open: Daily noon–midnight.

For the best in Argentinean-style steaks, try the Shorthorn Grill, a new and attractive restaurant largely decorated with cowhide. There's an open salad bar, and all dishes come with a baked potato and sour cream. There are sauces on your table, green and red-hot red. The menu is in both English and Spanish. Owner Esteban Diaz is proud of his restaurant and ensures that all requests are attended to. He also owns Le Club, one of our top nightspot recommendations.

"EL TORO" STEAKHOUSE RESTAURANT, Calama 339. Tel. 235-751.
Cuisine: STEAK. **Reservations:** Not accepted.
$ Prices: Appetizers $1–$1.50; main courses $2–$6.
Open: Daily lunch and dinner.

Ⓢ "El Toro" is probably the best value in a steakhouse that you could hope to find anywhere. The menu features a variety of steaks—including filet mignon and T-bones—prepared many different ways. Also on the menu are *chorizo* (sausage); *morcilla* (blood sausage); and numerous chicken dishes, including roasted chicken, chicken in wine sauce, and breaded chicken. There are also *parilladas* (an assortment of meat and sausage) for one or more persons. All orders come with salad and baked potato or french fries.

ELSEWHERE IN NEW CITY

COLUMBUS, Avenida Colón 1262. Tel. 551-857 or 231-811.
Cuisine: ARGENTINEAN/STEAK. **Reservations:** Recommended.
$ Prices: Appetizers $1–$3; main courses $5–$8; meals under $6.
Open: Lunch and dinner.

Ⓢ Many people consider the Columbus the best budget steakhouse in town. Cooked Argentinean-style over a charcoal grill, thick, juicy steaks are prepared to order and are served with two special hot sauces. Side dishes include fabulous coleslaw and potato salad. A delicious meal can total less than $6. Other locations include Avenida Tarqui 758, at 10 de Agosto (tel. 541-920), and Avenida Amazonas 1643, at Atahualpa (tel. 451-965).

RISTORANTE VECCHIA ROMA, Roca 618. Tel. 56-5659.
Cuisine: ITALIAN. **Reservations:** Not accepted.
$ Prices: Appetizers $1–$3; main courses $3–$6.
Open: Daily 8am–10pm.

Drop in at any hour of the day and enjoy the old-world comfort of the Vecchia Roma's main dining room. You'll swear you're sitting in New York City's Little Italy. The prices are comfortable, too, for dishes such as cannelloni, ravioli, and pizza. We particularly enjoyed a delicious chicken cacciatore. During warm weather, dine outdoors at curbside tables. The Vecchia Roma serves breakfast outdoors from 8am on, charging just $1.50 for a hearty American breakfast and under $2 for rolls and coffee. The restaurant is open for lunch, and dinner is served from 6 to 10pm. The management is friendly and courteous.

EL TORO PARTIDO, Leonidas Plaza and 9 de Octubre. Tel. 233-092.
 Cuisine: BRAZILIAN. **Reservations:** Recommended.
$ Prices: Appetizers $1–$3; main courses $4–$8. Major credit cards accepted.
 Open: Lunch and dinner.
This authentic Brazilian *rodizio churrascaría* is upstairs. The menu includes 10 types of meat and 18 salads—all you can eat for $6. Strolling musicians add to the fun. Head upstairs and try for a table that overlooks Avenida Amazonas.

CHIFA CHINA, Carrion 1274, at the corner of Versalles. Tel. 23-9954.
 Cuisine: CHINESE. **Reservations:** Not accepted.
$ Prices: Appetizers $1–$3; main courses $3–$6.
 Open: Lunch daily noon–3pm; dinner daily 6pm–midnight.
This is a good Chinese restaurant. Enter through a garden and a gate into a rather large dining area divided into several rooms, each with hanging lanterns. The lengthy bilingual menu features some 20 soups and many duck (*pato*) dishes. Squab is favored by the regulars. Dishes we like include the *bola de camerón con cangrejo* (shrimp balls with crabmeat) and the *gallina* (hen) concoctions.

CHURRASCARIA TROPEIRO, Veintimilla 546 and Avenida 6 de Diciembre. Tel. 54-8012 or 545-793.
 Cuisine: BRAZILIAN. **Reservations:** Recommended.
$ Prices: Appetizers $2–$5; main courses $6–$10. Major credit cards accepted.
 Open: Lunch and dinner.
Authentic Brazilian *churrasco* (barbecued beef slow-cooked over an open flame) is tops on the menu at the Churrascaría Tropeiro. It's served *rodizio* style, which means you'll be offered different cuts of beef and sausage until you say *no más*. A salad bar is included. *Feijoada*, the traditional pork-and-bean stew, is served on the weekends in keeping with Brazilian and Portuguese tradition. And, of course, no *rodizio* would be complete without a *caipirinha* (aguardiente and lime juice).

LAS CUEVAS DE LUIS CANDELAS, Alemania 1144. Tel. 23-3867.
 Cuisine: SPANISH. **Reservations:** Recommended.
$ Prices: Appetizers $1–$4; main courses $5–$9. Major credit cards accepted.
 Open: Daily lunch noon–4pm; dinner 6–11pm.
At our favorite restaurant in this area the "must" dish is the locally celebrated chateaubriand (steak marinated in wine sauce), a fine value for $6, including salad and vegetable. One afternoon when we were not particularly hungry, the owner/manager Luís Yepez Baca whipped up for us some scrambled eggs with herbs—marvelously light and tasty. The restaurant is located in a Spanish-colonial home on a residential street.

LAS REDES, Avenida Amazonas 845 at Veintimilla. Tel. 525-691.
 Cuisine: SEAFOOD. **Reservations:** Recommended.
$ Prices: Appetizers $3–$6; main courses $6–$12.
 Open: Lunch and dinner.
For the best in seafood, try Las Redes. The specialty of the house is *mariscal;* similar to paella, it's made with shellfish and rice and serves two to three. Another choice is the lobster casserole for two at $15.

TABERNA BAVARIA, Juan Leon Mera 1238, at the corner of Garcia. Tel. 23-3206.
 Cuisine: GERMAN. **Reservations:** Not accepted.
$ Prices: Appetizers $1–$5; main courses $4–$8.
 Open: Tues-Sun.
This is our favorite place for German food in Quito. The restaurant, opened in 1984,

is set in a large private home with a roaring fireplace. The food is authentic Bavaria, with appetizers such as leberwurst (liver pâté) and entrées such as *Gemischte wurstplatte* with home-fries and sauerkraut (mixed wurst platter) or *Huhnerbrustrollchen* (breast of chicken rolled with ham and spinach). Of course, there's also Wienerschnitzel. The ceilings are beamed, and the menu is in three languages, including English.

MORE CHOICES

ARLEQUIN, Avenida Orellana 155, across from the Hotel Quito. Tel. 239-993.
  Cuisine: INTERNATIONAL. **Reservations:** Recommended.
$ Prices: Appetizers $4; main courses $6–$10. Major credit cards accepted.
  Open: Mon–Fri 1–3pm and 8pm–1am; Sat 8pm–1am.

⭐ Opened in 1991, Arlequin is located in a lovely white-and-beige building, easily recognized by the harlequin figure outside. The menu, reasonably priced for a restaurant of this caliber, features international and regional dishes. There is also a very fine wine list. Appetizers include the *pâté de la casa* (the chef's own special recipe served with bacon and fresh mushrooms), *la gran fuente de arlequin* (fresh shellfish for at least two, served over ice), lobster bisque (in season), and many others. Among the many entrées are various lobster dishes (when available), *entrecôte doble de ajo* (entrecôte in a garlic sauce), *pato con higos a la Nueva Orleans* (deboned duck stuffed with a fig-and-cherry mousse), and regional dishes including *cebiches costeños* (a variety of cebiches prepared at your tableside) and *empanadas de verde o morocho* (typical empanadas made with plantains or white corn meal).

LA CASA DE MI ABUELA, Juan León Mera, near Pinta. Tel. 23-4383.
  Cuisine: INTERNATIONAL. **Reservations:** Recommended.
$ Prices: Appetizers $2–$5; main courses $6–$12. Major credit cards accepted.
  Open: Mon–Sat dinner; Sun lunch and dinner.

⭐ Bring a big appetite to "My Grandmother's House." Located in an old colonial home, this charming restaurant features succulent cuts of meat served in huge portions. Grandmother María reigns over the dining room and oversees the preparation of meals herself. We ordered a 400-gram filet mignon that covered the plate. Choose the Italian dishes if you want to shave a few pennies off your bill, or order a generous salad and soup. The dishes aren't cheap, but the atmosphere is well worth it! In addition to the careful preparation of your meal, Grandma will often provide a complimentary glass of wine or an after-dinner drink. Be sure to ring the bell; the front door is often locked.

LA CHOZA, Avenida 12 de Octubre 1821. Tel. 23-0839.
  Cuisine: ECUADORIAN. **Reservations:** Recommended.
$ Prices: Appetizers $1–$4: main courses $6–$8. Major credit cards accepted.
  Open: Lunch daily noon–3pm; dinner daily 7pm–3am.

⭐ This is a large, striking bilevel restaurant in a new building. The menu is changed daily, and the typical Ecuadorian dishes should satisfy the most fastidious palate. Try the *llapingachos* (cheese-and-potato dish), the *empanada de morocho*, and the *cebiche de camerón* (shrimp appetizer). Start with a potent rice cocktail called *chicha*, and don't miss trying the *rosero*, a delightful fruit drink. The elegant beamed ceiling is made of local bamboo called caoba wood. You enter via a 50-foot-long outdoor walkway, covered by a canopy of branches and straw which is illuminated at night with colored lights.

LA COSTA VASCA, Avenida 18 de Septiembre 553 and Paez. Tel. 56-4940.
  Cuisine: SPANISH. **Reservations:** Recommended.
$ Prices: Appetizers $3–$7; main courses $8–$15; meals for two $25. Major credit cards accepted.
  Open: Mon–Sat noon–3pm and 6–11pm; Sun noon–3pm.

Very popular for business lunches, La Costa Vasca is probably Quito's best Spanish restaurant. It specializes in Basque cooking, considered by many to be the best in Spain. Here we would recommend the *parrillada de mariscos* accompanied by a Spanish wine, from either the Rioja or Cataluna. Expect to spend around $25 for two, including wine and coffee.

RINCON DE FRANCIA, Roca 779, on the corner of 9 de Octubre. Tel. 23-2054.
   Cuisine: FRENCH. **Reservations:** Recommended.
$ **Prices:** Appetizers $5–$10; main courses $8–$15; meals from $15. Major credit cards accepted.
   Open: Mon–Fri lunch and dinner; Sat dinner only.
Perhaps Quito's finest restaurant—and a must—is Rincón de Francia. Chef/owner Gilles Blain is your host. A guitarist serenades you while you enjoy such favorites as coq au vin, chateaubriand, and *tournedos grille.* Expect to spend at least $13 per person. The decor and food are on a par with fine French restaurants worldwide.

LA TERRAZA DEL TARTARO, Veintimilla 106 and Amazonas. Tel. 52-7987.
   Cuisine: INTERNATIONAL. **Reservations:** Recommended.
$ **Prices:** Appetizers $4–$8; main courses $8–$15; dinner for two $28–$32. Major credit cards accepted.
   Open: Dinner only.
This place deserves an award for the restaurant with the best view of Quito; it's located in a penthouse 20 floors above the city. La Terraza offers not only a breathtaking view but also an international menu specializing in steaks. Dinner for two, including wine and dessert, will cost between $28 and $32.

OLD CITY

CAFÉ NIZA, Venezuela 624.
   Cuisine: LIGHT MEALS/SANDWICHES.
   Open: 7am–6pm.
At the busy Café Niza you can have a quick breakfast or light lunch. The Niza offers an assortment of simple sandwiches—hot or cold. A complete breakfast—large orange juice, two eggs, bread, and coffee—is a bargain at $1.25, tax included. Drop by in the late afternoon and linger over a pastry and coffee.

CHIFA CHANG, Chile 927.
   Cuisine: CHINESE/INTERNATIONAL.
$ **Prices:** Meals under $3.
   Open: Daily 7:30–11:30am and 2:30–6:30pm.
For a quick snack or complete meal, try Chifa Chang, two blocks below Plaza de la Independencia. It is a small complex consisting of an ice-cream bar, a pastry shop, and a cafeteria. The cafeteria offers a complete menu ranging from pizza and hamburgers to roasted chicken, *churrascos,* and rice dishes. Half the menu is devoted to Cantonese dishes, such as wonton soup, beef with vegetables, rice and beef, and chop suey.

THE MADRILLON, Chile 1270 and Benalcazar.
   Cuisine: SANDWICHES/SNACKS.
$ **Prices:** Complete meals $1–$4.50.
We recommend this soda fountain, one block from Plaza de la Independencia, for breakfast or a light lunch. A long, narrow eatery, with Formica-covered tables and a small, compact menu, it offers such items as orange juice, toast and butter, and coffee for 80¢; a ham or cheese sandwich for 75¢; and a hot chicken sandwich for 75¢. We

suggest the tasty tortilla (omelet) made of lobster, shrimp, or chicken and served with tomatoes and potatoes.

MANILA RESTAURANT AND CAFETERIA, Chile 1050. Tel. 51-2419.
   Cuisine: CHINESE/ECUADORIAN.
$ **Prices:** Appetizers 50¢–$2; main courses $2–$5.
   Open: Daily 7:30am–12:30pm and 2:30–6:30pm.
The Manila has a large, pleasant dining area both upstairs and downstairs. Their extensive menu (printed in both Spanish and English) features typical Ecuadorian dishes and Chinese selections at low prices. The Manila also serves cocktails, imported wine, and sangría.

QUITO VIEJO, Guayaquil.
   Cuisine: INTERNATIONAL/SANDWICHES.
$ **Prices:** Appetizers $.50–$1.50; main courses $2–$4.
   Open: 7am–11pm.
Just off the Plaza Bolívar, this is a good choice. Practically two restaurants in one, it has an informal cafeteria-style dining room in the front, good for breakfast or lunch, and a more formal one in the back with cloth tablecloths, napkins, and a piano bar. An American breakfast of juice, eggs, ham, toast, and coffee is $1, while a T-bone steak is $3. A cheeseburger and shake will cost a little over $1.75.

LAS CUEVAS DE LUIS CANDELAS, Benalcazar 709, on the corner of Calle Chile. Tel. 21-7710.
   Cuisine: SPANISH. **Reservations:** Recommended.
$ **Prices:** Appetizers $1–$4; main courses $5–$9. Major credit cards accepted.
   Open: Daily lunch noon–4pm; dinner 6–11pm.
This restaurant is designed to resemble a cave that owner/manager, Luís Yepez Baca, once visited in Spain; you'll head downstairs from the street level onto a simulated bridge and into either of the two small dining rooms. Bullfight (*toro*) murals, flamenco music, and a fireplace create an ideal atmosphere. In addition to the chateaubriand, consider the *langostina* (shrimp) *a la plancha* ($6.50) or the tortillas ($2), as well as any of the beef dishes. We recommend especially the mussels in garlic sauce at $2.75.

SPECIALTY DINING

LIGHT FARE IN NEW CITY   Snag a table at one of the sidewalk cafés that line Avenida Amazonas at Robles. You can snack on pizza, hamburgers, beer, or coffee and watch the passing scene. The most popular is **Mario's,** where the house specialty is *cena al maigo*—a hamburger or hot dog with french fries and beverage—for $1.25. The *cena al minuto*—chicken, salad, and coffee—is just $2.75. One block down is **Manolo,** where the sandwich is king. Next door is **El Chacarero,** a nice place for pastry and coffee. The low prices and fast but hearty fare attract a young crowd, mostly university students. At the corner, the **Hotel Almeda Real Cafeteria** also has sidewalk tables.

   At Roca 736 is a delightful *pasteleria* called **Chantilly.** Walk into the *pasteleria,* order coffee at the counter, and choose your favorite pastry or fresh-baked sweet roll. Upstairs is a cafeteria where you can order sandwiches for $1 and up or a full-course meal after 12:30pm. The Chantilly has tasty beef steaks, whitefish (*corvina*), or chicken in wine sauce for $5. Dine at attractive tables covered with crisp white cloths or linger over a drink at the bar. The Chantilly is open for breakfast and lunch Monday to Saturday. **Sandy's** is a delightful self-service cafeteria on the corner of Avenida Amazonas and Naciones Unidas; it's open Sunday to Friday 24 hours. You can choose fresh salads, fruit bowls, hot soups, and a variety of daily specials with vegetables.

The **Plazuela Café del Teatro,** alongside the Teatro Sucre on Marabi, is a great spot for a late-afternoon coffee or tea or an after-theater snack. It also features exhibits by local artists. It is open Monday to Saturday from 2pm to midnight and Sunday from noon to 7pm. **Pims,** at Calama 413, is a pub. It's quite small, but worth the wait for a table. It serves hamburgers, sandwiches, beer, and ice creams.

Pizza Nostra, on Amazonas and Washington, is a small place with inexpensive specials; a whole pizza for one and a glass of wine for $2. There are branches of **Pizza Hut** at Juan Leon Mera 566, on the corner of Carrion; Espejo 847, at the corner of Guayaquil; at the corner of Avenida Amazonas and Naciones Unidas; and in the atrium building at Avenida Gonzalez Suarez 894.

For any meal at rock-bottom prices, we highly recommend **El Americano,** a self-service bar at Avenida 10 de Agosto 674, open daily from 8am to midnight. The floors are bare and the tables have glass tops, but pick up a tray and get a half chicken dinner for 75¢ or pork chops for 50¢. There are noodle dishes (pasta), yogurt, and salads.

A popular chicken chain is **Pollo Gus,** where you can get a whole chicken for $2 (half a chicken is $1). They have self-service, and you sit on wooden benches in an immaculate dining room. You can watch the chickens roasting. Hamburgers are also available. A good Gus is at 10 de Agosto, at the corner of José Riofrio, across from El Americano. There are several Pollo Gus restaurants throughout the city.

The **Café Colón,** in the rear of the Hotel Colón lobby, is open 24 hours and offers sandwiches, soups, pizzas, and full-course meals in almost-elegant surroundings. The chairs are upholstered, and there are attractive murals of old Quito. On the expensive side for Quito, a four-course dinner here will run about $8.

King Chicken, at Avenida 10 de Agosto 2156, offers Kentucky-style fried chicken, plus hot dogs and shakes. Half a chicken with french fries is $3.50; fried fish is $2.50; hot dogs are 40¢; and shakes are 90¢. The complete menu is printed on placemats, and there is a breakfast special of juice, eggs, bread, and coffee for just $1. Adjoining King Chicken is an ice-cream and hot-dog stand.

McDonald's and Kentucky Fried Chicken (**Pollo Kentucky**) have established themselves in Quito. McDonald's is on Amazonas, at the corner of Lus Cordero (a Quarter Pounder is $2). Pollo Kentucky is on the corner of Avenida Amazonas and Naciones Unidas and in the Centro Comercial Inaquito.

---

6. ATTRACTIONS

Quito is one of the world's most scenic cities, and it is only a short trip to several Andean villages, where you can visit fascinating Indian markets.

THE TOP ATTRACTIONS

MUSEO NACIONAL DE ARTE COLONIAL, Cuenca and Mejía. Tel. 212-297.

Ecuador's best art can be found at this museum, which also features examples of Spanish-colonial furniture as part of its permanent exhibition. Enter into a colonial courtyard with fountains and plants. As fascinating as the paintings is the museum building itself, a fine example of colonial architecture.
Admission: 60¢.
Open: Mon–Fri 9am–4pm; Sat–Sun 10am–4pm.

MUSEO DEL BANCO CENTRAL DE ECUADOR, 10 de Agosto, at the corner of Briceno, on the fifth and sixth floors of the Central Bank of Ecuador Building.

⭐ For an outstanding look at pre-Columbian art, definitely stop in at this museum. The exhibition includes rare gold and silver coins, regal crowns, and colonial art and furniture. The fifth floor is replete with archeological discoveries and offers fascinating insights into the region's history. On the sixth floor you will find colonial art.
Admission: 50¢.
Open: Tues–Fri 9am–8pm; Sat–Sun 10am–5pm.

CASA DE LA CULTURA ECUATORIANA, at the corner of 9 de Octubre and Patria. Tel. 565-808, ext. 40–42.
The Casa de la Cultura is Ecuador's largest cultural organization. Permanent exhibits are on display in various salons throughout the facility, including 19th-century art in the Joaquin Pinto Salon, indigenous art in the Pedro Leon Salon, as well as the contemporary and Latin American art salons, the children's art gallery, the Galo Galecio Gallery of Engravings, and the Miguel de Santiago Salon. One of the museum's most popular exhibits is the Pedro Traversari Musical Instruments Salon, repository of an excellent collection of indigenous and Ecuadorian instruments, arranged in chronological order from pre-Columbian times to the present.
Open: Mon–Fri 8am–noon and 2–6pm.

JACINTO JIJON Y CAAMAÑO MUSEUM, Avenida 12 de Octubre 1436, in the Catholic University.
This museum features an excellent collection of Indian clothing, hunting implements, musical instruments, and assorted religious artifacts gathered in Ecuador and Peru by the founder, Jacinto Jijon y Caamaño. In one section paintings and sculptures by 17th- to 19th-century artists of the Quito school are displayed.
Admission: 10¢.
Open: Mon–Fri 8am–noon and 2–6pm.

MUSEO FRANCISCANO (MUSEO DEL CONVENTO DE SAN FRANCIS-CO), in the San Francisco Church building, at the Plaza San Francisco. Tel. 21-1124.
To enter this museum, climb up the flight of steps, heading toward the door on the right of the church facade. Once upstairs, knock on the convent door and a guide will appear to conduct you through the museum, which focuses on religious works from Ecuador's earliest colonial period.
Admission: 30¢.
Open: Mon–Sat 7am–noon and 3–6pm; Sun 9am–noon.

MUSEO MUNICIPAL ALBERTO MENA CAAMAÑO MUNICIPAL MUSE-UM, Espejo and Benalcazar. Tel. 210-863.
This museum is housed in what had been a Jesuit monastery until 1747, when Charles III of Spain banished the Jesuit order. During the Wars of Independence from Spain it served as an army headquarters and became known as "El Cuartel Real de Lima." This museum has a collection of paintings and sculptures from the era of independence.
Admission: 20¢.
Open: Tues–Fri 8:30am–4pm; Sat–Sun 9am–1pm.

MUSEO HISTORICO CASA DE SUCRE, Venezuela 573, at the corner of Sucre. Tel. 512-860.
The era of independence is also represented here, in a beautiful colonial home that once belonged to Mariscal Antonio Jose de Sucre, who liberated Ecuador from Spanish rule in 1882. Directed by the Ministry of National Defense, this museum displays weapons, uniforms, furniture, and documents.
Open: Tues–Fri 9am–3:30pm; Sat 9–11:30am; Sun 10am–1pm.

OBSERVATORIO ASTRONOMICO, in Alameda Park.
If you're fascinated by the heavens, drop by Quito's 19th-century observatory.

Make your appointment during the day for an evening peek at the stars. The winding stairway to the tower seems endless; watch the low bridge at the top.

Admission: Free.

Open: Sat 9am–noon.

GUAYASAMIN MUSEUM AND FOUNDATION, Jose Bosmediano (Bella Vista). Tel. 242-779 or 244-373.

⭐ With the help of his family, Ecuador's foremost artist, Oswaldo Guayasamín, established the Guayasamín Foundation in the mid-1970s in order to preserve Ecuador's cultural heritage. The Foundation (as well as his own work) emphasizes the principles of equality, free determination of the people, respect for human rights, and freedom of religion and thought.

Born in Quito in 1919, Guayasamín studied painting and sculpture in Quito's School of the Arts. But his style and aesthetic sensibility have their roots in the mestizo culture. Most of his paintings depict injustices suffered by the lower classes (Indians, mestizos, and blacks). His best-known works include the *Huacaynan* and *En la edad de ira* (In the Age of Anger), a series of more than 150 paintings that he bequeathed to the Ecuadorian people.

Guayasamín's works are on permanent exhibit in the Foundation building, where he also maintains his workshop. He has also created pre-Columbian–style metal sculptures in bronze and copper, figures in balsa wood and acrylic reminiscent of the bread dolls from Calderón, and jewelry using precious and semiprecious stones and metals inspired by pre-Columbian art and jewelry.

The Foundation also hosts temporary exhibits of other Ecuadorian as well as international artists. Many of the pieces displayed here, including some by Guayasamín, are for sale. The museum next door houses a fine collection of pre-Columbian ceramics and artifacts, including figurines, urns, and tools, as well as religious paintings and sculptures dating back to the colonial period. The complex also contains a restoration workshop for restoring pre-Columbian and colonial art, plus an art library.

Open: Daily 9am–12:30pm and 3–6:30pm. A taxi here from the New City should cost no more than $4.

A WALKING TOUR

Begin at **Plaza de la Independencia,** in the Old City, one of the loveliest squares in South America. The trees, shrubbery, and monuments all contribute to the calm beauty here. In the center of the plaza is a brilliant monument to the heroes of the August 10, 1809, "Cry of Independence" that sparked the beginning of the movement for independence from Spain. The largest structure in the plaza is the **cathedral** (open Monday to Saturday from 6 to 10am, Sunday from 6am to noon and 6 to 7pm), with its green cupolas. General Sucre is buried here, and Caspicara's famous painting *The Descent from the Cross* hangs inside.

On the northwest side of the plaza is the 19th-century **Government Palace,** and behind it Pichincha Mountain rises in the distance. There are two patios within the palace. The far wall of the second one is covered with a mural painted by Oswaldo Guayasamín in 1960. Native handcrafts are sold in a main-floor shop in the palace.

Amble south along Calle Garcia Moreno to Calle Sucre. At this intersection is **La Compañía de Jesus Church,** considered one of the most beautiful in South America. Construction of the church took place from 1605 to 1775. The interior decorations contain nearly 1½ tons of gold, while the exterior of the church is made of volcanic stone. Works from the Quitenean period are located throughout. The church can be visited Monday to Saturday from 6 to 11am and 4 to 7pm, Sunday from 6am to 12:45pm and 4 to 9pm.

Turn right on Sucre, and two blocks later, along narrow winding streets with adobe houses, is the **Iglesia de San Francisco,** the first church erected in South America following the Spanish conquest. It was built between 1536 and 1580 on the site of the Inca palaces of Augui Francisco Tupatauchi, son of Atahualpa. The church is rich in artworks, primarily from the Golden Century in Quito. Be sure to visit the Cantuna

❓ DID YOU KNOW . . . ?

- Originally founded in A.D. 1000, Quito is the oldest capital city in Latin America.
- August 10 is Ecuador's independence day; thus, a street was named in commemoration. The street called 6 de Diciembre celebrates modern Quito's founding in 1534 by Benalcazar.
- The highest mountain on the equator is Ecuador's volcano Cayambe at 19,285 feet.
- Charles Darwin's landmark trip to the Galápagos Islands in 1835 helped him to develop his theory of natural selection.
- Unique to the Galápagos Islands is the marine iguana, the only sea-feeding lizard in the world.
- The American writer Herman Melville visited the Galápagos Islands in 1841. He described them as more of "a group of rather extinct volcanoes than of isles, looking much as the world might after a penal conflagration."
- Central Ecuador's 17,159-foot Mt. Sangay is believed to be the most continuously active volcano in the Andes. The mountain is nearly always hidden by precipitation.

Chapel. Built in the 18th century, it was named for the Indian who, as legend has it, sold his soul to the devil in order to assure the church's completion. The church is open Monday to Thursday from 7am to noon and 3 to 6pm, Friday to Sunday from 7am to noon and 5 to 8pm. The chapel is open mornings only on Monday to Saturday and all day on Sunday.

Now head left on Cuenca to **Avenida 24 de Mayo,** which is the center of Quito's oldest section. Here the streets are steep, cobblestoned, and narrow. Many of the whitewashed homes have red-tile roofs and carriage lamps outside. Nearby, on 24 de Mayo, an Indian market (household goods) is held every Tuesday morning. Make a left and head downhill to **Calle Morales** (popularly known as **Calle de la Ronda**), a sightseeing must. The oldest and most picturesque street in Quito, Morales is a cobblestone, alleylike avenue that winds its way downhill into Avenida Guayaquil. Look for the Indian families gathered in front of the buildings and notice the Spanish-colonial architecture.

To leave this section, turn left on Guayaquil, a bustling shopping street that becomes 10 de Agosto in the New City. Guayaquil shopowners pile their goods on the sidewalks, and you may find yourself walking in the roadway. Along the way you'll pass the **Teatro Sucre** (at Manabi) and, three blocks later, the **National Library.** Just ahead is **Alameda Park,** which marks the beginning of the New City; the contrast between this area and the Old City is startling.

Surrounding the park are modern office buildings, attractive shops, private homes, and wide tree-lined streets. At the entrance to the park is a statue of Símon Bolívar and inside the park is an observatory. There is a well in front of the statue where Indian women fill huge pails.

Three blocks beyond Alameda Park is the huge six-square-block **Ejido Park.** Originally a botanical garden, it contains a great variety of trees, many of which are more than 100 years old. Here you can watch **Pelota de Guante,** a traditional Ecuadorian game similar to jai alai. The park is also home to a small art gallery that features temporary exhibits by national and foreign artists. Open-air art exhibits (with some works for sale) are held on the weekends. Theater groups often perform in the park on Saturday mornings. Its neighbor to the right (east) is the **Casa de la Cultura.**

Continuing on 10 de Agosto for four more blocks, you will come to Jorge Washington. Make a right at Paez (one block) and two blocks left is **Calle Roca,** a wealthy street that might have been designed by a medieval architect. The colors and shapes of the buildings are astonishing. One house appears to be a green mosque, another resembles a stone fortress, and one must be the only pink castle in the Western world. If you tire, take the Colón-Camal *colectivo* on 10 de Agosto back to the center of the Old City.

ORGANIZED TOURS

Organized tours of Quito are readily available through a number of agencies. The most reliable tour operator in Quito, and one of South America's finest, is **Metropoli-**

tan Touring at Avenida Amazonas 239 (tel. 56-0550). There are Metropolitan Touring offices in other Ecuadorian cities. Others worth trying are **Ecuadorian Tours** (the American Express agency here), at Avenida Amazonas 339 (tel. 56-0588); and **Turis Mundial,** at Amazonas 657 (tel. 54-6511). A 3-hour city tour costs about $11 for up to three people, with larger groups paying $4 per person. A group of 10 will pay $5 per person.

    Latin Tours, located next door to the Hostal Cumanda on Yanez Pinzon (tel. 56-8657), is a smaller agency. It offers city tours at prices comparable with those of the agencies above. But the groups will always be smaller, with no more than five or six. They also offer tours to the Indian markets and Cotopaxi.

7. SPORTS & RECREATION

SPORTS

BULLFIGHTING Bullfighting is held at the **Plaza Monumental** in Quito during the beginning of December to celebrate the anniversary of the founding of San Francisco de Quito. Well-known *toreros* from South America and Spain come to Quito to participate. Admission ranges from $5 to a high $50. You can easily get to the arena, which is in the New City on Avenida Juan de Ascaray by *colectivo* for 50¢ or by taxi (up to five passengers) for $5.

FUTBOL The main season for soccer is June to November. However, games are held every Sunday and on holidays throughout the year in various stadiums around the city. The best stadium for *futból* is the **Estadio Atahualpa,** where the admission charge for regular events ranges from a minimum of $3 to a top of $10. Special games will cost more. Check with your hotel clerk for schedules. To reach the stadium, take a taxi (up to five passengers) for $2 or a *colectivo* for 15¢.

STONEBALL A game that resembles volleyball but involves a 20-pound bat and a 2½-pound ball is *pelota de guante* (stoneball). Free matches are held on Saturday and Sunday afternoons at Barrio Vicentina near the American Embassy. Check with your hotel clerk.

RECREATION

Both novice and expert mountain climbers might want to contact the **Nuevos Horizontes Club,** Pasaje Royal and Calle Venezuela, in front of the Iglesia Compañía (tel. 21-5135). The club sponsors day-long and weekend hiking and climbing expeditions for a minimal cost. Keep in mind that the high elevation fatigues most visitors the first day or two—so don't rush into serious climbing until you have become somewhat acclimated.

8. SAVVY SHOPPING

Quito shops are noted for their exquisite handmade rugs with old Indian designs, intricately carved wooden masks and figurines, woolen goods, straw handbags, silver articles, and Panama hats.

    Many stores are located on Avenida Guayaquil around Plaza de la Independencia, but the best are in the New City, on Avenida Colón. Store hours are Monday to Friday from 9am to noon and 3 to 6:30pm and Saturday from 8:30 to noon. Some shops stay open Saturday afternoon.

    The most elegant shops in Quito are located at the rear of the lobby of the Hotel Colón Internacional. Do not expect to find inexpensive items; these shops carry good-value, high-quality (and high-priced) items. The **Bazaar** carries elegant gifts and **Paipaco** has popular art. There are also an antiques shop, **Antiguedades;** a branch of the **LibriMundi** bookshop; **Folklore Olga Fisch;** and an **H. Stern** jewelry shop. The Hotel Oro Verde has similar shops in its arcade.

The Mariscal-Sucre Airport has a good duty-free shop for departing passengers which offers perfume, liquor, handcrafts, and jewelry.

FOLKLORE-OLGA FISCH, Avenida Colón 260. Tel. 541-315.

★ One of our favorites is this store, which is not far from the Hotel Quito. (Other branches are located in the Hotel Colón and Hotel Oro Verde.) Its founder, Olga Fisch, who died at the age of 90 on December 30, 1990, was a loving collector of Ecuador's folk art and a key figure in the preservation of Indian handicrafts. A talented artist, she worked primarily in textiles, designing and weaving beautiful hand-knotted rugs inspired by early Indian motifs from pottery and other artifacts uncovered by archaeologists. In fact, it was she who taught the Indians, who at the time knew only how to draw, design and weave the rugs commonly seen today all over Ecuador.

Five of Olga Fisch's rugs hang on the wall at the United Nations in New York, 14 are in the Metropolitan Opera building at Lincoln Center, and others hang in museums throughout the world. Shortly after her death, a collection of her sketches and rugs was donated to the Banco Central Museum. The collection was exhibited by the Smithsonian in Washington, D.C., and in 15 other cities across the United States. The collection is now on permanent exhibit in a museum established in the apartment above the store where the artist lived. The collection includes sketches of Indian dancers and the creation of rugs.

Ms. Fisch's presence is felt throughout the shop. In addition to the handwoven rugs, for which Folklore is famous, it sells excellent quality old and modern Ecuadorian folk art in wood, leather, straw, copper, silver, and hand-woven materials. The prices range from $1 for an Indian reed flute to $2,000 for exquisitely polychromed 17th-century figures. Embroidered dresses cost $30 and up. There is an excellent selection of hand-woven and embroidered dresses, too. Don't leave without asking to see Mrs. Fisch's Ethnographic Section—El Galpón—where you'll find, under a thatched roof, representative pieces of folk art (most of which are not for sale).

To reach Folklore, take the Colón-Camal *colectivo* from Santo Domingo Square on Calle Flores.

OCEPA, Calle Jorge Washington, on the corner of Amazonas. Tel. 458-428.

This is probably the best handcraft outlet is Ocepa, with three shops around Quito. Weave your way among good-quality ponchos, woodcarvings, ceramics, purses, chess sets, and handmade jewelry—all in a broad range of prices. The other two branches are in New City at Calle Carrion, near Versalles, and downtown at Pasaje Espejo y Venezuela.

LA GUARAGUA, Jorge Washington 614. Tel. 520-347.

At La Guaragua browse amid the antique clocks, carvings, religious hats, and paintings, as well as the more popular native handcrafts. Prices are competitive, and the selection is large.

H. STERN, in the Hotels Colón, Oro Verde, and Quito and at the airport.

Gold and silver jewelry made in Ecuador—with or without gemstones—is a good value at the local H. Stern outlets. Prices vary widely, but the quality is uniform. Many of the most popular pieces are those inspired by the pre-Columbian designs on display at the Banco Central Museum. And for chess lovers, H. Stern carries a unique silver- and gold-plated handcrafted set. Other excellent values are in Colombian emeralds, sold at bargain prices.

HAMILTON C. LTD., Avenida Amazonas 171. Tel. 540-468.

The best in gold and silver, handmade and at low prices, can be found here.

Besides jewelry, tableware, and the like, the Hamilton sells other wares, such as a striking chess set made of Guayacan wood. Prices range from $1 to $100.

NAJAS, under the Government Palace (Palacio de Gobierno), in Plaza de la Independencia.

For inexpensive ($1 and up) masks, trinkets, and wood gifts, stop in at Najas. There are half a dozen similar stores here, but this seems the best.

COOSAS, Juan Leon Mera 834.

This shop specializes in T-shirts featuring colorful scenes from the Galápagos Islands. Coosas also has a fine selection of woven rugs and wallhangings.

GALERIA LATINA, Juan Leon Mera 833. Tel. 540-380.

This shop features two floors of beautiful South American handicrafts and jewelry, with the emphasis on Ecuador, of course.

GALERIA ARTES, 6 de Diciembre, on the corner of Veintimilla.

Situated in a pretty town house, this shop features a different selection of handcrafted items every three weeks. You'll find paintings and handcrafted jewelry in gold and silver, as well as pottery and antiques. Prices start at $10 and climb to $600. A nice touch is the cheese-and-wine room.

LA BODEGA, Juan Leon Mera 614. Tel. 23-2844.

For a wide selection of handcrafted items at the best low prices in Quito, La Bodega comes highly recommended.

GALERIA DE ARTE RUBEN POTOSI, in the Centro Comercial El Espiral, at the corner of Amazonas and Jorge Washington.

If you can't get to San Antonio de Ibarra, in this shop you can see the woodcarvings for which the village is famous. All the pieces are for sale, including some original works by Potosí himself.

INTI RAYMI, Amazonas 171. Tel. 502-482.

Inti Raymi is a great place to shop for something special for the folks at home. You'll find a fine selection of alpaca and woven rugs and bags, ceramic pieces, silver jewelry, and precious and semiprecious stones and jewelry.

LIBRIMUNDI, Juan Leon Mera 851. Tel. 234-791.

ART FORUM, Juan Leon Mera 870. Tel. 544-185.

The finest bookstore in Quito, LibriMundi is no ordinary bookshop. It is housed in a beautiful white building that is part bookshop/part café—the perfect gathering place for artistic and literary types. The café serves coffee, cappuccino, pastries, and sandwiches, both indoors and on the patio. The bookshop offers a fine selection of Ecuadorian literature as well as books in English. It specializes in books on Ecuador, including the Galápagos.

Directly across the street, Art Forum features temporary exhibits by Ecuadorian as well as international artists.

ARTESANAS YANZAR, Amazonas 515, on the corner of Roca.

This is the place if you're looking for alpaca rugs. That's all the store carries—in all different sizes, shapes, and colors.

QUIPUS, Amazonas 634.

Come here for authentic pre-Columbian figures, sweaters, and jewelry.

LA LLAMA, Amazonas 149.

One of our favorite shops is La Llama, where you can get all types of handcrafts in wood, ceramics, or textile. It's a good place to buy your Panama hats at prices from $20 to $60. Look for the llama logo on the sign.

ROPA DE CUERO, Amazonas 175.

Next door to La Llama is a terrific leather shop with items in antelope, suede, and regular leather—handbags, wallets, and travel bags. They export and will ship your purchase on request.

AN INDIAN SHOP

On our last trip to Quito, we were walking down Guayaquil, just beyond Sucre, toward the New City, when we were approached by two young Indians selling ponchos. After much pleading, they convinced us to go with them to their shop, "just to look" ("*para mirar, no más*"). The shop itself, located in a courtyard off Guayaquil, was lined with shelves overflowing with sweaters, tapestries, bags, ponchos—everything imaginable. Needless to say, we did some of the best bargaining of our lives there, and left with a lovely woolen poncho (for less than $10) and several odds and ends.

SHOPPING CENTERS

There are two major shopping centers in Quito. The largest is the **Centro Comercial El Bosque,** located at the intersection of Avenida Brasil and Carrajal. It boasts a wide variety of shops in a modern building. The **Centro Comercial Unicornio** has a good selection of stores, as well as a playing area for children.

9. EVENING ENTERTAINMENT

Quito is not one of South America's swinging night towns, and places go out of business here quickly. The big hotels are your best bets; there you can gamble away your sucres in slot machines and at blackjack tables. There are casinos at the hotels Colón, Quito, Alameda Real, Chalet Suisse, and Oro Verde. Each of these hotels has a cocktail lounge or nightclub. El Techo del Mundo, the Quito Hotel's top-floor restaurant, has a breathtaking view—the prices are also breathtaking, so stick to a drink.

THE PERFORMING ARTS

Concerts, operas, and plays—often performed by international touring companies—can be seen at the **Teatro Nacional Sucre,** Plaza del Teatro, between Guayaquil and Flores. However, tickets are high priced, frequently starting at $5 and sometimes running to $12. Check with your hotel clerk for schedules.

The U.S. community here (including many embassy people) sponsors a theater group called the **Pichincha Playhouse,** which stages plays at various locations. Their production of *South Pacific* was a "smashing" success.

THE ECUADORIAN FOLKLORE BALLET: "JACCHIGUA." Wednesdays at 7:30pm at the Teatro Nacional Sucre, Plaza del Teatro, between Guayaquil and Flores. For tickets and reservations contact Metropolitan Touring (tel. 560-550) or the Office of Tourism (tel. 527-074).

★ "*Jacchigua*" is the traditional cry of the Andean Indian on the final day of the harvest on the *haciendas* of the Andean highlands. As part of the "*Jacchigua*" festival, the Indians would kidnap the hacienda owner and his foreman and bind them with leather reins and carefully woven belts. They would be taken to the main patio of the hacienda, where they would then be decorated with the best of the harvest formed in the shape of a cross and attached to their shoulders. Then the Indian's celebration would begin. The captives would not be released until all of the food and drink had been consumed.

"*Jacchigua*" is an expression of both joy and sacrifice, encompassing an intangible series of concepts, ideas, and concerns of the Andean Indians. Rafael Camino, director of the Ecuadorian Folklore Ballet, has chosen "*Jacchigua*" as the fitting title of the EFB's colorful celebration of Ecuador's indigenous heritage. Sixty exceptional dancers perform a series of dances exploring the different indigenous cultures, legends, and celebrations of Ecuador.

THE CLUB & MUSIC SCENE
LIVE MUSIC

JUAN SEBASTIAN BAR, Avenida Calama 400. Tel. 546-955.
This is one of the nicest clubs in town, drawing a well-dressed, attractive crowd. The music goes on all night.

LA LICORNE, in the Hotel Colón Internacional, Avenida Amazonas.
The Hotel Colón boasts the ingratiating La Licorne (just beyond the casino downstairs), where the prices are right—$2 and up for drinks. There's good pop music, much of it via U.S. disks. Open Monday to Saturday from 9pm to 4am. **Admission:** $4–$8 minimum when there's a show.

PUSSYCAT, Calle Juan Rodríguez.
You can't miss this club. The sign over the door features a pipe-smoking shocking-pink pussycat. It's a marvelously noisy, psychedelic place. Drinks are $2.25, and you can revel until 4am.

RINCON QUITEÑO, Gonzalez Saurez 2500, in the lower level of the Hotel Quito.
This club has live music. You can spend the entire evening and nurse one drink for $2.50.

LA VIEJA TAVERNA, downstairs at Avenida Amazonas, at the corner of Pinto, in the Edificio Varig. Tel. 52-3724.
This advertises itself as a club/piano bar. Actually it's more. While there is a resident pianist, they have occasional shows with special guest performers. Pianist Joe Mont writes his own songs. There are a sunken dance floor and leather couches, and the music is loud. Open from 7:30pm to 2am.

DISCOS & DANCE CLUBS

AMADEUS, Coruña 1398, at the corner of Orellana. Tel. 230-831.
This is one of Quito's most elegant clubs. You could come here for dinner (French cuisine is the specialty) and spend the entire evening. There is a live show nightly, as well as a dance floor with videos and a game room.

BLUES, Amazonas 112. Tel. 451-313.
Blues is not a jazz club, but one of the hottest discos in town. A large dance floor, a great light show, and pulsating music make it hard to sit still here.

CAFE 3.30, Whimper 3.30. Tel. 237-210.
For a more subdued atmosphere, try Café 3.30. Here you can relax and listen or dance to soft music in very elegant surroundings. It is also a first-class international restaurant. Open Tuesday to Saturday.

GASOLINE, at the corner of Juan Leon Rodriguez and Juan León Mera.
Gasoline is another popular disco, especially with the younger set. It's a private club, but small and informal. The music here, mostly rock, is very danceable, although the dance floor is on the small side. You'll recognize it by the gas tank outside.

ICE PALACE, Reina Victoria 1138. Tel. 54-6035.
Head downstairs to the attractive dance floor with clinging couples surrounded by couches set up to afford privacy.

PIRAMIDE, Avenida Amazonas.
Another great club is set in a lovely private house. The club, which is always crowded, opens at 11pm with shows starting at midnight. The music here varies from boleros to Latin rock to salsa to *música folklórica*.

VOCU, Avenida Brasil, at the corner of Itaborda. Tel. 45-3273.

The most popular disco in Quito is a private club that's a 10-minute drive beyond the Channel 4 TV satellite station. Vocú is a large place that becomes active after midnight, when the club members start to arrive. There are couches all about, set on different levels, with a poolroom below and beyond the dance floor. Introduce yourself through the "speak-easy" window.

Admission: About $3.

PEÑAS FOLKLÓRICAS

Quito sports several *peñas* clubs where there is live folkloric music with audience participation. They are loud, fun, and inexpensive. Our favorite is **Peña Pacha Mama,** at Jorge Washington 530, which is open from 9pm to 3am. The blazing fireplace adds to the decor, particularly on a cold evening. Another one we like on Calama (the famous restaurant strip) is **Peña del Pasillo.** Farther out on 6 de Diciembre is **Peña Jatari Tambo,** which opens about 5pm. We can also recommend **La Lira Quiteña,** at Orellana and Amazonas, and **El Chucaro,** on Reina Victoria. These clubs are generally closed on Sunday and Monday.

PUBS

PAPILLON BAR, Diego de Almagro, at the corner of Santa Maria. Tel. 443-882.

This is one of Quito's most popular meeting places. Butterflies dominate the decor. The bar, though large, is always crowded, and, as you'd imagine, noisy. It's undoubtedly a great place to see the locals in action. Open daily from 5pm to 3am.

GALERIA CAFE PLANETA PICASSO, Cordero 932, at the corner of Diego de Almagro. Tel. 567-622.

Planeta Picasso is a unique two-floor nightspot in what was once a private home: a modern-art gallery, café, and bar all in one. Since it opened in November 1991, its popularity has grown quickly. Since much of the work exhibited is by young artists, it attracts a young artsy/bohemian crowd. Owner/manager Paul Jauregui is himself an artist and much of his work is displayed throughout the gallery. The decor is unique. Stars dot the ceilings and candlelit tables create a romantic ambience.

EL POBRE DIABLO, Santa Maria 338, at the corner of Juan Leon Mera. Tel. 231-982.

This new meeting place occupies an entire house where patrons gather to meet and converse with friends throughout many different rooms. Conversation is often intellectual in theme. For those not in the mood for talk, there's also the opportunity to pick up a game of chess. Furnishings, mostly wooden tables and chairs, are old yet functional. Tropical colors dominate, complemented by a thatched ceiling and original photos and paintings.

FOR MEN ONLY

If striptease is your cup of tea, visit **Hot Pants,** at La Niña and Avenida Amazonas. There is a large bar, with attractive "hostesses," as well as a small dance floor. A go-go dancer appears on a small round dance floor and gyrates herself nude. Open from 10pm on.

Another club is **Los Años Locos,** at Amazonas 1324 (tel. 54-2521), where the dancing girls also frequent the large bar area lined with men. The place is open until 3am on weekdays, later on weekends.

MORE ENTERTAINMENT

GAMBLING   If you like to gamble, Quito is for you. You bet as little as 70¢ and play black jack, roulette, or poker in rather elegant surroundings. One night we cashed $10 and played black jack at the Hotel Colón casino for 3½ hours. When we left (at 3am), we redeemed $8 in chips. The rules are similar to those in Las Vegas or Atlantic

City. The casinos at Hotels Quito, Colón, Alameda, and Oro Verde are open from 9pm to 4am.

10. THE GALAPAGOS ISLANDS

You may be as unimpressed at your first glimpse of the Galápagos Archipelago as we were. The islands look as if they're made of swirls of solidified mud, but it's actually lava, since the islands themselves are the tops of gigantic volcanoes. However, that first fleeting impression will be rapidly dispelled, for a visit to the Galápagos National Park is truly a unique experience. Even if you aren't a bird fancier and you think iguanas are repulsive, you'll find yourself fascinated by the animal life on these 13 islands, 600 miles in the Pacific Ocean off the Ecuadorian coast.

Having been formed by eruptions during the past million years (the most recent in 1968), the islands became slowly inhabited by creatures and plants brought by wind and the Humboldt Current. No large land mammals ever reached the islands, so reptiles are the dominant species, as they were all over the earth long ago. Because of the islands' isolation from the mainland of South America, and even from one another (by deep water and treacherous currents), these creatures developed uniquely. They adapted themselves to conditions on the islands and became different from their ancestors on the continent. No two islands have identical flora or fauna, although some of the animals are found on several of the islands. Also, there are creatures here that do not exist anywhere else on earth.

The young Charles Darwin came to these islands in 1835 on his scientifically equipped ship the *Beagle*. What he saw and recorded on his 5-week stay provided the basis for much of the information that Darwin published 30 years later in his momentous *Origin of Species*. In 1835 the fundamentalist view of the creation of the earth, only 6,000 years before, was prevalent. Species of animals and plants were seen as fixed, unchangable, immutable organisms in this young world. In spite of mounting geological evidence to the contrary, the fundamentalist views remained the accepted theory because those scientists who felt that the earth was far older and that creatures could adapt to their environment had no unquestionable evidence to support their claims. Darwin and others aboard the *Beagle* set out to collect evidence of evolution. Pressure was so great that Darwin didn't publish his findings until 30 years after his return to England.

It was a species of finches (now known as Darwin's finches) with 13 varieties that provided Darwin with the initial thrust. These finches were all clearly related to one another and to similar finches on the mainland. However, they all had developed independent characteristics. Some ate hard nuts and had developed stocky, powerful beaks to crack open the shells. Others ate soft fruit, and their beaks were of a different shape and were longer, while a third variety, known as the woodpecker finch, made itself a tool of cactus that it used to pry insects out of cracks in trees. As Darwin studied the finches, he noted the developmental changes. He also became aware of adaptation by the giant tortoises.

On one island, the vegetation eaten by the tortoise grows quite tall and the tortoise shells had evolved to permit these turtles to lift their heads to eat. Identical creatures on another island, where the vegetation hugs the ground, have shells that do not permit these tortoises to lift their heads. Other species studied by Darwin include land iguanas; marine iguanas; and such birds as the cormorant, which swims in search of food but has lost the ability to fly.

All these creatures, as well as others, still exist on the Galápagos Islands, and because there are no predators and few people come here, the creatures have no fear of one another or of people. Birds will land on an iguana's head, while crabs scurry alongside boobies. The extraordinary tameness of the animals is astonishing: They swim with you and approach you on land instead of moving away; even birds allow you to stand beside them.

That a place as peaceful and natural as the Galápagos can still exist in this modern world is a credit to the Ecuadorian government; the United Nations Educational, Scientific, and Cultural Organization (UNESCO); and the Charles Darwin Foundation. In 1959 they established the Galápagos as a national park and protected all native animals, reptiles, and birds. The Charles Darwin Research Station on Santa Cruz Island is staffed by scientists and conservationists. These organizations have set out to preserve those species endangered by outside influences. The tortoises, for example, had been captured for centuries by pirates and whalers and used for food. Several islands' tortoise communities were completely decimated. Also feral animals (domesticated animals allowed to run wild), brought to the islands by people trying to settle there and then abandoned when these people moved on, are a serious threat to the indigenous animals. Goats eat the vegetation, pigs and dogs attack the iguanas, while rats eat the eggs of tortoises and birds. These animals are being eradicated in order to preserve the natural environment.

By the way, *galápagos* is the Spanish word for "tortoises," and these giant animals can live 160 years. The islands have Spanish and English names, which makes for some confusion. Visitors to the islands are limited to 1,000 a month and may come only with prearranged groups. Tours vary from three to eight days, and what you'll see will vary with the tour you've chosen. All groups fly in from Guayaquil and Baltra (Seymour) Island, where a U.S. military base was established during World War II. You board your cruise ship here.

THE ISLANDS Here's a rundown on some of the islands. You should definitely do some preparatory reading before coming here.

James (Santiago) Island has a fur seal colony living in its black-lava rock formations. Sharing this home are sea lions, crabs, pelicans, and marine iguanas. Espumuilla Beach is great for swimming alongside the seals and observing diving birds and flamingoes. **Tower (Genovesa) Island** is a bird haven. The frigate bird with its bright-red throat, red-footed and masked boobies, doves, and gulls populate this island.

Plaza Island is tiny island heavily overgrown with thick brush and cactus. As you come ashore, you'll be welcomed by sea lions and land iguanas. On the cliffs you'll see blue-footed boobies, gulls, and many other sea birds. Snorkeling is good here. On **Hood (Española) Island** you'll see blue-footed boobies and lava lizards. During mating, the male lizards whistle while the females honk. Watch the albatross as he takes off from the rocks as if he were a jet plane.

Charles (Floreana) Island is one of the few permanently inhabited ones (5,000 nonscientists live on the Galápagos). Check the post office barrel, an unofficial post office opened by whalers in the 18th century, where mail was traditionally dropped to be picked up by a whaler going in a different direction. More than 50 volcanic cones dot the island. Graceful pink flamingoes inhabit one of the island's lagoons.

Indefatigable (Santa Cruz) is the location of the Research Center. You can visit it and see firsthand the work being done here. The island is rich in wildlife, with the largest number of finches, gulls, and mockingbirds living in its cactus forest. Among the reptiles that exist here are the giant land tortoises (galápagos), sea turtles, land iguanas, marine iguanas (the only seagoing lizard in the world), lava lizards, and the nonpoisonous Galápagos snake. Birds can be divided into two categories—sea birds and land birds. The Galápagos albatross, the Galápagos penguin, and the flightless cormorant are found nowhere else on earth. There are three species of boobies (red-footed, blue-footed, and masked), 13 species of finches, frigate birds, gulls, hawks, and mockingbirds. Mammals that are indigenous include sea lions and fur seals. All other animals were brought here later.

GETTING THERE While a visit here will far exceed your budget, it is certainly worth saving for, and we urge you to consider it. It's an unequaled experience, and you should definitely take advantage of your closeness to it. The easiest and most convenient way to tour the Galápagos is to book passage on one of the many cruise ships run by most of the larger tour operators. You must make your arrangements well in advance. The cost, of course, will depend on the length of the tour you select and the cruise ship you are on. We suggest that you contact various operators; ask for literature and then choose the tour that best suits your plans.

Metropolitan Touring, the first operator to offer tours to the islands, has a fleet of cruise ships and a number of itineraries. You can also get together a group of approximately 20 and charter a yacht (either a motor yacht or a schooner) to the Galápagos. You can contact **Metropolitan Touring** at C.P.O. Box 310 Quito, Ecuador, or call their U.S. representative, **Adventure Associates** (tel. toll-free 800/527-2500) for information.

Additional tour operators to the Galápagos include **Galápagos Inc.**, in Miami, which represents the Galápagos Explorer (tel. toll free 800/327-9854); **Nuevo Mundo Expeditions**, P.O. Box 402-A, Quito, Ecuador (tel. 55-2617; or 55-2816 at 2468 Avenida Amazonas); **Turis Mundial** (tel. 54-6511), in the Turis Mundial Building, 657 Avenida Amazonas; and **Ladatco,** a Miami-based tour operator that covers all of Latin America (tel. toll free 800/327-6162).

Although somewhat more complicated, it is also possible to arrange your own trip to the Galápagos. You can fly to Isla Baltra, just off Isla Santa Cruz, on Monday to Saturday mornings on **Tame** airlines. Be sure to book your flights in the United States, as costs may be lower and flights fill up quickly. Round-trip airfare is $400 from Quito and slightly less from Guayaquil. Confirm your flight when you first arrive in Ecuador. Remember that there is a $50 visitor's fee that you'll have to pay upon your arrival in Baltra.

From Baltra you must travel to Puerto Ayora, the main tourist center in the Galápagos. In the ticket lounge at the airport, you have to purchase a bus/ferry/bus ticket to Puerto Ayora, Isla Santa Cruz. The buses, however, are usually quite crowded. Before leaving Quito or Guayaquil, inquire at travel agencies about island tours and cruises. In Puerto Ayora, you can book cruises at the **Ingala** (National Galápagos Institute) office, but it's better to book in advance, as tours fill up quickly. There is also a government-run tourist office **(CETUR)**, but the schedule isn't reliable.

There are several good hotels to choose from on Puerto Ayora. Again, we advise you to book in advance. A few to choose from are the **Hostal El Delfin** the **Hostal Galápagos,** and the **Hostal Las Ninfas.** A couple of good restaurant choices are the **Garrapata Bar/Restaurant,** the **Casa Blanca** pizzeria, and the **Las Ninfas** restaurant, near the docks.

Background Reading Before you go, you should read *Darwin and the Beagle,* by Alan Moorehead, and *Galápagos: A Natural History Guide.* Both are available from the Complete Traveller Bookstore, 199 Madison Ave., New York, NY 10016. Mention this guidebook and receive a 10% discount.

11. SUGGESTED ITINERARIES

THE EQUATOR

⭐ The most popular excursion in Ecuador is the one that takes visitors 15 miles north of Quito to the monument that officially marks the imaginary line that girdles the globe. It was here in 1736 that members of a French Geodesic Mission led by Charles de la Condamine fixed the exact location of the equator to prove the Newtonian Theory that the earth flattened at the two poles and was widest at the equator. Their calculations coincided with those of the Indians, who centuries earlier had identified the trajectory of the sun's perpendicular rays, calling the equator **Inti Ñan** (the sun's pathway). During their eight-year stay, the members of the Geodesic Mission referred to what was then Quito as the "Land of the Equator," giving origin to the Republic of Ecuador referred to in the nation's first constitution in 1830.

The altitude at the equator is 7,700 feet, so temperatures are quite moderate. Travelers never tire of being photographed with one foot in the Northern Hemisphere and the other in the Southern Hemisphere. And if you are here on March 21 or September 21, you'll find that you cast no shadow, as the sun is directly overhead. A new tourist complex was inaugurated in 1992. In addition to the monument inaugurated 10 years earlier to replace the historical pyramid dedicated in 1936, the Equator Complex is home to a planetarium; an astronomical observatory; the Ethnographic Museum inside the monument; and the "Middle of the World" city, a true-to-life reproduction of a colonial settlement. Along the esplanade leading to the monument are busts of the members of the French Geodesic Mission. There are two restaurants in the complex: **La Posada** and **Vicentes.** Both specialize in typical Ecuadorian cooking and accept credit cards.

GETTING THERE Your best bet is via bus (a 30-minute, 20¢-trip each way). No. 22 buses marked MITAD DEL MUNDO ("Middle of the World") leave every half hour from the Panecillo (the hill that has a beautiful view of Quito). If you're in the Old City you can take the bus on Baha de Caraquez and 24 de Mayo; if you're in the modern part of Quito, buses leave every half hour from Avenida América.

The bus trip is worthwhile in itself—a chance to see the countryside and the surrounding villages (Pomasqui and San Antonio, two sleepy towns through which the bus passes, seem to have stopped in time).

Another way to reach the monument—where the plaque reads "0° 0' 0'''"—is by taxi, $15 for up to four passengers. Tour services charge $5 to $10 per person, depending on the number in the group and the type of transport used (bus or limousine).

INDIAN MARKETS

⭐ While you can glimpse Ecuadorian Indian life in Quito's old quarter, you must go to the countryside for a fuller view. Despite the fact that they are descended from the Incas, the Indians of Ecuador have developed entirely different customs, dress, and modes of living from the Indians of Peru and Bolivia. Your wisest plan is to combine a trip to the countryside with a visit to an Indian market; these are generally held Monday to Saturday. However, a trip to these delightful villages is worthwhile even on Sunday. There are markets in villages to both the north and south of Quito.

We have selected two routes, north and south, which you can travel individually with a rental car or with one of the local tour operators in Quito. Both are via the PanAmerican Highway. Also known as the Avenue of the Volcanoes, the PanAmerican Highway was the Inca's Royal Road connecting Quito to her sister city, Cuzco, in Peru.

IMBABURRA PROVINCE

The northern route travels through the province of Pichincha to Ibarra, capital of the province of Imbaburra. The highlight of this trip is the colorful market, held on Saturday, in Otavalo. If possible, plan to arrive in Otavalo Friday evening in order to be in Otavalo when the market begins at sunup on Saturday.

Following the highway north out of Quito, you'll cross the equator line at **Cayambe.** There is a small monument at the crossing (you can straddle the line here). In the distance, to the east, are the snow-covered Mt. Cayambe. Continuing onward, you next step should be the village of **Calderón,** 6.25 miles outside Quito. Residents produce the colorful bread dolls you see sold all over Quito. They are made of dough that is dyed and shaped in the form of animals and other figures. Traditionally, they are used as grave decorations.

Next en route is the village of **Peguche,** where the Otavalo Indians do their weaving. You can visit them in their workshops and watch as they weave the magnificent woolen shawls, ponchoes, and fabrics sold at the Saturday fair. If you can't make it to the fair, you can purchase directly from the workshop. Next is the Spanish-founded town of Otavalo, where there is a small market on Wednesday. We recommend that you be here for the Saturday fair that starts around 7:30am and lasts until 4pm.

OTAVALO   The village of Otavalo is 59 miles north of Quito. For centuries Indians from the nearby villages of Peguche, Agato, and Iluman have paraded into Otavalo at sunrise on Saturday morning to sell their handwoven articles. Their original and very colorful designs are known throughout the world. Traditionally this was perhaps the quietest Indian market in Ecuador. Bargaining (a must) was done in soft tones with no shouting, as in other markets. However, just as everything changes with time, this is no longer the case.

There are actually two markets in the village, one dealing in wool goods and the other in pottery, baskets, and handmade jewelry. The Indians are garbed quite colorfully, the women in bright skirts and shawls, and the men in equally bright colors and with braided hair. You should note that only members of the tribe wear traditional costumes. For a man this includes a felt hat over hair in a long braid, a reversible dark-blue or gray poncho, a pair of calf-length white pants, and sandals. A woman is attired in a blue-and-white cotton headcloth, an embroidered white blouse with a shawl, and a long navy-blue skirt. After the market closes there are cockfighting matches, and in June there is bullfighting.

If you plan to stay overnight in Otavalo, try the **AliShungu Hotel Restaurant** on the corner of Calles Quito and Quiroga (tel. 920-750); call ahead for reservations. All rooms include private bath. Breakfast, lunch, and dinner are served in the restaurant.

Nine miles beyond Otavalo is the artisan community of **Cotachi,** where residents work in leather, producing a wide variety of well-crafted leather goods at great prices.

You're final destination is **Ibarra,** a colonial city and capital of the province of Imbaburra. Also called the "White City," it is best known for its *helados de paila* (homemade ice cream made from fruit juice), *arropa de mora* (blackberry syrup), *nogadas* (walnut nougat), and *canelazo* (a typical drink made with cane liquor and cinnamon). There are many small artisan shops in the city. Just outside Ibarra is San Antonio de Ibarra, a small village whose residents are skilled woodcarvers.

If you'd like to stay overnight in Ibarra and spend a day exploring the surrounding countryside, a good choice would be the **Hosteria Rancho de Carolina,** just 2.5 miles outside the city on the PanAmerican Highway. Just as the name suggests, you'll enjoy the peace and quiet of the country, with plenty of open space and lovely gardens to wander through. Rooms, all with private bath, are spacious and comfortably furnished. For reservations call 955-215.

CHOTA VALLEY   Twenty-five miles outside Ibarra is the Chota Valley, inhabited by blacks whose ancestors were brought to Ecuador more than 400 years ago to work as slaves on haciendas. They still maintain the customs and traditions of their ancestors, including the round African huts they live in and their African folklore and dances.

LAKES OF IMBABURRA   Imbaburra is known as the province of the lakes. You'll pass the following during your trip:

Laguna San Pablo   Located just beyond the border of Pichincha and Imbaburra, San Pablo is the largest in the region. It lies at the foot of the mythical peak "Taita Imbaburra." Early in the morning you can see the Indians fishing here in reed canoes.

Cuicocha Lagoon   Centuries ago this lake formed the crater of an ancient volcano of the same name. Today it is part of the Cotachi-Cayapas ecological reserve. While it is not possible to visit the two islets in its center and explore the flora and fauna there, you can sail around the lagoon in launches provided by the tourist service. The Cuicocha Lagoon is located just outside Cotachi.

Lago Yahuarcocha   This lake is situated 11 miles outside Ibarra, and its name is a Quechua word meaning "Blood Lake." As the legend goes, during a fierce battle between the ancient Caranquis Indians, who once inhabited the region, and the Inca invaders, the waters turned red with the blood of the slain. Today the lake is best known for the racetrack surrounding it and the international events that take place there.

THE AVENUE OF THE VOLCANOES

The German scholar Alexander Von Humboldt appropriately named the PanAmerican Highway south of Quito the "Avenida de los Volcanos" because the Andean basins it travels are surrounded by the volcanoes and snow-capped mountains of the eastern and western cordilleras. Along the way, you'll drive through fields of lava boulders and past houses fashioned out of the light-gray lava rock.

Your first stop should be at the base of **Cotopaxi** in **Cotopaxi National Park.** The parklands were recently set aside as an ecological sanctuary to protect the fast-disappearing llama and other animals, such as bears, wolves, puma, and deer. At 19,700 feet, Cotopaxi is the world's highest active volcano. While here, be sure to keep your eyes open: Condors are occasionally spotted flying through the park.

An interesting side trip from Cotopaxi, although not as authentic as it once was, is the village of **Santo Domingo de los Colorados.** An unusual Indian community, the primitive Colorados reside in the jungle 7,000 feet below Quito. Every Sunday (the day you should visit), the tribespeople come to the town of Santo Domingo to buy and sell. The Indian men and women, who wear very little clothing, paint their torsos and hair with a red paste made from the achiote seed to ward off evil spirits. The village, in the midst of banana, coffee, and cacao plantations, is quite warm, so you should dress accordingly.

Note: On our last visit, very few Indians came to town. Those who did came to earn some money for being photographed.

Your next stop is the village of **Saquisili,** 45 miles south of Quito and home of the noisiest, wildest market in the vicinity. Every Thursday morning the Indians pour into the village to hawk their pottery, tablecloths, and wood etchings. Bargaining is intense and loud, so don't be bashful. Remember, it starts early and is usually over by noon.

The market is actually many markets in one. The main market covers two squares. You'll find such modern items as TV sets, radio, stereos, furniture, and costume jewelry. There is a live animal market where you'll see sheep, llamas, and cows roaming freely, as well as a fruit and artesanías market where you can bargain for the more traditional handwoven rugs, blankets, wallhangings, paintings, and Panama hats. These are actually made in Ecuador in the coastal cities of Montecristi and Jipijapa and most recently in Cuenca.

(Despite their loud bargaining, the Indians here are on the shy side and don't like to be photographed. If you wish to photograph them, do so indirectly. Pretend to be taking a picture of a large scene to avoid offending them.)

Latacunga, capital of the province of Cotopaxi, is next en route. It was originally a pre-Inca city that later became a colonial center. If you stop here be sure to visit the lovely cathedral that's full of excellent examples of colonial art, plus the Inca observatory and cemetery. A visit to the Tilipulo Monastery just a few miles outside Latacunga will give you some insight into monastic life during the colonial period.

Because one of the chief industries of Cotopaxi is agriculture, Latacunga is home to a farmer's market on Tuesday and Saturday. Produce stands throughout the city's plazas offer innumerous photo opportunities. The colorful displays of fruits and vegetables are only matched by the colorful dress of the Indians selling them.

If you visit the Tuesday market, we urge you to stay overnight and go to **Pujili** for the market there on Wednesday. The Indians trade mostly among themselves. However, you may be able to get some good buys on ceramics. Spend the night at either the **Hosteria Rumpibamba de las Rosas** in Salcedo (tel. 726-128) or the **Hosteria La Cienaga** (tel. 801-622). Both offer hacienda-type accommodations with activities such as horseback riding.

Continuing south on the PanAmerican Highway, you'll come to **Ambato,** 75 miles south of Quito, capital of the province of **Tungurahua** and host of the largest market in Ecuador (Monday only). Called the "Garden City of Ecuador" because of its fine orchards and magnificent summer homes, Ambato is famous for the flowers and fruit sold at its market. The city is also a center of leather production. You can buy handsome wool goods, ponchos, and wooden masks here as well. Because of its high elevation, many wealthy Ecuadorians have second homes in the area. While in Ambato be sure to visit **La Lira,** the 19th-century home of Juan Leon Mera, author of the Ecuadorian national anthem and a native son of Ambato.

Should you decide to stay overnight in Ambato, the **Hotel Ambato,** on the corner of Guayaquil and Rocafuerte (tel. 827-598), is a good choice. Rooms, all with private bath, are comfortably furnished. By the way, if you're shopping for leather goods and didn't make it to the market or find anything you liked, **Tsanara,** on the corner of Sucre (11-41) and Espejo, is the best shop in town. A branch of Tsanara is in the Hotel Ambato.

Just 25 miles outside Ambato is **Baños,** a favorite tourist destination best known for the healing powers of its thermal baths and the beauty of its landscape. Since it is a mere 38 miles from the rain forest, the vegetation and climate here are almost tropical. Orchids and waterfalls—including the **"Manta de la Novia"** ("The Bride's Veil") and *"La Virgen"*—dominate the landscape. On the way to Baños you'll pass **Salasaca,** a textile-manufacturing village best known for its original wallhangings.

From Ambato you travel on to **Riobamba,** capital of the state of Chimborazo, strategically located equidistant from Quito and Guayaquil. A worthwhile stop along the way is at the village of Guano, best known for the quality and originality of the rugs made there. Most are inspired by pre-Columbian designs.

The town of Riobamba, 4 hours from Quito, has a wonderful market on Saturday mornings. It gets underway very early (by 9am it's going strong), so it's best to go on Friday. Wake up early and head for the market, which is spread throughout the town's 11 plazas. Each plaza is reserved for a particular type of merchandise—interesting carvings in one, leather goods in another, and ponchos and sweaters in still another. Be sure to stroll through the streets of the Spanish-colonial city. Try to visit the **Museum of Colonial Art** located in the Cloister of the Sisters of the Immaculate Conception.

The **Centro Turístico y Hostería el Troje** (tel. 960-826; fax 964-572) is a good place to spend the night or even the weekend. All rooms have a private bath. In addition to the restaurant, bar, and Mirador Lounge with its great view of the surrounding mountains, recreational facilities include an indoor pool, tennis courts, a basketball court, bumper cars, a children's playground, and landscaped gardens.

INDIAN MARKETS BY BUS   It is possible to travel to the Indian villages by bus from Quito:

Ambato   Buses for Ambato leave from the Terminal Terrestre. The one-way fare is $2.50 for the 3-hour trip.

Otavalo and Ibarra   Buses for Otavalo leave frequently from Calle Manuel Larrea 1211. The one-way fare is $2.50 for the 2½-hour journey. Buy tickets in advance.

Santo Domingo de los Colorados   Transportes Occidentales and Transportes Esmeraldes operate regular bus trips from Avenida 24 de Mayo ($7 round trip). The journey takes 4 hours.

Saquisili   Buses leave from the Terrestre Terminal, charging $1.50 for the 90-minute trip. You can either travel to Saquisili directly or, for more frequent service, take the bus to Latacunga and then take a local bus to Saquisili.

CUENCA

Approximately 260 miles south of Quito via the PanAmerican Highway south, Cuenca is a fitting finale to your tour of the Indian villages and towns of Ecuador. Most Ecuadorians consider it their most beautiful city.

Built on an ancient Inca site, Cuenca is Ecuador's third-largest city. Yet its picturesque cobblestoned streets, red-roofed adobe houses, lovely ironworked balconies, and plazas still retain their Spanish-colonial charm. Dotting the skyline are churches, rather than the high-rise buildings normally found in large cities. The willow-lined Tomebamba River flows through the base of the city, adding to her tranquil ambience and colonial charm. The city is known for its colonial homes with overhanging balconies that hug the bluffs of the river. Cuenca is home to numerous churches, including the "new" **cathedral** in the Parque Calderón. Construction began in 1880 yet was never finished due to an architectural miscalculation. The cathedral bells remain on the ground outside the church. Just a few blocks away is the Convent of El Carmen, which has been preserved as it was in the late 1600s. Although it's not possible to visit the convent, the Bank of Ecuador has restored the **Monastery of the Conception** next door and opened it to the public. On display is a remarkable collection of religious artifacts from the colonial period, as well as everyday objects.

Also worth visiting are the **Municipal Museum**, best known for its displays of artifacts from the first inhabitants of the region (the Canari and Chordeleg cultures) and the **ICDAP Interamerican Museum**, which specializes in South American handicrafts. Handicrafts are one of the best reasons to visit Cuenca; and the best place to shop for them is at the **Thursday fair**. Thousands of Indians fill the city, concentrating themselves around the 9 de Octubre and 10 de Agosto plazas to sell their wares, including embroidered blouses, natural sheep-wool sweaters, gold and silver filigree jewelry, and weavings with tie-dyed patterns called *jkat*. You shouldn't leave Cuenca without at least one Panama hat. Contrary to popular belief, Panama hats were originally made in Montecristi (Ecuador not Panama) and sent to the workers constructing the Panama Canal. Cuenca is a leading producer of Panama hats.

If you have the time, the **Ingaparica Fortress** outside Cuenca makes an exciting day trip. The only remaining monument of the Inca Empire, it is believed to have been a religious and administrative center as well as a fortress. It was built by the Incas on top of a Canari settlement. There is an archaeological museum at the site. The Spanish pueblos on the outskirts of Cuenca are also worth visiting.

Should you decide to spend a few days in Cuenca, there are several good budget hotels in town. The **Hotel Paris Internacional** (tel. 827-181) is a slightly higher than budget selection ($45 for a double). The **Hotel La Laguna**, under the same management as the Hotel Oro Verde in Quito (tel. 831-200), is a beautiful five-star selection for a big splurge.

GETTING THERE As we mentioned above, if you're driving, you can reach Cuenca by continuing south on the PanAmerican Highway, which will take you the better part of a day to drive from Quito to Cuenca. You can also check buses to Cuenca at the Cumanda Terminal.

GUAYAQUIL

A bustling prosperous city with a pace much faster than Quito's, Guayaquil ("Pearl of the Pacific") is Ecuador's largest city and its most important seaport. The River Guayas is almost always congested with cargo boats bringing coffee, cocoa, pineapples, and, above all, bananas from the inland villages and plantations. Of interest here are the beautiful colonial homes on **Numa Pompilio Llona**, a narrow, twisting, cobblestone street in Las Peñas, the city's historic district and site of its founding at the foot of Cerro Santa Ana next to the river. In Las Peñas you should also visit the lovely **Colombus Plaza**, the **cathedral**, and the **Santo Domingo, La Merced**, and **San Francisco** churches.

The city is home to numerous monuments. The best known is the **Rotunda**, dedicated to South America's great liberators Simón Bolívar and José de San Martín. Also worth visiting is **El Mirador**, the city's lookout tower. Both are located on the riverside boulevard, Malecón Simón Bolívar.

Guayaquil also has its share of lovely museums, most emphasizing pre-colonial and colonial art. The **Municipal Museum**, on the corner of Sucre and Chile, has an unusual collection of shrunken heads, *Tzantzas*, made by tribes in Eastern Ecuador, as well as an exposition of presidential portraits and objects of value that belonged to some of the nation's late presidents. The **Anthropology Museum of the Banco**

Central, on the corner of Jose de Antepara and 9 de Octubre (tel. 329-785), features temporary and permanent art and anthropology exhibits.

Since the city is at sea level, not far from the equator, it is warm, so it's best to visit in the dry season (May to November), when the warm, rainless days give way to cool evenings. Locals are justifiably proud of the racetrack (**Hipódromo Santa Cecilia**), as well as the *futból* stadium, golf, tennis, and yachting clubs. Two hours farther is Ecuador's most popular resort—**Salinas**—where you can swim all year round and visit the posh gambling casino. This area is also famous for deep-sea fishing.

If you decide to stay in Guayaquil for a few days, you'll find a number of budget hotels from which to choose. The deluxe five-star **Hotel Oro Verde** is at Garcia Moreno and 9 de Octubre (tel. 327-999; fax 329-350). The **Hotel Rizzo,** at Calle Ballen 319 and Chile (tel. 325-210), is a more reasonabley priced, albeit less luxurious, selection.

GETTING THERE The most comfortable and inexpensive mode of travel is via the privately owned buses operated by **Trasandina** from its terminal at Terrestre. Buses leave daily on the 8-hour (300-mile) trip, and the fare is only $8 each way. Since tickets are in demand due to the relative comfort of the buses, you must purchase your seats at least one day, preferably two days, in advance. Another bus company with a Quito-to-Guayaquil trip is **Flota Imbaburra,** which also operates from the Terrestre Terminal. Again, buy your tickets ahead of time. Don't forget to bring a sandwich or two.

As a last resort, use the **public bus** that departs from the Panamericana Terminal. Tickets are $5 each way for a 10-hour, far-less-comfortable ride in older buses.

If you are on a tight schedule, your best option, budget permitting, is to fly to Guayaquil. You might have stopover privileges on your plane ticket. The flight to modern Bolívar Airport takes about half an hour.

CUENCA & GUAYAQUIL BY RAIL

Metropolitan Tours offers an exciting (and more comfortable) alternative for travel to Cuenca and Guayaquil, rail travel aboard Metropolitan's **Expreso** fleet of especially equipped rail cars.

The initial plans and attempts to construct a railway connecting Guayaquil and Quito date back to 1860. It was not until 1874 that the first locomotive reached the town of Milagro not far from Guayaquil. In 1895, after many difficult years, American engineers Archer Harman and Edward Morely, representatives of the company interested in building "the most difficult railroad in the world," were contacted. The Guayaquil and Quito Railway Company began construction in 1899.

Construction went smoothly until the tracks came to a huge obstacle outside the town of Alausi: a nearly perpendicular wall of rock called **"La Nariz del Diablo"** ("the devil's nose"). Numerous lives were lost in the construction of what is considered a masterpiece of railway engineering: a ziz-zag carved out of the rock allowing the train to reach the town of Alausi by advancing and backing up. The tracks reached Alausi by September 1902 and Riobamba in July 1905. On June 25, 1908, the train made a triumphal entrance into Quito.

In September 1915 construction of a line from Simbambe to Cuenca began. The railroad to Cuenca was officially inaugurated on March 6, 1965.

Today much of the railway is inoperable, with the exception of two tourist lines operated by Metropolitan Tours: Alausi-Guayaquil and Alausi-Cuenca. Regardless of your final destination, for the first leg of the journey you'll travel by bus to Riobamba, combining the trip to Cuenca or Guayaquil with a tour of the Indian villages. You'll travel south along the PanAmerican Highway with time to admire Cotopaxi and stops in Latacunga, Ambato, and Guano.

After spending the night in Riobamba, you'll continue by bus to Alausi, where you'll board the Expreso Metropolitan train to either Cuenca or Guayaquil. Both journeys begin with the breathtaking descent (7,655 feet) from Alausi to Devils Nose to continue almost perpendicularly down the 1,000-foot cliff to Sibambe. Here the train will turn toward your final destination, Cuenca or Guayaquil.

The Autoferro is an exciting way to travel to Cuenca or Guayaquil. The cost of the trip (based on double occupancy) is approximately $260 to Guayaquil and $400 to Cuenca; overnight accommodations and meals are included.

Note: As of this writing the railroad to Cuenca was operable only as far as the town of Chunchi, approximately 20 miles from Alausi. Check the status of repairs prior to booking a railtrip to Cuenca.

EXPLORING THE AMAZON

For those with time and money to spare, a visit to that most mysterious of places—the Amazon jungle—could be the highlight of your stay in Ecuador. Again, planning is necessary since the tour, offered by Metropolitan Touring, is a leisurely five-day cruise down the Napo River, headwaters of the Amazon, aboard a luxurious 180-ton floating hotel called a flotel. During the day you'll venture out via motor canoe to explore the world's deepest rain forest and visit the villages of the Yumbo Indians, the tribe that has lived here for centuries. Metropolitan provides well-trained guides who'll help you to discover and understand the flora and fauna of the region and translate so that you can barter with the Indians. The current rate (not including round-trip airfare from Quito)—with accommodations and meals aboard the flotel, lectures, and tour guides—for a two-berth cabin is about $395 per person; a four-berth cabin is $300. A double-berth cabin with single occupancy is $595. For information and reservations, contact **Metropolitan's Unseen Amazon,** P.O. Box 310 Quito (tel. 52-4400). In the United States, contact **Adventure Associates,** 13150 Coit Rd., Suite 110, Dallas, TX 75240 (tel. toll free 800/527-2500). A $50 deposit is required.

CHAPTER 10

BOGOTA, COLOMBIA

- **WHAT'S SPECIAL ABOUT BOGOTA**
1. **INTRODUCING BOGOTA & COLOMBIA**
- **WHAT THINGS COST IN BOGOTA**
2. **ORIENTATION**
3. **GETTING AROUND**
- **FAST FACTS: BOGOTA**
4. **WHERE TO STAY**
5. **WHERE TO DINE**
6. **ATTRACTIONS**
- **DID YOU KNOW . . . ?**
7. **SPORTS & RECREATION**
8. **SAVVY SHOPPING**
9. **EVENING ENTERTAINMENT**
10. **EASY EXCURSIONS**

From the instant you land at the sleek El Dorado International Airport, you'll feel a privileged guest in this warm, receptive city that has much to offer beyond Juan Valdez and his superb Colombian coffee.

While the people here are more imbued with the conservative traditions of old Spain than those in any other South American capital, nevertheless Bogotá is totally modern in its approach to tourism. The better hotels are on a par with good hotels in Lima and Santiago, and we have been able to locate fine budget choices in many parts of the city.

In common with much of South America, Bogotá is a city in transition. The greatest building boom in Bogotá's history is permanently altering this old, proud city that is slowly adjusting to a wave of high-rise luxury apartment houses and office structures. The skyline is unrecognizable to visitors absent for 5 or more years. The Pope's visit to Bogotá in 1968 accelerated the boom, with miles of new streets paved and many new hotels built in his honor.

While the largely *mestizo* population (Spanish and Indian mixture) is deeply traditional in religion, dress, and customs, there are indications that attitudes are changing among the young. Nowhere is this more evident than in the Zona Rosa's nightclubs, which are frequented by trendy, up-and-coming Bogotanos. Nevertheless, it is uncommon in Bogotá for women to venture out alone in the evenings or for men to be seen without ties and jackets. The handsome wool poncho, called a *ruana,* is a colorful costume that is worn by both men and women. The costume, apparently of Indian origin, has survived the Spanish invasion and conquest of the 1530s and is today a rather charming anachronism.

You'll find most Bogotanos reserved, not only toward strangers but even toward one another. The people here tend to be somewhat formal, but be patient; courtesy and good manners go a long way toward relaxed relationships. Most locals also tend to be home oriented, and if they have money, private club oriented. Emeralds and coffee are, of course, constant topics of conversation: Colombia mines 90% of the world's emeralds, and many experts insist that its coffee is the world's best.

WHAT'S SPECIAL ABOUT BOGOTÁ

Beaches
- ☐ Cartegena and Santa Marta, Caribbean beaches just a short flight from Bogotá.

Museums
- ☐ The Museo de Oro (Gold Museum), one of the continent's finest.
- ☐ The Museo de Arte Moderno, home of the country's largest collection of contemporary art.

Great Neighborhood
- ☐ The Candelaria, a living monument to Colombia's colonial past.

After Dark
- ☐ La Zona Rosa, a great place to catch young Bogotanos in action.

Plaza
- ☐ Plaza Bolívar, one of the most majestic in South America.

Shopping
- ☐ The colonial-style Hacienda Santa Barbara, one of the loveliest shopping centers in South America.

Natural Spectacles
- ☐ The salt mine and cathedral at Zipaquira contain enough salt to supply the world for 100 years.

1. INTRODUCING BOGOTA & COLOMBIA

BACKGROUND Archeological ruins; modern cities and colonial villages; white-sand beaches and snow-capped mountains; neverending plains and tropical jungles—all of this (and more) is Colombia. The fourth-largest country in South America (Brazil, Argentina, and Peru are bigger), it covers an area of 440,000 square miles in the northwest corner of the continent and has 1,800 miles of coastline, 1,000 of which are on the Caribbean Sea; the remaining 800 miles are on the Pacific Ocean.

When they enter Colombia, the Andean Mountains divide into three smaller ranges, or **cordilleras.** These in turn divide the country into four distinct regions:

Important Warning: The running battle between the government and the drug cartels in Colombia poses a significant danger for the traveler, especially in the provincial cities of Medellín and Cali, where the cartels seem to hold sway, and in the capital, Bogotá. Instances of violence continued as we went to press, with bombings in areas visited by tourists.

If you intend to visit Colombia, therefore, call the **U.S. Department of State's Citizens' Emergency Service** (tel. 202/647-5225) in Washington, D.C., on weekdays from 8:15am to 10pm, for an up-to-date report. If you're already in Colombia when you read this, inquire at your embassy in Bogotá about the safety situation in the capital and elsewhere in the country.

the Caribbean; the Amazon-Orinoco; the Pacific; and the Andean, the most densely populated of the four and home of Colombia's capital city, Santa Fe de Bogotá (popularly known as Bogotá).

The city of Bogotá was founded on August 6, 1538, by Spanish conquistador Gonzalo Jiménez de Quesada. Situated on the **Sabana de Bogotá,** a broad and fertile highland plain 8,500 feet above sea level, the land had been occupied by the Muisca Indians, one of the most advanced cultures in the region. The Muisca were talented goldsmiths and craftsmen who plied their crafts in worship of the gods. The legend of El Dorado originated in one of their most famous pieces, the Balsa Muisca, which, along with many other Muisca relics, is now part of the collection at the Museo Del Oro. It was the Legend of El Dorado that brought Jiménez de Quesada and the Spanish to the New World in search of gold.

As capital of the Vice-Royalty of Nueva Granada (the region comprising modern-day Venezuela, Panama, Colombia, and Ecuador), Bogotá played an important political role during the colonial period. The colonial-style churches and homes of the **Candelaría,** the city's historic district, are guardians of the three centuries of legends, anecdotes, and clandestine meetings that led to the country's independence from Spain in 1819. In 1830, Bogotá became the capital of Colombia.

Today, Bogotá is a rapidly expanding city with a population of nearly 6 million. Old meets new here as modern high rises and skyscrapers in the northern sector contrast sharply with the colonial splendor of the Candelaria and the majesty of the Plaza Bolívar.

THE PEOPLE The Colombian people are primarily *mestizo* whose roots go back to the country's original inhabitants, the Indians, the Spanish settlers and the black slaves who were brought over by the Spanish. Of the nation's 30 million inhabitants, 75% live in the Andean region; 21% live on the Caribbean Coast; and the remaining 4% live on the Pacific Coast and in the Amazon-Orinoco region.

A PRECAUTION Life in Colombia has quieted down considerably since the 1989 uprisings by Colombian drug cartels. Travelers needn't feel apprehensive toward visiting Bogotá or Cartagena. However, if you're planning to include Medellín in your itinerary, we advise you to call the U.S. State Department (202/647-5225) to check on the current situation prior to your departure.

The Colombian government does not tolerate the illicit possession of drugs. Dealers, pushers, and "mules" are given long prison terms. The mere possession of drugs is a serious crime. Under no circumstances should you have any drug in your possession for which you do not have a medical prescription.

WHAT THINGS COST IN BOGOTA	U.S. $
Cab from the airport to the city center	5.00
City bus fare	.20
Local telephone call	.10
Double with bath at Residencias Dorantes (budget)	14.00
Double with bath at the Hotel Inter-Bogotá (moderate)	30.00
Double with bath at the Hotel Presidente (deluxe)	55.00
Lunch at the Pasapoga (budget/moderate)	5.00
Dinner with wine at the La Guayacana (moderate)	10.00
Dinner with wine at Tramonti (splurge)	18.00
Cup of coffee	.35
Coca-Cola	.35
Average museum admission	.50

COLOMBIA

Caribbean Sea

N
0 _____ 200 mi
          321.9 km

PANAMA

Pacific
Ocean

Riohacha
Santa Marta
Barranquilla
Cartagena
Valledupar
Maicao

Sincelejo

VENEZUELA

Turbo
Río Cauca
Cucuta

Barrancabermeja
Bucaramanga

Río Atrato
Medellín
Arauca
Puerto
Carreño

Quiboló
Tunja
Río Meta
Río Orinoco

Río Magdalena
Manizales
Cartago
Armenia
Ibagle
★ BOGOTÁ
Villavicencio
Río Guaviare
Puerto
Inirida

Buenaventura

Guápi
Neiva

Popayán
San Jose
del Guaviare

Tumaco
Florencia
Río Apaporis
Mitú

Pasto

Ipiales
Puerto Asis

Leguizamo
Río Caquetá
BRAZIL

Río Putumayo

ECUADOR

PERU
Tarepacá

Letícia

IMPRESSIONS

Bogotá is a city of conversation. As you walk along you have to keep skirting couples or small groups, all absorbed in excited talk. . . . The cafés are crammed, too . . . [and] I have never seen so many bookshops anywhere.
—CHRISTOPHER ISHERWOOD, THE CONDOR AND THE COWS, 1949

Bogotá reminded us at times of a kind of Spanish-speaking Glasgow, not least in its heavy-lidded friendliness, a kind of take-a-drink-or-I'll-break-your-arm quality.
—WILLIAM MCILVANNEY, (LONDON) OBSERVER, MAY 28, 1978

2. ORIENTATION

ARRIVING

An example of Bogotá's accommodating approach to visitors is the treatment you receive upon arrival at the **El Dorado International Airport.** A **hotel reservation service** on the second floor is at your disposal. You can pick up maps and tourist information at the **Corporación Nacional de Turismo,** the National Tourist Office, nearby. A 20-minute cab ride (the only practical transportation to the city) puts you in downtown Bogotá for about $5. There are also minibuses that cost under $1 and will take you downtown.

TOURIST INFORMATION

In addition to its office in the airport, the Government Tourist Office, **Corporación Nacional de Turismo,** is at Calle 28, no. 13A-15, on the first floor (tel. 283-9466). Up-to-date information specific to Bogotá, including a schedule of events, is available from the **Instituto Distrital de Cultura y Turismo** at Calle 10, no. 3-6 (tel. 286-6555).

CITY LAYOUT

You'll find the city's sensible planning a great help in learning how to find your way about. Here are a few basic points to remember: The city is divided into north and south at Calle 1 (the north is the financial/commercial center; the south is exclusively residential). Streets here have three designations: **carreras**—the main, wide streets that run north-south (the main carrera is no. 7, where you'll find outstanding shops, restaurants, and theaters); **calles**—the east-west streets; and **avenidas**—the diagonal streets.

FINDING AN ADDRESS Getting lost in Bogotá is virtually impossible. Street addresses are so ingeniously clear, once you understand the system, that you can locate any number instantly in your mind. For example, the address of Colombia's most famous hotel, the Tequendama, is Carrera 10, no. 26-32. This immediately tells you that the hotel is on the 10th carrera, between Calles 26 and 27, at building no. 32. If an address is Calle 12, no. 4-35, this indicates that the building is on Calle 12, between Carreras 4 and 5, at no. 35. Avenidas are exempt from the system.
    Remember that on calles, even numbers are on the north, and on carreras, even numbers are on the east.

BOGOTÁ

Plaza de Toros de Santa Maria

Cemetery

Calle 26

Calle 25

Calle 24

Carrera 13A

Calle 23

Calle 22

Carrera 14 (Avenida Caracas)

Carrera 3A

Calle 20

Calle 21

Calle 19

Carrera 7

Carrera 5

Carrera 4

Calle 18

Railway Station

Calle 17

Calle 16

Carrera 13

Carrera 12

Carrera 10

Carrera 9

Carrera 8

Calle 15

Carrera 17

Carrera 16

Carrera 15

Avenida Jimenez de Quesada

Calle 14

Carrera 6

Calle 13

Calle 12

Calle 11

Carrera 11

Calle 10

Plaza de Bolivar

Plaza San Carlos

Calle 9

MAIN ARTERIES   The heart of Bogotá for visitors is a rectangle bounded on the south by the **Plaza de Bolívar** at Calle 10; on the north by the city's social hub, the Hotel Tequendama at **Calle 26;** on the west by the thoroughfare **Carrera 14** (also called **Caracas**); and on the east by **Carrera 4.**

The huge pigeon-filled **Plaza de Bolívar,** a major tourist attraction located between Carreras 7 and 8, is the bustling site of most political rallies (the oratory is a lot more restrained than in London's Hyde Park) and is home to the royal-like Cardinal's Palace, the imposing National Cathedral, and the stately Capitol Building and City Hall. Carrera 7, a lively thoroughfare crammed with shops and restaurants, as well as banks, airline offices, and churches, is a must on your first day in Bogotá.

A key cross street, intersecting with Carrera 7, is **Avenida Jimenez de Quesada** (called Avenida Jimenez here), which becomes **Calle 15** in the downtown area. Here you'll find the Hotel Continental, one of our choice recommendations, as well as Colombia's most important bank, the Banco de la República (Bank of the Republic). For a stunning view of Bogotá, follow Avenida Jimenez to **Mt. Monserrate,** particularly lovely at twilight. The mountain is a famous religious shrine where pilgrims from all over Colombia journey during important festivals.

Carreras 7 and 13 and Avenida Caracas are the major thoroughfares heading out from central Bogotá toward **Chapinero,** which begins at about Calle 50. This newer section is replete with lovely homes, shops, clubs, cinemas, and restaurants. Beyond Chapinero, at Calle 90, you enter **Chico,** which is the city's most modern and attractive residential district. Beyond Chico is **Unicentro,** an enormous shopping complex housing shops, restaurants, nightspots, and cinemas. Parking and babysitting services are available.

Heading farther from Center City, you'll come to **Santa Barbara,** another wealthy residential area and the site of several lively discos and clubs. Also in Santa Barbara is Bogotá's newest shopping center, one of the most modern in South America, the **Hacienda Santa Barbara.** The 19th and 21st centuries come together in this colonial hacienda, which was declared a national monument in 1985. Still preserving the beautiful gardens, plazas, and patios of its 19th-century origins, today the Hacienda Santa Barbara is home to modern cinemas, restaurants, a five-star hotel, and numerous open-air cafés.

3. GETTING AROUND

When you buy a ticket to fly within Colombia, be sure to pay in pesos. There is one rate for credit cards and another for pesos, and the difference here is not mere pennies.

BY BUS & COLECTIVO   Buses are plentiful and cheap—20¢ until 8pm. In the residential sections, the best way to travel is via *colectivo,* small Volkswagen buses that carry up to five passengers and charge 60¢.

BY TAXI   Cabs are reasonable and at night should be used exclusively. The rate is about 1¢ for each 100 yards, plus 60¢ at the flagdrop, with a slight extra charge at night. Stick to the green-and-ivory cabs and the yellow-and-black cabs that have RADIO TAXI written on them.

BY CAR   **Hertz** has branch offices at the airport and in the Tequendama Hotel arcade, at Carrera 10, near Calle 26 (tel. 284-1445). Rates typically are high—$25 per day plus 14¢ per kilometer for a Ford Falcon, and $20 per day plus 9¢ per kilometer for a VW. Weekly rates are $70 and 14¢ per kilometer for a Ford, and $48 and 9¢ per kilometer for a VW. **Avis** has a branch at Calle 99, no. 11–26 (tel. 610-4455).

Driving in Bogotá, as in many South American cities, tends to be more chaotic than what most Americans are used to. Since taxis are plentiful and reasonably priced, you may feel more comfortable riding in them while in the city.

BOGOTÁ

Airlines **Avianca** is at Carrera 7, no. 16–36 (tel. 241-2302). If you're considering traveling throughout Colombia, call for information regarding the Avianca Airpass. **American Airlines** is at Carrera 7, no. 26–20 (tel. 285-9560). The **Varig** office is at Carrera 10, no. 26-49 (tel. 285-3340).

American Express American Express is located at Calle 73, no. 8–60 (tel. 217-1300).

Area Code The country code for Colombia is 57; the city code for Bogotá is 1.

Babysitters The concierge in your hotel may be able to help you arrange for child care.

Business Hours Most **shops** are open from 9 or 10am until 7pm. **Banks** are open Monday to Thursday from 9am to 3pm and Friday until 3:30pm. There are branches of the **Banco Internacional de Colombia** in the Hotel Tequendama and at Carrera 10, No. 27–75. The **Banco de la República** is at Carrera 7 no. 7–43.

Car Rentals See "Getting Around" earlier in this chapter.

Cigarettes U.S. brands are relatively cheap—$1 for Philip Morris. Piel Roja (Red Skin), the local brand, is 50¢.

Climate The local weatherpeople have an easy task. To be accurate day after day, they need only remember to predict this: "Cloudy and mild, with a chance of brief afternoon showers." That in a nutshell is Bogotá's weather most of the year. Since Bogotá is just north of the equator, there are no distinct seasons. Yet temperatures are refreshingly moderate due to the city's elevation (8,600 feet above sea level). Afternoon temperatures range in the mid to upper 60s Fahrenheit all year round, while evening lows usually hover in the mid-40s.

No matter how clear the morning, always carry a light raincoat. Afternoon sprinkles can come up rather suddenly. If you plan to remain out into the evening, bring along a heavy sweater and lined raincoat.

Credit Cards VISA, American Express, Diners Club, and MasterCard are accepted virtually everywhere.

Crime See "Safety" below.

Currency The basic currency here is the *peso,* which has fallen in value from 310 to the U.S. dollar in our previous edition to 580 at press time. Prices for accommodations and food have fallen dramatically from those in the previous edition. Prices in this edition are based on 580 pesos to the dollar because the drop in prices cannot be allowed to continue. So it seems obvious that they will gravitate upward in the next two years. *You should use our listed price as a ballpark figure and add at least 10% in 1994.*

Note: The "$" sign is used in Colombia to indicate pesos (for example, 5 pesos is written $5). There are 100 centavos to a peso, and coins come in denominations of 5, 10, 20, and 50 centavos. Pesos are issued in $.50, $1, $2, and $5 coins and in $10, $20, $50, $100, $200, $500, $1,000, $2,000, and $5,000 bills. (Reminder: All prices quoted in this book are in *U.S.* dollars.)

Important note: Keep all receipts for dollars you have converted to pesos. You may have trouble changing pesos to dollars without them.

Currency Exchange Currency can be exchanged in the **Banco de La República,** the **Banco Internacional de Colombia,** larger hotels and at Exchange Offices, including **Exprinter** at Carrera 6, no. 14–64, and the **International Money Exchange** at Carrera 7, no. 32–29.

Dentists/Doctors Ask the concierge at your hotel or call the embassy for a list of English-speaking dentists and doctors.

Drugstores Ask the concierge at your hotel to direct you to a nearby drugstore.

Electricity The current for Bogotá is 110 volts.

Embassies/Consulates The **U.S. Embassy** is located at Calle 38, no.

8-61 (tel. 285-1300). The **United Kingdom Embassy** is at Calle 98, no. 9-03 (tel. 218-5111). The **Canadian Embassy** is at Calle 76, no. 11-52 (tel. 235-5066).

Emergencies   Call the **police** at 112; the **fire department** at 119; the **city ambulance** at 115; the **Red Cross** at 225-800; the **Toxicology Emergency Clinic** at 257-6818; and the **Tourist Police** at 334-2501, ext. 33.

Eyeglasses   The concierge at your hotel should be able to direct you to a nearby optician.

Hairdressers/Barbers   The **Centro de Estética Iosmar** is located in the Centro Internacional Tequendama at Carrera 10, no. 27-51, local 224 (tel. 284-8720).

Holidays

Feast of Saint Joseph	March 19
Ascension Day	May (varies)
Labor Day	May 1
Saint Peter and Saint Paul	June 29
Corpus Christi	May/June (varies)
Sacred Heart	June (varies)
Independence Day	July 20
Battle of Boyacá	August 7
Ascent of Our Lady	August 15
Columbus Day	October 12
Independence Day	November 11

Hospitals   For emergency care try any of the following: **Hospital San Ignacio,** Carrera 7, no. 40-62 (tel. 285-0540); **Hospital Militar Central,** Transversal 5, no. 49-00 (tel. 232-5333); or **Cruz Roja Colombiana** (Red Cross), Avenida 68, no. 66-31 (tel. 231-5623).

Information   See "Tourist Information" earlier in this chapter.

Language   Spanish is, of course, the national tongue. Nevertheless, a surprising number of Bogotanos speak English and speak it well.

Laundry/Dry Cleaning   The major hotels offer laundry and dry-cleaning services.

Luggage Storage/Lockers   If you plan to go on a short trip, you may be able to store your luggage at your hotel.

Newspapers/Magazines   No major English-language newspapers are available here. The best of the Spanish-language dailies is *El Tiempo*. Other papers include *El Espectador, El Nuevo Siglo, La Republica,* and *La Prensa*.

Photographic Needs   Most types of film are readily available. However, prices may be higher than at home.

Post Office   The main branch is at Carrera 7, near Calle 17 (Edificio Avianca). Avianca at the Tequendama Hotel receives mail.

Religious Services   Although Colombia is predominately Catholic, numerous faiths are represented in Bogotá. The concierge in your hotel should be able to help you find religious services in your faith. You should also check the local paper.

Restrooms   Restrooms in hotel lobbies are usually very accessible. Public restrooms are available in most museums, pubs, and restaurants.

Safety   Colombia's drug and crime problem (see "Important Warning" on page 299) has received a good deal of North American press attention. Indeed in our files we have innumerable letters sadly detailing incidents of stolen property and physical beatings, many in broad daylight, even on main streets. Pickpocketing and muggings are, of course, the biggest problem. The most popular attractions for the bandidos are watches, cameras, and jewelry. We suggest keeping your camera under wraps and your watch and other jewelry as inconspicuous as possible. (Home or in a hotel safe is the best place for expensive-looking watches and jewelry. Remember that it doesn't have to be the real thing to catch a thief's eye.)

Pickpockets ply their trade in crowded areas, particularly in elevators and buses. They often work in groups of three or more, subtly surrounding their victim as they empty his or her pockets. When on the bus, do not place bags on the floor between your legs as they may be pulled out by thieves sitting behind you. Tourists making the trip to the Monserrate are among the most common victims of street crimes. Check with the concierge at your hotel on recent conditions there.

Some thieves will even go so far as to pretend to be from the police or security forces. Do not talk to these people. Ignore them and walk away. Avoid wandering about after dark, and if you must, stick to main streets. Taxis are a bargain here. Use them.

Increased police vigilance is highly visible at tourist sites and government buildings throughout the country. Violence, however, perpetrated by the drug cartels continues and poses a significant danger to the traveler.

Shoe Repairs Ask the concierge in your hotel to direct you to the nearest shoe-repair shop.

Taxes As elsewhere in Latin America, Colombia charges foreign visitors an airport tax. For a stay of less than 60 days that tax is $17 ("Exención de Impuestos"), otherwise it goes up to $30. Make sure you make the length of your stay clear to the Customs agent upon your arrival.

Taxis See "Getting Around" earlier in this chapter.

Telegrams/Telexes There are two telecommunication centers in Bogotá from where you can make long-distance phone calls and send telexes and telegrams. One is located in the downtown area at Calle 17, no. 7-15 (tel. 234-8743); it's open weekdays from 8am to 7:45pm and holidays from 9am to 6:45pm. The other is located at Calle 90, no. 14-26, in office 102; it's open weekdays from 7am to 7:45pm.

Telephone Listen for the dial tone and then deposit an appropriate coin (under 10¢). The AT&T Direct Program is a great cost-saver for international calls. To reach the AT&T Direct operator, dial 980-110010.

Useful Telephone Numbers For information on the latest tourist events and shows, call 282-0000. To call a cab to the airport, call Radio Taxi at 211-1111. To call a city cab, call Coturismo at 282-9151 or Proturismo at 223-2111.

4. WHERE TO STAY

IN TOWN
DOUBLES FOR LESS THAN $30

HOTEL PANAMERICANO, Calle 15, no. 12-70. Tel. 281-2957. 50 rms (all with bath). TEL
$ Rates: $13.25 single; $15 double.
This three-story hotel has basic, carpeted accommodations. It also boasts a restaurant and laundry facilities. Head to the second floor for the reception desk.

HOTEL VIRGEN DEL CAMINO, Calle 18A, no. 14-33, off Avenida Caracas. Tel. 282-4450 or 282-4470. Some rooms with bath.
$ Rates: $9–$9.50 single without bath, $11 single with bath; $13–$13.50 double without bath, $15 double with bath.
This older five-story home offers clean, cozy rooms at moderate prices. There are no elevators, so ask for a room on one of the lower floors. The new management has maintained, if not improved, the fine attentive service you'll enjoy here.

RESIDENCIAS DORANTES, Calle 13, no. 5-07. Tel. 334-6640. 33 rms (some with bath).
$ Rates: $6 single without bath; $9 single with bath; $8 double without bath, $14 double with bath.

Located between Carreras 5 and 6, the Dorantes offers fine airy doubles. The owners seem to delight in polishing the furniture daily, so there often is the faint fragrance of polish in the bright rooms.

HOTEL MENENDEZ, Calle 20, no. 5-85. Tel. 243-3274. 18 rms (all with bath). TEL

$ Rates (including all meals): $9 single; $15 double.

The Menendez offers guests a comfortable lobby sitting room, complete with fireplace and TV, and rooms that are plainly furnished but clean and acceptable. The meals are exceptionally generous. Look for a gray building set back from the street and a small sign.

HOTEL RESIDENCIA SANTA FE, Calle 14, no. 4-48. Tel. 342-0560. 44 rms (all with bath). TEL

$ Rates: $10 single; $14 double; $16 per person room with all meals.

Fading fast, but still a good value, is this white-and-yellow colonial-style hotel, where you can have three meals included for a modest rate. The hotel is furnished in an old Spanish motif. Clean and airy, most rooms have awnings and window shutters. Apartments are also available.

MANILA HOTEL, Calle 17, no. 8-23. Tel. 243-9010. 19 rms (all with bath).

$ Rates: $10 single; $15 double.

This nine-story elevator hotel is located between Carreras 8 and 9, just around the corner from the Cordillera. The rooms are clean, though rather plain.

PENSION ALEMANA, Caracas, no. 25-15. Tel. 241-7590. No rooms with bath.

$ Rates (including breakfast): $15 double; $20 triple. Lower weekly rates can be negotiated.

An outstanding budget choice is the three-story Alemana, on Carrera 14, which differs from most pensions because it includes only breakfast in the rates. Enter on Caracas and ascend one flight, where you register. The large, bright rooms, all immaculate, with full-length mirrors, are an excellent value. Five public bathrooms, each with a shower and bidet, are more than adequate for the 17 guests. Breakfast, by the way, includes juice, toast, eggs, and coffee. Hostess Julia de Pinilla takes good care of her guests.

LOS CERROS, Avenida 19, no. 9-18. Tel. 283-8458. Fax 284-2031. 19 rms (all with bath). MINIBAR TV TEL

$ Rates: $22 single; $26 double.

This small hotel is three blocks from Carrera 7. The carpeted rooms in the four-floor Cerros make up for in comfort what they lack in size. The hotel has a small restaurant that offers all meals, plus a bar.

HOTEL CRISTAL, Calle 17, no. 7-92. Tel. 243-0030. Fax 292-1709. Telex 45-707. 28 rms (all with bath). TEL

$ Rates: $17 single; $25 double.

You'll enter the small ground-floor lobby and then an elevator will whisk you up to your room. The rooms, spread over 10 floors, are large and airy, with twin beds, couches, and sitting areas. The second-floor restaurant and bar are worth trying.

HOTEL DEL DUC, Calle 23, no. 9-38. Tel. 334-0085. Fax 284-5169. 56 rms (all with bath). TEL

$ Rates: $18 single; $24 double.

Just two blocks from Carrera 7, the eight-floor Del Duc has been open since 1966. The carpeted rooms have small sitting areas. A bar and restaurant are on the premises, and laundry service is available.

HOTEL ILE DE FRANCE, Calle 18, no. 14-56. Tel. 342-0684. 45 rms (all with bath). TEL

$ Rates: $13 single; $19 double; $24 two-bedroom flat.

This pension is between Carreras 14 and 15. A family of four can get a two-bedroom flat, with living room, kitchenette, and private bath. The three-story pension is not impressive in appearance, but it is well maintained by the owners, who live on the premises. Note the French scenes in the spacious dining hall.

HOTEL REGINA, Carrera 5, no. 15-16. Tel. 334-5135. 31 rms (all with bath). TV TEL

$ Rates: $15 single; $23 double. Major credit cards accepted.

A cozy find that we like for its *gemütlich* qualities is the eight-floor elevator Regina, between Calles 15 and 16. The friendly owners offer a choice of twin or double beds at no difference in cost. The Regina's rooms are spotless. A restaurant and cafetería, as well as a bar, are on the premises.

DOUBLES FOR LESS THAN $50

DANN COLONIAL, Calle 14, no. 4-21. Tel. 341-1680. Fax 334-9992. (all with bath). MINIBAR TV TEL

$ Rates: $35 single; $45 double. Major credit cards accepted.

⭐ The Dann Colonial is in the heart of Bogotá's colonial quarter, La Candelaría. The streets around it are narrow, and the buildings are red-roofed. The hotel itself is modern and very luxurious. The rates are not that high for a first-class hotel.

HOTEL BACATA, Calle 19, no. 5-20. Tel. 283-8300. Fax 281-7249. 277 rms (all with bath). TV TEL

$ Rates: $36 single; $46 double. Major credit cards accepted.

A newish near-luxury choice is the Bacata. Everything here is first class. Guests have private parking facilities. A good bar and restaurant are on the premises.

HOTEL CONTINENTAL, Avenida Jimenez, no. 4-16. Tel. 243-9773. Fax 334-3325. 175 rms (all with bath). TV TEL

$ Rates: $30 single; $33–$48 double. Major credit cards accepted.

⭐ A superb choice—worth every extra peso—is the almost-luxurious Continental, near Carrera 5. The Continental ranks just behind the magnificent Tequendama and Orquidea Real as the best hotel in Bogotá. This nine-story oasis offers spotless rooms with carpets that are scrupulously vacuumed daily. We stayed in a rear double during a recent visit and were delighted to find each evening that the maid had turned down our beds, scrubbed down the shower stall, and left us with fresh soap. The room had colorful draperies, a modern bureau, two end tables, and a comfortable double bed. The front doubles are more expensive than the rear ones.

The Continental also houses one of our recommended restaurants (the *arroz con pollo* is outstanding), a clean, quick-service coffee shop, and a relaxing cocktail lounge and bar. Lovely extras are the beauty parlor and the uniformed doorman.

HOTEL INTER-BOGOTA, Carrera 3a, no. 20-17. Tel. 334-6712. 30 rooms (all with bath). TV TEL

$ Rates: $20 single; $30 double. Major credit cards accepted.

The three-star Inter-Bogotá is especially fine, clean and well cared for. Windows all around offer lovely views of the surrounding mountains. The hotel has its own bar and restaurant and offers 24-hour room service.

SPLURGE CHOICES

HOTEL DANN INTERNATIONAL, Avenida 19, no. 5-72. Tel. 284-0100. Fax 282-3108. 150 rms (all with bath). MINIBAR TV TEL

$ Rates: $42 single; from $56 double. Major credit cards accepted.

The centrally located Dann International is out of our budget range but worth the money. This 13-floor luxury stop offers a restaurant, beauty parlor, barbershop, laundry, bar, and convention room. Rooms are carpeted and have drapes and modern furniture.

HOTEL PRESIDENTE, Calle 23, no. 9-45. Tel. 243-5020. Fax 284-5766. Telex 043112 HOTPR. 150 rms (all with bath). TV TEL
$ Rates: $45 single; from $55 double. Major credit cards accepted.

⭐ One of our great favorites in Bogotá, the charming Presidente is ideally located for nightlife, between Carreras 9 and 10. The carpeted rooms are clean and roomy. Continental breakfast is $3, $4 with eggs. Guests have use of the garage on the premises; there is a bar, and the restaurant is located on the upper level. One of our recommended nightspots is located here.

NUEVA GRANADA, Avenida Jimenez no. 4-77. Tel. 286-5877. Fax 284-5465. 110 rms (all with bath). TV TEL
$ Rates: $48 single; $56 double. Major credit cards accepted.
Opened in 1982, the Granada is a four-star luxury stop in the heart of downtown offering large modern rooms. It has its own restaurant and bar as well as a cafeteria for light meals; a barbershop for men and beauty salon for women; in-house medical assistance; and travel services, including currency, car-rental, and travel arrangements.

THE SUBURBS

As the city expands northward, progress follows. Modern shopping centers, beautiful private homes, restaurants, and boutiques have sprung up in the area beyond Calle 90, called Chico. This lovely sector of Bogotá is known for its highly regarded eye clinic, which draws patients from all over the world, who stay in the modern new hotels and pensions that have opened to meet the demand. For those who don't mind the 20-minute bus or taxi ride into downtown (longer at peak hours), a stay in the suburbs is an interesting way to experience a different side of this city.

PENSIONS

By far the best buys in the suburbs are the pensions, where the price of your room will often include three meals. And you'll be made to feel like a member of the family.

CHICO NORTE RESIDENCIAS, Carrera 22, no. 101-39. Tel. 236-5099. Most rooms with bath.
$ Rates: $30 room with 1 meal per person; $40 room with 3 meals per person.
This ranch-style home has a spacious living room where guests often congregate around a small modern fireplace. Rooms, located off the living room, are large, clean, and contemporary in decor.

HALIFAX, Calle 93, no. 15-93. Tel. 256-6143.
$ Rates: $45 room with 3 meals per person.
If the Chico Norte is full, check out the Halifax. Prices are somewhat higher for rooms that are similar in size and furnishings. Make reservations at least 2 weeks in advance.

5. WHERE TO DINE

Bogotanos dine relatively early in comparison to other South Americans—as early as 8pm. Most restaurants are closed by midnight. Colombians eat with gusto and prefer their evening meal to be generous in portion and rich in spices. Other meals are light. Meat and chicken dishes, highly seasoned and served with heaping cooked vegetables, are menu staples in most restaurants.

A superb national specialty—a must in your dining—is a marvelously tangy beef stew called *puchero* that brims with fresh vegetables, sausage, and chunks of chicken. Another must is the *arroz con pollo*—the best we've ever eaten—which is a long dinner-table jump from the chicken-and-rice dishes served elsewhere in South America or even in Madrid. The chicken, carefully boned and sharply seasoned, is mixed with four or five vegetables and rice and is usually served in a large bowl. You should also try the *ajiaco,* a deliciously filling soup made with three types of potatoes and served with cream, hard-boiled egg, corn, and avocado. Very traditional in Bogotá, it is served in most restaurants (you can always ask for seconds). Another specialty is *empanadas* (potato pies), eaten as a snack. The national beverage is *tinto,* a demitasse made with rich Colombian coffee (which we consider the world's best). U.S. style coffee is called *café,* coffee served with cream. But black is best.

Beer drinkers should rejoice here, for the Club Colombia brand is as good as the best coming out of U.S. breweries and is now sold in the United States.

In general, the better hotels have good restaurants, and most also operate inexpensive coffee shops or cafeterias.

Tip: Most restaurants close on Sunday, and your dining will be limited generally to hotel restaurants on that day. Also, service is not included in the bill. A 10% tip is generally appropriate.

IN TOWN
MEALS FOR LESS THAN $10

LA FONDA ANTIOQUEÑA, Calle 19, no. 5-98. Tel. 341-3747.
   Cuisine: COLOMBIAN. **Reservations:** Not accepted.
$ **Prices:** Appetizers $1–$2; main courses $3–$5.
   Open: Lunch and dinner.
This restaurant is typical of Colombia's "cowboy" region. Its tables are tree trunks, and the director's chairs are covered with cowhide. The foods are typical as well. Try *sancocho* with beef or chicken—it's a soup/stew with lots of vegetables and avocado. Enough for an entire meal, it costs only $3.75. Roast chicken, pork, and steak *à la caballo* (with eggs) are the most popular choices.

PASAPOGA RESTAURANTE, near Calle 12, off an alley leading from Carrera 7.
   Cuisine: COLOMBIAN.
$ **Prices:** Appetizers $1–$2; main courses $3–$6.
   Open: Lunch and dinner.
For a wonderful budget-priced meal, go to Pasapoga, where beefsteak *à la caballo* (fried egg on top) is only $4. There are daily menu specials from $2.50 to $5. The tables are covered with white cloths. Of the two dining rooms, the upstairs is a bit more cheerful. Both levels are usually jammed with working-class Bogotanos, so expect a short wait. If you're on foot, approach the Pasapoga from Carrera 7 and you'll come upon the small courtyard the restaurant faces. Another restaurant with the same name, at Calle 15, no. 9-35, offers an excellent Sunday brunch.

RESI BERLIN, Centro Internacional Tequendama. Tel. 234-2910.
   Cuisine: GERMAN.
$ **Prices:** Appetizers $1–$2; main courses $3–$6.
   Open: Daily noon–11pm.
This restaurant can be found in the Tequendama arcade across from the telegraph office. The Bavarian theme is carried out in the waiters' garb and the traditional sausage dishes. Each day there is a delicious specialty of the house for $3.50.

MEALS FOR LESS THAN $20

CAFETERIA EL VIRREY, in the Hotel Tequendama, Carrera 10, no. 26-21. Tel. 286-1111.
   Cuisine: INTERNATIONAL. **Reservations:** Recommended.
$ **Prices:** Appetizers $2–$5; main courses $4–$8. Major credit cards accepted.
   Open: Breakfast, lunch, and dinner.

When a North American and a Bogotano have a dinner date, they seem to wind up at the Hotel Tequendama's elegant Cafeteria El Virrey, on the main floor. While certainly not a cafeteria, the Virrey nevertheless offers some surprisingly reasonable values. For example, we've savored a fine fish filet (*filete de robalo*), served with a delicate mushroom sauce. A superb treat is the sirloin in pepper sauce, or the filet mignon, though you can order something lighter, such as a hamburger. After dinner, stroll through the Tequendama's lobby to see why this hotel is considered one of South America's finest.

CHALET SUIZO, Avenida 22, no. 39a-48. Tel. 245-6115.
   Cuisine: SWISS. **Reservations:** Recommended.
$ **Prices:** Appetizers $2–$5; main courses $4–$8. Major credit cards accepted.
   Open: Mon–Fri noon–4pm and 6:30–11:30pm; Sun noon–10pm.
At this intimate and clean restaurant, the grilled chicken (*medio pollo à la brasa*) is a fine value, especially since it includes french fries, salad, and vegetable. A small, tender baby beef is also available, as is a popular Swiss fondue. You'll find the wooden booths and unusual black-and-white horsehair chairs most comfortable.

EL FOGONAZO RESTAURANT, Carrera 7, no. 21-59. Tel. 342-7534.
   Cuisine: INTERNATIONAL.
$ **Prices:** Appetizers $2–$4; main courses $4–$8.
   Open: Lunch and dinner.
The *carne al Fogonazo* is a fine buy here, as are the *churrasco Argentino* and *arroz con pollo*. This is a bilevel restaurant with glass-topped tables and booths that doubles as a tearoom in the late afternoon. It has a stand-up section, too. El Fogonazo also serves pizza.

LA GIRALDA, Carrera 15, no. 33-21. Tel. 245-3350.
   Cuisine: SPANISH/COLOMBIAN.
$ **Prices:** Appetizers $1–$4; main courses $4–$7.
   Open: Lunch and dinner.
Located in front of the bullring, La Giralda is decorated accordingly with bullfighting posters and memorabilia. This small restaurant, reminiscent of a *mesón*, offers a variety of Spanish and Colombian specialties. Try the *arroz con pollo* or the *robalo con champinones* (halibut with mushrooms). The paella and the *cazuela de mariscos* (seafood casserole), although slightly more expensive, are both excellent choices. One order is enough for two people.

LA GRAN PARRILLA SANTA FE, Carrera 13, no. 13-49. Tel. 232-5906.
   Cuisine: COLOMBIAN/INTERNATIONAL.
$ **Prices:** Appetizers $1–$3; main courses $4–$7.
   Open: Lunch and dinner.
The dozen tables in this attractive small restaurant are crowded at lunchtime with government workers who are lured by the homemade soups, salads, and grilled meats. Steaks, pork chops, and *arroz con pollo* are very good.

LA GUAYACANA, Avenida Jimenez, between Carreras 3 and 4.
   Cuisine: SOUTH AMERICAN.
$ **Prices:** Appetizers $1–$4; main courses $7–$12.
   Open: Lunch and dinner.
This attractive restaurant has several intimate dining alcoves. Beamed ceilings and antique mirrors create a fine Spanish atmosphere. Recommended especially are the chicken dishes, charcoal-broiled steaks, and typical South American dishes.

LA HACIENDA RESTAURANT, in the Hotel Orquídea Real, Carrera 7, no. 32-16, 4th floor. Tel. 285-6020.
   Cuisine: COLOMBIAN/INTERNATIONAL. **Reservations:** Recommended.
$ **Prices:** Appetizers $2–$5; main courses $5–$12. Major credit cards accepted.
   Open: Mon–Fri 11:30am–11pm; Sat–Sun and hols 5pm–midnight.
This restaurant is in elegant surroundings that include strolling musicians and singers who entertain at each table. Surprisingly, rates are not astronomical. The chicken

parrillada is very good and reasonably priced. Pasta and omelette dishes will let you get by for a few dollars less than the steak and chicken platters.

RESTAURANTE HONG KONG, Calle 23, no. 5-98. Tel. 342-7304.
  Cuisine: CHINESE. **Reservations:** Recommended.
  $ Prices: Appetizers $1–$3; main courses $4–$8. Major credit cards accepted.
  Open: Daily noon–midnight.
You can savor chop suey, egg foo yung, and wonton soup, in this delightful Chinese eatery decorated with red Asian designs. Our favorite is the *arroz oriental*—fried rice with lobster, chicken, pork, and shrimp. Another branch is in Chico at Carrera 11, no. 92-51 (tel. 236-2758).

ROMANA CAFETERIA, Avenida Jiménez, no. 6-65. Tel. 334-8135.
  Cuisine: ITALIAN.
  $ Prices: Appetizers $1–$4; main courses $3–$7.
  Open: 8am–8pm.
This is a charming Italian spot with wood-paneled walls that make the decor worthy of a far more expensive restaurant. A particular bargain is the daily special, which includes an Italian-style meat or chicken dish, with vegetable, bread and butter, and beverage for $5. Open from 8am to 8pm. The Romana serves an expensive breakfast.

EL ZAGUAN DE LAS AGUAS, Calle 19, no. 5-62. Tel. 341-2336.
  Cuisine: COLOMBIAN. **Reservations:** Recommended.
  $ Prices: Appetizers $1–$4; main courses $3–$7. Major credit cards accepted.
  Open: Lunch and dinner.
This large colonial-style house has separate dining rooms. Try the *sancocho gallina*, *puchero*, or *arroz bogotano*. There is music and folkloric dancing nightly from 8pm to midnight, on Sunday from noon. Service and food are first class.

CASA VIEJA DE SAN DIEGO, Carrera 10, no. 26-50. Tel. 284-7359.
  Cuisine: COLOMBIAN. **Reservations:** Recommended.
  $ Prices: Appetizers $3–$5; main courses $6–$9. Major credit cards accepted.
  Open: Daily noon–midnight.
Housed in what was once the old San Diego cloister, the lovely Casa Vieja is an excellent choice if you want to sample native cuisine. The cloister's walkways, once quietly trodden by monks, have been converted into a picturesque dining area that looks out onto a pretty courtyard. We enjoyed the *puchero* (a hearty stew brimming over with sausage, beef, bananas, and vegetables). Served with soup, this dish is filling. The menu also features steak with grilled potatoes or creole steak, roast pork with apple sauce, jumbo creole prawns, and chicken with capers. A strolling musician sets a romantic mood while you dine. There are four Casa Vieja restaurants in Bogotá: downtown at Avenida Jimenez, no. 3-73 (tel. 334-6171); at Carrera 11, no. 89-08 (tel. 236-3421); and at Avenida Pepe Sierra 116, no. 20-50 (tel. 213-7855).

COZINEIRO RODIZIO BAR, Calle 38, no. 13-28. Tel. 245-9241.
  Cuisine: BRAZILIAN. **Reservations:** Recommended.
  $ Prices: Appetizers $3–$5; main courses $6–$10.
  Open: Lunch and dinner.
Cozineiro is a terrific *rodizio* that you can easily walk to from center city. (*Rodizios* are the Brazilian restaurants where waiters serve beef, chicken, lamb and chorizo from long skewers. They wander from table to table, each time with a different choice, won't stop until you do.) Going upstairs (the bar is on the main floor) as you walk to your table you can eye the huge circular salad bar. You can also order the meat à la carte. A plus is that there's a good disco on the corner.

LA FRAGATA, Carrera 13, no. 27-98, 2nd floor (Bavaria Building). Tel. 243-2959.
  Cuisine: SEAFOOD. **Reservations:** Recommended.
  $ Prices: Appetizers $2–$4; main courses $4–$9. MasterCard accepted.
  Open: Mon–Sat noon–11:30pm.

This elegant restaurant is decorated like a 19th-century ship (the bartender resembles Captain Bligh), complete with portholes and captain's couches. Try the *trucha salmonada* (trout), *lenguado* (sole), or *robalo* (haddock). There is another La Fragata in the World Trade Center, not far from the Hacienda Santa Barbara Shopping Center (tel. 222-8806).

REFUGIO ALPINO, Calle 23, no. 7-49. Tel. 284-6515.
   Cuisine: FRENCH/SWISS. **Reservations:** Recommended.
$ Prices: Appetizers $1–$4; main courses $5–$8.
   Open: Lunch and dinner.
This restaurant, between Carreras 7 and 8, serves superb food in a Swiss lodge–type setting. Ski scenes and hanging wine bottles make this small hideaway one of our favorites. Steak dishes we enjoy are entrecôte St. Moritz and *lomito alpino*. Fish platters and a well-prepared *arroz con pollo* are bargains. Piped-in music adds to the ambience, and the dozen or so tables are usually occupied by locals.

THE SUBURBS

Many of Bogotá's best dining spots are located in the suburbs; however, most will stretch your budget. In addition to the following, some of the successful restaurants in Bogotá have opened locations in the north as well: **La Fragata** can be found at Calle 100, no. 8a-55, on the twelfth floor; and a branch of Casa Vieja, called **Casa Vieja del Norte,** is located at Carrera 11, no. 89-08.

MEALS FOR LESS THAN $20

CACTUS, Carrera 15, no. 94-78, in Chico. Tel. 257-3032.
   Cuisine: INTERNATIONAL. **Reservations:** Recommended.
$ Prices: Appetizers $1–$4; main courses $4–$10. Major credit cards accepted.
   Open: Lunch and dinner.
A favorite in Chico, Bogotá's exclusive suburb, is a wonderfully modern restaurant that has a salad bar featuring 15 kinds of vegetables and is owned by a delightful young couple. The Cactus's waiters are all students, and the atmosphere is informal and friendly. Hanging plants, a skylight, chrome-and-leather chairs, and a raised wooden platform, creating two separate dining areas in the back, make this very attractive. Order a ¾-pound steak and accompany it with a bottle of chilled wine ($8.75—cheap by Colombian standards). Barbecued chicken is another Cactus specialty, as are hamburgers.

GRAN CHINA, Calle 77A, no. 11-72. Tel. 249-5938.
   Cuisine: CHINESE. **Reservations:** Recommended.
$ Prices: Appetizers $1–$4; main courses $4–$9.
   Open: Daily lunch and dinner.
Gran China's menu offers a wide selection of Pekinese and Szechuan dishes. The restaurant is a favorite among Bogotanos, so you may want to make reservations ahead.

LE PETIT BISTROT, Calle 76, no. 10-28. Tel. 249-4058.
   Cuisine: FRENCH. **Reservations:** Recommended.
$ Prices: Appetizers $2–$4; main courses $5–$9.
   Open: Lunch and dinner.
Flawless service in a refined European setting make this a fabulous choice for a special evening. The menu varies, but the cuisine is always French. The desserts are nothing short of magnificent.

MISTER RIBS, Avenida 82, no. 9-52. Tel. 257-9050.
   Cuisine: BARBECUE.
$ Prices: Appetizers $2–$4; main courses $4–$9. Major credit cards accepted.

Open: Noon–midnight.

Mister Ribs is without a doubt one of Bogotá's top rib eateries, serving barbecued chicken and beef dishes. It has a colonial atmosphere, brick walls, and a long bar with high wooden armchairs.

NIHONKAN, Calle 90, no. 11A-31. Tel. 236-1560.
   Cuisine: JAPANESE. **Reservations:** Recommended.
   $ Prices: Appetizers $1–$3; main courses $4–$8. Major credit cards accepted.
   Open: Mon–Sat noon–3pm and 7–11pm.

If you tire of Colombian cooking and want something a little more adventurous, why not opt for sushi at Bogotá's finest Japanese restaurant? Or order a Japanese steak prepared at your table. Specialties here include sushi, sashimi, teppanyaki, and shabu shabu.

O SOLE MIO, Calle 90, no. 17-48. Tel. 236-2426.
   Cuisine: ITALIAN.
   $ Prices: Appetizers $1–$3; main courses $4–$8. Major credit cards accepted.
   Open: Daily noon–3pm and 6–11pm.

O Sole Mío has the best pizza in town—it's crusty and covered with globs of thick cheese and any topping that strikes your fancy. They serve pasta, too, but stick to the pizza.

PIZZERIA NAPOLITANAS, Carrera 7, no. 59-10, Chapinero. Tel. 249-1302.
   Cuisine: ITALIAN.
   $ Prices: Appetizers $1–$3; main courses $3–$8.
   Open: Lunch and dinner.

The decor and cuisine are flawless here. You can have a huge chicken cacciatore platter or perhaps veal and beef, served with fresh vegetables and pasta side dishes. And if you like pizza, try it here. A favorite among regulars is pizza *con mariscos* (shellfish).

THE PLACE, Calle 94, no. 15-45. Tel. 257-9194.
   Cuisine: AMERICAN.
   $ Prices: Appetizers $1–$2; main courses $2–$5.
   Open: Daily noon–midnight.

The Place is an informal eatery known for its enormous hero sandwiches, but it also serves fine burgers and Tex-Mex finger foods. It's frequently crowded with young Bogotanos. Another branch is at Calle 118, no. 26-56.

SPLURGE CHOICES

GRAN VATEL, Carrera 7, no. 70-40. Tel. 255-8142.
   Cuisine: FRENCH/BELGIAN. **Reservations:** Recommended.
   $ Prices: Appetizers $3–$6; main courses $7–$12. Major credit cards accepted.
   Open: Dinner 7–11pm.

Few restaurants in the world can claim a more attractive setting than this—in a mansion that once was the home of former Colombian President Alfonso López. You enter through a garden to dine in any of several elegant rooms, each with a unique decor. Owner Madam Goerres is a gourmet's gourmet. The food is superb, and prices surprisingly are not astronomical. Try the hors d'oeuvres *variados* platter (for two), which includes meatloaf, salami, ham, pickles, and smoked trout. Then the *demipoulet Gran Vatel*, a chicken dish with sauce, or the *filet pargo cardinal*. Ismael, the headwaiter, will attend to your every need—he's been here for over 25 years.

TRAMONTI, Carrera 1, no. 93-50, Via a la Calera. Tel. 218-2400.
   Cuisine: INTERNATIONAL. **Reservations:** Recommended.
   $ Prices: Appetizers $2–$5; main courses $5–$12. Major credit cards accepted.
   Open: Daily noon–midnight.

⭐ Bogotá's most spectacular restaurant is located about a mile above the city. Named for a village in the mountains of northern Italy, Tramonti is, as the name suggests, "among mountains." And the view of the city is breathtaking, especially at dusk, so be sure to request a table with a view, which shouldn't be too hard to come by as there are windows all around.

Besides the view, the restaurant itself is, as owner Beatriz Orozco was proud to point out, a showcase. There are five dining rooms, all on different levels, in this chalet-type structure that has been built right into the side of the mountain. In fact, one of Tramonti's two bars, appropriately named Las Rocas, has the actual rock of the side of the mountain as its back wall!

The menu and wine list are as extensive as the restaurant is big. But don't worry—fires glowing in the fireplaces, the candles on the tables, and just the overall ambience of the restaurant, plus the excellent service, will make you feel as if you're in a much smaller and very intimate place. There's something here to please every palate, from a simple T-bone steak to lobster thermidor, with a highly recommended *ajiaco santafereño* and pasta dishes in between.

Tramonti is a definite must. If dinner is out of your budget, why not go up at teatime (3 to 6:30pm Monday to Friday)? It's also popular for drinks in the evening.

SPECIALTY DINING

LIGHT FARE Located across from the Teatro Jorge Eliecer Gaitan on Carrera 7, the 24-hour **Punto Rojo** is clearly one of Bogotá's best budget choices. A complete meal here is less than $4, and you won't go away hungry. This large self-service restaurant offers a wide selection of chicken, fish, meat, and rice dishes, as well as tempting desserts, salads, and sandwiches (*empareados*). Check for the daily specials, which include *sancocho con pollo, piquete mixto,* and *ajiaco bogotano.* With locations along the highways, Punto Rojo is a favorite pitstop for travelers.

You might also consider **Ramses,** on Carrera 7, between Calle 18 and 19, for a continental breakfast (about $1.75) or an inexpensive lunch. The leather booths are comfortable, and the atmosphere is cheerful. For a hefty lunch at a not-so-hefty price, try the executive lunch (*almuerzo ejecutivo*) at **La Plazuela,** on the Plaza Jimenez. A complete meal with soup, salad, main course, and dessert is just over $1.50. The restaurant is fairly small and sparsely decorated, the food simple yet filling.

Drop in for a quick pizza at **Domo Taberna and Pizza,** Carrera 7, no. 21-52. By the slice is 75¢ and up, depending on the toppings. **Jenos,** with branches all over town, is another option for pizza.

Another inexpensive lunch stop is **La Brasa Roja,** Calle 17, no. 8-76, where booths line the walls and whole chickens rotate over glowing coals. Chicken and french fries is $2.50. Yet another quick lunch stop is **PPC** (Pollo, Pizza, and Carne), Calle 22, no. 8-43. Pick up your whole pizza ($2.50), whole grilled chicken ($4.50), or sizzling steak ($3.50) and head to an upstairs table. You'll find other PPCs all over town.

Lechonería Tolimense, Carrera 7, no. 22-01, has a stand-up area as well as booths. The specialty is a variety of ice creams with exotic toppings. A newer, more modern Lechonería Tolimense has just opened on the next block in a small shopping arcade.

Crem Helado (literally "ice cream"), Avenida Caracas, no. 31-49, near Calle 31, is the closest reproduction of a Howard Johnson's available in South America. This modern beef haven features succulent burgers (with french fries, fried onions, and tomato) for $3.25. The slow service doesn't seem to deter the hundreds of young Bogotanos who flock here on evenings and weekends, particularly on Sunday, when it is one of the few places open. A nice touch is the phone in each booth that you use to call your order in. A fine value is the chicken in the basket at $4, and the fried shrimp, served with french fries and tomato, for $7.50. The chile con carne ($3.25) and tasty steak sandwiches (also $3.25) are other good values. Don't leave without sampling the oversized pineapple pie à la mode ($1.50). Open from 11am to midnight.

Fine inexpensive hamburgers and other fast foods are **Wimpy's** specialty. For as little as $1 you can have a hamburger, and a bacon-and-eggs burger is $1.75. Add 30¢ for the quarter-pounder (Wimpy-Maxi). There are several Wimpy's around town, the most convenient on Carrera 7, between Calles 23 and 24.

Broaster, at Carrera 13, no. 27-08, is another inexpensive breakfast, lunch, or dinner choice. Eggs run a bargain 80¢; with ham they are $1.25. Sandwiches start at $1.25, and a chicken-and-rice platter is only $3.75. Hamburgers are delicious at $1.25. Another location is on Carrera 13 at Avenida 39.

The **Koko Rico** chain, rather like Kentucky Fried Chicken, has several branches around town, with one on Carrera 7, no. 23, and another on Carrera 10, no. 24. Fried and roast chicken pieces, burgers, and hot-dog platters are all inexpensive. Eat-in or take-out. **Del Oeste Hamburgers,** at Carrera 10, is another inexpensive fast-food establishment, serving spaghetti, fried chicken, and sandwiches.

Great sandwiches are made to order any time at the **24 Horas Sandwich Shop.** This new arrival to the fast-food scene has locations at Carrera 13, no. 23-06, and on Avenida 13, not far from Calle 23. You can get American-style sandwiches on hero rolls or french bread for around $1.25.

Vegetarian fans should head over to **El Vegetariano,** at Calle 18, no. 5-74, where yogurt and dairy dishes are king. You can take advantage of the take-out service run by this nonprofit organization. Other branches are at Carrera 8, no. 21-39; and Calle 22, no. 8-89 (third floor). **El Champiñón** at Carrera 8, no. 16-36, is another good spot for vegetarian cooking.

Two unostentatious lunch places you might like to try if you're in the vicinity are the **San Martín,** Carrera 27, no. 64-20; and the **Restaurante Delphi,** Carrera 7 at Calle 22, opposite the Cinema Colombia. The two-floor San Martín offers roomy booths on the upper level. Stick to the daily special (about $1.50), which frequently includes clams, one of the better dishes here. The Delphi, open from 8am to midnight, is rather plain but features a filling six-course meal for $2.75.

TEA A late-afternoon culinary custom in Bogotá is tea and pastries—Bogotanos seem to devour enormous quantities of baked goods. An ideal spot for relaxing is the charming **La Suiza** ("The Swiss"), Calle 25, no. 9-41, which skillfully uses bright tablecloths and red-leather chairs. It will cost you $1 for a cream-filled pastry and tea or café. Closed Monday. If you're a coffee lover, don't miss **Oma,** a café/restaurant at Carrera 10, no. 27-91, in the modern Bavaria Building. Drop by in the late afternoon and linger over a cup of Colombia's finest, which can also be purchased by the pound and ground to your specifications.

There are a number of small cafés scattered around Plaza Jimenez. All are very popular with the Bogotanos and crowded at tea time. Or as a healthy alternative to pastries, stop in at the **Frutería Las Catorce,** also on Plaza Jimenez, for a refreshing fruit salad or shake (*crema de fruta*).

FOR PICNICS La Gran Via at Carrera 7, no. 17-48, offers a delightful alternative to restaurant dining. It is a gourmet grocery shop where you'll find a wide variety of cheeses, both imported and domestic; fresh baked breads; and other gourmet fare.

6. ATTRACTIONS

THE TOP MUSEUMS

MUSEO DEL ORO, Carrera 6 and Calle 16, no. 5-41. Tel. 281-3600.

 This is Bogotá's most famous museum, housed in a relatively new four-story structure. The magnificent collection of emeralds and 8,000 gold pieces includes exquisite arm bracelets, nose rings, crowns, bowls, whistles, and even

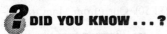

DID YOU KNOW . . . ?

- In June 1991 Colombia's new constitution restored the ancient name "Santa Fe de Bogotá" to the capital that until then had been known only as Bogotá.
- The capital city, Bogotá, is named after a Chibcha Indian chieftain by the same name who resisted the Spaniards.
- When the Spanish arrived in 1499, they found an Indian population that numbered between 1.5 and 2 million.
- By the late 1980s Indians constituted only 1% of the Colombian population.
- From the 17th to the 19th centuries, African slaves were legally imported to the country. Slavery was not abolished until independence from Spain in 1810.
- By the 1860s coffee had emerged as a key export crop. Today it accounts for 60% of the country's export earnings.
- More than 95% of the population has been baptized in the Catholic Church.
- Colombia is about twice as large as France.
- Buenaventura on the Pacific coast is the wettest city in the world, averaging 265 inches of precipitation annually.
- Over 90% of the world's emeralds come from Colombia.

gold and copper weapons. The English-speaking guide explains the historical significance of the treasures. Inexpensive copies of the collection's eye-catching gold masks are sold throughout the city. The collection traces its beginnings back to two early Indian tribes—the Quimbay and the Chibcha, who laboriously fashioned each piece for festivals. The conquistadors in the mid-16th century sent many of the finest pieces to Spain, where presumably they were melted down for gold bullion. An outer room features antique pottery (mostly funeral artifacts) from the same era—roughly 800 to 1,000 years ago.

Make sure you ask the guard on the third floor to open the vault, a dark room. Gradually the room is illuminated, and you'll realize you are completely surrounded by gold. The effect is overwhelming. Don't leave without viewing the world's four largest emeralds—the largest is 1,795 carats—on display here.

Admission: 75¢; children under 7 half price.

Open: Tues–Sat 9am–4pm; Sun and hol 9am–noon. Films in English are shown at 10am and 2:30pm (on Sunday at 11am).

MUSEO DE ARTE MODERNO, Calle 24, no. 6-55. Tel. 286-0466.

Works by outstanding Colombian artists, as well as other South American artists, are displayed here. Founded in 1955, it is home to the largest collection of contemporary art in the country.

Admission: 50¢.
Open: Tues–Sun 9am–7pm.

MUSEO DE ARTE COLONIAL, Carrera 6, no. 9-77. Tel. 241-6017.

This museum, which specializes in Spanish-colonial art (1650–1800), is between Calles 9 and 10. Erected behind mammoth 17th-century–style stone walls, it is marked by massive wooden doors and Moorish archways that lead into eight rooms, each housing paintings, sculpture, silver, or furniture.

Admission: 25¢.
Open: Tues–Sat 9:30am–6:30pm; Sun and hols 10am–5pm.

MUSEO DE ARTES Y TRADICIONES POPULARES, Carrera 8, no. 7-21. Tel. 284-5319.

This enchanting museum, in an old monastery near Plaza Bolívar, displays the handcrafts produced throughout Colombia. A small shop sells many of the handmade items on display at very good prices. Colorful woven baskets, rugs, woodcarvings, and ceramics make great home accessories. Stop in **Claustro de San Agustín** for a cool drink or a sandwich. The shop and restaurant are open every day.

Admission: 50¢.
Open: Tues–Sun 9am–5:30pm.

MUSEO NACIONAL, Carrera 7, no. 28-66. Tel. 334-2129.
The best historical museum is located between Calles 28 and 29. The building was once a prison—and it looks it. The formidable graystone walls could use sandblasting, or just blasting, to make the building resemble what it has been since 1948—a repository for historical documents relating to the Colombian revolution and a home for archeological finds as well.
Admission: Fri–Wed 15¢; Thurs free (children under 5 not admitted).
Open: Tues–Sat 9:30am–6:30pm; Sun 10am–5pm.

MUSEO DE 20 DE JULIO, Calle 11, no. 6-94. Tel. 334-4150.
If you'd like to see the famous press that was used to print Colombia's *Rights of Man* petition during the revolution, drop in at the charming Museo de 20 de Julio, near Carrera 7, which houses other remembrances of Colombia's bolt for freedom in the early 19th century. Often called **La Casa del Florero ("House of the Flower Vase")**, the museum was named after an incident on July 20, 1810, that helped trigger the revolution. It seems that the owner of the house then located on the site was severely lashed after refusing to lend a handsome flower vase to the Spaniards for use at a reception. The house and the vase thus became a symbol against tyranny. The museum is housed in an authentic early, 19th-century structure and presents a vivid example of the architecture of the period.
Admission: 25¢ adults, 10¢ children.
Open: Tues–Sat 9:30am–6:30pm, Sun 10am–5pm.

QUINTA DE BOLÍVAR, Calle 20, no. 3-23. Tel. 284-6819.
A quarter mile from the funicular at Mt. Monserrate is the widely visited home of Simón Bolívar, now a mansionlike museum of the colonial era. Built in 1800, the structure was given to Bolívar after the revolution, and he lived there from 1826 to 1828. The cannons are relics of the war of independence. In 1966 a summit meeting of the presidents of Chile, Venezuela, and Colombia was held here.
Admission: 35¢ adults, 10¢ children.
Open: Tues–Sun 10am–6pm.

MUSEO DE ARTE RELIGIOSO DEL BANCO DE LA REPUBLICA, Calle 11, no. 4-93. Tel. 243-7200.
The Museum of Religious Art does not have a permanent collection but exhibits works borrowed from monasteries and churches throughout Colombia. It is located in a lovely home in the Candelaría, Bogotá's colonial neighborhood.
Admission: 50¢.
Open: Mon–Fri 9am–5pm; Sat 9am–4pm; Sun 9am–noon.

MUSEO ARQUEOLOGICO, Carrera 6, no. 7-43. Tel. 282-0940.
The Archeological Museum is located in the house of the Marquis of St. George (Marques de San Jorge), one of the most beautiful buildings in the city. Recently remodeled, the original dates from the 17th century and houses one of the best pre-Columbian pottery collections in the world. Each whitewashed room is built around an inner patio, with gushing fountains and lush plants. There's an inexpensive restaurant for lunch only.
Admission: 50¢.
Open: Tues–Fri 9:30am–noon; Sat 1–5pm; Sun 10am–1pm.

CANO GALLERY, Carrera 13, no. 27-80. Tel. 242-8851.
This contains the private collection of artifacts gathered by the Cano family over the last 50 years. Gold, jewelry, ceramics, tombs, and semiprecious stones are on exhibit. Demonstrations of different methods used by the ancient artist are given, as are slide shows.
Admission: Free.
Open: Mon–Sat 9am–7pm.

MORE ATTRACTIONS

MT. MONSERRATE

Tourists from all over Colombia stream into Bogotá on Sunday for the trek to the top of 2,500-foot Mt. Monserrate. Not only is there a magnificent view of the capital, but the hillside takes on a festival air. Vendors hawking candy, food, and trinkets wind their way through picnicking families sprawled on the grass, drinking in the clean, crisp air. The Sabana plain, on which Bogotá rests, is visible for miles and miles beyond the city limits. Bogotá itself is fully visible, down to the red-tile roofs in the old section. Visible, too, is **Mt. Guadalupe,** accessible only by car, which is marked by a huge statue at the top. (*Warning:* Do not drive to Mt. Guadalupe unless you're part of an organized group tour. It's a lonely road with many reported crimes.)

You can enjoy a sandwich and soft drink at the mountaintop **Panorama** restaurant while viewing the countryside through the windows. Little wonder that families often travel up to eight hours to spend half that time here. There are many *artesanía* shops to browse in.

The world-famous church and shrine located here draws hundreds each week to the **Lord of Monserrate,** a statue in a glass case elevated on an altar. Many kiss the glass in penance and then pray in the neighboring chapel for escape from afflictions.

GETTING TO THE TOP You have two choices in your ascent—either a 7-minute ($2.75) funicular ride (100 passengers) that carries you through a 750-foot-long tunnel excavated out of the mountainside; or via a cable car called a *teleférico*, holding 40, that puts you at topside in 3 minutes for the same $2.75. The one-car *teleférico* is not only more comfortable but far more scenic, since it makes an outside ascent. Incidentally, the 80J slope near the peak on the funicular is literally breathtaking.

Note: The *teleférico* runs regularly—normally, every half hour—from 9am to 11pm every day. The funicular runs only on Sunday. Because of the current situation in Colombia, we do not recommend that you hike to the top of Monserrate.

THE PLANETARIUM, Calle 26, at the corner of Carrera 7. Tel. 243-9726.

The planetarium, located next to the bullring in the Parque de la Independencia not only offers fascinating views of the heavens but also is home to a large collection of works by Colombian artists and host to many temporary exhibitions.

Admission: 25¢.

Open: Tues–Fri 9am–5pm; Sat–Sun 10am–5pm. Shows are held at 11am and 3:15 and 5:15pm.

COOL FOR KIDS

EL SALITRE PARK, Calle 63, between Carrera 50 and Avenida 68.

A great place to go with the kids, this park has a playground and some rides as well as a small lake.

Open: Mon–Sat 8am–6pm.

JAIME DUQUE PARK, Central Road, via Tibitó (Autopista Norte, km 34).

The highlight here is the monorail that travels over a large relief map of Colombia, detailing the characteristic landscape of the different regions of the country. There is a mini amusement park here, as well as the Museum of Man, home to the largest collection of wax figures in Latin America.

Open: Sat noon–6:30pm; Sun and hols 10am–6:30pm.

MUNDO DE FANTASIA, Calle 19, between Carreras 6 and 7.

Located across from the Hotel Dann International, this mini amusement park (or Fantasy World) with games and rides is a convenient in-town place to take the kids.

RODEOLANDIA, Autopista Norte, Km 20 Chía. Tel. 676-0017.

The kids will love this one. It has a mini amusement park, lovely gardens, and rooms for children's parties. There is also a restaurant here.
Open: Sat noon–6pm; Sun and hols 10am–6pm.

WALKING TOURS

COLONIAL BOGOTA As in all our cities, we recommend a leisurely stroll through Bogotá on your first day here. Our walking tour can be wrapped up in about one hour and starts at the imposing **Plaza de Bolívar,** Carrera 7 between Calles 10 and 11. Here you roam about benches and statuary and resting Bogotanos. Look around at the magnificent Athenian-style **Capitol** building, where Congress convenes, and the 400-year-old **National Cathedral** (built in 1572 but renovated several times since), graced with jewel-encrusted monstrances and the famous **Chapel of El Sagrario.** Dominating the plaza is an enormous statue of Simón Bolívar. (Paradoxically, Colombians fervently hail Bolívar for freeing them from Spain. Yet, this country clings to more of old Spain's traditions than any other Latin American nation.)

Leading away from the plaza are the steep, narrow streets of the famous **Barrio de la Candelaría,** the nucleus of the city during colonial days. Here you'll get a glimpse into early Bogotá, for this area has hardly changed in 200 years. Typically, the buildings here are one- or two-story brown adobes with barred windows, massive wooden doors, and red-tile roofs. Inner cobblestone courtyards seem to be standard in many homes. Look carefully at the street signs. The faded colonial designations over the modern street names are still visible.

Stroll up Calle 10 and after half a block you'll find yourself in the lovely **Plaza San Carlos,** studded with palm trees and surrounded on three sides by historic structures dating back to the 1600s. Owned and preserved by the University of America Foundation, the buildings include the house of Bolívar's mistress, Dona Manuela Saenz, and the printing shop where the famous *Rights of Man* was printed just prior to Colombia's revolution in 1810. A bigger-than-life reproduction of the text covers the far wall of the plaza. Be sure to take a peek inside the **Church of San Ignacio,** opposite the plaza.

Another block up, beyond Carrera 6, is the striking **San Carlos Palace,** home of Colombia's president, where handsomely uniformed guards parade in precise routines that never seem to vary. The palace, which houses much of Colombia's prized art, is open to the public. A few steps down from the main entrance to the palace is the window through which Bolívar fled to avoid being assassinated. Visiting hours are Monday to Friday from 9am to 5pm. Admission is free. Across the street is the **Teatro Colón,** Bogotá's cultural center, which houses in one structure the city's ballet, opera, and theater companies. (See "Evening Entertainment" for specifics.)

Turn right on Carrera 6 and just beyond Calle 11 you'll find a small jewel—the nine-room **Museo de 20 de Julio,** a perfect example of Spanish-colonial architecture. Just beyond the museum is Bogotá's main shopping thoroughfare, bustling **Carrera 7,** normally jammed with pedestrians and cars. Head right on Carrera 7; four blocks down is a main intersection, at Avenida Jimenez. Off to the right is the sleekly modern **Banco de la República,** and behind it at Carrera 6 and Calle 16 is the remarkable **Museo del Oro** (Gold Museum). On your left is the venerable **San Francisco Church.** Now four centuries old, it is a magnificent example of Latin American baroque architecture.

You have the choice now of continuing along Carrera 7 to the Tequendama Hotel and the pink bullring just beyond it; or you might amble along Avenida Jimenez to either Carrera 10 or 14. Both these streets wind up at the Tequendama as well. If you prefer browsing in shops, stick to Carrera 7.

MODERN BOGOTA To see the other side of Bogotá—new, fresh, and modern— set aside one afternoon and head out to Carrera 15 and Calle 76. Start at the **Centro Comercial El Lago,** a shopping center with fine boutiques and a La Fragata restaurant branch. After browsing, head back to Carrera 15 and head out toward the higher numbers. You'll pass modern boutiques, tea shops, restaurants, private homes, and clubs. Plan to walk to Calle 95. At Calle 90 you enter Chico, Bogotá's chicest area.

Unicentro, one of the largest and most modern shopping centers in South America, is located on Calle 127 and Carrera 15. The bilevel center is a complex of department stores, boutiques, restaurants, movie theaters, and nightspots. You can nosh on pizza at Pizza Nostra or Little John's or sample a knockwurst at Taberna Baur or the Plaza Café. Edelweiss is a rather nice German restaurant, and Uni-club is the deluxe eatery here. A bus (30¢) or a taxi ($3) will take you there from downtown.

Hacienda Santa Barbara, Bogotá's new shopping center, is located in a stunning 19th-century hacienda in this residential area (Carrera 7, no. 115–60). It has branch stores of well-known international boutiques as well as restaurants and cinemas.

7. SPORTS & RECREATION

SPORTS

BULLFIGHTING First-class bullfighting can be seen between December and February at the **Plaza de Toros de Santa María,** at Carrera 6 and Calle 26, every Saturday and Sunday beginning at 3pm. The best seat (*barrera*) can cost as much as $25, but you can get a bleacher ticket (*sol*) for $6.35. Novices take over from March to November, and you can see a fair match for $5 general admission. Off-season top tickets are only $10.

FUTBOL On most Sunday afternoons starting at 3pm, local sports fans who are not at the bullring are certainly at **El Campin Stadium,** Avenida 57, near Carrera 28, where 40,000 *futból* (soccer) devotees are packed into the 30,000-seat park. The best seat is $6.25, with general admission at 75¢. Take a cab ($1).

THE TRACK Another Sunday (and Thursday) afternoon event that draws the sports-minded is racing at the **Hipódromo Techo,** located on the Avenida de las Americas (a cab costs under $1 and is recommended). A day at the races will run you under $10 allowing for the admission, the minimum bet (*apuesto*) per race, and transportation. Races are on Thursday and Sunday, and the festivities get under way at 10am. A new racetrack, **Los Andes,** has opened north of the city. Admission is $1.50 (tel. 272-3243 for information).

TEJO A popular Indian game that loosely resembles horseshoes, *tejo* is played by farm workers in the rear of small rural taverns and restaurants. If you take an excursion, you'll see the game being played in the countryside. Some games are played near the bullring.

RECREATION

Although there is no outdoor swimming in Bogotá, you can take an excursion to the warmer climates, particularly **Giradot** ($10 round trip for a 3-hour bus ride), where you can swim in a hotel pool. Even closer is **Melgar,** 1½ hours away.

8. SAVVY SHOPPING

Emeralds are the thing here—see "Emeralds" below for information about judging and buying them. Other fine buys in Bogotá are wood handicrafts, ceramics, brass and copper pieces, and Indian masks.

Most stores are open Monday to Friday from 9am to noon and 2 to 7pm (Saturday from 9am to noon and 2 to 7pm; however, Saturday hours vary from store to store, so check ahead). Unicentro and Hacienda Santa Barbara shops are open from 10am to 7pm.

A BEST BUY — THE WORLD'S BEST COFFEE

Using Juan Valdez, the National Federation of Coffee Growers of Colombia (Federacafe, for short) spends a great deal of money promoting the viewpoint that this country's coffee is the best anywhere. More than 80% of the foreign exchange pouring into Colombia derives from overseas coffee sales. Federacafe represents 200,000 coffee growers, most of whom have coffee plantations of under 8 acres. Four out of five coffee farms are owner-operated. The federation bolsters the coffee industry by curtailing foreign sales during high-supply periods when ruinous price wars could develop. Moreover, the organization supports local prices by buying the farmers' coffee when prices fall below a certain level. The purchased coffee is stored until world demand picks up, when it is sold at better prices.

As an indication of the size of this country's coffee market, keep in mind that the United States buys about $250 million worth of Colombian coffee annually.

SHOPPING FROM A TO Z
ANTIQUES
ANTIGUEDADES, Carrera 7, no. 10-66.
Antiguedades has both originals and reproductions. Although the outlet is small, the values and quality are high.

JOYERÍA CLASICA, Avenida Jimenez, no. 5-06.
For antique items in pottery—some as old as 2,000 years—try Joyería Clasica. Prices range from $6 to $100. Also on display are silver and gold jewelry items, coins, and ruanas.

ARTESANIAS
Colombia's handicrafts vary by region. Colorful hammocks, straw hats, baskets, and carnival masks are produced in villages along the Caribbean, while the Andean region is best known for beautiful ceramic items, including scaled-down reproductions of typical rural houses and markets as well as knitted garments, blankets, and tapestries handmade from pure wool.

ARTESANIAS DE COLOMBIA, at the Iglesia de Las Aguas, Carrera 3, no. 18-60. Tel. 284-03095.
For the best in handmade leather, wool, straw, or ceramics, try this nonprofit establishment. The outlet is worth browsing around, for the large variety of attractive items from all over Colombia. Prices are rock-bottom. Open Monday to Friday from 10am to 7pm and Saturday from 9am to 2pm. A more convenient outlet is on Carrera 10 (no. 26-50). Another branch is located in the San Felipe fortress in Cartagena.

ASSOCIACION COLOMBIANA DE PROMOCION ARTESANAL, Carrera 8, no. 7-21, beyond Plaza Bolívar.
Actually a museum of *artesanías,* the setting is in a magnificent Spanish-colonial house, set around a patio. Choose from the matted rugs, wicker items, colonial art, baskets, dolls, pottery, wood, and much more. Prices start at as little as $1.

CASA GRISON, Carrera 10, no. 26.
Casa Grison has an unusual assortment of copper mobiles, gaily painted ceramic salt and pepper shakers, and beautiful brass urns.

MUSEO DEL COBRE (Copper Museum), Avenida Jimenez, no. 14-40.
Consider purchasing brass and copper artesanías here. True to its name, this is more of a museum than a shop. Spread over three floors, the copper and brass items range from souvenirs to large pitchers, pots, plates, and candlesticks.

EMERALDS (ESMERALDAS)

Colombia is the world's greatest source of emeralds, the brilliant-green gems that rank above diamonds in the jewelry hierarchy. The finest varieties come from the mines of Muzo, Cosquez, Gachala, and Chivor.

The most important attribute of an emerald is its color. It varies from light to very dark green; the most desirable and rarest shade is an intensive dark green without noticeable blue or yellow tint. Emeralds are not free from imperfections. In fact the ever-present crystallization marks (called *jardín* by connoisseurs) produce the velvet effect of the true emerald; and irregular light reflections through the crystallization cause the special glimmer, found only in emeralds, often called "green fire."

In the evaluation of emeralds, size is also of great importance, as the larger gems, which are translucent and of good color, are very rare. All factors considered, unset emeralds can range from as little as $50 up to $10,000 and more per karat. In general, unset polished stones offer the best values. As emeralds are difficult to evaluate, a guarantee is offered only by reliable jewelers up to date on gem research. So shop carefully.

For the best orientation, your first stop should be the **Jewelry Center** stores, Calle 12 between Carreras 6 and 7, which feature extensive selections in all price ranges. Definitely browse here from store to store to get a feel for prices and design. Then try browsing in the shops on and around Carrera 10, between Calles 26 and 30. When you've "done" the jewelry centers, your next stop should be H. Stern.

H. STERN, in the Hotel Tequendama, Carrera 10, no. 26-71. Tel. 283-2819.

This international jewelry concern features the highest-quality emeralds and offers an emerald guarantee accepted worldwide. You'll find items from $100 up to $5,000 and even higher. And 18-karat gold rings with small emeralds start at $150. Popular men's items are the 18-karat gold tie tacks with top-quality small emeralds. Browse all you want—there's no sales pressure here. If you make a purchase, you get an incredible one-year money-back guarantee. (The New York branch, at 645 Fifth Avenue, will refund your money.)

Other H. Stern outlets are in the Hacienda Santa Barbara Shopping Center (tel. 612-1895); the Orquidea Real Hotel; at the airport; and at the Puente Aereo Avianca, the Avianca airshuttle between Bogotá, Cali, and Medellín.

JOYERÍA EL LAGO, Carrera 7, no. 16-46, in the Edificio Avianca.

Here you can pick up interesting replicas in gold of items from the Gold Museum. Earrings, rings, and tie pins are big sellers. El Lago also has an outlet in the Edificio Bavaria, at Carrera 10, no. 27-63.

WILLIS F. BRONKIE, in the Edificio Bavaria, Carrera 9, no. 74-08, Office 1203. Tel. 211-4621.

This store has a large selection of choice unpolished and polished stones, women's rings, earrings, and bracelets, and a varied men's selection as well. Ask to see the film about emerald mining and production. Outstanding buys include rings with rough emeralds from $50, bracelet charms with rough emeralds for $25, and earrings from $30 and up. Other good buys are gold-finished emerald tie pins and tie tacks. There is a branch of Willis F. Bronkie in the Hacienda Santa Barbara Shopping Center.

FASHIONS

LULIETH, in the Hotel Dann, Avenida 19.

An interesting boutique for men and women is Lulieth. The men's shop is upstairs on the left; women should try the downstairs shop. There are excellent values in macramé shawls and ruanas.

LEATHER

Bogotá is home to a great many leather shops whose prices range from fairly inexpensive to expensive. A good choice is **Boots N' Bags** with branches in the

Hotel Tequendama; in the Unicentro and Hacienda Santa Barbara Shopping Centers; and at Calle 19, no. 5-35. **Cuerolandia** is nearby on Calle 19, no. 4-90, with additional branches in the Hotels Tequendama and the Bogotá Royal. **Tapir** is at Calle 19, no. 4-24 (tel. 282-8296).

PRE-COLOMBIAN ART

Bogotá is the place for collectors of ceramics dating back 2,000 years or so. The ceramics are primarily funeral objects that have been retrieved from tombs. The Indians believed in life after death, and many of the possessions of the deceased were buried with him or her in the belief that they would be necessary in the afterlife. They were buried as deep as 30 feet in order to be preserved against dampness. Many shops selling these items are scattered throughout the city.

JAIME ERRAZURIZ, in the lobby of the Hotel Tequendama, Carrera 10, no. 26-71. Tel. 334-1961.

Your first stop should definitely be at the exposition of Chilean-born Jaime Errazuriz, on the ramp in the main entrance to the hotel. While prices here are not low, the quality is high, and you need not worry about misrepresentations. You can buy small figures for as little as $15. Mr. Errazuriz is one of Colombia's great authorities on pre-Colombian art. He is a lecturer on the subject and has written books on the Tumaco culture. Incidentally, you'll receive a certificate identifying and authenticating your purchase. Jaime has another shop in the old city in Cartegena and has proudly announced the opening of third shop in his native Chile, on Avenida Suecia, in the Providencia section of Santiago.

PRE-COLOMBIANOS SAN DIEGO SHOP, in the Tequendama Center.

This large shop (not the jewelry store in the hotel) has a wide selection of ceramic pieces, jewelry, and stones. The Galera Cano shop nearby is another excellent source for ceramics but is especially proud of their gold reproductions of jewelry.

RECORDS

For the best selection of records and tapes, stop in at any of the **Bambuco** branches along Carrera 7.

9. EVENING ENTERTAINMENT

THE PERFORMING ARTS

THEATERS

TEATRO COLÓN, Calle 10, no. 5-32. Tel. 241-6141.

This old but elegant theater houses every important opera, ballet, concert, and play presented in Bogotá. We saw an impressive performance of *Carmen* here. During one of our visits we were fortunate enough to catch the Venezuelan National Ballet, which was superb. We paid $4 for a good orchestra seat; balcony tickets run as low as $1. The custom here is for two performances per evening, at 6:30 and 9:30pm. Check your hotel clerk for the current attraction and pick up your tickets at the box office.

Prices: Tickets $1–$4.

TEATRO MUNICIPAL, Carrera 7.

Another fine theater, this is between Calles 22 and 23 (box office in front of the theater). For the latest information, check with your hotel clerk.

DINNER WITH MUSIC

GIPSY, Calle 82, no. 13-39. Tel. 257-8772.

Gipsy is a wonderful new addition to Bogotá's list of world-class restaurants. The menu features an extensive selection of nouvelle Colombian dishes, most original creations of Gipsy's master chief. Our recommendations include the pork loin in tamarind sauce, the beef loin in feijoa sauce, and the hage duck. The crayfish caviar in mushroom sauce appetizer is truly exquisite. You'll dine by firelight to the accompaniment of soft bossa nova and jazz in Gipsy's lovely dining room with its indoor gardens and hearth. Open Monday to Saturday noon to midnight.

AS DE COPAS, Carrera 13 and Calle 59, in Chapinero. Tel. 249-0710.

The flamenco beat floods the atmosphere at the candlelit As De Copas, located farther out from center city, where the food is as Spanish as the music. Situated off a small street, the Copas is marked by a large sign that highlights a guitar, the dominant instrument in the 9:15pm nightly music. Try the *langostino* (shrimp) for $6 or the *arroz con pollo* for $5; drinks are a high $3.50. A show kicks off nightly at midnight, and there is dancing. Open for lunch; closing time is 3am.

TIERRA COLOMBIA, Carrera 10, no. 27-27. Tel. 234-9525.

Here you can catch a colorful *folklorico* show while dining on native fare. There's an excellent selection of *típico* and international dishes, and the show here is first rate. However, a word of caution is necessary: Prices are high! The Tierra Colombia must be planned as "big night out" only. Reservations are a must.

LAS RAMBLAS, Avenida 13, no. 79-90, in Centro Comercial Los Heroes. Tel. 257-4370.

Another good spot to enjoy a colorful *folklórico* show while dining on native fare is Las Ramblas, known for its enormous and delicious paellas. These, made with lobster chunks, chicken, and sausage, or a variety of shellfish are a perfect dinner, especially with a bottle of good Chilean wine. The show, which starts at 9pm, often features folk dancers and singers.

GREENHOUSE, Calle 73, no. 10-70.

Greenhouse is a lovely restaurant; plants all around will make you feel as if you were in a greenhouse. There's live music in the evenings and, management permitting, you can dance until dawn. The kitchen is open until 11pm.

THE CLUB & MUSIC SCENE
DISCOS & DANCE CLUBS

Once a town that slept at night, Bogotá now has a nightlife scene that is starting to come into its own. The city's hottest clubs are in the area known as **La Zona Rosa,** the Pink Zone. This strip of Calle 82, between Carreras 11 and 15, is filled with discos, bars, restaurants, and chic boutiques—all of which cater to affluent young Bogotanos. Most of the clubs here play the same music as is heard in their North American and European counterparts, primarily house, rap, and hip hop. Doors usually open around 9pm. The most popular clubs in this area include:

Bar La Rockola, Carrera 11, no. 84-18.
La Cave Bar, Carrera 13, no. 82-25. Tel. 257-9934.
Friday's Bar Restaurante, Calle 82, no. 12-18. Tel. 218-2610.
Up & Down Bar, Carrera 13, no. 81-29. Tel. 218-1163.
Keops Club, Calle 96, no. 10-54. Tel. 218-2258.
Michelangelo, Calle 94, no. 11-46.
Stefanos, Carrera 7, no. 133-95.

MARIACHI CLUBS

In Chapinero, next to one another are three mariachi clubs where the nightly crowds attest to the good food, camaraderie, and fun. **El Gran Garibaldi,** at Carrera 7, no. 59-56 (street level), is probably the most popular of the three. Next door is **La Ronda,** at no. 59-34. Upstairs is **Rafael,** at no. 59-30. Each club has a two-drink minimum per person, and drinks run about $2.50 to $3. The orchestra starts at 9pm. Each club has beamed ceilings and a Mexican decor.

A mariachi club downtown that serves up authentic Mexican food and lively music is **Guadalajara,** at Carrera 7, no. 30-04. Customers here sing along with the strolling musicians who wear sombreros and serapes. Occasionally on a Saturday night there will be a cockfight.

If you like flamenco music, try the **Club Cacique** at the Hotel El Presidente. You can enjoy your cocktails for $2 to $3 while seated in a black-leather chair in this intimate club (no cover or minimum). A three-piece flamenco group entertains you.

CLUBS WITH A VIEW

CLUB MASSEI, Via a la Calera at Km 4. Tel. 610-4664.

To escape civilization, yet keep the lights of Bogotá in view at the same time, jump in a cab and go on safari at Club Massei, located in the wilds above Bogotá. But don't expect to find solitude here. Massei is one of Bogotá's hottest clubs and attracts a mixed crowd of yuppies and students.

Using the wide-open plains of Africa as his theme, owner Rafael Alba took advantage of the excellent location when he built Massei. The club is spacious, with tables set up on various levels surrounding the dance floor in the center. Windows covering the entire side of the club facing Bogotá give it an open feeling, not to mention a magnificent view of the city. The African theme is even carried over to the cocktails. One that sticks in our minds, "La Jirafa" (The Giraffe) is a potent mixture of rum, vodka, crème de café, and tropical juices. Most drinks are $3.50, but you'll pay more for the exotic ones.

SALON MONSERRATE, on the 17th floor of the Hotel Tequendama, Carrera 10, no. 26-21. Tel. 286-1111, ext. 2112.

If you can't get to our out of town choices, this is a fine compromise, located on the rooftop of the Hotel Tequendama. Rest assured that the setting and service will be impeccable.

TRAMONTI, Carrera 1, no. 93-50, Via a la Calera. Tel. 218-6460.

Tramonti is the ideal place for after-dinner relaxation. You can sit endlessly, nursing a drink or two while you admire the lights of Bogotá below or the stars above.

THE BAR SCENE

For that late-afternoon cocktail, by all means meet at the lobby bar of the **Orquidea Real Hotel,** at Carrera 7, no. 32-16. Great after a day of sightseeing are the comfortable leather chairs or couches. Drinks run about $3.50.

More reserved is the intimate **Bar Chispas,** on the main floor of the Tequendama Hotel, where you can have a quiet cocktail until 2am (3am on weekends). While drinks are about $3 each, there is no cover or minimum. Recorded music provides pleasant background in a lovely, relaxed atmosphere.

The **Den,** Carrera 14, no. 85-24, is a good choice if you're looking for a place to relax and have a drink. Its homey interior and friendly atmosphere make it a favorite after-work meeting place. **Lloyd's Pub,** on Calle 94, at Carrera 14, (tel. 610-3169), is also a favorite watering hole among Bogotanos. There's often live music.

MORE ENTERTAINMENT

MOVIES Colombians cannot seem to get enough of English-language films; consequently almost every downtown theater seems to feature one U.S. or British flick. Stick to Carrera 7 for the best movie houses. Admission is about $1. For schedules, check the cinema section of *El Tiempo,* the local daily here.

GAMBLING Gambling has become discreetly popular in Bogotá. There are no big casinos or Vegas-type shows, but lots of small clubs have opened for roulette, blackjack, and other games (no slot machines). Our favorites are **C R Casino,** in fashionable Chico at Carrera 14, no. 90-23; and **Casino Versailles,** at Carrera 10, no. 27, in Tequendama arcade. **El Caesar,** at Calle 93A, no. 14-11, draws the high rollers. The city's newest casino, the **Casino Monseignor** in the Hotel Orquídea Real on Carrera 7, no. 32-16, does have slot machines.

10. EASY EXCURSIONS

ZIPAQUIRA

How about a visit to an underground cathedral located in a salt mine half a mile below ground? One of the wonders of Latin America is the huge **Zipaquira Cathedral,** which draws thousands of worshipers and tourists each week to this town (pop. 30,000), 35 miles from Bogotá. The region, which has vast salt resources, is noted, too, for the finest beef cattle in Colombia. The country's better restaurants and private clubs serve Zipaquira beef, exclusively. But salt was the major economic bulwark for many years, and as a tribute to the blessings it brought to the community, a cathedral was erected in a salt mine. Visitors flock here from throughout the continent to worship at an altar carved out of salt rock within walls made of salt. Roads have been built into the mine and cars drive right to the cathedral. We're told there's enough salt in the mine to supply the world for 100 years. Open Monday to Friday from 10am to 1pm and Sunday and holidays until 4pm.

GETTING THERE The least expensive way is by bus ($3 each way), which takes 1½ hours from downtown Bogotá and passes through the lovely northern residential section and into the countryside, where Indians and donkeys are a common sight. From anywhere along Avenida Caracas (Carrera 14), take a bus marked ZIPA that will be heading north toward the higher-numbered streets. The fare is collected en route, and you exit at the town square. The walk from the village to the cathedral is uphill and will take you less than half an hour. If you prefer, an inexpensive cab ride will take you right into the mine for $2. You can easily walk back to the center of town.

If you prefer a package tour, any travel agency will handle it for you ($16 per person). Ask your desk clerk.

TEQUENDAMA WATERFALL

Nineteen miles south of Bogotá, over the southern highway, are the 450-foot **Bogotá River Falls,** which for years were a major tourist attraction. Sadly, they opened a hydroelectric plant up the river from the falls in 1975. Since then the falls have literally been turned off. They are still worth a trip, as the area is very beautiful. You'll also enjoy seeing the turn-of-the-century hotel that sits on a precipice. It is closed to the public for that reason; but for those with a romantic nature, it's fun to gaze at the hotel and imagine what it was like in its heyday, when it served as a honeymoon spot for wealthy newlyweds.

GETTING THERE Make the 40-minute trip to the falls on a modern bus operated by **Flota Macarena** ($2.50 round trip). The buses leave every half hour, starting at 4:30am, from the new bus terminal that has been built south of the city—Terminal de Transportes Terrestres, at Calle 33B, no. 69-35. It's quite impressive, with shops and restaurants. To reach the terminal, look for the special bus stop at Calle 13, no. 15.

MONOLITHS IN SAN AGUSTIN

Some 300 miles southeast of Bogotá lies Colombia's archeological equivalent of Peru's Machú Picchú—the monolith-strewn ruins of San Agustín, which archeologists trace back to the time of the Golden Age of Greece (500 B.C.). This incredible site has yielded thousands of sculptures, ranging in height from a foot or so to 10 feet and more, as well as temples and shrines and tombs. The sculptures were first written about in the mid-18th century, but it wasn't until 1913 that serious digging began

(Machú Picchú was uncovered by Hiram Bingham in 1911). In 1935 the Colombian government wisely purchased the sites containing the principal ruins.

THE RUINS Hundreds of stone statues, most of which were originally buried (many in tombs), have been uncovered. The ruins are scattered over a large area. Your first day should be set aside for a visit to **Parque Arqueologico de San Agustín,** where the principal monuments are located, the most famous of which is the huge **Fuente de Lavapatas** (foot-washing fountain), a ceremonial fountain carved by natives in the bare rock. A brook winds its way through the carved human and animal figures (monkeys, serpents, and lizards). Many anthropologists speculate that the site was probably used for sacrificial ceremonies. A great deal has been learned of the lifestyle of the original inhabitants from these numerous sculptures.

The archeological park, about 2 miles from San Agustín, also has a museum (with stone and ceramic objects) and the **Forest of Statues** (approximately 35 in all) located along the path amid the forest. These statues typically are excavated funeral art. Before leaving this area, make sure to visit the **Doble Yo** ("Double I") sculpture on the Alto de Lavapatas, one of the many samples of a statue containing a second face (sometimes that of an animal). There are many efforts psychologically to explain this art as representing man's alter ego.

Your next visit should be to **El Alto de Los Idolos,** near San José, 18 miles from the park. Here you'll find huge statues and colorfully decorated tombs. Most of the finds here were uncovered after 1970.

Time permitting, you should then consider heading for **Alto de Las Piedras,** which is located beyond Alto de Los Idolos on the road that passes San José de Isnos to Pitalito. This "hill of stones" contains some marvelous statues. Note **La Gordita,** literally a fat woman, but actually a symbol of fertility, as well as the **Doble Yo statue.** There are more sites to see, and the Government Tourist Office in San Agustín will offer all the assistance you'll need.

The best way to tour the park is to rent a Jeep in San Agustín or Neiva and drive along the tree-lined paths that meander through the park crossing small streams. The statues pop up all along the road. Other exploring options include horseback and foot power. Don't forget to buy a map and guidebook (sort of in English) at the entrance or at the tourist office in town.

GETTING THERE Many travelers head to San Agustín via organized tours. Any travel agent would be glad to make these arrangements for you. Check with your hotel clerk. Do-it-yourselfers should note that there is air service from Bogotá to Neiva. Schedules vary. A good airline is **Aires,** at Carrera 13, no. 35-39 (tel. 257-3000), in Bogotá. From Neiva you can rent a car or Jeep for the trip to San Agustín.

The road from Neiva passes through **Garzon** (halfway between Neiva and San Agustín) and Pitalito (an hour—20 miles—from San Agustín). Neiva is approximately 180 miles from San Agustín and 6 hours away by auto. The roads are fair. (Public buses take some 8 hours and cost about $10 to San Agustín.)

Another way is to go via bus or special taxi directly from Bogotá. **Coomotor,** at Carrera 25, no. 15-36, operates buses that leave on the hour from 4am to 10am. The trip takes 12 hours, and the one-way fare is $18. Your hotel clerk will give you the information you need about the *taxis verdes,* which offer service to San Agustín from Bogotá via Neiva.

WHERE TO STAY You have your choice of staying in San Agustín itself or in nearby Neiva, Garzon, or Pitalito. In San Agustín, you can stay at the 27-room **Hotel Yalconia** (tel. 37-3013), where doubles run $28 and singles are $25. This state-run hostelry has a pool and is right near the park. Many budget travelers prefer the more rustic **Hotel Osoguaico** (tel. 73069), which is about half a mile from the park. Boasting a restaurant, sauna, and campsites, the Osoguaico charges $10 per double for its 29 rooms. The **Hotel Central,** at Calle 3, no. 10-44, offers 25 clean and well-maintained rooms, with private bath, for $6 single and $10 double.

In Pitalito, your first choice should be the **Hotel Calamo,** located in the heart of town at Carrera 5, no. 5-41 (tel. 6-0600), which offers air-conditioned rooms, a pool, and a restaurant in a modern setting. Each of the 24 double rooms costs $20. The **Pigoanza,** nearby at Calle 6, no. 4-42 (tel. 6-0430), has bathless rooms at $7 double; it's rather basic. The **Timanco,** at 1 Sur Via a San Agustín (tel. 6-0666), has 22 rooms, all with private bath, at $15.

In Neiva, the three best stops are the 97-room **Hotel Plaza,** at Calle 7, no. 4-62 (tel. 2-3980), which has a pool and a disco. Rooms are air-conditioned and run $15 for a double. The nearby **Hotel Arayaco,** at Calle 8, no. 3-26 (tel. 2-6695), has 50 air-conditioned rooms. Doubles here are $19, and singles are $14. Finally, the **Americano,** at Salida del Sur No. 5 (tel. 2-7778), is a three-star hotel with a pool and steambath. Most rooms are air-conditioned. Doubles run $20, with singles at $15.

CHAPTER 11

WHERE COLOMBIANS PLAY

1. CARTAGENA
2. SANTA MARTA
3. SAN ANDRES ISLAND

At the top of Colombia, on the Caribbean, are two resort cities, Cartagena and Santa Marta—only an hour from Bogotá by air—where Colombians throng for holidays and long weekends. A third Latin playground is San Andrés Island, perched in the Caribbean off the coast of Nicaragua some 480 miles northwest of the Colombian mainland. North Americans are discovering all three for different reasons: Cartagena for its Spanish-colonial ambience amid walled fortifications; Santa Marta for its splendid beaches; and San Andrés for its primitive remoteness and marvelous fishing and snorkeling. All are warm year-round. If rates in these towns seem high compared with those in Bogotá, keep in mind that these are resort areas and cater to tourists year-round.

GETTING THERE **Avianca,** the Colombian airline, has one flight (5 hours) a week from New York to Cartagena. At other times, or to go to Santa Marta, fly to the northern coastal city of Barranquilla, then hop a 15-minute shuttle flight east to Santa Marta or west to Cartagena. From Barranquilla, it takes one hour to fly to San Andrés.

ORIENTATION Keep in mind that both Cartagena and Santa Marta use the carrera and calle street system of Bogotá. For example, if a restaurant is at Carrera 4, no. 8-10, this tells you the place is on the fourth carrera, between Calles 8 and 9 at building no. 10. If the address is Calle 6, no. 4-20, then you know that your destination is on the sixth Calle, between Carreras 4 and 5, at building no. 20. Avenidas are exempt from the system. In Cartagena's Old City, however, many streets retain their colonial names.

Important Warning: The running battle between the government and the drug cartels in Colombia poses a significant danger for the traveler, especially in the provincial cities of Medellín and Cali, where the cartels seem to hold sway, and in the capital, Bogotá. Instances of violence continued as we went to press, with bombings in areas visited by tourists.

If you intend to visit Colombia, therefore, call the **U.S. Department of State's Citizens' Emergency Service** (tel. 202/647-5225) in Washington, D.C., on weekdays from 8:15am to 10pm, for an up-to-date report. If you're already in Colombia when you read this, inquire at your embassy in Bogotá about the safety situation in the capital and elsewhere in the country.

1. CARTAGENA

765 miles N of Bogotá

GETTING THERE   By Plane   Chances are you'll fly here from Bogotá, in which case you will fly directly to Cartagena's **Rafael Núñez Airport** in just over one hour. A desk at the airport will call a hotel for you. When you buy your ticket at Avianca in Bogotá, check the price in pesos before paying with a credit card. There is often a big difference in price, and the difference is not in your favor. A round-trip ticket was $140 at the time of this writing.

ESSENTIALS   Fast Facts   There's an **Avianca** office in the Pierino Shopping Center, Laguito, and you should reconfirm your flights here (*note:* imperative for flights within Colombia). The post office is on Avenida Urdaneta, near Avianca. Other than the *cambios* at the major hotels, a good one is the **Banco de la República,** in the Plaza Bolívar in the walled city. **Citibank** is another, near the plaza. If you need a pharmacy, the **Droguería Nueva York** has two well-stocked branches on Avenida San Martín and another on Calle Román downtown. The large one on San Martín is open 24 hours, and there's another one near Pierino Gallo. For picnic lunches or sightseeing excursions, buy your fixings at the market in the Edificio Seguro Bolívar. The **Government Tourist Office** is in the historic home of the Marqués de Valdehoyos on Carrera 3. Maps and brochures (some in English) are available.

Getting Around   Buses (20¢) and cabs (inexpensive) are joined by horse-drawn carriages (get one in front of the Del Caribe—$4 an hour). If you're planning to rent a car, **Hertz** and **National** both have offices in the airport as well as in Bocagrande. Hertz is at Avenida San Martín, No. 6-84 (tel. 65-2852); National is on the corner of Avenida San Martín and Calle 10 (tel. 65-1164).

Much larger than its coastal neighbor, Santa Marta, the walled city of Cartagena is a Caribbean city, where the people (called Costeños, "people of the coast") are much darker than Bogotanos. This is not surprising since the sun beats down ceaselessly, as it does throughout the Caribbean. Afternoon temperatures hover in the upper 80s and 90s Fahrenheit most of the year, while evenings cool down pleasantly. (By the way, there are no real seasons as such. The December to March period is considered summer, but it simply is the dry season. It is more humid June to September.)

The fascinating aspects of Cartagena are the fortresslike walls that surround the city (originally built as protection against pirates) and the faithfully preserved streets and houses of the inner city. Carefully restored, the walls today are much as they were 300 years ago, as is the city itself. Also, there are good beaches with flat, dark sand. The nice balance between history and the beaches gives Cartagena a certain tourist magnetism.

BACKGROUND

One of the oldest cities in the Western Hemisphere, Cartagena was founded by Spanish conquistador Don Pedro de Heredia in 1533, on the site of a small village known as Calamari. Shortly thereafter it became the central depository and port for the gold and riches unearthed by the Spanish explorers in the New World. Gold and

---

IMPRESSIONS

When Colombians spoke about the past I often had the sense of being in a place where history tended to sink, even as it happened, into the traceless solitude of autosuggestion.
—JOAN DIDION, THE WHITE ALBUM, 1979

emeralds were shipped from Cartagena to King Felipe II in Madrid along the legendary ocean highway known as the "Spanish Main."

After the original village was destroyed by fire in 1552, Heredia, who was governor at the time, ordered the city rebuilt with brick, tile, and stone. While a suitable precaution against fire, this was not enough to protect the city against raiding English buccaneers and pirates. The city had met its first defeat in 1544 at the hands of French pirate Robert Baal, who was followed by John Hawkins and the brothers Jean and Martin Côtes; and, of course, the most infamous of all was Sir Francis Drake in 1568. This was to be the last major defeat suffered by the Spaniards. By the middle of the 17th century they had completed construction of a series of 29 forts throughout the city (16 of which are still standing) and had enclosed the city within a protective coral wall, 40 feet high and 60 feet wide.

Cartagena declared its independence from Spain on November 11, 1811, only to be captured by Spanish loyalist troops led by Pablo Morillo 4 years later. With the defeat of the Spanish by Simón Bolívar in 1821, Cartagena was granted permanent independence.

Today Cartagena, located in the state of Bolívar, is the sixth-largest city in Colombia with a population of 530,000. Tourism is one of its top-three industries, and, in keeping with its past, it is an important world center for the emerald industry. UNESCO has awarded the city the designation of World Cultural Heritage Site.

A CAUTIONARY NOTE We have received several letters regarding purse snatchings and pickpockets in the walled city. Virtually every one of these crimes occurred after dark. Crime is serious business no matter what time of day. However, with a little common sense, many of these unpleasant incidents can be avoided. Don't wander around the walled city after dark—it is not well lighted. If you go into the city for dinner, have the restaurant call a cab for you. Don't wear expensive jewelry downtown and leave valuables in your hotel.

ORIENTATION

Hop a cab from Cartagena's modern international airport. The $3.50 ride is a good opportunity to get a feel for the city. First you pass through new suburban areas with neat small homes and manicured lawns, then you skirt the barrios where the poor have only a rickety shack between themselves and the pounding sun, and finally you pass the center of Old Cartagena, where there was once an inner wall designed to separate the wealthy from everyone else. Note, too, the dock area and outdoor markets.

Eventually your cab will slide onto the peninsula of **Bocagrande,** where most of our recommended hotels, restaurants, and beaches are located. But sightseeing will be in the **Old City,** thereby balancing your trip here nicely.

To orient yourself quickly, keep in mind that Cartagena has a large outer wall encircling the Old City, designed originally to keep out the previously mentioned marauding visitors as well as Henry Morgan and Captain Kidd. Each block in the Old City is known by its colonial name, noted on a corner plaque.

MAIN STREETS IN THE OLD CITY Key avenues to familiarize yourself with are **Avenida Venezuela,** which cuts through the Old City from the **Tower of the Clock** northeast to **Cabrero Lake.** Southwest of the tower the street is called **Avenida Blas de Lezo,** which leads to Bocagrande, where most of our recommended hotels are. Following are some important landmarks.

La Puerta del Reloj Actually a gate with a clock on top of it, this spot once served as the entranceway for residents to pass through the old inner wall that in colonial times separated well-to-do homes from the poorer working-class sections. The clock tower was added in the 19th century. As the main entrance to the walled district, the archway leads into the Plaza de los Coches (Carriage Plaza). Now the inner wall has been leveled, except for the area around the clock, and there is free access between all parts of the Old City. The Tower of the Clock is a natural meeting place.

Plaza de la Independencia   Located near the dock area, near the Tower of the Clock, this plaza is actually a small park. Note the outdoor markets nearby.

Plaza de Los Coches   Just beyond the Tower of the Clock in the original inner city, this area has some interesting shops and arcades. The slave market was held here during colonial times.

Plaza Bolívar   Inside the inner city, this small park was named in honor of Simón Bolívar, whose equestrian statue stands in the center. **El Palacio de la Inquisición,** the city's most important example of colonial-style architecture is located here.

Plaza de las Bóvedas   The 47 archways and 23 rooms that make up this plaza were built in 1798. This area was initially used by the Spaniards as barracks and to store provisions and ammunition, only to be turned into dungeons after independence was declared. Today they are home to art galleries, bars, cafés, and handicraft shops. It's located in the northern section of the walled city, between the Santa Clara and the La Tenaza forts. Here is where you get a fine view of Cartagena Bay from atop the outside wall.

Calle Larga   This wide street travels along the dock area and the Centro de Convenciones to the yellow Puente Romana, which connects the mainland with the island of La Manga.

El Monumento a la India Catalina   According to popular legend, Catalina was a beautiful and brave Indian woman from Galerazamba who was captured by Alonso de Ojeda in 1509 and taken to Central America by Diego de Nicueza, where she was sold as a slave in Santo Domingo. She returned to Cartagena in 1533 as Don Pedro de Heredia's interpreter. One of the city's newest monuments, she stands opposite the Puente Chambacú as a proud symbol of the city's Indian ancestry.

BOCAGRANDE   The major street here is **Avenida San Martín.** Most hotels and restaurants are on it, and the bus runs along it, too. San Martín is Carrera 2; the beach street is Carrera 1. The calles are numbered with the lowest numbers at the Hotel del Caribe and the higher near the Old City. The bayfront thoroughfare is Avenida Chile. **El Laguito** is a small peninsula off the tip of Bocagrande, behind the Caribe Hotel. Produced by a vigorous landfill project that took several years, it now has private homes, restaurants, shopping centers, and the Hilton and Las Velas hotels.

WHAT TO SEE & DO

THE TOP ATTRACTIONS

In addition to the sights listed below, you might want to catch a taxi and ask the driver to take you across to **La Manga** and drive along the **Calle Real de la Manga.** The private homes along here are beautiful examples of Cartagena's splendor at the turn of the century. One of the most beautiful is the home of the Romana family. Teresita Romana, author of the best-selling cookbook *Cartagena en la Olla* and one of the family's few surviving members, will be more than happy to show you around. There is a beautiful tile fountain in the front garden, and the huge back patio stretches all the way to the next street.

SAN FELIPE FORTRESS, San Lázaro Hill.

✪   Built between 1536 and 1657, the San Felipe Fortress is considered the masterpiece of Spanish military engineering in the New World. This massive fort commands a magnificent view of the approaches to Cartagena, sitting 135 feet above sea level on the summit of the San Lázaro Hill. Besides its imposing size and strategic location, the fortress features an ingenious network of subterranean tunnels and galleries that you may visit with a guide. A sound-and-light show re-creates the era Saturdays at 8pm (in Spanish only). Admission is $1. A very good handcraft store is located here, Artesanías de Colombia; part of a government-operated chain, it has another shop in Plaza Bolívar.

SAN FERNANDO CASTLE and THE SAN JOSE FORT, Bocachica.

⭐ Since they are located on opposite sides of the entrance to the bay of Cartagena, crossfire from the San Fernando Castle and San José Fort proved an effective deterrent to enemy attacks.

The horseshoe-shaped San Fernando is located on a small penninsula on the island of Tierrabomba. Well-preserved despite its construction some 200 years ago, this fort protected Bocachica when a sandbar closed the Bocagrande entrance to the Bay of Cartagena. Check out the vaults and dungeons. The castle features two main bulwarks connected by a circular rampart.

Recently restored, the 18th-century San José Fort in Bocachica consists of a battery of 21 cannons as well as a powderhouse. Note the ingenious system of valves, designed to control the force of waves and tides.

FORT SAN SEBASTIAN DE PASTELILLO, La Manga.

Completed in 1743, this battlement complemented San Felipe Fortress. It is home today to the Cartagena Fishing Club and to a fine restaurant, Club de Pesca.

EL MUSEO DE ORO, Plaza Bolívar.

To celebrate Colombia's vast cultural heritage, the Banco de la República has founded museums throughout the country. Each displays pre-Columbian goldworks and ceramics of its particular region. Cartagena's museum is devoted to pieces from the Caribbean and is located in a lovingly restored colonial manor.

LA POPA MONASTERY.

A lovely cloister with stone columns and brick archways, this church and convent is located on a hill overlooking the entire city. Founded in 1607 by the Agustín Fathers, it is still used as chapel and monastery. The view from the hill is stirring. (If you're ever here on February 2, Feast Day, be sure to see the candlelight procession.)

Admission: 75¢.

Transportation: Take any bus marked POPA from the Old City and hike up the hill. Or have a cab take you all of the way up for $3 round trip.

WALKING TOURS

We recommend at least two visits to the Old City during your stay here. Accordingly, we've outlined two walking tours that will give you a good feel for the city. Streets generally are crowded with peddlers, cars, and pedestrians. It's a good idea to try to make one visit on a weekday and the other during the weekend.

THE INNER CITY The inner city was originally the area located within the outer protective walls. An inner wall, now leveled for the most part, segregated the wealthy from the poor sections of the inner city. Start your stroll at the city's main gate, called **La Puerta del Reloj,** marked by three gates and its famous Clock Tower. This is the **Plaza de Los Coches,** which is filled with vendors selling mostly homemade candy. Turn left at the gate; a short distance up is the city's largest plaza, the **Plaza de la Aduana** (Customs Square), so called because the original customs house was here. In colonial times it served as the Plaza de Armas and home to many government offices as well as Pedro de Heredia's mansion. Look for the statue of Columbus there.

Continue along the wall area to the 17th-century **Iglesia y Monasterio de San Pedro de Claver** (Church and Monastery of San Pedro Claver), which honors a great priest, now a saint, who devoted his life to ministering to the needs of the African slaves imported by the Spanish to Cartagena. Streets here are extremely narrow—wide enough in some places for only one person. **Santa Teresa** and **Calle de Boloco** are typical.

Nearby is the **Plaza Bolívar,** a large plaza in El Centro, once the wealthiest section of the city. Notice that the houses are two stories high and have ornate carvings and overhanging terraces. The **Palacio de la Inquisición** (Inquisition Palace)—dating from 1776—still stands in the west end of the plaza. Its massive doors are ornately etched, with the Inquisition's coat-of-arms above. Thirteen secret dungeons were hidden in the depths of the building next door, which also was home to the inquisitors. Today the palace is home to the Anthropological, Colonial, and Inquisition museums. Across the street is the **Casa Skandia,** named after the Swiss insurance company that restored it. Feel free to step inside the courtyard for a glimpse of 18th-century Cartagena. On the other end of the plaza is the pink-hued **Basilica Menor,** the city cathedral. Construction, which started in 1575, suffered a major setback at the hands of Sir Francis Drake in 1586. If you look up at the outer wall here you'll see a sunclock dating back some 300 years.

Continue along **Calle Santo Domingo** one block to the city's oldest religious building, the **Santo Domingo Church and Convent,** which date back to the 16th century. Note the oddly shaped steeple. Inside, the statue of the Virgin Mary has a gold-and-emerald crown. At this point the street becomes **Calle Factoría,** which leads to the outer walls and also the **Plaza de La Merced,** site of an old church now used as a theater. Climb up the outer wall nearby and take in the breathtaking view of the bay. Follow the promenade to the **Plaza Bovedas,** where 22 cells were used as prisons in colonial times and now are used as shops for souvenirs and handcrafts. Continue following the wall and shortly you'll find yourself back on Avenida Venezuela, not far from Boca del Puente, where you began.

THE OUTER WALLED CITY This tour carries you through parts of the outer walled city. It was once called the Getsemaní Barrio, and here the working classes lived in one-story houses called *casas bajas.* It remains a working-class area. Start your tour at the **Puerta del Reloj** (Clock Tower) near the dock area and stop at the nearby **Parque Centenario,** where you'll see a series of busts called the **Callejón de Los Martires,** commemorating the city's heroes in the fight for independence from Spain. Here, too, is an outdoor flea market. Just beyond the dock is the wide **Calle Larga,** the major street of the barrio, which leads to the yellow **Puente Romano** (Roman bridge) leading to the island of **Manga,** formerly a fort, now a well-to-do suburb. From the bridge you get a good view of **San Felipe Fortress** and **La Popa Hill.** Walk along Calle Larga to the bridge, but instead of crossing it, follow the outer wall (which you'll find yourself on) to the left along Calle Lomba until you reach another old bridge, called **Paseo Heredia.** At this point there is a grassy knoll housing a touching monument called **Los Zapatos Viejos** ("old shoes"), a loving tribute to Colombia's great poet, Luís Lopez de Mesa. The poet once compared Cartagena to a pair of comfortable old shoes. The poem and a symbolic pair of shoes are here. Cross the bridge to San Felipe Fortress, which stands 135 feet above sea level. It was the highest of the many forts built here and thus was strategic in the area's defense.

At this point you can bus it back to the Tower of the Clock along Avenida Venezuela. The same bus usually continues past the tower to Bocagrande.

WHERE TO STAY

You should definitely stay on Bocagrande. The nicer hotels, better restaurants, and nightspots are there, and it's cooler and has far less commercial traffic. It is safe to walk on Bocagrande at night. There are always lots of people at the sidewalk cafés. We are quoting rates for Cartagena's high seasons—December 15 to April 30 and June 15 to August 31. At other times you can expect to pay about 25% less.

Hotels in Cartagena add several unusual charges to your bill without informing you when you check in. We have seen "security tax," "telephone tax," and a variety of other such charges. Several readers have written us about extra charges for singles who were placed in a double room without being informed of the extra charges. Check your rates very carefully and ask about these extras.

Note: There are a few hotels located near the Old City—one in the Plaza Bolívar itself. We do not, however, recommend that you stay downtown or on Marbella beach. We have received some letters from readers about purse, watch, and camera snatchings downtown at night. While this can and does happen in any city, we feel that walking to and from your hotel is something you should be able to feel unconcerned about.

HOTEL ARRECIFE, Carrera 3, no. 5-66. Tel. 65-7208. Fax 65-7210.
$ Rates: $16.50 single; $20 double.

The Arrecife is a good value, only one block from Avenida San Martín, on a quiet residential block. The rooms are clean, and the service is friendly.

RESIDENCIA BOCAGRANDE, Carrera 2, no. 7-187. Tel. 65-6418. Fax 65-4437. 50 rms (all with bath). A/C TEL
$ Rates: $16 single; $21 double.

This three-star hotel offers cozy, spotless rooms. Enter through the door on Calle 8. It has its own small restaurant, great for breakfast before heading off to the beach, as well as a lovely outdoor courtyard.

HOTEL BARLOVENTO, Carrera 3, no. 6-23. Tel. 65-3965. Fax 65-5726. Telex 037805. 48 rms (all with bath). A/C MINIBAR TV TEL
$ Rates: $38 single: $47 double. Major credit cards accepted.
The Barlovento is very fairly priced, located not far from the beach. Rooms are comfortably furnished. Facilities include a bar, restaurant, and pool.

HOTEL BAHIA, Calle 4, at the corner of Carrera 4. Tel. 65-0316. Fax 65-6170. 66 rms (all with bath). A/C TEL
$ Rates: $40 single; $48 double.

An old favorite is the Bahía, which has a comfortable lobby, a round pool, a backyard, and innocuous furnishings. Nice people run it.

CAPILLA DEL MAR, Avenida 1 at Calle 8. Tel. 65-1140. Fax 65-5145. Telex 037739 HCM CO. 190 rms (all with bath). A/C MINIBAR TV TEL
$ Rates: $50 single; $60 double. Major credit cards accepted.
No relation to the restaurant of the same name, this 21-floor hotel has a small pool and sundeck on the roof. There are a good restaurant and a health club on the premises. The service here is only fair, which is disappointing considering the prices. Rooms have stocked refrigerators. Watch out for extra charges.

HOTEL CASAGRANDE, Carrera 1, no. 9-128. Tel. 65-3943. Fax 65-6806. 24 rms, 6 apts (all with bath) A/C TV TEL
$ Rates: $45 double. Major credit cards accepted.

The Casagrande is a lovely colonial-style home surrounded by beautiful tropical gardens. Friendly, personalized service will make you feel at home here. The hotel is located just one block from the beach and not far from the walled city. The Casagrande has its own restaurant and snack bar.

HOTEL EL DORADO, Avenida San Martín, no. 4-41. Tel. 65-0211 or 65-0830. Fax 65-0479. Telex 37625. 326 rms (all with bath). A/C MINIBAR TV TEL
$ Rates: $42 single; $55 double. Major credit cards accepted.
Since it opened in 1976, El Dorado has expanded considerably. Today it boasts all the amenities of a luxury hotel, including a small shopping arcade, two restaurants, two cafeterias, a disco, a pool and room service. Despite its growth, guests here still enjoy the personalized service of a smaller hotel.

LAS VELAS HOTEL, Calle Las Velas, no. 1-60. Tel. 65-0000. Fax 65-0530. Telex 037715 HTCLV. All rooms with bath. A/C MINIBAR TV TEL
$ Rates: $45 single; $50 double. Major credit cards accepted.
Las Velas Hotel is a favorite among the more reasonable deluxe choices. On Laguito, Las Velas is small enough to be called intimate. The lovely pool is set in a quiet inner courtyard, and the slide is fun for young and old. The hotel is on a secluded part of the beach, too. There's a good restaurant (serving kosher food) in the hotel, and most rooms have an ocean view or a view of the walled city.

HOTEL PLAYA, Avenida San Martín, no. 4-87. Tel. 65-0552. Fax 65-0036. Telex 37849 PLAYA CO. 86 rms (all with bath). TEL
$ Rates: $24 single with fan; $32 double with fan.

An excellent moderately priced choice is the four-story Hotel Playa, where you can bed down in a plainly furnished but clean room. A nice bar with a terrace is on the second floor. Air-conditioned rooms are $5 to $10 more.

ROYAL PARK, Avenida 3, Calle 7, no. 171. Tel. 65-5507. 30 rms (all with bath). A/C
$ Rates: $23 single; $30 double.
Located a few blocks from the beach, the four-floor Royal Park is decorated in modern bright colors and towering plants. It has a snack bar and restaurant, plus the coldest lobby in Cartagena.

RESIDENCIAS

A number of family-run *residencias* are located in Bocagrande. Most are located in private houses a few blocks from the beach. They are uniformly small; most have a few tables for breakfast, a TV in the lobby, and a porch to rock on. Your room will be small and basically furnished, but almost all have private bath and most have air conditioning.

LEONELA, Carrera 3, no. 7-142. Tel. 65-4761. All rooms with bath.
$ Rates: $16 single; $20 double.
Leonela is slightly less expensive than other *residencias* because it's a block farther away from the beach. It has a well-regarded restaurant and bar in front.

HOTEL RESIDENCIAS PUNTA CANOA, Calle 7, no. 2-50. Tel. 65-4179. 13 rms (all with bath).
$ Rates: $20 double without air conditioning, $24 double with air conditioning.
Under new management, Punta Canoas is the most attractive *residencia* we found. The rooms spread over two floors are clean and sunny, and the lobby has comfy furniture and Spanish-colonial decor. You have the option to take it with meals, but we think you'd have more fun eating out. Arrangements can be made for long stays. For a reservation, write Gustavo Suarez Sandino, Apartado Aereo 02007 Laguito, Bocagrande Cartagena.

HOSTAL RESIDENCIAS INTERNACIONAL, Avenida San Martín, no. 4-110. Tel. 65-2675. All rooms with bath.
$ Rates: $15 single; $22 double.
The rooms in this recently opened pension are small, each furnished with a bed, nightstand, and table. The staff is friendly and helpful. Most rooms are air conditioned.

SPLURGE CHOICES

HOTEL CARIBE, Carrera 1, no. 2-87. Tel. 65-0155. Fax 65-3707. Telex 37811 OHTCR CO. 199 rms (all with bath). A/C MINIBAR TV TEL
$ Rates: $80–$92 single; $92–$112 double. Major credit cards accepted.
Once the center of social activity in Cartagena, the Caribe retains its colonial charm and dedication to excellence. It has been refurbished, and its facilities now include a completely modern fitness center in addition to the lovely gardens, huge pool and sundeck, and good restaurant at poolside. Several restaurants, a bar and disco, and folkloric and international shows round out the evening activities. Accommodations in the smaller, more modern buildings cost more than those in the colonial main building.

HOTEL CARTAGENA REAL, Avenida Malecon, no. 1-150. Tel. 65-5590. Fax 65-4163. Telex 37795. 75 suites (all with bath). A/C MINIBAR TV TEL
$ Rates: $80 double.
The Cartagena Real offers the luxury of a suite for the price of a single room (although basic facilities make up the difference). Each suite includes a separate living room and bedroom, plus a balcony with hammocks. The hotel has a pool, restaurant, and cocktail lounge.

**HOTEL COSTA DEL SOL, Avenida 1, at the corner of Calle 9. Tel.
65-0866.** Fax 65-3755. 126 rms (all with bath). A/C MINIBAR TV TEL
$ Rates: $100 double.

The ultramodern Costa del Sol, the newest arrival to Bocagrande, was designed to
take full advantage of a spectacular beachfront location with windows all around and
a rooftop pool and terrace. Rooms have been painstakingly furnished with comfort in
mind.

WHERE TO DINE

Since Cartagena is a coastal city, seafood is the thing here. Highly recommended is the
red snapper (*pargo*), prepared in a variety of ways. As the city has developed into an
international tourist center, a wide variety of restaurants has opened, and you can find
French, Italian, Arabian, Spanish, Colombian, and good old American steakhouses all
within the boundaries of Bocagrande.

CAPILLA DEL MAR, Carrera 5, no. 8-59, Bocagrande. Tel. 655-001.
   Cuisine: SEAFOOD. **Reservations:** Required.
$ Prices: Appetizers $3–$6; main courses $6–$12. Major credit cards accepted.
   Open: Tues–Sun lunch 12:30–3:30pm; dinner 7–11pm.

Cartagena's most famous restaurant, and one that would stand out anywhere, is
Capilla Del Mar, now in a lovely house overlooking the bay, three blocks from
San Martín. The restaurant has a porch and several dining rooms cooled by
ceiling fans and bay breezes. Michelle and Pierre Daguet, a brother-and-sister team,
owned this restaurant for 25 years. After Pierre's death, Michelle ran the restaurant
alone for a number of years, until her death just recently. Now the restaurant is owned
and run by the staff, as had been arranged before the Daguets passed away. The fare is
seafood and, while international, leans a little toward French.

We highly recommend the *cazuela de mariscos* (seafood casserole) and the *arroz
con mariscos* (rice with seafood). The *cazuela* was the best we've had anywhere. Be
sure to try a rum sour before dinner. And save room for dessert: The coconut pie and
baba au rum are both excellent. Service is slow, making dinner here a great way to
spend a relaxed evening.

**CLUB DE PESCA, Fuerte de San Sebastián de Pastelillo, La Manga. Tel.
66-1239.**
   Cuisine: SEAFOOD. **Reservations:** Recommended.
$ Prices: Appetizers $3–$7; main courses $8–$15. Major credit cards accepted.
   Open: Daily 11am–11pm.

The Club de Pesca is located in the historic Fort San Sebastian on the nearby
island of La Manga. You can reach it in a 15-minute walk from the downtown
dock area or a $2 cab ride from Bocagrande. A fun way to go is to rent a horse
and buggy (bargain over the price—figure $5 to $6—but you get a long picturesque
ride). The view of the bay is relaxing, and you eat outdoors under the shade of a huge
old caucho tree that has probably been there longer than the restaurant, with the
guard towers and gun embankments of the fortress around you. All this combined
with the candle on the table will make this an evening you'll never forget. Any of the
fish dishes are recommended and start as low as $8. Lobster dishes are a high $15, but
the large and delicious shrimp are less.

**BODEGON DE LA CANDELARIA, Calle de las Damas, in the Walled City.
Tel. 64-7251.**
   Cuisine: SEAFOOD. **Reservations:** Recommended.
$ Prices: Appetizers $5–$9; main courses $9–$16. Major credit cards accepted.
   Open: Daily 6:30–midnight.

Another special choice is located in a romantic 16th-century house in the
walled city. Legend has it that it was in this house that the Virgen of the
Candelaria appeared to Fray Alonso of the Cross and instructed him to build
the Monastery of the Popa. Bodegón is administered by the Cartagena Hilton Hotel

and furnished with colonial antiques and early wine-making equipment. Its menu is virtually all fish and shellfish. Half an avocado comes stuffed with shrimp, squid, snails, and claws, accompanied by a delicate pink sauce. Hot lobster is served with a mustard sauce and cold lobster with a sherry sauce—both are fabulous. Try the fried shrimp with grated coconut.

RESTAURANTE DE DORIS, Carrera 4, no. 9-73, Bocagrande. Tel. 53-808.
   Cuisine: SEAFOOD. **Reservations:** Recommended.
 $ **Prices:** Appetizers $4–$8; main courses $8–$14. Major credit cards accepted.
   Open: 6:30–11pm.

Doris herself will be here to greet you and make you feel at home. This restaurant is located in a spacious house overlooking the bay in Bocagrande. Here you have the choice of dining indoors or out on the balcony. Once you're settled, Doris will be at your table to take your order. The *langosto de la casa* (lobster served in a pink sauce with rice, vegetables, almonds, and pine nuts) and lobster *minarete* (served with three sauces) are both excellent. If you're really hungry, try the Fiesta Marinera, an incredible seafood platter.

BOCAGRANDE

LA OLLA CARTAGENERA, Avenida San Martín, no. 5-100. Tel. 653-861.
   Cuisine: COLOMBIAN. **Reservations:** Recommended.
 $ **Prices:** Appetizers $2–$5; main courses $4–$10. Major credit cards accepted.
   Open: Lunch and dinner.
La Olla Cartagenera is one of the loveliest eateries here. Walk through the unimpressive storefront to the beautiful garden covered with a tin roof. A spraying fountain stands in the courtyard surrounded by tables and flowering plants. Grilled meats, fish, and shellfish dishes dominate the menu, and prices here are the same as at less impressive restaurants.

LA FONDA ANTIOQUEÑA, Avenida San Martín, no. 6-164. Tel. 65-1392.
   Cuisine: COLOMBIAN.
 $ **Prices:** Appetizers $1–$3; main courses under $9. Major credit cards accepted.
   Open: Lunch and dinner.
One of the best in town, this is a typical restaurant from Colombia's "west," with cowhide chairs and tables hewn from tree trunks. Steaks and other grilled meats are served with typical sauces made from hot peppers and avocados. You can eat inside the fan-cooled dining room or out back in the garden. Chorizos (sausages) are very tasty with drinks, and you should sample a *sancocho* (soup-stew) of chicken or beef with a lot of vegetables. Grilled pork chops are excellent. Beer, wine, and drinks are served.

GIOVANNI O SOLE MIO, San Martín, no. 4-66. Tel. 655-671.
   Cuisine: ITALIAN.
 $ **Prices:** Pizza $3–$10; main courses under $8.
   Open: Lunch and dinner.
Owned by a husband-and-wife team, O Sole Mío specializes in pizzas in four sizes and with a variety of ingredients. The pizza is much like what you'd find in New York, with a slightly thick, chewy crust. Booths, checkered tablecloths, and posters provide the decor. Other Italian foods are served as well.

DA TERESA, Avenida 4, at Calle 8. Tel. 652-907.
   Cuisine: ITALIAN.
 $ **Prices:** Appetizers $1–3; main courses $3–$6.
   Open: Lunch and dinner.

Da Teresa is set in a private house a little off the beaten path. All the food is cooked to order, and Teresa is quite a cook! It's like eating at home. Prices for most items are less than those on the main drag.

CHEF JULIAN, Avenida San Martín, no. 9-61. Tel. 655-220.

Cuisine: SEAFOOD. **Reservations:** Recommended.
$ Prices: Appetizers $1–$4; main courses $6–$9.
Open: 6:30–11pm.

This attractive colonial-style dining room is in a private house, marked with an old-fashioned lamppost outside. Julian also has an outdoor garden. The specialties are three lobster halves, each with a different sauce, and the best paella in Cartagena.

CREPES N' WAFFLES, Avenida Almirante Brion, no. 1-98 (Laguito).

Cuisine: INTERNATIONAL.
$ Prices: Light meal/snack under $5.
Open: 11am–midnight.

Here you can order stuffed crêpes (with shrimp, chicken curry, and ham and cheese). Waffles and ice cream make a cool afternoon pick-me-up.

LOS PINOS, Avenida San Martín, No. 8-164.

Cuisine: INTERNATIONAL.
$ Prices: Appetizers $1–$3; main courses $3–$6.
Open: 11am–midnight.

Los Pinos is quite large and has a huge menu. There are indoor tables, but the sidewalk café is nicer. This is a great budget restaurant for enjoying the likes of pasta, steak Cartagena style, barbecued meat, or *arroz con pollo.*

NAUTILUS, Avenida San Martín, no. 9-1456. Tel. 653-964.

Cuisine: SEAFOOD. **Reservations:** Recommended.
$ Prices: Appetizers $1–$5; main courses $5–$10.
Open: Lunch and dinner.

Nautilus was built to look like a ship with portholes, fishnets, and ballast on the walls and diving gear on the floor. Even the waiters are dressed as sailors. Each table has a nautical map and comfortable chairs. Organ music sets the mood while you dine on *ceviche* ($5.50), fried *pargo* ($6), and calamari ($5). Bend as you enter—the door is very low.

MEE WAH, San Martín, no. 8-33. Tel. 651-310.

Cuisine: CHINESE/CREOLE.
$ Prices: Appetizers $1–$3; main courses $4–$10. Major credit cards accepted.
Open: Lunch and dinner.

If you're in the mood for Chinese/Creole dishes, try Mee Wah, where you have a choice of five dining rooms. Specialties include *vuc kai* (chicken Cantonese) and *vag tiac ja* (shrimp and ham in an onion sauce).

OLD CITY

MARCEL, Calle de la Inquisicion. Tel. 64-7058.

Cuisine: FRENCH. **Reservations:** Recommended.
$ Prices: Appetizers $5–$8; main courses $8–$12. Major credit cards accepted.
Open: Dinner only.

For French cuisine and ambience in the middle of the walled city, try Marcel, in the recently restored Casa Skandia. Be warned that Marcel is significantly more expensive than our other choices.

PACO'S RESTAURANTE Y TABERNA, Plaza Santo Domingo. Tel. 644-294.

Cuisine: SEAFOOD. **Reservations:** Recommended.
$ Prices: Appetizers $2–$5; main courses $5–$9.
Open: Mon–Fri noon–midnight; Sat–Sun and hols 7pm–midnight.

One of our recommended nightspots, Paco's also boasts a very good kitchen. Tapas are the specialty of the house, but the complete meals are excellent. Seafood is the specialty. Come for dinner and stay for the entertainment.

SPECIALTY DINING

LIGHT FARE   There's a **Kiko Riko Chicken House** on Avenida Venezuela, with a **Presto** (like McDonald's) across the street. They both have tables and take-out service for picnic lunches. **Whopper King,** a few blocks away, is on a par with the first two. They all serve burgers, fried chicken, hot dogs, and drinks. **El Torito** and **La Papa Loca,** on the corner of San Martín and Calle 10, is another good place for a light meal. You'll have your choice of indoor or outdoor tables and Mexican or fast food.

   Pizzería Margarita is a small eatery serving only pizza. Located on the water's edge on Laguito near Las Velas, Margarita puts all kinds of ingredients onto its thin crisp dough base. A pizza for one starts at $3 and goes up to $6 with many toppings. Order a tall cool beer and enjoy a tasty light lunch. Other branches are on San Martín and Calle 5 and in the Bocagrande Shopping Center.

   Small sandwich and soft-drink places abound through Bocagrande. They serve heros, some sandwiches, ice-cold beer, and soda. Try **Sandwiches Cubanos,** a take-out with branches on San Martín (no. 5-32) and all over town. **Pío Kiko** and **La Piragua,** next door on Avenida San Martín, take over the entire sidewalk with their bridge tables and chairs, serving rotisseried chicken, sandwiches, and drinks. These are nice places to sit at night when a live combo plays on the bandstand into the wee hours.

   Try **Pipos,** on Laguito and at Avenida San Martín, at Calle 8, for ice cream. **Palacio de las Frutas** is a good stop for a drink of freshly squeezed orange or pineapple juice. Mango and coconut drinks are popular, too. The **Heladeria Arabe,** on Avenida San Martín, at Calle 7, is a good breakfast stop. The tea and sweet pastries are delicious. **Robin Hood** is a good choice for ice cream. Cartagena's best ice cream is at **La Fuente,** on Avenida San Martín between Calles 8 and 9.

SAVVY SHOPPING

If you're going to be in Bogotá, you're probably better off shopping there. The selection is larger and the prices are a bit lower. Most shops in Cartagena are branches of well-known Bogotá firms. The one exception is handcrafts, since these are locally produced.

SHOPPING CENTERS

Pierino Gallo on Laguito, is a modern two-story center with chic shops and airline offices. Coffee and refreshments are served in the patio. Two fine jewelry stores are here: **H. Stern,** famous for its Brazilian gemstones in a variety of colors, as well as emeralds; and **Joyeria Cesareo,** known for emeralds. Another Stern shop is in the Hilton Hotel. *Típico* clothing and handcrafts can be purchased at the **Tropicano Típicos.** The center also houses the Bank of Colombia, the Casino del Caribe, and the Royal Night Club, plus other fashionable shops.

   El Pueblito, on San Martín at Calle 6, will be of little interest to the tourist. There are toy and record shops and service stores. The bar-and-disco complex behind it on the beach is a good spot to head to at night.

   Centro Comercial Bocagrande, on San Martín at Calle 8, is the newest center in Bocagrande, large and modern, with several levels, fashionable shops, and, best of all, movie theaters that sometimes have English flicks. **Ventatom Artesanía,** located on the street level of this center, is one of the best handcraft shops in Cartagena. Start your browsing here.

SHOPPING A TO Z
Artesanias

ARTESANÍAS DE COLOMBIA, in the Plaza Bolívar.
   Make your first stop the Artesanías de Colombia shop, part of a nonprofit chain located in different parts of the country. The big things here are the large wallhangings

($12 to $15), some in tree shapes. (The same items were triple the price in Bloomingdale's in New York.) You can also find a good selection of straw mats, handbags, belts, ceramic pieces, and ruanas. Soft leather duffel bags and cases are good buys. Another branch is on Avenida San Martín and Calle 5.

ARTEXPO, in the Inquisition Palace, Plaza Bolívar.
This very small shop across the plaza has a wide selection of handcrafts and costume jewelry. It is run by a Peace Corpsman. A fun buy here is a "Colombia" T-shirt in blazing color for $4.

COLOMBIAN TOURIST SHOP, Calle Roman, no. 5.
Here you can buy stuffed alligators for $3, a great gift for children. This is a place for souvenir-type buys.

TROPICANA, Avenida San Martín, near Calle 5.
Tropicana is a large store. Nice buys here are colorful hammocks, placemat sets, and wooden masks. They carry a large selection of the soft leather bags and suitcases made in Colombia.

LA VILLA REAL, Plaza de las Bóvedas, local 10. Tel. 64-4305.
La Villa Real offers a wonderful selection of handmade items. Embroidery and leatherwork is the specialty here.

Leather
LAND, San Martín at Calle 7.
Land leather goods are considered Colombia's finest. Very soft and worked in the same manner as leathers from Italy, they are fashioned into handbags, luggage, briefcases, and less expensive accessories. Another Land outlet is in the Pierino Center (second floor).

Pre-Columbian Art
ARTESANIAS SIGLO XVIII, in the Shopping Arcade of the Cartagena Hilton.
Featured here is a marvelous selection of original pre-Colombian artifacts as well as excellent reproductions. Lovely handicrafts are for sale here as well.

GALERIA CANO, in the Pierino Gallo Shopping Center, Laguito.
This outstanding gallery features pre-Columbian artifacts and reproductions and beautifully crafted jewelry in Indian motifs. Another branch is located in the Hilton. The main store is in Bogotá.

LA TIENDA, Avenida San Martín, near Calle 5.
La Tienda has reproductions of antique mirrors and pre-Columbian artifacts.

VALDIVIA, Calle Santo Domingo, no. 33-94.
Archeologist/owner Michel Brenon, a specialist in the pre-Columbian cultures of Ecuador, will fill you in on the background of any piece you may be interested in. Prices start at $10, and all pieces come with a certificate of authenticity.

EVENING ENTERTAINMENT
CLUBS & DISCOS
LA ESCOLLERA, Carrera 1, at the corner of Calle 5, just off Avenida San Martín, Bocagrande. Tel. 653-030.
Across the street from the beach, La Escollera was first recommended to us by someone in Panama. Cartagenians and tourists alike come here to dance to international and tropical rhythms until dawn. Balconies overlooking the large dance floor provide a break from the crowds.

MINERVA and EL GIRATORIO, in the Hotel Capilla del Mar, Carrera 1 at Calle 8. Tel. 651-140.

Residents and regular visitors to Cartagena will be quick to tell you that Minerva is the best disco in town. Located on the ground level of the Hotel Capilla del Mar, it spans both indoors and out. Indoors is air-conditioned, of course. Patrons crowd the large video dance floor where they move to the pulsating rhythms of the latest international and tropical hits. Sitting areas with couchettes provide a haven from dance floor.

El Giratorio, on the 21st floor, provides a quiet alternative. Enjoy a drink, quiet conversation, and the twinkle of the city lights below as the bar slowly revolves to the soothing coastal music performed by the Hotel Orchestra. There is also a small dance floor.

NAUTILUS VIDEO BAR DISCO, Avenida San Martín, no. 9-96.
This place is very popular with the younger crowd, who come here to catch their favorite videos. The overflow from the Escollera usually winds up here.

PACOS RESTAURANT AND TAVERN, Plaza Santo Domingo. Tel. 644-294.
Pacos is inside the walled city—why not travel here by horse and buggy? It's a great place to relax over a cold beer after a long day of sightseeing. And if you're hungry, try the tapas. The grilled shrimp and the squid are both delicious. Live music is provided every night by Los Veteranos del Ritmo (the Rhythm Veterans), a delightful group of men ranging in age from 57 to 72. Nick, Paco's English proprietor, who came to Cartagena years ago on an engineering contract and never made it back home, is always around to make you feel comfortable and to fill you in on all the local happenings.

PORTOBELLO CLUB, San Martín at Calle 9.
A sedate club, this draws an older, well-dressed, sophisticated crowd. The music varies from disco to Latin and back. Drinks here run $4.

TABERNA LA QUEMADA, Calle de la Amargura, at the corner of Ladrinal. Tel. 645-612.
Just off the Plaza de la Aduana, this establishment has live jazz every night. A replica of the English taverns of the early 19th century, it was built for the filming of *Burn!*, directed by Gillo Pontecorvo and starring Marlon Brando, Evaristo Marquez, and Renato Salvatori. The walls are covered with photographs of scenes from the movie. Taberna La Quemada is also inside the walled city, so you may want to travel here by horse and buggy.

EL TORMENTIN, on the top floor of the Hotel Las Velas, Calle Las Velas, no. 1-60. Tel. 650-000.
If you like a view with your drink and dancing, El Tormentin is a good spot. It has a view of the harbor and the walled city, and occasionally features live music.
Admission: $5 minimum.

A CASINO

One of Latin America's best casinos is located in Cartagena, the ✪ **Casino del Caribe,** in the Pierino Gallo Shopping Center beyond the Hotel Caribe. It's red-carpeted and comfortably air-conditioned. Buy your chips (*fichas*) and *buena suerte*. Open from 4pm until 4am. Since our last edition, a couple of new casinos have opened. There is the new **Casino Turístico** on Avenida San Martín and the very lovely **Casino Royale** in the Hotel Caribe.

MORE ENTERTAINMENT

Grab a folding chair at **La Piragua,** at San Martín and Calle 8, and listen to the music while sipping a cool beer or soft drink. Rent a **buggy** and ride around Bocagrande and the walled city. Bargain over the price. **El Laguito,** at San Martín and Calle 5, is a store filled with pinball machines and other electronic games. Games are 10¢.

EASY EXCURSIONS

Consider a day trip to the **Rosario Islands,** 2½ hours away over the open sea. The unspoiled islands, site of vacation homes and villas, have sandy beaches and an intact coral reef populated by colorful tropical fish. The $30 fee includes the 5-hour boat ride and lunch. Bring your own snorkel gear or rent equipment for an additional fee. The boat leaves at 8am and returns at 5pm. Bring lots of suntan lotion. Buy your ticket the day before at **Yates Alcatraz,** Avenida San Martín, no. 6-134 (tel. 653-442). Diving trips to the islands are offered by **El Caracol** on Calle 5, no. 12-53 (tel. 654-649).

Or you can take an hour's boat ride to **Bocachica,** a charming fishing village on the island of Tierrabomba in the bay. Both the San Fernando and San José forts are nearby. Snow-white beaches, turquoise waters, and quaint seafood restaurants are another reason for coming here. The *Alcatraz* leaves from the dock in front of the clock tower—$5 round trip. Smaller boats leaving from the same site cost $3 round trip. You can buy your tickets for any of the boats at the dock or make arrangements with Acuatur in front of the Hotel Caribe. Boats leave between 9:30 and 10:30am. Waterskiing can also be arranged here.

A must is the small fishing village of **Boquilla,** just 15 minutes from Cartagena by cab. Nestled among coconut and palm trees, this quaint hamlet provides a respite from the noise and crowds of the modern civilization. The people here live in much the same way as their grandparents did. The beaches and inexpensive seafood restaurants here are lovely.

---

2. SANTA MARTA

770 miles N of Bogotá

GETTING THERE By Plane The **Avianca** shuttle travels daily from the coastal city of Barranquilla to Santa Marta or you can fly Avianca direct from Bogotá to Santa Marta. Just be sure to check the price before purchasing your ticket with a credit card. Remember that there is often a big difference in price that probably won't be in your favor.

By Bus Expreso Brasilia S. A. buses leave daily from Cartagena to Santa Marta. For schedule and fare information in Cartagena, go to their office at Avenida Pedro de Heredia, 20D-5, or call 661-692. Their office in Santa Marta is on the corner of Calle 24 and Avenida Bavaria (tel. 234-088). Many travel agencies offer day and overnight trips from Cartagena to Santa Marta. **Tesoro Tours** at Avenida San Martín, no. 6-134 (tel. 654-713) and **GEMA Tours,** in the lobby of the Cartagena Hilton (tel. 650-208), may be worth checking into.

By Car It's possible to drive from Cartagena to Santa Marta. The trip along the coast should take you around 4 hours. Be sure to get up-to-date highway maps before you go.

ESSENTIALS Fast Facts Buses are plentiful, clean, cheap, and recommended. They cost 25¢ from downtown, at Carrera 1, Calle 11 (stops all along Carrera 1), to the Hotel Tamaca. Buses leave when full. An electric train "Rodatren," travels up Carrera 3 and down Carrera 2, and you can get on and off at different points (50¢). Its schedule is irregular, but it stops at 11pm. The largest bank here is **Banco de la Republica,** at Carrera 5, Calle 17. For a pharmacy, the **Droguería Nueva York,** at Carrera 2 on Calle 10, in Rodadero, and in Plaza Bolívar downtown, is convenient. The tour agency TMA, on Carrera 4, no. 14-35, is your best bet. The Ley chain (similar to Woolworth's) has a store at Carrera 5 downtown.

Developed around a graceful bay with calm blue waters, Santa Marta is blessed with natural beaches that would be the envy of any resort city. Ten minutes away on inviting Rodadero Beach are good hotels and restaurants. The towering Andes, complete with snow-tipped peaks, are a magnificent backdrop for the city.

The oldest city in Colombia, Santa Marta was founded on July 29, 1525, by Spanish conquistador Rodrigo de Bastidas. Prior to the arrival of the Spanish, the region was inhabited by the Tayrona Indians, one of the most advanced cultures in the new world. The principal ruins of the Tayrona civilization were discovered in 1976 and are known as **The Lost City of the Sierra Nevada of Santa Marta.** It is a week's journey on foot from Santa Marta to the lost city. The smaller **Pueblito** ruins are located in the Tayrona National Park, not far from Santa Marta.

During the colonial period Santa Marta was overshadowed by Cartagena. However, it was once the Spanish center in the battle against Simón Bolívar and the revolutionaries, who finally liberated the city in 1821. And it was here that Bolívar came when his federation plan for South America collapsed. He died in Santa Marta in 1830. Today, Santa Marta is the capital of the state of Magdalena and one of the leading cities on the Caribbean.

As befits a Caribbean city, the weather is warm and "swimmable" the year round. Humidity rises in June through September.

ORIENTATION

Rodadero Beach is the resort area of Santa Marta. Located 15 minutes from Simón Bolívar Airport by cab, it's the place to stay when coming to Santa Marta. The finer hotels, better restaurants, and nightspots are here. Maps and tourist information should be available at the **Corporación Nacional de Turismo,** in the Edificio Claustro del Seminario on Carrera 2, no. 16-44 (tel. 35-773); the **Promotora de Turismo,** in the same building (tel. 36-053); or the Municipal Tourist Office (**Oficina Municipal de Turismo**), at Calle 14, no. 3-80 (tel. 36-195).

RODADERO'S MAIN ARTERIES   Carrera 1 is the avenue that runs along the beach; it's closed to traffic, and part of it is a promenade. **Carrera 2** is the major thoroughfare of the community; it's residential and commercial. The calles (streets) are numbered, with the higher numbers at the Hotel Tamaca end of the beach. The area is small, having only a dozen streets and even fewer avenues.

DOWNTOWN SANTA MARTA'S MAIN ARTERIES   The downtown area is 10 minutes by auto beyond Rodadero Beach. **Carrera 1** runs along the beach and has benches and trees. Be there one evening at sunset—lovely. **Quinta Avenida** (Fifth Avenue), four blocks away, is the major shopping street, and banks and airline offices are here as well. **Paseo Bastides,** which is named for the city's founder, is a lovely promenade extending from Calle 15 and Carrera 1 along the beach to the dock area. The calles (streets) are colonial and often only wide enough to walk single file.

WHAT TO SEE & DO

CITY SIGHTS   While in the city you should try to visit the **Cathedral** or **Basílica Menor,** on the Plaza Bolívar. It is the final resting place of the city's founding father, Rodrigo de Bastidas. The former **Casa de la Aduana** (Customs House) on Calle 14, at the corner of Carrera 2, is now home to the city's Anthropological and Ethnological Museum, which contains an interesting collection of Tayrona goldwork.

SAN PEDRO ALEJANDRINO ESTATE   About 3 miles outside the city is the Quinta de San Pedro Alejandrino, where Simón Bolívar died on December 17, 1830. The house has been rebuilt in colonial style and today contains many relics of Bolívar's life, including his bed, chair, desk, and clock (stopped at 1:03, the time he died). A statue of Bolívar at age 28 is here, too. On the grounds is a memorial building, reminiscent in some ways of the Lincoln Memorial in Washington, D.C. The Bolívar Museum of Contemporary Art is also here.

To get here, take a bus from Fifth Avenue (Avenida Quinta) that says MAMATOCO (25¢). It goes through much of the city as well. Open daily from 9am to 5:30pm.

PUNTA BETIN   Punta Betin is a peninsula that juts out into the bay, with nice views of the city. The area houses a small aquarium and several seafood restaurants (good red snapper). To get here, take a cab ($1.25). The aquarium is open from 8:30am to noon and 2 to 6pm daily; admission is 50¢.

TAYRONA PARK On the coastal road (Troncal del Caribe) 20 miles east of Santa Marta is the picturesque fishing village of **Taganga** and the beginning of the **✪ Tayrona National Park.** The entrance to the park is just past Taganga at **El Zaíno.** Of the park's 37,000 acres, 30,000 are land. The remaining 7,000 acres correspond to the marine strip, an area of solitary beaches and coves. The **Concha** and **Cañaveral** beaches are the most popular with restaurants and facilities nearby. If you'd like to stay in the park, not far from Cañaveral there are 10 "ecohabs," cabins built in Tayronian style that can be reserved for a maximum of three nights. To do so you must contact the National Institute for Renewable Natural Resources (INDERNA) in Bogotá at least one month in advance. The Tayrona ruins of El Pueblo are a three-hour hike from Cañaveral.

The Beaches The best is Rodadero Beach, 10 minutes from center city. Beaches are free, with calm waters that are ideal for year-round swimming and boating. You can swim at Center City Beach, too. It extends virtually the entire length of the city. This area is more crowded on weekends.

A Festival In July, the city celebrates the 4-day **Festival of the Sea.** A queen is crowned; there are fireworks and dancing in the parks and just about everywhere else. Waterskiers from all over Latin America come to compete.

Sports and Recreation The **Gaira Golf Course** allows tourists to play its nine-hole course. Bicycles can be rented at Rodadero at $2.75 per hour. Paddleboats and waterskis are rented on the beach near the Hotel Tamaca; per hour, boats are $2.50; skis run $7 to $14.

WHERE TO STAY
RODADERO BEACH

HOTEL CAÑAVERAL, Carrera 2, no. 11-65. Tel. 227-002. 60 rms (all with bath). A/C
$ Rates: $15 single; $22 double.
The Cañaveral is an attractive choice. A five-story white building, it has modern, attractive furnishings and an elevator.

HOTEL LA RIVIERA, Carrera 2, no. 5-42. Tel. 227-666. Some rooms with bath.
$ Rates: $13.50 single without air conditioning, $15 single with air conditioning; $19.50 double without air conditioning, $22 double with air conditioning.
This hotel was built in 1973 on a quiet street and is only a two-block walk to the beach promenade. Many rooms have terraces. If you write for a reservation, specify with or without air conditioning.

HOTEL EL RODADERO, Calle 11, no. 1-29. Tel. 227-262. 45 rms (all with bath).
$ Rates: $17 single; $25 double.
The El Rodadero looks much larger than it is. The halls go off in all directions from the desk. Furnishings are adequate but not very attractive, and most rooms have air conditioners.

HOTEL LA SIERRA, Carrera 1. Tel. 9-47. Fax 27960. 74 rms (all with bath). A/C MINIBAR TV TEL
$ Rates: $30 single; $40 double. Major credit cards accepted.
A brightly lit lobby with a busy restaurant and coffee shop make this an "up" place to stay. Located on the promenade and always busy, the ten-floor Sierra has comfortably furnished rooms, with many facing the bay.

HOTEL LILLIAM, El Rodadero. Tel. 227-699. 53 rms (all with bath). A/C

$ Rates: $17 single, $24 single with 3 meals; $22 double, $32 double with 3 meals. Located on Carrera 2, the Lilliam is a fine choice and has been a popular stop with our readers. There are no frills, but you'll find very clean, comfortable rooms and a very friendly and helpful staff. The lobby restaurant is open for all meals.

HOTEL TAMACA, Carrera 2, no. 11A-98. Tel. 227-015. 72 rms (all with bath). A/C
$ Rates: $21 single; $30 double.
A fine choice here is the five-story Tamaca, located on the beachfront. Try to get a room facing the bay—lovely at dusk. The Tamaca is at the end of the beach near the native-style rancho restaurants, a natural sand slide into the sea, and the newest modern apartment houses of Rodadero. The attractive doubles are furnished in Spanish-colonial style. There are restaurants, a bar, a beauty shop, and a casino.

CENTER CITY

HOTEL ANDREA DORIA, Calle 18, no. 1C-90. Tel. 234-329. 12 rms (all with bath).
$ Rates: $9.50 single; $12.75 double.
Friendly management and very reasonable rates more than make up for any lack of extra creature comforts here. Although basic, rooms are clean and well cared for.

RESIDENCIA MIRAMAR, Carrera 1, no. 18-23. Tel. 237-238. 31 rms (all with bath).
$ Rates: $9.50 single without air conditioning, $12 single with air conditioning; $11.50 double without air conditioning, $14 single with air conditioning.
This is an inexpensive choice. Again accommodations here are very basic.

SPLURGE CHOICES

HOTEL IROTAMA, Km 14, Vía a Barranquilla 598. Tel. 234-000. 36 bungalows, 48 efficiencies, 28 rms (all with bath). A/C MINIBAR TV TEL
$ Rates: $50–$68 double; $60–$78 triple; from $63 efficiency. Major credit cards accepted.
Our favorite splurge stop is the Irotama, 5 minutes from the airport on its own beach. The original hotel has small bungalows built in an arc away from the main house along the beach; the bungalows have sitting areas, bedrooms, and bath (shower), with air conditioning.
The brilliant-blue swimmable waters have proved so popular that another section has been added. Known as Irotama II, this section has 48 apartment-type rooms, each with a refrigerator. They are moderately decorated and are air-conditioned—good for families. This area has a pool.
The Irotama has an indoor air-conditioned restaurant and an outdoor restaurant on the porch of the main house. Lunch is served on a patio at the beach.

SANTAMAR, Vía al Aeropuerto Km 8, Pozos Colorados. Tel. 350-770. 130 rms (all with bath). A/C MINIBAR TV TEL
$ Rates: $55 single; $68–$80 double or cabin. Major credit cards accepted.
One of the city's newest hotels is the SantaMar, 10 minutes from the airport on the way to Santa Marta. Rooms are beautifully furnished, with an emphasis on comfort. They have outdoor hammocks for lounging, plus a pool, a tennis court, and a disco.

WHERE TO DINE

Many visitors seem to eat at their hotels, but Santa Marta has some very good restaurants. We suggest having breakfast in your hotel, a light lunch on the beach or at a "rancho," and dinner at one of our suggested restaurants. All are informal and you won't need reservations.

By the way, all along the beach street are small snack shops ideal for breakfast or a light lunch. They serve hot dogs, fried chicken and fish, sandwiches, and soft drinks.

RODADERO BEACH

PORTOFINO, Carrera 1.
Cuisine: ITALIAN.
Open: Lunch and dinner.
Owned by a Neapolitan family, the Portofino was originally located downtown. It has an air-conditioned dining room, but on cool evenings we like the covered terrace— dimly lit and very relaxing. We invariably eat some pasta ($3.75) or *carne pizzaiola* (slightly higher). They have some exotic octopus dishes as well. Not everything on the menu is Italian.

LOS CUMBIEROS, Carrera 2, near Calle 3.
Cuisine: FRENCH.
Open: Lunch and dinner.
One of the most attractively decorated restaurants here, the colorful Cumbieros is French style, with white wrought-iron touches. We think you'll like the interesting menu; the *salade niçoise,* steak *pimienta,* and *pollo normandie* are outstanding.

RESTAURANT LOS DELFINES, Carrera 2, near Calle 9.
Cuisine: SEAFOOD.
Open: Lunch and dinner.
The menu here features *arroz langostinos* (large shrimp with rice) and *cazuela de mariscos.* Los Delfines has both indoor and patio dining.

EL CONQUISTADOR, in the Hotel Tamaca, Carrera 2.
Cuisine: INTERNATIONAL.
Open: Dinner only, daily 7–10pm.
This classy restaurant has a modern decor and air conditioning. You can dine on trout, pargo, seafood brochette, or any number of meat and poultry dishes. Expect to send a little extra here.

RESTAURANTE CAPRI, Carrera 1.
Cuisine: SEAFOOD/COLOMBIAN.
Open: Lunch and dinner.
Restaurant Capri (at the other end of the beach) is another attractive choice. It has a bar and an outdoor patio, as well as a wood-paneled air-conditioned dining room. Seafood and Colombian dishes (*arroz con pollo* at $4.50) are featured.

KAREY, Calle 9A, no. 1-19.
Cuisine: INTERNATIONAL.
Open: Lunch and dinner.
Karey is a small eatery with a cozy atmosphere. The menu is eclectic but has something to suit everyone's taste. Prices start at $5 for pasta dishes and run higher for meats.

LA RODADITA, Carrera 2, Calle 7.
Cuisine: SEAFOOD.
Open: Lunch and dinner.
Since many fishing villages are in the area, the catch here is always fresh and prepared a number of ways.

EL CARACOL, Carrera 2, near Calle 3.
Open: 11am–10pm.
This is a snail-shaped restaurant of white stucco, with bright-orange plastic tables and chairs. With a breakfast of juice, eggs, toast, and coffee for $1.25, and light lunches for

$2.25, you can't beat it. *Arroz con pollo* ($2.50) and *bistec à la criolla* ($3) are typical dinner choices.

MI RANCHITO, on the beach near the Hotel Tamaca.
   Open: All day.

Ⓢ   In this thatch-roofed native restaurant, you can get fine *criolla* food at prices ranging from $1.75 and up per platter. Look for toucans and parrots on the premises.

CENTER CITY

Sorrento Pizzería and **Fuente De Soda** are at Carrera 1, and the tables on the sidewalks in front are big hangouts for locals and young tourists. Sandwiches, pizza, and ice cream are served.

PANAMERICAN, Calle 18, no. 1C-10. Tel. 32-900.
   Cuisine: CONTINENTAL.
   Open: Lunch and dinner.

★   The best restaurant downtown has a lovely view of the bay. Steaks, pork, and chicken dishes start at $6. Desserts are delicious pastries and fruits. Expect to spend a little more here.

EL TURISTA, Carrera 1, Calle 22.
   Cuisine: INTERNATIONAL.
   Open: Lunch and dinner.

This attractive restaurant is opposite the city's main hospital. The dining room is semioutdoors—with a roof but no sides. Ocean breezes keep things cool. Set in a white colonial house, the Turista specializes in fried snapper as well as *arroz con pollo*. The half chicken is a good buy.

LA BRASA RESTAURANT, Carrera 1, no. 17-05.
   Cuisine: SEAFOOD.
   Open: Lunch and dinner.
La Brasa has three separate dining areas—an indoor area, some outdoor tables under a covered roof, and a patio area in the center.

FONDA DE LAS COLONIAS, Carrera 1, Calle 18.
   Cuisine: COLOMBIAN/INTERNATIONAL.
   Open: Lunch and dinner.
This long, narrow restaurant has overhead fans and booths like an ice-cream parlor along the thatched walls. A variety of dishes is on the menu, with *criolla* foods in the lead.

LA REAL PARRILLA Y PIZZERA, Carrera 2, Calle 22.
   Cuisine: ARGENTINEAN/PIZZA.
   Open: Lunch and dinner.
This white-stucco restaurant is very popular with locals and is crowded on weekends. The meats are grilled Argentine style.

SAVVY SHOPPING

Santa Marta does not have many good shops, and if you're traveling in Colombia you can do better elsewhere. **Artesanía,** at Carrera 2, at Calle 7, in Rodadero, is the nicest store we found for some carved masks, woven wallhangings, and leather goods. The **Del Caribe** in the Plaza Bolívar is the best store in downtown Santa Marta for souvenir-type articles. Small outdoor stalls selling fresh fruit, cooked food, and sundries are located at Carrera 3, near Calle 7.

EVENING ENTERTAINMENT

The most popular evening pastime is gambling, and the place to catch the action is at the air-conditioned **Casino Tamaca,** on the main floor of the hotel. Informality in dress is the key. It's open from 9pm to 2am every night. There are 10¢ slot machines and black jack, roulette, and dice tables. The minimum bet is 50¢.

Drop in at **Roberto of the Tropics,** at Calle 9, near Carrera 1, and say hello to Robert Selnick of New York, who owns it. With wicker chairs and tables and a gleaming dance floor, Roberto's is the most attractive bar in Rodadero. With your drink ($2.75) comes a spicy guacamole dip. Ask Roberto about the discos, since they seem to close quickly here. At this writing, the three most popular are **El Pulpo,** in Edificio Los Corales; **El Molino,** at Carrera 2, at Calle 7; and **Puppy,** in the Edificio Irora.

Guigo's Piano Bar offers dim lighting and oldtime tunes as well as the latest in American music. It's a nice place for a quiet drink.

---

3. SAN ANDRES ISLAND

500 miles NW of Colombia; 150 miles E of Nicaragua

GETTING THERE   By Plane   Avianca flies to San Andrés from Cartagena and Bogotá. You can check schedules and prices in the Avianca office in either city. You can also fly to San Andrés from Barranquilla. The airport on San Andrés is the Sesquicentenario.

ESSENTIALS   Avianca is located in an office building a block and a half from the ocean on Avenida Duarte Blum. The post office is right next door to Avianca. The tourist office is located on Avenida Colombia (tel. 23-832).

Travel brochures talk a great deal about unspoiled beaches, but rarely do the facts fit the prose. However, at tiny San Andrés Island, in the Caribbean, the beaches are truly virginal. Together with the islands of Old Providence and Santa Catalina, San Andrés forms the San Andrés and Old Providence Archipelago, a Colombian possession whose history is very different from that of the mainland. It is full of bloody disputes and struggles between the islands original British colonists and the Spanish.

Although they had been discovered much earlier, the islands were first colonized by a group of English Puritans and Jamaican woodcutters who settled there with their slaves. Because of their strategic location along the routes travelled by the Spanish galleons, they provided a great base for pirates and English bucaneers as well as a great hideout. According to popular legend English pirate Henry Morgan chose San Andrés as his base and hid his treasure there. (Incidentally, his treasure has never been found.) In 1793 England recognized Spain's sovereignty over the islands, and in 1822 the islands became part of the independent republic Gran Colombia. In 1953 San Andrés was declared a free port, initiating a stream of immigration from the mainland. During that same period, regular air service was established by Avianca.

Although Spanish is the official language, English (primarily Caribbean) is widely spoken here, a leftover, presumably, from the days of the British occupation. Gambling is legal here, and there are two fine casinos as well as several nightclubs.

The island—only 7½ miles at its widest point—is shaped like a seahorse. Coral reefs surround it, as well as the neighboring islands of Providencia and Santa Catalina. Waters are perfect for snorkeling and scuba-diving. There are only two towns—San Andrés and San Luís. Essentially underdeveloped, the island depends heavily on tourism. Temperatures are virtually perfect—afternoons in the upper 80s and low 90s and evenings pleasantly in the 70s.

ORIENTATION

Your flight lands at a jetport only 5 minutes or so by cab ($2.75) from town. It's actually near enough to walk if you're light of luggage. The main street is **Avenida de la Playa,** which parallels the beaches. Most hotels are located here, as are the better restaurants. Key shopping streets are **Avenida Las Américas, Avenida 20 de Julio,** and **Avenida Costa Rica.**

A Spanish-made Fiat (called a Seat) now rents for $20 for 4 hours, with gasoline included and unlimited mileage. See **Portofino** on Avenida Colombia.

WHAT TO SEE & DO

Most of the island is uninhabited. The eye sees little more than tall palms, thick bush and grass, and the brilliantly blue ocean. The nicest homes on the island are in the **Sarie Bay** section near the airport. To see the island, consider renting a bicycle for about $3 a day. A taxi runs about $3.50 per hour.

Morgan's Cave, where Henry the pirate was said to have stored his treasures, is near Sarie Bay. Water fills the cave periodically, but you can climb down to it from the roadway. It's 50¢ to enter. At the tip of the island is a **Blow Hole (Hoyo Soplador),** where water rushes in at such force that it shoots 30 feet into the air.

San Luís, the island's other village, houses many of the locals, who depend on fishing for their living. There's a beach here. You can also admire the local architecture. One of the best examples is the **Emmanuel Baptist Church,** which dates back to 1874. Stop for lunch at the Sound Bay Beach Restaurant.

JOHNNY CAY It's 10 minutes by motor launch to this small coral island where the swimming and snorkeling are as perfect as we've seen anywhere in Latin America. The sand is thick and multicolored due to the coral. You can walk around the tiny reef in 10 minutes. A snack bar sells soft drinks, but you should bring a picnic lunch. Pick up the launch at the dock near the Tiuna Hotel ($3 round trip). You can rent snorkeling equipment and a boat at the **Hansa Club** for $20 per hour.

ACUARIO Not far from Johnny Cay is a natural aquarium where snorkelers endlessly explore the marine life and coral. A motorboat from Tiuna Hotel takes you there in under 15 minutes ($6 round trip).

SPORTS & RECREATION A charming double bike, with canopy, is yours for $3 an hour. Conventional two-wheelers are $2 per hour at the stand across from the Hotel Casablanca. There are four tennis courts for rent located near the Hotel Isleno on the beach. Watersports equipment can be rented at the Hansa Club Villas or at the Sea Horse Inn. Snorkeling, scuba-diving, and deep-sea fishing are available through the larger hotels and Baha Marina. The cost is $15 per hour.

WHERE TO STAY

HOTEL TIUNA, Avenida Colombia, no. 3-59. Tel. 23-235. All rooms with bath.
$ Rates: $20 single; $30 double.

This beachfront three-star hotel is lovely. Request a room with a terrace facing the beach.

ABACOA, Apartado Aereo 16. Tel. 24-133. 100 rms (all with bath).
$ Rates: $55 double. Major credit cards accepted.
This fine hotel is located right on the beach. A new wing, with air-conditioned rooms, was added some years ago. The Abacoa has a fine restaurant and a casino.

AQUARIUM, Avenida Colombia 1-19. Tel. 26-923. Fax 3994. 108 rms (all with bath). A/C MINIBAR
$ Rates: $52 single; from $64 double. Major credit cards accepted.
One of the newer hotels on the island is Aquarium, which sits right on Punta Hasa at the edge of the bay. It's actually a series of connected three-story circular buildings, all with dome roofs, built along the shore and in the bay itself. The restaurant, bar, pool, and shops are in these unique buildings as well.

CASABLANCA, Avenida Costa Rica, no. 1-40. Tel. 25-451. All rooms with bath. A/C MINIBAR

$ Rates: $47 double; $120 suite for up to four. Major credit cards accepted.

⭐ The Casablanca is a lovely beachfront hotel. The doubles are spacious and have small refrigerators. The hotel has a small pool and dining room. If you're traveling in a small group, a suite here may be worth the price.

EL ISLEÑO, Avenida la Playa, no. 5-117. Tel. 23-990. Fax 3126. 42 rms (all with bath). A/C MINIBAR TV TEL

$ Rates (including 2 meals): $35 single; $45 double. Major credit cards accepted.

⭐ The Isleño is one of the best hotels in this area and is located right on the beach. All the rooms are good sized and overlook the beach.

WHERE TO DINE

EL OASIS, Avenida Colombia.
Cuisine: SEAFOOD.
Open: Lunch and dinner.

⭐ An Argentine owns El Oasis, but the cuisine is strictly nautical—and superb. Sea breezes make dining here refreshing. Fishnets, diving bells, and wicker chairs shape the atmosphere. The potent rum-based cocktails put you in the right frame of mind to sample the house specialty: lobster in coconut sauce ($8). Meat dishes are excellent—try the chateaubriand—as are the fish platters.

LA CARRETA, Avenida Colombia.
Cuisine: INTERNATIONAL.
Open: Lunch and dinner.

For a wide variety of menu, with meat and poultry dishes leading the way, try La Carreta. The steaks are charcoal-broiled and quite good.

LA FONDA ANTIOQUENA, Avenida de la Playa.
Cuisine: COLOMBIAN.
Open: Lunch and dinner.

Although the menu in this charming restaurant is somewhat limited, the food and service are quite good. A large restaurant extending out over the water, La Fonda is popular. A continental breakfast costs $1.50, while a full American breakfast with two eggs and *arepa* (corn cakes) costs just 30¢ more. Your second cup of coffee is free, and the usual 10% service charge is not added to the check. At dinnertime, lobster dishes command the highest prices.

LA TORTUGA, Avenida Colombia.
Cuisine: SEAFOOD.
Open: Lunch and dinner.

For tasty seafood, head to the "Turtle," where shellfish is king and prices are reasonable.

PIZZERIA DE GIOVANNI, Tel. 6073.
Cuisine: ITALIAN.
Open: Lunch and dinner.

If you just have to have pizza, head to this restaurant in front of the Cañon de Morgan.

EVENING ENTERTAINMENT

There are two casinos worth exploring, both in hotels. The **Casino Hotel Abacoa,** open Tuesday to Sunday from 9pm to 3am, requires neither jacket nor tie. The Casa Dorada houses the other casino, with much the same rules. You have a choice of roulette, black jack, or a high-rolling game called *punta y banca*. The roulette tables accept 50¢ bets.

For music with a dance beat, downtown is a branch of **La Escollera,** Cartagena's popular disco. If its too crowded for you, there is a disco in the Hotel Casa Dorada.

CHAPTER 12
PANAMA CITY, PANAMA

- **WHAT'S SPECIAL ABOUT PANAMA CITY**
1. **INTRODUCING PANAMA CITY & PANAMA**
- **WHAT THINGS COST IN PANAMA CITY**
2. **ORIENTATION**
3. **GETTING AROUND**
- **FAST FACTS: PANAMA CITY**
4. **WHERE TO STAY**
5. **WHERE TO DINE**
6. **ATTRACTIONS**
- **DID YOU KNOW . . .?**
7. **SPORTS & RECREATION**
8. **SAVVY SHOPPING**
9. **EVENING ENTERTAINMENT**
10. **EASY EXCURSIONS**

Panama City immediately conjures up in most people a vision of hacking through a dense subtropical jungle to glimpse a view of a 50-mile "ditch." This, we suspect, derives from the hazy Hollywood view that comes through via old James Cagney–Pat O'Brien films.

If the canal and the "jungle" image come to mind first (complete with U.S. expatriate losers trying to find a way home), forget it. It is inaccurate and may deter you from making this intriguing stopover at no additional transportation cost.

What can you expect in this city of over 800,000 located on the Pacific and yet only 90 minutes by auto from the Atlantic? Well, for one thing, it's a night town, with plush gambling casinos and swinging nightclubs that don't really get moving until well after 11pm. For another, Panama City is truly international, with North and South Americans, Asians, and Europeans mingling on congested downtown streets along with Hindu shopkeepers and Panama's large black population.

You certainly will not want to leave this beehive of a city without scooping up some of the Western world's great bargains in linen, silk, or china. Japanese imports, particularly electronics, cameras, VCRs, and computers, are extremely good values here.

Then, of course, there is that tribute to early 20th-century engineering skill—the Panama Canal, 15 minutes by bus from downtown Panama City. The Canal Area (formerly the Canal Zone), which embraces many separate communities, links the Atlantic and the Pacific across 50 miles of what was once jungle. Visitors still marvel at the fantastic feat of flooding the giant locks to raise huge ocean liners so they can sail across the above-sea-level isthmus. A trip here is a must.

Panama is rightly called the "Gateway City to South America," bordering as it does on Colombia. Flights depart from Panama to virtually every major South American destination. United and COPA, the Panamanian National airline, have daily service from Miami to Panama with connecting flights to New York. American Airlines flies here, too.

You can stop here either at the beginning of your trip or on your way home. We prefer an end-of-trip stop so we don't have to tote our bargains with us and because we can usually count on good weather. Even in the rainy season (May to November) you can count on sunshine each morning. Panamanian lore has it that only on 14 days in the last 16 years was there no sunshine at all.

We are happy to report that since the U.S. military operations in Panama in December 1989, and the subsequent surrender to U.S. authorities of President

WHAT'S SPECIAL ABOUT PANAMA CITY

Beaches
- ☐ Seemingly endless expanses of white sand and crystalline waters make Taboga, Contadora, and San Blas veritable island paradises.

Monuments
- ☐ The monument to Nuñez de Balboa is a startling tribute to the discoverer of the Pacific.

Building
- ☐ The Teatro Nacional is a scaled-down version of La Scala in Milan.

Museums
- ☐ The Anthropological and the Panamanian Man Museums both offer a fascinating look into the country's past.

Ace Attraction
- ☐ The Panama Canal is a glowing testimony to engineering genius (and human perseverance).

Shopping
- ☐ Bargain hunting in Panama and the Free Zone in Colón is virtually without equal.

Manuel Noriega, friendly relations have been restored between the United States and Panama. We visited Panama in 1990 and again in 1992 to update this edition and found Panama City, for the most part, just as we had left it after our last visit in 1988.

A CAUTIONARY NOTE   Panama is currently suffering a severe economic crisis; as a result, street crime is on the rise. However, as long as you exercise good judgment, there is no need to be alarmed. Jewelry and all valuables should be locked in the hotel safe. Stick to the main streets and keep cameras out of view when walking around the city. Unless it's absolutely necessary to carry a purse, don't. Also, it's advisable to travel by taxi when going out in the evening.

1. INTRODUCING PANAMA CITY & PANAMA

Modern-day Panama City is actually the second of two Panamas, the first Hispanic colony in the Pacific. The first was founded on August 15, 1519, by Pedro Arias Dávila, alias Pedrarias the Cruel, 18 years after Columbus discovered the Atlantic coast of Panama. Arias Dávila's nickname was well deserved. It was he who murdered

---

IMPRESSIONS

Panama: The Bridge Between the Oceans.
—NATIONAL SLOGAN

[The Panama Canal] is the greatest liberty Man has ever taken with Nature.
—JAMES BRYCE, *SOUTH AMERICA*, 1912

Vasco Núñez de Balboa, discoverer of the Pacific, in 1513 and who initiated the slaughter of 57 of the region's 60 indigenous peoples.

The original Panama served as an important base for the Spanish during their conquest of the Americas. Francisco Pizarro began the plunder of the Inca from Panama, and the city quickly became a depository for stolen treasure before it was shipped by galleon to Spain. The city also became an important base for the slave trade as well as transatlantic commerce between Europe and the New World. So great was the city's wealth that it was the target of many an attack by pirates and buccaneers until finally, in 1671, Henry Morgan looted and burned it.

The second Panama, colonial Panama, was rebuilt at a site 4 miles away on a rocky peninsula and surrounded by a fortified wall for further protection. Time passed uneventfully from then on. Panama was granted independence from Spain in 1821 and subsequently formed the Republic of Greater Colombia with modern-day Colombia and Venezuela. In 1903, with the help of the United States, Panama separated from Colombia when it signed the Hay-Bunau-Varilla Treaty. This treaty granted the United States permanent and exclusive use of the Canal Zone.

WHAT THINGS COST IN PANAMA CITY	U.S. $
Cab from the airport to the city center	10.00
City bus fare	.25
Local telephone call	.10
Double with bath at the Hotel Acapulco (budget)	22.00
Double with bath at the Hotel Caribe (moderate)	45.00
Double with bath at the Hotel El Continental (deluxe)	70.00
Full meal at the Cafeteria Manolo (budget)	5.00
Dinner at Restaurant Las Américas (moderate)	8.00
Dinner with wine at Lesseps (expensive)	15.00
Dinner with wine at El Casco Viejo (splurge)	20.00
Average museum admission	.50
Cup of coffee	.35
Coca-Cola	.35

2. ORIENTATION

You'll be surprised at the hubbub that permeates this city, with office employees, shoppers, government officials, and visitors threading their way at a no-nonsense pace through traffic-clogged downtown streets. This is no sleepy city. While most downtown buildings are old, a vast government rebuilding project is dramatically altering the face of the city.

You'll no doubt be impressed, as we were, by the building boom and the endless parade of horn-blowing, gaily decorated privately owned buses that swarm the streets.

ARRIVING

After landing at modern **Tocumen International Airport,** 30 minutes from center city, head to the government-operated tourist counter (IPAT) there, which is open daily from 8am to midnight. Any of the polite clerks will gladly call a hotel for you to make a reservation at no charge. The only practical way into center city is via taxi, which

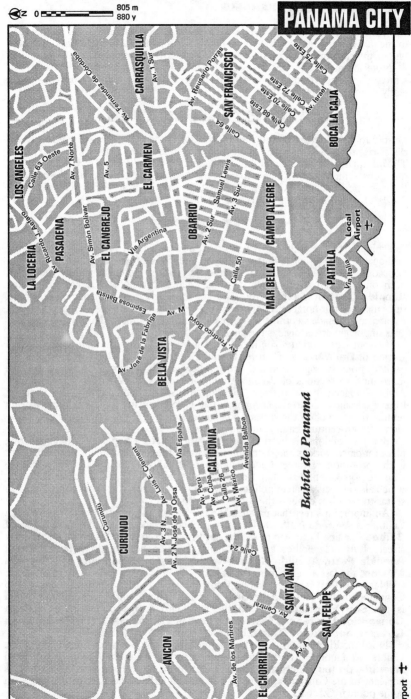

PANAMA CITY

0 ⊂🧭z

805 m
880 y

CARRASQUILLA

Av. Fernandez de Córdoba

Av. 1 Sur

SAN FRANCISCO

Av. Reusario Porras

Calle 15 Este

Calle 72 Este

Av. Israel

Calle 70 Este

Calle 68 Este

BOCA LA CAJA

LOS ANGELES

Calle 63 Oeste

Av. 7 Norte

Av. 5

EL CARMEN

Calle 64

LA LOCERIA

Av. Ricardo J. Alfaro

PASADENA

Av. Simón Bolívar

EL CANGREJO

Vía Argentina

OBARRIO

Samuel Lewis

Av. 3 Sur

CAMPO ALEGRE

Local Airport ✈

PATTILLA

Vía Italia

Av. 2 Sur

Calle 50

MAR BELLA

Espinosa Batista

Av. José de la Fábrega

Av. M

Av. Frederico Boyd

BELLA VISTA

Bahía de Panamá

Vía España

CALIDONIA

Av. Luis E. Clemente

Av. Perú

Av. Cuba

Calle 26

Av. México

Avenida Balboa

CURUNDU

Cununú

Av. 3 N.

Av. 2 N. José de la Ossa

Calle 24

Calle 25

SANTA ANA

SAN FELIPE

ANCON

Av. de los Mártires

EL CHORRILLO

Av. Central

Av. A

Airport ✈

will cost you $20 for up to three persons to the same destination. To save money head to the taxi desk, where you'll be linked with a group of four or five other travelers in one of the cabs operating as a *colectivo*. Fare is $10 each this way.

Note: Because of the recent escalation of drug trafficking through Panama, bag searches by Customs officers have become quite commonplace. Just be patient—there really is little else you can do.

TOURIST INFORMATION

Be sure to pick up maps and tourist information at the **IPAT (Instituto Panameño de Turismo),** the government tourist office, counter in the airport when you arrive. The information is quite comprehensive and the clerks will gladly answer any of your questions. Otherwise, you'll have to go to the main office located outside the center of town in the Centro De Convenciones ATLAPA on Via Israel in San Francisco (tel. 26-7000). You'll need to take a cab to get here.

CITY LAYOUT

Ten minutes before your cab reaches the downtown area, you'll pass through the fashionable suburbs of **Campo Alegre** and **El Cangrejo,** which house two luxurious hotels—El Continental on your left and the Hotel Panamá on your right, both on the main street of Via España. Keep in mind that Via España—called **Avenida Central** in center city—is a key thoroughfare for orientation purposes, since many of our hotel selections are on or near this busy street. On most maps Via España and Avenida Central are designated jointly as **Avenida 7a** (Seventh Avenue). This important street divides the city east and west.

As your cab continues south on Via España you'll pass through the residential section of **Bella Vista.** Then ready yourself for a view of **Calidonia,** one of the capital's poorest neighborhoods. Situated between the **Plaza 5 de Mayo** and the more modern sections of Panama City, Calidonia is noted for its many children. Autos—clogged in the narrow, winding streets—outdoor vendors, and shouting lottery salesmen add to the cacophony that is so peculiarly Calidonia. Slowly being rebuilt, this area offers the visitor a sometimes startling, always fascinating alternative view of 20th-century Latin America.

Beyond Calidonia is bustling **Santa Ana Plaza,** a popular midday gathering place for office workers and shoeshine boys in the heart of downtown. An oddity here is the profusion of rather good Chinese restaurants—Panama City has a sizable Chinese population. Busy shops, outdoor stalls, and office buildings circle the plaza, which also attracts amateur politicos and the resultant speechmaking. Santa Ana also seems to be a bus depot—the supply is endless.

An important street that parallels the Bay of Panama, five blocks east of Avenida Central, is **Avenida Balboa.** The most prominent landmark here is the **Statue of Balboa** (the first European to see the Pacific). Between Avenida Central and the bay street of Avenida Balboa are these major avenues, heading down from Central: **Avenida Perú, Avenida Cuba, Avenida Justo Arosemena,** and **Avenida México,** the last a block from the bay.

Nearby is **Paitilla,** the local airport from which small aircraft will wing you to Contadora in the Pacific and the San Blas Islands in the Atlantic. East of Punta Paitilla is the **San Francisco** area on the bay. This area also houses the **Atlapa Convention Center** and **Marriott Hotel** on Via Israel. IPAT, **the Panamanian Government Tourist Office,** is in the Atlapa building (tel. 26-7000).

North of El Cangrejo is the **Los Angeles** section, home of Lung Fung, a fine Chinese restaurant. Another important street is **Avenida Tivoli,** also called **Avenida de los Martires,** formerly Cuatro de Julio (Fourth of July), which is adjacent to the Canal area. Many fine shops and airline offices are here, along with some popular G.I. bars.

The Panama Canal visitors' area at Miraflores Locks is a short bus ride from downtown (we'll have more to say about this "must" side trip later).

The better budget hotels and restaurants are scattered throughout the city, unlike in most other Latin American cities.

3. GETTING AROUND

BY BUS   The city has a very comprehensive bus system that can get you just about anywhere you want to go in the city. Buses are marked with their final destination and the fare is 25¢. To avoid mishaps tell the driver where you want to get off when you board.

BY TAXI   Cabs here have no meters, so you must set the price in advance. Fares vary with the number of passengers and the distance to be traveled. For example, within a single zone a lone passenger would be charged $2.25, while four passengers would pay $6. A trip into a second zone would cost one passenger an additional $1.50 and four passengers an additional $3.75. The rate is $5 for the first hour and $3 for each subsequent hour. You can bargain before you get into the cab. There are small and large cabs—small ones charging less.

BY CAR   You must be at least 18 years old and hold a valid license to rent a car. All the major international companies are here, and there are local rental agencies, too. Shop around for the best price. For prices and location nearest you, call **Budget** at 63-8777; **Dollar** at 61-7773; and **National** at 64-8277 or 69-1921. These and local agencies have offices at the airport. Gasoline is quite expensive—over $2.35 a gallon.

FAST FACTS *PANAMA CITY*

American Express   The American Express office is in the Banco Exterior Building on Avenida Balboa (tel. 63-5888).
Area Code   The area code for Panama is 507.
Babysitters   The concierge in your hotel may be able to help you arrange for child care.
Banks   Panama is an international banking center, with over 120 banks. Banks do not have fixed hours, so make sure to check on hours at the branch you want to use.
Business Hours   Most **stores** are open daily from 9am to 6pm; some close on Sundays.
Car Rentals   See "Getting Around" earlier in this chapter.
Climate   The climate, while warm, is seldom hot, and the evenings are surprisingly cool. Although humidity can be high and somewhat uncomfortable from June to September, midday temperatures are equivalent to Miami Beach's summer readings—in the 80°-to-85° range—and are perfect year round for swimming. There is little climate variation here between the dry season (December to May) and the rainy season (June to November). The Atlantic side of Panama (Colón) receives almost twice as much rain as the Pacific (Panama City) side.
Crime   See "Safety" below.
Currency   As for currency, there is virtually no difference between Panama and the United States, since the basic money unit here is the U.S. dollar, called the *balboa.* Five dollars is written B/5, meaning 5 balboas, and the paper currency is the U.S. $5 bill. There are local coins in 1¢, 5¢, 10¢, 25¢, and 50¢ denominations, although U.S. coins circulate freely.
Tip: Local silver dollars are collectors' items and as such are worth considerably more than $1. So, if you come across one, hold on to it.
Dentists/Doctors   Contact the embassy for a list of English-speaking dentists or doctors.

Drugstores The **Farmacia Arrocha,** with several locations throughout the city, is open 24 hours a day.

Electricity Panama has the same 110-volt current as the United States. No adapter is necessary.

Embassies/Consulates The **U.S. Embassy** is at Avenida Balboa and Calle 37 (tel. 27-1777); open weekdays from 8am to noon and 1 to 4pm.

Emergencies In case of emergency, contact the concierge in your hotel or go to the front desk of any of the larger hotels for assistance.

Eyeglasses The concierge in your hotel should be able to direct you to a nearby optician.

Hairdressers/Barbers The concierge in your hotel should be able to direct you to a nearby hairdresser.

Holidays

Day of the Martyrs	January 9
Carnival Tuesday	Tuesday before Ash Wednesday
Labor Day	May 1
Revolution Day	October 11
Memorial Day	November 2
Independence from Colombia	November 3
Flag Day	November 4
Mother's Day	December 8

Information See "Tourist Information" earlier in this chapter.

Kosher Foods Panama's sizable Jewish community buys its provisions at **Comisariato Kosher,** a supermarket in Albert Einstein Plaza, off Calle 65, in El Cangrejo; it's closed Saturday, open Sunday. Here they have salamis, gefilte fish, herring, and much more. There's another kosher supermarket in the Bal Harbour Shopping Center.

Language While Spanish is the official tongue, many residents speak English. We are constantly surprised to hear bus drivers respond to questions in flawless British-accented English. The city's international character, deriving from the former Canal Zone influence, explains the English-language emphasis.

Note: Panamanians refer to this city as Panama and never as Panama City. Don't let this confuse you when asking directions.

Laundry/Dry Cleaning Most of the major hotels offer laundry and dry-cleaning services.

Luggage Storage/Lockers If you're planning to take a short trip, you'll probably be able to store your belongings in your hotel. Check on this before you finalize your arrangements.

Newspapers/Magazines The *International Herald Tribune* and the *Miami Herald* are available at the larger hotels and at some newsstands. *Time* magazine is $1.95 (international edition).

Photographic Needs You'll find film to be readily available here.

Post Office All post offices, including the Balboa branch in the Canal Area, are open Monday to Saturday from 7am to 6pm. Airmail to the United States is 60¢, to Europe 75¢.

Religious Services Although Catholicism is the predominant religion, many faiths are represented in Panama. Contact the concierge in your hotel or check the local papers for services of your faith.

Restrooms Most restaurants, museums, and nightclubs provide restrooms for patrons. There are also restrooms near the reception areas of the larger hotels.

Safety Just as in most major cities today, street crime has become prevalent in Panama. Do as you would do anywhere else and exercise at all times the same common-sense caution. Avoid walking the streets after dark, stay out of suspicious areas, and leave all your valuables at home.

Shoe Repairs You can get a quick shine in the Plaza Santa Ana. For more serious repairs, the concierge in your hotel should be able to direct you to a nearby shop.

Taxes   Prepare to pay an airport tax of $15 per person when flying out of Panama.

Taxis   See "Getting Around" earlier in this chapter.

Telegrams/Telexes/Faxes   Major hotels provide fax and telex services. This can also be handled at an INTEL office.

Telephone   Local calls are 10¢. You can dial direct from many hotels here, or the operator will make the call for you. Check on the charge added by the hotel before placing the call. You can also call from an INTEL office. AT&T Direct is a great cost saver. To get an AT&T Direct line, dial 109.

Television   Channel 8 broadcasts in English, with news at 6 and 10pm nightly. You can catch U.S. films and TV shows, including *Sesame Street* (no commercials). English-language newspapers carry listings daily. The station is part of the U.S. Southern Command Network. Many hotels also carry CNN.

Time   Panama's time zone Eastern Standard Time.

Tipping   Service is not included in your hotel or restaurant bill. A 10% to 15% tip is standard.

4. WHERE TO STAY

Panama is a small city, but one with quite an unusual number of good-value hotels in all price ranges. Remember to add 10% tourist tax. Most hotels have a late (2 to 3pm) checkout time.

PANAMA

DOUBLES FOR LESS THAN $30

HOTEL ACAPULCO, Calle 30 Este, between Avenidas Cuba and Perú. Tel. 25-3832. Fax 27-2032. 55 rooms (all with bath). A/C TV
$ Rates: $20 single; $22 double.

The Hotel Acapulco offers simply furnished rooms in the heart of the commercial district at a very good price. The bar and restaurant and the friendly management will make your stay here a pleasant one.

EL HOTEL COLON, Transveral 1, no. 7-55, at the corner of Calle B and 12 Oeste. Tel. 28-8510. 45 rms (all with bath).
$ Rates: $14–$19 single; $18–$22 double; $24–$26 triple.
Near Santa Ana Park, one block off Avenida Central, is the colonial-style Colón. You may want to rent an airy room with shutters, a bath and shower, a telephone, air conditioning, and a balcony; or you may opt for a cheaper room without air conditioning. This four-story elevator hotel has blue mosaic tile on the lobby walls and offers a small rooftop patio overlooking the Pacific. On a clear day the canal is visible. A Dairy Queen cafeteria is next door. If you plan a stay of a week or longer, by all means negotiate for a better rate.

HOTEL IDEAL, Calle 17 Oeste, no. 15-55. Tel. 62-2400. 170 rms (some with bath).
$ Rates: $16–$19 single; $21–$24 double; from $25 triple. **Parking:** Free.

The four-story Ideal, located several blocks off Avenida Central and not far from the Canal Area, offers guests the option of paying more for private bath and air conditioning. You may choose to have a fan if you don't want air conditioning. The cheapest rooms are the ones without baths, air conditioning, or fans, but they do have sinks. An annex with less desirable rooms has lower rates. The management offers a 5% discount for a one-week stay and a 10% reduction for a month's visit. Each room contains worn leather chairs (couches in some cases), along with a dressing table and comfortable beds. A TV in the lobby is a bonus. A self-service restaurant, a boîte, a dining room, a pool, a barbershop, a beauty parlor, and a laundry are on the premises.

HOTEL RIAZOR, Calle 16 Oeste, no. 15-105. Tel. 28-0986. 46 rms (some with bath).
$ Rates: $12–$13 single with bath; $18–$19 double with bath; $24–$25 triple with bath.
Near Avenida Central, the Riazor offers clean, comfortable, colonial-style lodging and roomy doubles. Air conditioning costs a dollar. Some bathless rooms with double beds instead of twin beds are cheaper. The large rooms have dressers, chairs, stall showers, and telephone. The lobby, one floor above street level, is partially covered with a skylight, which adds some brightness. A restaurant and bar are on the premises.

HOTEL 2 MARES, Calle 30, between Avenida Cuba and Perú. Tel. 27-6150. 87 rooms (all with bath). AC TV
$ Rates: $22 single; $25 double.
The 2 Mares is an excellent value in this price range, with rooms that are modern and comfortably furnished. Extras include a fitness center with sauna, a pool, a bar and restaurant, and a nightclub.

DOUBLES FOR LESS THAN $60

HOTEL COSTA INN, Avenida Perú and Calle 30. Tel. 27-1522. Fax 25-1281. 155 rms (all with bath). A/C TV TEL
$ Rates: $38 single; $45 double. Major credit cards accepted.
The Costa Inn has rooms that are spacious and tastefully furnished. There are a bar and restaurant within the hotel and room service is available 24 hours. Television is cable, and some U.S. stations are available.

EUROPA HOTEL, Via España 33. Tel. 63-6369. Fax 63-6749. Telex 3573 EUROPHTL PG. 100 rms (all with bath). A/C TV TEL
$ Rates: $45 single; $50 double.
In front of the Bella Vista Theater is another good choice. Rooms are carpeted, comfortably furnished, and always in demand. The pool and bar are popular, as is the cafeteria.

GRAN HOTEL SOLOY, Avenida Perú y Calle 30. Tel. 27-1133. Fax 27-0884. Telex 2509. 200 rms (all with bath). A/C MINIBAR TV TEL
$ Rates: $50 double. Major credit cards accepted.
This 20-story choice is located in downtown Panama, but not in a heavy traffic area. From its roof pool you can see the city and the Panama Canal. The Soloy has a fine restaurant and casino.

HOTEL BELLA VISTA, Via España 31. Tel. 64-4029. 40 rms (all with bath). A/C
$ Rates: $28 single; $30 double.
This hotel was converted from a pension that we'd been recommending for years. Now we recommend the hotel. Look for the red sign outside and climb one flight to the registration desk. An outside porch is for guest use. Next door is the popular Gran Muralla (Chinese) Restaurant.

HOTEL CARIBE, Calle 28 and Avenida Peru. Tel. 25-0404. Fax 27-3115. 150 rms (all with bath). A/C TEL
$ Rates: $40 single; $45 double. Major credit cards accepted.

One of the best hotels in this category is the ten-floor Caribe. A bonus is the location, one block from a huge public pool. The rooms are small but comfortable. A coffee shop and bar are on the premises.

HOTEL ROMA, Avenida Justo Arosemana, at Calle 38. Tel. 27-3844. Fax 27-3711. 150 rms (all with bath). A/C MINIBAR TV TEL
$ Rates: $40 single; $49.50 double. Major credit cards accepted.

The recently renovated Hotel Roma boasts beautifully furnished rooms. A cafetería, two restaurants, a pool with its own bar, and a piano bar with live entertainment are all on the premises. Mauricio, the hotel representative from the InterClub Travel Service, is a great source of information and will be glad to recommend restaurants or nightclubs. He can also arrange a three-hour guided tour of the Old City, Panama Viejo, and the canal. The cost of the tour is $17 per person for two or $30 to $35 if you're alone.

DOUBLES FOR LESS THAN $90

HOTEL EL CONTINENTAL, Via España. Tel. 63-9999. Telex 368-2699. P.O. Box 8475 Panama 5. 240 rms (all with bath). A/C TEL
$ Rates: $65 single; $70 double. Major credit cards accepted.

The Continental is conveniently located in the commercial-and-banking sector. It has a terrific seafood restaurant, a swinging disco, a casino, and a coffee shop. The pool and sundeck are small. There is another Continental located by the airport.

HOTEL Y CASINO GRANADA, Calle Eusebio Morales. Tel. 64-4900. Fax 64-0930. Telex 3682699 CONTINEN PG. 175 rms (all with bath). A/C MINIBAR TV TEL
$ Rates: $72 single; $82 double. Major credit cards accepted.

Within easy walking distance of the Via España (one block) is the deluxe Granada. Its rooms are attractively and comfortably decorated. The Granada has a pool, a coffee shop, and a casino and cocktail lounge.

COLONIAL PANAMA

COLONIAL, Calle 4 in the Plaza Bolívar. Tel. 62-3858. Some rooms with bath.
$ Rates: $9 single; $11 double.

The Colonial is an interesting old hotel with all the amenities of a deluxe stop; however, they have not all aged well. There are a small pool, restaurant, and bar.

HOTEL CENTRAL, in Plaza Catedral. Tel. 68-8044. 145 rms (some with bath).
$ Rates: $7 single without bath, $10 single with bath; $11 double without bath, $13 double with bath.

The large, once-first-class Central could have been the setting for an old Hollywood film, complete with ceiling fans. This fading three-story palace, once the city's leading hotel, now somewhat dilapidated, offers extremely large rooms, all with balconies and wicker chairs. There is an elevator.

A PENSION

PENSION AMERICA, Avenida Justo Arosemena, no. 33-54, near Calle 34. Tel. 25-1140. Some rooms with bath.
$ Rates: $11–$13 single without bath, $14–$16 single with bath; $14–$16 double without bath, $17–$19 double with bath.

The Pensión America is still going strong and has actually expanded. This large pink house, located on a quiet residential street two blocks from Avenida Balboa, has many plants and trees on the grounds. The rooms are modestly furnished but clean. Three public bathrooms are reserved for guests. Rooms with air conditioning cost more.

RESIDENTIAL HOTELS

If you enjoy living in an apartment with the services of a hotel, you might consider one of Panama's several fine apartment-hotels. In these establishments you get an apartment with a kitchen, stove, refrigerator, sitting area, and bedroom. Maid service is included. You can save your food dollars by shopping in the supermarkets and eating in. A fine idea for families.

APART-HOTEL AMBASSADOR, Calle D, El Cangrejo near the local airport. Tel. 63-7274. Fax 64-7872. 40 suites (all with bath). A/C TV TEL
$ Rates (including continental breakfast): $77 studio; $88 suite. Major credit cards accepted.
A lovely rooftop pool with terrace, a fitness center, and meeting facilities are the extras you'll enjoy at the Apart-hotel Ambassador. Great for those planning a lengthy stay in Panama, the Ambassador offers modern suites and suites and studios, complete with fully equipped kitchens. The Ambassador is located just off Via España close to some of the city's finest restaurants and nightspots. Reserve ahead of time (write to Apartado Postal 5364, Zona 5, Panama).

COSTA DEL SOL APART-HOTEL, Vía España y Avenida Federico Boyd. Tel. 23-7111. Fax 23-6636. 242 suites (all with bath). A/C TV TEL
$ Rates: $85 per day. Weekly and monthly rates available. Major credit cards accepted.
The Costa del Sol boasts many of the amenities of a resort hotel: an elegant lobby; a world-class restaurant and bar often featuring live entertainment; a tennis court, jogging area, and saunas; plus a lovely rooftop terrace and pool. Self-service laundry facilities are available on every floor. The Costa del Sol is within easy walking distance of the banking district, shopping, many fine restaurants and nightspots. Write ahead for reservations to P.O. Box 8572, Panama 5.

TOWER HOUSE SUITES, Calle 51, no. 36, Bella Vista. Tel. 69-2244. Fax 69-2869. All suites with bath. A/C TV TEL
$ Rates (including continental breakfast): $42–$48. Major credit cards accepted.
Tower House's location in the heart of the banking center makes it an ideal choice for business travelers. Facilities include a fitness center, pool, convention center, and restaurant. Room service is available 24 hours.

A SPLURGE CHOICE

PLAZA PAITILLA INN, Vía Italia and Winston Churchhill, on Punta Paitilla. Tel. 69-2408. Fax 23-1470. 280 rms (all with bath). A/C MINIBAR TV TEL
$ Rates: $105 double. Major credit cards accepted.
The Holiday Inn has come under new management and is now the Plaza Paitilla Inn. It's the only hotel in town with an ocean view (actually of the bay); rooms are in a 20-story round tower, which also houses a pool, tennis courts, and a disco.

5. WHERE TO DINE

Panama's restaurants come in all categories and are scattered throughout the city. While there are a sufficient number of good eateries in our price range, Panama's finer restaurants are rather more expensive. Since you'll want to sample them, save money on breakfast and lunch by eating in our recommended cafeterias and small restaurants. The least expensive choices are the fast-food places that have proliferated here. Restaurants charge no tax, and tips are not included in your bill: A tip is customary. Dining hours follow U.S. patterns. Keep in mind that many restaurants in town close on Sunday or Monday, so it's a good idea to call before setting out.

Italian foods are very popular here, with pasta dishes and pizza the best-sellers. New Chinese restaurants seem to pop up each time we revisit Panama. Over the past few years restaurants serving a variety of foods have opened throughout the city, but most are a cut above budget levels. You can enjoy Spanish, Colombian, Peruvian, Japanese, and Korean specialties if you're prudent when ordering. The seafood here is outstanding, in both the variety of dishes served and the high quality of the preparation. *Panama* means "abundance of fish," and this is not a misnomer.

Note: Panama is not the place to wander idly into a restaurant in search of some exotic fare. Stick to the well-known places, where you can't go wrong.

Now for some of our favorite Panamanian dishes. **Sancocho** is a popular soup/stew, almost a meal in itself—an excellent lunch. **Ropa vieja** is a blend of shredded beef and vegetables, served with rice and *plátano* (plantain). **Ceviche** is marinated raw fish in a delicious sauce. Panama's dinner hour generally ends by 10pm, although many places close earlier. So if you're planning a very late meal, call first.

AMERICAN LEGION, Fort Amador.
Cuisine: NORTH AMERICAN.
$ Prices: Complete meals for $4–$8.
Open: Lunch and dinner.
The restaurant at the American Legion has as its lure a fantastic view of the Panama Canal. You can look out one of the large glass windows fronting the Bridge of the Americas and watch the ships passing into the canal or into the ocean. There's a large bar, too, so you can stop in just for a drink. You'll need a cab to get here.

CAFETERIA MANOLO, Via Argentina. Tel. 64-3965.
Cuisine: INTERNATIONAL.
$ Prices: Full meal around $5.
Open: All day.

This cafeteria is always crowded and lively. You'll find fresh vegetables, steaming beef and fish dishes, and *churros* (powdered doughnuts)—almost as good as those in Buenos Aires and only 60¢. Another branch is on Vía España.

LA CASCADA, Avenida Balboa, between Calles 25 and 26. Tel. 62-1297.
Cuisine: INTERNATIONAL. **Reservations:** Recommended.
$ Prices: Appetizers $1–$3; main courses $4–$10.
Open: Dinner only, Mon–Sat 4:30–11pm.

La Cascada is an unusual open-air restaurant with life-size figures of animals peering out of abundant greenery and water cascading down a high rock wall; it draws a happy-go-lucky crowd of both adults and children. Portions are very large and the food is very tasty.

COSTA AZUL, Calle Ricardo Arias 11.
Cuisine: INTERNATIONAL.
$ Prices: Appetizers $1–$3; main courses $2–$8.
Open: Lunch and dinner.
Costa Azul, an inexpensive restaurant with outdoor and indoor tables as well as counter service, is a good choice for all meals. The outdoor tables on the roof-covered deck are jammed with locals enjoying the daily specials, which include omelets and chicken dishes as well as steaks. Sandwiches and soups are available too.

HOTEL IDEAL CAFETERIA, Calle 17 Este, no. 15-55, near Avenida Central.
Cuisine: INTERNATIONAL.
$ Prices: Appetizers $1–$3; main courses $2–$8.
Open: 6am–midnight.
Here you'll find one of the city's most inexpensive eateries, perfect for all meals as well as late-night snacks. Well known for its exceptional desserts, it's more of a restaurant than a cafeteria as we know it. Whole dinners start at $7, which is very inexpensive for Panama.

MANDARIN, Avenida Cuba and Calle 33.

Cuisine: CHINESE.
$ **Prices:** Dinner $6–$11.
Open: Lunch and dinner.
Try the air-conditioned Mandarin, behind the Tribunal Electoral in a quiet residential area. Most attractive in decor, the Mandarin features wood paneling, red-leather booths, and spotless tablecloths. Specializing in northern Chinese food, this charming restaurant offers a choice of four family dinners ranging from $6 to $11 per person, depending on your party's size. Beef consommé, chow mein, shrimp in a tomato sauce, egg foo yung, and hot-and-spicy chicken dishes are all worth sampling.

NAPOLI, Calle Estudiante and Calle 1. Tel. 62-2446.
Cuisine: ITALIAN.
$ **Prices:** Appetizers $1–$2.50; main courses $3–$8.
Open: Mon–Sat 10:30am–11pm.
A good Italian eatery is the bustling Napoli, near the Instituto Nacional in the center of town, which seems filled with students every time we stop by. The indoor-outdoor Napoli is proud of its clams parmigiana and chicken *cazadore* (cacciatore, that is). Lower down on the price scale are pizzas and sandwiches. The menu is bilingual and offers a wide variety of low-priced fare. A good breakfast will cost about $1.75.

RESTAURANT DE LAS AMERICAS, Avenida 1 Sur y Calle 57, in the suburb of Obarrio, near the Teatro Opera. Tel. 23-4676.
Cuisine: PANAMANIAN. **Reservations:** Recommended.
$ **Prices:** Five-course dinners $6.25–$12.
Open: Daily 11am–10pm.
⭐ This modern and clean establishment is a typical Panamanian restaurant—with bilingual menus to ease your language problems. Look for the circular red neon sign. In this spacious, brightly lit spot you have a choice of indoor or outdoor dining. Stick with the executive menu, which offers splendid five-course dinners at reasonable prices. For example, you can have crisp antipasto, seafood chowder, pepper steak with rice and peas, flan (pudding), and marvelous coffee for $9.

SORRENTO, Via Porras at Calle 69. Tel. 26-6980.
Cuisine: ITALIAN.
$ **Prices:** Appetizers $1–$3; main courses $3–$6.
Open: Wed–Mon 11:30am–midnight.
Sorrento serves delicious pizzas and other Italian fare as well. There is a branch of Sorrento on Calle Ricardo Arias.

RESTAURANTE BAR PANAMAR, Calle 50 Final, in San Francisco de la Caleta. Tel. 26-0892.
Cuisine: SEAFOOD. **Reservations:** Recommended. **Taxi:** $1.50 from the commercial center.
$ **Prices:** Appetizers $3–$6; main courses $5–$12. Major credit cards accepted.
Open: Noon–midnight.
⭐ For a seaside setting and excellent seafood, try the Club Panamar. The shrimp and lobster dishes are superb. You might choose shrimp Creole, baby red snapper, filet *corvina alemendrine*, or lobster thermidor. You have a choice of eating in the air-conditioned salon or the outdoor garden. Ask manager Victor Sierra to show you the huge refrigerators filled with fresh fish.

LA FONDA ANTIOQUEÑA, Vía Cincuentenario. Tel. 21-1268.
Cuisine: COLOMBIAN.
$ **Prices:** Appetizers $2–$5; main courses $4–$9.
Open: Lunch and dinner.
A tavern typical of the cattle-raising areas of Colombia has been reproduced here amid the ruins of Old Panama. Spend the afternoon exploring the area, then stop for dinner. Grilled meats are the specialties, but we prefer the grilled fish. *Bistec a caballo* (steak with eggs on top) is very popular. Try a *chorizo* (typical sausage) with a cocktail. The restaurant is a popular nightspot, with a jukebox that's kept busy all evening.

LESSEPS, Via España and Calle 46, in La Cresta. Tel. 23-0749.
  Cuisine: FRENCH. **Reservations:** Recommended.
  $ Prices: Appetizers $3–$6; main courses $6–$10. Major credit cards accepted.
  Open: Sun–Fri lunch and dinner; Sat dinner only.
Travel back to the beginning of the century in Lesseps, where exquisite French cuisine is served in an art nouveau setting. You are sure to enjoy the special bar atmosphere, even more so if you try the Brigitte Bardot or the Panama cocktail.

MARBELLA, Avenida Balboa and Calle 30. Tel. 25 0065.
  Cuisine: SPANISH. **Reservations:** Recommended.
  $ Prices: Appetizers $2–$4; main courses $5–$10.
  Open: Lunch and dinner.
Marbella, a former private home that faces the bay, is a small restaurant where you can dine on paella, *arroz marinera*, and tortillas. The sidewalk terrace is popular on cool evenings, and the large windows offer excellent views of the bay.

EL PAVO REAL, Calle 51, in Campo Alegre. Tel. 69-0504.
  Cuisine: INTERNATIONAL. **Reservations:** Recommended.
  $ Prices: Appetizers $1–$3; main courses $5–$10.
  Open: Mon–Sat noon–midnight.
⭐ El Pavo Real is an eatery with a SoHo atmosphere. The owner, Sarah, is very friendly and will be more than happy to recommend something from her menu, which includes a delicious selection of homemade pâtés, quiches, and stuffed crêpes, plus more filling entrées such as steaks, pasta, and seafood. There is also a help-yourself salad bar. A good spot for a light dinner or lunch.

TINAJAS, Calle 51, no. 22, in Bella Vista. Tel. 69-3840.
  Cuisine: PANAMANIAN. **Reservations:** Recommended.
  $ Prices: Appetizers $2–$5; main courses $6–$10. Major credit cards accepted.
  Open: Dinner only.
⭐ For a delicious Panamanian dinner plus a folklore show, make reservations for dinner here. The restaurant is located in a private house; the decor is ranch-style Spanish; and the seafood stew, tamales, and Panamanian-style shrimp are excellent. There is a $5 cover charge for the show, which goes on at 9pm on Tuesday, Thursday, Friday, and Saturday. A small shop sells handcrafts, but you probably can do better elsewhere.

TORITOS, Calle Miguel Brosella. Tel. 60-0735.
  Cuisine: MEXICAN. **Reservations:** Recommended.
  $ Prices: Appetizers $1–$3; main courses $3–$7.
  Open: Lunch and dinner.
If you're in the mood for Mexican, try Toritos. It also has its own disco, Piramides. Tequila cocktails are one of the specialties of the house.

EL TRAPICHE, Via Argentina, near the Café Manolo. Tel. 69-4353.
  Cuisine: PANAMANIAN.
  $ Prices: Appetizers $1–$3; main courses $3–$7.
  Open: Lunch and dinner.
Tasty Panamanian food is served at this small but popular eatery. The restaurant itself, which specializes in the cuisine of the central provinces, is modeled after a *trapiche*, an old-world sugar mill still used in some parts of the country to squeeze the juice (*guarepo*) from the sugarcane. Be sure to try the *en hojaldra* (flour fritters filled with chicken or meat), *mondogo* (seasoned tripe), and *gallo pinto* (rice-and-bean casserole). A sidewalk terrace is popular with Panamanians, but we prefer to eat inside.

SPLURGE CHOICES

EL CASCO VIEJO, Calle 50 in the Mansión Danté, across from Plaza New York, in Bella Vista. Tel. 23-3316.
  Cuisine: FRENCH. **Reservations:** Recommended.
  $ Prices: Appetizers $4–$6; main courses $8–$14. Major credit cards accepted.

Open: Lunch and dinner.

One of our favorite restaurants in Panama has moved to a more convenient location in the more modern part of town. The French food served here, however, has remained of the same excellent quality.

EL CORTIJO, Calle Morales, across from the Hotel Granada. Tel. 69-6387.
Cuisine: SPANISH. **Reservations:** Recommended.
$ Prices: Appetizers $4–$8; main courses $8–$14; average dinner $20. Major credit cards accepted.
Open: Lunch and dinner.

Another of Panama's finest restaurants, this is set in a beautiful whitewashed building that would be at home in Seville (in Spain, a *cortijo* is a ranch). Spanish dishes are the specialties, with seafood used in many. Try a delicious paella.

GINZA TEPPANYAKI, Calle D and Avenida Morales, near the Granada Hotel. Tel. 69-1389.
Cuisine: JAPANESE. **Reservations:** Recommended.
$ Prices: Appetizers $3–$6; main courses $10–$15. Major credit cards accepted.
Open: Lunch and dinner.

This Japanese steakhouse is one of the finest in the city. Two ferocious stone dragons guard the entrance to the Chinese lantern–bedecked house. Join other diners at a long rectangular table, where your dinner will be cooked on a hot tray built into the table. Steak, chicken, shrimp, and other shellfish are popular selections. Dinners include soup and dessert.

SARTI'S, Calle Ricardo Arias, just beyond the Continental Hotel. Tel. 23-7664.
Cuisine: ITALIAN. **Reservations:** Recommended.
$ Prices: Appetizers $3–$6; main courses $6–$15. Major credit cards accepted.
Open: Lunch and dinner.

Sarti's is a small, expensive restaurant that serves some of the best Italian dishes in Panama. Here we suggest that you stick to the pasta and pizza platters to keep down your costs—perhaps ravioli, lasagne, or ham-and-pepperoni pizza.

SPECIALTY DINING

LIGHT FARE Your best bet for a scenic breakfast or lunch is the popular **El Boulevard,** at Calle 31, on Avenida Balboa, facing the Bay of Panama. We look forward to their breakfast of ham and eggs, toast, and coffee for $2.50; a continental breakfast is only $1.25. For lunch, the sandwiches are popular ($2 to $3.50). For heavier fare, try the pepper steak ($3.25) or chicken in the basket ($2.50). Cocktails are an inexpensive $1 to $2.25. A good-priced breakfast is served, starting at 7am, at **Café Manolo,** on Vía España.

Niko's Café, open 24 hours, is a budget traveler's delight, serving a wide variety of fare at low prices. Many Panamanians eat lunch here. Look for the Supermarket El Rey on Via España. A fine breakfast spot is **Delirys,** located under the Charlot Pub on Avenida M. Icaza, near the Continental Hotel. Head downstairs to the cafetería-style restaurant, pour your own juice, and make your selections from the counter. If you're like us, you will dine al fresco; others choose to eat at the indoor tables.

El Vegetariano Mireya, on Calle Ricardo Arias, is open daily and serves fresh-fruit salads and drinks, delicious sandwiches on home-baked wheat bread, yogurts, and vegetable hot plates. It's a small restaurant where the specials change daily.

Romanaccio Cafetería and Pizzería, in the Centro Comercial La Galería on Vía Ricardo J. Alfaro, is a great lunch or dinner choice. The food is well prepared, spicy, and hot. Thronged with shoppers and workers from the nearby banks at lunchtime, Romanaccio quiets down at dinner. Italian specialties are the biggest draws, but there are beef and fish dishes as well as heroes and desserts. Romanaccio is so popular it has opened a second eatery in the Centro Comercial Marbella in Paitilla.

？DID YOU KNOW . . . ?

- In 1534 Charles I of Spain ordered the first survey of a proposed canal route through the Isthmus of Panama.
- Frenchman Ferdinand de Lesseps was the first to start digging a canal across the Isthmus. Construction began in 1879, but after 40,000 laborers were killed, the project was abandoned.
- Panama leased the United States the 10-mile-wide canal zone for a down payment of $10,000,000.
- The highest Canal toll is $120,439.20, paid by the *Star Princess* on October 5, 1990. The lowest toll is 36¢, paid in 1928 by adventure author Richard Halliburton for swimming the canal.
- Gatun Lake was the largest artificial lake in the world until Lake Mead was formed by the construction of the Hoover Dam.
- The three major tribes of Indians in Panama are the Guaymi, Cuna, and the Choco.
- Scholars suggest that there may have been about 500,000 Indians from 60 tribes living on the Isthmus in the 1500s.
- In 1610, the population of Panama City consisted of about 4,800 people: 3,500 were African slaves, 150 were free blacks, and 1,150 were Spaniards.
- The Church of Nata, built in 1522, is believed to be the oldest church still in use on the mainland of the Americas.
- Many of Panama's blacks are descendants of laborers who were brought into the country in the early 1900s from the West Indies to build the Panama Canal.
- The first railroad to cross the isthmus was completed in 1855 by a group of New York financiers.
- *Bajareque* is the Panamanian word used to describe the mist in the air where the winds from the Atlantic and Pacific meet.

Open for all three meals, it's quieter and dining is more leisurely.

A **Domino's Pizza** has just opened on the corner of Vía Brasil and Calle 50. They'll deliver to your hotel room. (Remember, 30 minutes or it's free.) For breakfast or hamburgers, look no further than **McDonald's,** with six branches all over town. The most popular is the outlet on Vía España across from the Continental Hotel. Another one is on Calle 3 de Noviembre, near the Hotel International. A Quarter Pounder (*cuarto de libra*) is $1.10 (add 15¢ for cheese). A Big Mac is $1.25. Fried chicken is available here, too. Look for the familiar yellow sign. Other fast-food stops include **Burger King,** on Vía España; **Popeye's,** for fried chicken, on Vía España; and **Mr. Pollo** and **Big Mama's,** on Calle R. J. Alfaro.

The late Colonel Sander's **Kentucky Fried Chicken (Pollo Kentucky)** is equally well represented around town. The most convenient location is on Vía España in the Obarrio section. Prices and selection are similar to those in the United States.

Panama has several **Dairy Queens,** somewhat different from their U.S. counterparts because they have outdoor tables and serve sandwiches as well as milk shakes. Some of the nicer branches are near Paitilla Airport, on Avenida Central at Calle 17, and on Vía España. Besides ice cream, they serve hamburgers, fried chicken, and similar fare.

Dunkin' Donuts, next to Kentucky Fried Chicken, on Vía España (at Galerías Obarrio), is open daily from 8am to 11pm. A wide variety of doughnuts are sold for takeout, but you can enjoy them at one of the shop's counters with coffee or tea. Remember also that many of Panama's larger hotels have 24-hour cafeterias.

6. ATTRACTIONS

THE TOP ATTRACTION
THE PANAMA CANAL

THE CANAL AREA The Canal Area, formerly the Canal Zone, a 50-mile-long, 10-mile-wide strip of territory surrounding the Panama Canal, was from 1914 to 1979 a chunk of North America in Panama. When the canal was constructed, a treaty was signed granting the United States jurisdiction over the zone, in order for it to operate the canal, until the year 2000. The Canal Zone was as typical of Middle America as Columbus, Ohio—maybe more so. Teenagers in fashion jeans on 10-speed bicycles and slim, tanned matrons hitting drop shots amid magnificently manicured green lawns and smart modern homes are the pictures of the zone that stand out in my mind. These were the families of U.S. engineers and administrators of the Panama Canal Company, which operates the canal. Most had lived here all their lives and for several generations. The Canal Zone was the only home they had ever known. However, building and maintaining a bit of the United States in the midst of Panama created a great deal of unrest and was a constant source of friction between the two nations. The anger was exacerbated by the history of the signing of the original treaty and by the striking difference in the standard of living between Zonians and many Panamanians.

The dividing line at **Avenida de los Martires** (formerly Tivoli and before that Fourth of July) made the differences immediately and painfully obvious. This, a poor section of the city, with buildings crowded together, badly in need of paint and repair, was directly across the street from an immaculate, green oasis. After years of negotiation, a revised treaty was signed in 1979 by President Jimmy Carter and Gen. Omar Torrijos. The treaty abolished the former Canal organization, which had included the Panama Canal Company and the Canal Zone. In its place, a Panama Canal Commission was established. This, a U.S.-government agency, is responsible for the overall management of the canal until the year 2000, when the treaty expires and the entire operation is turned over to Panama. More Panamanians have become involved in the canal's operation, and the commissioner is now Panamanian.

Of course, "Zonians" were saddened by the treaty, which meant the loss of their special way of life. Many families have returned to the mainland. The Canal Area is very different but is still a fascinating place to visit.

(Engineering friends of ours assure us that no one today could build the Panama Canal any better than it was built in the early part of this century. Construction people the world over still come here to marvel at the brilliance and skill of the U.S. Army Corps of Engineers in building this remarkable "ditch," which took 10 years (1904–14) and cost $525 million. The cost today would run into the billions. Over 300,000 visitors view the canal each year.)

HISTORY   To appreciate the engineering genius behind the canal's creation, remember that most of it was constructed above sea level. The hard-rock base of the isthmus would have made it far too expensive to lower the land surface to the level of the Atlantic and Pacific oceans. Therefore, it was decided by George Washington Goethals and his engineers to build the canal above sea level via an ingenious use of locks. These locks would raise (or lower) the canal's water level to allow ships to enter, and later leave, the 23½-mile-long **Lake Gatún,** in the center of the isthmus. Lake Gatún, among the world's largest freshwater lakes, is 85 feet above sea level, which means that the canal had to be designed to enable ships to reach that height.

Today, a typical ship might require 8 hours to make the 40-mile canal journey, plus the 10 extra miles covering the approach and the exit. Moreover, the Panama Canal today is the world's only multilock canal that can handle two-way traffic. In contrast, the Suez Canal, whose opening predated the Panama Canal's, has no locks, since it is at sea level. Yet, the Suez Canal can process only one-way traffic.

A SHIP'S JOURNEY   Let's trace a typical ship along its 8-hour journey across the 40-mile-long canal, plus the 10 miles of approach and exit.

Assuming the vessel enters on the Pacific side—where there are three separate sets of locks—the first "stop" will be the locks in Miraflores, a Canal Area community quite close to Panama City. (Below we describe the best way to reach and tour Miraflores Locks.) A special ship's captain, employed by the Panama Canal Commission, takes over the helm and guides the craft through the locks. A fascinating sight in Miraflores is seeing the ship rise as water rushes into the locks. At first only the stacks are visible; then the top deck, then the lower decks; and finally the hull glides into view.

At Miraflores, all vessels are raised precisely 54 feet above sea level—in two equal lifts of 27 feet. Proceeding past Miraflores, the ship is raised the remaining distance of 31 feet in the Canal Area community of Pedro Miguel. The escalating vessel has now reached Lake Gatún and a few hours later is ready for its 85-foot descent to sea level, which takes place in three equal stages in a trio of locks in Gatún on the Atlantic side. The cost is measured per ton—it's a bargain, considering the cost and time required for the alternative route around Cape Horn. Incidentally, you can observe the entire canal via a Panama City–Colón trip, which we recommend below.

The 52 thousand gallons of water used per ship is all freshwater, which accounts for the locks' durability over the last half century. Stored in reservoirs and flowing by the force of gravity only, the water passes as needed from and into Lake Gatún.

Oddity: The canal runs north-south, not east-west, as is commonly believed.

TOURING MIRAFLORES LOCKS   If you're touring Panama, the best site for a look at the canal is from Miraflores, a short bus ride away. Getting here is no problem. Simply hop the Balboa bus from any major Via España intersection. Ask to be dropped at the post office in Balboa (a 15-minute ride). You change here (near the post office) for another bus (a brightly colored North American model)—marked PEDRO MIGUEL, GAMBOA, or PARASO (each is a Canal Area community). You pay 60¢ as you enter the bus. Be sure to *avoid* the Clayton bus. Ask to be dropped at Miraflores Locks, a 10-minute ride, and then you have a pleasant 15-minute stroll to the tourist area. The driver will point the way. Plan to arrive after noon, when traffic is greatest.

A taxi from downtown Panama will run you $10 an hour, and the cabby will wait for the return trip. There are no Canal Area cabs, so don't plan on hopping a taxi from the Balboa post office. Admission is free to the visitors' area, which is open daily from 9am to 5pm. Once past the imposing gates, follow the white arrows up to the Observation Tower, where there are grandstand seats overlooking the canal. It is a stunning sight. On the arm of each chair is a map detailing the entire canal—including each of the locks and Lake Gatún. Well-informed bilingual guides deliver a recitation of the canal's history and operation. And here is where you can glimpse the striking elevation of a vessel as it enters the lock.

Tip: A great photo is the before-and-after shot of a vessel entering and then leaving the Miraflores Locks.

Unfortunately, the canal is too busy to permit ferry rides through it, but **Argo Tours** (tel. 64-3549) runs a launch tour through the canal on Saturday during the dry season (November to May). The launch *Fantasía del Mar* is comfortable, and drinks and light fare are available. Expect to pay about $35, $20 for kids under 12.

If you aren't able to cruise the canal, the next best way to see the canal is a scenic 90-minute bus or car ride across the isthmus (see the excursion to Colón). The Canal Area now has a population of 40,000, most involved in the operation of the canal. Major towns on the Pacific (Panama City) side are Ancón, Balboa, and Gamboa, while on the Colón (Atlantic) side Cristobál and Gatún are the largest towns.

You'll also enjoy a visit to the Panama Canal Commission Administration Building, a high, domed edifice atop a hill in Balboa Heights, open daily from 7:15am to 4:15pm daily; entrance is free. The murals vividly depict the construction of the canal.

For an interesting and concise historical background, you should pick up a copy of *The Path Between the Seas* by David McCullough.

PANAMA CANAL RAIN FOREST ADVENTURE   Even more fascinating than a canal cruise is to cruise the canal and enter the **Barro Colorado Island Nature Monument,** the rain forest bordering the Panama Canal. This remarkable world of huge moss-covered trees, multicolored birds, and unusual tropical wildlife is managed by the Smithsonian Tropical Research Institute. The trip runs Thursdays through Sundays throughout the year and includes transportation to and from your hotel (6am pickup with a 3pm return), a bilingual naturalist guide, a bag lunch, binoculars, and ponchos. For reservations or more information, contact Eco-Tours in the Centro Comercial La Alhambra, Local 6a, El Dorado (tel. 36-3575; fax 36-3550).

MORE ATTRACTIONS

When you stroll along the Promenade, Avenida Balboa, your eye is caught by a startling testimonial to the discoverer of the Pacific in 1513. The explorer is standing on a globe, held up by four men who symbolize the races of humans.

PANAMÁ VIEJA (OLD PANAMA).

Four miles from the present site of Panama City, right on the Pacific, is Panamá Vieja, where the city was originally settled in 1519, as an embarkation point for the numerous expeditions to South America. The city was an important storage point for gold and other treasures from Peru, which were transported across Panama via the historic **Las Cruces** trail (Camino Real) to the Atlantic and then onto Madrid.

Panamá Vieja was easy prey for pirates, and there were never-ending raids. In 1671, Henry Morgan sacked the city, and it was moved 4 miles inland to its present location behind protective walls. Today, Panamá Vieja is a ruin, standing mutely on the Pacific, a monument to a majestic past. Many of the famous landmarks are standing and have been identified from a map drawn by an engineer in 1609. The four main buildings are grouped near the **cathedral** (the tallest structure). Down the road is the **Convent of San José,** which housed the famous golden altar that was saved from the pirates and later moved to its present location. Many of the ruins are unidentified since they were built subsequent to 1609.

At the far end (a 10-minute walk) is the 350-year-old **Puenta del Rey** (King's Bridge), the stone span that linked the city to Las Cruces trail. The Panamanian Tourist Bureau publishes an excellent pamphlet (with annotated maps) about the ruin. The pamphlets are sold at hotel newsstands.

GETTING THERE A visit here is a must, and the most comfortable mode of transportation is by cab. The charge is $8 an hour (the ride each way is only 10 minutes), but four people can be accommodated, so if you can round up a carload, the per-person charge is kept to a minimum. You can also get near the ruin by local bus. Take any bus marked PMA VIEJO (yellow-and-blue bus). The fare is 75¢. The bus driver will point you in the right direction.

MUSEUMS

ANTHROPOLOGICAL MUSEUM REINA TORRES DE ARAUZ (Anthropological Museum), Avenida Central and Plaza 5 de Mayo. Tel. 62-0415.

★ This eclectic museum, housed in an impressive building with stone pillars, is one of Latin America's finest and most interesting. You can view pre-Columbian ceramics, tools, pottery, monoliths, and much more. On the first floor we enjoyed viewing the monolith from Barriles, near Volcan, of the priest on the shoulders of a nude man bearing a necklace. There are six rooms spread over three floors. Don't miss the Gold Room on the mezzanine, which is a small version of Bogotá's famous Gold Museum. Interesting, too, are the funereal remains on display. There are collections of Hindu, African, and even Sephardic Jewish artifacts. The museum was inaugurated in December 1976.

Admission: 50¢ adults, 25¢ children.
Open: Tues–Sat 10am–6pm; Sun 3–5:30pm.

MUSEO DEL ARTE RELIGIOSO COLONIAL (Museum of Colonial Religious Art), Church of Santo Domingo, Calle 3, on Avenida A.

Located downtown (near the flat arch), this museum features historic religious art that is interesting from both its artistic and its historical perspective. It is housed in chapel in the Church of Santo Domingo, which dates back to 1756. You can also tour the interior of the church, including the interior patio and cloister. The convent has recently been restored and has a small archaeological museum.

Open: Tues–Sat 10am–4pm; Sun 3–6pm.

MUSEO DE HISTORIA DE PANAMA (Museum of Panamanian History), in the Municipal Palace, Avenida Central between Calles 7 and 8. Tel. 25-6231.

History buffs will enjoy this museum. Its four rooms cover Panamanian history through the present, with emphasis on the colonial periods and republican periods as well as the treaty with the United States for construction of the canal.

Admission: 50¢.
Open: Tues–Sat 10am–6pm, Sun 3–6pm.

MUSEO AFRO-ANTILLANO (Afro-Antillian Museum), Calle 24 and Avenida Justo Arosemena. Tel. 62-5348.

The experience of the Afro-Antillian group who helped to construct the Panama Canal is documented through photographs and domestic objects in this small museum. Artifacts from Haiti, Jamaica, and Martinique are also displayed here. This is located in the original Christian Mission building.
Admission: 50¢.
Open: Tues–Sat 10am–6pm. Call the museum for Sunday hours.

MUSEO DEL HOMBRE PANAMEÑO (Panamanian Man Museum), Avenida 7 at Plaza Cinco de Mayo.

Gold and historical artifacts demonstrating Panama's rich cultural heritage are displayed throughout four rooms here.
Admission: $1.
Open: Tues–Sat 10am–6pm; Sunday 3–6pm.

A WALKING TOUR

As we recommend in all cities in this guidebook, you should start familiarizing yourself with Panama City on foot. Inveterate walkers that we are, we first experienced the diversities that Panama City offers via a two-hour stroll early one morning during our initial trip. An ideal starting point is **Santa Ana Plaza**—where the shoeshine boys won't take no for an answer. By all means treat yourself to a shine (it will cost you all of 25¢). The boy—sometimes rather middle-aged—will spot you as a Gringo instantly and might offer a colorful broken-English, arm-waving description of the busy shops and office buildings that surround the plaza. He might even offer to act as your guide.

Stroll around the plaza and its church and then wander leisurely down **Calle 13,** the city's busiest street. Shops, outdoor stalls, grocery stores, and Chinese restaurants vie for your attention. Poke around the stalls—you may be able to find a good-quality piece of embroidery or native pottery. However, the best shopping bargains are to be found on Avenida Central and Avenida 4 de Julio.

Four blocks down in the bustling dock area there is a huge public market that sells fresh fish. (Incidentally, the stretch between Santa Ana Plaza and the dock area is jokingly referred to by residents as *"Sal si puedes,"* which means, loosely, "Get out if you can." The name derives from the ease with which one can get lost in this hectic section.) At the dock area, pick up **Avenida Alfaro** and stroll to your right (south). You'll pass old but well-maintained Spanish-style homes with ornate balconies and courtyards modeled after 16th-century colonial Spain. Just beyond Calle 5 is the stunning white **Presidential Palace,** called the Palace of the Herons, because five of these graceful birds (actually small flamingos) have free run of the grounds. Normally the white creatures congregate around a large fountain in the center of the marble lobby. Visitors are permitted.

Continue along Avenida Alfaro to Calle 4 and turn right into the **Plaza Bolívar,** a lovely, peaceful square dominated by a statue of Simón Bolívar. All Latin American countries took part in the dedication of this statue. A few steps from the plaza, at Calle 3a, are three older but important structures: the **National Palace,** which houses government offices; the famous **San Francisco Church;** and the famous **Teatro Nacional** (National Theater), a restored jewel. Be sure to take a few minutes to step inside and admire the interior of this Renaissance-style theater. Completed in 1909, El Teatro Nacional was designed by the same architect who designed La Scala in Milan, the world-famous Ruggieri. It is in fact a scaled-down version of La Scala, with only three balconies to La Scala's five. The fresco on the ceiling is *El Nacimiento de la República* (*The Birth of the Republic*), by Roberto Luís, a Panamanian educated in Paris.

Continue left on the short block back to Avenida Central to the **Paseo de Las Bóvedas** (Promenade of the Dungeons). Built on the ruins of an old sea wall, which once protected the city from pirates, this historic walkway houses some private homes.

At the end of the street is the **Plaza Francia** (French Plaza), which sits at the city's most southerly tip. Here are the **Palace of Justice,** old dungeons for pirates, and a variety of monuments and statuary erected to honor the French, who were the first to attempt to build the Panama Canal. The French Embassy is located here. Relax on one of the many benches nearby for a few minutes amid the well-kept trees and shrubbery, where you can observe children avidly playing *futból.*

Return along Avenida 8a. At Calle 3a is an old stone-and-brick arch between two walls that served to show U.S. engineers that the area is earthquake-free and therefore that the canal could be built through Panama. The flat arch still stands as originally built. Also here is the **Museum of Colonial Religious Art.** Retrace your steps along Avenida Central to **Plaza Catedral,** also called Plaza de la Independencia, which houses the city's major cathedral as well as numerous busts of the city's founders.

Pick up Calle 7a (not to be confused with Avenida 7, which is Avenida Central) and you will stroll by the walls of the city's old church. At Calle 8, the next block, is the famous **Church of San José,** which was rebuilt here after Henry Morgan's pirates sacked and burned much of Panama Viejo (Old Panama) in 1671. The church's famous gold altar, which had been painted to disguise its value from the pirates, was undamaged by the flames, and it was transferred to the new church in present-day Panama. If the front door is locked, stroll around to the side entrance (to your right) and ring the bell. A priest will admit you.

Stroll back to Avenida Central and you'll find yourself a few blocks from Santa Ana Plaza.

7. SPORTS & RECREATION

Panamanians, like most Latin Americans, enjoy athletics, but whereas in most southern climes *futból* (soccer) is the favored sport, here it is the track that captures the heart and mind.

SPORTS

BASEBALL Practically a national sport here between December and February, baseball demonstrates the historic influence of the United States via the former Canal Zone. Panamanians are fiercely partisan to their teams, which play a brand of ball roughly equivalent to a top minor-league team in North America. Players here seem somewhat smaller and less powerful but certainly faster than their U.S. counterparts. Admission to the **Estadio Justo de Arosemena,** near Balboa, the major stadium here, is $1 to $3. Check with your hotel clerk for home-team schedules and the bus to take you there.

BOXING A weekend draw here are local prize fights at the **Gimnasio Nuevo Panamá.** Top price is $8 to $10, and your hotel clerk should know the nightly card. By the way, Roberto Duran is a Panamanian, and several other Panamanian boxers have held world championships as well.

HORSE RACING If ponies hold the slightest attraction for you—and even if they don't—a must in Panama is a weekend visit to the **Hipódromo Presidente Remon,** the city's major track, located in the suburb of Río Abajo, near the airport. Admission to the grandstand is a paltry 75¢ (occasionally, when business is slow, tourists are admitted free—show your Tourist Card); the minimum bet is $2. All bets are to win or place. It's open Thursday, Saturday, Sunday, and holidays only; the action starts at 1pm. (By the way, four of the world's most famous jockeys, past and present—Gustines, Baeza, Pincay, and Velásquez—are Panamanians. Also, local horses are widely sought for stud purposes.) To reach the track, take the Río Abajo bus (50¢) along Via España. Remember that you'll be heading toward the airport. A small taxi will run about $2.50 per person.

LOTERÍA NACIONAL A national craze in Panama is the national lottery, which benefits hospitals and other charities. Cash prizes can run up to a healthy $1,000 for a mere 55¢ investment on a 4-digit number. There are 10,000 separate 4-digit numbers, but 100 tickets on each combination are sold. A smaller 2-digit drawing with a $12 top prize is available for 35¢. The odds are much better, but the take is smaller.

A major event here every Sunday morning is the noon drawing for the 4-digit lottery winners, held on an outdoor stage at Lottery Plaza, between Avenida Cuba and Avenida Perú. Television cameras zero in on the festive proceedings, which are hosted by local dignitaries. The poor throng the area with that constant hope that lightning will strike and presto! riches. The smaller lottery drawings are conducted at noon Wednesday at the same place. But, as you might expect, far fewer Panamanians attend this ritual. If you're interested in buying a chance, just look for the street vendors throughout the city, who will be only too pleased to take your money. Winnings are tax exempt.

8. SAVVY SHOPPING

Due to extremely low import duties, you can purchase goods from Hong Kong, Japan, Europe, and even the United States at bargain levels in Panama. You'll find, for example, that Japanese electronics are priced well below what you might pay in a large U.S. discount store.

Caution: Before citing the best buys here, we must state that *bargaining is a must,* particularly in the Hindu-owned shops, where price negotiations are taken as much for granted as they are in the flea markets of Paris and Rome. Therefore, never accept the first or even the second price offered—unless you're splurging in a first-class shop where prices are marked and fixed. We watched a determined Brazilian bargain for an ivory chess set until the price came down to a good buy at $85—from $150. As a gift, we purchased a British pipe for $12 that was originally at $35.

Many shops, as an inducement to tourists, advertise boldly that their goods are "duty free." This is not true; although duties are low, they still exist. Panama's taxes are also quite low, which is another consumer bonus. Some stores are licensed to sell duty free and your purchases will be delivered to the airport. Check with the owner. This usually applies to high-priced electronic goods and not to handcrafts, linens, and so forth.

Avenida Central from Plaza 5 de Mayo to Santa Ana Plaza has many good shops, and others can be found on **Calle J.** New shopping centers have sprung up all along Avenida España and near major hotels. These shops are worth checking out.

The best shopping centers in town are **El Dorado,** near Calle 50, the **New York Plaza,** at the Calle 50, and the **Bal Harbour** and **Plaza Paitilla,** in Punta Paitilla.

In general, your best buys in Panama are in linens, cameras, tape recorders, portable radios, antiques, silks, Asian ivory figurines, and French perfume. In addition, Panamanian handcrafts make particularly inexpensive and often original gifts, especially the *molas.*

SHOPPING A TO Z
CAMERAS & ELECTRONICS

When shopping for cameras or electronics bargaining is an absolute must. Prices vary tremendously, so you should as a first step do some comparison-shopping to get a feel for prices and quality.

AUDIO FOTO INTERNACIONAL SHOP, Avenida Central 151.
This is a good place to start your research. You can buy a Japanese Walkman for as little as $15, but prices rise as the quality rises. Shortwave radios and "boxes" start at $35. Camera prices vary, so shop carefully and avoid hasty buys. Near Foto

Internacional are several Hindu-owned shops that sell similar lines. Another branch is in the Plaza Regency building, on Plaza España.

FOTOKINA, Avenida Central, Plaza 5 de Mayo.
Fotokina is also good for stereos, radios, cassettes, and tape recorders.

KARDONSKI HERMANOS, Avenida Central, no. 10A-53, off the main street.
If you want to get rock-bottom prices on stereos, radios, cassettes, and tape recorders, head to Kardonski Hermanos—actually a wholesaler. Enter the side door and head upstairs to the showroom. A salesperson will write up your selection by model number without a price. Head downstairs and Polish-born Señor Kardonski will establish your price. He's honest, but mild bargaining may help. If you don't find what you want here, try Fotokina (above).

TOBY'S, Avenida Central 122.
Mr. Cohen, the proprietor, claims to sell novelties "from the universe." Recommended are the radios and tape recorders. Good buys are also available in Japanese watches and electronic goods and all Sony products, too. A branch is in El Panama Hotel.

LINENS

CASA DE LOS MANTELES, Avenida de los Martires, no. 21-60.
The best linen shop we found in Panama is Casa de los Manteles (Linen House), which was highly recommended by Panamanian friends. However, there is *no bargaining here*—the shop charges one price and one price only for its quality goods, many hand-embroidered and appliquéed. We purchased a lovely linen tablecloth—a 108-inch oval—plus 12 napkins for $70. Prices start as low as $20 for cloths made of linen or fine cotton. Don't pass up the finely crafted sheets, luncheon sets, napkins, and beaded handbags. In general, prices here are about half of what they would be in New York.

NATIVE ART

Reproductions of *huacas* (decorative pre-Columbian artifacts found in Indian burial grounds) make unusual gifts. **Reprosa** is the firm that created the process by which these items are cast. While the originals were in gold, these modern versions are in sterling silver, some with a gold overlay. If you're really enthralled, you can buy an 18-karat gold one. Reprosa shops can be found in El Panama Hotel and the Marriott, but the main store is on Avenida Samuel Lewis near the Sanctuario Nacional Church.

ARTESANIAS NACIONALES, Avenida A, in Panamá Vieja.
Panamanian handcrafts, as well as those from all parts of Latin America, are on sale at this small shop, alongside the San José Church.

FLORY SALTZMAN'S SHOP, in the Via Veneto building, Via España.
You can order *molas* by mail from this shop, which is near El Panama Hotel (mailing address: Apartado 1719, Balboa). Señora Saltzman has a wonderful selection in a variety of sizes.

MERCADO PUBLICO, Sal Si Puedes off Avenida Central.
Here you'll find Panamanian handcrafts; offer half the price and then go up a bit. But leave your purse at home and exercise extreme caution, as pickpocketing and muggings are very frequent.

PIÑATAS

For the child back home or with you, stop in at one of these shops; piñatas make great party gifts, but don't forget to choose one in a size you can carry home easily: **Piñatas Especiales** is at Avenida Justo Arosemena and Calle 39; **Piñatas Flormarily** is on Calle 55, near Via Argentina.

SILKS

CASA SALIH, Avenida Central 125.
For silks, your best buys are at Casa Salih, where lovely bed jackets or kimonos are only $15. Other good buys are in silk blouses, perfumes, alligator bags, incense, wooden boxes, and ivory pieces. Since goods are displayed without price tags, this is your invitation to bargain—so, don't be shy about it.

WOODCARVINGS

SOL DE LA INDIA, Avenida Central 123.
At this shop you can pick up rosewood figurines for $7, carving sets for $5, ivory Buddhas for $12, and superb ivory chess sets for $14 and up, way up. A nice gift is a set of hand-woven cocktail napkins, 12 for $3.25. Remember to bargain here, although the shop advertises itself as a one-price store.

FAR EASTERN GOODS

CASA HONG KONG, Calle J.
This is an Asian shop you should visit, but there's *no bargaining* here. It's around the corner from Casa Tokyo.

CASA TOKYO, Avenida Central.
You should check out this Asian shop.

SALOMON'S STORES, two branches on Avenida Central.
Salomon's stores offer a wide range of Asian goods, brass and rosewood furniture, as well as perfumes and linens. A third branch is in the Hotel Continental.

MISCELLANEA

P. JHANGIMAL, Avenida de los Martires, near Plaza 5 de Mayo.
In this high-quality Hindu-owned shop, Japanese pearls run as low as $12. Lovely ivory jewelry boxes are priced at $15, while French perfumes, Swiss watches, and transistor radios are priced as low as $13.

MARCOS, Avenida Central 129, at Calle J.
One of the most popular Panama stores is Marcos. Here you can get just about anything that is sold in Panama at competitive prices, whether it is sweaters, silks, perfumes, appliances, or pipes. This is a good place to browse.

9. EVENING ENTERTAINMENT

Panamanians like to step out at night, and the evening action here centers around the government-supervised gambling casinos and the many nightclubs. For a more sedate evening, there are theater performances and concerts of quite good quality.

THE PERFORMING ARTS

Several hotels have Panamanian buffets and folk shows. These are very enjoyable—the dancing and the costumes are lovely, and you should certainly see one. One of the most notable is at the **Plaza Paitilla Inn** on Wednesday nights. *Miercoles Típicos* feature typical Panamanian food, live folkloric music and dances, and even a cockfight. **Tinajas,** already mentioned above under "Where to Dine," offers a show on several nights a week at 9:30pm.

THE CLUB & MUSIC SCENE

Panamanian nightclubs really swing, but you must be selective. You can really get stung badly here if you wander about, casually dropping in on clubs indiscriminately. Clip joints, complete with ladies who'll promise you anything for a price, abound. Avoid them if you value your wallet.

DISCOS

BACCHUS, Via España, at Calle 52. Tel. 63-9004.

An older crowd gravitates to Bacchus, which is like a cocktail lounge with a dance floor. Bacchus boasts a Karaoke room, which they've imported from Japan. It permits guests to entertain, using the machine as background music.

BUS PALLADIUM, Calle A. de La Guardia 5. Tel. 69-4892.

A large whitewashed private house is home to the hottest disco in Panama. It draws a spirited young crowd of Panamanians and tourists. Open from 8pm until the last dancer drags out.

MAGIC, Calle 50. Tel. 63-6885.

Another spot popular with Panama's yuppies and students is gleaming Magic, housed in a large private building. Psychedelic lighting creates a with-it atmosphere, and the well-dressed crowd rocks and drinks till the wee hours. Drinks run about $4.

PATATUS, in the New York Plaza Shopping Center. Tel. 64-8467.

A huge antique white convertible is in the middle of the action at this popular disco. Especially popular with the younger crowd, it is arranged almost like a stadium, with seats on different levels all around the large dance floor. There's always a crowd on the dance floor. When you take a break, you can sit back and watch the videos. **Admission:** $5.

PIRAMYD DISCOTHEQUE, in the Toritos Restaurant, in El Dorado Shopping Center. Tel. 60-6062.

At this popular nightspot, there are nightly drink specials as well as live entertainment. The club is open Tuesday to Saturday.

STELARIS DISCO, in the Marriott Caesar Park Hotel. Tel. 26-4077.

This is one of the city's most popular night haunts. The crowd, a mix of trendy Panamanians and hotel guests, swings till the action winds down. One drawback is the stiff cover charge. The consolation to that are the two happy hours nightly; the first is from 8 to 10pm and the second is at midnight. Open Thursday to Saturday from 8pm to 3:30am. **Admission:** $7.50 men, $3.50 women.

LIVE MUSIC

In addition to the following, don't forget the hotel lounge areas, which frequently feature evening "happy hours", live music, and small dance floors. Most popular are the **Inna Nega,** in the Plaza Paitilla Inn; the **Mai Tai,** in the Gran Hotel Soloy; and **Mi Rincón,** in the Marriott Caesar Park.

CLUB AKASAKA, Vía España and Calle 52E. Tel. 69-3291.

Patrons are the entertainment at the Karaoke show at the Club Akasaka. An elegant atmosphere, attentive service, fine Japanese cuisine, and the opportunity to belt out your favorite tune in Cantonese, English, Japanese, or Spanish set Akasaka apart from the other clubs in town. If singing is not for you, there is also a dance floor.

COCO, in the Hotel El Panamá, Vía España 111, at Eusebio A. Morales. Tel. 69-5000.

Located on the lower level of the new Hotel El Panamá, this is a very lovely pub with live music nightly. If you're in the mood to dance, try the Bar Partenon Disco on the ninth floor. It's open Thursday, Friday, and Saturday.

CUBARES, Calle 52 and Vía España. Tel. 64-8905.

This fine Cuban restaurant next door to the Bacchus Disco is a favorite nightime meeting place. There are a small dance floor with videos and occasional live entertainment. Thursday is ladies night; and there is a happy hour on Friday, featuring door prizes.

LA HUACA, Calle Ricardo Arias.

Swinging doors lead to La Huaca, a thoroughly relaxing lounge decorated in ranch style, located next door to Sarti. A fine place to stop for a nightcap or some quiet conversation, it has piped-in music, comfortable seating, and an interesting decor. Open until 2am.

LE PALACE, Calle 52. Tel. 69-1844.

An upscale crowd gathers at the elegant Le Palace, which is not far from the Hotel El Ejecutivo. Seats and felt couches are arranged facing the large stage to assure everyone of a good seat for the nightly musical shows. Beautiful dancers and cordial service make an evening here one of the highlights of a visit to Panama.

Admission: Varies depending on entertainment.

EL RINCONCITO DEL LESSEPS, in Lesseps Restaurant, Vía España and Calle 36. Tel. 23-0749.

Lesseps, one of the city's finest restaurants, has added live music to the menu on Wednesday through Saturday. Wednesday, Friday, and Saturday are jazz and swing nights featuring New Orleans–type jazz. Thursday is ladies night, when ladies receive a free welcome cocktail; the rest are half-price. Romantic Mexican guitar music sets the mood.

EL SOTANO, in the Hotel El Continental, Vía España. Tel. 63-9999.

"The Basement" is a club that sways to the sounds of the large Wurlitzer organ that plays nightly for dancing as well as listening. It's not church music. Drinks run $3.

Admission: Free.

FOR MEN ONLY

Panama has its places for men seeking a female companion to share a drink or two. You can choose from B-girl bars, strip joints, or legal bordellos. Any cab driver will be happy to escort you to any of the several bordellos around town.

Let's start on and around Calle J, just off Avenida de los Martires (formerly Avenida Tivoli). Check out the **Bar Ovalo Inn,** the **Paris,** and **Five Stars.** Nearby, the **Ancón Inn,** the self-proclaimed "Paradise of Single Men," also offers to cash G.I. checks—wonder why? Drinks are $1 to $2. **Bar Relax** and **Taberna Don Quixote,** both on Via España, feature strippers, brassy bands, and B-girls. Drinks in both start at $3.

MORE ENTERTAINMENT

MOVIES Panamanians are film buffs, and 20 or so theaters scattered about the city offer first-run North American and European features. Admission ranges from 50¢ to $3. Among the best downtown film houses are the **Presidente, Lux, Metro, Opera, Central, Bella Vista, Majestic, Plaza Galerías Obarrio, Aries 1 & 2, Cinema Arte, Plaza,** and **Multicines America.**

CASINOS It's one thing to gamble away your money in a rundown casino, such as in Nice. It is quite a different experience to lighten your checkbook in elegant surroundings such as in Monte Carlo or in the two swankest hotels here—the **Marriott Caesar Park** and the **El Panamá.** Both plush hostelries offer action equal to what we've seen in Las Vegas in tempo, style, and hard cash. Glance across the green-felt tables in either casino and be awed by the exquisite Latin women, often in evening dress, and their cool, suave white-jacketed escorts. However, informal attire is okay, so don't feel obligated to wear a jacket or tie.

The best part of this highly recommended evening is that admission is free, so it need cost you nothing. If you care to bet, you must buy at least $5 worth of chips. Minimum table bets are $1; however, the omnipresent one-armed bandits accept coins and will methodically relieve you of your money in smaller doses. Other casinos are located at these hotels: **Continental, Granada, Soloy, Doral, Plaza Paitilla,** and the **Caribe.**

---

10. EASY EXCURSIONS

COLON

A trip to Panama's second city, Colón, is well worth it, if only to get a better idea and view of the workings of the Panama Canal. The city lies 50 miles north of Panama on the Atlantic coast. Colón's **Front Street** is famous for its many stores specializing in perfumes, china, and ivory products, as well as electronic equipment. But don't go there only to shop. Go there also to view the canal, the Canal Area, and the magnificent lakes in between.

GETTING THERE The trip is more than half the fun. The best way to go is by the Panama Railroad, which has five departures on Monday to Friday (only three on weekends). Schedules are usually available at the post office in Balboa or in most of the big hotels. Trains depart from Balboa (a five-minute walk from the post office); sit on the left side of the train while going to Colón to get your best view of the canal. The seats are like those of the old trolleys in the United States; if you have a party of four, they can be reversed to face one another. The trip takes 1½ hours and costs $2.50 round trip. You can buy your tickets on the train if the booth at the station is closed. There are second-class compartments (hardback seats) at cheaper prices.

Note: At the time of this writing, the train to Colón was out of service. This leaves you the option of either renting a car or going by bus. Express buses to Colón leave from in front of the Almacén Picolo on Calle O in Caledonia. A round-trip ticket costs only $3. Be sure to plan ahead. IPAT or the concierge at your hotel should be able to give you up-to-date schedule information.

WHAT TO SEE & DO The maritime importance of Colón will strike you in the form of the numerous steamship offices near the station. The Canal Area portion of Colón is called **Cristóbal.**

Colón houses one of the most luxurious (and historic) hotels of Panama, the **Washington Conquistador,** at Calle Segunda. The **Free Zone,** located in the eastern part of Colón, has given the city an enormous economic importance, due to its tax-free status. If you have the time, tour the zone, open until 3:30pm—but keep in mind that this is an area of wholesale distributors and many do not sell retail.

On Front Street are several fine shops in which you might wish to browse. Famous is the **Bazar Frances,** for porcelain, including Hummel figures, as well as Lalique mirrors. Nearby are **Aldao,** for Monte Cristi (Panama hats); **Bazar Gandhi** (a wide assortment of items); and **Benny** (specializes in Japanese watches).

Gambling casinos are in the Washington Conquistador Hotel and Hotel Sotelo. *Note:* While walking through Colón's streets, you'll observe many nightclubs and bars. These establishments cater primarily to the seamen who pass through.

WHERE TO STAY After touring the city and Free Zone, you'll find that there is not much more to Colón. You would probably be happier visiting the city and returning to Panama that same day. However, if you do opt to stay overnight, three recommended hotels in Colón are the **Sotelo** (doubles at $28), the **García** (doubles for $20), and the **Carlton** (doubles at $45).

WHERE TO DINE If you want to have lunch in Colón, try the **Café Nacional** on

11th Street, between Amador Guerrero and Herrera, or **La Fortuna** nearby. La Fortuna offers tasty Chinese food as well as international dishes. **Pizzería Siciliana,** on Front Street, makes the best pizza in town. More formal dining is in the **Washington Conquistador** dining room.

PORTOBELO

One of the first Spanish settlements on the isthmus was Nombre de Díos, on the Atlantic side. Panamá Vieja became a transfer site for the shipment of gold from Peru to Spain. From Panamá Vieja the gold was shipped overland to Nombre de Díos, then on to Spain. In 1572 Drake destroyed Nombre de Díos. Thereafter the Spanish built in a more protected area a fortress city that they named Portobelo. Five separate fortresses were built.

Modern Portobelo houses 300 families. But tourists flock here to view the fortresses, the historic relics, and the church. Musts are **Fort San Gerónimo, Fort San Fernando,** the **Customshouse,** and the **Black Christ Statue**—in the town's church. Also, take a launch to **Isla Grande** and explore the beaches there. If you'd like to stay overnight, arrange for accommodations at **Cabanas Jackson** (tel. 47-9128).

Note: As of this writing, the railroad from Panama to Colón is out of service. If you don't rent an auto, take a local bus heading to **Colón** from in front of the Almacén Picolo in Caledonia. Tell the driver you want to change buses in Sabanitas, where you'll catch the local bus to Portobelo, about 25 miles northeast of Colón.

TABOGA

This "island of flowers," a mere one-hour launch ride from Balboa in the Canal Area, is one of the few vacation places anywhere where the government travel literature does full justice to its joys. Nestled in the Pacific 12 miles from the mainland, Taboga gave us one of our loveliest days in all our travels to Latin America and Europe. As expected, the beaches are endless, the sun is ceaseless, and the tropical vegetation provides glorious color. But beyond this, there are a serenity and a well-ordered beauty here that seem to seduce visitors into a gentle state of relaxed joy. We cannot too strongly recommend a side trip here for a day or even two, if you can spare the time. Evenings are delightfully cool (and quiet), while the afternoons are a sun-worshipper's delight. And there are no automobiles here.

GETTING THERE

The launch, which charges $2.50 each way per adult and $1.25 for children, leaves from Pier 18 in the Canal Area community of Balboa. Take the Balboa bus to the post office. It's only a short walk from there (directly ahead). Look for the sign TABOGA—LAUNCH LANDING. The pier is on the left. On Monday to Friday the ferry leaves at 8:30am and 4pm. On weekends and holidays an additional ferry leaves at 11:30am. Try to avoid a weekend visit, for the ferries and facilities are overcrowded. Call **Argo Tours** (tel. 64-3549) for more information.

WHERE TO STAY

HOTEL CHU. Tel. 50-2035. 30 rms (some with bath).
$ Rates: $25 single with bath; $38 double with bath.
If the Taboga's prices seem too high (see below), try the island's only other choice, named for the Chinese family who own and run the establishment. The hotel is located a quarter of a mile to the left of where your boat docks. Meals are served on the terrace. Rooms without baths are $5 less.

HOTEL TABOGA. Tel. 50-2122. 30 rms (all with bath). A/C
$ Rates: $50 double.
On our first trip here we missed the last boat back—partly by design—and stayed at the charming and unspoiled Taboga, owned by the Panama Institute of Tourism. The

two-story Taboga, located near the dock, is well worth the $50. Keep in mind that only the second-floor rooms are air-conditioned, but most evenings are cool enough for comfortable sleeping with the help of an open window only. The grounds are superbly landscaped with flowers, shrubbery, and trees. Our room was rustic, with twin beds, a bureau, and a private bath.

SAN BLAS ISLANDS [KUNA INDIANS]

★ Twenty-five minutes by air from Panama City are the San Blas Islands, an archipelago of some 365 islands stretching for 200 miles off Panama's Caribbean coastline. As you might suspect, many of the islands are barely visible from the air, so tiny they house only a few palm trees and a patch of sand. Others, somewhat larger, do have homes with families, while still others are small villages, with a general store, a school, and possibly even an athletic field.

The bronze-hued, short-in-stature Kuna Indians have lived here for centuries, with little change in customs, traditions, or lifestyles. Except in one way. Since many Kuna men work on the mainland, they and their sons have adopted Western-style clothing. The male Kunas speak Spanish, some English, and their native Kuna tongue. Females speak only Kuna.

The Kunas have adopted a form of communal sharing that has served them quite well. The land on all the islands is owned communally. However, the palm trees are privately held, and this is vital since the coconut is the accepted currency, with a value of about 25¢ each. Trees, therefore, are so valuable that families hire caretakers to watch over their trees on a particular island. Normally one family owns all the trees on a small island.

MOLAS AND KUNA WOMEN As a result of the new interest in *mola* designs (reverse appliqué embroidery), Kuna women have achieved a certain fame in fashion circles. The designs, used to make throw pillows, bedspreads, and curtains, are sold in many better U.S. department stores. Most *molas* are on red cloth. Black and green are used frequently to accent the design. Unusual and imaginative, *molas* represent individual expression of Kuna women. Quality varies with the sewer's skill.

Kuna women are their own best advertisements. They wear their own *molas* as blouses and then add wraparound ankle-length skirts. Accenting the threads are bracelets and anklets. A lovely ring is worn through the nose, and the feet are shoeless. Wealthier women wear heavy gold necklaces as well. Finally, add a scarf to cover the close-cropped hair and a black-painted stripe down the bridge of the nose and you have a picture of a well-dressed Kuna woman. Fascinating and authentic (no tourist show here).

VISITING THE ISLANDS Regular day trips are available to several of the San Blas Islands. **ANSA** (tel. 26-7891) offers daily service to the Porvenir Airport, where you can rent a canoe or flat-bottomed boat to make your visit. Make sure to pick up a *mola* while here. If you want to stay over, your options are quite limited. Try for the **Posada Anai** (tel. 20-6596 or 20-0746), on Wichub Walla Island. The 14-room two-story hotel has a small pool and electric lights; a few rooms even have baths. Rates are a whopping $110 for a double. A second option is the **Hotel San Blas,** on Nalunega Island, where your accommodation is a candlelit thatched hut, open-air showers, and a bathroom you must hike to. The hotel charges $20 per person and will take you fishing, snorkeling, and island-hopping. Finally, there is the 10-room **Las Palmeras,** on Narganá (tel. 22-3096). Obviously, food is included at all three. They're primitive, but lots of fun.

Eco-Tours offers an overnight excursion to the San Blas Islands, including accommodations at the Dolphin Island Lodge on Uaguitupo, tours to neighboring islands, snorkeling, meals, and airfare for $149 per person during the week and $175 on the weekend. For further information and reservations, contact Eco-Tours in the Centro Comercial La Alhambra, Local 6a, El Dorado, Panama (tel. 36-3575; fax 36-3550). Eco-Tours is the first company in Panama dedicated solely to nature tourism.

CONTADORA ISLAND

In the Bay of Panama, in the Pacific Ocean, sits this pearl of an island, fifth-largest of the over 220 in the **Las Perlas Islands Archipelago.** Less than a half-hour flight from Panama, you can easily make this a day trip; or as a big splurge, stay overnight at the 210-room **Caesar Park Contadora** (P.O. Box 1880 Panama 1; tel. 69-5269; fax 69-4721), a favorite resort of the Panamanian jet set. Rates are about $120 for a double. Tours are available. Check with your hotel clerk for current information.

Head here for a delightful day of swimming. You can get a locker at the Contadora (about $15—good for four people). In addition to swimming, sports fans come here for the snorkeling, scuba-diving, and sailing. The luxurious Contadora has a popular casino. The late Shah of Iran spent some of his time in exile on this island.

Aero Perlas (tel. 69-4555) and **ANSA** (tel. 26-7891) operate regular flights to Contadora daily from 8am to 5pm. Call for schedule information and reservations.

PANAMA'S BEACHES

Considering Panama's delightful climate, you might wish to swim at a nearby beach. Apart from Taboga Island, the only other beach in the area is on **Naos Island,** at the end of the causeway from Fort Amador, a 15-minute drive from Plaza de Mayo. Enjoy swimming on the small beach and watch the ships moving through the canal. Admission is $1, and there are changing facilities. You can rent a beach chair, and a small cafeteria serves the usual beach foods.

If you rent a car, you can explore some of the country's lovely beaches stretching along the Pacific Coast. **Gorgona Beach,** 46 miles away, is closest and is followed by **Coronado, San Carlos, Río Mar,** and **Corona.** All have tourist facilities. At Gorgona you can rent a cabin complete with kitchen at Cabanas Gorgona. Stay at the **Playa Río Mar Hotel** at Río Mar. A double with private bath is $39 during the weekend (50% discount on the second night) and $20 during the week. Coronado is the most developed, with restaurants, villas for rent, and an 18-hole golf course. To get to the beaches, just cross the Bridge of the Americas onto the PanAmerican Highway, an easy road to drive.

CHAPTER 13

LIMA, PERU

1. **INTRODUCING LIMA & PERU**
- **WHAT'S SPECIAL ABOUT LIMA**
- **WHAT THINGS COST IN LIMA**
2. **ORIENTATION**
3. **GETTING AROUND**
- **FAST FACTS: LIMA**
4. **WHERE TO STAY**
5. **WHERE TO DINE**
6. **ATTRACTIONS**
- **DID YOU KNOW . . .?**
7. **SPORTS & RECREATION**
8. **SAVVY SHOPPING**
9. **EVENING ENTERTAINMENT**
10. **EASY EXCURSIONS**
11. **SUGGESTED ITINERARIES**

Lima is among the most cosmopolitan of western South American cities. The downtown area, dotted with skyscrapers, gives way in the south to well-planned suburbs that resemble U.S. suburban communities. Some 8 miles to the west is Lima's seaport city of Callao and the modern Jorge Chavez International Airport.

1. INTRODUCING LIMA & PERU

BACKGROUND Francisco Pizarro, revered as a hero in Peru, landed here in 1532 with some 200 men. His goal was gold. He believed that an advanced Indian civilization was living in the mountains, led by their king (Inca), who had access to enormous stores of gold and silver.

The Inca Empire (which now refers to the entire population) extended from the mountains of Colombia south through Ecuador and Peru and parts of Bolivia, Chile, and even Argentina.

Some 5 years earlier, in 1527, this vast territory

A WARNING ON PERU

As we went to press, the situation in Peru, marked by continuing terrorist violence, had become so dangerous to tourists that the U.S. Department of State warned U.S. citizens not to travel there. The reason was a sudden increase in bombing attacks, in heavily touristed areas in Lima and elsewhere, by the Maoist guerrilla group known as *Sendero Luminoso* (Shining Path). Peruvian authorities warned of a "very bloody" period ahead as the rebels vowed to intensify their campaign of terror, despite a state of emergency declared earlier by the government.

If you plan to travel to Peru, therefore, be sure to call the **U.S. Department of State's Citizens' Emergency Service** (tel. 202/647-5225) in Washington, D.C., on weekdays from 8:15am to 10pm, for an up-to-date report of the situation in Peru. If, however, you're already in Peru when you read this, inquire at the U.S. Embassy—or at your own country's embassy if you're not a U.S. citizen—for news as well as advice regarding the current situation and what you should do to avoid unnecessary risk to your safety.

WHAT'S SPECIAL ABOUT LIMA

Archeological Finds

- ☐ The Pachacamac ruins, some 20 miles outside Lima, which offer an excellent introduction to pre-Inca and Inca civilizations.
- ☐ The lines at Nasca, one of the world's most pondered mysteries.
- ☐ Machú Picchú, the "Lost City of the Incas," which is a testament to the magnificence of the Inca culture.

Buildings

- ☐ The church of San Francisco, a beautiful example of baroque architecture.

Museums

- ☐ The Museo del Oro, which offers a glimpse of Inca civilization as well as its Spanish conquerors.
- ☐ The Rafael Larco Herrera Museum, home to a remarkable collection of 2,000-year-old mummies.

Plaza

- ☐ The Plaza de Arma, the most majestic in South America.

Nightlife

- ☐ Sachun in Miraflores, which offers a remarkable panorama of Peru's cultural diversity.

---

had been united under the rule of the Inca, Huayna Capac. Upon his death, the empire was divided between his two sons. Huascar ruled the southern kingdom from Cuzco, and his half-brother, Atahualpa, ruled the northern kingdom from Quitu (now Quito, Ecuador). Shortly thereafter a civil war erupted, since each brother wanted to be the sole ruler of a united empire.

Fortunately for Pizarro, this war was in progress when he arrived. He and his men worked their way up the steep mountain toward Cajamarca in Peru. Atahualpa, given advance warning of Pizarro's arrival, was convinced that the Sun God had sent a white god to aid him in his struggle with his half-brother.

When Atahualpa and Pizarro met, the Inca was in awe of the white-skinned Spaniards and their horses, which were unknown in his world. When the king told his troops to lay down their arms, the Spaniards slaughtered thousands of Indians and imprisoned the king. But he was promised his freedom if the Indians would fill one room with gold and two others with silver. After this was done, Pizarro ordered Atahualpa—believed to be the son of the Sun God by his followers—strangled to death.

Since Huascar had already been killed in battle, the Indians were now leaderless and, for all practical purposes, defeated. Pizarro pushed on to Cuzco and sacked it. He then realized that for this territory to become an important Spanish colony, a seaport would be required. Thus, Pizarro marched back to the sea and, in 1535, founded Lima and the port of Callao (pronounced "*cay*-ow"). He established Lima inland, so that Callao could act as a buffer in case of foreign attack.

Pizarro named Lima the "City of Kings" and set about to create a true Spanish capital. He deliberately excluded all Inca influences, and therefore today, unlike Cuzco and Quito, Lima has no Inca temples or ruins. Instead, the city's older quarter is rich in Spanish colonial architecture.

IMPRESSIONS

The main thing to say about Lima, even today, is that it was the dominant Spanish city in South America for three hundred years. It still has the overtones of an imperial metropolis, and it still utterly dominates Peru.
—JOHN GUNTHER, *INSIDE SOUTH AMERICA,* 1967

There are, however, nearby Indian ruins to which you can take several short excursions. And, of course, the true magnificence of the Inca world still reveals itself in Cuzco and Machú Picchú, described in Chapter 14.

Warning! Peru (population about 22 million) is currently going through one of the most troubled periods in its history. Because of continuing terrorist activities by the leftist movement known as *Sendero Luminoso* (Shining Path), both in the countryside and in Lima, the government of President Alberto Fujimori declared a state of emergency in 1992. We advise you, therefore, to exercise *extreme caution* in visiting Lima or any other place in Peru.

WHAT THINGS COST IN LIMA	U.S. $
Taxi from the airport to the suburbs	$13.00
Trans Hotel jitney to downtown	10.00
Taxi to downtown	20.00
Colectivo from the suburbs to downtown	1.00
Bus from the suburbs to downtown	.50
Double with bath at the Hostal Alameda (budget)	20.00
Double with bath at the Residencial Collacocha (moderate)	30.00
Double with bath at the Tampu Diplomat (deluxe)	65.00
Lunch at the Café Galeria (budget)	4.00
Prix-fixe dinner at Faison (budget)	5.50
Dinner with wine at Blue Moon (moderate)	12.00
Dinner with wine at La Rosa Nautica (splurge)	20.00
Museum admission	3.00

2. ORIENTATION

ARRIVING

Chances are you'll arrive at the **Jorge Chavez International Airport,** 10 miles from downtown Lima. From the moment you step past Immigration, you'll be beset by hucksters representing center-city hotels. Check the proffered brochures and rate cards to determine exact hotel prices, which, as we've stressed, can change suddenly. The **Mont Blanc** travel services is one of the reputable agencies at the airport. They will make hotel reservations and arrange transportation for you.

If you plan to stay at one of our recommended center-city hotels rather than at one of our preferred suburban pensions, you have three choices of transportation downtown. A **taxi** ($15–$23) is most convenient. Be sure to establish the fare in advance since drivers often try to charge a higher price and will expect you to negotiate.

To save a few dollars, use the convenient **Trans Hotel jitneys,** which pull up right in front of the airport terminal and provide regular service to downtown hotels for $10. The day before leaving Lima, call Trans Hotel for door-to-door service from your hotel to the airport (tel. 46-9872 or 51-8011).

Another way to reach your downtown hotel is via a *colectivo,* which will drop you near the centrally located Plaza San Martín for $10. The *colectivo,* actually a four-door sedan, is advantageous since it makes no intermediate stops. However, if you have much luggage, you may have a wait since drivers give preference to people without bags. When you need to return to the airport, these five-passenger cabs leave regularly from the **Galería Internacional,** Avenida Nicolas de Pierola 733, between 6am and 9pm.

To reach our suburban pensions directly from the airport, take either a taxi ($11 to $13) or the Trans Hotel bus marked MIRAFLORES ($6). The Miraflores bus will drop you at a hotel in any one of the suburban areas. Or you can take the *colectivo* to Plaza San Martín and then pick up a suburban *colectivo*. Again, luggage could present a problem.

TOURIST INFORMATION

Free tourist information and assistance are available from the **Peruvian Official Tourism Bureau** (government operated), at Jirón de la Unión (Belen) 1066 (tel. 32-3559). They are open Monday to Friday from 9am to 6pm and Saturday from 9am to 1pm.

CITY LAYOUT

MAIN ARTERIES   There are two important plazas in Lima: **Plaza San Martín** and **Plaza de Armas.** The Plaza de Armas, in the older quarter of the city, was where Pizarro founded Lima and where he laid a cornerstone for the city's huge cathedral. The remains of Pizarro are preserved in a glass coffin in the cathedral.

Plaza San Martín is located on the important main street, the **Colmena,** which cuts through the heart of the city and houses hotels, restaurants, and many of the major airline offices and skyscrapers.

The two plazas are five blocks apart and connected by a key shopping street, **Jirón de la Unión.** The word *jirón* describes a series of streets—in this case, a series of blocks on Union Street. The use of that word is a result, again, of an action by Pizarro. Originally, he decided that every individual block in Lima would have its own name—that of one of the conquistadors. But as the city grew, it became too complicated to remember the names of the many blocks. And so groups of streets were given a name prefaced by the *jirón,* or series. Yet the original names were retained. Thus, along Jirón de la Unión the colonial name of each street is noted on street signs below the Jirón de la Unión designation. Ignore the colonial names since nobody uses them anymore.

Two final important streets are **Tacna-Wilson Diagonal** and **Avenida Abancay.** While locals use the convenient Tacna-Wilson designation, actually the bustling thoroughfare embraces two connecting streets: Avenida Wilson, which runs from the suburbs to the Colmena, and Avenida Tacna, which stretches from the Colmena to its terminus at the Rimac River.

Four blocks from the Plaza San Martín (away from Tacna-Wilson) is the traffic-clogged **Avenida Abancay.** Heavily commercial, Abancay houses several super-budget hotels and restaurants.

NEIGHBORHOODS IN BRIEF   Handsome private homes, swank modern shopping centers, drive-in restaurants, movie theaters, and fashionable schools mark three suburban areas outside Lima.

Each of the suburbs has a number of pensions (offering room and all meals at modest prices) and small hostels (called hostals) that we heartily recommend. Whether you stay here or not, you should visit these areas; you will be astonished by the in well-ordered, modern look.

To reach the suburbs, take either a *colectivo* (a comfortable, cheap taxi that operates as a jitney) or bus no. 2. Both depart from near the Plaza San Martín and travel along the four-lane highway called **Arequipa,** the main route between the near suburbs and center city.

Downtown's closest suburb is **Lince;** it is starting to resemble Lima, which is pushing out from its congested center. Next is **San Isidro,** a fashionable residential area with modern shopping centers, good restaurants, and upbeat nightclubs. Finally comes **Miraflores,** which is only 15 to 20 minutes away, depending on traffic. You may want to spend most of your time in Miraflores, which has the best restaurants, hotels, and nightspots. The principal avenues in Miraflores are **Avenida José Pardo** and its extension, **Avenida Ricardo Palma.** Avenida Arequipa runs perpendicularly to those avenues. Two important streets that cut across Miraflores are **Oscar Benavides** and **Avenida José Larco.** Beyond Miraflores are the summer beach areas of **Costa Verde, Barranco, Chorrillos,** and **La Herradura.**

Callao The principal port of Peru, founded by Pizarro, is 8 miles west of Lima. The **Real Felipe Fortress** still stands as testimony to the Spanish-English conflicts of yesterday. The main avenue, **Avenida Saenz Peña,** leads to the Real Felipe Fort. Avenida Guardia Chalaca and Avenida Argentina head to the docks. Nearby **La Punta** is a popular summer beach area.

3. GETTING AROUND

BY BUS Buses are cheap (about 50¢) but terribly crowded most of the time. You'll get used to seeing passengers hanging on to the outside back railing at precarious angles. They do this primarily because it is the only way to get aboard. This is not true for the modern Volvo buses that run from Plaza San Martín along the Arequipa, particularly the S.M.-Arequipa no. 2 line. Bus stops are designated **Paradero de Omnibus.**

BY TAXI It's best to use the cabs parked in front of major hotels or have the hotel clerk phone a car service. Most cabs do not have meters. Establish the price with the driver in advance, based on distance to be traveled. Don't be afraid to try bargaining for a better rate; it sometimes helps. The city has been divided into zones, and rates are based on these. The minimum fare for a trip in the downtown area is $3 to $4. Evening rates are higher. To hail a cab, wave your arms and hiss loudly.

BY CAR Car rentals in Lima are relatively expensive. A two-year-old Volkswagen or Hillman will cost you $50 per day, plus 20¢ per kilometer (.62 miles). Weekly rates are about $100, plus 15¢ per kilometer. Shop around and compare prices. Rental agencies include **Hertz,** at the airport (tel. 51-8199); **Avis,** in the Sheraton Hotel (tel. 32-7146) and at the airport (tel. 52-9570); and **Budget,** in the Sheraton (tel. 31-5002) and in San Isidro at Moreyra 514 (tel. 41-1129). **Dollar** has a branch in Miraflores, on La Paz 430 (tel. 44-9920), and another at the airport (tel. 52-6741). Airport branches are usually open 24 hours. Driving in Lima, particularly downtown where there are no traffic lights, is chaotic at best. Cabs are preferable here.

BY COLECTIVO These jitneylike taxis are the best and least expensive way to move around Lima. They accommodate five passengers and make regular stops. When seats are available, the driver holds up his fingers to indicate how many passengers he can take. Fares average about $1. The most important *colectivo* routes for our purposes are those that head from Plaza San Martín out on Arequipa to the suburbs of Lince, San Isidro, and Miraflores.

FAST LIMA

Airlines Airline offices are open Monday to Friday from 9am to 5pm. You can telephone them on Saturday from 9am to 1pm. **American Airlines'** office is in San Isidro at Juan de Arona 830 (tel. 42-8555). **Varig** is also in San Isidro in the Torre Real Building (office 803–804) at Camino Real 456 (tel. 42-4278). **Faucett** is downtown at Inca Garcilaso de la Vega 865 (tel. 33-6364). **LanChile** is at Avenida José Pardo in

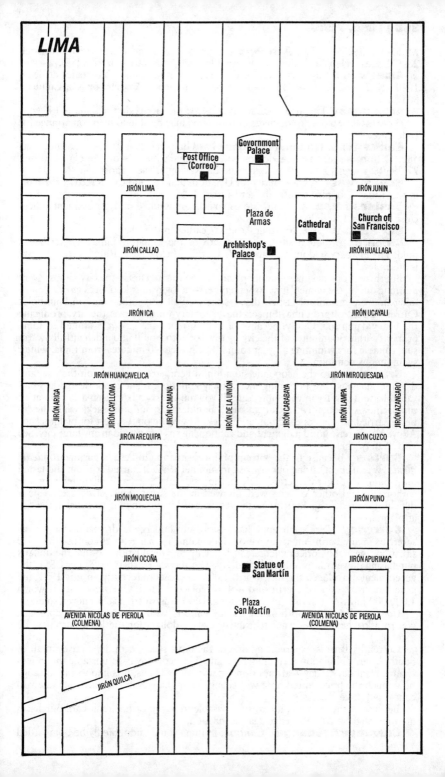

Miraflores (tel. 47-6682). **AeroPeru** has an office on the Plaza San Martín (tel. 28-5721), as well as in Miraflores at Avenida José Pardo 601 (tel. 47-8255).

American Express American Express is in the Lima Tours office at Belen 1040 (tel. 27-6624). **Cook's** has a Lima office on Ocona. **Exprinter** is at Colmena 805.

Area Code The area code for Peru is 51; the city code for Lima is 14.

Babysitters The concierge in your hotel may be able to help you arrange for child care.

Banks **First National City Bank** has a branch in San Isidro, at Las Begonias 580. **Citibank** has an office downtown on Avenida Nicolás de Piêrola 1070 (tel. 27-3930). There is a branch of Banco de La Nación at the airport.

Bookstores A good outlet for U.S. books and periodicals is **ABC Librería,** in the Todos Shopping Center in San Isidro.

Business Hours Many stores, offices, museums, and government offices close between 1 and 3pm.

Car Rentals See "Getting Around" earlier in this chapter.

Climate Although situated 12° south of the Equator, Lima is nevertheless mild. The mercury seldom rises above 80°F or dips below 50°F. Rain is rare. The city is at sea level.

But there is one peculiar weather phenomenon that occurs in the city almost every morning during the winter (June to September)—a foggy mist known as *garúa*. It may dissipate by afternoon or last all day. As the cold air above the Peruvian Humboldt Current moves toward Lima, it meets the customary warm air over the city, producing the heavy damp fog. Oddly, because of rain currents, the *garúa* is limited to Lima proper. Within 30 minutes of the city by train or auto, you'll find a delightfully warm sun, suitable for swimming all year round. In Chosica, 40 minutes from Lima, winter swimming is common.

Crime Due to the economic situation in Peru, street crime is on the rise, and daytime muggings are becoming increasingly common. It's a good idea to leave all valuables and jewelry in your hotel safe. If you must carry a bag, keep it in sight at all times; thieves frequently slit camera bags, shoulderbags, and knapsacks while they're being carried on someone's shoulder or back. Always be on the alert for pickpockets. Above all, exercise good judgment and caution, just as you would in any large city. See also "Safety" below.

Curfew Because of the current political situation in Peru, a curfew (*toque de queda*) was in effect during our last visit in summer 1992. It started at 10pm and lasted until 5am. During this period only authorized cabs (virtually all hotel cabs are authorized) and other vehicles were allowed in the street. This, of course, made it difficult for the average Limeño (as the resident of Lima is known) to travel in the city at night.

Currency Peru's currency has historically undergone dramatic changes, as severe as in any Latin American nation. Fluctuating exchange rates confuse the price situation. Inevitably, prices fluctuate in line with any revaluation, so that the dollar's purchasing power rarely shifts markedly. When the *sol* reached 5,000 per US$1, the government introduced the *inti*, worth 1,000 soles. More recently, in July 1991, the government introduced the **nuevo sol** to replace the inti. One *nuevo sol* is worth 1,000,000 intis. At the time of this writing, US$1 was worth $1.25 nuevos soles.

Caution: Endless **cambistas,** moneychangers with calculators, will approach you to ask whether you want to exchange your dollars for the local currency. Be careful!

Currently, Peru is experiencing one of the most severe economic crises in all of South America. Inflation is running rampant. The economy is so unstable that prices change from day to day—always rising, never falling. Thus, it is impossible to gauge how much the prices listed here will change or if changes in the exchange rate will cancel out price increases.

Because of the inflation, it may be advisable to pay in cash. Credit-card purchases are increased by 20% to hedge against inflation.

Currency Exchange *Caution:* In Lima you'll undoubtedly be bombarded by people who want to change money in the street. *Don't!* You'll do just as well at the many travel agencies and exchange offices scattered throughout the center of the city.

Dentists/Doctors   Ask the concierge in your hotel or contact the embassy for a list of English-speaking dentists and doctors.

Drugstores   U.S.-manufactured drugs are plentiful in Lima. A good pharmacy is **Botica Inglesa,** at Cailloma 336, where English is spoken. Just as in most South American cities, pharmacies in Lima operate under the **Farmacia de Turno** system, in which one pharmacy in every neighborhood stays open 24 hours. The concierge in your hotel should be able to direct you to the open pharmacy in your neighborhood.

Electricity   The current is 220 volts AC at 60 cycles. Some hotels have specially marked 110-volt outlets in bathrooms.

Embassies/Consulates   The **U.S. Consulate** is located at Grimaldo del Solar 346, in Miraflores (tel. 44-3621). The **United Kingdom Consulate** is on the 11th floor of the Washington Building, downtown at Natalio Sanchez 125 (tel. 33-5032); it's open Monday to Thursday from 8:45am to 1:15pm.

Emergencies   The Emergency **Police** can be reached by dialing 115. For emergency **medical attention,** call 40-3570. The **fire department** can be reached at 32-3332. The **tourist police** are located at Avenida Salaverry 1158 (tel. 71-4579).

Eyeglasses   You'll find opticians located throughout the city. The concierge at your hotel should be able to direct you to one nearby.

Hairdressers/Barbers   The **Helena Rubinstein Salons** in Miraflores, at Schell 411 (tel. 44-4144) and Alcanfores 393 (tel. 44-0300), are great for a simple trim or an all-out beauty trip. **Peluqueria Arturo,** at Pasaje Tarata 285 (tel. 44-2255), also in Miraflores, is a good choice for men.

Health   As of this writing, cholera had reached near-epidemic proportions in Peru. So long as you exercise caution, your chances of contracting cholera are low (see our list of health precautions in Chapter 1).

Holidays

New Year's Day	January 1
Easter	Varies
Labor Day	May 1
St. Peter and St. Paul Day	June 29
Independence Day	July 27–29
Santa Rosa Day	August 30
National Dignity Day	October 3
Immaculate Conception	December 8
Christmas Day	December 25

Hospitals   Most major hotels have a doctor on call. The following clinics have 24-hour emergency assistance and usually have an English-speaking staff member on duty: **Clinica Anglo-Americana,** Avenida Salazar in San Isidro (tel. 40-3570); **Clinica Internacional,** Washington 475 downtown (tel. 28-8060); **Clinica San Borja,** Avenida del Aire 333 in San Borja (tel. 75-3141); and **Clinica Ricardo Palma,** in San Isidro at Avenida Javier Prado Este 1066 (tel. 41-6064).

Information   See "Tourist Information" earlier in this chapter.

Laundry/Dry Cleaning   Many hotels offer laundry and dry-cleaning service.

Luggage Storage/Lockers   If you're planning a short trip, you may be able to store your things at your hotel until you return.

Newspapers/Magazines   The weekly English-language *Lima Times* (50¢) is available at most newsstands. The stands in the Bolívar, Sheraton, and Crillon hotels sell the *International Herald Tribune,* the *Wall Street Journal,* and the *Miami Herald* for $4. *Time* and *Newsweek* are available anywhere.

Photographic Needs   Film is significantly more expensive in Peru than at home. When purchasing film here, be sure to check the expiration date. The following places are considered off limits to photographers: parts of mines, civilian airports, railroad stations, military barracks, military instruction centers, naval bases, air bases, public water and energy plants, PIP stations, police stations, oil wells, and petroleum refineries.

Post Office   The main post office is past the Haiti Restaurant, two blocks from Plaza de Armas, on Conde de Superunda. It is open Monday to Saturday from 8am to 6pm and Sunday from 8am to noon. There are other branches in San Isidro on Libertadores 325 and in Miraflores at Petit Thouars 5201; both are open Monday to Friday from 8am to 7:30pm.

Religious Services   Peru is predominantly Catholic. The concierge at your hotel should be able to inform you of the availability and schedule of services in your faith.

Restrooms   The restrooms in hotel lobbies are usually the most convenient. Museums and restaurants, however, also generally have restrooms.

Safety   Many readers have written to us expressing concern about safety in Peru, specifically because of continuing terrorism by the Maoist group called *Sendero Luminoso* (Shining Path). For years the terrorists had confined their attacks to the area around Ayacucho, a town in southern Peru. But now they have spread their activities to the capital, Lima, and elsewhere in their campaign to overthrow the existing social and political order in Peru. As a result, in 1992 the government of President Alberto Fujimori declared a state of emergency; soldiers and armed police were posted in many places to guard against attacks. Yet, despite the increased security, the danger posed by the terrorists remains serious. We advise you, therefore, to exercise *extreme caution* at all times, *even in highly touristed areas.*

See also "A Warning on Peru" at the beginning of this chapter for a further discussion of the serious safety problem in Peru.

Shoe Repairs   The concierge in your hotel should be able to direct you to a nearby shoe-repair shop.

Taxes   A $17.40 airport tax must be paid in dollars upon departure. There's a $4.50 tax on domestic flights, plus a $2 municipal tax at all airports, except the one in Lima.

Taxis   See "Getting Around" earlier in this chapter.

Telegrams/Telexes/Faxes   Most of the major hotels offer telex and fax services.

Telephone   To make a phone call, purchase tokens called *rings*. Each *ring* allows 3 minutes of talking. To place international calls, dial 108 for the international operator. AT&T Direct Service is available at centers throughout the city. Ask the concierge in your hotel to direct you to the nearest one.

Useful Telephone Numbers   Diners Club has an office in San Isidro at Canaval y Moreyra 535 (tel. 41-4272); office hours are Monday to Friday from 9am to 1:30pm and 2:30 to 6pm. MasterCard also has an office in San Isidro at Miguel Seminario 320 (tel. 44-1891); it's open Monday to Friday from 9am to 5pm. VISA is represented at the Banco de Crédito downtown, at Jirón Lampa 499 (tel. 27-5600); it's open Monday to Friday from 8:30 to 11:30am.

4. WHERE TO STAY

The best budget accommodations in Lima are, without doubt, the pensions located in private homes in the suburbs. Here a couple can get a sparkling-clean room in a U.S.-style split-level home for about $15 per person per day, breakfast included.

We strongly urge visitors to Lima to stick to our suburban selections and not stay in downtown Lima. Lima's finest restaurants and nightlife are no longer downtown but have gravitated to the suburbs—namely, Miraflores and San Isidro. Furthermore, street crime has reached a crisis level downtown. Although street crime is less severe in the suburbs, you should always exercise extreme caution. However, for travelers who do want to stay downtown, we will include several center city selections. Government Tourist Hotels are operated by **Entur Perú**, at Los Nogales 249 in San Isidro (tel. 42-8626). You can make reservations through any travel agent.

Note: Hotel rooms are at a premium in July and October—Peru's busiest vacation months. Contact the hotel well ahead for reservations.

CENTER CITY

CLARIDGE HOTEL, Jirón Cailloma 437. Tel. 28-3680. 60 rms (all with shower). TEL
$ Rates (including tax and service): $12 single; $15–$18 double; $20 triple.
An eight-floor elevator hotel, the Claridge was once *the* choice hotel in Lima. But, over time, as newer hotels were built elsewhere, and as the suburbs boomed, the Claridge lost its glitter. Yet it still offers good value. The large rooms, traditionally furnished, all have ample sitting alcoves. The Claridge also houses an inexpensive top-floor restaurant that is open Monday to Saturday for breakfast and lunch. On our last visit, the hotel needed a good painting—so ask to see your room before you check in.

CONTINENTAL, Jirón Puno 196. Tel. 27-5890. Fax 27-7282. 90 rms (all with bath). TEL
$ Rates: From $20 single; from $30 double. Major credit cards accepted.
The Continental offers comfort and a top-floor restaurant, where you can have a continental breakfast for under $2.50. All in all, it's a cheerful surprise in Lima, where many older hotels need painting.

HOSTAL MONT BLANC, Jirón Emilio Fernández 640. Tel. 24-7762. All rooms with bath.
$ Rates (including continental breakfast): $15 single; $22 double; $26 triple.
This delightful hostal is located in a quiet residential area, just 15 minutes from the center. If you want to stay downtown, we strongly suggest the Mont Blanc as your first choice. In operation since 1988, this large, comfortable home was formerly the family residence of owner Hugo Paredes. He and his family will make you feel right at home. All rooms are large and fully carpeted, with comfortable beds.

HOSTAL RENACIMIENTO, Parque Hernan Velarde 52-54. Tel. 31-8461. All rooms with bath.
$ Rates (including breakfast): $12 single; $20 double.
This is one of our most comfortable downtown choices—an elegant Italian-style mansion, with beautiful gardens, just a 10-minute walk from downtown. The rooms are clean and comfortable, and the management is very hospitable.

HOTEL SAVOY, Cailloma 224. Tel. 28-3520. Fax 33-0840. 224 rms (all with bath). A/C MINIBAR TEL
$ Rates: $35 single; $45 double. Major credit cards accepted.
The Savoy, although not as luxurious as it once was, offers good value. The hotel has a roof bar and restaurant that is open during the summer—a delightful spot for a leisurely lunch, with a terrific view of the city. *Folklórico* shows are also held under the stars in nice weather. Other pluses are the hotel's two restaurants and convenient transportation to the airport for $5.

EL PLAZA HOTEL, Nicolas de Pierola (Colmena) 850. Tel. 28-6270. Telex 25943 PE. 56 rms (all with bath). A/C TEL
$ Rates: $30 single; $36 double. Major credit cards accepted.
For modern comfort, be sure to check out El Plaza, across from the well-known

Bolívar. The rooms are just what you would expect in a newer hotel: fully carpeted, clean, bright, and comfortable. The restaurant is open for all three meals—with à la carte dishes only.

A YOUTH HOSTEL

ALBERQUE JUVENIL KARINA, Jirón Charcay 617. Tel. 32-3562. 70 beds (communal bath).

$ Rates: $5 per person.

The young in spirit may want to try the youth hostel. The rooms are dormitory-style, with bunk beds, but the 70 guests lodged on 3 floors enjoy clean surroundings and attentive care. The fourth floor houses the cafeteria, which overlooks the downtown area. Be aware that the hostal is not located in a very good neighborhood.

SPLURGE CHOICES

GRAN HOTEL BOLIVAR, Plaza San Martín 864. Tel. 27-6400. Fax 33-8626. 184 rms (all with bath). A/C MINIBAR TV TEL

$ Rates: $60 single; $70 double. Major credit cards accepted.

The English-style Bolívar was formerly one of the city's premier hotels; it still features attentive service and comfortable accommodations. Facilities include three restaurants, a lovely tearoom (afternoon tea here is a must) and two bars. The location, however, is a major drawback.

HOTEL CRILLON, La Colmena 589. Tel. 28-3290. Fax 32-5920. 515 rms (all with bath). A/C TEL

$ Rates: $75 single; $95 double. Major credit cards accepted.

The Crillon is one of the most modern of the downtown hotels. Guests have their choice of four top-notch restaurants, including the Skyroom with its unparelleled view of Lima. Thoughtful service and attention to small details are the rule here. However, its location is also a liability.

THE SUBURBS

DOUBLES FOR LESS THAN $40

COLUMBUS HOTEL, Arequipa 1421. Tel. 71-0129. 45 rms (all with bath).

$ Rates: $17 single; $29 double.

This colonial-style hotel is a good choice; each room has carpeting.

HOSTAL ALAMEDA, Avenida José Pardo 931, Miraflores. Tel. 47-9806226. All rooms with bath. TEL

$ Rates: (including continental breakfast): $20 single; $25 double.

Ⓢ Beautifully furnished sitting areas, a lovely garden, and a friendly management will make your stay at the colonial-style Alameda a pleasant one. The rooms here are quite spacious.

HOSTAL COLONIAL INN, Comandante Espinar 310, Miraflores. Tel. 46-6666. Fax 45-6937. 15 rms (all with bath). TV TEL

$ Rates: $15 single; $26 double. Major credit cards accepted.

Ⓢ This is a comfortable, attractive inn, at the intersection of Espinar and Enrique Palacios. The decor is Spanish modern, with beamed ceilings and tile floors. Continental breakfast is an additional $1.75, while an all-out American-style breakfast is just over $2. A plus is the dining room, which serves fine food and is open until 11pm.

HOTEL ELDORAL, Avenida José Pardo 486, Miraflores. Tel. 47-6305. Fax 46-8344. 37 rms (all with bath). MINIBAR TEL

$ Rates: $32 single; $37 double.

The five-story Eldoral, which opened in 1983, offers first-class carpeted rooms with kitchenettes. The hotel has a pool and laundry service. For the price of a single or double, it's a great value.

RESIDENCIAL COLLACOCHA, Andrés Reyes 100, San Isidro. Tel. 42-3900. Fax 42-4160. 30 rms (all with bath).
$ Rates: $25 single; $30 double.
A modern and comfortable colonial structure on the corner of Andres 100, the Collacocha (opened in 1976) has carpeting and drapes in each room. There are balconies and large Spanish windows on each of its three stories. Breakfast can be purchased here.

DOUBLES FOR LESS THAN $70

ARIOSTO, Bolívar 769, Miraflores. Tel. 44-1414. Fax 44-3955. Telex 21195. 104 rms (all with bath). TEL
$ Rates (including tax): $35 single; $45 double; $55 suite.
The Ariosto will delight you with its authentic Spanish ambience, complete with tile floors, stucco walls, and an appealing restaurant and bar situated around an open courtyard that is reminiscent of a Peruvian coastal farm. The Ariosto's management is friendly and helpful. Services include laundry, medical assistance, airport bus, and plane and tour information—all the nice touches of a first-class hotel. Several rooms have balconies overlooking the courtyard, and the suites have parlor areas.

COUNTRY CLUB, Calle Los Eucalyptos, San Isidro. Tel. 40-4060. 76 rms (all with bath). A/C MINIBAR TV TEL
$ Rates: $45 single; $60 double. Major credit cards accepted.
If you insist on first-class accommodations, head for the rustic Country Club, where you'll find a Spanish-colonial setting, complete with two pools and tennis, basketball, and volleyball courts. A golf course is across the road. Situated on 30 acres in a secluded suburban setting amid palm trees and manicured lawns, this hotel—once a private club—rents many rooms with sitting alcoves, at rates that are high but appropriate. There are several restaurants on the premises, including an outdoor snack bar at poolside. The pools, including one for kids, are open to club members, who give the grounds a resort ambience on hot days. For nightime entertainment, the management has recently added a casino and game room.
Note: Consider the Country Club only in summer (December to March). The weather can be chilly and dreary in the winter (June to September).

TAMPU DIPLOMAT, Alcanfores 290. Tel 47-8776. Fax 46-6767. Telex 21618 HOTDIPLO. 125 rms (all with bath). A/C TV TEL
$ Rates: $50 single; $62 double.
The five-star Diplomat has spacious and comfortable rooms. Guests here pamper themselves at the spa with its modern exercise equipment, sauna and Jacuzzi, masseur, and hairdresser. The Le Gourmet and Las Alturas restaurants specialize in international and Peruvian cuisine, while the Café Andino and Bambu bar are great places to unwind.

PENSIONS

ELLA FRIEDRICH GUEST HOUSE, Arequipa 3090. Tel. 22-7041. 8 rms (none with bath).
$ Rates (including breakfast): $20 double.
This cheerful, comfortable pension, on the corner of Tradiciones, has carpeting in all

rooms and paintings on most walls. A relaxing spot is the second-floor couch and TV area, where guests congregate for evening conversation. There are three large guest bathrooms. Breakfast is the only meal served.

HOSTAL BEECH, Libertadores 145, San Isidro. Tel. 42-8716. 22 rms (all with bath). **Transportation:** Bus no. 1 to Camino Real, near Libertadores; or the *colectivo* to the 3300 block of Arequipa, near the Petroperu Service Station. Turn right, walk four blocks to Libertadores; the hotel is on the left.
$ Rates (including breakfast): $16 single; $25 double.

The Beech, formerly owned by Audrey Beech, is on our "best value" list. All rooms are immaculate and attractively furnished, and there is a lovely garden in back. You can have your laundry done for a small extra charge.

HOSTAL FRANCIA, Samuel Velardi 185, San Isidro. Tel. 61-754.
$ Rates (including breakfast and tax): $27 single; $30 double.
This fine choice has comfortable rooms, with a pool and a bar. Señora Dora Salas, your gracious hostess, will attend to all your needs.

PENSION ALEMANA, Arequipa 4704, Miraflores. Tel. 45-6999. 15 rms (some with bath).
$ Rates (including breakfast): $12 single without bath, $25 single with bath; $30 double with bath.
At the homey and comfortable Alemana, all rooms are well furnished. Lunch and dinner ($7 each) must be ordered in the morning. The large dining room overlooks a garden, and attractive alpaca rugs cover many walls. The Alemana has no outdoor sign, so ask the *colectivo* driver to let you off at block no. 4600 and look for the white house on the corner of Tarapaca.

RESIDENCIAL 28 DE JULIO, 28 de Julio 531. Tel. 44-3680. Fax 46-9677.
All rooms with bath.
$ Rates: $22 single; $32 double.
Formerly a private home, this sunny yellow house is set back off the street. Enter through a gate to the well-kept front yard, which sports a lawn table with umbrella. The delightful two-story Residencial has rooms opening onto a garden patio. Prices are somewhat high, but the management aims to please (English is spoken).

SPLURGE CHOICES

MIRAFLORES CESAR, at the corner of La Paz and Diez Canseco. Tel. 44-1212. Fax 14-4440. Telex 21348 CESARHOT. 150 rms (all with bath). A/C MINIBAR TV TEL
$ Rates (including tax): $130 single; $145 double. Major credit cards accepted.

Only 30 minutes by taxi from the airport, the five-star Cesar is in the heart of Miraflores, not far from El Suche Shopping Center. This area has an abundance of *artesanías*, boutiques, and restaurants. Opened in 1978, the Cesar offers all the amenities of a first-class luxury hotel. Breakfast is extra and can be enjoyed in your room or at the hotel's European-style café, La Vereda.

If you plan a special night out, try the hotel's rooftop restaurant, La Azotea, where you can enjoy a spectacular view of the city. Dinner, without many extras, runs about $20. Or you can head over to the Sunset Bar, where you can nurse a drink for $3 while watching the sun set over Lima. The bar is open Monday to Saturday from 11am to 1am.

CONDADO MIRAFLORES, Alconfores 465, Miraflores. Tel. 44-1890. Fax 44-1981. Telex 21219 PE-CONDADO. 75 rms (all with bath). A/C TV TEL
$ Rates: $79 single; $90 double. Major credit cards accepted.
The four-star Spanish-style Condado in El Suche Shopping Center has large and

tastefully furnished rooms, with lots of plants and bright accessories. The hotel boasts several restaurants and a discotheque.

EL PARDO HOTEL, Avenida José Pardo 420, Miraflores. Tel. 47-0283. Fax 44-2171. 120 rms (all with bath). A/C MINIBAR TV TEL
$ Rates: $80 single; $90–$100 double. Major credit cards accepted.
Modern and first-class, the 10-story Pardo has piped-in music and wall-to-wall carpeting in each room. Some doubles have small terraces and two double beds. Other luxury touches are a pool and roof garden, cocktail lounge, restaurant, snack bar, and gymnasium and sauna. A popular fast-food operation is also part of the hotel complex. Dining in the hotel's restaurant is low-key and elegant.

MARIA ANGOLA, Avenida La Paz 610. Tel. 44-1280. Fax 46-2860. Telex 21380. 56 rms (all with bath). A/C TV TEL
$ Rates: $70 single; $82 double. Major credit cards accepted.
The four-star Angola is quite modern, with a computerized system throughout. Your room key is a card. Rooms are thickly carpeted, and furnishings are in the rich Spanish mode. On the roof are a pool and a sauna. This is a good stop for business travelers, since it has a telex system.

AN "APART-HOTEL"

APART-HOTEL LOS GALGOS, Alanfores 329, Miraflores. Tel. 44-3975. Fax 47-8199. Telex 21244 PE. 24 apts (all with bath). A/C TV TEL
$ Rates: $70 single; $80 double.
If you're planning to stay in Lima for a week or more, an apart-hotel may be good for you. Los Galgos offers comfortably furnished one- and two-bedroom apartments, some with terraces. Guests have access to the roof garden with a Jacuzzi. The hotel has a small coffee shop and bar and offers 24-hour room service.

A YOUTH HOSTEL

ALBERGUE JUVENIL INTERNACIONAL, Casimiro Ulloa 328, Miraflo-res. Tel. 46-5488.
$ Rates: $5 per person.
This is an excellent choice for the young at heart or for those on a tight budget who don't mind communal-style (but clean) accommodations. It's housed in a big, bright building with its own pool and garden. The management is friendly.

5. WHERE TO DINE

Lima can be an expensive city for dining; many of the attractive restaurants in the city center and suburbs are priced way beyond our budget.

It is important to understand something about dining habits and customs in Lima. Breakfast is light, usually consisting of coffee and rolls with butter or marmalade. Lunch, served from 1 to 2:30pm, is moderately heavy. At the 5pm "tea hour" what is actually served is coffee or something stronger, such as the popular pisco sour (grape brandy with the customary sour mix). Pisco is available at $5 a bottle. Dinner is late, after 9pm.

Food specialties that you should try include *anticuchos de corazones,* an appetizer of grilled chicken hearts served on a skewer; *chicharrones de pollo,* chopped grilled chicken; and *picantes de camarones* or *pollo,* pieces of shrimp or chicken cooked in a sharp chili sauce. As a main course, *aji de gallina,* chicken served in a lightly piquant cream sauce, is a fine choice, as is *lomo saltado,* morsels of beef sautéed with onions and peppers and served with fried potatoes and rice. If you have the chance, try *pachamanca,* a typical dish of the sierra. It's a delicious stew of meats and vegetables, cooked together in pots over heated stones that are dug into the ground. Also try *picarrones,* deep-fried sweet-potato batter served with molasses.

Peru's tropical fruits make great desserts. One of the most common and delicious is *chirimoya,* a large sweet and fleshy green fruit commonly served as *merengue de chirimoya.* The nutlike *lucuma* is especially good in ice cream and cakes. The cactus fruit *tuna,* which is sweet and firm, is best served plain.

Don't be surprised to find many Chinese dishes on menus here; there is a large Asian population in Lima.

The ubiquitous Coca-Cola and Pepsi-Cola are here, of course, along with an even more popular tasty local soft drink, Inca Kola.

Since menus are frequently posted in the windows of restaurants, you can look before you enter. A 31% tax is added to all bills.

CENTER CITY

CAFE GALERIA, 120 Galerías Boza. Tel. 28-8770.
  Cuisine: INTERNATIONAL.
  $ Prices: Light meal $2.75; three-course lunch $4.
  Open: All day.

Our favorite breakfast stop is this rather plain café in the busy Boza's arcade that runs between Jirón de la Unión and Carabaya, half a block from the Plaza San Martín. Here you can get a hearty breakfast of two eggs, toast, and coffee for $2.25. Inexpensive sandwiches and hot plates are available for lunch. The eight tables outside the café in the arcade attract streams of persistent shoeshine boys. To avoid them, sit at a booth inside.

LA CASA VASCA, Colmena 134. Tel. 23-6690.
  Cuisine: SPANISH.
  $ Prices: Appetizers $2–$5; main courses $6–$9.
  Open: Lunch and dinner.
At this good, informal Spanish restaurant near the Hotel Crillon, we recommend the *tortilla Española,* the *langostinas al ajillo* (crayfish), or the *corvina* (whitefish). There are small booths and tables.

CHIFA LUNG WHA, Jirón Huancavelica 218, at the corner of Camana.
  Cuisine: CHINESE.
  $ Prices: Appetizers $1–$3; main courses $3–$6.
  Open: Lunch and dinner.
Popular at lunchtime, this restaurant has tables and booths that are scattered around one dining room. Wontons are served in soup or fried, and there are shrimp and chicken dishes, along with Peking duck.

GIANNINO'S, Calle Rufino Torrico 899. Tel. 31-4978.
  Cuisine: PERUVIAN/ITALIAN.
  $ Prices: Appetizers $1–$3; main courses $3–$8.
  Open: Mon–Fri 8–11pm; Sat 3–7pm.
This charming bistro-style restaurant specializes in both Peruvian and Italian cookery. Tasty pizza and pasta are served, along with fish dishes. The three-course lunch (with coffee) costs $5.

HAITI, Conde de Superunda 144. Tel. 28-3351.
  Cuisine: LIGHT MEALS.
  $ Prices: $3–$5.
  Open: Mon–Sat 9am–10pm; Sun 9:30am–10pm.

S The Haiti is a busy breakfast, lunch, and late-evening spot. Resembling a Greenwich Village coffeehouse or a Left Bank café, it may serve the best coffee in downtown Lima. Part of a chain owned by the Haiti Coffee Corp. (a large coffee-growing company), this eatery overlooks the Plaza de Armas, which at night is beautifully illuminated. The outside tables make snacking pleasant. Try the quarter chicken with salad and potato or perhaps a sandwich. The best value is the fixed-price ($3.50) lunch, which may include chicken and rice, dessert, and coffee. There's another branch in Miraflores at Avenida Diagonal 160.

JAMBOREE SNACK, in the Via Veneto arcade, Jirón de la Unión 835. Tel. 27-1250.
   Cuisine: INTERNATIONAL.
$ Prices: Light and full meals $2–$8.
   Open: Breakfast, lunch, and dinner.
Located at the end of the Via Veneto arcade, the Jamboree Snack has a tempting assortment of sandwiches and hot plates at low prices. You can fill up here late in the day on chicken and rice ($4.50), beef steak with fried potatoes ($5.50), or a cold-cut platter ($3), and easily skip a costly dinner. The most expensive dishes on the menu—lemon chicken and a tender beef filet—are less than $8, tax included.

LUCKY STAR, Nicolas de Pierola.
   Cuisine: INTERNATIONAL.
$ Prices: Soup and sandwiches $2–$4; full meals $5–$8.
   Open: Breakfast, lunch, and dinner.
This is an excellent choice for breakfast and lunch and even a light quick dinner. It's spotless, bright, and cheerful. Service is quick at the counter or the booths. Sandwiches and large steaming bowls of soup are offered; served with bread and butter, they're a full meal. Fish platters, steak dishes, wine, and cocktails are also available.

PIZZERIA AMERICANA, Colmena 514.
   Cuisine: ITALIAN.
$ Prices: Pizzas $1.25–$6; pasta and hamburgers $3–$6.
   Open: Lunch and dinner.
This is a favorite with the students who attend the university nearby. Comfortable straw chairs and glass-topped tables are always crowded for lunch. Pizzas start at $1.25 (tomato and cheese for one), and $4 will buy a large eight-slice pie. Add 75¢ for each additional topping. Ravioli and spaghetti dishes are also served, as are hamburgers.

RESTAURANT RAIMONDI, Jirón A. Quesada 158.
   Cuisine: INTERNATIONAL.
$ Prices: Light meals $2–$4; full meals $5–$8.
   Open: Daily 8am–11pm.
S Perhaps the largest servings in Lima can be found here, between Calle Carabaya and Union, four blocks from Plaza San Martín. The *churrasco* (steak) with french fries is delicious and filling. An even better value is the *corvina* (whitefish) or the quarter chicken (*pollo*) for the same price; both come with salad, potato, or rice. Enter into a small stand-up area (where you can have a sandwich) and then go left into the first of two dining rooms, which seat about 100 patrons.

SAN MARTÍN PARRILLADA, Nicolas de Pierola 890. Tel. 24-7140.
   Cuisine: ARGENTINE. **Reservations:** Recommended.
$ Prices: Appetizers $2–$4; main courses $5–$10.
   Open: Lunch and dinner.
Located on Colmena and San Martín Plaza, this is an attractive bilevel Argentinean restaurant. Prices are a little high, but if you are selective you can keep costs at an acceptable level. The meat and salads are excellent.

LAS TRECE MONEDAS, Jirón Ancash 536. Tel. 27-6547.
   Cuisine: SWISS/PERUVIAN. **Reservations:** Recommended.

$ Prices: Appetizers $3–$5; main courses $8–$12. Major credit cards accepted.
Open: Lunch and dinner.

★ For a memorable treat, have one meal (preferably dinner) at Las Trece Monedas ("The Thirteen Coins"), half a block off Avenida Abancay. Specialties include the tempting French (Swiss) and Creole dishes. Of particular interest to the foreign visitor is the 250-year-old mansion that houses the restaurant. It was built in the colonial period and still retains its original ceilings and panels. All around are examples of Spanish life: goblets 300 to 400 years old, antique paintings, wooden floors, and a carriage (in the garden entrance) fit for a marquis. If you're in a French mood, try the *canard à l'orange*. Typical *criolla* dishes include *ceviche de corvina* and *anticuchos mixtos al gusto*. Try crêpes Suzette for dessert.

THE SUBURBS

BIMBOS BURGER GRILL, Benevides in Miraflores.
Cuisine: HAMBURGERS/SANDWICHES.
$ Prices: Hamburgers $3.50; hot dogs $2; sandwiches $1–$3.
Open: Lunch and dinner.

⑤ As we've been told by more than one Limeño, the best burgers in town are served at Bimbos Burger Grill. The place is a popular hangout for the younger set.

BLUE MOON, Pumacahua 2526, Lince. Tel. 70-1190.
Cuisine: ITALIAN. **Reservations:** Recommended.
$ Prices: Appetizers $1–$5; main courses $6–$12.
Open: Until 2am.
Blue Moon is a quaint neighborhood-style bistro. Entrées range from fettuccine Alfredo to veal scallopine bolognese to chateaubriand. The antipasto caprichoso makes a great light meal. For dessert try the *chirimoya alegre* or the *tartuffo siciliano*.

BOOM, Avenida Diez Canseco.
Cuisine: INTERNATIONAL.
$ Prices: Full meals $4.50–$6.
Open: Noon–11pm.
This is a colorful ice-cream and burger eatery, with oversize booths and counters. Two three-course fixed-price meals are served daily; they cost $4.50 and $6, with apéritif or wine included.

CHIFA MIRAFLORES, Ricardo Palma 322, Miraflores.
Cuisine: CHINESE.
$ Prices: Appetizers 75¢–$2; main courses $3–$6.
Open: Lunch and dinner.
Chinese lanterns provide a bit of color; otherwise, the decor here is rather drab. The food is well prepared and inexpensive.

CHIFA PACIFICO, Avenida Diagonal 150. Tel. 47-8522.
Cuisine: CHINESE.
$ Prices: Appetizers $1–$3; main courses $3–$6.
Open: Lunch and dinner.
Above the Haiti restaurant, one flight up (look for the Cine Pacfico), is a place for lovers of Chinese food. Typical, good-quality food can be enjoyed while watching the bustling Miraflores street scene.

CHURRERIA MANOLO, Avenida Larco 608, Miraflores. Tel. 44-2244.
Cuisine: SPANISH/INTERNATIONAL.
$ Prices: Light meals $2–$5.
Open: 7am–10pm.

Try this informal eatery for delicious burgers and ice-cream concoctions. This is a good spot to sample *churros:* long, thin fried cakes, often served with a cup of very thick hot chocolate; they are also great with coffee.

LA CRÊPERIE, Avenida La Paz 635, Miraflores. Tel. 44-1800.
    Cuisine: CRÊPES.
    $ Prices: $3–$8. Major credit cards accepted.
    Open: Daily 12:30–3pm and 7–11:30pm.
An old French country chalet, with polished brass, copper pots, and antiques, is home to La Crêperie. The menu is limited to soups and 32 varieties of crêpes, which come stuffed with cheese and bacon, anchovies, shrimp, and asparagus. Dessert crêpes are $2.50. You'll find homestyle Italian cooking in a friendly setting here. Pizza, pasta, meat and fish are all on the menu.

CHEESE & WINE RESTAURANT, in the El Alamo Shopping Center, at the
    corner of Avenida La Paz and Diez Canseco, Miraflores.
    Cuisine: WINE/CHEESE.
    $ Prices: Cheese boards $6–$12.
    Open: Mon–Sat 12:30–3pm and 7pm–midnight.
The Cheese & Wine Restaurant is tucked away upstairs in this interesting shopping arcade. The atmosphere is delightful, reminiscent of that in an old wine cellar. The restaurant offers six kinds of local cheese, along with a carafe of excellent red or white Peruvian wine. Portions are small, so don't go with a full-size appetite. Try the fondue.

CHIFA MANDARIN, Juan de Arona 887, San Isidro. Tel. 42-3766.
    Cuisine: CHINESE.
    $ Prices: Appetizers $1–$3; main courses $5–$10.
    Open: Daily noon–11:30pm.
At this restaurant squab is a house specialty. Have a drink in the lower-level rear bar and garden, then proceed upstairs for the *pichon* (squab) *con champignon* or *pato con jenjibre,* a delicious duck delicacy. Popular, too, are the *camarón* (shrimp) dishes. There are also a dozen soups to choose from. Private booths offer complete privacy for your party.

EL CORTIJO, República de Panamá 675 (Barranco). Tel. 45-4481.
    Cuisine: ARGENTINE. **Reservations:** Recommended.
    $ Prices: Appetizers $2–$5; main courses $6–$12.
    Open: Daily noon–midnight.
Resembling an Argentine *parrillada* restaurant, complete with large grill, the Cortijo specializes in steak and chicken at prices that can run your check up if you're not careful. We strongly urge you to just order chicken here. One good value is the *medio pollo* (half chicken), served with french fries; it's crisply grilled and marvelously seasoned.

DON ADOLFO, Manuel Bañon 295, San Isidro. Tel. 22-6681.
    Cuisine: SEAFOOD. **Reservations:** Recommended.
    $ Prices: Appetizers $2–$5; main courses $5–$8.
    Open: Noon–3pm and 7:30–11pm.
For excellent seafood, head to Don Adolfo, where lobster, crab, and oysters are the specialty. A complete dinner costs $10, including tax. *Corvina*—very fresh—is $6; *sopa de camarones* is $4.50.

FAISON RESTAURANT, Avenida Diez Canseco 119, Miraflores.
    Cuisine: INTERNATIONAL.
    $ Prices: Full meal $4–$8.
    Open: Lunch and dinner.
The best budget restaurant in this exciting area is very clean; its dozen tables are filled by students, trim matrons, and families. The menu changes daily, but for $5.50 you

402 • LIMA, PERU

can have a three-course meal that is tasty and varied. The appetizers include soup or stuffed avocados, and the entrées consist of fowl, pork, and beef dishes, as well as vegetarian plates. Desserts vary. There is an à la carte menu, too. This restaurant is so popular that a second branch recently opened nearby at Calle Bellavista 258.

FUENTE DE SODA DE PILAR, 123 Pancho Fuerro.
  Cuisine: SANDWICHES/SNACKS.
$ Prices: Light meal $2–$5.
  Open: Until midnight.
This late-night snackery is across from Los Condes de San Isidro restaurant. It is a typical fast-food operation where fried chicken is king. Local residents consume it eagerly, ordering seconds and thirds unashamedly. You can't beat the prices.

MEDITERRANEO CHICKEN, Benavides 420, Miraflores. Tel. 47-9431.
  Cuisine: CHICKEN.
$ Prices: Full meal $6.
  Open: Lunch and dinner.
We discovered this chain of chicken restaurants during our most recent trip. They claim to have the fattest, biggest, and tastiest chickens. There is a second branch in San Isidro on the second block of Conquistadores (tel. 41-5522) and another downtown at the corner of Quilca and Camaná 901 (tel. 23-7541).

NAUTILUS, Ricardo Palma, Miraflores.
  Cuisine: PERUVIAN.
$ Prices: Appetizers $1–$3; main courses $4–$7.
  Open: Lunch and dinner.
This may be the best *criollo* restaurant in Lima, across from the Vivaldi *confitería*, specializing in *mariscos* (shellfish). Look for the blue-and-white sign and the yellow-and-blue awning.

LAS TEJAS, Diez Canseco 340. Tel. 44-4360.
  Cuisine: PERUVIAN. **Reservations:** Recommended.
$ Prices: Appetizers $1–$3; main courses $4–$8.
  Open: Lunch and dinner.
Adjoining El Alamo Shopping Center, this *criolla* is reasonably priced and therefore usually busy. Try for one of the outdoor tables if the dining rooms are crowded. *Anticuchos*, shish kebabs, *ceviche* of corvina, *humitas,* tamales, and *choclo* are the stars of the menu.

LA PIZZERIA, Avenida Oscar Benavides 322. Tel. 46-7793.
  Cuisine: ITALIAN.
$ Prices: Appetizers $1–$3; main courses $6–$10. Major credit cards accepted.
  Open: Daily noon–midnight.
This popular restaurant is invariably jammed on weekends with young couples. Chicken and pasta dishes, pizza, and sandwiches are featured. Service is fast.

MATSUEI, Canada 236. Tel. 72-2282.
  Cuisine: JAPANESE. **Reservations:** Recommended.
$ Prices: Appetizers $3–$5; main courses $7–$12.
  Open: Lunch and dinner.
This is Lima's finest Japanese restaurant. Though we suggest that you avoid the sushi and sashimi, the tempura and steak are very good.

MANOS MORENOS, El Suche 640, Miraflores. Tel. 45-5592.
  Cuisine: PERUVIAN/INTERNATIONAL. **Reservations:** Recommended.
$ Prices: Appetizers $3–$5; main courses $7–$12.
  Open: Lunch and dinner.
This is a fine new restaurant. We found it during our most recent visit and can recommend the *aji de gallina* (chicken in a cream sauce) and the *lomo saltado con arroz y choclo* (beef sautéed in onion and tomato, served with rice and corn).

RESTAURANTE LA CALESA, M. Bañon 255, San Isidro. Tel. 40-5568.
Cuisine: INTERNATIONAL. **Reservations:** Recommended.
$ Prices: Appetizers $1–$4; main courses $5–$12. Major credit cards accepted.
Open: Lunch and dinner.
Our favorite restaurant in the Centro Commercial shopping arcade is also popular with local businesspeople at lunch. It is restful and intimate, with wooden tables, some benches, and bright-orange tablecloths. The food is excellent. Prices range from an economical $5 for fettuccine, and $6.50 for fish dishes to $8 and up for tender, juicy beef. If you're not particularly hungry, try a bowl of delicious creamed vegetable soup, served with a miniloaf of bread ($2.50).

EL RODIZIO, Ovalo Gutiérrez, at the corner of Santa Cruz, Miraflores.
Tel. 45-0889.
Cuisine: BRAZILIAN. **Reservations:** Recommended.
$ Prices: Main course with salad bar $8–$14. Major credit cards accepted.
Open: 1pm–1am.
This restaurant offers an excellent selection of meats. They are grilled in the Brazilian *rodizio* style over an open flame. The aroma alone will whet your appetite.

LA TRATTORIA, Manuel Bonilla 106, Miraflores. Tel. 46-7002.
Cuisine: ITALIAN. **Reservations:** Recommended.
$ Prices: Appetizers $1–$5; main courses $7–$12. Major credit cards accepted.
Open: Mon–Sat 1pm–3:30pm and 8–11pm.
This is a great choice for authentic Italian cooking. While you're there, be on the lookout for owner Hugo Plebison, one of Peru's best-loved television personalities.

A SPLURGE CHOICE

TODO FRESCO, Miguel Dasso 110, San Isidro. Tel. 40-7955.
Cuisine: SEAFOOD. **Reservations:** Recommended.
$ Prices: Appetizers $3–$6; main courses $9–$22. Major credit cards accepted.
Open: Lunch and dinner.
This is Lima's most-talked-about seafood restaurant. Located seven blocks to the right of the 3700 block of Arequipa, Todo Fresco is surprisingly unpretentious, with Formica-topped tables (no cloths) and rather plain decor. However, gourmets—quasi, pseudo, or actual—should point their forks directly at the lobster thermidor, which is a high $24 but sweetly succulent. Other not-to-be-missed dishes are oysters (*picantes de mariscos*) and any of several shrimp platters. For better value, stick to the daily special. There is another Todo Fresco at Avenida Petit Thouars 32.

SPECIALTY DINING
AFTERNOON TEA OR COFFEE

Downtown, the delightful **Café D'Onofrio,** Pasaje Olaya 145, located in an arcade near the Plaza de Armas, is ideal for a late-afternoon refreshments. Catering largely to well-to-do shoppers, this café offers wonderful service, bright-pink tablecloths in one room, and comfortable booths in the rear room. Prices can run high—$1.25 for an ice-cream soda—but the quality is excellent.

Drop into the **Pastelería Kudan,** on the Colmena for a cup of tea and delicious pastry or small sandwiches. **Don Pepos,** on the Plaza San Martín, is also an inviting stop for pastries. For an ice-cream break, head to **Galería El Centro,** on Avenida Belen, near Plaza San Martín.

If you're out shopping or walking in Miraflores, you may want to enjoy a lovely interlude at the homey **La Tiendecita Blanca**—a café located on the wide Avenida Larco at 111 opposite the Haiti. In warm weather there are outside tables, where you can relax amid well-dressed matrons and local businessmen. Many patrons speak English. Savor a strawberry tart ($2.50) while gazing at the chic men and women.

For a taste of Paris in Peru, visit the **Vivaldi.** Its cheerful orange-and-blue canopy over a cluster of outdoor tables is most inviting. Indoors, you'll find mirrored walls and glass-topped tables—an elegant setting for your afternoon tea, cappuccino, ice cream, pastry, or apéritif. Cocktails are also served. The Vivaldi, located at Ricardo Palma 2258 in Miraflores, is open until 2am.

Liverpool, at Alameda Ricardo Palma 250, is a pub-style restaurant with indoor and outdoor tables. It attracts a regular following for late-afternoon tea and sandwiches as well as for dinner. It has the best salad bar in town. The restaurant is open from noon to 4pm for lunch. A sandwich, salad, dessert, and beverage cost $5. For dinner you can fill your plate with salad and order a main course (beef, fish, or fowl) for under $12.

Another fine place for afternoon tea, cookies, or a sandwich is **Cherry,** at Avenida Jose Larco 835, in Miraflores. You can choose between comfortable indoor and outdoor dining. Look for the red-and-white awning.

For some delicious ice cream, stop by **Donofrio's Shop,** on Avenida Diez Canseco, near Miraflores Park. The ice cream is very much like Häagen-Dazs. Eat in or take out.

FAST FOOD

A lunch spot that resembles McDonald's is **MacTambo,** with locations in Lince, San Isidro, and Miraflores. Some branches have curb service, while others have inside counters and tables. Sandwiches ($2.50) are delicious, and the super dogs ($2.15) and burgers come with all the extras. Mac Pollo (the chicken plate) and Mac Plato (the breakfast special) are both under $3. **Kentucky Fried Chicken** has several branches here, with one on Avenida Arequipa, in San Isidro, and others on Avenida Schell and Comandante Espinar, in Miraflores. If you prefer your chicken roasted, $2 will get you half a roasted chicken at **Pollos Broaster** just off the Plaza San Martín at Jirón de la Unión 739. There's a **Pizza Hut** next door to the KFC on Comandante Espinar, in Miraflores, as well as on the Plaza San Martín downtown.

PIZZA

Calle San Ramón, a three-block diagonal street leading from Miraflores Park, is the place to go for good pizza or hearty Italian food. There are at least six restaurants on the block offering these foods, with several others in the immediate vicinity. **Don Corleone** has a counter and sells by the slice. The others are all attractive, tables-only restaurants. **Parking Pizza** has a branch on either side of the street. Pizzas are sold by the quarter, half, or whole. A quarter portion of cheese pie is $1, while the whole pie is $4. With additional ingredients it can run up to $6. Ravioli, lasagne, and fettuccine are also served. **La Glorietta, El Pizzaton, Las Pizzas Bar, Mr. Pizza, Mama Leone's,** and **Al Capone's** have virtually identical menus and prices.

DINING BY THE SEA

COSTA VERDE RESTAURANT, Playa Barranquito. Tel. 41-4084.
   Cuisine: SEAFOOD. **Reservations:** Recommended.
   $ Prices: Appetizers $3–$6; main courses $8–$20. Major credit cards accepted.
   Open: Daily noon–midnight.
In this indoor/outdoor restaurant you can watch the fishermen haul in the day's catch. The Costa Verde serves mainly seafood, although it also offers some excellent beef dishes. The lobster dishes are excellent. This is the perfect place to watch the sunset over the Pacific while sipping an exotic cocktail.

LA ERMITA, Avenida Bajada de Baños 340, Barranco. Tel. 67-1791.
   Cuisine: INTERNATIONAL. **Reservations:** Recommended.

$ Prices: Appetizers $2–$5; main courses $6–$12.
Open: 12:30pm–midnight.

For an intimate evening for two, your first choice should be El Puente. If you're looking for a little romance, this restaurant, nestled underneath El Puente de los Suspiros, provides the perfect setting.

LA ROSA NAUTICA, Espigon 4, Costa Verde, Miraflores. Tel. 47-6765.
Cuisine: SEAFOOD. **Reservations:** Recommended.
$ Prices: Appetizers $3–$6; main courses $8–$20. Major credit cards accepted.
Open: Daily 12:30pm–2am.

Built on a pier over the water, Rosa Náutica serves fresh seafood and Peruvian-style beef. The bar is decorated with a nautical theme. There's music and dancing at the disco next door on Friday and Saturday nights. Expect to spend at least $18 per person.

RINCON GAUCHO, Parque Salazar, Miraflores. Tel. 47-4778.
Cuisine: ARGENTINE. **Reservations:** Recommended.
$ Prices: Full meals $8–$14.
Open: Tues–Sun lunch and dinner.

Of our listings, Rincón Gaucho, nestled on the beach, is the closest to the city. The view is incomparable, and so is the *parrillada,* grilled Argentinean-style at your table and served with green and red sauces.

6. ATTRACTIONS

THE TOP ATTRACTIONS

TORRE TAGLE PALACE, Jirón Ucayali 358.

Peru's Foreign Office Building, off Avenida San Pedro near the Plaza de Armas, was at one time the palace of the Marquis of Torre Tagle, who in 1735 built this handsome structure, an outstanding example of Spanish architecture. Many of its rooms are closed to visitors, as they are used as offices. Note the intricately carved mahogany balconies and the massive carved doors. You enter through an open courtyard.

Admission: Free, but it is customary to tip the guard.
Open: Mon–Fri 9am–5pm.

COURT OF THE INQUISITION, Avenida Abancay.

In Plaza Bolívar are two buildings you should definitely visit. The larger one is the National Congress, and the other, to the right of Bolívar's statue, is the infamous Court of the Inquisition, where heretics were tried during the dark period between 1570 and 1820.

As you enter the court's main hall, you'll see up front the seven red-felt chairs of the judges behind a mahogany table. To the right is the witness box. Thick, ornately carved wooden beams criss-cross just beneath the high ceiling. It's usually eerily quiet here, and it doesn't require too much imagination to hear a heretic asking forgiveness for his sins.

Admission: Free, but it is customary to tip the guard.
Open: Mon–Sat 9am–7pm.

CHURCH OF SAN FRANCISCO, Jirón Lampa, at the corner of Ancash.

Probably the most beautiful church in Lima is the baroque Church of San Francisco, two blocks from the Plaza de Armas. Completed in 1674, the structure has strong Arabic influences in its design. When inside, look closely at

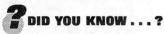

DID YOU KNOW . . . ?

- Only 6.8% of Peru's land can produce crops.
- At 15,806 feet above sea level, Galera Station (below Mt. Meiggs) is the highest standard-gauge railroad station in the world.
- Lima was originally called *Ciudad de los Reyes* (City of the Kings), because it was founded by Europeans on January 6, 1535—Three Kings Day.
- The name *Lima* is said to be a corruption of the Quechua word *Rimac*, which means "He Who Speaks," referring to an Indian oracle at the site.
- In 1862 the 200-ton Scottish steamer *Yaraui* sailed to the port of Mollendo, where it was dismantled and Indians carried it across the Andes by hand to Puno, where it was reconstructed. It still sails there today.
- The versatile penca plant is used by Indians to make hats, rope, thread, and even roofing.
- At 10,574 feet deep, El Cañón de Colca is the deepest canyon in the world.

the gold monstrance that was made in Cuzco some 300 years ago. The jewels are quite real. There are also several famous paintings in the church. The adjoining monastery, which admits men only, is famous for its tilework and paneled ceiling.

Admission: Free.

Open: Daily 10am–1pm and 3–6pm.

MUSEUM OF ANTHROPOLOGY AND ARCHEOLOGY, Plaza Bolívar. Tel. 63-5070.

This museum, dedicated to the study of the aborigines of Peru, is located in the small Plaza Bolívar, in the suburb of Pueblo Libre. Don't confuse this plaza with the much larger plaza of the same name near Plaza de Armas.

On display here are ancient woven capes, shawls, and ceramic objects that predate the Incas. But there are Inca relics here, as well as artifacts from the Paracas, Chavin, and Pachacamac cultures. The oldest, the Paracas, date back to 500 B.C., which would make them contemporaries of the ancient Greeks about the time of their Golden Age. In the Inca room is a fine scale model of Machú Picchú, the famous "Lost City" of the Incas that was not discovered until 1911.

This museum is a must if you are going on to the Inca country of Cuzco and Machú Picchú. But even if you have been there already, the museum will help you better appreciate what you witnessed.

Dining note: For a fine lunch or snack break during your museum hopping, stop at the multilevel modern **Restaurant Piselli**, at Calle La Mar 215, on the corner of Avenida Brasil, one block from where the *colectivo* drops you. Through clever use of plants and water, an outdoor feel has been created. Sit at a mezzanine table overlooking the lower-level dining area and order the *corvina*, whitefish in an asparagus sauce ($5), or the *cordero*, lamb in a wine sauce ($6). Steaks (*churrasco*) are good values at $6 per platter. If you're snacking, try the *tortas* (tarts) for $2.50. Open Monday to Saturday from 11am to midnight, Sunday until 4pm.

To get here, take the Pueblo Libre *colectivo* from Plaza San Martín. You'll be dropped at Avenida Brasil, three blocks from the museum. Or you can hop a slower omnibus at Plaza San Martín and ask to be dropped at the museum. Cabs are $3 each way.

Admission: $4, plus 65¢ to take photos.

Open: Mon–Sat 9am–5pm; Sun 9am–1pm.

MUSEO ARQUEOLOGICO RAFAEL LARCO HERRERA, Avenida Bolívar 1515, Pueblo Libre. Tel. 61-1312.

Ten minutes by *colectivo* from the Museum of Anthropology and Archeology is the famous privately owned Herrera Museum—noted for its erotica (artistic, of course). But, for us, the room on the main level directly ahead of the entrance is what makes the museum well worth a visit. Twelve 2,000-year-old mummies, some shockingly "alive," are in glass cases, most with their faces exposed. Incredibly, parts of some faces are perfectly preserved, while others are hideous skulls. Most are dressed in ceremonial garb. One appears to have had a fatal chest wound, perhaps from a spear. There are several child mummies, too.

There are invaluable gold and silver jewelry pieces from Indian civilizations in an adjoining room that is sealed by a massive metal door. You enter into what appears to be a vault—and that's what it is. Check out the huge colorless pearl on the left. Another room (the one on your left from the courtyard) has a fine collection of rocks, minerals, and ceramic pieces.

After exploring the three rooms on the main level, head back outside and follow the wide brick pathway down to the lower level. At last you are in the midst of hundreds of rather small ceramic pieces, most showing Indian figures in various stages—and contortions—of coupling (animals, apparently, were much favored).

You enter the museum grounds from Avenida Bolívar and wind your way up the brick pathway to the entrance. To get here, take the green-and-white microbus no. 37, which runs along the Avenida Emancipacíon. It will be marked CLEMENT. Ask to be dropped at the Museo Rafael Larco Herrera, a 3-mile trip. From the Museum of Anthropology and Archeology (10 minutes away), take the Avenida Bolívar *colectivo* at Plaza Bolívar, checking first to make sure it goes past the Herrera Museum. If you're heading to the Museum of Anthropology and Archeology from the Herrera Museum, take any *colectivo* heading to your right as you leave the grounds. Exit at Plaza Bolívar.

Admission: $4.50.
Open: Mon-Sat 9am-1pm and 3-6pm.

MUSEO DEL ORO DEL PERU, Alonso de Molina 1100, Monterrico. Tel. 35-2917.

✪ The Spanish colonial era is re-created magnificently in this Gold Museum, where perfectly restored armor, cannon, pistols, swords, and other armaments are handsomely displayed.

The lower level is devoted to the artifacts of Inca and Indian civilizations, with spears and shields and marvelously crafted gold and jewelry pieces imaginatively mounted. Some of the pieces go back 3,000 years.

To get here, first take a *colectivo* from the Plaza San Martín to the center of Miraflores. Ask to be dropped where you can get the *colectivo* to Monterrico. Tell the driver of the second *colectivo* "Museo del Oro, por favor," and he'll leave you a block or so from the museum (about 50¢ each way). You can also take bus no. 2 to Miraflores and get off at the intersection of Arequipa and Angamos. On Angamos, catch microbus no. 72 to Monterico and ask to get off at the Museo del Oro (50¢ round trip). A cab from Miraflores will run you about $5 and take 15 minutes. The trip by public transportation is about one hour.

Admission: $6.
Open: Daily noon-7pm.

NATIONAL MUSEUM OF ART, Paseo Colón. Tel. 23-4732.

The magnificent art of ancient Peru, which dates from the Paracas civilization of 2,500 years ago, is on display at the National Museum. The building was the official palace of the International Exhibition held here in 1868. Instead of having the structure leveled, the government made it a repository of the country's artistic treasures. You'll find silver goblets, ceramics, tapestries, and Spanish-colonial furniture, as well as delicately worked jewelry and ivory fans. The exhibits include artwork from every period in Peru's history—right up to the excellent collection of contemporary art.

Admission: $1.75.
Open: Tues-Sun 9am-5pm.

A WALKING TOUR

It is fitting that you start your foot pilgrimage through Lima where Pizarro started his—at the **Plaza de Armas.** It was here, in 1535, that Pizarro founded what he called the "City of Kings." The Indians later renamed it Lima, their name for the Rimac River that flows through the town. Today, this is the heart of the capital's older section, a haven for sightseers.

Floodlit at night, this plaza ranks with Plaza de la Independencia in Quito as the most beautiful in South America. The surrounding buildings are blessed with superb wooden balconies that are intricately carved. The massive **cathedral** here, which houses the remains of Pizarro in a glass coffin on public view, has been rebuilt several times. The altars are coated with pure silver, and the wall mosaics bear his coat-of-arms.

Next to the cathedral is the **Archbishop's Palace,** and not far from there, in the plaza, is the **Government Palace,** which is the presidential residence. Precisely at 12:45pm every day the Changing of the Guard takes place, a ritual that involves blaring trumpets and clanking swords. The red-uniformed guards, trained originally by Prussian officers, goosestep in perfect timing. The bronze fountain in the plaza's center has been there for over 300 years.

If you sit on one of the benches, expect to be surrounded by shoeshine boys who won't give up easily. The kids will ask you endless questions, and if you know any Spanish at all, you'll have a lot of fun while learning firsthand about life in Peru.

After strolling around the plaza, follow **Jirón de la Unión** out of it toward Plaza San Martín. You'll be on the main shopping street, which is closed to traffic for a part of each day to give pedestrians freedom of the way. If you feel like bargain hunting, see the shopping section later in this chapter. When you reach **Plaza San Martín,** after a five-block walk, you'll be entering the modern part of Lima. The plaza is surrounded by lavish hotels and several theaters. Opposite the Bolívar Hotel you can catch the *colectivos* to the suburbs. As you wander around the plaza, note the equestrian **Statue of San Martín** (San Martín helped liberate Peru from Spain in 1821).

The main thoroughfare, **Nicolas de Pierola** (the **Colmena**), leads into the plaza, but don't turn onto it. Instead, pick up Jirón de la Unión again, on the other side of the plaza, and continue for two more blocks until you come to the **Paseo de la República,** a wide tree-lined promenade that houses the **Palace of Justice.** To your right are the Sheraton Hotel and the civic center—a good spot for browsing in the shops. Benches line the center, and there are numerous sculptured llamas, the national animal, made of marble and bronze. Occasionally, you'll see Indian families sprawled on the grass enjoying the midday sun. On your right is the **Museum of Italian Art,** which houses copies of famous Italian paintings.

When you reach the end of República after several blocks, you'll be at the **Plaza Grau.** Turn right on Paseo Colon (also called 9 de Deciembre), a mile-long street that is the home of Peru's **Museum of Art.** Nearby is the **Parque Neptuno,** where you might like to rest. Three blocks farther along is the circular **Plaza Bolognesi,** housing a good deal of statuary. Many streets branch out from the plaza. Turn left onto **Avenida Guzmán Blanco** for three blocks to the **Statue of Jorge Chavez,** the famous Peruvian aviator for whom the airport was named. Across the street is the attractive **Campo de Marte,** a popular children-filled park that is the site of frequent parades and celebrations. Pause here a minute and relax as the locals do.

To return to Plaza San Martín, either walk back or hop on any bus heading that way.

ORGANIZED TOURS

Lima Tours, at Belen 1040 (tel. 27-6624), and **Dasatour,** at Josê del Llano Zapata 331, ninth floor, in Miraflores (tel. 41-5045), are the recommended services. Both operate half-day tours of modern and colonial Lima (about $20) and excursions to Pachacamac ($35), to Chosica ($30), and to mountain villages across to Peru's Central Highway ($60 per person in groups of four or more).

An incredibly knowledgeable guide who speaks English is Mariella Samame Marcazzolo, who works for **El Dorado Travel Agency,** at Jirón de la Unión 1015 (tel. 52-0143).

If your idea of travel is breaking away from the pack and setting out for out-of-the-way destinations on your own or with just a few other adventurous souls, then try **Overland Expeditions,** in the Hostal Mont Blanc, at Jirón Emilio Fernandez 640 (tel. 24-7762). Founder Hugo Paredes specializes in designing unique trekking expeditions to exciting destinations not offered by conventional tour companies. Expeditions can last from one to several weeks, depending on what you're looking for. Even if you decide to go on your own, he can arrange for contacts en route to make sure your needs are well taken care of.

Among the destinations unique to Overland Expeditions are **Markahuasi,** where you'll marvel at incredible rock formations and wonder about prehistoric civilizations; **Aray,** home of a pre-Columbian fortress and of the magnificent condor; **Rupac,** ancient seat of the pre-Incan Atawillos culture; and **Lachay,** one of Peru's most important natural reserves, located 70 miles north of Lima, in the middle of Peru's coastal desert. Tents and camping equipment are provided whenever necessary.

7. SPORTS & RECREATION

Lima is one of the few cities south of Mexico where you can take in a **bullfight** on a regularly scheduled basis. Some cities in South America permit an occasional bullfight event, but Lima schedules one every Sunday and holiday afternoon in October and November at the **Plaza Acho** bullring, located in the older Rimac section just across the Rimac River. The toreadors, imported from Spain, pack the stadium for every event and predictably are absolute heroes in Peru. Posters all over the city will remind you of the coming attraction.

Despite their high price ($15 to $20), tickets are much in demand and are available at most hotels. Be sure to ask for seats in the shade. To reach the ring, take a taxi ($3) or walk via Abancay across the Rimac River Bridge. The stadium is visible from the span, which links center-city Lima with a poorer section of the city.

Women can pamper themselves at **Gymnasio Helena Rubinstein,** at Shell 411, in Miraflores (tel. 44-4414). Open daily from 8am to 8pm, it features aerobics, exercise machines, and a Turkish bath. The instruction equipment and surroundings are first class.

THE TRACK Easily one of the finest tracks in the world is the **Hipódromo de Monterico,** 30 minutes outside of Lima. Owned by the fashionable Jockey Club, the track holds races all year round on Saturday, Sunday, and holidays at 1:30pm and on Tuesday and Thursday at 6pm. Admission is $1, and the minimum bet is $1. Take a *colectivo* from Plaza San Martín (50¢) or a cab ($4). On race days a special bus, marked HIPODROMO, departs from the plaza, too.

FUTBOL In Peru, as elsewhere south of the border, *futbol* (soccer) is the national sport, and every weekend throughout the year 45,000 frantic fans jam the **Estadio Nacional,** which offers seats for $5 and up ($15 and up for better seats). Take the suburban *colectivo* from Plaza San Martín, which passes the stadium. You can easily walk here from any point downtown, though.

BEACHES The best nearby resort is **La Herradura,** a short distance from the suburb of Miraflores, on the Pacific. Between October and May, there is swimming virtually every day, and even in the winter (June to September) there are days warm enough for an ocean dip. While not a major resort, it nevertheless has a good deal of physical beauty, mainly because of the mountains that close in from east and south. From Miraflores, hop a taxi ($7) for the 20-minute trip. But avoid weekends, when roads and beaches are jammed. Other, closer beaches are **Costa Verde, Barranco,** and **Chorrillos**—but Herradura is probably the best.

Avid swimmers should head to **Chosica,** 25 miles east of Lima, in the Rimac Valley, where there is swimming all year round. Many wealthy Peruvians have vacation homes here, and it's a popular weekend retreat. It is a good way to escape the June through August *garúa,* or mist, in Lima. Chosica can be reached by *colectivo* (catch one on Nicolas de Pierola) or by bus no. 200A, which leaves from the 1500 block on

Nicolas de Pierola. You can also hop the train to Huancayo, which leaves from Desamparados Station Monday to Saturday at 7:40am and stops at Chosica. You pick up the return train at 3:30pm. One-way fare is about $2. Lima Tours, as well as several other travel agencies, offers bus tours to Chosica and to the nearby Cajamarquilla Indian ruins (not from December to March, when the heat makes the trip uncomfortable).

8. SAVVY SHOPPING

Your best bargain bets in Lima are native handcrafts, silver jewelry, and alpaca rugs. The designs, as you might expect, are largely of Inca influence. Remember that if an item is made of pure silver, the number 925 must appear on the back. Store hours are Monday to Saturday from 10am to 1pm and from 3 to 7pm. Many souvenir shops are open later.

SHOPPING CENTERS

Two fine shopping centers in Miraflores are **El Suche** and **El Alamo**. Both are on La Paz, not far from the Condado Hotel. The **Camino Real** and **Todos** shopping centers in San Isidro are also quite good.

Without question, the best shopping values in Lima are to be found at the **Centro Artesanal de Pueblo Libre,** more commonly known as **La Marina,** a kind of shopping center run by Indian families in Pueblo Libre. There are 26 semienclosed independent stalls that offer an enormous variety of gold, copper, and silver jewelry; alpaca rugs; leather goods; wall plaques; handcrafts; ponchos; and miscellany. Many items are handmade. Bring your Spanish dictionary: English is not spoken here. And service is sometimes downright indifferent; be patient, however.

SEVERAL TIPS

Before buying item one, browse through the 26 stalls to get a feel for price and quality. Start on your left at Stall 1, called **Tumi** (most stalls have no names, only numbers), and slowly wind your way around the horseshoe-shaped area. Then return to those stalls that impressed you and start bargaining furiously.

Be sure that alpaca rugs and garments are 100% alpaca and not alpaca mixed with wool. You can tell by feel and by price differentials (wool mixtures are at least 25% cheaper).

Since nothing is shipped from here, be sure to buy only what you can comfortably carry with you back to your hotel and aboard your flight home.

HOURS & HOW TO GET THERE

La Marina is open daily from 6am to 10pm. To get there, hop on the San Felipe bus from Plaza San Martín heading toward the airport (the shopping center is actually midway between San Isidro and the airport). Ask the driver to drop you at the center, which is on the main road, Avenida Marina at the 1000 block. (Tell the driver "*Cuadra Diez,*" pronounced "*Kwah*-drah *Dee*-ez.") A cab will run you about $5.

SHOPPING FROM A TO Z
DOWNTOWN

There are several handicraft shops and many silver and jewelry shops on the pedestrian-only Jirón de la Unión, between Plaza San Martín and Plaza de Armas. It's best to browse several shops, and don't forget to bargain.

Antiques

CASA PARACAS, Jirón de la Unión 713.

The large Casa Paracas houses many antiques (*antiguedades*), such as pottery and artifacts. Some items are claimed to be over 5,000 years old. There are wares in all price ranges. Come in and browse, but be careful about your purchases.

Handicrafts

ARTESANÍAS HUAMANQAQA, Jirón de la Unión.

This shop is spread over several floors and has many handcrafted decorative items from all over Peru. These include Sulca wallhangings, Paucar weavings, and Quinua and Shipibo ceramics. The Krikor mirrors and attractive light fixtures are especially good buys.

ART NUSTA, Jirón de la Unión 1045.

This long, narrow shop carries all types of handcrafted items, including Inca-motif ties ($3), alpaca rugs from $25, ornately carved bookracks, and woolen ponchos ($15 to $30). Puno bulls are $3, $5, and $8, depending on size. English is spoken here.

GALERIA EL CENTRO, Avenida Belen.

The Galería El Centro, near Plaza San Martín, has 24 handcraft shops, all small and most run by the artisans themselves. Knitted sweaters, scarves, and ponchos are good buys, as are gilt mirrors and gaily painted ones starting at $8. It is also home to a very good ice-cream parlor.

INCA PRODUCTS, Jirón de la Unión 838.

This is a good place to start your browsing, since it has a large selection. Alpaca rugs, which have gone way up in price and are not as well made as they once were, start at $75. Hand-knit sweaters with Peruvian motifs are a good buy at $25.

Silver

CASA WAKO, Jirón de la Unión 841. Tel. 28-8661.

We've always had good luck with the values at this large store, where you can get a wide variety of silver pins in striking Inca designs ranging from $17 to $40.

OLD CUZCO, Jirón de la Unión 823.

This store has an excellent collection of silver. Candlesticks ($40); plates ($20); and a variety of bells, ashtrays, and the like make good gifts.

VICKY'S ARTESANIA, Colmena 783.

This is one of our favorite silver shops downtown. Besides a wide variety of silver items, there are crystal displays worth your attention.

H. STERN, in the Sheraton, Bolívar, Cesar Miraflores hotels; at the international airport; and in the Gold Museum.

For the best in gemstones, such as aquamarine, topaz, and tourmaline, visit H. Stern. A very beautiful branch is located in a pavilion at the Museo de Oro. You'll find an extensive selection of silver and 18-karat gold reproductions of the fabulous pieces of pre-Columbian art, such as ceremonial masks and *collar de tumis* (tumi necklaces), which you'll admire in the actual museum. The spirit of the pre-Columbian cultures has been remarkably reproduced in every piece.

THE SUBURBS

Alpaca

ALPACA 111 S. A., Avenida Larco 859, Miraflores. Tel. 47-7163.

Alpaca 111 S. A. has an extensive selection of alpaca weavings, hand-knit sweaters and scarves, yarns, and leather clothing. There are additional branches in Cuzco, at Ruinas 472 (tel. 23-6322); in Arequipa; and in the Camino Real Shopping Center in San Isidro.

CINSA, Avenida Argentina 2458. Tel. 52-6065.

For over 35 years, Cinsa has been creating beautiful alpaca sweaters and fabrics, most for export to major fashion centers around the world. Another showroom is at Avenida Benevides (block 51).

HELEN HAMANN'S, Taena 370, Miraflores.
There are several small boutiques in the suburbs where you can get high-quality and high-fashion alpaca sweaters or even the yarn itself if you'd rather knit your own. Helen Hamann's hand-knit sweaters in alpaca and cotton are exported to some of the finest boutiques and department stores of the world.

Antiques

EL ARCON, La Paz 646 No. 12, Miraflores. Tel. 47-6149.
El Arcon specializes in antique silverware. Collectors are sure to find something worth taking home. A lovely handicraft selection make this a fine place to shop for gifts.

Artwork

ARTE ANTIGUO PERUANO, Avenida La Paz 588, Miraflores.
For reproductions and authentic antique works of art, try this store. There are many works from the Cuzco school of art available, including candelabras, mirrors, and frames.

KUNTUR HUASI, Ocharan 182, Miraflores. Tel. 44-0557.
This is a lovely gallery dedicated to temporary exhibits of high-quality folk arts and crafts by local artists. It is open Monday to Saturday from 2 to 7pm and will open Sunday by appointment.

Artesanías

ANTISUYOS, Tacna 460, Miraflores. Tel. 47-2557.
Antisuyos offers a complete selection of traditional handicrafts from over 30 native Amazonian tribes, as well as weavings from Taquile, Pomata, and Cajamarca and pottery from Chulucanas. If you're looking for an interesting gift, you'll be sure to find something here.

ARTESANIAS MIBEKAS, in El Alamo Shopping Center, Miraflores.
This shop has an excellent assortment of hand-knitted alpaca sweaters, tapestries, ponchos, rugs, coats, ceramics, copper, Indian blankets, and erotic art from the Mochica and Chinua cultures.

ARTESANIAS PERUANAS, Avenida Orrantia 610, San Isidro.
This shop, with four locations in Lima, is your best stop for handcrafts. Only the finest-quality authentic Peruvian crafts are on display and for sale. The atmosphere is rather like that of an art gallery, with beautifully hung exhibits of silverwork, enamel, rugs, knitted goods, and lovely ceramic pieces displayed in the garden. Prices are as good as, if not better than, those downtown; there's less high pressure, too. Other branches are at Avenidas Perez Aranibar 749 and José Pardos 450 in Miraflores and the market adjoining the Hotel Sheraton downtown. Credit cards are accepted.

EL ARTESANO, Diez Canseco 498, Miraflores. Tel. 44-0346.
This interesting gallery specializes in ceramics from Chulucanas and tapestries from Ayacucho.

EXPORTADORES DEL INCA, Avenida Orrantia 1235, San Isidro.
This shop, in a private home, has an excellent selection of unusual handicrafts in ceramic, straw, and wool. Christmas decorations are lovely gifts, and they're for sale most of the year. Check out the unusual giraffe-head vases and the ceramic band of musicians, plus the unique items from the jungles of Peru. Open Monday to Friday from 8am to 4:30pm.

LA GRINGA, La Paz 522, Miraflores. Tel. 41-1704.
La Gringa, on the corner of La Paz and Díez Canseco, offers a wide selection of authentic Peruvian arts and crafts.

SILVANIA PRINTS, Los Conquistadores 915, San Isidro. Tel. 22-6440.

⭐ High-quality cotton and linen yard goods in Inca and pre-Inca designs can be purchased here. Owner Silvia Lawson, who was educated in the United States, also sells ready-made blouses, dresses, scarves, and bikinis, as well as tablecloths, placemats, and cloth bags. She hasn't neglected menswear: Ties, sport shirts, and swim trunks are fast-moving items. Prices are reasonable, considering the high quality. Blouses, for example, that might sell for $40 to $50 in the United States are $35 here. The designs are copies from the textile and ceramic artifacts found in Peru. Ideal gifts are the print purses ($7.75), bright-colored scarves ($15.50), and ponchos ($25).

An additional shop is at the Miraflores Cesar hotel, Diez Canseco 337, in Miraflores.

URPI, Avenida La Paz 592, Miraflores.

For fine pottery, woodcarvings, alpaca sweaters, and leather, try Urpi. It's a small shop brimming with Peruvian handcrafts of top quality.

9. EVENING ENTERTAINMENT

For a quick orientation to Lima's nightlife, check the Sunday edition of *El Comercio*, Lima's large Spanish-language daily, which lists cultural and sporting events for the upcoming week. The English-language newspaper *Lima Times* does not have as comprehensive a listing of cultural events as *El Comercio*.

THE PERFORMING ARTS

AMAUTA ARENA, Avenida Venezuela, Chacra Ros.

This indoor arena seats 9,000 and has diverse bookings ranging from the Moscow Ballet to the circus and Peruvian festivals. Check the Sunday *El Comercio* for programs.

Prices: Vary by performance.

TEATRO MUNICIPAL, Jirón Ica 323.

For fine concerts and ballet, head to the Municipal Theater, near Cailloma, three blocks from Plaza de Armas. A good balcony seat runs $8.

Prices: Tickets $6–$12.

TEATRO SEGURA, in Plazuela del Teatro.

A second hall for concerts is the Teatro Segura, two blocks from the Teatro Municipal. Check *El Comercio* for programs.

Prices: Vary by performance.

FOLKLÓRICO

For a dip into Peruvian folklore via music and dance, catch a *folklórico* show on Monday evenings at the **Teatro Municipal,** Jirón Ica 323. We're partial to the *marinera,* a mating dance marked by a handkerchief in the hand. The cheapest seats at the Teatro Municipal are up near the rafters ($2.35). Seats downstairs run $3 to $3.75. Locally popular is the delightful folkloric show that goes up Wednesday, Friday, and Saturday at 9pm at a small restaurant called **Wifala.** The $3 admission includes a beer.

THE BAR & CLUB SCENE

Lima has several late-evening clubs (most are couples only), where the dancers and bands are uninhibited. The fast-moving and fast-spending young set gravitates to a number of suburban clubs, largely in San Isidro and Miraflores. Remember that street crime in Peru is on the rise. Nowhere is this more true than in the center of Lima, especially after dark. The suburbs—Miraflores and San Isidro—are relatively safe. Please exercise extreme caution.

DOWNTOWN

HOTEL CRILLON, La Colmena 589. Tel. 28-3290.
Spend one evening at the Skyroom, where the orchestra keeps the dance floor crowded until 1am. When you're tired, look out over the skyline of Lima through the panoramic windows on three sides. When you get off the elevator on the 20th floor, stroll casually straight ahead toward the couches, where you can lounge comfortably much of the evening for the price of a single drink (about $3.50, plus tax). If you sit at a table, you'll be expected to drink more.

There is a *folklórico* show here on Tuesday to Sunday night at 8pm. Native artists perform typical Peruvian music and dances. And, when the show is over, you can dance to the hot Latin-Caribbean rhythms of the Skyroom orchestra.

THE SUBURBS

Several high-priced private clubs have opened in San Isidro, attracting a fairly exclusive crowd. Although you don't have to be a member to get in, there is a selection process at the door.

As a preface to the after-dark hours, drop in for a cocktail in the late afternoon or early evening at the **Orient Express Bar,** in the El Suche Shopping Center. You'll spot it by the train platform in the entrance. Another romantic choice is **Le Bistro,** nearby. After dinner you'll probably want to visit one (or more) of the nightclubs.

Two popular first stops in San Isidro are **Onion's Pub,** next door to Keops, and **Pub Los Olivos.**

CASABLANCA PUB, Emilio Cavenecia 162, San Isidro. Tel. 22-5247.
A fun crowd gathers here, mostly to talk and joke with friends. Photos of antique autos decorate the walls. Other than that furnishings are fairly simple wooden tables and chairs. There's a large bar. Light food is served, and you may be able to squeeze in a game of darts.
  Admission: $15.
  Open: Mon–Sat until 2 or 3am.

CLUB LAS ROCAS, Rivera Navarrete 821, San Isidro. Tel. 42-0960.
Here the decor is strictly jungle, with waterfalls and primitive masks. Head downstairs, pass over the bridge and waterfall, and enter the intimate romantic club where there are stained-glass windows with tropical-bird designs.

EL ESCARABAJO, Avenida Nicholas Arriola 270, Santa Catalina.
El Escarabajo sets the tempo for the younger generation nightly, rising to a crescendo well after midnight. Gazing down on the circular bar is a rather benevolent-looking beetle (*el escarabajo* himself). The dance area is dark and crowded. Prices are steep—$3.50 for a drink, plus a $6-per-person minimum on weekends. Look for the beetle (more like a ladybug) outside.

FACES, Centro Comercial Camino Real, Sotáno (lower level), San Isidro. Tel. 41-1133.
You'll almost feel as if you're at the Harvard Club at this fancy English pub in San Isidro. Rich leather and wood dominate. The bar area is fairly large and very nice. There is even a coat check. Open Tuesday to Saturday until 5am.

KEOPS, Camino Real 149, San Isidro.
Not far from the Camino Real Shopping Center, Keops is a somewhat exclusive private club that attracts a young crowd.

MIDNIGHT, Miguel Dasso 143. Tel. 40-8221.

Its innovative use of glass sets Midnight apart from all the discos we've visited. Comfortable couches are scattered around the ever-crowded dance floor. Dim lighting reflected on the glass creates a mystical ambience.

LA MIEL, Avenida José Pardo 120. Tel. 45-3699.

Pass through the heavy wooden doors in the lobby of the El Pacífico Pardo building and head downstairs to La Miel. This large dance club sports a black-and-red motif. Because it's popular, you'll need a reservation on the weekend. There's often a $15 minimum here.

LA MONELLA, Diez Canseco 148, Miraflores.

La Monella is relatively traditional, couples only. As you descend into the disco you'll find yourself at the circular mirrored bar. You have your choice of dance floors: The left side of the disco is larger and holds more people, the right is more intimate. Drinks start at $3.

RAIZING DISCOTHEQUE, Camino Real 111, San Isidro.

This is a full-fledged disco complete with strobe lights and a separate area for quieter moments. There's a fairly large bar area as well. Open Tuesday to Saturday from 8pm to 4am.

RED AND BLUE, in the Grand Hotel Miraflores, Avenida 28 de Julio 151, Tel. 47-9641.

A younger crowd gravitates to the Red and Blue downstairs at the Grand Hotel Miraflores. Although far from fancy, the dance floor is large.

LA ROSA NAUTICA, Espigon 4, Costa Verde, Miraflores. Tel. 47-0057.

Not only is La Rosa Nautica one of Lima's finest restaurants, but also it is one of the city's loveliest nightclubs. Located in a building apart from the restaurant, the sides are open to take full advantage of the Pacific breezes. Patrons can sit and listen to the waves as they roll into shore or dance to live music. A terrific way to spend an evening under the stars. (The **Costa Verde** in Barranco has a similar discotheque; however, the music is not live.) Open Friday and Saturday nights.

SEXES, Miguel Dasso 160, San Isidro. Tel. 40-9871.

A large dance floor is the main attraction here. The latest hit music, primarily from the States, draws a younger crowd. Always busy. Open Tuesday to Thursday until 3am, Saturday and Sunday until 5am.

Creole Clubs

Lima really comes alive in the creole clubs, where the rhythms, dancers, decor, and cuisine come together in one cacophonous wonder. These clubs get going late— usually after 9pm—and wind up near dawn. The food is typically Peruvian, particularly the *corvina* (whitefish) and the various *churrasco* (steak) and *pollo* (chicken) dishes.

SACHUN, Avenida del Ejército 657, Miraflores. Tel. 41-0123

The rich cultural legacy of Peru is celebrated in song and dance every night at Sachun. It's no easy task to fit a country's worth of entertainment into one evening, but through hard work and ingenuity, the Sachun brothers have managed to do just that. The evening's performance kicks off with elegant dances from the coast, including the Limeñan Marinera. Also known as the *Mozamala*, it is Peru's national dance. In the southern coastal valleys outside Lima, Creole rhythms were combined with an African beat by the black slaves brought by the Spanish conquistadors to work the cotton fields there. Peru's black folklore was born during the colonial period and lives on in dance.

The scene changes to the Andean Highlands and the highly charged dances of its indigenous residents. Many of these dances, which are still performed today, have their roots in the Spanish conquest of the Incan Empire and openly poke fun at the strange habits of the Spanish conquistadors. The most common of these dances are the *diablada,* the *llameranda,* and the *chonguinada.* The folkloric portion of the show winds up with the languid sounds and movements of the jungle. The serene and fluid movements of the dancers' bodies imitate the swaying of palm trees in a tropical breeze and the ebb and flow of the waters of the great Amazon.

The audience also gets a turn on the dance floor. Sachun's house bands are just as adept at merengue, salsa, romantic boleros, and popular music. Top entertainment is provided by the best-loved Peruvian singers and comics. We guarantee you a fabulous evening here.

LA CASA DE EDITH, Ignacio de Merino 250, Miraflores. Tel. 41-0612.

Edith offers a nightly 2½-hour show featuring fine creole-style entertainment. In one dance, called the *alcatraz,* two couples in *típico* garb chase around after one another, trying to ignite a cloth tailpiece with a lighted candle. But the climax comes when a member of the audience is invited to grab a candle and start chasing also. Also, there are the inevitable comics, singers, and folk dancers, all appropriately tireless.

Invariably jammed on Friday and Saturday evenings, Edith is best and less expensive during the week (closed on Sunday). Come around 10pm. There's a special $16 package price that includes the steep cover charge ($6.50 per person on weekends, $5.50 during the week), one drink, and a full-course meal (three dishes, dessert, and coffee).

HATUCHAY, 228 Trujillo.

For folkloric music, head to Hatuchay, just across the river, on Trujillo. Admission is $3, and drinks run about $2. Although it caters to tour groups, the music is great and incorporates rhythms not only from Peru but from all of South America. There's plenty of room for dancing, so don't be shy.

BARRANCO

A somewhat bohemian crowd gravitates to the outlying suburb of Barranco, home to many of Peru's finest artists and poets. Dancing and drinking are the norm at the many *peñas* located here. The music usually starts at around 9:30pm and lasts well into the wee hours. *Warning:* Leave your jewelry and other valuables in the safe at your hotel.

Los Balcones de Barranco, at 294 Grau, is an excellent choice if you like to have dinner and then enjoy one of Lima's finest *típico* shows and music in one place. **El Otro Sitio,** at 317 Sucre, is another good choice for creole cuisine and live music. Less formal choices are **El Buho Pub,** at Sucre 315; **Don Porfirio,** at Pasaje, Tumbes 109; **La Estación de Barranco,** at Pedro de Osma 112; and **Taberna 1900,** at Grau 268. There's dinner with music nightly at **El Boulevard de Barranco,** at Sanchez Carrion 135. The best shows are on the weekends. Several rock groups were performing here during our last visit. If jazz and contemporary music are more to your liking, stop in at **La Casona de Barranco,** at Grau 329.

El Cosario Pub, under the Puente de Suspiros (Bridge of Sighs) at Bajada de los Baños 343 (tel. 67-1886), is a lively pub with a nautical theme. Outdoor tables make this a great choice for a late-afternoon respite.

Café Teatro

A popular form of entertainment in Lima these days is *café teatro.* Similar to our own small café theaters, the *café teatro* serves up comedy sketches, short dramas, and musical revues while you sip a drink or a cup of coffee and nibble sandwiches or pastries. The price of admission is about $10. Much of the humor might escape you because the sketches are usually in Spanish; however, you can't help but enjoy the enthusiasm of the performers and audience. The night we visited, we caught a comedy team and acting troupe from Spain. The refreshments served at a *café teatro* are often native to the country of the performer. For example, we enjoyed Spanish meat pies for $3. Small round tables are clustered around a tiny stage, and the performers use piano accompaniment. A good *café teatro* in Miraflores is the **Palacio Atanea.**

OTHER ENTERTAINMENT

MOVIES   First-run U.S. films (undubbed) are shown in about 12 downtown theaters. Prices range from $2 (balcony) to $3.50 (best orchestra seat). Seats are reserved. Most of the better movie houses are now located in Miraflores. They are very crowded, so go early. There are also English-language films on TV.

CASINOS   A couple of casinos have recently opened shop in Lima. The first is in the **Grand Hotel Miraflores,** next door to the Red and Blue disco; it's open Monday to Friday from 5pm to 2am (5am on the weekends) and features black jack and roulette. Slightly nicer is the casino in the **✪ Country Club Hotel.** It is open Monday to Friday from 5pm to 2am (until 3am Friday and Saturday). Gamers have their choice of black jack, roulette, or the infamous one-armed bandits. Each game is in a separate room.

---

10. EASY EXCURSIONS

CALLAO

Peru's largest port is Callao, 8 miles west of Lima, and the most interesting attraction here is the famous **Real Felipe Fortress,** which at one time protected this city and Lima from British raids. Sir Francis Drake sacked Callao in the 16th century but failed to get past the fortress on the road to Lima. This was also where the Spanish royalists made their last stand against Símon Bolívar and his liberators from in 1824 to 1826.

In the fortress is a small museum called the **Museo Histórico Militar** (tel. 29-1505); it is usually open on Tuesday, Wednesday, and Friday from 9am to noon and 3 to 5pm, Saturday and Sunday from 2 to 5:30pm. The hours of admission frequently change, so call first to get the latest schedule. Admission is free.

Callao is easily reached by microbus no. 71 in 30 minutes from Nicolas de Pierola, in front of the Gran Hotel Bolívar. The bus marked LIMA–LA PUNTA, which charges 50¢ each way, stops at a sign reading: LIMA–CALLAO–LA PUNTA–LINEA 56. An alternative is to travel via *colectivo* (Lima-Callao) for 50¢. Pick it up near the Bolívar.

At the southern tip of Callao is La Punta ("The Point"), a popular summer (December to February) resort noted for its many fine summer homes and ocean swimming.

THE PACHACAMAC RUINS & MUSEUM

✪ These stunning ruins, 20 miles south of Lima in the Lurin Valley, were once pyramids built by pre-Inca Indian tribes to satisfy an omnipotent god. Upon the same structures the Incas later constructed their own temples and pyramids, dedicated to the sun god and to the moon, which they filled with silver and gold objects. Sadly, the conquistadors, led by Francisco Pizarro's brother, Gonzalo, killed the Inca priests, destroyed the religious idols, and looted the temples.

Much, however, of the era's history has now been pieced together by archeological discoveries in this century. Indeed, so many relics and artifacts were uncovered that a museum was erected on the site to house them. Mummies, pottery, original woven textiles, and many silver objects can be seen here. Daily hours are 9am to 5pm, and admission is $2.

CBS Tours, at Miguel Dasso 132, in San Isidro (tel. 70-4090), operates daily tours, leaving at 9:30am to the area for $18 per person, which includes a private auto tour to both the museum and the ruins. Other services offering a similar tour for the same price include **Lima Tours**, with offices at Pardo 392 in Miraflores, Los Rosales 440 in San Isidro, and Belen 1040 downtown; **Receptour,** at Jacinto Lara 195; and **Condor Travel** in the Lima Sheraton.

To save money, you can go on your own. Buses leave from Plaza Santa Catalina every half hour, and the one-way cost is about $3. Get off at kilometer 31 of the Southern Panamerican Hwy. There is an admission of $2. The trip takes around an hour.

EL PUEBLO HYATT HOTEL [LA GRANJA AZUL]

This smashing restaurant/resort complex (tel. 35-0777) has long been a favorite of ours. La Granja Azul, as many natives still call it, is located on the road to Chosica in Santa Clara and is well worth the 10-mile trip. Once simply a restaurant specializing in exotic cocktails and chicken-only dishes, it has evolved into a planned Peruvian village–cum–resort—embracing a 250-room Spanish-colonial inn complete with tennis courts; pools; horseback riding; and a full health club with sauna, gymnasium, and bowling alley. A golf course is open to guests. A funicular railway carries guests from the restaurant area to secluded cottages with private pools.

This newly created village features a multitude of shops (Silvania Prints and Artesana have outlets here), discos, a movie house, a piano bar, three restaurants, a museum, a conference hall, and even a chapel. Plus marvelous vistas of the Andes—all in brilliant sunshine most of the year (no *garúa* here).

If you can't stay overnight, plan a Sunday day trip to see the folklore show. The grounds surely are worth it, and you can dine in one of six dining rooms in the restaurant, where you can order unlimited barbecued chicken for $15. Chicken is actually what La Granja Azul built its reputation on, and some 30 years later it is still barbecued the same way—on hickory logs. If you like, you can drink your day away; huge, potent drinks are served in coconut husks, among other exotic containers. But prices are steep—up to $5 for cocktails. All breads and pastries are baked on the premises and are first rate.

GETTING THERE   There is now a free shuttle-bus service to and from El Pueblo, with pickup at many of our recommended hotels ($2 each way). Check your hotel for the schedule. Another inexpensive way to reach this resort complex is via bus no. 202V, marked SANTA CLARA, which leaves from the Parque Universitario, not far from Plaza San Martín. It costs $2 round trip. It will drop you in Santa Clara, a short walk from the village. A taxi at $15 each way is high, but five passengers can share the cost.

WHERE TO STAY   Doubles at El Pueblo run $115 (tax included). Singles are $95. All rooms come with private bath. Bungalows are $150 for two people, $165 for four. For full American Plan (all three meals), add an additional $25 to the room rate. Modified American Plan (breakfast and dinner) is an additional $15. A continental breakfast will cost $6; an American breakfast is $8. On Friday and Saturday evenings, the nightlife pulses frenetically when the under-30 set moves in.

NASCA

More and more tourists are drawn each year to the magical lines of Nasca—the site where an ancient civilization carved, with absolute precision, huge animals, birds, human figures, and geometric lines into a rock plateau that extends for miles. Visible only from the air, these amazing drawings and lines (known as von Däniken's runways) suggests that a highly developed knowledge of hydraulic engineering and astronomy existed in pre-Inca times.

We have taken this excursion and can only share our absolute awe in viewing this amazing work of art. We promise you that the experience will haunt you long after your trip is over. Were the lines actually an airstrip? Did a knowledge of aeronautics exist in pre-Inca times? If so, can we draw the conclusion that a civilization as sophisticated technologically as our own, or more so, existed so many thousands of years ago?

GETTING THERE   Numerous tours are now available to the area. **Lima Tours** offers a three-day package that includes viewing the lines and sightseeing in Ica and Paracas, the nearest villages, at a cost of $325 per person.

The budget traveler can put together a do-it-yourself excursion by taking a *colectivo* from the **Señor de Loren** office, at Avenida Abancay 1167 (tel. 28-0630). *Colectivos* depart from Lima to Nasca at 7am and 2pm, with a round trip costing $25. Señor de Loren also offers service to Ica.

It's possible to do the trip all in one day by leaving at 4am, but it's a very long day. Driving time to Nasca alone is 7 hours, and there can be delays in waiting for the *colectivos* to fill (they prefer to leave with six people, although you can offer to pay the extra fare if you're only one person short).

You can also take the bus to Nasca. Your best options are the Tepsa and Ormeno bus lines. Check with both companies for current schedules and be sure to pick up your ticket a day in advance. **Tepsa** is located at Paseo de la República 129 (tel. 27-6077); **Ormeño** is at Carlos Zavala 177 (tel. 27-5679).

WHERE TO STAY   For big-splurge living, check into the new **Las Dunas** resort, just 3 hours by car from Lima, on the Panamerican Highway, in Ica. A lush oasis among sand dunes, Las Dunas serves as a center for those wishing to spend a few days in the area to view the lines, sample local wines (Ica is known for the manufacture of red, rosé, and white wines), and check out the important archeological sights and museums in both Ica and Paracas. Best of all, the resort has direct flights over the Nasca lines from their own airstrip. A sparkling white Spanish structure, Las Dunas offers ultramodern accommodations, with pools, tennis courts, and horseback riding. For reservations and current rate information, write to Las Dunas, Avenida Rivera Navarrete 889, Office 208, in San Isidro. In Lima call 42-3090 or 42-3091. In the United States call American Express (tel. toll free 800/327-7737).

Two additional choices are the **Hotel de la Borda,** on kilometer 447 of the Panamerican Highway (tel. 40-8430 in Lima for reservations); and **La Maison Suisse,** also on kilometer 447 of the Panamerican Highway (tel. 28-2243 in Lima for reservations).

11. SUGGESTED ITINERARIES

Peru is an exciting and diverse country, the perfect destination for the adventurous traveler. Visitors to Peru often find themselves at remote jungle outposts or trekking through the Andean highlands. Of course, one of the most magnificent destinations in Peru, and even South America for that matter, is Cuzco and Macchú Picchú (see Chapter 14).

THE JUNGLE

IQUITOS   About 1,000 miles from Lima, Iquitos sits on the Amazon River, 2,300 miles upriver from the Atlantic Ocean. Iquitos is reached by flying one of **Faucett's** nonstop flights from Miami (three days a week) or from Lima (two flights daily). The city, dating from the mid-18th century, has had a roller-coaster existence, much like its sister city, Manaus, on the Brazilian Amazon. At its height, during the rubber boom, huge steamers loaded at its docks, and the city had magnificent hotels and an opera house. When it became cheaper to buy rubber in Malaysia, the boom died and with it went the glory of Iquitos. The city is certainly worth strolling through (bring lots of insect repellent), especially the Plaza de Armas and the market.

The government-run **Hotel de Turistas** (tel. 42-8626 in Lima for reservations) is a great choice, especially since its bar is a popular hangout. The **Hostal Caravelle** (tel. 32-5828 in Lima for reservations) is also a popular choice. Most visitors head out of Iquitos to **Explorama Lodge,** 50 miles downriver. It offers clean and comfortable accommodations and surprisingly good food. Tours from Explorama to visit the jungle and its inhabitants (animal and tribal) are first rate. Write for information to **Exploraciones Amazónicas,** Box 446, Iquitos, Peru. Leave yourself lots of time, because mail is slow. In Lima call 24-4764.

Another popular spot to stay is the new **Amazon Lodge,** a modern village of thatch-roofed huts on the Momon River, a tributary of the Amazon. Amazon Lodge is only a 90-minute ride downriver from Iquitos. Trips from here are also well organized and well run. For more information, write to Lima Tours, Box 4340, Lima, Peru; or to Amazon Village, 5805 N. W. Blue Lagoon Dr., Miami, FL 33126 (tel. 305/261-3024). Faucett Airlines offers package tours from Miami and others from Lima. You should contact them at Suite 450, 1150 N. W. 72nd Ave., Miami, FL 33126.

PUCALLPA On the River Ucayali, Pucallpa is Peru's second most popular jungle destination, in the center of the country's oil-exploration activities. Use the city as a jumping-off point for trips along the nearby lake, which was once part of the river. Close by is a village lived in by the Shipibos tribe. Their huts are made of open-sided wood and palm leaf and are raised from the ground to avoid snakes. Barter for one of their unusual glazed pots or an 8-foot blowgun. Other tribes live nearby. Although a frontier town in the midst of the jungle, Pucallpa is only a one-hour flight from Lima. Contact Faucett for more information (see above).

There are several lodgings in Pucallpa, including a government tourist hotel at Jr. San Martín 552. The best restaurant is in the **Hostal Inambu.**

HUANCAYO

A 3-day excursion, well worth the time if you have it, is the 192-mile trip to Huancayo, a typical mountain village 10,000 feet up in the Andes, which has the most famous market in Peru. At the first sign of dawn on Sunday, the Indians come in from the countryside laden with alpaca rugs, hats and slippers, food, pottery, woven baskets, gourds, and jewelry. The goods are spread on the ground in the town square and then the bargaining begins—serious, low-key, and persistent. You'll hear little of the shrill wrangling common to the Rome and Paris flea markets. Instead, conversation is businesslike, limited to numbers representing nuevo soles. The price is given, the customer counters, the dealer drops his or her price, and the deal is consummated.

Getting to Huancayo is much of the excitement. The train, in its 9-hour journey from Lima, winds its way through the highest reaches of the Peruvian Andes and at one point rolls along at a height of 15,800 feet. Some airplanes cruise at that altitude, so it is little wonder that the railway brags that its tracks are the "highest in the world." You'll cross over no fewer than 59 bridges and through 66 tunnels to reach Huancayo.

Enafer Perú line has daily trains to Huancayo. Check on schedules from Lima at the Desamparados station, at Jirón Ancash 207 (tel. 28-9440). We recommend that you leave on Saturday and return on Monday. Get your ticket at the station a day before your trip. Remember that train travel in Peru is rudimentary at best. Travel first class but don't expect luxury. *And hold on to your belongings* (luggage should be kept to a minimum).

Several bus companies make the trip as well. These include **Mariscal Caceres,** at Avenida 28 de Julio 2195 (tel. 24-2456 or 31-4729); **Etusca,** at Prolongacion Huanaco 1582 (tel. 23-3247); **Hidalgo,** at Avenida 28 de Julio 1750; and **Los Andes,** at Avenida 28 de Julio (tel. 23-0660).

Entur, at Los Nogales 249 in San Isidro (tel. 42-8626), will make reservations for you to stay at the **Turista Hotel.** Rates were $35 for doubles and $25 for singles the last time we investigated, but check for recent changes.

If you prefer, any travel agency will make arrangements for you. If you cannot make it to Huancayo and yet are interested in seeing an Indian mountain village, make sure you include the market in **Pisac,** near Cuzco.

MOVING ON

Two domestic airlines—Faucett and Aeroperú—fly to Cuzco from Lima. Flying time is one hour. **Faucett** at Inca Garcilaso de la Vega 865 (tel. 33-6364) is the more reliable of the two. **Aeroperú** has an office in Plaza San Martín (tel. 28-5721) and in Miraflores at Avenida José Pardo 601 (tel. 47-8333). Each has two daily flights to Cuzco, leaving at approximately 7am. Neither airline accepts traveler's checks, but both accept credit cards. Make sure to check on the rate in nuevo soles before you pay.

CHAPTER 14

CUZCO & MACHÚ PICCHÚ

- **WHAT'S SPECIAL ABOUT CUZCO & MACHÚ PICCHÚ**
1. **INTRODUCING CUZCO & MACHÚ PICCHÚ**
2. **ORIENTATION**
3. **GETTING AROUND**
- **FAST FACTS: CUZCO**
4. **WHERE TO STAY**
5. **WHERE TO DINE**
6. **ATTRACTIONS**
7. **SAVVY SHOPPING**
8. **EVENING ENTERTAINMENT**
9. **EASY EXCURSIONS**
10. **MOVING ON**
11. **MACHÚ PICCHÚ— THE LOST CITY OF THE INCAS**

Cuzco, a magic name among the Indians who lived in the Andes 500 years ago, and Machú Picchú, the incredible Lost City of the Incas, are still magic names today. The two Peruvian cities, one occupied by Indians living as they did centuries ago, the other a magnificently preserved testament to the genius of the Incas, represent South America at its peak of traveler fascination and excitement. In personal terms, nowhere else—Athens, Budapest, Rome, or Tangiers—have we ever been so completely captivated as in Cuzco and Machú Picchú; when we first gazed upon the latter site, the sheer beauty of it left us in wonderment.

Cuzco was the fabled gold-laden capital of the Inca world when that world extended from what is now Chile and Argentina north through Bolivia, Peru, Ecuador, and Colombia. In some respects, the city—350 miles southeast of Lima—has hardly changed at all since it was razed and rebuilt by Pizarro's conquistadors, beginning in 1533.

Most historians believe that Machú Picchú is the legendary city where a small band of Incas fled during the Spanish occupation of Cuzco. When it

A WARNING ON PERU

As we went to press, the situation in Peru, marked by continuing terrorist violence, had become so dangerous to tourists that the U.S. Department of State warned U.S. citizens not to travel there. The reason was a sudden increase in bombing attacks, in heavily touristed areas in Lima and elsewhere, by the Maoist guerrilla group known as *Sendero Luminoso* (Shining Path). Peruvian authorities warned of a "very bloody" period ahead as the rebels vowed to intensify their campaign of terror, despite a state of emergency declared earlier by the government.

If you plan to travel to Peru, therefore, be sure to call the **U.S. Department of State's Citizens' Emergency Service** (tel. 202/647-5225) in Washington, D.C., on weekdays from 8:15am to 10pm, for an up-to-date report of the situation in Peru. If, however, you're already in Peru when you read this, inquire at the U.S. Embassy—or at your own country's embassy if you're not a U.S. citizen—for news as well as advice regarding the current situation and what you should do to avoid unnecessary risk to your safety.

WHAT'S SPECIAL ABOUT CUZCO & MACHÚ PICCHÚ

Architecture
☐ In Cuzco Spanish-colonial structures were seemingly superimposed on the ruins of the original Inca settlement, yet vestiges of the original structures remain.

Monuments
☐ Machú Picchú, Ollantaytambo, Pisac, and Sacsayhuaman are monuments to the valor, engineering genius, and ingenuity of the Inca.

Museum
☐ Cuzco's Museum of Religious Art is home to a fascinating collection of paintings from the Cuzco school.

The People
☐ Despite the influx of tourists from the developed world, for the most part the Indians of Cuzco have held firm to their traditional way of life.

Natural Spectacles
☐ Nowhere is the majesty of the Andes more apparent than at Machú Picchú.

was unearthed in 1911, after years of labor, it instantly became the most famous sight in Peru. It deserves to be listed among the great sights of the world. Situated 75 miles north of Cuzco, this wondrous place, where the sun hardly ceases to shine, retains all its glory for the visitor. We cannot urge you too strongly to make this and Cuzco absolute musts in your South American trip.

1. INTRODUCING CUZCO & MACHÚ PICCHÚ

When the Spanish arrived here, Cuzco was the largest and most important city in the Western Hemisphere. Its population today is 99% Indian and 1% *mestizo* (a mixture of Indian and Spanish).

The conquistadors were looking for gold, and there was more of it here than even their most wild-eyed dreamers foresaw. Pizarro found temples filled with gold, and monuments and ritual baths made of the yellow metal. After looting the city, the Spanish leveled it, sparing only a few buildings and the city walls. On the ruins the conquerors built a settlement of churches, residences, and military buildings, all of colonial design. A Spanish city was thus transplanted to the New World; one culture was destroyed and another superimposed on the rubble. The identical transformation took place in Quito, another Inca center to the north, a year or so later.

Today, this city—more than 2 miles in elevation—is an unusual combination of Spanish colonial in its architecture and old Indian in its culture. You'll find that the Indians here have not altered their dress, methods of farming, or traditions for over four centuries! And yet many of them are in almost daily contact with the so-called civilized world of Lima, Rio, Buenos Aires, and Chicago, via the stream of visitors that flock here. Tradition does not die easily in Cuzco.

The color brown seems to dominate the city. The surrounding mountains, the earth, the homes, the cobblestone streets, the women's skirts, the men's hats, and

IMPRESSIONS

There is no sense in my trying to describe Cuzco; I should only be quoting from the guidebook. . . . What remains with you is the sense of a great outrage, magnificent but unforgivable. The Spaniards tore down the Inca temples and grafted splendid churches and mansions on to their foundations. This is one of the most beautiful monuments to bigotry and sheer stupid brutality in the whole world.
—CHRISTOPHER ISHERWOOD, *THE CONDOR AND THE COWS*, 1949

the complexion of the people all seem to blend into a single reddish brown hue. It is as if, over the centuries, varying shades of brown have blended and reblended until now there is only the single shade. And it is as if, finally, the city and its people have become one. The ever-present sun is the catalyst, and after a day or two you'll find—if you're fair—that your complexion has started to turn a reddish brown.

The smell of history is stronger here for us than it has ever been at the Colosseum in Rome or the Parthenon in Athens. Rome and Athens today are modern Western capitals, and the historical remains of their stunning pasts are anachronisms in their present-day settings. In Cuzco the past and present are inseparable. They confront each other in the streets, in the homes, and in the traditions. The only anachronisms are the tourists and the planes that wing into the Velasco Asete Airport. Even the newer hotels blend into the whole.

Moreover, the meaning of Cuzco has greater impact when you remember that the Inca civilization was abruptly strangled in a single year—at its zenith—while the Roman and Greek cultures died more leisurely, after long, full lives.

No one knows what heights the Incas might have scaled in world history. You'll wonder that, too, as you stroll past the Inca walls, the stonework, and the intricate centuries-old terracing on their farms that enables the soil to retain precious moisture for many months. And then look hard at the shoeless Indian women in their high stovepipe hats as they tote enormous loads on their sturdy backs.

BACKGROUND   The Incas, who began stirring from their home in Cuzco in about the year A.D. 1000, quickly conquered Indian tribes south in what is now Chile and north in what is today Colombia. The empire flourished for over 500 years, during which time the Incas imposed their own social order on the conquered people. They worshiped the sun, source of all light and warmth, and encouraged their subjects to worship it. The sun god's representative on earth was the Sapa Inca. Originally, the term *Inca* applied only to the ruler. The Spaniards extended it to the nobles and priests, and it has since come to mean the entire race.

Subject peoples were assigned land to work and assorted tasks, such as weaving, potterymaking, and constructing fortresses. One-third of the harvest was stored in granaries against the threat of famine. Another third was devoted to upkeep of the sacred temples, erected to honor the sun god. The final third remained with the conquered people.

Superb builders, the Incas constructed networks of roads, bridges, tunnels, aqueducts, irrigation ditches, and stone stairways—all without benefit of the wheel, which they apparently never developed. Their terracing system to retain water for farming is still used today.

The language of the Incas was the Quechua tongue, imposed on all their subjects. It's still the dominant language of 5 million Indians on the west coast of South America.

The history of the era is sketchy, since the Incas developed no written language, not even hieroglyphics. Meager records were kept on knotted llama cords called *quipas,* hardly enough to form a basis for understanding the civilization. Historians rely on the accounts left by the conquistadors and missionaries.

2. ORIENTATION

ARRIVING If you fly from Lima, you'll probably take one of the two popular Faucett flights that leave each morning and arrive in Cuzco in about an hour. Alternatively, you might take the Aeroperú flight, which also leaves Lima daily, in the morning. The times of these flights are always subject to change, so check carefully before you go.

Whichever flight you choose, sit on the left-hand side of the plane to gain the better view of the Andes as you approach Cuzco. After you land at the **Velasco Asete Airport,** crowds of Indian tradesmen will surround the aircraft offering to sell you souvenirs or rugs or even a package tour. A polite but firm no is your wisest reaction. *Important:* Confirm your return flight to Lima when you arrive in Cuzco.

Take a taxi to your hotel, but arrange the price in advance because there are no cab meters here; pay no more than $5. Ask the cab to wait while you're checking to see if the hotel has room for you. Or phone from the airport to make a reservation.

TOURIST INFORMATION There is a **Government Tourist Office** at the airport that has a list of hotels and their current prices. Check with them before heading into town. The office at Portal Belen 115, in the Plaza de Armas, is open Monday to Friday from 8am to 5:30pm and Saturday from 8:30am to 12:30pm. The office in the airport is open until noon every day. The tourist office has some literature (not much in English), and it can answer questions about train schedules and the like.

You'll get a lot of enthusiastic advice from the **University Tourism Students.** They've recently opened a small office in the courtyard of the Compañía de Jesus. Someone should be there to answer questions Monday to Friday from 8am to noon and 3 to 6pm. No question is too insignificant. The students are eager to put their studies into practice and will do their best to get you on the right track.

Faucett Airways, one of the two airlines that fly to Cuzco, acts as a clearing agent for all other airlines. To change a reservation, inform the Faucett clerk on Avenida del Sol, opposite the Ollanta Hotel, who will wire his Lima office. That office will pass your message on to your airline. A confirming message will be sent to you in care of the Faucett office here. There is no charge for the service.

Warning: Cuzco, like La Paz and Quito, is a high-in-the-mountains, thin-air city, and therefore you should move slowly your first day here, eat lightly, and rest frequently. Otherwise, the tourist's ailment—*soroche*—will cause headaches and lightheadedness.

CITY LAYOUT Cuzco is a small city, so you'll orient yourself quickly. The city center is the **Plaza de Armas,** site of Inca walls and temples that have withstood the conquistadors, 2 earthquakes, and 400 years of sun and wind.

The main street leading through the city is **Avenida del Sol,** an uphill thoroughfare that runs from the airport to Plaza de Armas. Most of our hotels and restaurants are on or near Avenida del Sol, not far from the plaza. The Puno railroad station is at the bottom of Avenida del Sol. Follow **Calle Loreto,** a narrow street lined with Inca walls, out of the plaza to visit the remains of the massive Inca **Temple of the Sun,** a must sight. It's two blocks downhill from the plaza, between Avenida del Sol and Pampa del Castillo.

Follow **Avenida Santa Clara** uphill out of the plaza. Three blocks away is the **Plaza San Francisco,** which marks the start of the Indian quarter of Cuzco. It may sound strange to mention an Indian quarter in a city that is 99% Indian; however, the differences in garb and in the quality of life, and especially customs, are immediately obvious as you pass through the arch. Three blocks into the area is the sprawling Indian market that is adjacent to the railroad station, from which you'll get your train to Machú Picchú.

Note: The market has become a favorite haunt of skilled pickpockets. We've received letters detailing slashed purses and camera snatchings. Leave valuables and cash in your hotel.

3. GETTING AROUND

Cabs here have no meters, so establish all fares in advance. Tipping is not expected. The trip from the airport is $3. Owners of the newest cabs belong to a group called Comité de Servicio Aeropuerto. Most cabs in the group are four-door U.S. sedans.

FAST   CUZCO

American Express   The American Express representative in Cuzco is at Lima Tours, Portal de Harinas 177 (tel. 22-8431).

Babysitters   The concierge at your hotel may be able to help you arrange for child care.

Bookstores   The **Mini Shop,** at Portal Confituria 217 or Heladeros 132, has a wide selection of books on Cuzco, Peru, and South America in a number of languages.

Business Hours   Business hours in Cuzco are the same as those in Lima. Since most businesses cater to the tourists, however, many shops do not close at midday.

Climate   The climate of Cuzco is similar to that of La Paz, but warmer. The sun shines brilliantly much of the year, and afternoon temperatures hover in the 60s Fahrenheit. Evening lows are in the 40s, and winds are constant but not strong. Bring a raincoat in November and May to June. Most important, though, heed our warning on the thin air, which can cause you to become fatigued easily. Indeed, our best suggestion for you is to dine lightly and rest often on the first day. However, if you've come here from La Paz or Quito, you should experience no discomfort. You should carry a sweater with you no matter how warm it may seem, since the temperature shifts rapidly.

Currency   At the time of this writing, US $1 was worth 1.19 nuevo soles. For more information see Chapter 9.

Currency Exchange   There are banks and exchange houses in Cuzco where you can change money.

Dentists/Doctors   The concierge at your hotel should be able to help you find a dentist or a doctor.

Drugstores   The concierge at your hotel should be able to direct you to a nearby pharmacy.

Emergencies   The tourist police are located next door to the Tourist Office in the Plaza de Armas. In case of an emergency call 22-1961.

Holidays

San Sebastian Procession	January 20
Lord of the Earthquakes Festival	Easter Monday
Vigil of the Cross	May 2–3
Independence Day	July 28
Santorantikuy (Buying of Saints)	December 24

Hospitals   The **Regional Hospital** is on Avenida de la Cultura (tel. 22-1131).

Information   See "Tourist Information" earlier in this chapter.

Laundry/Dry Cleaning   **Lavanderías Imperial,** Espaderos 136 at the corner of Uriel Garcia (formerly Suecia), offers same-day service.

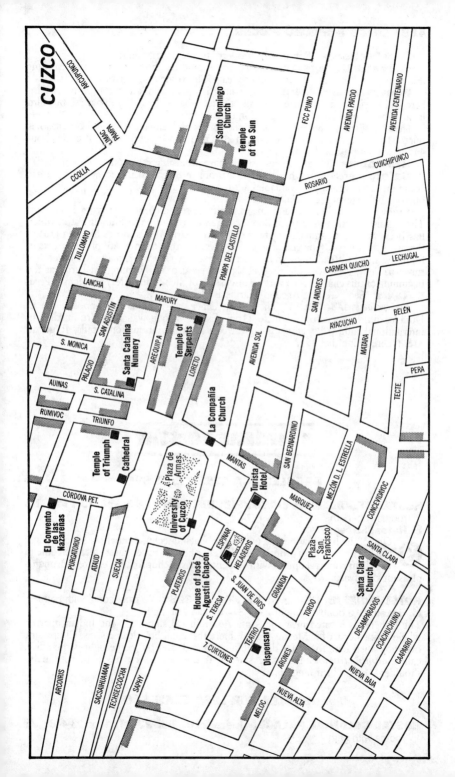

Lost Property   Report lost property to the Tourist Police.

Luggage Storage/Lockers   You should be able to arrange to leave your things at your hotel should you plan to leave Cuzco for a few days.

Photographic Needs   A UV filter is recommended at this altitude. Film here will be significantly more expensive than it is back home. If you have to buy film locally, be sure to check the expiration date.

Post Office   The post office, on the corner of Avenida del Sol and Garcilaso, is open Monday to Saturday from 8am to 7pm and Sunday until noon. It costs about 49¢ to send a postcard.

Restrooms   Hotel lobbies usually have accessible restrooms.

Safety   Street crime has become a problem in Cuzco in recent years, so use common sense. Leave your valuables at home, use a moneybelt, and keep a close eye on your belongings—especially when you're in a crowd.

Safety in Peru, however, has come to signify more than protection from petty theft. The Maoist guerrilla movement known as *Sendero Luminoso* (Shining Path), which has been waging a campaign of terror since the early 1980s, poses an even greater threat to the tourist. Guerrilla leaders have warned that tourists are prime targets in bombing attacks. Readers are thus advised to exercise *extreme caution* whenever they travel in Peru, even to archeological sights. See also "A Warning on Peru" at the beginning of this chapter for a further discussion of the serious safety problem in Peru.

Taxis   See "Getting Around" earlier in this chapter.

Telephone/Telexes   The ENTEL Office, on Avenida Sol opposite the El Dorado Inn, is open from 7am to 11pm. Expect a long wait if you're making an international call. AT&T Direct is a great cost saver for international calls. To get an AT&T Direct line dial 191.

4. WHERE TO STAY

DOUBLES FOR LESS THAN $20

HOSTAL RESIDENCIAL MACHÚPICCHÚ, Quera 282. Tel. 23-1111. No rooms with bath.
$ Rates: $5 per person.

One of the best low-budget buys is the Machúpicchú, a cut above super-budget level. The motherly proprietress does her best to make guests feel welcome in the clean rooms. Popular with students, the Machúpicchú is entered through a pleasant courtyard.

HOTEL IMPERIO, Chaparro 121. Tel. 22-8981. 40 rms (some with bath).
$ Rates: $10 double without bath, $14 double with bath.
The Imperio is located near the Santa Ana railroad station, in the Indian quarter, where trains depart for Machú Picchú. Here the small but clean rooms, all upstairs, overlook a garden. You enter through a courtyard, and off to the right is the office, called *administración*. Don't be startled if the desk clerk has a parrot on his shoulder—he's a bird fancier.

DOUBLES FOR LESS THAN $30

HOSTAL COLONIAL PALACE, Quera 270. Tel. 23-2151 or **23-4481.** All rooms with bath.

$ Rates: $20 single; $25 double; $30 triple.

At the Palace you'll feel as if you've stepped back in time to a colonial estate (with modern amenities). All the carpeted rooms open onto a beautiful courtyard. (However, rooms can get a little chilly on colder days.) The hostal has its own restaurant and bar and offers laundry and medical service.

HOSTAL MANTAS, Calle Mantas 115. Tel. 23-1431. 20 rms (all with bath).
$ Rates: $10 single; $16.50 double.
Better than basic is what you'll find at the Mantas, less than a block from Plaza de Armas. All rooms are carpeted and have heaters. There is a restaurant on the main floor, as well as a bar. Head up one flight.

HOSTAL RESIDENCIAL LOS MARQUESES, Calle Garcilaso 256. Tel. 23-2512. 16 rms (all with bath).
$ Rates: $16 single; $21 double; $24 triple.

This is the most historically intriguing hotel here. A converted 300-year-old hacienda, the fantastic Los Marqueses has been lovingly restored, and much of the original mahogany and other woodwork can be seen in doors, paneling, and banisters. In fact, the massive, intricately etched doors to each room, as well as the colonial floor chests and closets, make a visit here mandatory, whether you're a guest or not. All rooms are off a common courtyard and have been redone in exquisite taste. They are large, each with its own floor chest and hot-water heater. However, Los Marqueses may not be to everyone's taste (many of the rooms are windowless, and the baths could be upgraded).

HOSTAL TAMBO REAL, Calle Belen 588. Tel. 22-1621. 18 rms (all with bath).
$ Rates: $12 single; $20 double; $26 triple.
Two blocks from the railroad station you'll find this small, comfortable hotel. The three-story Tambo Real offers carpeting and nicely draped windows in each room.

HOTEL EL SOL, San Andres 338A. Tel. 22-6421. All rooms with bath.
$ Rates: $13 single; $19 double.
El Sol is a fairly new hotel. All rooms have heating. The hotel offers laundry service and has a bar and restaurant on the premises.

HOTEL VIRREY, Portal Comercial 165. Tel. 22-1771. All rooms with bath.
$ Rates: $15 single; $22 double; $30 triple. Continental breakfast $1.50 extra.
For ideal location, it would be hard to top the Virrey, situated in Plaza de Armas. The carpeted rooms are very spacious, clean, and cheerful, with red-and-white bedspreads; even the bathrooms are large. The decor in this three-story hotel is comfortable, and the management friendly and helpful. Try to get an upper room for a full view of the plaza.

DOUBLES FOR LESS THAN $40

HOSTAL EL SOLAR, Plaza San Francisco Tel. 23-2451. 18 rms (all with bath).
$ Rates: $25 single; $30 double; $32 triple.
The two-story El Solar is an old colonial-style hotel with its own special charm. Here you'll find spacious rooms, many with balconies overlooking the plaza, opening onto a pleasant courtyard. All are carpeted, with nicely draped windows and electric heaters. Note that several of the rooms have no windows. We're sure you'll want a view of the plaza, so check your room first.

HOSTAL WIRAQOCHA, Plaza de Armas at Mantas. Tel. 22-1283. 28 rms (all with bath).
$ Rates: $22 single; $30 double. Extra bed $8.

For a hard-to-beat combination of comfort, friendliness, and good location, head for the four-story Wiraqocha, where many rooms command an excellent view of the Plaza de Armas. Located at the corner of Plaza de Armas, at Mantas, the Wiraqocha is a family-run affair. Owner Arturo Samanex and his wife take great pride in their hostal and couldn't be kindlier or more helpful. The rooms have comfortable beds, rugs, writing tables, and heaters. One flight down is a restaurant, and there's a soda fountain on the main floor for snacks. The large public sitting room is a homey spot. Don't skip heading to the roof, where you can sunbathe and enjoy a breathtaking view of the city's cupolas silhouetted against the clearly visible Andes.

HOTEL CONQUISTADOR, Santa Catalina Angosta 149. Tel. 22-4461. 28 rms (all with bath).
$ Rates: $21 single; $30 double.
Just a few steps from Plaza de Armas is the Conquistador, opened in 1973. The rooms are small but well furnished, with wall-to-wall carpeting, floor-to-ceiling drapes, and electric heaters. There are no elevators, so foot-weary travelers should avoid the third floor. For those who don't mind the climb, the third floor is cheerful and sunny because it's covered with a skylight. The hotel has a bar, restaurant, and comfortable sitting area.

HOTEL INTI, Matara 260. Tel. 22-8401. All rooms with bath.
$ Rates: (including breakfast): $18 single; $24 double.
The Hotel Inti, which opened its doors in 1976, is an attractive modern building offering clean, sunny rooms—all fully carpeted. Enter the lobby and check out the shop to the left featuring native handcrafts. The Inti has an attractive dining room, with a cozy brick fireplace, where the specialties of the house are trout, chicken, and beef (special, too, is the complete dinner for $7, including tax). All rooms have bright-green bedspreads and matching drapes.

HOTEL TAMBO, Ayacucho 233. Tel. 22-3221. 43 rms (all with bath).
$ Rates: $22 single; $30 double. Extra bed $8.
Opened in 1973, the modern two-story Tambo is sparkling white, with a red-tile roof. It has a large, colorful lobby with a carpeted staircase, wrought-iron grillwork, and graceful arches. Try the on-premises restaurant and enjoy the 24-hour room service.

PENSIONS

HOSTAL RAYMI, Avenida Pardo 954. Tel. 22-5141. 15 rms (all with bath).
$ Rates (including breakfast): $12 single; $18 double.
This attractive two-story green house is not far from Leonard's Lodgings (below). The Raymi's rooms have wall-to-wall carpeting, and most baths contain a full tub and a vanity sink. The hotel has a dining room, coffee shop, and bar.

LEONARD'S LODGINGS, Avenida Pardo 820. Tel. 23-2831. 14 rms (none with bath).
$ Rates (including breakfast): $12 per person.
Business is booming here, and we think this charming hostal deserves every bit of the attention. Californian Bill Leonard and his Peruvian wife, Luisa, have created an inviting home away from home at their pension, located just beyond the post office, on Avenida Sol. You get a cozy, comfortable room in the Leonard home and a North American breakfast. Bill and Luisa have the facility of making a guest feel instantly like a family member. They have added more guest rooms, in addition to the nine spotless and simply furnished rooms available when we were there. A bonus is that Luisa (who speaks English) is a folklore scholar and fluent in several Indian tongues. Also, she can advise you where to buy what and how much to pay. When writing, address your letter to the Leonards, at Apartado 559, Cuzco.

SPLURGE CHOICES

ALHAMBRA II, Avenida del Sol 596. Tel. 22-4899. All rooms with bath.

$ Rates: $40 single; $57 double. Continental breakfast $3 extra; American breakfast $4.50 extra.

The Alhambra II is a Spanish-colonial style hotel. Its comfortable lobby with plush couches around the sparkling fireplace gives a cozy, friendly feeling. Rooms are spacious and immaculate.

EL DORADO INN, Avenida del Sol 395. Tel. 23-3112. All rooms with bath.
$ Rates: $40 single; $55 double.

On the site of the old El Dorado is the spiffy, newer building. This three-story white hotel boasts a sauna, a wading pool, a beauty shop, a boutique, and a small solarium on every floor. It has a modern elevator in the middle of the lobby. Order a pisco sour (just under $1) from the bar and sip it leisurely in front of the open fireplace. Strolling musicians set a romantic mood. El Dorado's restaurant serves first-class meals.

HOTEL CUZCO, Heladeros 150. Tel. 22-4821. All rooms with bath.
$ Rates: $40 single; $56 double.

Once the only deluxe hotel in town, the Hotel Cuzco is one of 31 government-owned hostelries in Peru. They were built when there were few privately owned hotels for tourists. Large and homey, the aging but still proud Cuzco has a willing staff and is built round a small inner garden. Check out the handsome bar, whose rich wood paneling and large windows make it an inviting place for a leisurely drink. A roaring fire in the lobby's main sitting area draws guests every evening.

HOTEL ROYAL INKA, Plaza Regocijo 299. Tel. 23-1067. 36 rms, 3 suites (all with bath).
$ Rates: $36 single; $48 double; $62.50 suite (with breakfast).

The Royal Inka is owned by a Peruvian who owns three restaurants in New York. He has imported everything, from pots and pans to stainless steel, to make the Royal Inka's kitchen the most modern in Peru. The chef has prepared a variety of dishes to be served in the elegant dining room. Off the lobby is a small bar with a jukebox. Suites are duplex. The other rooms are on four floors, with no elevator.

SAN AGUSTIN, Calle Maruri and San Agustín 390. Tel. 23-1001. 65 rms (all with bath).
$ Rates: $40 single; $55 double.

The renovated three-floor San Agustín has carpeted whitewashed rooms with small sitting areas and heaters. It has an elevator, which is rare here. The San Agustín has a good restaurant, a lovely private bar, and a coffee shop.

5. WHERE TO DINE

If your hotel has a dining room, chances are you'll use it often. However, Cuzco has many interesting restaurants, offering good food at budget prices. Remember that you should eat lightly when you first arrive to give your system time to adjust to the altitude.

BREAKFAST & LUNCH

CHEF VICTOR, Portal de Panes, Plaza de Armas.
   Cuisine: INTERNATIONAL.
$ Prices: Full meals $2.50–$8.
   Open: All day.

Students from Cuzco University seem to fill the counters and tables at the two Chef Victor restaurants, which stand virtually adjacent to one another. Sandwiches, hamburgers, hot dogs, and drinks are the fastest movers. The Victors also have beef, fish, and chicken dishes, soups, pastas, and eggs.

GOVINDA, Espaderos 136.
  Cuisine: VEGETARIAN.
  $ Prices: Four-course lunch $2.50.
  Open: Lunch and dinner.
This restaurant, formerly at Procuradores, has moved into larger quarters. Run by Hare Krishnas, it offers a four-course lunch, homemade breads, cheeses, and yogurts.

PICCOLO RESTAURANT, Portal de Panes.
  Cuisine: INTERNATIONAL.
  $ Prices: Light meals $2.50–$4.
  Open: All day.
The Piccolo, in Plaza de Armas, attracts a cosmopolitan crowd that keeps the oval counter busy. Students meet here to enjoy the *fuente de soda* (light food) and low prices. A good hamburger, ham and eggs, sandwiches, omelets, spaghetti, soup, and juices make up the menu.

EL SUMAK, Mantas 117.
  Cuisine: INTERNATIONAL.
  $ Prices: Light meals $1.75–$3; full meals $3–$6.
  Open: Mon–Sat 9am–11pm.
For low-cost fare and fast counter and table service, head to the Sumak, near Plaza de Armas. The menu features "light eating" at prices that the budget traveler can well appreciate. It's a good place to grab a quick breakfast— scrambled eggs; a cheese omelet; or ham, cheese, and eggs. A beef steak with french fries is a low $4. Don't skip the dessert pancakes with mangoes, bananas, or honey.

TRATTORIA ADRIANO, Mantas 105.
  Cuisine: ITALIAN.
  $ Prices: Meals $3–$7.
  Open: 8am–midnight.
A popular stop for light dining is the Adriano, just off Plaza de Armas. The Trattoria serves hamburgers, sandwiches, and pasta dishes at low prices. At night, stick to the pasta if you're on a tight budget.

DINNER

PIZZERIA LA MAMMA. Portal Escribanos 177.
  Cuisine: PIZZA.
  $ Prices: Full pie $4.25–$6; pasta $1.50–$3.
  Open: 9am–11pm.
Pizzeria La Mamma in Plaza Regocijo, is a bright, cheerful restaurant, with checkered cloths, wicker chairs, and hanging planters. Pizza is served by the slice or the pie ($4.25 for cheese and tomato sauce). Add 50¢ for any extras. La Mamma also serves lasagne, spaghetti plates, and empanadas.

RESTAURANTE CAFFE PIAZZA, Portal Panes 139.
  Cuisine: INTERNATIONAL/ITALIAN.
  $ Prices: Appetizers $1–$2; main courses $2–$5.
  Open: Lunch and dinner.
At this restaurant on Plaza de Armas, you'll be greeted with a complimentary pisco sour. When we were there, we enjoyed the *trucha a la chorillana,* grilled trout with tomatoes and onions. Meat dishes are a little more expensive. Live music is an excellent accompaniment to a meal here.

RESTAURANT PAITITI, Portal de Carrizos 270. Plaza de Armas.
   Cuisine: INTERNATIONAL.
$ Prices: Appetizers $1–$2; main courses $2.75–$5.
   Open: Lunch and dinner.
Walk through the Portal Carrizos to the Paititi, where Spanish-style tables and chairs coexist happily with an old Inca wallhanging and an ancient map. The bilingual menu offers beef and fish dishes, pizza, soups, and omelets. A hamburger with french fries and beer or soda is only $2.75.

ROMA, Portal de Panes 105.
   Cuisine: INTERNATIONAL.
$ Prices: Appetizers $1–$2.50; main courses $2–$8.
   Open: 8am–11pm.
In Plaza de Armas is the Roma, which offers an extensive menu. You have a choice of dining on the main floor or up in the balcony, which is somewhat quieter and warmer. Either way, you'll be handed a large menu, which lists 70 items, including 20 soups, and a lengthy wine list. The most expensive dish is *lomo a la Roma* (steak), which is as filling a platter as you're likely to find in Cuzco. The stuffed avocado is also a treat, with a variety of fish, cheese, and vegetables. And finally, we've enjoyed the *bisted a la parrilla* (fried beef steak served with potatoes). The *menu familiar* ("family menu") is a best buy for $4: You get a four-course lunch or dinner, including soup, meat or fish, fruit, and coffee.

TUMI RESTAURANT, Portal Belen 115.
   Cuisine: INTERNATIONAL.
$ Prices: Appetizers $1–$3; main courses $4–$10.
   Open: Lunch and dinner.
A popular stop for lunch, dinner, or late-afternoon coffee is the Tumi, on Plaza de Armas, with bright-red tablecloths and ladderback chairs. The prices are right, too. Start with an appetizer, such as avocado vinaigrette or shrimp cocktail. Sample a delicious beef steak or another house specialty, the trout with garlic sauce—a real bargain at $4. In fact, the most expensive dish, the chateaubriand, is still a buy at $9.50. Sandwiches and omelets are available for about $1. The Tumi offers up exotic specialty drinks, such as the Cuba or Peru Libre.

SPECIALTY DINING

LOCAL FAVORITES If you're feeling strong enough to sample local fare, then venture into a *quinta. Quintas* are small restaurants that specialize in nothing but native cuisine. You'll sample dishes the likes of which you've probably never seen before, such as *cuy al horno* (baked guinea pig), *k'acchi de setas* (a Quechua dish made from wild mushrooms, which are available only during the rainy season, from December to March); *queso kapiche* (best in November and December, it is made with green broad beans, boiled potatoes, milk, red or yellow chiles, and cheese); *chuño* or *cola* (a year-round dish, it's a filling soup of sausages, rice, chickpeas, and potatoes, thickened with *chuño,* dried potato flour); and *recotos rellenos* (hot bell peppers stuffed with minced meat, peanuts, raisins, and green peas, which are then coated with eggs and fried). Among the *quintas* recommended to us by a local guide are **La Tranquera,** on Plaza Tupac Amaru; **Quinta Eullalia** (open for lunch only), on Choquechaca 384; and **El Mirado,** on Avenida Argentina, overlooking the city.
   If you want to try *chicharrones,* small bits of pork fried in lard, there's a series of *chicharronerías* on Pampa del Castillo—nicknamed *"el lugar de los chicharrones"* (the place of the chicharrones) by the locals—just off Calle Loreto.

CAFES Two small cafés have opened in town. The more interesting is **Varayoc,** in Plaza Regocijo. A poor man's literary café, it has several tattered magazines and newspapers in a variety of languages in a rack on the wall (drop off any printed material you don't feel like carting home). Good for breakfast and sandwich foods, it's open daily from 8am to 11pm. The other is **Café Allyu,** in the Portal de Carnes. Cuzco's finest café, it caters to a more highbrowed clientele than does the Varayoc.

6. ATTRACTIONS

A mandatory **tourist ticket** went into operation in Cuzco in 1982. For a $10 fee you can visit the cathedral, temples, and museums of the city; the four major ruins on the outskirts of Cuzco—Tambomachay, Kenko, Puka Pukara, and Sacsayhuaman; and the ruins at the Sacred Valley—Ollantaytambo and the ruins near the town of Pisac. The ticket can be purchased at the Tourist Office in the Plaza de Armas.

THE TOP ATTRACTIONS
THE INDIAN MARKET

One of the busiest spots in Cuzco is the colorful open-air Indian market. The streets are packed with vehicles and with people browsing and buying at the red-roofed stalls. The market extends for several blocks along Calle Tupac Amaru—just a short uphill walk from Plaza San Francisco—and spills over from the street into the railroad station. The street stalls are full of interesting items, ranging from the banal (cheap trinkets) to the beautiful (fine handcrafted alpaca rugs). Selling in the Indian quarter is a family affair; bargaining is a must. Be prepared for down-home earthiness: There are food stalls in abundance, and the butchers proudly display whole carcasses hanging from the hooks. The clothing items are of special interest; good-quality wool sweaters—hand-knit and bearing Indian motifs—can be purchased, as well as ponchos, hats, and mittens. There are hand-carved wood and metal pieces, too. The items vary in quality and craftsmanship, so it's a good idea to inspect the merchandise carefully. You can do this market by taxi, but to really feel its vibes you should hoof it. *Note:* The market is a favorite haunt of pickpockets. Be alert! Leave all valuables at your hotel. And save your shopping for some of the smaller markets in our shopping section.

MUSEUMS
MUSEUM OF ARCHEOLOGY, Calle Tigre.

✪ The Museum of Archeology, two blocks from the Plaza de Armas, is a small (nine-room) home of antiquity crammed with Inca and pre-Inca stonework, mummies, and woven textiles. Four-foot-tall vases, extracted from the Inca ruins, are on the enclosed porches that overlook an open courtyard. One room is loaded with hand implements used by the Incas to weave textiles and to construct temples. Room 5, devoted to the burial rites of the Incas, has several mummies on view, and Room 4 houses relics of the Paracas Indians, who predated the Incas. (At the time of this writing, the Archeology Museum was temporarily closed. Some exhibits had been moved to the Museum of Regional History.)
    Open: Mon–Fri 8am–noon and 3–6pm; Sat 9am–noon.

MUSEO HISTORICO REGIONAL, Palace of the Admiral on Calle Tucuman.
    Located in a restored colonial mansion, the Regional History Museum is home to a fine collection of paintings from the colonial period, as well as pre-Columbian artifacts.
    Open: Mon–Fri 8am–noon and 3–6pm; Sat 9am–noon.

MUSEO DE SANTA CATALINA, Plazoleta Santa Catalina.
    On display here is colonial art, primarily religious, from the convent's private collection.
    Open: Mon–Sat 8am–6pm.

MUSEO DE ARTE RELIGIOSO, at the corner of Hatunrumiyoc and Herejes.
One of the loveliest buildings in Cuzco, the Museum of Religious Art was originally the palace of the Marques de Buenavista. Today it is home to a fine collection of paintings from the Cuzco school of art, which prevailed during the 16th, 17th, and 18th centuries.
Open: Mon–Sat 9am–12:30pm and 3–5:30pm; Sun 3–5:30pm.

ARCHITECTURE

EL CONVENTO DE LAS NAZARENAS [Convent of the Nazarenes], Calle Palacio.
Behind the cathedral is the Convent of the Nazarenes, a fine example of the blending of Inca and Spanish architecture. The stones of this building were taken from the Temple of the Serpents, while the walls above the stonework are adobe. The original conquistador owner had his Inca builders etch two mermaids into the stonework above the doorway.

SANTA CATALINA NUNNERY, Calle Santa Catalina.
Located at Arequipa, a block from Plaza de Armas, is another example of a Spanish and Inca mixture. The convent's walls were built of stones from the Inca House of the Chosen Women.

LA CASA DE CONCHA, Calle Santa Catalina.
This private home is a good example of an 18th-century colonial palace. The upper walls are true colonial, with hanging balconies; the lower walls are of Inca stone.

HOUSE OF JOSÉ AGUSTÍN CHACON, Heladeros.
This house has an exquisite doorway made of Inca stone. Señor Chacon was executed by the Spanish in 1815 for his underground effort in behalf of the liberation movement.

HOUSE OF GARCILASO DE LA VEGA, Heladeros.
Another historical residence you may like to visit is the house across from the Turista, home of the famous Inca historian, who was born here in 1539.

NEARBY ATTRACTIONS

INCA RUINS Just outside the city are four imposing Inca ruins, all on the main highway that leads to Pisac, a small village 20 miles away, best noted for its Sunday and Thursday markets. Seeing all four ruins will take half a day at most and can be nicely combined with a trip to Pisac.
The most impressive of the quartet is also the nearest—**Sacsayhuaman,** 1 mile from Plaza de Armas, which was a huge fortress and parade ground for Inca warriors, as well as an important religious site. A remarkable engineering achievement, the 1,000-foot-long structure was built of stone blocks, some weighing 300 tons, which were fitted together so perfectly that today a razor blade cannot be inserted between the sections. No cement or mortar was used. The stones, cut from a quarry a mile away, were transported by levers, since both the wheel and the pulley were unknown to the Incas. Climb to the top for a stunning view of the city below and the surrounding mountains. (An even better view of the city is from the nearby **Christ Statue.**) Llama and sheep graze in the nearby fields.
Five miles from the city is **Tambomachay.** Known as the "Baño del Inca," it was used by the Incas as a ritual bath. The Incas worshiped water as one of the elements of life and held ritual baths quite frequently. Cold water gushes down the wall into what was the bathing area. The water source has yet to be found. Again, huge stone blocks were used in the construction.
The last two ruins, located just before Tambomachay, are the **Puka-Pukara Fortress,** which was actually a *tambo,* a travel lodge for the Incas, and the **Kenko Amphitheater.** From the top of Pucara you again have a wonderful view of the

countryside. Kenko, far more interesting, has an underground network of tunnels and cellars. The stone altar here was used for animal sacrifices.

A WALKING TOUR

Start at the most logical point—the **Plaza de Armas,** the center of the city both now and when it was the Inca capital. Five centuries ago the square was twice its current size, divided in two by the Sapphi River, which now flows beneath the buildings on the side of the plaza opposite the cathedral. The part of the plaza that remains today was called **Huakaypata.** Loosely translated, this means "weeping square," so named for the mourning that would occur there when a ruling Inca had died. The major religious temples, all filled with gold and silver, were located here.

Pizarro's sacking of Cuzco in 1533, followed by earthquakes and armed revolts in subsequent years, destroyed most of the Inca and early Spanish structures, but the walls of the old Inca city are still intact near the plaza. Pause a moment in the plaza—there are benches all around—to observe the Indian families walking through the area. The women are multiskirted, with stovepipe hats perched atop their jet-black hair. Many carry huge loads on their backs or lead donkeys laden with enormous burdens of food and wood. At midday you see children trudging through the square with pails of hot food, which they are taking to their fathers at work in the fields and stores.

Facing the square is the largest structure in Cuzco, the **cathedral,** which took 94 years to build. The Spanish began the project in 1560 and did not complete it until 1654. The stones used in building the cathedral were culled from the destroyed Inca temple **Quishuarcancha** that had stood on the site. The cathedral contains almost 400 colonial period paintings, many of which are from the Cuzco school. Be on the lookout for Marco Zapata's depiction of the Last Supper, in which *cuy* (guinea pig, the main course at the Inca's sacred feasts) is the featured meal; a painting of a very pregnant Virgin Mary; and a group of cherubs who, unable to fly, are hanging on to the curtains for dear life. The cathedral is also home to the largest bell in South America, the María Angola, cast in 1659. As the story goes, the bell is named for the black woman who put 25 pounds of gold into the crucible after 2 unsuccessful castings. The third was a success! The tolling of María Angola can be heard from as far away as 40 kilometers.

Adjoining the cathedral, to its right, is the totally intact **Temple of Triumph,** the first Christian church built in Cuzco. It was constructed by Pizarro's three brothers to celebrate the crushing of the 1536 Inca revolt led by Manco Capac. They built it on the site of the *Suntur Huasi,* the main Inca Armory and where the Spanish had been trapped during Manco Capac's initial attack. According to popular legend, the thatched roof of the Suntur Huasi caught fire when the Incas burned the city. The fire was extinguished by the Virgin Mary accompanied by Saint James on horseback. The Incas were terrorized by the vision and fled. Inside the church are two inscriptions, a painting and a statue depicting the miracle. Many historians believe that after this defeat, Capac fled to the mountain retreat now called Machú Picchú—the fabled Lost City of the Incas. Before his defeat, he and his followers had laid siege to Cuzco for a year.

On the south side of the plaza is Cuzco's finest church, **La Compañía,** which was built over the ruins of **Amarucancha,** the Inca Temple of the Serpents, where the last great Inca ruler, Huayna Capac, had resided. After an earthquake in 1650, it was rebuilt in its present form. Note the intricately etched gold altars and handsome wooden dome. Check the paintings for a view of the dress and architecture of 16th-century Cuzco. One portrait depicts the wedding of an Indian princess and a Spanish nobleman. Adjacent to the church is the **University of Cuzco,** founded by Simón Bolívar after Peru's liberation in 1821.

We continually return to this plaza just to sit and contemplate its historic importance. But on a recent visit we were reminded that historical artifacts are truly fragile things. For many years an Indian statue commanded the central position atop the fountain. No Inca warrior this, however, but, rather, a U.S. model, feathers and all.

We were told that the statue was that of Chief Powhatan (remember his famous daughter?) and had ended up in Cuzco because of a shipping error. Nevertheless, the stately Indian suited his home, even if it was the wrong continent, and had become, in its own way, a part of Cuzco's history. Now the warrior is gone—lost during a labor dispute—and has been replaced by a very incongruous white flamingo.

Now stroll along a true Inca street, **Calle Loreto,** which runs alongside La Compañía. This narrow cobblestone street is lined on both sides with Inca walls, on top of which adobe homes have been built. On your right will be the rear ruins of the **Temple of the Serpents** and on your left the remains of **Acllahuasi, the Inca House of the Women of the Sun.** This was the residence of the Chosen Women of the Incas, who were reared and trained for marriage to the ruler and certain high-ranking noblemen. The Incas were polygamous. A block down Loreto, the street becomes **Pampa del Castillo,** where a small market is open daily.

Farther on is the **Temple of Korichancha,** renamed the Temple of Santo Domingo by the Spaniards. It is on the site of the sacred Inca Temple of the Sun, built in the 12th century, the largest and most important structure in the Inca kingdom. When the Spanish arrived, it housed most of the gold later taken by the conquistadores. Within the temple were five subtemples in honor of the sun, moon, stars, lightning, and rainbow. A sixth room was the residence of the temple keepers.

It wasn't until 1950, when a tremendous earthquake rocked Cuzco, that the walls of the temple were uncovered virtually intact. The Santo Domingo church has been rebuilt around the temple's walls, so that visitors have a clear view of the temple remains. Most of the nearby walls and streets are Inca in origin.

Head back to Plaza de Armas on any street from here. They all converge at the square. At the plaza, turn left and stroll along **Mantas,** beyond Plaza San Francisco, through the arch of the Old City. On your left you'll see the **Cuzco Indian Market,** a bustling place much of the time, with fruit and household goods trading hands.

ORGANIZED TOURS

There are several reliable tour operators in Cuzco. They run modern minibuses and seem well organized. Their tours include English-speaking guides. Private-car tours are also available if you want to pay the price. Rates seem fixed, although they do vary a bit. You can save money by hiring a car and driver if you speak Spanish.

Lima Tours (American Express), at Portal de Harinas 177 (tel. 22-8431), are the largest tour operators in Peru. They run a half-day tour of Cuzco and the nearby ruins that leaves daily at 2pm and returns at 5:30pm. It costs $18 per person. Pisac, Sacred Valley, and Ollantaytambo tours run $35 per person. **Receptur,** in the Hotel Libertador, is another reputable tour operator. Tours to Machú Picchú cost $90 per person; the cost includes the train, a minibus to go up the hill, and lunch, plus entrance to the ruins. **Condor Travel** at Heladeros 164 (tel. 22-5921), is another good choice.

Several local tour operators will provide a guide and include the four nearby ruins in a city tour. However, the tour lasts only 3½ hours, which will not leave you enough time to see the ruins as you should. Take this option only if your time is extremely limited. You can take a tour of the ruins for a half day and see them all well, and then you can make a visit to Pisac. Both tours cost $35 per person.

An interesting alternative is to see the ruins on horseback. Make arrangements through **K'Antu Tours,** at Portal Corrizos 258, Plaza de Armas (tel. 23-2021). The 4-hour tour costs about $10.

7. SAVVY SHOPPING

Best buys in Cuzco are knitted sweaters, scarves, leg warmers, and knee socks. Alpaca and llama rugs are still available, but the good-quality items have risen in price. Handcrafts and silver pieces are also good values.

A great shopping street is **Calle Triunfo,** which leads from Plaza de Armas. It has an artisan's market, called **Yachay Wasi,** that has inexpensive knitted goods and alpaca rugs. A small market has opened in Plaza de Armas, adjacent to the Lourdes Church. Its stalls feature knitted goods.

In previous editions, we strongly recommended the **Indian market,** on Santa Clara, as one of the best places to shop. Times have changed, and in terms of quality and price you'll do just as well at the shops in town. You should come here to look rather than to buy. As we've stressed in our coverage of Peru, the country has come upon extremely hard times economically. Street crime has skyrocketed, especially pickpocketings and muggings. Both are especially common in marketplaces, such as Cuzco's Indian market. So, if you want to visit the market, we strongly suggest that you don't do so alone and that you leave all your valuables in your hotel safe. If you insist on taking your camera with you, hold on to it securely.

SHOPPING A TO Z

ALPACA CRAFTS A good first stop is the smart **Bazaar Huasi,** near Parque Espinar. Good-quality alpaca rugs range from $125 on up, depending on size. Nice gift items are the alpaca seat mats at $3 each. *Artesanías,* too, can be found here, from $2 and up. **Inca Wasi,** at Plateros 344, has lovely knitted sweaters and scarves. If you'd rather knit your own alpaca sweater, stop in at **Alpacas 111,** on Heladeros, to pick up some alpaca yarn.

For the finest sweaters in the city, don't miss the **Bazar Paracas,** at Santa Catalina Angosta 163 (tel. 3535). You can have an alpaca sweater made to order. This store stocks sweaters in all sizes, even extra large; if you don't find one to your choosing, the owner will whip one up for you within 24 hours. The shop also features a good selection of silver jewelry, ponchos, pillow covers, and other Indian handicrafts.

ANTIQUES Two antiques shops worth browsing in are **Artesanías Peruanas** and **Makiwan,** on the second floor of the Portal Confituras. For beautiful pre-Columbian, colonial, and modern-style Peruvian pieces in copper, crystal, and wood, as well as for gold and silver jewelry and antiques, stop in at **Farah Artesanías Peruanas,** just off Plaza Regocijo, at Heladeros 106. The management boasts of the store's exclusive selection.

ARTWORK Check out the original art at **Mérida,** at Portal Espinar 288, on the corner of Espaderos. You'll also find the usual tourist items, rugs, and alpaca here as well. **Josefina Olivera**'s shop, at Santa Clara 501, has some fine weavings, as does **Narciso Vilcahuaman,** in Plaza Regocijo.

When you're on Calle Triunfo, take the time to peruse the exhibits at the **Galería García,** at no. 122. On display here are works by local artists, depicting various scenes of regional life, especially the Indians in Cuzco. Owner Agusto García is an artist himself and one of Cuzco's finest teachers. Almost all the pieces are for sale. Prices range from $10 to $350.

ARTESANIAS Don't miss the Cuzco branch of **Eppa,** the fine handcraft shops that are located throughout Peru. In a large store at Plateros 359 (half a block from Plaza de Armas), you'll find the widest variety of crafts. Browse here before heading elsewhere. Stunning woven wall tapestries of Indian life start at $12. Gilt mirrors, for as little as $2, make unusual gifts. Knitted sweaters, scarves, mittens, and leg warmers are brightly colored and will make you a hit on the ski slopes.

An excellent store for ceramics is **Cerámica Ruiz Coro,** at Triunfo 387. **Ramac Maki** and **Hirca,** both off Triunfo, also have unusual handcraft items. A shop for silver and pottery is the **Bazar Pisac,** at Portal Comercio 189, in Plaza de Armas. Ponchos and sweaters, too, are available, at prices comparable to Paracas. **Souvenirs Teqsemayo,** at Teccsecocha 432, near the Archeological Museum, has some things not seen elsewhere.

An excellent alternative to the Indian market is **El Indio,** a large shop offering a seemingly endless selection of sweaters, weavings, alpaca rugs, and ceramics. You should also stroll through the **Feria Artesanal Korikancha,** an open-air market with numerous stalls, selling everything you expect to find in Cuzco. Both are located on Avenida Sol, across from the Alhambra II Hotel. There's another **Feria Artesanal** at the corner of San Andres and Quera. Along Calle Triunfo you'll find **Feria Artesanal Inka,** as well as numerous other small shops, selling similar goods.

JEWELRY   Along Calle Plateros (*platero* means "silversmith"), you'll find one boutique after another selling handcrafted jewelry made of Peruvian silver. Many of them double as the workshop of the silversmith. You can find some very unusual and beautiful pieces here. You'll find 18-karat gold and silver pieces in modern and Incan designs at **H. Ormachea**'s workshop, at Plateros 372. Be forewarned: We guarantee that you'll fall in love with at least one of Señor Ormachea's original pieces.

There's an excellent selection of jewelry inlaid with Peruvian turquoise at **Leoncio Cerro Acharia's** showroom, at Plateros 334. If you still haven't found what you're looking for, **Artesanías Chami Perú,** at Plateros 392, the workshop of Lolo Chavez Miranda, will probably have it for you. He has an excellent selection of silver and bronze necklaces, earrings, and bracelets.

Artesanías Victor's, at Calle Procuradores 344, is the place to go if you're looking for earrings. All four walls are solid earrings, from corner to corner, in this small shop. You'll find also some very lovely necklaces and bracelets here, at reasonable prices.

8. EVENING ENTERTAINMENT

The town generally closes up early because most tourists are tuckered out after a day of tramping through Inca ruins and retire early.

THE PERFORMING ARTS

TIPICO SHOWS

CENTRO QOSQO, Avenida del Sol. Tel. 3708.
First choice is here, at this new 604-seat theater near the new post office. All performers are students at the University of Cuzco, and their enthusiasm is contagious. We're partial to the *cueca* dance (look for the handkerchiefs at the shoulder). The 90-minute shows start at 6:40pm sharp.

Admission: Tickets are about $5, but many hotels have signs posted, offering a package that includes round-trip transportation. Walk it and save.

INTI RAYMI, Calle Saphy 605.
When strolling through Plaza de Armas during the day, you'll undoubtedly be approached by local students selling discounted tickets to their nightly folkloric show here at Inti Raymi. The show starts at 6:45pm and runs until about 8pm, making this a good pre-dinner and pre-*peña* activity.

DINNER SHOWS

EL TRUCO, Calle Regocijo.
The Three Musketeers would have felt right at home at this bilevel restaurant resembling an old Spanish cave, located across from the Turista Hotel. You'll enjoy the "swashbuckling" atmosphere suggested by the Spanish arches, whitewashed walls, bare wooden floors, high ceilings, and red cloth–covered tables. The food is good and inexpensive: Rice with shrimp is $1.75; *arroz con pollo* is $2; *riñones parrilla* are $1.75; pancake desserts are $1.35; and a pisco sour is 95¢.

Every evening El Truco features live-entertainment shows at 8:30pm, for which there is a $1.25 cover charge if you don't have dinner here. You'll be transported back in time as you listen to the native instruments: the *hena* (flute), the *changa charango* (small guitar), and the *tambor* (drum).

THE BAR & CLUB SCENE

In addition to the establishments listed below, there are **Camino Real** and **Dancin' Days,** both on Avenida de la Cultura, a five-minute cab ride from downtown. They're somewhat out of the way but similar in style and atmosphere to Las Quenas and Muki (below). The El Dorado Inn at Avenida del Sol 395 (tel. 23-2573) also has a fine disco, the **Caribbean Disco Club.**

KAMI KASE, Plaza Regocijo.

The name here says it all, as does it's slogan: "*El lugar de los locos responsables*" ("The place for responsible crazy people"). There's folkloric music at 11pm, and then the night really gets going with hard rock blasting from midnight to 3am. It's a favorite hangout for university students.

LAS QUENAS, Avenida del Sol 954. Tel. 22-4322.

This is the classiest disco in town, located in front of the Hotel Savoy. Looking like the inside of a spaceship, the disco has green booths enclosing tiny tables. The white walls are sculptured, and the dance floor is long and centrally located. The music starts at 8pm and goes strong until 3am nightly. There's a two-drink minimum, with drinks running $2.50 and up.

MUKI, Santa Catalina.

Muki, just off Plaza de Armas, is a lively popular hangout for couples only. The white walls and many small coves will make you think that you've stepped into a cozy snow cave. Check out the original Inca walls on the right as you enter. Muki opens at 8pm, and the action goes on well into the late-night hours. Drinks are $2 to $3.

PEÑA DO RE MI, Portal Confiturías 233.

If you need a respite from the noise at neighboring *peña* Qhatuchay (below), try this smaller and quieter place just across the hall. There's another Do Re Mi, on Calle Tres Cruces, with live music and folkloric dancing nightly. More popular with tourists, however, than with the locals, it also doubles as a restaurant.

QHATUCHAY, Portal Confiturías 233.

There's much dancing, clapping, and pure enjoyment at Qhatuchay, as local couples clear an area around the bar to dance to the native rhythms that are so much a part of their heritage. Qhatuchay is so popular that on weekend nights you'll find people sitting *under* the bar—every table is taken. The drink to sample is Kaipi, a concoction of pisco, lemon, ice, and cinnamon.

9. EASY EXCURSIONS

THE SACRED VALLEY: PISAC & OLLANTAYTAMBO

The Urubamba Valley was the heart of the Inca Empire. Points to visit are Pisac and Ollantaytambo, with a short stop at the village of Tarabamba. Cross the Urubamba here and spend a few minutes at the village of Pichinjoto. The cliffs and mountains above this village are thickly encrusted with salt deposits, which have created an overhang. The small village is poised right below the overhang—in fact, you can't see it at all until you are right there.

PISAC

On Thursday and Sunday mornings, in the village of Pisac (20 miles from Cuzco), an Indian market takes place that you should make every effort to see. (The market on Thursday tends to be quieter and more *típico*.) The vendors spread their wares on the ground, and all around the town square are colorful arrays of alpaca rugs, hats, and mittens, knitted wool caps, gourds, vases, native jewelry, fruits, vegetables, and metals. Best buys are the alpaca items and the jewelry. But bargain, by all means. We recently purchased an unusually carved gourd for $2.50 and a pair of alpaca slippers for $5.

A highlight each Sunday is the formal procession through town to the local church by 12 mayors from the neighboring villages. Accompanying them are musicians, who blow into a reedlike instrument that resembles a recorder.

Another fascinating aspect of Pisac is the Indian dress, quite different from that of Cuzco. The women wear red skirts and flat, round red hats; the men are garbed in brown trousers and jackets and multicolored knit caps. And everyone is shoeless, with the result that the bottoms of their feet are like smooth stone.

To get a real feel for the town, walk through the narrow unpaved streets and observe the homes and the shops. The cows there are surely among the thinnest in the world. Donkeys, llamas, and pigs are other wandering animal life you'll see.

Above the city, on a mountainside, are an Inca fortress and other ruins. They are within walking distance. The healthy hike should take you about an hour. You'll need your Tourist Ticket to visit the ruins. This is the largest fortress city, or *Pucara*, as it is called in Quechua, of the Incas. Yet strangely enough, there are no written accounts of its existence.

GETTING THERE   The best way to reach Pisac is by taxi, which will cost you about $45. Five passengers will be accommodated for the one price, so gather a party and share the cost. Establish the cab fare in advance; the driver will wait for you, and you needn't be concerned about taking the time to wander through Pisac. But try to return to the cab when the market closes. If you're lucky, your driver will speak enough English to describe the sights. To make the most of your day, leave Cuzco by 9am.

The picturesque ride out carries you over a winding road that leads up into the mountains. When you want to snap a picture or two, ask the driver to stop. A must is the view of the village of Pisac with the ruins on the mountainside behind it. The Urubamba river runs alongside the village. The Incas converted much of it into a canal to create the largest pre-Columbian canal in the Americas. As we indicated earlier, you can combine this trip with visits to the ruins outside Cuzco. The cab fare should again be the same—about $45.

Organized tours are available to Pisac on Sunday and Thursday. They leave for the market at 9am and return at 12:30pm. On nonmarket days, you can explore the Pisac ruins. Cost is $25 per person either way. Groups travel by minibus. You can combine your visit to Pisac with a visit to the Sacred Valley of the Incas. You follow the newly paved road to Ollantaytambo, about 35 miles away. Cabs will run about $60 for this trip. Tours run $35 per person (lunch included); they leave at 9am and return at 5:30.

Another way to reach Pisac is by bus, which departs two blocks from Plaza de Armas, on Calle Saphi, on Sunday at 6am and returns in the early afternoon. The cost is less than $10 round trip, but the four buses are ancient vehicles, packed with Indian families. If you're really hardy, you can take one of the open-air trucks that leave sporadically from the plaza. Passengers are jammed into the rear for the stand-up ride.

WHERE TO DINE   The Pisac market is over by midday, and you'll probably be hungry by then. Stop for lunch at **Chongo Chico,** a converted hacienda about half a mile from the central square on the road leading to the Inca Ruins. The food is superior and many of the furnishings are handmade.

OLLANTAYTAMBO

Ollantaytambo, about 35 miles from Pisac, is reached by a paved road. Strategically located at the northern end of the Sacred Valley, it was from this fortress that the Incas defended Cuzco from attacks by other tribes. Ollantaytambo is a true Inca town, not rebuilt by the Spanish. The square has several narrow streets leading from it, one of which is called the "Avenue of the Hundred Windows." The town was the site of a great battle during the Manco Inca rebellion in 1536. Although they put up a valiant fight, the Inca were grossly outnumbered due to the return of Diego de Almagro's troops from Chile. Sensing imminent defeat, Manco led his followers to their last fortress at Vilcabamba, now known as Machú Picchú. You'll want to visit the ruins and the valley nearby, where the "Bath of the Princess" lies. It's a natural spring still running over a rock that was shaped to form a waterfall.

WHERE TO STAY & DINE　If you have the time and the interest, you can spend some time in the Sacred Valley. With many more tourists visiting the area, several small, rather basic hotels and dormitories have opened:

Centro Vacacional, Jirón Cabo Alonzo. Tel. 22-7191. Rates: $8 per person.
In Urubamba, the government-run Centro is the most popular stop. It resembles a motel, but it has a pool and small bungalows are the accommodations, with four or five beds to a room. Breakfast is $1.50; lunch and dinner are each under $5.

Hostal Alhambra III, 123 Plaza Manco II, Yucay. Tel. 22-4076. All rooms with bath. Rates: $40 single; $50 double.
The nicest accommodations in the area are at the Hostal Alhambra III, at Yucay (a tiny village on the Pisac road). This restored Dominican monastery has a score of rooms, all with balconies overlooking the courtyard. Dinner will cost about $12; fish is the house specialty. The people you meet here are a cross section of the world. German professors, Swedish backpackers, French archeologists, and American journalists all gather in the tiny dining room to swap Inca tales and drink pisco.

Restaurant Hotel Parador, Ollantaytambo. Rates: $8 per person.
The Parador, in Plaza de Armas, is owned by a charming Italian gentleman and his Peruvian wife. They offer three large dormitories, each of which has four beds. You can add $10 for two meals daily: There is no other place to eat at. The Italian influence is felt in the kitchen, where pizza is the pièce de résistance.

RIVER RAFTING & TREKKING

You can explore the Sacred Valley by rafting down the Urubamba River and can trek the Inca trails all the way from Cuzco to Machú Picchú. Treks to Machú Picchú take six days or more. Some treks involve mules. Check with **Expediciones Mayuc,** on Calle Procuradores 354 (tel. 23-2666), for information. **Explorandes,** at Urb. Magisterio N-17 (tel. 22-6599), and **APU Expediciones,** at Portal de Carnes 236 (tel. 23-5408), also offer trekking expeditions.

JUNGLE TOURS

For something a little different, try a tour of the jungle. Bill Leonard's guided tours through the Amazon jungle were extremely popular with visitors here—alas, Bill (of Leonard's Lodgings) no longer leads them himself. He has turned the reins over to his nephew, Hugo Pepper, a charming and knowledgeable young man. Hugo, operating his **Naranja Tours** from Procuradores 372, leads tours of various lengths and experiences.

　　Hugo provides guides who take groups of 4 to 10 people to the beautiful **Madre de Dios** area, some 150 miles north of Cuzco. Traveling by Jeep, and with all supplies provided, you can watch the sun come up from the 12,500-foot Tres Cruces Mountain—the display of colors is staggering. You'll also explore the jungle itself—visiting a Franciscan mission deep in the jungle's interior and getting a glimpse of Indian life available nowhere else. You'll wind up at the Leonards' jungle outpost on the Madre de Dios River—the comfortable Hacienda Erica, a sprawling ranch adapted for travelers. In this exotic jungle setting, you can enjoy river fishing (the trout are huge) and boating.

These tours operate only April through October. Longer tours to the National Park at Manu are even more exciting. Write to Hugo for the latest information.

Cuzco Tours Amazonico, at Procuradores 48, is another excellent group to deal with. Their Cuzco Amazonico lodge is downriver from Puerto Maldonado.

10. MOVING ON

Here's some information necessary for those going to La Paz. There is a really pleasurable way to travel to La Paz via bus and boat. We have already waxed enthusiastic about this journey—flip to the end of Chapter 8. Buses with comfortable seats and restroom facilities depart on Tuesday, Thursday, and Sunday at 6pm. It's an enjoyable direct trip, which will have you in Puno, at Lake Titicaca, for an early (5am) breakfast. You'll cross the lake by barge, have lunch at the Copacabana at 11am, and finally arrive in La Paz at 5:30pm. This congenial trip is made merrier by bar service on the bus.

The buses are operated by **Transturin** (tel. 2317), located at Portal Harinas 191 (second floor), in Plaza de Armas. The one-way fare is about $100 (breakfast and lunch included).

There is also daily train service to Puno, from which you can catch either one of the buses that are run irregularly by the Morales Bus Company or a taxi to La Paz.

11. MACHÚ PICCHÚ — THE LOST CITY OF THE INCAS

We have been to Europe over two dozen times and have traveled through North Africa, the Far East, Australia, much of the United States and Canada, and South America. If we were asked to cite the single most exciting moments of our travels, we would fairly shout (with no hesitation): *Machú Picchú!* No other city, monument, relic, mountain, or valley on this earth will affect you quite the way Machú Picchú does as you first stroll casually around a bend high in the Andes and suddenly come full face upon the glory of this wondrous city.

GETTING THERE You have two choices: a tour or a do-it-yourself trip. Many travelers prefer the convenience of a tour, and this can be arranged through the travel agents of **Receptour** or **Limatour** in Cuzco. The cost for a one-day excursion—via train and microbus—is a high $90 to $100. This includes the admission, all fares, a guide, and lunch at the Turista.

However, we strongly urge you to try doing it yourself—you'll wind up saving about $25. The only difference will be the absence of a guide and no prepaid lunch. We suggest that you bring your lunch along.

IMPRESSIONS

What a breathtaking place! You seem to be climbing into a larger world, a landscape built by titans in a fit of sheer megalomania.
—CHRISTOPHER ISHERWOOD, *THE CONDOR AND THE COWS,* 1949, ON MACHÚ PICCHÚ

The train—called the "Tourist Train," since it is the same one the tour people use—leaves from the San Pedro (Santa Ana) Station, near the Hotel Imperio, at 6:15am each day. Since seats are limited, tickets must be purchased a day ahead. These tickets are now sold in a booklet for $75; the booklet also contains your round-trip bus tickets (up and down the mountain) and entrance ticket to the ruins.

The train will drop you off at the base of the mountain, 3,000 feet below Machú Picchú, at about 9:30am. Look up and see if you can spot it. A microbus will then carry you up the winding road to the city in about 20 minutes. The view on either side is stunning. You'll remain there from about 10am until 3pm, when the buses start to load up again to catch the 4:20pm train for the return trip. You will be back in Cuzco by 7pm, exhilarated as if you had just conquered the highest mountain peak or skied the steepest trail in the Alps.

Early risers may prefer the local train used by the natives, which departs at 5:30am. Since this train is not an express, it stops at each station, where Indians board to barter and sell their handmade goods. In addition, you will save at least $8 when you take this early train. And best of all, you will arrive in Machú Picchú before the tourist train and therefore will be able to tour the ruins all by yourself before the crowds arrive.

Note: The train passes through a number of Indian villages and farms and through the sacred **Valley of the Incas** in the Urubamba River Valley. At a midpoint stop, Indians sell bananas and other fruit.

WHAT TO PACK The city requires nothing from you other than film. Bring as much as you have. We shot six rolls on our first visit and then tried to buy more from other travelers. No one was selling any.

As for clothing, you'll need a light sweater and comfortable walking shoes. If you're there during the rainy season, you may want to consider a light raincoat. You might want to take along a sandwich or two. You can get a fixed-price lunch at the adjacent **Turista Hotel** for $12. However, if you're not spending the night, this will take a good bite out of the limited time you have to tour the ruins.

BACKGROUND For centuries historians believed that a small band of Incas established a mountain kingdom not far from Cuzco after an unsuccessful effort to overthrow the Spanish in 1536. But it wasn't until 1911 that an unheard-of Yale professor named Hiram Bingham uncovered support for this thesis by discovering a remarkably preserved city high in the mountains, 75 miles north of Cuzco. Bingham, who later became a senator from Connecticut, promptly named the city Machú Picchú, after one of the two mountain peaks nearby, and declared unequivocally that this was the Lost City of the Incas.

Abuse swirled about the scholar's head after the pronouncement, largely from other scholars, who disputed his interpretation that this was the site of the lost Inca kingdom. But Bingham insisted he was correct and in subsequent years many other historians rallied to his support. Today, there is no serious challenge to his thesis. In his fascinating study, *The Lost City of the Incas,* Bingham reconstructs the founding of the city in this fashion:

The Spanish, after crushing the Incas in 1533 and razing Cuzco, installed a puppet Inca ruler, Manco Capac, who believed that the Spanish truly meant to reinstate the Inca dynasty as they had promised.

When Manco Capac realized instead that Spanish control was to continue, he and his followers revolted in 1535. After laying siege to Cuzco for a year, the Incas were finally forced to flee before the superior firepower of the conquistadors. They settled in two areas in the mountains 75 miles from Cuzco.

One, the fortress city of Vitcos, was quickly located by the Spanish and destroyed. The other, the Royal City of Vilcabamba, which became the home of Manco Capac, was never located by the Spanish, although try they did.

Vilcabamba was situated between two mountain peaks—Machú Picchú and Huayna Picchú—on a plateau about 3,000 feet above the Urubamba River Valley. Here, the Incas built homes and temples and intricate terracing for farming. In all, about 1,000 Incas lived here until the last Inca ruler died in 1571. After that, for reasons no one has been able to fathom, the city was abandoned.

And not until 340 years later, when Professor Bingham made his discovery, was the city unearthed. The Peruvian government appropriated funds to reclaim the area from the tremendous overgrowth. But there has been no formal restoration work done beyond the clearing of earth and bush from the structures. Only the roofs of the buildings, which were made of straw, are missing. Otherwise the condition of the buildings is astonishing.

Machú Picchú, said Bingham, was a self-sustaining community that grew its own food and produced its own goods. As far as is known, there was no regular contact with other Incas.

Key to the successful farming methods were the elaborate terraces cut into the sides of the city and into the mountainside above. These were so designed—in a horizontal pattern, about 4 feet apart—that rainwater was retained for long periods. So successful was the terrace design—which is also seen today in Cuzco, Pisac, and along the Urubamba Valley—that the retained water over the centuries softened the earth and the city slowly receded into the ground.

Bingham made his discovery by laboriously tracing every legend, rumor, and document that came to his attention. His persistence led to one of the great archeological finds of the 20th century, one still largely unfamiliar to many sophisticated travelers.

THE GENERAL IMPRESSION   When you come around the bend in the road and see the city stretched out in front of you, you'll be struck by the incredible vastness of the scene and the absolute quiet. Your eyes will sweep across row upon row of neat gray buildings, and you'll look beyond the city to the distant peak of Huayna Picchú, which is regularly climbed by hearty travelers. It is connected to the city. To the left of it is a smaller peak.

As you turn slowly, in the brilliant sunlight, you'll see behind you the larger peak, Machú Picchú. Slowly thread your way down into the city itself and then work quietly through the buildings. You'll catch your breath again when you peer over either side of the plateau to view the Urubamba River and Valley 3,000 feet below.

In the highest area of the city are the temples, among them the sacred **Temple of the Sun,** with its famous sundial, used by the Incas to "tie down" the sun symbolically at the winter solstice each year. Expert astronomers and mathematicians, the Incas believed that on June 21—the day of the winter solstice in the Southern Hemisphere—the sun was farthest away from the earth. The Incas sought to prevent the sun, which they worshiped, from "escaping" by roping a huge gold disk to the sundial. (They were successful every year.) Inspect the dial. It is in almost perfect condition, a testament to Inca craftsmanship. And be sure to have your photo taken here.

In equally good condition is the circular **Temple of the Chosen Women.** Not far from that is the cemetery, the source of a great unsolved mystery: Of the hundreds of skeletons uncovered here, only a few are male, and all of these are from young boys or old men. The Incas in other areas buried males and females in the same cemeteries, which have been found by archeologists. But not here.

Wind your way through the city using the 100 or more perfect stairways constructed by the Incas. And as you walk you may realize gradually that you are in a kind of semitrance, as if drugged by the beauty and the enchantment. You'll probably be astonished to find that 4 hours have passed and it is time to catch the bus for your return trip.

SOLVING THE MYSTERY   We mentioned above that the Spanish could not locate this city. Let's clear up that mystery now. The fact is that from below the plateau on which Machú Picchú rests, the city is invisible. And this was by design. The Incas arranged the placement of buildings and terraces so that they could not be seen from below (and they succeeded brilliantly). Even today the city cannot be seen until you actually come upon it directly.

These days, 18 men (and 4 alpaca) care for the grounds that went untended for so long.

WHERE TO STAY   If you have the time, we wholeheartedly recommend that you spend at least one night in Machú Picchú. Seeing the ruins at sunrise is truly incredible, and the morning sun is great for picture taking. Plus, you'll have some quiet time here before the tourist train arrives and again after it leaves.

The government-operated **Hotel de Turistas** is really quite nice. All the comfortable rooms have private baths. Doubles are $55, with singles only slightly less at $52. To make reservations ahead of time, in Lima call or go to the Entur Peru office at Los Nogales 249 in San Isidro (tel. 42-8626). You can also reserve ahead through a travel agent. If the Turista is full, you might spend the night in one of the three very basic hostals located on the main street in Aguas Calientes, a small town about half a mile from the Machú Picchú station. For the most part, these hostals are spotless, with hot water; rates are $15. A good one to try is the **Hotel Albergue Aguas Calientes** (tel. 72-1928).

A word of advice: If you do opt to stay overnight at either the youth hostel or the Turista, be sure to change enough money for your stay ahead of time. If you exchange here, you may wind up getting half of what you would get in Lima or Cuzco.

RECOMMENDED READING   Two books you should read before or during your trip are *The Conquest of the Incas* by John Hemming and *Cut Stones and Crossroads* by Ronald Wright. Both are available at the Complete Traveller Bookstore, 199 Madison Ave., New York, NY 10016 (tel. 212/685-9007). Mention this guidebook for a 10% discount.

APPENDIX

A. USEFUL VOCABULARY

As you certainly know by now, Portuguese is the language of Brazil, while Spanish—or, more accurately, "Castellano"—is spoken almost everywhere else in South America. Although it helps tremendously to know either Spanish or Portuguese, you'll find that English is the second language of the educated South American and that you'll have no trouble being understood. Certainly, the hotels have at least one clerk apiece who speaks English, many restaurants have bilingual menus, and many shops have an English-speaking salesperson.

Nevertheless, the knowledge of a few phrases will help you considerably, as will translation of the menu terms you're most likely to encounter. That's what follows now—first for Portuguese, then for Spanish, with phonetic pronunciations set forth in parentheses following most words.

PORTUGUESE
NUMERALS

1	**Um** (oohn)	15	**Quinze** (*keen*-zay)	60	**Sessenta** (se-*sen*-tah)
2	**Dois** (doys)	16	**Dezesseis** (dayse-*says*)	70	**Setenta** (set-*ten*-tah)
3	**Três** (trays)	17	**Dezessete** (dayse-*set*-tay)	80	**Oitenta** (oy-*ten*-tah)
4	**Quatro** (*kwa*tro)	18	**Dezoito** (dayss-*oy*-to)	90	**Noventa** (no-*ven*-tah)
5	**Cinco** (*seen*ko)	19	**Dezenove** (dayse-*no*-vay)	100	**Cem** (sayn)
6	**Seis** (says)	20	**Vinte** (*veen*-tay)		**Cento** (*sen*-to)
7	**Sete** (*set*-tay)	30	**Trinta** (*treen*-tah)	200	**Duzentos** (do-*zen*-tos)
8	**Oito** (*oy*-to)	40	**Quarenta** (kwa-*ren*-tah)	1,000	**Mil** (meel)
9	**Nove** (*no*-vay)	50	**Cinquenta** (seen-*kwen*-tah)		
10	**Dez** (dayss)				
11	**Onze** (*un*-zay)				
12	**Doze** (*do*-zay)				
13	**Treze** (*tray*-say)				
14	**Quatorze** (kwa-*tor*-zay)				

DAYS OF THE WEEK

Sunday	**Domingo**	do-*meen*-go
Monday	**Segunda-Feira**	say-*goon*-da *fay*-ra
Tuesday	**Terça-Feira**	*tayr*-sa *fay*-ra
Wednesday	**Quarta-Feira**	*kwar*-ta *fay*-ra
Thursday	**Quinta-Feira**	*keen*-ta *fay*-ra
Friday	**Sexta-Feira**	*says*-ta *fay*-ra
Saturday	**Sábado**	*sa*-ba-do

USEFUL EXPRESSIONS

Very good	**Muito bém**	Moo-*eeto* ben
Good night	**Boa noite**	*Bo*-ah *noy*te
Good afternoon	**Boa tarde**	*Bo*-ah *tahr*de
Why, because	**Porque**	Por-*keh*
The day	**O dia**	O *dee*-ah
Where is . . . ?	**Onde está . . . ?**	*Ohn*de esta . . . ?
Hotel	**Hotel**	O-*tel*

Restaurant	Restaurante	Res-ta-oo-*rahn*-tay
Toilet	Toucador	To-ca-*dohr*
Airport	Aeroporto	Ah-airo-*por*-to
Post office	Correio	Kor-*ay*-yo
Beach	Praia	*Pray*-ya
Taxi	Taxi	*Tak*-see
I want . . .	Quero . . .	*Ke*-ro . . .
Mr.	Senhor	Seyn-*nor*
Mrs.	Senhora	Seyn-*nyor*-a
Miss	Senhorita	Seyn-nyor-*ee*-ta
Hello	Olá	Oh-*la*
When?	Quando?	*Kwan*-do
The check	A conta	A *kon*-ta
To eat	Comer	Coh-*mer*
A room with bath	Quarto con banho	*Kwar*-to kon *ban*-yo
Here	Aqui	A-*kee*
How much?	Quanto custa?	*Kwan*-toh *kus*-ta
Less expensive	Mais barato	Mays ba-*ra*-to
Good	Bom	Bon
Yesterday	Ontem	*Oyn*-ten
Today	Hoje	O-zjeh
Tomorrow	Amanhã	A-man-*yan*
What is . . . ?	Que é . . . ?	Keh *eh* . . . ?
What time is it?	Que horas são?	*Keh* oh-rahs sown?
It is cold	Faz frio	Fahs *free*-o
It is hot	Faz calor	Fahs ka-*lor*
It's sunny	Faz sol	Fahs sol
Left	Esquerdo	Ez-*ker*-do
Right	Direita	Dee-*ray*-ta
Yes, sir	Sim, senhor	Seen, sen-*yohr*
No	Não	Noun
Thank you	Obrigado	O-bree-*ga*-do
Please	Por favor	Por fa-*vor*
Money	Dinheiro	Deen-*yay*-ro
Until tomorrow	Até amanhã	Atay a-man-*yan*
Red	Vermelho	Ver-*mel*-yo
White	Branco	*Bran*-ko

RESTAURANT TERMS

Waiter	O garção	Oh gar-*sown*
Menu	Cardápio	Kar-*dap*-yo
Please bring me the check	O favor de me trazer a conta	Oh fa-*vor* day may tra-*zer* ah *kon*-ta
Breakfast	Café	Kah-*fay*
Lunch	Almôço	Al-*mo*-soo
Dinner	Jantar	Zhan-*tar*

SOUPS—*SOPAS*

Caldo de carne Meat bouillon
Caldo de cebola Onion soup
Caldo de verde Vegetable soup
Creme de espargos Cream of asparagus soup

Sopa de galinha Chicken soup
Sopa de tomate Tomato soup

CONDIMENTS—*CONDIMENTOS*

Açúcar Sugar
Geléia Marmalade

Manteiga Butter
Pão Bread

Pimenta Pepper

Sal Salt

SANDWICHES

Americana Hot open combination
sandwich, ham-cheese, egg salad
Misto Ham and cheese

Presunto Ham
Queijo Cheese
Queijo presunto Ham and cheese

MEATS—*CARNES*

Alcatra Roast beef
Bife Beef steak
Carne de porco Pork
Carne de vaca Beef
Chorizo Sausage
Churrasco Barbecue
Churrasco mixto Mixed barbecued
grill
Cordeiro Lamb
Costeletas de carneiro Lamb
chops

Filet mignon Filet mignon
Frango Seasoned chicken and Spanish
rice
Galinha Chicken
Língue Tongue
Pato Duck
Perú Turkey
Rosbife Roast beef
Salsichão Sausage

FISH—*PEIXES*

Bacalhau Codfish
Camarão Shrimp
Lagosta Lobster

Linguado Sole
Ostras Oysters
Sardinhas Sardines

EGGS—*OVOS*

**Ovos estrelados com batatas
fritas** Fried eggs with fried potatoes
Legumes Vegetables
Presunto Ham

Queijo frito Grilled cheese
Omelete Omelet
Ovos mexidos Scrambled eggs
Ovos quentes Soft boiled eggs

SALAD—*SALADA*

Salada de alface Lettuce salad
Salada de batata Potato salad
Salada mixta Mixed salad

**Salada de maionaise de
galinha** Chicken salad
Salada tomate Tomato salad

VEGETABLES—*LEGUMES*

Alface Lettuce
Arroz Rice
Batatas Potato
Fritas Fried
Puré Mashed
Cebola Onion

Cenouras Carrots
Couve-flor Cauliflower
Espinafre Spinach
Farofa Farfel
Feijão verde Stringbeans
Repôlho Cabbage

DESSERT—*SÔBRE MESA*

Fruta Fruit
Mamão Papaya (Brazilian)
Pasteis Cake
Pêssego Melba Peach Melba
Pudim Custard

Queijo Cheese
Sorvete Ice cream
Salada de frutas Fruit salad
Torta Pie
Torta de Maçã Apple pie

BEVERAGES—*BEBIDAS*

Água Water
Água mineral Mineral water

Cacao Cocoa
Café-puro Black coffee

Café com leite Coffee with milk
Cerveja Beer
Chá Tea

Chocolate Chocolate
Leite Milk
Suco Juice

FRUIT—*FRUTA*

Fruta Fruit
Abacate Avocado
Abacaxi Pineapple
Banana Banana
Laranja Orange
Lamão Lemon

Maçã Apple
Morango Strawberry
Pêra Pear
Pêssego Peach
Uvas Grapes

SPANISH

USEFUL EXPRESSIONS

Good day	**Buenos días**	*Bway*-nohss *dee*-ahss
How are you?	**Cómo está usted?**	*Koh*-moh es-*tah* oos-*ted?*
Very well	**Muy bien**	Mwee byen
Thank you	**Gracias**	*Grah*-see-ahss
Good-bye	**Adiós**	A-dee-*ohss*
Yes	**Sí**	See
No	**No**	Noh
Excuse me	**Perdóneme**	Pehr-*doh*-neh-may
When?	**Cuando?**	*Kwahn*-doh
Yesterday	**Ayer**	Ah-*yayr*
Today	**Hoy**	Oy
Tomorrow	**Mañana**	Man-*yah*-nah
Where are you going?	**A dónde va usted?**	Ah *dohn*-day vah oos-*ted?*
Where is . . . ?	**Dónde está . . . ?**	*Dohn*-day ess-*tah* . . . ?
the station	**la estación**	la ess-tah-*syohn*
a hotel	**un hotel**	oon hoh-*tel*
a restaurant	**un restaurante**	oon res-tow-*rahn*-tay
the toilet	**el retrete**	ell ray-*tray*-tay
the shop	**la tienda**	lah tee-*en*-dah
the market	**el mercado**	ell mayr-*kah*-doh
post office	**el correo**	ell koh-*rray*-oh
I want a single room	**Quiero un cuarto individual**	Kee-*ay*-roh oon *quahr*-toh in-de-ve-doo-*ahl*
a double room	**un cuarto para dos personas**	oon *quahr*-toh *pah*-rah dohss payr-*sohn*-ahss
with bath	**con baño**	kohn *bahn*-yoh
without bath	**sin baño**	seen *bahn*-yoh
How much is it?	**Cuánto?**	*Kwahn*-toh?
Too much	**Es demasiado**	Ayss day-mah-see-*ah*-doh
Cheaper	**Mas barato**	Mahss bah-*rah*-toh
Better	**Mejor**	Meh-*hohr*
I don't like it	**No me gusta**	No may *goos*-tah
Money	**Dinero**	Din-*ay*-ro
My name is . . .	**Mi nombre es . . .**	Mee *nohm*-bray ayss . . .
Black	**Negro**	*Nay*-groh
Red	**Rojo**	*Roh*-hoh
Blue	**Azul**	Ah-*zool*

White	**Blanco**	*Blahn*-koh
Green	**Verde**	*Vayr*-day
Yellow	**Amarillo**	Ah-ma-*ree*-yoh

NUMERALS

1	**Uno** (*Oo*-no)	15	**Quince** (*Keen*-say)	60	**Sesenta**
2	**Dos** (Doss)	16	**Dieciseis**		(Say-*sen*-tah)
3	**Tres** (Trayss)		(Dyes-ee-*sayss*)	70	**Setenta**
4	**Cuatro** (*Kwah*-tro)	17	**Diecisiete**		(Say-*ten*-tah)
5	**Cinco** (*Seen*-ko)		(Dyes-ee-*sye*-tah)	80	**Ochenta**
6	**Seis** (Sayss)	18	**Dieciocho**		(Oh-*chen*-tah)
7	**Siete** (*Syeh*-tay)		(Dyes-ee-*oh*-choh)	90	**Noventa**
8	**Ocho** (*oh*-choh)	19	**Diecinueve**		(No-*ben*-tah)
9	**Nueve** (*Nway*-bay)		(Dyes-ee-*nway*-bay)	100	**Cien** (Syen)
10	**Diez** (Dyes)	20	**Veinte** (*Bayn*-tay)	200	**Doscientos**
11	**Once** (*Ohn*-say)	30	**Treinta** (*Trayn*-tah)		(Dose-*syen*-tohs)
12	**Doce** (*Doy*-say)	40	**Cuarenta**	1,000	**Mil** (Meel)
13	**Trece** (*Tray*-say)		(Kwah-*ran*-tah)		
14	**Catorce**	50	**Cincuenta**		
	(Kah-*tor*-say)		(Seen-*kwen*-tah)		

DAYS OF THE WEEK

Sunday	**Domingo**	Doh-*meen*-goh
Monday	**Lunes**	*Loo*-nayss
Tuesday	**Martes**	*Mahr*-tayss
Wednesday	**Miércoles**	Mee-*ayr*-koh-layss
Thursday	**Jueves**	Hoo-*ay*-vayss
Friday	**Viernes**	Vee-*ayr*-nayss
Saturday	**Sábado**	*Sah*-bah-doh

RESTAURANT TERMS

Breakfast	**El desayuno**	Ell day-sah-*yoo*-noh
Lunch	**El almuerzo**	Ell ahl-moo-*ayr*-so
Dinner	**La comida**	Lah koh-*mee*-dah
The check	**La cuenta**	Lah *quen*-tah
Water	**Agua**	*Ah*-gwah
The waiter	**Mozo**	*Moh*-so

SOUPS — *SOPAS*

Arroz al caldo Consommé with rice
Caldo de gallina Chicken soup
Consomméa la reina Consommé with egg
Crema de esparragos Asparagus soup

Crema de tomates Tomato soup
Sopa de cebolla Onion soup
Sopa de gallina Chicken soup

MEAT — *CARNE*

Aves Poultry
Bife Baby beef
Carne asado Prime ribs (also barbecued beef)
Chuleta Chops
Chivito Kid (goat)
Chorizos Sausage
Churrasco Tenderloin

Cordero Lamb
Gallina Chicken
Higado Liver
Jamón Ham
Lengua Tongue
Lomo Porterhouse
Milanese Veal
Parrillada Barbecued beef

Pavo Turkey
Pollo Chicken
Salchica Sausage

Ternera Veal
Tocino Bacon

FISH — *PESCADO*

Albacora Swordfish
Almejas Clams
Anchoa Anchovy
Atún Tuna
Calamares Squid
Camarones Shrimp
Choritos Mussels

Congrio Eel
Corvina White bass
Erizos Sea urchin
Langostinos Lobster
Ostras Oysters
Ostiones Scallops

EGGS — *HUEVOS*

Fritos Fried
Pasados por agua Boiled

Revueltos Scrambled
Tortilla Omelet

BEVERAGES — *BEBIDAS*

Agua Water
Agua mineral Bottled mineral water
Café Coffee
Cerveza Beer

Jugo de naranja Orange juice
Leche Milk
Té Tea
Vino Wine

DESSERTS — *POSTRES*

Postre Dessert
Dulce Sweetmeat, cake
Flan Custard
Helado Ice cream

Macedonia Fruit salad
Panqueques Pancakes
Torta Cake

CONDIMENTS & OTHERS — *CONDIMENTOS & OTROS*

Aceite Oil
Ajo Garlic
Azúcar Sugar
Hielo Ice
Mantequilla Butter

Mermeladas Jam
Pan Bread
Panecillo Rolls
Sal Salt
Tostada Toast

B. METRIC MEASURES

LENGTH

1 millimeter (mm)	=	.04 inches (*or* less than ⅟16 inch)
1 centimeter (cm)	=	.39 inches (*or* just under ½ inch)
1 meter (m)	=	39 inches (*or* about 1.1 yards)
1 kilometer (km)	=	.62 mile (*or* about ⅔ mile)

To convert kilometers to miles, multiply the number of kilometers by 0.62. Also use to convert speeds from kilometers per hour (kmph) to miles per hour (m.p.h.).
To convert miles to kilometers, multiply the number of miles by 1.61. Also use to convert speeds from m.p.h. to kmph.

CAPACITY

1 liter (l)	=	33.92 ounces	=	2.1 pints	=	1.06 quarts
	=	0.26 U.S. gallons				
1 Imperial gallon	=	1.2 U.S. gallons				

To convert liters to U.S. gallons, multiply the number of liters by 0.26.
To convert U.S. gallons to liters, multiply the number of gallons by 3.79.
To convert Imperial gallons to U.S. gallons, multiply the number of Imperial gallons by 1.2.
To convert U.S. gallons to Imperial gallons, multiply the number of U.S. gallons by 0.83.

WEIGHT

1 gram (g)	=	0.035 ounces (*or* about a paper clip's weight)
1 kilogram (kg)	=	35.2 ounces
	=	2.2 pounds
1 metric ton	=	2,205 pounds = 1.1 short ton

To convert kilograms to pounds, multiply the number of kilograms by 2.2.
To convert pounds to kilograms, multiply the number of pounds by 0.45.

AREA

1 hectare (ha)	=	2.47 acres
1 square kilometer (km²)	=	247 acres = .39 square miles

To convert hectares to acres, multiply the number of hectares by 2.47.
To convert acres to hectares, multiply the number of acres by 0.41.
To convert aquare kilometers to square miles, multiply the number of square kilometers by 0.39.
To convert square miles to square kilometers, multiply the number of square miles by 2.6.

TEMPERATURE

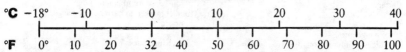

To convert degrees Celsius to degrees Fahrenheit, multiply °C by 9, divide by 5, and add 32 (example: 20°C × 9/5 + 32 = 68°F).
To convert degrees Fahrenheit to degrees Celsius, subtract 32 from °F, multiply by 5, then divide by 9 (example: 85°F − 32 × 5/9 = 29.4°C).

INDEX

GENERAL INFORMATION

Air travel, 9–10
  airlines, 10
  budget fares, 10
  stopovers, 10
American Express, 7
Argentina:
  exchange rates, 6
  sources of information, 3
Asunción, 2

Black market, in currency exchange, 6
Boat travel and cruises, 10
Bolivia:
  exchange rates, 6
  sources of information, 3
Brazil:
  exchange rates, 7
  sources of information, 3
Bryce, James, 3
Buenos Aires, 1–2

Caracas, 2
Cartagena, 2
Cash, 5–7
Chile:
  exchange rates, 7
  sources of information, 3
Cholera, 8
Clothing, packing, 8–9
Colombia:
  exchange rates, 7
  sources of information, 3
Consulates, 3–4
Credit cards, 7
Currency, 5–7
  exchange, 6–7
Customs, 4

Diners Club, 7
Documents for entry, 4

Ecuador:
  exchange rates, 7
  sources of information, 3
Embassies and consulates, 3–4
Entry requirements, 4

Ferguson, J. Halchro, 3

Glossary of terms, 384–89

Health concerns and precautions, 7–8
  medical aid, 7–8
  preparations, 8
  vaccination certificates, 4

Immunizations, 4, 8
Impressions, of South America, 3

Information sources, 3–4
Insurance, 8
International Association for Medical Assistance to
    Travelers (IAMAT), 7–8

La Paz, 2
Laundry, 9
Luggage, 8–9

Margarita, 2
MasterCard, 7
Measurements, converting, 389–90
Medical aid, 7–8
Money, 5–7

Package tours, 10
Packing for your trip, 8–9
Panama:
  exchange rates, 7
  sources of information, 3
Paraguay:
  exchange rates, 7
  sources of information, 3
Parallel market, in currency exchange, 6
Passport, 4
Peru:
  exchange rates, 7
  sources of information, 3
Planning and preparing for your trip:
  entry requirements, 4
  getting to. see Traveling
  health concerns and precautions, 7–8
  information sources, 3–4
  money, 4, 6–7
  packing, 8–9
Portuguese phrases and terms, 384–87

Quito, 1

Restaurants, glossary of terms used in, 385–89
Rio de Janeiro, 1–2

Shipping, 4
Shopping, 2
  shipping purchases home, 4
South America, 1–3
  impressions of, 3
  map, 5
Spanish phrases and terms, 387–89

Theroux, Paul, 3
Tourist cards, 4
Tourist information, 3–4
Tours, package, 9
Traveler's checks, 7
Traveling, 9–10
  package tours, 10
  by plane, 9–10
  by ship, 10

Uruguay:
 exchange rates, 7
 sources of information, 4

Vaccination certificates, 4
Venezuela:

exchange rates, 7
sources of information, 4
Visa, 4, 7
Vocabulary, 384–89

Yellow fever vaccination, 4, 8

DESTINATIONS

AMAZON (ECUADOR), 297
AMBATO (ECUADOR), 293–4
ANGELS FALLS (VENEZUELA), 51
ASUNCIÓN (PARAGUAY), 210–29
accommodations:
 Adelia, Hotel, in town, 216
 Asunción Palace Hotel, in town, 217
 Continental Hotel, in town,* 217
 Cristal, 229
 Embajador, Hotel, in town, 216
 Excelsior Hotel Paraguay (S), 217
 Gran Hotel Armele, in town, 217
 Gran Hotel Del Paraguay, near town,* 218
 Guarani, in town, 217–18
 Ita Enramada, Hotel, near town, 218
 La Española, Hotel, in town, ($), 216
 Nanduti Hotel, in town, ($), 216–17
 Novotel, 229
 Tirol Hotel, 229
 Zaphir Hotel, in town,* 217
evening entertainment, 226–7
excursions from:
 Chaco, 229–30
 Golden or Central Circuit, 227–8
 Iguassu Falls, 230
 Jesuit ruins, 228–9
 Villa Florida, 227
Fast Facts, 214–16
restaurants, 218–22
ARGENTINEAN
 Restaurant-Choperia la Manija, 219–20
BRAZILIAN
 Restaurant-Choperia la Manija, 219–20
CONFITERÍAS
 Confitería Imagen, 221
 Confitería Ventura, 221
 Di Trevi, 221
 San Marcos, 221
 Vendôme Shopping Center, 221
DINING WITH A SHOW
 Gran Hotel del Paraguay, 221–2
 El Jardín de la Cerveza, 221
 Tayi Poty, 221
 Yguazu, 221
FRENCH
 Le Gran Café,* 219
GERMAN
 Bistro, 220
 Restaurante El Caballito Blanco, 220
 Restaurante Westfalia, 220
 San Marcos, 220

ICE CREAM
 Helados Pucavy, 221
INTERNATIONAL
 Don Quixote Restaurant, 219
ITALIAN
 Il Capo, 218–19
LIGHT FARE
 American Fried Chicken Paraguay, 220
 Bar Restaurant Asunción, 220
 Café Metro, 220
 Confitería Alemana, 220
 Lido Bar, 220
 Pergola di Bolsi, 220
 La Recova, 220
 Restaurant Mundo, 220
PARAGUAYAN
 Exedra, ($), 219
 Le Gran Café,* 219
 La Pergola di Bolsi, ($),* 219
 La Preferida, 219
shopping, 225–6
sights and attractions:, 222–5
 Andrés Barbero Museum, * 222
 Bellas Artes, Museo de, 222
 Botanical Gardens, 222
 Casa de la Independencia,* 222, 224
 Cathedral, 224–5
 Center of Visual Arts, 223
 Contemporary Art, Museum of, 223
 Histórico Militar, Museo, 222
 Monseñor Juan Soforiano Bogarin Museum, 222
 Museo del Barro (Museum of Clay), 223
 Palacio de Gobierno, 224
 Panteón de los Héroes, 223
transportation, 214
walking tour, 223–5

BELO HORIZONTE (BRAZIL), 101–2
BOGOTÁ (COLOMBIA), 298–330
accommodations:
 Bacata, Hotel, 309
 Los Cerros, 308
 Continental, Hotel,* 309
 Cristal, Hotel, 308
 Dann Colonial,* 309
 Dann International, Hotel, 309
 Del Duc, Hotel, 308
 Halifax, in suburbs (R), 310
 Ile de France, Hotel, 308–9
 Inter-Bogotá, Hotel, 309
 Manila Hotel, 308

KEY TO ABBREVIATIONS: *HC* = Hotel Casino; *P* = Pension; *R* = Residential Hotel; *S* = Splurge Choice; *YH* = Youth Hostel; *$* = Super-special Value; * = An Author's Favorite

BOGOTÁ (COLOMBIA) *(cont'd)*
Menendez, Hotel,($), 308
Nueva Granada, 310
Panamericano, Hotel, 307
Pensión Alemana ($), 308
El Presidente, Hotel,* 310
Regina, Hotel, 309
Residencia Santa Fe, Hotel, 308
Residencias Dorantes, 307-8
Virgen del Camino, Hotel, ($), 307
climate, 305
evening entertainment, 325-8
excursions from:
Monoliths in San Agustín, 328-9
Tequendama Waterfall, 328
Zipaquira,* 328
Fast Facts, 305-7
historical and cultural background, 299-301
language, 306
map, 303
orientation, 302, 304
picnic supplies, 317
restaurants, 310-17
picnic supplies, 317
AFTERNOON TEA
Oma, 317
La Suiza, 317
AMERICAN
The Place, in suburbs, 315
BARBECUE
Mister Ribs, in suburbs, 314-15
BELGIAN
Gran Vatel, in suburbs (S), 315
BRAZILIAN
Cozineiro Rodizio Bar, in town, 313
CAFE
Frutería Las Catorce, 317
CHINESE
Gran China, in suburbs, 314
Restaurante Hong Kong, in town, 313
COLOMBIAN
Casa Vieja de San Diego, in town,* 313
La Fonda Antioqueña, in town, 311
La Giralda, in town, 312
La Gran Parrilla Santa Fe, in town, 312
La Hacienda Restaurant, in town, 312-13
Pasapoga Restaurante, in town, ($), 311
El Zaguan de las Aguas, in town, 313
FRENCH
Gran Vatel, in suburbs (S), 315
Le Petit Bistrot, in suburbs, 314
Refugio Alpino, in town, 314
GERMAN
Resi Berlin, in town, 311
ICE CREAM
Crem Helado, in town, 316-17
INTERNATIONAL
Cactus, in the suburbs, 314
Cafeteria El Virrey, in town, 311-12
El Fogonazo Restaurant, in town, 312
La Gran Parrilla Santa Fe, in town, 312
La Hacienda Restaurant, in town, 312-13
Tramonti, in suburbs (S),* 315-16
ITALIAN
O Sole Mio, in suburbs, 315
Pizzeria Napolitanas, in suburbs, 315
Romana Cafeteria, in town,($), 313
JAPANESE
Nihonkan, in suburbs, 315

LIGHT FARE
La Brasa Roja, in town, 316
Broaster, in town, 317
Crem Helado, in town, 316-17
Del Oeste Hamburgers, 317
Domo Taberna and Pizza, in town, 316
Jenos, in town, 316
Koko Rico, 317
Lechonería Tolimense, in town, 316
La Plazuela, in town, 316
PPC, in town, 316
Punto Rojo, in town, 316
Ramses, in town, 316
Restaurante Delphi, 317
San Martín, 317
24 Horas Sandwich Shop, 317
Wimpy's, in town, 317
SEAFOOD
La Fragata, in town, 313-14
SOUTH AMERICAN
La Guayacana, in town, 312
SPANISH
La Giralda, in town, 312
SWISS
Chalet Suizo, in town, 312
Refugio Alpino, in town, 314
VEGETARIAN
El Champiñón, 317
El Vegetariano, 317
safety concerns, 299-300, 306-7
shopping, 322-5
sights and attractions:
Cano Gallery, 319
for children, 320-1
Mt. Monserrate, 320
Museo Arqueológico, 319
Museo de Arte Colonial, 318
Museo de Arte Moderno, 318
Museo de Arte Religioso del Banco de la
￢ República, 319
Museo de Artes y Tradiciones Populares, 318
Museo Nacional, 319
Museo del Oro,* 317-18
Museo de 20 de Julio, 319
Quinta de Bolívar, 319
sports, 322
transportation, 304
walking tours, 321-2
warning concerning, 299
what's special about, 299
BOGOTÁ RIVER FALLS (COLOMBIA), 328
BRASILIA (BRAZIL), 100-1
BUENOS AIRES (ARGENTINA), 134-73
accommodations:
Camino Real Hotel, Avenida Florida area,($),
144
Carsson, Hotel, Avenida Florida area (S), 145
Castelar, Avenida de Mayo area,* 148-9
Central Córdoba, Hotel, Plaza San Martín
area,($), 146
Du Helder, Avenida de Mayo area,($), 148
Eibar Hotel, Avenida Florida area, 144-5
Gran Hotel Argentino, Avenida de Mayo area,*
148
Gran Hotel Buenos Aires, Plaza San Martín area
(S), 147
Gran Hotel Dora, Plaza San Martín area (S), 147
Gran Hotel Hispano, Avenida de Mayo area,
148
Gran Hotel Orly, Plaza San Martín area, 146

BUENOS AIRES (ARGENTINA) *(cont'd)*
Gran Hotel San Carlos, Avenida de Mayo area,* 147–8
Grand Hotel, "Broadway" area, 145–6
King's Hotel, "Broadway" area,(\$), 145
Liberty Hotel, "Broadway" area, 145
Novel, Avenida de Mayo area, 148
Principado, Hotel, Plaza San Martín area, 146
Promenade, Plaza San Martín area, 146
Regidor, Hotel, Plaza San Martín area, 146
Regis, "Broadway" area, 145
Ritz, Avenida de Mayo area, 148
Rochester Hotel, Plaza San Martín area (S), 147
San Antonio, Plaza San Martín area, 147
Suipacha Palace, Avenida de Mayo area, 148
Tres Sargentos, Hotel, Plaza San Martín area, 146
Victory, Hotel, Plaza San Martín area,* 146–7
Waldorf, Plaza San Martín area, 147
airport, 138
arriving in, 138
from Montevideo, 133
climate, 135
cost of everyday items in, 136, 138
currency, 136, 142
evening entertainment, 166–71
La Boca, 170
discos and dance clubs, 168–9
for gay men and lesbians, 169
jazz clubs, 169
for men only, 169–70
movies, 170
nightclubs and cabarets, 167–8
opera, 167
Fast Facts, 142–4
geography of Argentina, 134–5
history of Argentina, 135–6
itineraries from, 157, 171–3
gaucho country, 171
Iguasu Falls, 172–3
Mar del Plata, 171–2
Montevideo, 173
San Carlos de Bariloche, 172
Valle de Las Leñas, 172
maps:
Argentina, 137
Buenos Aires, 141
movies, 170
orientation, 138–40
people of Argentina, 136
restaurants, 149–56
late-night dining by the sea, 170–1
specialty dining, 154–6
ARGENTINEAN
La Cabana, Belgrano (S),* 153
La Churrasquita, "Broadway" area,(\$), 149
Las Deliciosas Papas Fritas, "Broadway" area,* 149–50
La Estancia, "Broadway" area,* 150
El Mundo, "Broadway" area, 150
La Nazarenas, "Broadway" area, 150
El Palacio de la Papa Frita, "Broadway" area, 150
Parilla Las Tejas, "Broadway" area, 151
La Posta del Gaucho, "Broadway" area, 150
Sorrento, "Broadway" area, 150–1
La Tranquera, Nuñez, 153
CAFE
La Biela, Recoleta, 152, 155
Café de la Paix, Recoleta, 151–2
Café Gran Victoria, Recoleta, 152
Confitería Jockey Club, 155

Confitería Obelilsco, 155
Lord Gin, 155
New Park Lane, Recoleta, 152
Open Plaza, Recoleta, 152
CAFETERIAS
Auto Service Grill, "Broadway" area, 154
Las Brases, "Broadway" area, 154
Café Parisien, "Broadway" area, 154
Florida Garden, "Broadway" area, 154
Grill Oriente, "Broadway" area, 154
Mimo's Bar, "Broadway" area, 154
Oriente, "Broadway" area, 154
Via Florida, "Broadway" area, 154
CHINESE
Chino Central, "Broadway" area, 151
CONFITERÍAS
Café Petit Colón, "Broadway" area, 155
Confitería del Molino, "Broadway" area, 155
Confitería Ideal, "Broadway" area, 155
Confitería My House, "Broadway" area, 155
Gran Café Tortoni, "Broadway" area, 155
Queen Bess, "Broadway" area, 155
Richmond Tea Room, "Broadway" area, 155
St. James, "Broadway" area, 155
CONTINENTAL
El Comite, San Telmo (S), 154
ENGLISH
London Grill (S), 154
FAST FOOD
Chéburger, "Broadway" area, 156
Frankfurt, 156
McDonald's, "Broadway" area, 156
Di Pappo, 156
Di Pappo d'Or, 156
Pumpernic, "Broadway" area, 156
FRENCH
Au Bec Fin, Recoleta (S), 153
GERMAN
ABC'(S), 153
Otto Cervecería, "Broadway" area, 151
INTERNATIONAL
El Aguila, Nuñez, 153
Arturito, "Broadway" area, 149
Au Bec Fin, Recoleta (S), 153
Café la Barra, "Broadway" area,(\$), 151
Clarks, Recoleta,* 152
Don Juan, Recoleta, 152
Fridays, "Broadway" area, 151
Happenings, Recoleta,* 152
Harpers, Recoleta,* 152
Lola, Recoleta,* 152
ITALIAN
La Churrasquita, "Broadway" area,(\$), 149
Ristorante Subito, "Broadway" area, 151
Ristorante Tommaso, Recoleta,* 152
Sorrento, "Broadway" area, 150–1
NOUVELLE CUISINE
Gato Dumas, Recoleta,* 152–3
PIZZA
Los Immortales, 156
Pizza Hut, 156
Pizza Roma, 156
SPANISH
Don Juan, Recoleta, 152
VEGETARIAN
Granix Restaurant Vegetariano, 155
La Huertan, 155
La Lecherisima, 155
Yin Yang, 155

BUENOS AIRES (ARGENTINA) (cont'd)
WHISKERÍAS
La Barra, "Broadway" area, 156
Café Paris, "Broadway" area, 156
Exedra, "Broadway" area, 156
Park Lane, "Broadway" area, 155–6
shopping, 163–6
sights and attractions:
Arte Hispano-Americano, Museo de, 158–9
Avellaneda Bridge, 157
La Boca (Little Italy),* 157
Botanical Gardens (Jardín Botánico), 160
Cabildo, 160
Casa Rosada, 160
Centro Cultural Las Malvinas, 160
Hipódromo de Palermo, 158, 162
Histórico Nacional, Museo, 158
Instituto Nacional Sanmartiniano, 159
Jockey Club, 158
Lavalle Stadium, 162–3
Luna Park, 162
Mitre, Museo, 159
Museo Municipal de Motivos Argentinos "José Hernandez, 159
Museo Nacional de Bellas Artes,* 158
Museo Nacional Histórico del Cabildo de la Ciudad de Buenos Aires y de la Revolución de Mayo, 159
National Congress, 157
Palermo Park (Bosques de Palermo), 159–60
Palermo Zoo (Jardín Zoológico),* 159–60
Plaza de Mayo, 160
Recoleta Cemetery, 160
recreation, 162–3
River Plate Stadium, 162
San Martín Cathedral, 160
suburbia, 158
sports and recreation, 161–3
student travelers, 169
tours, 171–3
tours, organized, 161
transportation in, 140, 142
traveling to, from Montevideo, 133
walking tour, 160–1

CALLAO (PERU), 417
CANAIMA (VENEZUELA), 51
CARACAS (VENEZUELA), 11–51
accommodations:
Las Americas, Hotel, Sabana Grande area,* 22
Aventura Caracas, San Bernardino area, 24
Avila, Hotel, San Bernardino area,* 24
Broadway, Hotel, Sabana Grande area, 22–3
Bruno, Hotel, Sabana Grande area, 21
Los Caobos, Hotel, Sabana Grande area,($), 21
Caracas Hilton, Altamira (S),* 25
CCCT Hotel, Altamira, 25
Coliseo, Hotel, Sabana Grande area (S), 22
El Condor, Hotel, Sabana Grande area, 22
Crillon, Hotel, Sabana Grande area (S), 23
Cristal Hotel, Sabana Grande area, 21
Eraso, Hotel, San Bernardino area, 23
Eurobuilding,($), 25
Fioremar, Hotel, El Litoral, 26
La Floresta, Hotel (S), 24
Jolly Inn, Sabana Grande area,($), 21
King's Inn, Sabana Grande area, 23
Kursaal Hotel, Sabana Grande area,* 23
Luna, Hotel, Sabana Grande area (S), 22
Macuto, Hotel, El Litoral,($), 27

Macuto Sheraton (S),* 27
Mari, Hotel, Sabana Grande area, 21
Melia Caribe (S), 27
Las Mercedes, Hotel, San Bernardino area, 24
Miriam, Hotel, Sabana Grande area,($), 21
Montpark, Hotel, Sabana Grande area, 22
Odeon, Hotel, Sabana Grande area, 21
Paseo Las Mercedes Hotel, 26
Las Quince Letras, Hotel,* 26
President, Hotel, Los Caobos, 25
Residencia Montserrat, Hotel, 24–5
Residencias Anauco Hilton, 26
Royal, Hotel, Sabana Grande area, 22
Royal Atlantic, Hotel, El Litoral, 27
Santa Fe Suites, Hotel, 26
Sava, Hotel, Sabana Grande area,($), 21
Savoy Hotel, Sabana Grande area (S), 23
Tamanaco, Hotel, 25
Tampa, Hotel, Sabana Grande area, (S), 23
Tanasu, Hotel, Sabana Grande area, 21–2
Tiburon, Hotel, Sabana Grande area, 22
Villa Verde, Sabana Grande area, 22
Waldorf, Hotel, San Bernardino area,($), 24
addresses, 16
arriving in, 14–15
beaches, 48–50
climate, 12
cost of everyday items in, 14
currency, 18–19
evening entertainment, 45–7
excursions from:
Canaima and Angel Falls, 51
Colonial Tovar,* 47–8
Maracay, 47
Margarita Island, 48–51
Merida, 51
Fast Facts, 18–20
maps:
Caracas, 17
Venezuela, 13
organized tours, 42
orientation, 14–16
restaurants, 27–38
local budget bets, 34–5
specialty dining, 34–8
splurge choices, 36–7
ARGENTINEAN
La Estancia, La Castellana (S), 36
CAFE
Café Memphis, Sabana Grande, 35–6
Checheres, Sabana Grande (R), 37
CHINESE
Gran China, Las Mercedes, 30–1
Hong Kong Chef, El Litoral, 37
CONTINENTAL
Gazebo, Las Mercedes,* 30
DELICATESSEN
Charcutería Tovar, Sabana Grande, 34–5
FAST FOOD
Arturos, 35
Doña Arepa, 34
Fiesta del Parque, Parque Central, 35
Papagallo, Sabana Grande, 34
Plaza Broadway, Sabana Grande, 34
Tropiburger, 35
FRENCH
Gazebo, Las Mercedes,* 30
Girafe, El Rosal, 29
Petite Bistro de Jacques, Las Mercedes,* 31

CARACAS (VENEZUELA) *(cont'd)*
GERMAN
Cervecería Berlin, Chacaito, 28
Fritz & Franz, El Rosal, 29
Rincón de Baviera, San Bernardino, 34
INDIAN
Delicatesses Indu, Sabana Grande, 32
INTERNATIONAL
La Cazuela, Sabana Grande, 32
El Carrizo, La Castellana (*S*),* 36
Cervecería Berlin, Chacaito, 28
Cervecería Juan Griego, Sabana Grande, 32
The Cookery, El Litoral, 37
Gaggia, Plaza Bolívar,$ 32
La Mansion, El Risal (*S*), 37
Parrillada Onassis, Bello Monte,($), 28
El Tinajero de los Helechos, Las Mercedes, 31
ITALIAN
Castellino, Avenida Francisco Solano, 35
Il Foro Romano, Bello Campo (*S*), 36
Il Mulino Rosso, Avenida Francisco Solano, 33
El Pollo Italiano, Avenida Francisco Solano, 33
Restaurante/Piano Bar Franco, Avenida Francisco
Solano, 33
Sorrento, Avenida Francisco Solano,* 33–4
La Vie Emilia Ristorante, Las Mercedes (*S*), 36–7
JAPANESE
Shogun Restaurant, El Rosal, 30
MEXICAN
El Tizon, Bello Campo, 28
MIDDLE EASTERN
Kibbe, Las Mercedes, 31
NORTH AMERICAN
Weekends, Altamira, 35
PASTA
Da Peppino, La Floresta, 30
Da Sandra, Avenida Francisco Solano,($), 33
Mamma Mia, Las Mercedes, 31
La Strada del Sole, Las Mercedes, 31
PERUVIAN
El Tizon, Bello Campo, 28
PIZZA
Da Peppino, La Floresta, 30
Da Sandra, Avenida Francisco Solano,($), 33
Mamma Mia, Las Mercedes, 31
Pida Pizza, Sabana Grande,* 32
Pizza House, El Rosal, 29–30
La Strada del Sole, Las Mercedes, 31
SEAFOOD
La Barba Roja, El Rosal, 28–9
Bodegón del Bogavante Marisquera, El Rosal, 29
Cervecería Maracaibo, Altamira, 28
Las Quince Letras, El Litoral,* 37–8
SPANISH
La Caleta, Sabana Grande, 35
Cervecería Juan Griego, Sabana Grande, 32
Don Sancho, El Rosal, 29
La Gran Paella del Caribe, El Litoral, 37
La Huerta, Sabana Grande, 32
Restaurant Nueva Esparta, Sabana Grande, 32–3
Tasca Grutas de San Antonio, Sabana Grande,
33
STEAK
Lee Hamilton Steak House, La Castellana (*S*), 36
SWISS
La Petit Suisse, Las Mercedes, 31
TEX-MEX
Dallas: Texas Café, Las Mercedes, 30
VEGETARIAN
Kibbe, Las Mercedes, 31

VENEZUELAN
El Jardin II, San Bernardino,* 34
Los Pilones, El Rosal, 29
Portón de Timotes, El Litoral, 38
El Portón El Rosal,* 35
El Tejar, El Rosal,($), 30
La Tinaja, Sabana Grande, 33
shopping, 43–5
sights and attractions: 38–42
Altamira and La Castellana, 39
Arte Colonial, Museo del, 40–1
Arte Contemporáneo de Caracas Sofia Imber,
Museo de, 41
Bellas Artes, Museo de, 41
Bolívar Museum,* 41
Casa Natal, 41
Ciencia Natural, Museo de, 41
Mt. Avila Peak, 40
Parque Zoológico de Caricuao, 42
Sabana Grande, 39
El Silencio, 38–9
University City, 41–2
walking tour, 38–9
sports and recreation, 42–3
transportation, 16, 18
traveling to, 14–15
what's special about, 12
CARTAGENA (COLOMBIA), 332–45
accommodations:
Arrecife, Hotel,($), 337
Bahía, Hotel,* 337
Barlovento, Hotel, 337
Capilla del Mar, 337
Caribe, Hotel (*S*), 338
El Caribe (*S*), 338
Cartagena Real, Hotel, 338
Casagrande, Hotel,* 337
Costa Del Sol, Hotel, 339
El Dorado, Hotel, 337
Hostal Residencia Internacional (*R*), 338
Leonela (*R*), 338
Playa, Hotel, 337–8
Residencia Bocagrande,($), 337
Residencias Punta Canoa, Hotel,($), 338
Royal Park, 338
Las Velas Hotel, 337
arriving in, 332
crime, 333
evening entertainment, 343–4
excursions from, 345
orientation, 333–4
restaurants, 339–42
CHINESE
Mee Wah, Bocagrande, 341
COLOMBIAN
La Fonda Antioqueña, Bocagrande, 340
La Olla Cartagenera, Bocagrande, 340
CREOLE
Mee Wah, Bocagrande, 341
FRENCH
Marcel, Old City, 341
ICE CREAM
La Fuente, 342
Pipos, 342
Robin Hood, 342
INTERNATIONAL
Crepes n' Waffles, Bocagrande, 341
Los Pinos, Bocagrande, 341
ITALIAN
Da Teresa, Bocagrande,$ 340

CARTAGENA (COLOMBIA) (cont'd)
Giovanni O Sole Mio, Bocagrande, 340
LIGHT FARE
Heladeria Arabe, 342
Kiko Riko Chicken House, 342
Palacio de las Frutas, 342
La Papa Loca, 342
Pio Kiko, 342
Pipos, 342
La Piragua, 342
Pizzería Margarita, 342
Sandwiches Cubanos, 342
El Torito, 342
Whopper King, 342
PIZZA
Pizzería Margarita, 342
SEAFOOD
Bodegón de la Candelaria,* 339-40
Capilla del Mar,* 339
Chef Julian, Bocagrande, 340-1
Club de Pesca,* 339
Nautilus, Bocagrande, 341
Paco's Restaurante y Taberna, Old City,* 341
Restaurante de Doris,* 340
shopping, 342-3
sights and attractions, 334-6
CHILEAN LAKE REGION (CHILE), 208-9
CHILLAN (CHILE), 208
CHOTA VALLEY (ECUADOR), 292
CHULUMANI (BOLIVIA), 257-8
COLONIA TOVAR (VENEZUELA), 47-8
COLON (PANAMA), 380-1
EL COLORADO (CHILE), 205
CONTADORA ISLAND (PANAMA), 383
COPACABANA (BOLIVIA), 256-7
COROICO (BOLIVIA), 258
COSTA VERDE (BRAZIL), 94-5
COTOPAXI VOLCANO NATIONAL PARK (ECUADOR), 293
CUENCA (ECUADOR), 294-5
CUZCO (PERU), 422-43
accommodations:
Alhambra II (S), 430-1
Colonial Palace, Hostal, 428-9
Conquistador, Hotel, 430
Cuzco, Hotel (S), 431
El Dorado Inn (S), 431
El Sol, Hotel, 429
El Solar, Hostal, 429
Imperio, Hotel, 428
Inti, Hotel, 430
Leonard's Lodgings (P), 430
Mantas, Hostal, 429
Raymi, Hostal, (P), 430
Residencial Los Marqueses, Hostal, 429
Residencial Machupicchu, Hostal, 428
Royal Inka, Hotel (S), 431
San Agustin (S), 431
Tambo, Hotel, 430
Tambo Real, Hostal, 429
Virrey, Hotel, 429
Wiraqocha, Hostal, 429-30
climate, 426
departure information, 443
excursions from, 440-3
fast facts, 426-28
getting to, 425
history of, 423-4
map, 427
nightlife, 439-40

orientation, 425-6
restaurants, 431-4
shopping, 437-9
sights and activities, 434-7
tourist information, 425

EASTER ISLAND (CHILE), 203-5
EQUATOR (ECUADOR), 290-1

FARELLONES (CHILE), 205

GALAPAGOS ISLANDS (ECUADOR), 288-90
GUAYAQUIL (ECUADOR), 295-6

HUANCAYO (PERU), 420-1
HUATAJATA (BOLIVIA), 257

IGUAÇU FALLS: see IGUASSU FALLS
IGUASSU (IGUAÇU) FALLS (ARGENTINA/BRAZIL), 103, 172-3, 230
IMBABURRA PROVINCE (ECUADOR), 291-2
IQUITOS (PERU), 419-20
ITAIPU DAM (BRAZIL), 103
ITAPARICA ISLAND (BRAZIL), 100

LA PARVA (CHILE), 205
LA PAZ (BOLIVIA), 231-60
accommodations:
Alem, Hotel, Indian Quarter,($), 239
Austria, Hotel, near Plaza Murillo,($), 238
Avenida, Hotel, near Plaza Murillo, 238
Calacoto, Hotel, near Plaza Murillo, 238
Continental, Hotel, Indian Quarter, 239
Cris, Hostal, San Francisco Church area,($), 239
Eldorado, Hotel, near Miraflores Fútbol Stadium, 240
España, Hotel, Prado,* 237-8
Gloria, Hotel, near Plaza Murillo,* 240
Grand Hotel, San Francisco Church area, 238-9
Hostería Claudia, Prado, 227
Latino, Hotel, near Plaza Murillo,($), 238
Libertador, Hotel, near Miraflores Futbol Stadium, 240
Milton, Hotel, Indian Quarter,* 239
Las Palmas, Hotel, Santa Cruz, 259
Panamericano, Hotel, Indian Quarter, 239
La Paz, Hotel, Chulumani, 258
La Paz Hotel (S), 240
Plaza, Hotel, San Francisco Church area, 239
Plaza, Prado,* 241
Prefectural, Hotel, Oruro, 258-9
Presidente, Hotel, near Miraflores Fútbol Stadium (S), 241
La Quinta, Hotel, Santa Cruz, 259
Residencial 6 de Agosto, Prado, 238
Sagarnaga, Hotel, Indian Quarter,* 239-40
San Bartolomé, Motel, Chulumani, 258
Sucre Palace Hotel, Prado, 240
Los Tajibos, Hotel, Santa Cruz, 259
Terminal, Hotel, Oruro, 258
arriving in, 233
climate, 232, 234
currency, 236
evening entertainment, 252-5
excursions from, 255-60
Fast Facts, 234, 236-7
fútbol, 250
getting around, 234, 236
map, 235

LA PAZ (BOLIVIA) *(cont'd)*
orientation, 232–4
performing arts, 249
restaurants, 241–6
ARGENTINEAN
  Churrasqueria el Arriero, near Plaza Isabel la
    Católica, 244
  Churrasqueria el Tropero, around Plaza Murillo,
    243
  Gringo Limon, near Plaza Isabel la Católica,* 244
BOLIVIAN
  La Casa del Corregidor, San Francisco Church
    area,* 243
  Giorggisimo, near Prado, 242
  Gringo Limon, near Plaza Isabel la Católica,* 244
  Peña Andina, near Prado,* 243
  El Refugio, near Plaza Isabel la Católica, 244
CHINESE
  Chifa Emy, near Plaza Isabel la Católica, 244
  Hong Kong, near Prado, 242
CONFITERIAS
  Confitería Club de La Paz, 245
  Confitería La Florida, 245
  Confitería Rayito del Sol, 245
  Confitería Tokio, 245
  Il Fiore, 245
  Kremrik, 245
  Monaco, 245
CONTINENTAL
  Giorggisimo, near Prado, 242
ECUADORIAN
  Los Escudos de la Paz, near Prado, 242
FAST FOOD
  California Donuts and Burgers, 245
  Denny's, 245
  Luigi's Pub & Pizzeria, 246
  Naira Crêperie, 246
  Quickes Pizza, 246
  Sancho Panza, 246
  Tops, 246
  Tutti Fruti, 246
  Venezia Pizza a la Piedra, 246
ICE CREAM
  Il Fiore, 245
  Max Bieber's, 245
INTERNATIONAL
  Alaya (S), 244
  Cafe Ciudad, near Prado, 241
  El Internacional, around Plaza Murillo,* 243
  Eli's, near the Prado,(S), 242
  Gargantua, near Prado,($), 242
  Los Lobos Balnearios Restaurant, in countryside,
    244
  Marilyn's, around Plaza Murillo, 243
  Monaco Restaurant, near Prado, 242–3
  Utama (S),* 245
ITALIAN
  Circulo Italiano, near Prado, 242
  Pronto Ristorante, near Prado, 243
PIZZA
  Luigi's Pub & Pizzeria, 246
  Naira Crêperie, 246
  Quickes Pizza, 246
  Venezia Pizza a la Piedra, 246
SWISS
  La Suisse (S), 244–5
shopping, 250–2
sights and attractions:
  Calle Buenos Aires, 247
  Calle Sagarnaga, 234, 247–8

Carnival of Oruro, 258
Casa de la Cultura, 249
Casa de Murillo, 249
Costumbrista Juan de Vargas, Museo, 249
Galería Artesanal Las Brujas, 247
Histórico Litoral, Museo, 249
Indian Quarter, 246–8
Indian shops, 247–8
Juan de Vargas Museum, 249
Litoral Historical Museum, 249
markets, 246–7
Monticulo Park, 248
Museo de Metales Preciosos y Precolombinos,
  248
Museo Nacional de Etnografía y Folklore, 249
National Art Museum,* 249
National Ethnography and Folklore Museum, 249
Open-Air Museum, 248
Plaza San Francisco, 234
Precious and Pre-Columbian Metal Museum,*
  238
Valley of the Moon, 248
skiing, 249–50
what's special about, 232
EL LITORAL (VENEZUELA), 42
LIMA (PERU), 384–421
accommodations:
  Alameda, Hostal, Miraflores, 394
  Albergue Juvenil Internacional, Miraflores, (YH),
    397
  Albergue Juvenil Karina (YH), 394
  Ariosto, Miraflores, 395
  Apart-Hotel Los Galgos, Miraflores, 397
  Beech, Hostal, suburbs (P), 396
  Claridge Hotel, Center City, 393
  Colonial Inn, Hostal, Miraflores, 394
  Columbus Hotel, 394
  Condado Miraflores, Miraflores (S), 396
  Continental, Center City, 393
  Country Club, San Isidro (S), 395
  Crillon, Hotel, Center City (S), 394
  Eldoral Hotel, Miraflores, 394
  Ella Friedrich Guest House, suburbs (P), 395–6
  El Pardo Hotel, Miraflores (S), 397
  El Plaza Hotel, Center City, 393
  Francia, Hostal, San Isidro (P), 396
  Gran Hotel Bolívar, Center City, 394
  Maria Angola, (S), 397
  Miraflores Cesar, Miraflores, 396
  Mont Blanc, Hostal, Center City, 393
  Pension Alemana, suburbs (P), 396
  Renacimiento, Hostal, Center City, 393
  Residencial 28 de Julio, Miraflores (P), 396
  Residencial Collacocha, San Isidro, 395
  Savoy, Hotel, Center City, 393
  Tampu Diplomat, 395
climate, 390
curfew, 390
excursions from:
  Callao, 417
  El Pueblo Hyatt Hotel (La Granja Azul), 418
  Huancayo, 420–1
  Iquitos, 419–20
  Nasca, 418
  Pachacamac Ruins and Museum, 417–18
  Pucallpa, 273
fast facts, 388–92
history of, 384–6
map, 389
nightlife, 413–17

LIMA (PERU) (cont'd)
orientation, 386–8
restaurants, 397–405
shopping, 411–13
sights and activities:
Arquologico Rafael Larco Herrera, Museo, 406–7
Church of San Francisco, 405–6
Court of the Inquisition, 405
Museum of Anthropology and Archeology, 406
National Museum of Art, 407
Oro del Perú, Museo del, 407
Torre Tagle Palace, 405
sports, 409–10
transportation, 388
walking tour, 407–8

MACHÚ PICCHÚ (PERU), 422–3, 443–6
books about, 312
getting to, 443–4
history of, 444–5
what to bring, 444
MADRE DE DIOS (PERU), 442–3
MARACAY (VENEZUELA), 47
MAR DEL PLATA (ARGENTINA), 171–2
MARGARITA ISLAND (VENEZUELA), 48–51
accommodations, 50
beaches, 48–50
evening entertainment, 50
getting there, 48–51
orientation, 48
sights and activities, 48–50
MERIDA (VENEZUELA), 51
MONTEVIDEO (URUGUAY), 103–33
accommodations:
Los Angeles, Hotel, Plaza de la Indepencia area, 114
Aramaya, Hotel, Plaza Libertad (Cagancha) area, 114
Artigas Hotel, Plaza Matríz area, 116
Ateneo, Plaza de la Independencia area,($), 113
Balfer, Hotel, Plaza Libertad (Cagancha) area, 114–15
California Hotel, Plaza Libertad (Cagancha) area, 114
Casino Carrasco Hotel, Carrasco,(HC), 117
Cervantes, Hotel, Plaza de la Independencia area,($), 113
Claridge, Avenida Mercedes, 115–16
Columbia Palace Hotel, Plaza Matríz area (S),* 116
Cottage, Hotel, Carrasco, 117
Crillon, Hotel, Plaza de la Independencia area,* 114
Español, Hotel, Plaza de la Independencia area, 114
Gran Hotel America, Plaza Libertad (Cagancha) area, 115
Gran Hotel America, Plaza Libertad (Cagancha) area (S), 115
Gran Hotel Ermitage, Playa Pocitos, 117
Hostería Del Lago, Carrasco (S), 117
Kings, Hotel, Plaza de la Independencia area,($), 113–14
Klee, Hotel, Plaza`Libertad (Cagancha) area,* 115
Lafayette, Hotel, Plaza Libertad area, 115
Lancaster, Plaza Libertad (Cagancha) area,* 115
Oceania, Punta Gorda,* 117

Oxford Hotel, Plaza Libertad (Cagancha) area, 115
Parque Hotel Casino, Playa Ramírez (HC), 116–17
Presidente, Hotel Plaza Libertad (Cagancha) area, 115
Reina, Hotel, Plaza Matríz area, 116
Victoria Plaza, Plaza de la Independencia area sports (S),* 114
arriving in, 108
climate, 110
cost of everyday items in, 106
evening entertainment, 128–31
excursions from, 131–3
Fast Facts, 110–13
maps:
Montevideo, 111
Uruguay, 107
orientation, 108–9
restaurants, 117–23
specialty dining, 121–3
CONFITERÍAS
Café de la Paix, 122
Confitería Francesca, 121
Giorgio's, 122
Horniman's Tea Room, 121
Oro del Rhin, 121
Las Palmas, 122
FRENCH
Club de Golf del Uruguay (S), 122
Doña Flor, center of town (S),* 122–3
L'Etoile (S), 122
Le Gavroche (S), 123
GERMAN
Otto, center of town, 120
HAMBURGERS
Pumpernic, center of town,($), 119
INTERNATIONAL
Bar Anticuario, center of town, 119–20
Conaprole, center of town, 118
Del Aguila, center of town,* 120
Makao, Punta Gorda (S), 122
Le Rendezvous, at beach, 121
Restaurant del Ferrocarril (S),* 123
Restaurant Morini, center of town, 120
Restaurant Panoramico (S), 123
Short Horn Grill (S), 122
La Vascongada, center of town,($), 120–1
ITALIAN
Club de Golf del Uruguay (S), 122
LIGHT FARE
Cervecería La Pasiva, center of town,($), 118
El Chivito de Oro, center of town, 118
PARRILLADA
Rodo Park, at beach,($), 121
PASTA
El Gatto Rosso, center of town, 118
PASTRIES
The Manchester, center of town, 119
PIZZA
El Gatto Rosso, center of town, 118
Hispano Bar, center of town, 118
Pumpernic, center of town,($), 119
SANDWICHES
Cervecería La Pasiva, center of town,($), 118
Hispano Bar, center of town, 118
The Manchester, center of town, 119
Pumpernic, center of town,($), 119
SEAFOOD
La Azotea, at beach, 121

MONTEVIDEO (URUGUAY) (cont'd)
Rodo Park, at beach,($) 121
Sea Garden Restaurant, at beach, 121
SPANISH
La Genovesa, center of town, 120
SWISS
Bungalow Suizo, center of town, 119
URUGUAYAN
La Azotea, at beach, 121
Las Brasas, center of town, 119
Conaprole, center of town, 118
El David, center of town,* 119
El Fogón, center of town, 120
Lokotas, center of town, 118–19
VEGETARIAN
Restaurante la Vegetariana, center of town, 120
shopping, 126–8
sights and attractions, 123–5
sports and recreational activities, 126
tours, organized, 108, 125–6
transportation in, 109–10
traveling to, from Buenos Aires, 173
walking tour, 125
what's special about, 106

NASCA (PERU), 418

OTAVALO (ECUADOR), 292
OLLANTAYTAMBO (PERU), 441–2
OURO PRETO (BRAZIL), 101

**PACHACMAC RUINS AND MUSEUM
 (PERU),** 417–18
PANAMA CANAL (PANAMA), 369–71
PANAMA CITY (PANAMA), 354–83
accommodations:
Acapulco, Hotel ($), 361
Apart-Hotel Ambassador (R), 364
Bella Vista, Hotel, 362
Caribe Hotel, 362–3
Central, Hotel, 363
Chu, Hotel (Taboga Island), 381
Colonial ($), 363
El Continental, Hotel,* 363
Costa del Sol Apart-Hotel (R), 364
Costa Inn, Hotel, 362
Europa Hotel, 362
Granada, Hotel y Casino, 363
Gran Hotel Soloy, 362
El Hotel Colón, 361
Ideal, Hotel ($), 361–2
Plaza Paitilla Inn (S), 364
Riazor, Hotel, 362
Roma, Hotel,* 363
Taboga, Hotel (Taboga Island), 381–2
Tower House Suites (R), 364
airport arrival, 356–7
climate, 359
crime, 360
currency, 359
evening entertainment, 377–80
excursions from:
beaches, 383
Colón, 380–1
Contadora Island, 383
Portobelo, 381
San Blas Islands (Kuna Indians), 382–3
Taboga, 381
language, 360
Lotería Nacional, 375
map, 357

orientation, 356, 358–9
restaurants, 364–9
CHINESE
Mandarin, 365–6
COLOMBIAN
La Fonda Antioqueña, 366
FRENCH
El Casco Viejo (S), 367–8
Lesseps, 367
INTERNATIONAL
Cafeteria Manolo,($) 365
La Cascada,* 365
Costa Azul, 365
Hotel Ideal Cafeteria, 365
El Pavo Real,* 367
ITALIAN
Napoli, 366
Sarti's (S), 368
Sorrento, 366
JAPANESE
Ginza Teppanyaki (S), 368
LIGHT FARE
Big Mama's, 369
El Boulevard, 368
Burger King, 369
Café Manolo, 368
Dairy Queen, 369
Delirys, 368
Domino's Pizza, 369
Dunkin' Donuts, 369
Kentucky Fried Chicken, 369
McDonald's, 369
Mr. Pollo, 369
Niko's Café, 368
Popeye's, 369
Romanaccio Cafeteria and Pizzeria, 368–9
El Vegetariano Mireya, 368
MEXICAN
Toritos, 367
NORTH AMERICAN
American Legion, 365
PANAMANIAN
Restaurant de las Americas,* 366
Tinajas,* 367
El Trapiche, 367
PIZZA
Domino's Pizza, 369
Romanaccio Cafeteria and Pizzeria, 368–9
SEAFOOD
Restaurante Bar Panamar,* 366
SPANISH
El Cortijo (S), 368
Marbella, 367
shopping, 375–7
sights and attractions:
Afro-Antillano, Museo, 373
Anthropological Museum Reina Torres de
 Arauz,* 372
Museo del Arte Religioso Colonial, 372
Museo de Historia de Panama, 372
Museo del, Hombre Panameño, 373
Panama Viejo (Old Panama), 372
sports and recreation, 374–5
transportation, 359
walking tour, 373–4
what's special about, 355
PAQUETA ISLAND (BRAZIL), 94
PARATI (BRAZIL), 95
PATAGONIA (MAGALLENES) (CHILE),
209

PETROPOLIS (BRAZIL), 87
PISAC (PERU), 441
PORTILLO (CHILE), 205-6
PORTOBELO (PANAMA), 381
PUNTA DEL ESTE (URUGUAY), 131-3

QUITO (ECUADOR), 261-97
accommodations:
    Alameda Real, New City, 269
    Los Alpes, Hostel, New City,* 269
    Amaranta Internacional, Hotel, New City (R), 271
    Ambassador, Hotel, New City, 269
    Los Andes Hostal Residencial, New City, 268
    La Casona, Old City,* 271
    Chalet Suisse, Hotel, New City, 269
    Colonial, Hotel, Old City, 270
    Cumanda, Hostal, Old City ($), 270
    Embassy, Hotel, Calle Presidente Wilson, 271
    Embassy, Hotel, Old City (R), 271
    Galaxie Hotel Suites, Old City (R), 271
    Gran Casino, Old City, 270
    Gran Casino II, Old City, ($), 270
    Hostal Florencia, New City ($), 268
    Hostal Los Maderos, New City ($), 268
    Majestic, Hotel, New City,* 268
    Paris Internacional, Hotel, Cuenca, 295
    Plaza, Hotel, Old City, 270
    Quito, Best Western Hotel (S), 269-70
    Real Audiencia, Hotel, Old City, 270-1
    República, Hotel, New City, 269
    Residencia Santa Clara, New City, 268
    Santa Maria, Hotel, New City, 269
    Tambo Real, New City, 269
    Viena Internacional, Hotel, Old City, 271
climate, 266
currency, 266
evening entertainment, 285-8
Fast Facts, 266-8
history of, 261-2
itineraries from, 290-7
    Amazon jungle, 297
    Cotopaxi Volcano, 293
    Cuenca,* 294-5
    Equator, 290-1
    Galápagos Islands, 288-90
    Guayaquil, 295-6
    Indian markets,* 291-4
map, 265
museums, 278-80
orientation, 262-4
restaurants, 272-8
ARGENTINEAN
    Columbus ($), 273
    Shorthorn Grill, on Calama Street, 273
BRAZILIAN
    Churrascaria Tropeiro, 274
    El Toro Partido, 274
CEBICHE
    El Cebiche, on Calama Street, 272
CHINESE
    Chifa Chang, Old City, 276
    Chifa China, 274
    Manila Restaurant and Cafeteria, Old City, 277
ECUADORIAN
    La Choza,* 275
    Manila Restaurant and Cafeteria, Old City, 277
ENGLISH
    Dickens, on Calama Street, 272
FRENCH
    La Creperie, on Calama Street, 272

    Rincón de Francia, 276
GERMAN
    Taberna Bavaria, 274-5
INTERNATIONAL
    Arlequin,* 275
    La Casa de Mi Abuela,* 275
    Chifa Chang, Old City, 276
    Excalibur, on Calama Street,* 273
    Juan Sebastian Bar, on Calama Street, 273
    Quito Viejo, Old City, 277
    La Terraza del Tartaro, 276
ITALIAN
    Ristorante Vecchia Roma ($), 273-4
LIGHT FARE
    El Americano, New City, 278
    El Chacarero, New City, 277
    Café Colón, New City, 278
    Café Niza, Old City, 276
    Chantilly, New City, 277
    Hotel Almeda Real Cafeteria, New City, 277
    King Chicken, New City, 278
    Manolo, New City, 277
    Mario's, New City, 277
    McDonald's, New City, 278
    Pims, New City, 278
    Pizza Hut, New City, 278
    Pizza Nostra, New City, 278
    Plazuela Café del Teatro, New City, 278
    Pollo Gus, New City, 278
    Sandy's, New City, 277
PIZZA
    Pizza Hut, New City, 278
    Pizza Nostra, New City, 278
SANDWICHES
    Café Niza, Old City, 276
    The Madrillon, Old City, 276-7
SEAFOOD
    El Cebiche, on Calama Street, 272
    Las Redes, 274
SPANISH
    La Costa Vasca, 275-6
    Las Cuevas de Luis Candelas,* 274
    Las Cuevas de Luis Candelas, Old City, 277
STEAK
    Columbus ($), 273
    El Toro Steakhouse Restaurant, on Calama Street ($), 273
    Hereford Grill Steak House, on Calama Street, 272
    Pims, on Calama Street, 272
SWISS
    Le Chalet Suisse, on Calama Street,* 272
shopping, 282-5
sights and attractions, 278-82
    Casa de la Cultura Ecuatoriana, 279
    Casa de Sucre, Museo Histórico, 279
    Guayasamin Museum and Foundation, 280
    Jacinto Jijon y Caamaño Museum, 279
    Museo del Banco Central de Ecuador,* 278-9
    Museo Franciscano, (Museo del Convento de San Francisco), 279
    Museo Municipal Alberto Mena Caamaño (Municipal Museum), 279
    Museo Nacional de Arte Colonial, 278
    Observatorio Astronómico, 279-80
sports, 282
tours, organized, 281-2
transportation, 264, 266
walking tour, 280-1

RIOBAMBA (ECUADOR), 294
RIO DE JANEIRO (BRAZIL), 53-104
accommodations:
Acapulco, Hotel, Copacabana, 68
Aeroporto Othon, Hotel, Center City (*S*), 65
Albergue da Juventude Bello (*YH*), 72
Ambassador, Center City,* 64
Ambassador Santos Dumont, Hotel, Center City, 65
Angrense, Hotel, Copacabana, 67
APA, Hotel, Copacabana, 68
Apart-Hotel, Copacabana, 72
Arpoador Inn, Ipanema, 70
Bandeirante, Hotel, Copacabana, 68
Belas Artes, Hotel, Center City, 63
Biarritz Hotel, Copacabana (*$*), 68
Bragança, Hotel, Center City, 63
Canada, Hotel, Copacabana(*$*), 67
Carlton, Hotel, Leblon, 70
Casa do Estudante do Brasil, Copacabana (*YH*), 72
Castro Alves, Hotel, Copacabana (*S*), 68, 70
Caxambu, Hotel, Flamengo Beach, 65
Club Rio, Rio (*S*), 72
Copa Linda, Hotel, Copacabana, 67
Copamar, Hotel, Copacabana, 68
Everest Park Hotel, Ipanema,* 70
Flamengo Palace, Flamengo Beach, 66
Florida, Flamengo Beach, 66
Globo, Hotel, Center City, 63
Gloria, Hotel, Flamengo Beach,* 66-7
Granada, Hotel, Center City, 64
Grande Hotel Novo Mundo, Flamengo Beach, 66
Grande Hotel O.K., Center City (*$*), 63
Grande Hotel Presidente, Center City (*$*), 63
Grande Hotel São Francisco, Center City, 64
Guanabara Palace, Center City,* 65
Imperial Hotel, Flamengo Beach, 66
Inglês, Hotel, Flamengo Beach, 66
Ipanema Inn, Ipanema, 70
Itajuba, Center City, 64-5
Marialva, Center City (*$*), 64
Mengo, Hotel, Flamengo Beach, 65
Nelba, Hotel, Center City, 64
Nice, Hotel, Center City, 63
Paulistano, Hotel, Center City, 64
Plaza Copacabana Hotel, Copacabana (*S*), 70
Pousada do Garuda, Santa Teresa (*YH*), 72
Praia Leme, Hotel, Copacabana, 67-8
Praia Lido, Copacabana, 68
Regina Hotel, Flamengo Beach, 66
Rio Flat Service, Leblon, 72
Toledo Hotel, Copacabana, 68
Vermont, Hotel, Ipanema, 70
airport, 54
beaches, 87, 94-5
carnival, 87-8
climate, 53, 58
cost of everyday items in, 53-4
currency, 58
entry requirements, 60
evening entertainment, 91-4
excursions from:
Belo Horizonte, 101
Brasília, 100-1
Buzios,* 94-5
Costa Verde, 94-5
ecological trips, 104
Iguaçu (Iguassu) Falls, 103
Paqueta Island,* 94

Salvador (Bahía), 95-100
São Paulo, 102-4
Vidigal and São Conrado, 82
Fast Facts, 58, 60-2
itineraries from, 82, 100-4
language, 61
maps:
Brazil, 55
Copacabana and Leme, 69
Ipanema and Leblon, 71
Rio de Janeiro, 59
orientation, 54-7
restaurants, 72-82
specialty dining, 81-2
BAHIAN
Chalé, Ipanema and Leblon (*S*),* 80
Oxala, Center City (*$*), 75
Restaurant Moenda, Copacabana Beach,* 78
BARBECUE
Churrascaria Copacabana, Copacabana Beach, 77
Churrascaria Jardim, Copacabana Beach, 77
Churrascolandia, Center City, 74-5
Cruzeiro do Sul, Center City, 73
Majorica, Flamengo Beach, 75
Marius, Copacabana Beach,* 77
Porcao Churrascaria, Ipanema and Leblon (*$*), 80
Rian, Copacabana Beach, 78
BRAZILIAN
Alvaro's Bar, Ipanema and Leblon, 78
Arataca, Copacabana Beach, 76
Aurora, Flamengo Beach, 75
Cafe Lamas, Flamengo Beach (*$*), 75
Le Coin, Ipanema and Leblon, 78
Final do Leblon, Ipanema and Leblon, 79
A Grelha, Ipanema and Leblon, 79
Janina, Flamengo Beach, 75
La Mole, Copacabana Beach, 76
Leiteria Mineira, Center City,* 74
Parque Recreio, Flamengo Beach, 75
CHINESE
Mr. Zee, Ipanema and Leblon (*S*), 80
Restaurante Oriento, Copacabana Beach, 76
CONFEITARÍAS
Colombo,* 81-2
CONTINENTAL
Antiquarius, Ipanema and Leblon (*S*), 80
DELICATESSEN
Delicat's, Ipanema and Leblon, 78-9
FAST FOOD
Bob's, Center City, 81
Bob's, Ipanema and Leblon, 81
Boninos, Copacabana Beach, 81
Bonis, Copacabana Beach, 81
Cervantes, Copacabana Beach, 81
Chaplin, Ipanema and Leblon, 81
Cupim Minas, Copacabana Beach, 81
Insalate, Center City, 81
Lanches Cerejinha, Center City, 81
Lojas Americanas, Copacabana Beach, 81
Polis Sucos, Ipanema and Leblon, 81
Top Top, Copacabana Beach, 81
FRENCH
Le Mazot, Copacabana Beach,* 77
GERMAN
Bar Luiz, Center City, 73
Ficha, Center City, 73
HEALTH/NATURAL FOOD
Celeiro, Ipanema and Leblon, 78
Sabor Saude, Ipanema and Leblon, 79

RIO DE JANEIRO (BRAZIL) (cont'd)
INTERNATIONAL
  Albacora, Ipanema and Leblon (S), 80
  Arosa Lanchonette, Copacabana Beach ($), 76
  Café do Teatro, Center City, 74
  Chicken House, Center City ($), 73
  Le Coin, Ipanema and Leblon, 78
  Esquina-Sabor Brasil, Center City ($), 73
  Final do Leblon, Ipanema and Leblon, 79
  Rio's, Flamengo Beach (S),* 76
  Terraco Atlântico, Copacabana Beach,* 78
ITALIAN
  Cantina Bella Roma, Copacabana Beach, 76
  Il Capo, Ipanema and Leblon, 79
  Grottammare, Ipanema and Leblon (S),* 80
  Río Napolis, Ipanema and Leblon, 79
KOSHER
  Delicat's, Ipanema and Leblon, 78–9
MEXICAN
  Lagoa Charlies, Ipanema and Leblon, 79–80
PIZZA
  Mister Pizza, Center City, 74
PORTUGUESE
  Bismarque, Flamengo Beach, 75
SANDWICHES
  Gordon's, Ipanema and Leblon, 79
SEAFOOD
  Grottammare, Ipanema and Leblon (S),* 80
  Restaurante A Marisqueira, Copacabana Beach,*
    77–8
  Shirley, Copacabana Beach,* 76–7
SPANISH
  Shirley, Copacabana Beach,* 76–7
SWISS
  Le Mazot, Copacabana Beach,* 77
VEGETARIAN
  Health's, Center City, 73–4
  Natural, Center City, 74
shopping, 88–91
sights and attractions, 82–7
  beaches, 82–3
  Botanical Gardens, 86
  Carmen Miranda Museum,* 85–6
  Chacara do Ceu Museum, 86
  Corcovado,* 83–4
  in countryside near Río, 87
  cruises, 87
  favelas, 86
  Hippie Fair, 99, 102
  Indian Museum, 85
  Joquei Club racetrack, 86
  Modern Art, Museum of, 85
  mountains, 83–4
  Museum of National History, 85
  Museum of the Republic, 85
  Quinta de Boa Vista, 86
  Santa Teresa, 86
  Sugarloaf (Pão de Açúcar),* 83
  Monument to World War II Heroes, 85
  Tijuca Forest, 87
special and free events, 87–8
sports and recreational activities, 88
taxis, 57–8
telephone, 62
transportation, 57–8
walking tour, 84
what's special about, 53

**THE SACRED VALLEY, URABAMBA
(PERU)**, 440–3

SALVADOR (BAHÍA) (BRAZIL), 95–100
accommodations, 98–9
arriving in, 95
capoeira, 99–100
evening entertainment, 99
excursions from, 100
folklore and religion, 95–6, 99–100
map, 97
sights and activities, 96, 99–100
**SAN AGUSTÍN MONOLITHS (COLOM-
BIA)**, 328–30
SAN ANDRÉS ISLAND (COLOMBIA),
  351–3
accommodations, 352–3
arriving in, 351
evening entertainment, 353
getting there, 351–3
orientation, 351–2
restaurants, 353
  La Carreta (international), 353
  La Fonda Antioquena (Colombian), 353
  El Oasis (seafood), * 353
  Pizzeria de Giovanni (Italian), 353
  La Tortuga (seafood), 353
sights and activities, 352
SAN BLAS ISLANDS (PANAMA), 382–3
**SAN CARLOS DE BARILOCHE (ARGEN-
TINA)**, 172
SANTA CRUZ (BOLIVIA), 259–60
SANTA MARTA (COLOMBIA), 345–51
accommodations, 347–8
accommodations:
  Andrea Doria, Hotel, 348
  Cañaveral, Hotel, 347
  Irotama, Hotel (S),* 348
  Lilliam Hotel,* 347–8
  Residencia Miramar, 348
  La Riviera, Hotel, 347
  El Rodadero, Hotel, 347
  Santamar (S), 348
  La Sierra, Hotel, 347
  Tamaca, Hotel, 348
beaches, 347
climate, 345–51
evening entertainment, 350–1
getting there, 345–51
orientation, 346
restaurants, 348–50
  La Brasa Restaurant, Center City (seafood), 350
  El Caracol, Rodadero Beach (light fare), 349–50
  El Conquistador, Rodadero Beach (international),
    349
  Los Cumbieros, Rodadero Beach (French),* 349
  Fonda de las Colonias, Center City (Colombian/
    international), 350
  Fuente de Soda, Center City (café), 350
  Karey, Rodadero Beach (international), 349
  Mi Ranchito, Rodadero Beach (criolla),* 350
  Panamerican, Center City (continental),* 350
  Portofino, Rodadero Beach (Italian), 349
  La Real Parrilla y Pizzería, Center City
    (Argentinean/pizza), 350
  Restaurant Los Delfines, Rodadero Beach (sea-
    food), 349
  Restaurante Capri, Rodadero Beach (seafood/
    Colombian), 349
  La Rodadita, Rodadero Beach (seafood), 349
  Sorrento Pizzería, Center City (pizza), 350
  El Turista, Center City (international), 350
shopping, 346

SANTA MARTA (COLOMBIA) (cont'd)
sights and activities, 346–7
SANTIAGO (CHILE), 174–209
accommodations:
Aloha Hotel, Providencia, 186
Calicanto, Hotel, Plaza de Armas area, 183
Castellon, Hotel, Viña del Mar, 206
City Hotel, Plaza de Armas area,* 183
Colorado Apart Hotel, Portillo, 206
Conquistador, Hotel, downtown, 186
Don Tito, Hotel de, near Santa Lucia Hill, 185
Edificio San Rafael, Alameda area, 184
España, Hotel, Plaza de Armas area ($), 183
Foresta Hotel, near Santa Lucia Hill,* 185
Fundador, Hotel, downtown, 186
Hanga Roa, Easter Island, 204–5
Hotu Matua, Hotel, Easter Island, 205
Iorana Korna, Easter Island, 205
Libertador Hotel, Alameda area ($), 184
Monte Bianco, Hotel, near Avenida Providencia, 185
O'Higgins, Viña del Mar, 207
Orly, Hotel, near Avenida Providencia, 185
Panamericano, Plaza de Armas area, 184
Parque, Hostal del, near Santa Lucia Hill, 185–6
Portillo, Hotel, Portillo, 206
Presidente, Hotel, near Avenida Providencia, 185
Residencial Londres, near Iglesia de San Francisco ($), 185
Ritz, Hotel, Plaza de Armas area, 183–4
Riviera, Hotel, Alameda area, 184
San Martín, Viña del Mar, 207
San Sebastian II, Providencia, 186
Santa Lucia, Plaza de Armas area (S),* 184
Tupahue Hotel, downtown, 186
currency, 180
evening entertainment, 201–3
excursions from:
Chilean Lake Region, 208–9
Easter Island, 203–5
Patagonia (Magallenes), 209
ski country, 205–8
Termas de Chillan, 208
Viña del Mar, 206–8
Fast Facts, 179–83
map, 176, 181
orientation, 175–6
restaurants, 186–93
specialty dining, 191–3
ARGENTINEAN
Don Carlos, downtown, 188–9
El Parron, 190
AUSTRIAN
La Jacaranda, downtown,* 188
CHILEAN
Los Adobes de Argomedo, downtown,* 188
Los Buenos Muchachos, Providencia and beyond,* 189
Chez Henry, downtown ($), 187
Eladio, downtown, 187–8
Hosteria Las Delicias, Las Condes, 190–1
CHINESE
Canton, downtown, 187
Palacio Danubio Azul, Providencia and beyond, 189–90
CONTINENTAL
Les Assassins, downtown, 187
ESPRESSO
Café Caribe, 193

Café de Brasil, 193
Haiti, 193
FAST FOOD
La Pavita, Providencia and beyond($), 189
FRENCH
Les Assassins, downtown, 187
Chez Louis, Las Condes, 191
La Jacaranda, downtown,* 188
INTERNATIONAL
El Carillon, downtown ($), 188
El Club Gran Avenida, Providencia and beyond (S), 190
El Giratorio, Providencia and beyond, 190
Salvaje, Providencia and beyond, 189
Steak House, downtown, 188
ITALIAN
Chez Henry, downtown ($), 187
Di Carla, downtown, 187
Le Due Torri, downtown (S), 189
San Marco Trattoria, downtown, 188
LIGHT FARE
Bar Nacional, 192
Bravíssimo, 191
Burger Inn, 192
Café Danté, downtown, 191
Café do Brasil, 192
Centro Pizza, downtown, 191
Charlie's, 192
Domus Quick Lunch, 192
Fritz, downtown, 191
Fuente Alemana, 191
Gatsby, 192
Kentucky Fried Chicken, 192
McDonald's, 192
La Merced, downtown, 191
Mermoz, downtown, 191
La Naranja, 191
El Naturista, 191–2
Nuria Quick Lunch, Santa Lucia Hill, 192
Papa Pollo, downtown, 191
Paparazzi, downtown, 191
Pizza Hut, 192
Pizza Inn, 192
Savory, 191
Silvestre, downtown, 191
El 27 de Nueva York, 192
ONCE
Café Colonia, 192
Café Paula, 192
Café Santos, 192–3
PIZZA
La Pizza Nostra, Providencia and beyond, 189
POLYNESIAN
Bali Hai, Las Condes, 191
SEAFOOD
Aqui Esta Coco, Providencia and beyond, 190
Coco Loco, Providencia and beyond, 190
La Jacaranda, downtown,* 188
STEAK
Hereford Grill, Las Condes, 191
SWISS
Casa Suiza, downtown, 187
VEGETARIAN
El Naturista, 191–2
El Vegetariano, 192
shopping, 189–201
sights and attractions:
Ahu Akivi, Easter Island, 204
Arte Colonial, Museo de, 195
Biblioteca Nacional, 197

SANTIAGO (CHILE) *(cont'd)*
La Casa Colorada, 196
Cerro San Cristobal and the Parque Metro-politano, 193-4
Cerro Santa Lucia, 197
Church of San Francisco, 196
Estación Mapocho, 196
Glacier Cruises, Patagonia, 209
Museo Precolombino, 195
Mundo Mágico, 195
Museo, Histórico Nacional,* 195
Museo Nacional de Historia Natural and Quinta Normal Park, 194
Orongo, Easter Island, 204
El Palacio Cousiño, 195-6
Palacio de Bellas Artes,* 194-5
Palacio de la Moneda, 196
Plaza de Armas, 196
Plaza de Bulnes, 196
Plaza de la Constitución, 196
Plaza de Libertad, 196
Rana Raraku, Easter Island, 204
Rano Kau, Easter Island, 204
Teatro Municipal, 197

University of Chile, 196
Viña Canepa, 197
Viña Concha y Toro, 197
Viña Undurraga, 197-8
walking tour, 196-7
sports, 198
transportation, 179
SANTO DOMINGO DE LOS COLORA-DOS (ECUADOR), 294
SAQUISILI (ECUADOR), 293
SÃO PAULO (BRAZIL), 102-4

TABOGA (PANAMA), 381
TITICACA, LAKE (BOLIVIA-PERU), 256-7, 260
TIWANACU (BOLIVIA), 255-6

VALLE DE LAS LEÑAS (ARGENTINA), 172
VALLE NEVADO (CHILE), 205
VALPARAÍSO (CHILE), 208
VIÑA DEL MAR (CHILE), 206-8

ZIPAQUIRA CATHEDRAL (COLOMBIA), 328

Now Save Money on All Your Travels by Joining
FROMMER'S ™ TRAVEL BOOK CLUB
The World's Best Travel Guides at Membership Prices

FROMMER'S TRAVEL BOOK CLUB is your ticket to successful travel! Open up a world of travel information and simplify your travel planning when you join ranks with thousands of value-conscious travelers who are members of the FROMMER'S TRAVEL BOOK CLUB. Join today and you'll be entitled to all the privileges that come from belonging to the club that offers you travel guides for less to more than 100 destinations worldwide. Annual membership is only $25 (U.S.) or $35 (Canada and all foreign).

The Advantages of Membership

1. Your choice of three free FROMMER'S TRAVEL GUIDES. You can pick two from our FROMMER'S COUNTRY and REGIONAL GUIDES (listed under Comprehensive, $-A-Day, and Family) and one from our FROMMER'S CITY GUIDES (listed under City and City $-A-Day).
2. Your own subscription to **TRIPS & TRAVEL** quarterly newsletter.
3. You're entitled to a **30% discount** on your order of any additional books offered by FROMMER'S TRAVEL BOOK CLUB.
4. You're offered (at a small additional fee) our **Domestic Trip Routing Kits.**

Our quarterly newsletter **TRIPS & TRAVEL** offers practical information on the best buys in travel, the "hottest" vacation spots, the latest travel trends, world-class events and much, much more.

Our **Domestic Trip Routing Kits** are available for any North American destination. We'll send you a detailed map highlighting the best route to take to your destination—you can request direct or scenic routes.

Here's all you have to do to join:
Send in your membership fee of $25 ($35 Canada and foreign) with your name and address on the form below along with your selections as part of your membership package to **FROMMER'S TRAVEL BOOK CLUB, P.O. Box 473, Mt. Morris, IL 61054-0473.** Remember to check off 2 FROMMER'S COUNTRY and REGIONAL GUIDES and 1 FROMMER'S CITY GUIDE on the pages following.

If you would like to order additional books, please select the books you would like and send a check for the total amount (please add sales tax in the states noted below), plus $2 per book for shipping and handling ($3 per book for all foreign orders) to:

FROMMER'S TRAVEL BOOK CLUB
P.O. Box 473
Mt. Morris, IL 61054-0473
1-815-734-1104

[　] **YES.** I want to take advantage of this opportunity to join FROMMER'S TRAVEL BOOK CLUB.
[　] **My check is enclosed.** Dollar amount enclosed＿＿＿＿＿＿＿＿*
　　　　　(all payments in U.S. funds only)

Name＿＿＿＿＿＿＿＿＿＿＿＿＿＿＿＿＿＿＿＿＿＿＿＿＿＿＿＿＿
Address＿＿＿＿＿＿＿＿＿＿＿＿＿＿＿＿＿＿＿＿＿＿＿＿＿＿＿＿
City＿＿＿＿＿＿＿＿＿＿＿＿＿＿＿＿＿ State＿＿＿ Zip＿＿＿＿

To ensure that all orders are processed efficiently, please apply sales tax in the following areas: CA, CT, FL, IL, NJ, NY, TN, WA, and CANADA.

*With membership, shipping and handling will be paid by FROMMER'S TRAVEL BOOK CLUB for the three free books you select as part of your membership. Please add $2 per book for shipping and handling for any additional books purchased ($3 per book for all foreign orders).

Allow 4-6 weeks for delivery. Prices of books, membership fee, and publication dates are subject to change without notice.

Please Send Me the Books Checked Below

FROMMER'S COMPREHENSIVE GUIDES

(Guides listing facilities from budget to deluxe, with emphasis on the medium-priced)

	Retail Price	Code		Retail Price	Code
☐ Acapulco/Ixtapa/Taxco 1993–94	$15.00	C120	☐ Jamaica/Barbados 1993–94	$15.00	C105
☐ Alaska 1990–91	$15.00	C001	☐ Japan 1992–93	$19.00	C020
☐ Arizona 1993–94	$18.00	C101	☐ Morocco 1992–93	$18.00	C021
☐ Australia 1992–93	$18.00	C002	☐ Nepal 1992–93	$18.00	C038
☐ Austria 1993–94	$19.00	C119	☐ New England 1993	$17.00	C114
☐ Austria/Hungary 1991–92	$15.00	C003	☐ New Mexico 1993–94	$15.00	C117
☐ Belgium/Holland/ Luxembourg 1993–94	$18.00	C106	☐ New York State 1992–93	$19.00	C025
			☐ Northwest 1991–92	$17.00	C026
☐ Bermuda/Bahamas 1992–93	$17.00	C005	☐ Portugal 1992–93	$16.00	C027
			☐ Puerto Rico 1993–94	$15.00	C103
☐ Brazil, 3rd Edition	$20.00	C111	☐ Puerto Vallarta/Manzanillo/ Guadalajara 1992–93	$14.00	C028
☐ California 1993	$18.00	C112			
☐ Canada 1992–93	$18.00	C009	☐ Scandinavia 1993–94	$19.00	C118
☐ Caribbean 1993	$18.00	C102	☐ Scotland 1992–93	$16.00	C040
☐ Carolinas/Georgia 1992–93	$17.00	C034	☐ Skiing Europe 1989–90	$15.00	C030
☐ Colorado 1993–94	$16.00	C100	☐ South Pacific 1992–93	$20.00	C031
☐ Cruises 1993–94	$19.00	C107	☐ Spain 1993–94	$19.00	C115
☐ DE/MD/PA & NJ Shore 1992–93	$19.00	C012	☐ Switzerland/Liechtenstein 1992–93	$19.00	C032
☐ Egypt 1990–91	$15.00	C013	☐ Thailand 1992–93	$20.00	C033
☐ England 1993	$18.00	C109	☐ U.S.A. 1993–94	$19.00	C116
☐ Florida 1993	$18.00	C104	☐ Virgin Islands 1992–93	$13.00	C036
☐ France 1992–93	$20.00	C017	☐ Virginia 1992–93	$14.00	C037
☐ Germany 1993	$19.00	C108	☐ Yucatán 1993–94	$18.00	C110
☐ Italy 1993	$19.00	C113			

FROMMER'S $-A-DAY GUIDES

(Guides to low-cost tourist accommodations and facilities)

	Retail Price	Code		Retail Price	Code
☐ Australia on $45 1993–94	$18.00	D102	☐ Mexico on $50 1993	$19.00	D105
☐ Costa Rica/Guatemala/ Belize on $35 1993–94	$17.00	D108	☐ New York on $70 1992–93	$16.00	D016
			☐ New Zealand on $45 1993–94	$18.00	D103
☐ Eastern Europe on $25 1991–92	$17.00	D005	☐ Scotland/Wales on $50 1992–93	$18.00	D019
☐ England on $60 1993	$18.00	D107			
☐ Europe on $45 1993	$19.00	D106	☐ South America on $40 1993–94	$19.00	D109
☐ Greece on $45 1993–94	$19.00	D100			
☐ Hawaii on $75 1993	$19.00	D104	☐ Turkey on $40 1992–93	$22.00	D023
☐ India on $40 1992–93	$20.00	D010	☐ Washington, D.C. on $40 1992–93	$17.00	D024
☐ Ireland on $40 1992–93	$17.00	D011			
☐ Israel on $45 1993–94	$18.00	D101			

FROMMER'S CITY $-A-DAY GUIDES

(Pocket-size guides with an emphasis on low-cost tourist accommodations and facilities)

	Retail Price	Code		Retail Price	Code
☐ Berlin on $40 1992–93	$12.00	D002	☐ Madrid on $50 1992–93	$13.00	D014
☐ Copenhagen on $50 1992–93	$12.00	D003	☐ Paris on $45 1992–93	$12.00	D018
			☐ Stockholm on $50 1992–93	$13.00	D022
☐ London on $45 1992–93	$12.00	D013			

FROMMER'S TOURING GUIDES
(Color-illustrated guides that include walking tours,
cultural and historic sights, and practical information)

	Retail Price	Code		Retail Price	Code
☐ Amsterdam	$11.00	T001	☐ New York	$11.00	T008
☐ Barcelona	$14.00	T015	☐ Rome	$11.00	T010
☐ Brazil	$11.00	T003	☐ Scotland	$10.00	T011
☐ Florence	$ 9.00	T005	☐ Sicily	$15.00	T017
☐ Hong Kong/Singapore/ Macau	$11.00	T006	☐ Thailand	$13.00	T012
			☐ Tokyo	$15.00	T016
☐ Kenya	$14.00	T018	☐ Venice	$ 9.00	T014
☐ London	$13.00	T007			

FROMMER'S FAMILY GUIDES

	Retail Price	Code		Retail Price	Code
☐ California with Kids	$17.00	F001	☐ San Francisco with Kids	$17.00	F004
☐ Los Angeles with Kids	$17.00	F002	☐ Washington, D.C. with Kids	$17.00	F005
☐ New York City with Kids	$18.00	F003			

FROMMER'S CITY GUIDES
(Pocket-size guides to sightseeing and tourist accommodations
and facilities in all price ranges)

	Retail Price	Code		Retail Price	Code
☐ Amsterdam 1993–94	$13.00	S110	☐ Miami 1993–94	$13.00	S118
☐ Athens, 9th Edition	$13.00	S114	☐ Minneapolis/St. Paul, 3rd Edition	$13.00	S119
☐ Atlanta 1993–94	$13.00	S112			
☐ Atlantic City/Cape May 1991–92	$ 9.00	S004	☐ Montréal/Québec City 1993–94	$13.00	S125
☐ Bangkok 1992–93	$13.00	S005	☐ New Orleans 1993–94	$13.00	S103
☐ Barcelona/Majorca/ Minorca/Ibiza 1993–94	$13.00	S115	☐ New York 1993	$13.00	S120
			☐ Orlando 1993	$13.00	S101
☐ Berlin 1993–94	$13.00	S116	☐ Paris 1993–94	$13.00	S109
☐ Boston 1993–94	$13.00	S117	☐ Philadelphia 1993–94	$13.00	S113
☐ Cancún/Cozumel/Yucatán 1991–92	$ 9.00	S010	☐ Rio 1991–92	$ 9.00	S029
			☐ Rome 1993–94	$13.00	S111
☐ Chicago 1993–94	$13.00	S122	☐ Salt Lake City 1991–92	$ 9.00	S031
☐ Denver/Boulder/Colorado Springs 1990–91	$ 8.00	S012	☐ San Diego 1993–94	$13.00	S107
			☐ San Francisco 1993	$13.00	S104
☐ Dublin 1993–94	$13.00	S128	☐ Santa Fe/Taos/Albuquerque 1993–94	$13.00	S108
☐ Hawaii 1992	$12.00	S014			
☐ Hong Kong 1992–93	$12.00	S015	☐ Seattle/Portland 1992–93	$12.00	S035
☐ Honolulu/Oahu 1993	$13.00	S106	☐ St. Louis/Kansas City 1993–94	$13.00	S127
☐ Las Vegas 1993–94	$13.00	S121			
☐ Lisbon/Madrid/Costa del Sol 1991–92	$ 9.00	S017	☐ Sydney 1993–94	$13.00	S129
			☐ Tampa/St. Petersburg 1993–94	$13.00	S105
☐ London 1993	$13.00	S100			
☐ Los Angeles 1993–94	$13.00	S123	☐ Tokyo 1992–93	$13.00	S039
☐ Madrid/Costa del Sol 1993–94	$13.00	S124	☐ Toronto 1993–94	$13.00	S126
			☐ Vancouver/Victoria 1990–91	$ 8.00	S041
☐ Mexico City/Acapulco 1991–92	$ 9.00	S020	☐ Washington, D.C. 1993	$13.00	S102

Other Titles Available at Membership Prices

SPECIAL EDITIONS

	Retail Price	Code		Retail Price	Code
☐ Bed & Breakfast North America	$15.00	P002	☐ Where to Stay U.S.A.	$14.00	P015
☐ Caribbean Hideaways	$16.00	P005			
☐ Marilyn Wood's Wonderful Weekends (within a 250-mile radius of NYC)	$12.00	P017			

GAULT MILLAU'S "BEST OF" GUIDES
(The only guides that distinguish the truly superlative from the merely overrated)

	Retail Price	Code		Retail Price	Code
☐ Chicago	$16.00	G002	☐ New England	$16.00	G010
☐ Florida	$17.00	G003	☐ New Orleans	$17.00	G011
☐ France	$17.00	G004	☐ New York	$17.00	G012
☐ Germany	$18.00	G018	☐ Paris	$17.00	G013
☐ Hawaii	$17.00	G006	☐ San Francisco	$17.00	G014
☐ Hong Kong	$17.00	G007	☐ Thailand	$18.00	G019
☐ London	$17.00	G009	☐ Toronto	$17.00	G020
☐ Los Angeles	$17.00	G005	☐ Washington, D.C.	$17.00	G017

THE REAL GUIDES
(Opinionated, politically aware guides for youthful budget-minded travelers)

	Retail Price	Code		Retail Price	Code
☐ Able to Travel	$20.00	R112	☐ Kenya	$12.95	R015
☐ Amsterdam	$13.00	R100	☐ Mexico	$11.95	R016
☐ Barcelona	$13.00	R101	☐ Morocco	$14.00	R017
☐ Belgium/Holland/ Luxembourg	$16.00	R031	☐ Nepal	$14.00	R018
			☐ New York	$13.00	R019
☐ Berlin	$11.95	R002	☐ Paris	$13.00	R020
☐ Brazil	$13.95	R003	☐ Peru	$12.95	R021
☐ California & the West Coast	$17.00	R121	☐ Poland	$13.95	R022
☐ Canada	$15.00	R103	☐ Portugal	$15.00	R023
☐ Czechoslovakia	$14.00	R005	☐ Prague	$15.00	R113
☐ Egypt	$19.00	R105	☐ San Francisco & the Bay Area	$11.95	R024
☐ Europe	$18.00	R122			
☐ Florida	$14.00	R006	☐ Scandinavia	$14.95	R025
☐ France	$18.00	R106	☐ Spain	$16.00	R026
☐ Germany	$18.00	R107	☐ Thailand	$17.00	R119
☐ Greece	$18.00	R108	☐ Tunisia	$17.00	R115
☐ Guatemala/Belize	$14.00	R010	☐ Turkey	$13.95	R027
☐ Hong Kong/Macau	$11.95	R011	☐ U.S.A.	$18.00	R117
☐ Hungary	$14.00	R118	☐ Venice	$11.95	R028
☐ Ireland	$17.00	R120	☐ Women Travel	$12.95	R029
☐ Italy	$13.95	R014	☐ Yugoslavia	$12.95	R030